TEACHER PREP

MERRILL PRENTICE HALL

Teacher Preparation Classroom

Your Class. Their Careers. Our Future. Will your students be prepared?

We invite you to explore our new, innovative and engaging website and all that it has to offer you, your course, and tomorrow's educators! Preview this site today at *www.prenhall.com/teacherprep/demo*. Just click on "go" on the login page to begin your exploration

Organized around the major courses pre-service teachers take, the Teacher Preparation site provides media, student/teacher artifacts, strategies, research articles, and other resources to equip your students with the quality tools needed to excel in their courses and prepare them for their first classroom.

This ultimate on-line education resource will provide you and your students access to:

Online Video Library. More than 250 video clips—each tied to a course topic and framed by learning goals and Praxis-type questions—capture real teachers and students working in real classrooms.

Student and Teacher Artifacts. More than 200 student and teacher classroom artifacts—each tied to a course topic and framed by learning goals and application questions— provide a wealth of materials and experiences to help your students observe children's developmental learning.

Lesson Plan Builder. Step-by-step guidelines and lesson plan examples support students as they learn to build high-quality lesson plans.

Articles and Readings. Over 500 articles from ASCD's renowned journal *Educational Leadership*. The site also includes *Research Navigator,* a searchable database of additional educational journals.

Strategies and Lessons. Over 500 research supported instructional strategies appropriate for a wide range of grade levels and content areas.

Licensure and Career Tools. Resources devoted to helping your students pass their licensure exam, learn standards, law, and public policies, plan a teaching portfolio, and survive their first year of teaching.

Introduction to Teaching
Becoming a Professional

Third Edition

Donald Kauchak
University of Utah

Paul Eggen
University of North Florida

Upper Saddle River, New Jersey
Columbus, Ohio

Library of Congress Cataloging-in-Publication Data

Kauchak, Donald
  Introduction to teaching : becoming a professional / Don Kauchak, Paul
Eggen.--3rd ed.
      p. cm.
  Includes bibliographical references and index.
  ISBN-13: 978-0-13-199455-3 (alk. paper)
  ISBN-10: 0-13-199455-7 (alk. paper)
  1. Teachers. 2. Teaching--Vocational guidance. 3. Education--United
States. I. Eggen, Paul D. II. Title.
  LB1775.K37 2008
  371.1--dc22

                                      2007000857

Vice President and Executive Publisher: Jeffery W. Johnston
Executive Editor: Darcy Betts Prybella
Development Editor: Amy Nelson
Production Editor: Alexandrina Benedicto Wolf
Design Coordinator: Diane C. Lorenzo
Text Designer: Kristina D. Holmes
Cover Designer: Ali Mohrman
Cover Image: Superstock
Photo Coordinator: Valerie Schultz
Production Manager: Susan W. Hannahs
Director of Marketing: David Gesell
Marketing Coordinator: Brian Mounts

This book was set in Galliard by Carlisle Publishing Services. It was printed and bound by R.R. Donnelley & Sons
Company. The cover was printed by Phoenix Color Corp.

Praxis™ is a registered trademark of Educational Testing Service (ETS). This textbook is not endorsed or approved by ETS.

Photo Credits: Andreanna Seymore/Stone/Getty Images, p. 1; Michael Newman/PhotoEdit Inc., p. 71; www.comstock.com,
p. 147; Will Hart/PhotoEdit Inc., p. 309.

Pearson Education Ltd.   Pearson Education Australia Pty. Limited
Pearson Education Singapore Pte. Ltd   Pearson Education North Asia Ltd.
Pearson Education Canada, Ltd.   Pearson Educación de Mexico, S.A. de C.V.
Pearson Education–Japan   Pearson Education Malaysia Pte. Ltd.

                                    10 9 8 7 6 5 4
                          ISBN-13: 978-0-13-199455-3
                          ISBN-10:   0-13-199455-7

Keys to Success on the Praxis™ and Other Professional Teaching Licensure Exams

This text is designed to help you succeed on the Praxis™ Principles of Learning and Teaching (PLT) Exam as well as state-specific tests. As of January 2006, thirty-two states use Praxis exams as part of their teacher licensing requirement; the vast majority of the other states have developed teacher licensure tests that are very similar to the Praxis tests in both format and content. Most states, including those that use the Praxis exams, test prospective teachers' knowledge of subject matter and grasp of basic skills as well as teachers' knowledge of basic principles of learning and teaching. The four Praxis PLT exams are divided by grade level, one each for teachers seeking licensure for Early Childhood, and grades K–6, 5–9, and 7–12. We focus this discussion on how to succeed on the Praxis PLT exam, but the same basic knowledge and test-taking strategies apply to state-specific tests.

To find out which test your state is currently using, go to either this text's Companion Website (*www.prenhall.com/kauchak*), which contains the addresses, phone numbers, and e-mail addresses of each state licensure office, or to the website developed by the University of Kentucky, which has the licensure requirements and Web addresses for all 50 states (*www.uky.edu/education/tep/usecert.html*).

The Praxis PLT exam has two parts (Educational Testing Service, 2006). One consists of 24 multiple-choice questions similar to those in the Kauchak and Eggen test bank and Companion Website interactive Practice Quizzes that accompany this text. The second part is based on four cases, which you will be asked to read and analyze, similar to the cases at the beginning and end of each chapter in this text. Three short-answer questions follow each case.

We have designed this text to help you succeed on the Praxis™ PLT exam by including cases and case-based questions at the end of each chapter and by providing feedback to these end-of-chapter questions on the Companion Website at *www.prenhall.com/kauchak*.

The PLT covers four broad content areas:

Students as Learners (multiple-choice and short-answer question; 33 percent of total test)

- Student development and the learning process
- Students as diverse learners
- Student motivation and the learning environment

Instruction and Assessment (multiple-choice and short-answer questions; 33 percent of total test)

- Instructional strategies
- Planning instruction
- Assessment strategies

Teacher Professionalism (multiple-choice and short-answer questions; 22 percent of total test)

- The reflective practitioner
- The larger community

Communication Techniques (short-answer questions; 11 percent of total test)

- Basic, effective verbal and nonverbal communication techniques
- Effect of cultural and gender differences on communications in the classroom
- Types of communications and interactions that can stimulate discussion in different ways for particular purposes

Preparing for the Exam

Plan ahead and acquaint yourself with the topics in the test. The Educational Testing Service booklet *Test at a Glance* (available online at *www.ets.org/praxis* or free by mail) includes detailed descriptions of topics covered in each of the four content categories as well as sample test questions. Study this booklet carefully, and take the sample tests available on this website and in their print materials. Analyze the different kinds of questions asked and the feedback and criteria provided. Follow the same procedures for state-specific exams.

Using This Text to Succeed on the PLT

What strategies should you employ as you use the exercises in this text to prepare for your licensure exam? Experts offer the following suggestions (Educational Testing Service, 2006):

Read the test directions carefully. Make sure you understand the test formats, what is being asked of you, and the time restrictions for each section.

Answer all parts of the question. For instance, if the question asks you to identify five characteristics of professionalism that were demonstrated in a case, be sure that your response includes all five.

Demonstrate an understanding of the theory or pedagogical concepts related to the question. As you analyze the case in writing, be sure to discuss key elements of the relevant concept or theory.

Demonstrate a thorough understanding of the case. In your answers be sure to discuss the case in general, as well as specific details within the case that relate to the question.

Repeat key words from the question. This helps to focus your response and communicates to the reader that you are directly responding to essential elements of the question. For example, if asked to list three important elements of student diversity, write, "Three important elements of student diversity are a, b, and c."

Support your answer with details. By specifically referring to the case and identifying the concepts that are being demonstrated, you will provide documentation for your answer.

Before you write a response, organize and outline your thoughts so they clearly represent your best thinking.

After you've written your own answers to the case-based questions that appear at the end of each chapter in this text, you can receive feedback by going to the *Preparing for Your Licensure Exam* module for each chapter on the Companion Website at *www.prenhall.com/kauchak*.

For additional help in preparing for the Praxis exams, you might want to purchase a copy of the *Principles of Learning and Teaching Study Guide* published by the Educational Testing Service. To find information for purchasing the study guide, go to the ETS website at *www.ets.org/praxis*.

References

Educational Testing Service (2006). *Tests at a glance: Praxis II subject assessments/Principles of learning and teaching.* Available online: *http://www.ets.org/praxis/prxtest:html* Accessed 8/12/06.

Correlation Matrix for the Praxis™ Principles of Learning and Teaching Exam

Knowledge Covered in the Praxis™ Principles of Learning and Teaching Exam	Chapter Topic Aligned With Knowledge Covered in the Praxis™ Principles of Learning and Teaching Exam	
I. Students as Learners (approximately 33% of total test)		
A. Student development and the learning process	Ch. 1 Ch. 7 Ch. 10 Ch. 11 Ch. 12	Creating productive learning environments Developmental characteristics of students Early childhood programs, elementary schools, junior highs, middle schools, and high schools What is an effective school? Curriculum and the professional teacher A focus on learners The human dimension of productive learning environments Developing learner responsibility Models of instruction Principles of learning
B. Students as diverse learners	Ch. 3 Ch. 4 **Each Chapter**	Cultural diversity Gender Ability differences Learning styles Students with exceptionalities Changes in student families Changes in socioeconomic patterns Changes in our students Students placed at-risk Exploring Diversity
C. Student motivation and the learning environment	Ch. 1 Ch. 3 Ch. 4 Ch. 11 Ch. 12	Creating productive learning environments Culturally responsive teaching Language diversity in the classroom Gender and schooling: Implications for teachers Learning styles: Implications for teachers Students with exceptionalities: Implications for teachers Effective teachers for students placed at-risk Personal teaching efficacy Caring Positive teacher expectations Modeling and enthusiasm Classroom management: Creating safe and supportive learning environments Creating a positive classroom climate Questioning Feedback

(continued)

II. Instruction and Assessment (approximately 33% of total test)		
A. Instructional strategies	Ch. 3	Culturally responsive teaching
		Language diversity in the classroom
		Gender and schooling: Implications for teachers
		Learning styles: Implications for teachers
		Students with exceptionalities: Implications for teachers
	Ch. 4	Effective teachers for students placed at-risk
	Ch. 12	Specifying learning objectives
		Questioning
		Direct instruction
		Lecture discussions
		Cooperative learning
		Guided discovery
	Ch. 13	Technology and instruction
		Drill and practice
		Tutorials
		Using technology to teach problem-solving and higher-level thinking skills
		Word processing: Using technology to teach writing
		Using the Internet as an instructional tool
B. Planning instruction	Ch. 1	Creating productive learning environments
		Accountability and high-stakes testing
	Ch. 3	Culturally responsive teaching
		Language diversity in the classroom
		Gender and schooling: Implications for teachers
		Learning styles: Implications for teachers
		Students with exceptionalities: Implications for teachers
	Ch. 4	Effective teachers for students placed at-risk
	Ch. 10	Curriculum in the elementary schools
		Curriculum in middle schools
		Curriculum in junior high and high schools
		Standards and accountability
	Ch. 12	Planning for effective teaching
		Planning in a standards-based environment
	Ch. 13	Preparing instructional materials
		Quality of available software
		Instructional alignment
		Accountability and time constraints
C. Assessment strategies	Ch. 1	Accountability and high-stakes testing
	Ch. 7	Frequent monitoring of student progress
	Ch. 10	Standards and accountability
	Ch. 12	Planning for assessment
	Ch. 13	Using technology to assess student learning

(continued)

III. Teacher Professionalism (approximately 22% of total test)		
A. The reflective practitioner	**Ch. 1**	Characteristics of professionalism
		Emphasis on decision making and reflection
		INTASC: Standards in teacher education
	Ch. 2	Induction and mentoring programs
		Teacher evaluation
		Becoming involved in professional organizations
		Becoming a teacher-leader
		National Board for Professional Teaching Standards
	Each Chapter	
		Decision Making: Defining Yourself as a Professional
B. The larger community	**Ch. 1**	Working with parents and other caregivers
		Collaborating with colleagues
	Ch. 2	Becoming involved in professional organizations
		Becoming a teacher-leader
	Ch. 4	It takes a village: The community-based approach to working with children placed at-risk
	Ch. 7	Strong parental involvement
	Ch. 11	Benefits of parental involvement
		Strategies for involving parents
	Ch. 13	Communication with parents
IV. Communication Techniques (approximately 11% of the test)		
A. Effective verbal and nonverbal communication	**Ch. 1**	Creating productive learning environments
		Collaborative colleague
	Ch. 3	Accommodating cultural interaction patterns
		Instructional responses to learning styles
	Ch. 4	Effective teachers for students placed at-risk
	Ch. 11	Positive teacher expectations
		Communication
		Questioning
	Ch. 13	The Internet as a communication tool
B. Cultural and gender differences in communication	**Ch. 3**	Culturally responsive teaching
		Language diversity in the classroom
		Gender and schooling: Implications for teachers
		Learning styles: Implications for teachers
		Students with exceptionalities: Implications for teachers
	Ch. 4	Effective teachers for students placed at-risk
	Ch. 11	Positive teacher expectations
	Ch. 12	Questioning
C. Stimulating discussion and responses in the classroom	**Ch. 1**	Creating productive learning environments
	Ch. 3	Culturally responsive teaching
		Instructional responses to learning styles
	Ch. 4	Effective teachers for students placed at-risk
	Ch. 12	Questioning
		Lecture discussion
		Cooperative learning
		Guided discovery

Preface

Welcome to the Third Edition!

This third edition of *Introduction to Teaching: Becoming a Professional* continues to introduce beginning education students to the real world of students, teachers, classrooms, and schools through an **integrated case-based approach**. This approach maximizes student understanding of new concepts by providing concrete frames of reference in every chapter. This new edition also offers the reader a **Guided Learning approach** based on solid principles of learning and teaching to help students understand important new educational concepts. As in the first two editions, this text continues to highlight the importance of understanding **diversity** and adapting teaching to meet the needs of diverse students. This third edition also emphasizes the challenges and rewards of **teaching in an urban setting**; the icon at the left identifies where these urban discussions occur. All in all, this emphasis on understanding these realities of students, teachers, classrooms, and schools helps readers answer two fundamental questions:

- Do I want to become a teacher?
- What kind of teacher do I want to become?

A Case-Based Approach

The book introduces readers to the real world of teaching through the use of case studies woven throughout the book. These compelling classroom snapshots help the reader understand new educational concepts by connecting them to the real world of classrooms and schools. Each chapter begins with a case study that provides the framework for the discussion that follows. Case study logos (as shown below) identify cases and vignettes that are integrated throughout every chapter to provide concrete frames of reference for educational concepts. When located at the top of the page, these case study logos let readers know that a case (or cases) is referenced within the discussion.

 Elementary   *Middle*   *Secondary*

Text Themes

The book is organized around three themes, which provide the threads that bind the topics of the chapters together.

- **Professionalism**
- **Diversity**
- **Reform**

Professionalism

Professionalism strongly emphasizes the importance of acquiring knowledge in the process of becoming a professional and the ability to use this knowledge to make decisions in ill-defined situations. The text encourages readers to explore what it means to be a professional teacher and to apply professionalism to their own careers through the following chapter features:

NEW! *Chapter 11, Creating Productive Learning Environments,* emphasizes the human dimension of teaching, illustrates the importance of well-managed classrooms, and offers strategies for involving parents in their children's education.

NEW! *Professional Knowledge: Test Yourself!* allows readers to test their knowledge of chapter content before reading the chapter by taking an interactive survey. We provide specific feedback throughout every chapter.

Decision Making: Defining Yourself as a Professional feature is located at the end of every chapter and helps students consider the implications for a situation related to chapter topics. Readers then decide what they would do in the situation and explore the implications for their development as a professional educator.

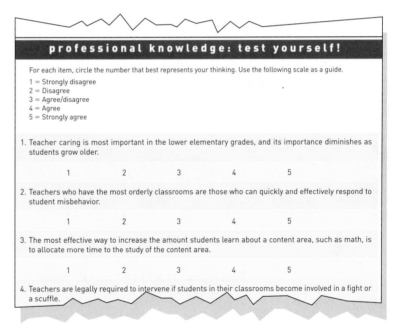

professional knowledge: test yourself!

For each item, circle the number that best represents your thinking. Use the following scale as a guide.

1 = Strongly disagree
2 = Disagree
3 = Agree/disagree
4 = Agree
5 = Strongly agree

1. Teacher caring is most important in the lower elementary grades, and its importance diminishes as students grow older.

       1   2   3   4   5

2. Teachers who have the most orderly classrooms are those who can quickly and effectively respond to student misbehavior.

       1   2   3   4   5

3. The most effective way to increase the amount students learn about a content area, such as math, is to allocate more time to the study of the content area.

       1   2   3   4   5

4. Teachers are legally required to intervene if students in their classrooms become involved in a fight or a scuffle.

Preparing for Your Licensure Exam is a case-based, end-of-chapter feature that helps readers prepare to successfully pass the Praxis II™ exam as well as individual state licensure exams. Readers can take an online exam and receive immediate feedback on the Companion Website (*www.prenhall.com/kauchak*).

- **NEW!** *State-Specific Education Materials* also offers future educators in Florida, Georgia, and Texas the ability to explore state-specific educational content and standards while applying text content through state-specific activities.

Professionalism

 NEW! *Becoming a Professional* **DVD** offers two different video features to expand readers' understanding and connection to chapter content:

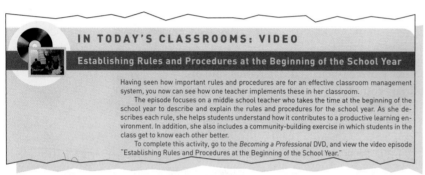

IN TODAY'S CLASSROOMS: VIDEO

Establishing Rules and Procedures at the Beginning of the School Year

Having seen how important rules and procedures are for an effective classroom management system, you now can see how one teacher implements these in her classroom.

The episode focuses on a middle school teacher who takes the time at the beginning of the school year to describe and explain the rules and procedures for the school year. As she describes each rule, she helps students understand how it contributes to a productive learning environment. In addition, she also includes a community-building exercise in which students in the class get to know each other better.

To complete this activity, go to the *Becoming a Professional* DVD, and view the video episode "Establishing Rules and Procedures at the Beginning of the School Year."

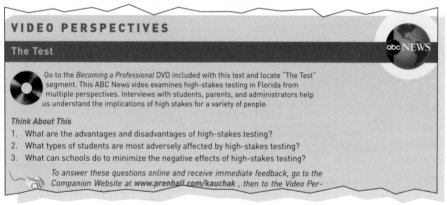

VIDEO PERSPECTIVES

The Test

abc NEWS

Go to the *Becoming a Professional* DVD included with this text and locate "The Test" segment. This ABC News video examines high-stakes testing in Florida from multiple perspectives. Interviews with students, parents, and administrators help us understand the implications of high stakes for a variety of people.

Think About This

1. What are the advantages and disadvantages of high-stakes testing?
2. What types of students are most adversely affected by high-stakes testing?
3. What can schools do to minimize the negative effects of high-stakes testing?

To answer these questions online and receive immediate feedback, go to the Companion Website at www.prenhall.com/kauchak, then to the Video Per-

- **In Today's Classrooms** video clips and in-text feature provide realistic glimpses of teachers working in real classrooms. Students read a summary of the real-world, unscripted, and unrehearsed video episodes, view the video on the DVD; and then respond to online questions by applying what they've seen to the content of the chapter (Chapters 1–3, 6, 7, and 10–13).

- **ABC News** *Video* **and the in-text** *Video Perspectives* features bring to life current and controversial educational issues discussed throughout the text. Readers then have an opportunity to answer questions and apply their responses to their professional philosophy or engage in group discussion (Chapters 1, 4, 5, 8, and 9).

Developing as a Professional: Online Activities are located at the end of every chapter and include the following:

- *Going Into Schools,* a feature on the Companion Website, invites readers to apply the information in each chapter to themselves and school settings. Through focused observations and interviews, readers connect to the schools and classrooms in which they'll teach.

- *Virtual Field Experience: Using Teacher Prep to Explore the Profession* allows readers who do not have a formal field experience component as part of their course to explore issues and topics through Merrill/Prentice Hall's interactive Teacher Prep Website (access code included) through video, artifacts, and research articles (Chapters 1, 3, and 11–13).

- *Online Portfolio Activities* are connected to INTASC standards and encourage readers to evaluate their own professional growth. Activities include visiting the websites of professional organizations, beginning readers' work on their philosophy of education, as well as connecting with local districts and state offices of education. The first portfolio activity in each chapter involves a *Personal Journal Reflection* that asks readers to think about chapter content in terms of their own strengths and goals. Students are able to record their reflection's on the text's Companion Website.

Diversity

Culture, language, ability differences, gender, and exceptionalities are just some areas of diversity that require both teacher understanding and the ability to adapt classroom practices to maximize student learning.

Readers explore today's diverse classrooms and the implications of diversity for classroom teaching through these special features:

NEW! *Teaching in Urban Settings* discussions allow students to learn about the challenges and rewards of teaching in an urban setting and how effective teachers adapt their teaching to meet the needs of students in urban areas. Margin icons identify where these discussions occur.

Exploring Diversity features help readers examine diversity issues in today's classrooms in more depth, consider diversity's important educational implications, and apply the issues to their own teaching philosophy.

exploring diversity

Communicating with Parents

Classrooms with large numbers of students from diverse backgrounds present unique communication challenges. Lower parent participation in school activities is often associated with families that are members of cultural minorities, lower-socioeconomic status (SES) and having a child enrolled in either special education or English-as-a-second-language programs (Tiedt & Tiedt, 2005; C. Weinstein & Mignano, 2003). Each factor makes communication between home and school more challenging, both for parents and teachers.

Economic, Cultural, and Language Barriers

Economics, culture, and language can all create barriers that limit the involvement of minority and low-SES parents in school activities (Barton et al., 2004; Gollnick & Chinn, 2006). Low-SES parents frequently lack resources—such as child care, transportation, Internet access, and even telephones—that allow them to engage in school activities. Multiple jobs often prevent parents from helping their children with homework. In addition, high rates of family mobility can create obstacles to effective parent–school communication (Nakagawa et al., 2002).

Cultural differences can sometimes be misinterpreted. Be-

Latino parents hesitate to become involved in matters they believe are best handled by the school, but teachers sometimes misinterpret this deference to authority as apathy (C. Weinstein & Mignano, 2003).

Language can be another barrier. Parents of bilingual students may not speak English, which leaves the child responsible for interpreting communications sent home by teachers. Homework also poses a special problem because parents cannot interpret assignments or provide help, and schools sometimes compound the difficulty by using educational jargon when they send letters home.

Involving Minority Parents

Teachers can narrow the home–school gap by offering parents specific strategies for working with their children (Epstein, 2001). Let's see how one teacher does this:

Nancy Collins, a middle school English teacher, has students who speak five different native languages in her class. During the first 2 days of school, she prepares a letter to parents, and with the help of her students, translates it into their native languages. The letter begins by describing how pleased she was to have students from

Reform

Standards, accountability, and testing—both teachers and students now encounter all of these as solutions to both educational and societal problems. Throughout the text, we explore the implications of the No Child Left Behind Act, a sweeping federal reform effort that has already changed schools and will continue to shape the profession for new teachers. Readers learn about additional reform issues in the following feature:

Teaching in an Era of Reform frames a specific reform issue in every chapter as it relates to chapter content and asks readers to make a personal evaluation of its potential.

teaching in an era of reform

Assertive Discipline

In their work with teachers, Lee and Marlene Canter (Canter & Canter, 1976, 2001) observed many classrooms that were chaotic, with students out of control. In response they developed a classroom management system called Assertive Discipline which was designed to address this problem.

What Is Assertive Discipline?

Assertive discipline is a comprehensive approach to classroom management that clearly specifies both teachers' and students' rights and responsibilities (Charles, 2005; Manning & Bucher, 2003). According to assertive discipline advocates, teachers have the right to teach in classrooms that are free from disruptions, and students have the right to learn in classrooms that are orderly and free from interruptions. Teachers create an orderly classroom by clearly communicating classroom rules and consistently enforcing the rules with consequences specified in advance. For example, if talking without being given permission is against classroom rules, the first instance of talking results in a consequence, such as the student's name on the board; a second infraction results in a check by the student's name, and a third leads to detention. The specific rules and consequences depend [...]

compare the following teacher responses to a student who is talking instead of beginning an in-class assignment.

Assertive: John, you need to stop talking and begin your assignment, NOW. That's a check by your name. One more and you stay in for recess.

Hostile: John, how many times do I have to tell you to stop talking and get to work. Your misbehavior is driving me crazy!

Nonassertive: John, I don't know what I'm going to do with you. Please stop talking.

The assertive response clearly identifies the misbehavior and communicates the consequences for misbehaving. The other two don't clearly address the misbehavior, nor do they describe consequences for continuing to misbehave.

The Issue

Assertive discipline is a successful but controversial approach to classroom management. Advocates laud the clear definition of teacher and student roles and responsibilities. Teachers are there to teach and students are there to learn, they argue, and the teacher has the right to establish and implement a man-agement [...] that all [...] lace.

For Every Student's Success

The Guided Learning Approach

To make the third edition of the text more usable and reader friendly, we have adopted a *Guided Learning approach* to present the content. This approach is designed to maximize readers' understanding of content. Grounded in basic principles of learning and teaching, the text provides readers with structure, opportunities to actively process the chapter content, feedback, and reviews—each an essential factor for learning from both text and classroom activities. The *Guided Learning approach* has the following features:

Specific Learning Objectives are linked to each of the major headings in the chapters.

Check Your Understanding questions at the end of each major section are directly aligned with the learning objective for that section. Readers can get feedback for these questions in Appendix A, which is located in the back of the text.

Making Connections questions throughout the text help integrate chapter topics with topics already studied. The *Making Connections* questions and feedback are on the Companion Website (*www.prenhall.com/kauchak*.)

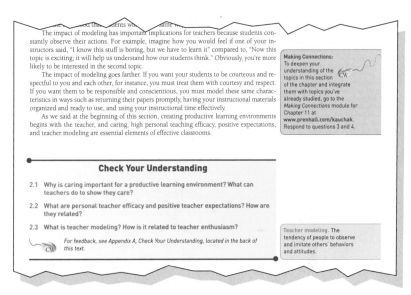

Meeting Your Learning Objectives section at the end of each chapter restates the learning objectives and provides a bulleted summary of the topics covered in each section.

Important Concepts section at the end of each chapter lists key terms and identifies the page on which each term is located and defined.

We hope the *Guided Learning approach* will make readers' understanding of the teaching profession deeper and more meaningful.

Student Supplements

We designed the following features and materials to offer students the resources to succeed in their coursework as well as in their first classroom.

Becoming a Professional **DVD** Two sets of videos, *In Today's Classrooms* videos and *ABC News Videos,* are included on the DVD with this text, allowing readers to view the videos outside of class.

Companion Website This text's Companion Website is located at *www.prenhall.com/kauchak*. The Companion Website provides readers with resources and immediate feedback on exercises and other activities linked to the text. In addition, these activities, projects, and resources enhance and extend chapter content to real-world issues and concepts. Each chapter on the Companion Website contains the following modules (or sections), unless specified otherwise:

- *Chapter Overview, Web Links, and Exploring Diversity Web Links*
- *Self-Assessment* Multiple-choice quizzes with automatic grading provide immediate feedback for students.
- **NEW!** *Making Connections* Readers can answer these chapter-integrated questions online and receive immediate feedback.
- **NEW!** *Professional Knowledge: Test Yourself!* Readers can print out and test their knowledge of chapter content before reading the chapter by taking an interactive survey. Specific feedback is provided throughout every chapter.
- *ABC News Video Perspectives* Thought-provoking questions correspond to the issue-based ABC News Video segments that appear within the text (in Chapters 1, 4, 5, 8, and 9).
- *In Today's Classrooms* Readers can answer critical-thinking questions that connect the *In Today's Classrooms* videos to chapter content (in Chapters 1–3, 6, 7, and 10–13).
- *Preparing for Your Licensure Exam Feedback* Answers are provided to the case-based exercises that are similar to those found on the Praxis™ exam and most state licensure exams.
- **NEW!** *State-Specific Education Materials* Future educators in Florida, Georgia, and Texas can explore state-specific educational content and standards, and apply text content through state-specific activities.
- *Developing as a Professional: Online Activities*

    Going Into Schools
    Virtual Field Experience—including connection to Merrill/Prentice Hall's
      Teacher Prep Website
    Online Portfolio Activities

OneKey Course Management Content OneKey is Merrill/Prentice Hall's exclusive new online resource for students and instructors. OneKey is available in the nationally hosted CourseCompass platform, as well as WebCT and Blackboard.

For more information about *OneKey* please contact your local Merrill/Prentice Hall representative before placing your textbook order.

For Every Professor's Success

The text has the following ancillary materials to assist instructors in their attempts to maximize learning for all students:

Instructor's CD

- **Instructor's Manual/Media Guide and Test Bank** provides concrete chapter-by-chapter instructional and media resources.
- **PowerPoint™ Slides** are also available on the Companion Website and the Instructor Resource Center.
- **Computerized Test Bank** questions give professors access to Multiple-Choice, Critical-Thinking, and Extended Response questions for each chapter. These questions are also available online in the Instructor Resource Center.

Becoming a Professional DVD

- **In Today's Classrooms** case videos are featured in Chapters 1–3, 6, 7, and 10–13.
- **ABC News Video Library** ABC News *Video Perspectives* are featured in Chapters 1, 4, 5, 8, and 9.

Instructor Resource Center

Instructor supplements can also be accessed at our Instructor Resource Center located at *www.prenhall.com*. The Instructor Resource Center opens the door to a variety of print and media resources in downloadable, digital format. Resources available for instructors include

- Instructor Manual/Media Guide and Test Bank
- Computerized Test Bank
- PowerPoint slides
- Request and/or review OneKey, WebCT, and Blackboard course content
- Instructions for downloading a Blackboard or Web CT e-pack

Your one-time registration opens the door to Merrill/Prentice Hall's premium digital resources. You will not have additional forms to fill out or multiple usernames and passwords to remember to access new titles and/or editions. Register today, and maximize your time at every stage of course preparation.

For instructors who have adopted this text and would like to receive book-specific supplements, please contact your Merrill/Prentice Hall sales representative, call Faculty Services at 1-800-526-0485, or e-mail us at *Merrill.marketing@pearsoned.com*. We look forward to hearing from you.

Brief Contents

Contents

Special Features

Video Perspectives

Chapter	Topic

Decision Making: Defining Yourself as a Professional

Chapter	Topic

Teacher Prep Website

Chapter	Topic

Becoming a Professional DVD

ABC News *Video* and *Video Perspectives*

Now available on the DVD included with every copy of *Introduction to Teaching: Becoming a Professional*, Third Edition!

Engage your readers through ABC News video segments, available on the *Becoming a Professional* DVD, focusing on controversial educational issues that illustrate chapter content relevancy and bring chapter content to life. ABC News *Video Perspectives* sections within the text indicate when a video is available and offer a short summary of each episode with discussion questions.

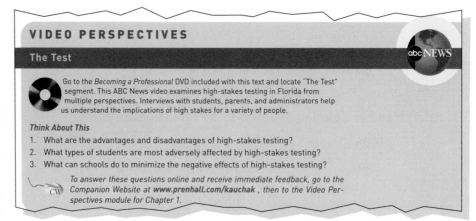

VIDEO PERSPECTIVES

The Test

Go to the *Becoming a Professional* DVD included with this text and locate "The Test" segment. This ABC News video examines high-stakes testing in Florida from multiple perspectives. Interviews with students, parents, and administrators help us understand the implications of high stakes for a variety of people.

Think About This
1. What are the advantages and disadvantages of high-stakes testing?
2. What types of students are most adversely affected by high-stakes testing?
3. What can schools do to minimize the negative effects of high-stakes testing?

To answer these questions online and receive immediate feedback, go to the Companion Website at **www.prenhall.com/kauchak**, then to the Video Perspectives module for Chapter 1.

CHAPTER 1 *Do I Want to Be a Teacher?*
The Test examines the effects of accountability and high-stakes testing in the state of Florida. **Running Time:** 19:44

CHAPTER 4 *Changes in American Society: Their Influences on Today's Schools*
The In Crowd and Social Cruelty analyzes social cruelty and bullying from the perspectives of students at different grade levels. **Running Time:** 38:00

Action, Reaction, and Zero Tolerance examines the effects of zero tolerance policies on schools and students. **Running Time:** 19:31

CHAPTER 5 *Education in the United States: Its Historical Roots*
The Reunion focuses on the reunion of the first group of Black and White students to integrate a wealthy Cleveland suburban school during the Civil Rights Era of U.S. history. **Running Time:** 39:01

CHAPTER 8 *Governance and Finance: Regulating and Funding Schools*
Failing Grade analyzes how financial problems and administrative mismanagement contribute to the problems of an urban school district. **Running Time:** 20:43

CHAPTER 9 *School Law: Ethical and Legal Influences on Teaching*
A Battle Between Faith and Science examines the controversies surrounding the teaching of evolution and creationism in a small town in Pennsylvania. **Running Time:** 19:42

In Today's Classrooms: Videos and Features

Included on the *Becoming a Professional* DVD, *In Today's Classrooms* video clips offer real-life, unrehearsed video cases and present students with a glimpse into the world of professional teachers. *In Today's Classrooms* boxed features throughout the text connect the video episodes to chapter content. Activities and guided reflection questions enable students to explore topics and determine how these concepts and experiences relate to them as professionals.

CHAPTER 1 *Do I Want to Be a Teacher?*
The Multiple Roles of Teachers focuses on a middle school teacher involved in instruction, collaborating with colleagues during a team meeting, and working with parents during a parent–teacher conference. **Running Time:** 12:41

CHAPTER 2 *Developing as a Professional*
Succeeding in Your First Year of Teaching analyzes the experiences of a first-year middle school teacher as she describes the ups and downs, successes, and challenges of surviving and thriving during the beginning of a professional career. **Running Time:** 7:40

CHAPTER 3 *Helping Diverse Learners Succeed in Today's Classrooms*
Culturally Responsive Teaching describes how a fourth-grade teacher adjusts her teaching to accommodate the religious beliefs of a Muslim girl in her classroom. **Running Time:** 5:00

CHAPTER 6 *Educational Philosophy: The Intellectual Foundations of American Education*
Examining Philosophies of Teaching analyzes how different philosophies of teaching result in very different approaches to teaching social studies at the secondary level. **Running Time:** 10:30

CHAPTER 7 *The Organization of American Schools*
The Principal's View of Professionalism focuses on what one middle school principal looks for when he interviews new teachers. **Running Time:** 8:00

CHAPTER 10 *The Curriculum in an Era of Standards and Accountability*
Curriculum, Standards, and Accountability examines the influence of standards and accountability on a second-grade teacher's curriculum. **Running Time:** 12:41

CHAPTER 11 *Creating Productive Learning Environments*
Establishing Rules and Procedures at the Beginning of the School Year describes how one teacher establishes rules and procedures to make her classroom a productive learning environment. **Running Time:** 11:00

CHAPTER 12 *Effective Instruction in American Schools*
Essential Teaching Skills in an Urban Classroom illustrates how essential teaching skills can be integrated into the science classroom. **Running Time:** 14:05

CHAPTER 13 *Technology in American Schools*
Integrating Technology Into Instruction examines how teachers integrate databases and PowerPoint presentations into their instruction. **Running Time:** 5:00

About the Authors

Donald Kauchak

Don has taught and worked in schools in nine different states and in higher education for 35 years. He has published in a number of scholarly journals, including the *Journal of Educational Research*, *Journal of Teacher Education*, *Teaching and Teacher Education*, *Phi Delta Kappan*, and *Educational Leadership*. In addition to this text, he has co-authored or co-edited six other books on education. He has also been a principal investigator on federal and state grants examining teacher development and evaluation practices, and presents regularly at the American Educational Research Association.

Don strongly believes in the contribution that public schools make to our democracy, and his two children benefited greatly from their experiences in state-supported K–12 schools and public institutions of higher education.

Paul Eggen

Paul has worked in higher education for 35 years. He is a consultant to public schools in his university's service area and has provided support to teachers in 12 different states. Paul has also worked with teachers in international schools in 23 countries, including Africa, South Asia, the Middle East, Central America, South America, Europe, and Japan. He has published several articles in national journals, is the co-author or co-editor of six other books, and presents regularly at national and international conferences.

Paul is strongly committed to public education. His wife is a middle school teacher in a public school; his two children are graduates of public schools and state-supported universities.

Acknowledgments

A project such as this text is the result of the collective effort of many people that we would like to both thank and acknowledge. First, special thanks to our editor, Deb Stollenwerk; she believed in this project from the beginning and supported us in innumerable ways. Amy Nelson, our developmental editor, brought energy and dedication to the project and helped turn our ideas into reality. Luanne Dreyer Elliot, our copy editor, made this the cleanest and clearest edition, yet. Alex Wolf, our production editor, conscientiously steered the final project to completion, ensuring the highest level of text quality. Darcy Betts, our link to instructors, helped us craft our thoughts into a text that will hopefully help teachers develop to their fullest potential. We are deeply grateful for all their efforts.

In addition we would like to acknowledge all the reviewers who helped us understand what students and instructors need and want: Adel T. Al-Bataineh, Illinois State University; Harriet Arnold, University of the Pacific; Virginia Batchelor, Medaille College; Bruce Butknecht, University of North Florida; Debra DeFoor, Purdue University North Central; John Huss, Northern Kentucky University; Marcia Janson, Pennsylvania State University, Erie; Lisa Kunkleman, Baker College-Flint; Cindy Marble, Arizona State University–East Campus; Jacqueline L. Mason, Northwestern State University; David A. Meckly, University of Nevada at Las Vegas; Jane Newaak, Appalachian State University; David Pratt, Purdue University North Central; Ann Selleck, Lansing Community College; Geoff Quick, Lansing Community College; and Mack Welford, Roanoke College.

Finally, we would appreciate your feedback about the text, as well as any of the supplements that accompany it. Please feel free to contact either of us at don.kauchak@gmail.com or peggen@comcast.net. We promise to respond to you.

THE TEACHING PROFESSION

Do I Want to Be a Teacher?

Chapter Outline

Rewards and Challenges in Teaching
  Rewards in Teaching • Challenges in Teaching

The Teaching Profession
  Characteristics of Professionalism • Are
  Teachers Professionals? • Putting Teacher
  Professionalism into Perspective

Diversity: The Changing Face of U.S.
Classrooms

The Modern Reform Movement in Education
  Changes in Teacher Preparation • INTASC:
  Standards in Teacher Education • Teaching in an
  Era of Reform

Learning Objectives

After you have completed your study of this chapter,
you should be able to:

1. Describe the major rewards and
   challenges of teaching.

2. Describe the different characteristics of
   professionalism, and explain how they
   relate to teaching.

3. Identify the different dimensions of
   learner diversity, and explain why
   understanding different teaching and
   learning environments is important for
   beginning teachers.

4. Explain how the current reform
   movement in education is changing the
   teaching profession.

Case Studies

  Elementary

 Middle

Secondary

Andy Sacks/Getty Images Inc.–Stone Allstock

"Do I want to be a teacher?" This question is probably on your mind as you begin your study of this book. In this chapter, we hope to help you begin answering the question by providing you with information about the teaching profession. As you read the following case studies, think about each teacher's experiences and how they compare to your own.

I always liked working with kids. I enjoyed watching my little brother when my mom ran errands, and I often helped out with summer youth programs. In high school I started thinking about being a music teacher, since I enjoyed playing the piano and singing in choral groups.

Then, I went to college and one of my courses required us to be a high school teacher's aide. I worked with a music teacher but never felt like I really fit in. Luckily, in a second course I had a chance to work in an elementary school. I went home after the first day and thought, "Yes, this is it."

There have been ups and downs, of course. My first job was in an urban second-grade classroom with 26 kids. Fortunately, I had an aide who spoke Spanish, and she was a huge help, since several of my students were still struggling to learn English.

Now here I am, 10 years later, married with a family of my own, and I still love teaching. The first few years were a bit of a struggle, but I learned so much. Now I've got my own student teacher and am eager to help her figure it all out. (Amy Carson, first-grade teacher in an urban elementary school)

Before I became a teacher, I worked for 20 years in the pharmaceutical industry, first in a research lab and then as a project manager. It was challenging, and I made a good salary, but I began to feel that there was more to life than making money for some big company.

A couple years ago I read a book in which the author described the difference between a person's "job" and a person's "work." Your job is how you make money; your work is how you contribute to the world. It began to crystallize everything for me. Business, for me, was a job, but I didn't really have any "work."

Then, I thought about my high school chemistry teacher, and I remembered how much he loved that stuff. I began to think about teaching, and, to make a long story short, I went back to school, and this time I did what I've always wanted to do. Of course it's tough some days. The kids can be "off the wall," and I periodically feel like I'm drowning in paperwork. But, when you see the lightbulb go on for someone, it's all worth it. Now, my job and my work are the same thing. (Matt Shepard, high school science teacher in a suburban high school and recent entry into teaching)

Some of you probably have characteristics similar to both Amy and Matt. You're intelligent and introspective, and you've had a number of life experiences. You've thought about teaching but aren't sure if it's for you or where you might fit in the profession. Others of you are less certain, still in the process of deciding what you want to do with your life. You enjoyed your school experiences, and most of your ideas about teaching are based on them. The idea of working with young people is attractive, but you're still not sure.

To begin answering the question "Do I want to be a teacher?" let's consider some reasons people go into teaching by responding to the accompanying survey on page 5.

We gave the same survey to other prospective teachers, averaged their responses, and ranked them from most (1) to least (9) important reasons for becoming a teacher. Table 1.1 summarizes the results. Let's see how yours compare.

We see from Table 1.1 that the desire to work with young people (Item 5) and wanting to contribute to society (Item 6) were survey participants' two most important reasons for considering teaching. These reasons are consistent with Amy's and Matt's thinking, and they're also consistent with polls of teachers over a nearly 25-year period (National Education Association, 1997).

A Public Agenda poll of new teachers found similar results, with 86 percent of new teachers viewing teaching as "a true sense of calling," 75 percent considering teaching a lifelong choice, and 68 percent reporting teaching as very satisfying. In addition, an amazing 96 percent of beginning teachers reported that teaching is work they love to do (Wadsworth, 2001).

Let's look more closely at the reasons people go into teaching.

Rewards and Challenges in Teaching

People go into teaching because it's rewarding, and, as with any occupation, it can also be challenging. We examine both in this section.

Rewards in Teaching

Intrinsic rewards. Rewards that come from within oneself and are personally satisfying for emotional or intellectual reasons.

Extrinsic rewards. Rewards that come from outside oneself, such as job security and vacations.

The rewards in teaching can be either **intrinsic**, those that come within oneself and are personally satisfying for emotional or intellectual reasons, or **extrinsic**, those that come from the outside, such as job security and vacations. Let's look at each.

Intrinsic Rewards

Many people become teachers because of intrinsic rewards, which fall into two broad categories—emotional and intellectual.

professional knowledge: test yourself!

For each item, circle the number that best represents your thinking. Use the following scale as a guide.

1 = Strongly disagree
2 = Disagree
3 = Uncertain
4 = Agree
5 = Strongly agree

1. Job security is a major reason I'm considering becoming a teacher.

   1   2   3   4   5

2. My family has strongly influenced my decision to teach.

   1   2   3   4   5

3. Long summer vacations are important to me as I consider teaching as a career.

   1   2   3   4   5

4. I've never really considered any other occupation besides teaching.

   1   2   3   4   5

5. My desire to work with young people is an important reason I'm considering becoming a teacher.

   1   2   3   4   5

6. I'm thinking of teaching because I'd like to contribute to our society.

   1   2   3   4   5

7. My interest in a subject matter field is a major reason I'm thinking about becoming a teacher.

   1   2   3   4   5

8. I'm considering entering teaching because of the influence of a former elementary or secondary teacher.

   1   2   3   4   5

9. I'm considering teaching because of the opportunity for a lifetime of self-growth.

   1   2   3   4   5

This is available in a downloadable format on the Companion Website for personal portfolio use.

TABLE 1.1   Responses to Interest in Teaching Inventory

Survey Rank	Item Focus	Average Response of Students	Item
1	Work with youth	4.6	5
2	Value to society	4.5	6
3	Self-growth	3.9	9
4	Content interest	3.8	7
5	Influence of teachers	3.6	8
6	Job security	3.1	1
7	Summer vacations	2.9	3
8	Family influence	2.8	2
9	Other careers not considered	1.9	4

Emotional Rewards. To begin this section, let's look at some true stories that teachers have shared.

Kasia, 23, calls her boyfriend, Jeff. It's "Teacher Appreciation Week" at her middle school, and she has just received a dozen roses from a group of her seventh-grade science students.

"I was always on them about whispering too," she excitedly tells Jeff. "I maybe would have expected this from my fifth-period class, but never from this bunch.

"Let me read the note I got from them," she continues. She reads,

"Thank you for all that you've done for us and for all the wonderful things that you've teached [sic] us. You are truly an amazing teacher. Thank you again."

Happy Teacher Appreciation Week,
Sincerely, Alicia, Rosa, Shannon, Tina, Stephanie, Melissa, Jessica, and Becca

"That's wonderful," Jeff laughs. "Good thing you're not their English teacher."
"I know. I showed Isabel [the students' English teacher] the note, and she broke up. 'So much for grammar,' she said."

Miguel Rodriguez, 42, another middle school teacher, received the following note from one of his students.

Mr. Rodriguez,

I wanted to think of some creative way to thank you for being the best teacher I ever had. (But I couldn't.)

Even though all the geography skills I'll ever use in my life I learned in second grade, I just wanted to say thanks for teaching me how to really prepare for life in the years to come.

Every day I looked forward to coming to your class (and not just because of Mike [a boy in the class]). I always enjoyed your class, because there was a hidden message about life in there somewhere.

Your [sic] my very favorite teacher and you've taught me some of the best lessons in life I could ever learn. Thank you so much.

A grateful student,
Erica Jacobs

P.S. No, I didn't write this to raise my grade.

These notes and the flowers Kasia received symbolize some of the emotional rewards in teaching. "They're what keep you going," Miguel commented matter-of-factly while discussing his enjoyment of his work.

Sharon, a veteran first-grade teacher, also describes emotional rewards in her work. "The beginning of the day gets me going," she said, smiling, when she described her continued commitment to her career. "I stand at the door, and the kids give me a hug, a high five, or a handshake when they come in the room. Even if the previous day was a bad one, all those little faces are enough to get me started all over again."

Sometimes students show their affection in strange ways, as this middle school teacher experienced:

> *Joanne, a first-year teacher, entered her classroom first thing in the morning on her birthday. Her students had arranged with the custodian to gain access to her room and had moved all the desks to the center of the room and had wrapped them with tape and toilet paper. How would you react?*
>
> *Joanne was delighted. "I called [the perpetrators] out of class and had them come down and [another teacher] took a picture of them standing out in the middle of it all. I left it here all day. I made them sit on the floor. It was really fun. It was really a fun day." (Bullough, 1989, p. 86)*

It helps to have a sense of humor when you teach. All teachers reap emotional rewards from their work with students, whether they are wide-eyed first graders, middle school students like Erica Jacobs, or high school seniors struggling to become adults.

Intellectual Rewards.   While emotional rewards motivate them as well, many people choose to teach because they are interested in a certain content area and want to share their interest and excitement with others (Liston, 2004).

> *David Ling, a high school physics teacher, enthusiastically begins his class: "Think about these questions and try to figure out what they have in common," and he then writes the following on the board:*

> *Why do we have seatbelts in our cars?*
> *Why does an automatic washer have holes in the drum?*
> *How does a dog shake the water off itself when it comes out of a pond?*

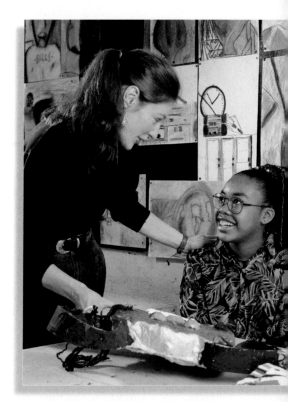

> *The students look at the list, and after several seconds David continues, "Now, what have we been studying?"*
>
> *"Inertia," Taneka responds after hesitating briefly.*
>
> *"Exactly," David says, smiling. "So let's review for a minute. What is inertia? . . . Go ahead, Dana."*
>
> *"The tendency . . . of something moving to keep on moving . . . straight."*
>
> *"Or something not moving to remain still," Jamal adds.*
>
> *"Excellent," David responds with a nod. "Now, let's answer the questions on the board using the idea of inertia."*
>
> *With David's guidance, the students conclude that if their cars suddenly stop, their bodies tend to keep moving because of inertia, and seatbelts stop them, so they don't get hurt. They also decide that inertia separates water from clothes in the washer because the water goes straight out through the holes in the drum, but the clothes are kept in it. Finally, they determine that as the dog shakes one way, and then stops, the water keeps moving, and the same thing happens when it shakes the other way. So the dog uses the principle of inertia to shake the water from itself.*
>
> *"Neat," Rebecca says. "Where'd you get that stuff, Mr. Ling?"*

Teachers' interactions with their students provide a major source of intrinsic rewards. (Tom Watson/Merrill)

"Oh, I thought up the questions over time," David replies. "The more I study, the more examples I find. . . . That's what we're here for. We study science so we can learn how the world around us works."

Our survey, discussed earlier (Table 1.1), found that "the opportunity for a lifetime of self-growth" and "interest in a subject matter field" were reasons for considering teaching, ranking 3 and 4 out of 9. Learning more about the world and seeing students get excited about the same things we do are some of the intellectual rewards of teaching. One teacher candidate commented, "I would like to think that contact with me would . . . deepen their confidence in their own thinking and make them more curious about the world" (Richardson & Watt, 2005, p. 485). Not surprisingly, these intellectual rewards also help keep veteran teachers in the field. One researcher studying exemplary veteran teachers concluded, "Without exception, intellectual stimulation is a burning need of the teachers I interviewed" (Williams, 2003, p. 72).

Extrinsic Rewards

Extrinsic rewards also attract people to teaching. For example, job security and summer vacations ranked sixth and seventh, respectively, in the survey.

The job security found in teaching is greater than in most other occupations. For example, after a short probation period—usually about 3 years—teachers are typically awarded tenure. Originally designed to attract good people and protect them from political pressures, tenure provides teachers with job security. (You will study teacher tenure in detail in Chapter 9.)

For some, working in a profession with long vacations is rewarding. According to an old joke, a student asked to identify three reasons for going into teaching responded, "June, July, and August." In addition, teachers have vacations throughout the year at times when vacations are most attractive—the Friday after Thanksgiving, the winter holiday season, and spring break, for example.

In addition to job security and desirable vacations, teachers enjoy convenient work schedules and occupational status. Teachers' schedules are similar to those of students, so, for example, teachers' own children don't go home to empty houses after school. Additionally, despite perceptions to the contrary, the teaching profession enjoys considerable occupational status (National Education Association, 2002). If you have doubts, consider how parents feel as they approach a parent–teacher conference. They want nothing more than to hear that everything is okay in school and that their child is growing academically and socially. Into no other profession's hands is so much care of young people placed.

Teachers' salaries are another extrinsic reward that both motivate teachers to enter and to leave the profession. While low compared to other professions, teacher salaries, when combined with benefits and favorable work schedules, provide a major extrinsic reward for entering the profession. However, low salaries are often cited as a major reason for leaving the profession after several years of teaching (Ingersoll & Smith, 2003). Salaries are improving, however. For instance, the average teacher salary in the United States for 2003–2004 was $46,597, ranging from a high of $56,516 in Connecticut to a low of $33,236 in South Dakota. In the same year, the average beginning salary was almost $32,000. Table 1.2 lists the average and beginning teacher salaries for each state in 2003–2004.

Union officials call the salary picture a "mixed bag" (American Federation of Teachers, 2004). While teacher salaries have risen an average of 3 percent the last 5 years, they still fall well below the starting salaries of other occupations such as engineering ($50,033) and accounting ($40,779).

Your beginning salary will depend on a number of factors, such as the local cost of living and the location of the school district. As you'll see in Chapter 8, local property taxes are the major funding source for schools, so teachers' salaries depend, in large part, on property values. Also, urban districts typically have higher salaries than their rural counterparts because of a higher cost of living. Though money isn't everything, research shows that higher

TABLE 1.2   Beginning and Average Teacher Salaries for U.S. States in 2003–2004

State	Average Salary	Beginning Salary
Alabama	$38,282	$30,973
Alaska	51,136	40,027
Arizona	42,324	28,236
Arkansas	39,226	26,129
California	56,444	35,135
Colorado	43,318	31,296
Connecticut	56,516	34,462
Delaware	51,112	34,566
Florida	40,598	30,696
Georgia	45,848	35,116
Hawaii	45,456	37,615
Idaho	40,111	25,908
Illinois	53,820	35,114
Indiana	45,791	29,784
Iowa	38,381	26,967
Kansas	38,622	28,530
Kentucky	39,831	28,416
Louisiana	37,123	29,655
Maine	39,864	25,901
Maryland	50,303	33,760
Massachusetts	53,274	34,041
Michigan	54,474	34,377
Minnesota	45,010	30,772
Mississippi	36,217	28,106
Missouri	38,247	28,938
Montana	37,184	24,032
Nebraska	39,635	28,527
Nevada	43,211	27,942
New Hampshire	42,689	27,367
New Jersey	53,663	37,061
New Mexico	38,469	31,920
New York	55,181	36,400

(continued)

TABLE 1.2   Beginning and Average Teacher Salaries for U.S. States in 2003–2004
(continued)

State	Average Salary	Beginning Salary
North Carolina	43,211	27,572
North Dakota	35,411	24,108
Ohio	47,791	28,692
Oklahoma	35,061	29,473
Oregon	47,829	33,396
Pennsylvania	52,640	34,140
Rhode Island	54,809	32,902
South Carolina	41,162	27,883
South Dakota	33,236	25,504
Tennessee	40,318	30,449
Texas	40,476	32,741
Utah	38,976	26,130
Vermont	43,009	25,819
Virginia	43,936	32,437
Washington	45,437	30,159
West Virginia	38,496	26,692
Wisconsin	41,687	23,952
Wyoming	39,537	28,900
U.S. AVERAGE	$46,597	$31,704

Source: American Federation of Teachers (2004).

salaries are related to teachers' staying longer in the profession in general, as well as remaining in a particular district or location (Guarino, Santibañez, & Daley, 2006).

Other economic factors also influence the attractiveness of teaching. For example, annual salary increases are virtually guaranteed, and, as we said earlier in the chapter, vacation periods are ideal. Medical, dental, and retirement benefits are usually provided, and job security is high. In addition, teachers are often paid supplements for extra duties, such as club sponsorships, coaching, chairing departments (e.g., chairing the English department in a middle school), and mentoring beginning teachers. In schools with year-round schedules, teachers work 11 months of the year versus 9 or 10 and are paid accordingly.

Challenges in Teaching

Teaching can be rewarding, but it is also challenging. The complexities of classrooms and the multiple roles that teachers perform are two of those challenges.

Complexities of Classrooms

"Classrooms are complex" is an understatement. Teachers make literally hundreds of decisions every day, and many must be made with nearly split-second timing (Kennedy, 2006). What does it feel like to actually teach and make these decisions? Let's look at different teachers' experiences.

Ken, an elementary teacher, shares the following incident in his teaching journal:

March 3: My class is sitting in a circle. I look up and notice one of the girls, Sylvia, is crying. Joey, she claims, has called her a fat jerk. The rest of the students all look at me to watch my response. I consider the alternatives: send Joey to hallway and talk to him in a few minutes; have Joey sit next to me; ask Joey to apologize; direct Sylvia to get a thick skin; ask Sylvia, "How can you solve this problem?"; send Joey to principal; have Joey write an apology letter; ask Joey, "Why did you do this?"; ignore the situation completely; keep Sylvia and Joey in for recess for dialogue; put Joey's name on the board; yell at Joey; send Sylvia and Joey to hallway to work out problem; tell them to return to their seats and write in journals about problem.

It took me about 10 seconds to run through these alternatives, and after each one I thought of reasons why it wasn't a good idea. By the time I look up at Sylvia after this brief introspection, she had stopped crying and was chattering away with a friend about something else. On surface, the problem had gone away. (Winograd, 1998, p. 296)

Joanne, a first-year middle school English teacher, has the following experience the first day back after a 4-day holiday. The students are excited and difficult to settle down. They talk about their weekends, some wander in late, and others are listless as she tries to get class started.

Finally, she can begin, but keeping them on task is a struggle. They don't listen to her directions, and their questions, complaints, and requests for help seem never-ending.

Joanne limps through the day, and as the end appears in sight, she nearly explodes. While her back is turned, one student throws a sponge ball across the room, another jumps up to catch it and knocks his desk over with a clatter. The rest of the class erupts into laughter, and Joanne says loudly, "Everyone settle down this instant, or there will be after-school detention." This seems to work. "If every day was like this, I'm not sure I would make it," she sighs after her students have finally left for the day.

Two high school student teachers discuss their frustrations in taking attendance on the day of a special school dance held during regular class hours:

Cheryl: *One boy comes in, he's dressed up. He says, "I have to go to the dance." Comes in early and tells me. Good kid. I'm like, "OK, that's fine Aaron." Then, Kent comes in five minutes late. This is tall Kent, has his own band and never lets me mark him tardy even though he's always tardy, "I'm going to the dance!" After I've already started class! "Ahem. Thank you, Kent. Please sit down." So he's wanting to leave but I can't let him go because he just interrupted my class and . . . I was so mad at him. So I say, "Do you have a ticket?" And he's like, "Well, yeah," and pulls out a ticket that goes to the movie he went to on Friday night and I say, "No, that's not the right ticket."*

Dani: *What color was it?*

Cheryl: *Pink.*

Dani: *What was the color for the . . . ?*

Cheryl: *The other guy who was legit had a gray one. But then, then, I don't know. And I mean WHO KNOWS! I said, "You're not on my excused list" but neither was the other guy and I'm like . . .*

Dani: *I didn't even get an excused list! I didn't even know this dance was—I kind of heard something over the intercom. (Dulude-Lay, 2000, p. 4)*

Figure 1.1   Characteristics of Classrooms

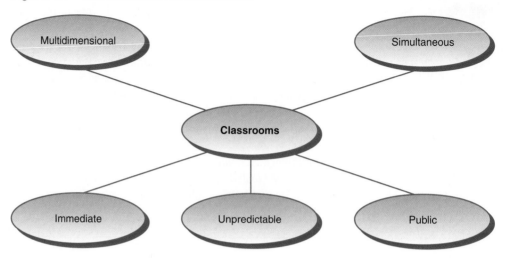

Each of these vignettes illustrates the challenging and sometimes frustrating world of teaching. Researchers have identified several characteristics of classrooms that contribute to this complexity (W. Doyle, 1986):

- Classrooms are multidimensional. Large numbers of events and tasks take place because so many people are in a classroom.
- Classroom events are simultaneous. The events and tasks happen at the same time.
- Classroom events are immediate. Events occur rapidly, sometimes too rapidly.
- Classrooms are unpredictable. Events often take unexpected turns.
- Classrooms are public. Teachers do their jobs in "fishbowls" with people constantly observing their actions.

These characteristics are outlined in Figure 1.1 and discussed in the following sections.

Classrooms Are Multidimensional.   Think about all the different roles you'll perform today. You're a student, a friend, a coworker, and perhaps even a parent. Your life is multidimensional. A classroom is as well; when you teach, you'll need to attend to a number of different events and perform various roles. For instance, while working with one group of students, you'll need to monitor other groups working on assignments. Students will request permission for routine activities, such as going to the bathroom, and learners with special needs may be pulled out of your classroom for extra help. Some students will be attentive and involved in your learning activities, whereas others will drift off and may even be disruptive. Ken found this out when he tried to begin his lesson.

Announcements, assemblies, and other school functions also add to the complexity. For example, Cheryl and Dani had to adjust their plans because of the dance. "If I only had time to teach," is a common teacher lament.

Classroom Events Are Simultaneous.   Many classroom events occur at the same time. For example, while Ken and Joanne were trying to teach, management problems arose. And, as Cheryl and Dani were trying to take roll and begin class, students came in needing immediate attention, asking questions, showing hall passes, and presenting admission slips. Knowing which problem to attend to first can be challenging, if not bewildering.

Classroom Events Are Immediate.   Experts estimate that teachers make somewhere between 800 and 1,500 decisions every day (Jackson, 1968; Murray, 1986). Beyond the sheer numbers, the need to make decisions *right now* adds to the demands on a teacher. Sylvia was crying; Ken needed to decide whether or not to intervene. Kent came in with a bogus hall pass; Cheryl needed to decide whether or not to honor it. And they needed to decide "*right* *now."* The immediacy of classroom life requires challenging, split-second decision making.

Classrooms Are Unpredictable.   *One first-grade teacher, attempting to involve students in a lesson about a story they had read about shoes, brought a shoe into class. Pulling it out of a bag, she began, "What can you tell me about this shoe?"*

"It's red," Mike responded.

The shoe was black—there was no sign of red on it anywhere!

Effective teachers plan carefully, but even this may not be enough. Planning for this child's response was impossible. Similarly, Ken couldn't anticipate the incident between Joey and Sylvia, and the same is true for many of the events in Joanne's, Cheryl's, and Dani's classrooms. Often, teachers have little time for thoughtful analysis and consideration of alternatives. After the fact, it is often easy to see what should have been done, but in the heat of the moment, a teacher must respond immediately to unanticipated events. Classrooms are exciting, unpredictable places—a major reason people find teaching both exhilarating and challenging.

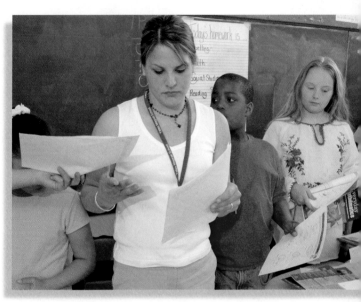

Classrooms are complex learning environments in which many events occur simultaneously. (© Ellen B. Senisi/Ellen Senisi)

Classrooms Are Public.   The fact that we teach in front of people is obvious. In a sense, we're on stage, and our triumphs and mistakes occur in public for all to see. As we work with students, we are bound to make mistakes, and our actions can have unintended consequences. Ken ignored Joey's (allegedly) calling Sylvia a "fat jerk." Did he unintentionally communicate that verbal abuse is acceptable? Cheryl considered allowing one student to slip out of her class with a bogus pass. If she had, would other students try the same thing? A "fishbowl" is an apt metaphor for teaching; as we swim through our day, both students and other teachers watch us and form judgments about our actions.

Will your first year of teaching necessarily consist of a series of unpredictable situations? Probably. Learning to teach is a journey filled with unanticipated events, and your first year will be exhausting, at times overwhelming, and frequently exhilarating. One book about the experiences of first-year teachers is aptly named *The Roller Coaster Year* (K. Ryan, 1992). It may help to remember, however, that thousands of other beginning teachers have not only survived but flourished.

The Multiple Roles of Teaching

The multiple professional roles that teachers perform is a second factor that makes teaching so challenging. Three of the most important include:

- Creating productive learning environments
- Working with parents and other caregivers
- Collaborating with colleagues

Creating Productive Learning Environments.   Creating a productive learning environment is a teacher's most essential role. A productive learning environment is one that is safe and inviting, focuses on learning, and provides opportunities for social and personal growth. In productive learning environments, students feel safe, both physically and emotionally, and the day-to-day routines—including the values, expectations, learning experiences, and both spoken and unspoken rules and conventions—are designed to help students learn and grow (Weinstein, 2007). Creating productive learning environments is so important that we devote an entire chapter (11) to the topic.

Working with Parents and Other Caregivers.   Learning should be a cooperative venture, with teachers, students, and parents/caregivers working together. Because the home environment has such a powerful influence on learning, teachers need to develop strategies to increase parental involvement in their children's academic life. These strategies should go beyond traditional once-a-year parent–teacher conferences and should actively involve parents, encouraging them to monitor and help with homework, limit television viewing, and read to their young children (Epstein, 2001; Marzano, 2003).

Students benefit from home–school cooperation in several ways:

- Greater willingness to do homework
- Higher long-term achievement
- More positive attitudes and behaviors
- Better attendance and graduation rates
- Greater enrollment in postsecondary education (Garcia, 2004; Hong & Ho, 2005)

These outcomes result from parents' increased participation in school activities, higher expectations for their children's achievement, and teachers' increased understanding of learners' home environments. Deciding how to respond to a student's disruptive behavior is easier, for example, when his teachers know that his mother or father has lost a job, his parents are going through a divorce, or a family member is ill.

Parent–teacher collaboration can also have long-term benefits for teachers. Teachers who encourage parental involvement have more positive feelings about teaching and their school, and they also have higher expectations for parents and rate them as being more helpful and more likely to follow through on teacher requests (Epstein, 2001).

Virtually all schools have formal communication channels, such as open houses (usually occurring within the first 2 weeks of the school year when teachers introduce themselves and describe general guidelines); interim progress reports, which tell parents about their youngsters' achievements at the midpoint of each grading period; parent–teacher conferences; and, of course, report cards. (We examine strategies for promoting parental involvement in Chapter 11.)

Making Connections:
To deepen your CW understanding of the topics in this section of the chapter and integrate them with topics you've already studied, go to the *Making Connections* module for Chapter 1 at **www.prenhall.com/kauchak**. Respond to questions 1–3.

Collaborating with Colleagues.   A third major teacher role is collaborating with colleagues. Teachers spend considerable time and effort collaborating with their colleagues, during which effective teachers make cooperative decisions about topics such as curriculum, assessment, grading, and teaching strategies. Administrators assess teachers' ability and inclination to collaborate in the initial job interview, and many principals view collaboration as one of the most essential characteristics of effective teachers.

At the beginning of the chapter, we said that our goal in writing it was to help you decide whether or not you want to be a teacher. Being aware of the rewards and challenges in teaching and teachers' multiple roles can help you make this decision.

IN TODAY'S CLASSROOMS: VIDEO

The Multiple Roles of Teachers

Having read about the multiple roles that teachers perform, you now can see one teacher immersed in these roles. The episode focuses on a middle school teacher involved in instruction, collaborating with colleagues in a team meeting, and working with parents during a parent–teacher conference.

To view this video, go to the *Becoming a Professional* DVD included with this text, click on *In Today's Classrooms*, and then this chapter's video: *The Multiple Roles of Teachers.*

To answer questions about the video online and receive immediate feedback, go to the Companion Website at **www.prenhall.com/kauchak**, *then to the* In Today's Classroom *module for Chapter 1.*

Check Your Understanding

1.1   What are the major rewards in teaching?

1.2   What are the major challenges in teaching?

1.3   Identify the four most often cited reasons to enter teaching.

 For feedback, go to Appendix A, Check Your Understanding, *located in the back of this text.*

The Teaching Profession

What does it mean to be a professional? Are teachers professionals? In the last 20 years, attempts to answer these questions have increased (Labaree, 2004, 2006; Neville, Sherman, & Cohen, 2005). Advocates contend that developing teaching into a true profession comparable to medicine and law would benefit teachers, students, and their parents. For teachers it would mean better preparation programs and higher standards for performance and ethics. For students and their parents, increased professionalism could result in parents more fully trusting teachers to help their children grow and develop. We believe in the potential of professionalization to transform teaching in many positive ways and have made it a major theme of this text. But let's examine the issue further.

Characteristics of Professionalism

Why are occupations such as medicine and law considered professions? Researchers examining these and other established professions have identified the following characteristics of **professionalism**:

- A specialized body of knowledge
- Autonomy
- Emphasis on decision making and reflection
- Ethical standards for conduct (Labaree, 2004; Neville et al., 2005)

These characteristics are discussed in the following sections.

A Specialized Body of Knowledge

Professionals understand and utilize a specialized body of knowledge in serving their clients (see Figure 1.2 on page 16). A physician, for example, understands and can recognize symptoms of diseases and other ailments and can prescribe medications, surgical procedures, or other forms of therapy to eliminate both the symptoms and their causes. People seek the advice and help of physicians because of their specialized knowledge.

Do teachers possess specialized knowledge? Researchers believe the answer is yes and suggest that this knowledge exists in four forms (Borko & Putnam, 1996):

- *Knowledge of content:* A thorough understanding of the content they will be teaching such as math, science, geography, or literature. Research shows that content knowledge influences both what and how teachers teach (T. Smith, Desimone, & Ueno, 2005).
- *Pedagogical content knowledge:* The ability to illustrate abstract concepts, such as equivalent fractions in math or nationalism in history, in ways that are understandable to students.

Professionalism. An occupation characterized by a specialized body of knowledge with emphasis on autonomy, decision making, reflection, and ethical standards for conduct.

Figure 1.2   Professionalism Requires a Specialized Body of Knowledge

- *General pedagogical knowledge:* Knowledge of general principles of teaching and learning, such as the ability to maintain an orderly and learning-focused classroom or to guide student learning with questions.
- *Knowledge of learners and learning:* Knowledge of theories of development and learning, such as understanding that learners, even in high school, tend to be egocentric, seeing the world from their own perspectives and ignoring the views of others.

To these we add knowledge of the profession, which includes an understanding of the social, historical and philosophical, and organizational and legal aspects of teaching, together with the ability and inclination to continue learning. These different dimensions of knowledge allow teachers to make professional decisions in complex, ill-defined situations.

The ability and inclination to continue learning is also essential for professionals. Just as physicians must continually upgrade their knowledge of medications, surgical procedures, and therapies, teachers must stay abreast of research in their field. For instance, intuition suggests that we encourage students who aren't successful to work harder, but research indicates that this can be counterproductive. Young children generally believe they are already working hard, so they're bewildered by the suggestion, and older students often believe that an admonition to work hard is an indicator of low ability (Brophy, 2004; Pintrich & Schunk, 2002). Teachers who are aware of this research encourage students to change the *way* they study instead of the *amount* they study. Without this professional knowledge, teachers wouldn't be able to adapt their instruction to best meet students' needs. Much of this text is designed to help you develop your knowledge of the profession.

Extended Training for Licensure.   Extended training for licensure is required to develop these different forms of professional knowledge. As with physicians, lawyers, and engineers, teachers must earn a license that allows them to practice their profession. The license is intended to certify that the teacher is competent, and, as with other professions, teachers must periodically renew their license to confirm that they are staying current in their fields. Teachers need at least a bachelor's degree before licensure, and in many states they must complete the degree in a content area, such as math or English, before they begin teacher-preparation experiences (Darling-Hammond & Bransford, 2005). Licensure also requires clinical experiences, such as internships, which are designed to ensure that teachers can apply the professional knowledge they have acquired in the real world of schools.

Autonomy

Autonomy. The capacity to control one's own professional life.

With knowledge also comes **autonomy**, the capacity to control one's own professional life. Professionals have the authority to make decisions based on their specialized knowledge

Figure 1.3   Professionalism Requires Autonomy

(see Figure 1.3). When a person sees a physician because of stomach pains, for example, no set of standards mandates specific treatments or medications; doctors have the authority to treat patients as they see fit. Some researchers suggest that teaching isn't a profession because states and districts, instead of teachers, prescribe what teachers teach (the **curriculum**) as well as how student understanding is measured (**assessment**) (van den Berg, 2002).

Indeed, states and districts prescribe **standards**, statements specifying what students should know and what skills they should have upon completing an area of study, and districts often require students to meet these standards before allowing them to move from one grade to another or graduate from high school (McCombs, 2005). However, in spite of these mandates, teachers still have a great deal of control over what is taught, how they teach it,

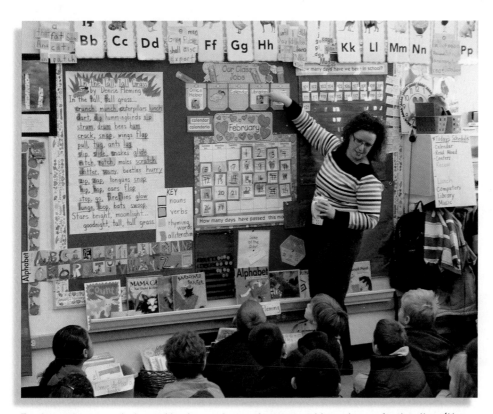

Teacher autonomy to design and implement instruction comes with teacher professionalism. (Hope Madden/Merrill)

Curriculum. What teachers teach.

Assessment. How student understanding is measured.

Standards. Statements specifying what students should know and what skills they should have upon completing an area of study.

and how students are assessed. Autonomy gives teachers the freedom to make professional decisions in their classrooms.

Emphasis on Decision Making and Reflection

As we saw earlier in the chapter, classrooms are complex, and teachers must make an enormous number of decisions in ill-defined situations. For example, Ken had to decide if he should ignore the incident when Sylvia accused Joey of calling her a fat jerk, or if he should intervene. And if he decided to intervene, what should this intervention be? Should he take Joey out of the classroom and talk to him? Make him apologize? Write a note to Sylvia? Call his parents? And, what if Sylvia wasn't telling the truth, or misunderstood what Joey said?

David Ling, in his lesson on inertia, had to decide how to begin his lesson, what examples to use, what students to call on and in what order, how long he would give them to answer, what kind of follow-up question he would ask if they were unable to answer, and a host of other decisions.

Making decisions in situations such as these is one of the differences between a professional and a **technician**, a person who uses specific skills to complete well-defined tasks, such as an electrician wiring an outlet (Sandholtz & Reilly, 2004). **Decision making**, by contrast, involves problem solving in ill-defined situations and is based on professional knowledge. This text attempts to help you develop your professional decision-making abilities by providing a "Decision Making: Defining Yourself as a Professional" exercise at the end of each chapter.

But how do teachers know if they have made good decisions? They receive little feedback about the effectiveness of their work. They are observed by administrators a few times a year at most, and they receive only vague, sketchy, and uncertain feedback from students and parents. In addition, they get virtually no feedback from their colleagues, unless the school has a peer coaching or mentoring program (Gilbert, 2005; Wayne, Youngs, & Fleischman, 2005). To develop as a professional, teachers must be able to continually assess their own classroom actions.

Reflection provides teachers with opportunities to think about and improve their practice. (Mary Kate Denny/PhotoEdit Inc.)

The ability to conduct this self-assessment requires that teachers develop a disposition for continually and critically examining their work. This is the essence of a simple, yet powerful idea called **reflection** (Lee, 2004; Schon, 1983), the act of thinking about and analyzing your actions. Reflective teachers are thoughtful, analytical, even self-critical about their teaching. They plan lessons thoughtfully and take the time to analyze and critique them afterward.

Reflection is important in teaching not only because it improves our effectiveness but also because it helps us develop as professionals (Bransford et al., 2005; Hammerness, Darling-Hammond, & Bransford, 2005). By analyzing their work, reflective professionals develop a coherent philosophy of teaching that helps them integrate theory and practice and continually refine their teaching (Rodgers, 2002) (see Figure 1.4).

Professional Ethics

Professionals also have ethical standards for conduct. To understand what this means, consider the following scenarios:

An ardent advocate of gun control, you believe that access to guns should be strictly regulated, and you have said so in class. Eric, one of your students, brings a newspaper editorial to school that makes a compelling argument against gun control. Because of your beliefs, you don't allow the student to share the editorial with the class.

Technician. A person who uses specific skills to complete well-defined tasks.

Decision making. Problem solving in ill-defined situations, based on professional knowledge.

Reflection. The process of teachers' thinking about and analyzing their work to assess its effectiveness.

Figure 1.4   Professionalism Requires Decision Making and Reflection

Greg is a very difficult student in one of your classes. He is continually disruptive and periodically shouts insults at other students and sometimes even at you. You've tried everything you know to control his behavior, but you've been unsuccessful. Finally, in exasperation one day, you walk up to him while he is talking, clap your hands together, and say angrily, "Greg, I've had it with you! You can't keep your mouth closed for more than 1 minute, and you're an embarrassment to yourself and the other students in this class. I don't want to hear another sound out of you the rest of the period." Surprisingly, Greg sits quietly for the remainder of the period. Now, finding that anger seems to be the only way to keep Greg from being disruptive, you sometimes use it to manage his behavior.

Have you behaved "ethically" in these examples? How do you know? **Ethics** are sets of moral standards for acceptable professional behavior, and all professions have codes of ethics intended to guide professionals as they make decisions about how to act (see Figure 1.5). In its code of ethics, the National Education Association (NEA), the largest professional organization in education, addresses the behavior of teachers working with their students (see Figure 1.6).

Figure 1.5   Professionalism Requires Ethical Standards for Conduct

Ethics. Sets of moral standards for acceptable professional behavior.

Figure 1.6 National Education Association Code of Ethics

Preamble

   The educator, believing in the worth and dignity of each human being, recognizes the supreme importance of the pursuit of truth, devotion to excellence, and the nurture of democratic principle. Essential to these goals is the protection of freedom to learn and to teach and the guarantee of equal educational opportunity for all. The educator accepts the responsibility to adhere to the highest ethical standards.

   The educator recognizes the magnitude of the responsibility inherent in the teaching process. The desire for the respect and confidence of one's colleagues, of students, of parents, and the members of the community provides the incentive to attain and maintain the highest possible degree of ethical conduct. The Code of Ethics of the Education Profession indicates the aspiration of all educators and provides standards by which to judge conduct.

   The remedies specified by the NEA and/or its affiliates for the violation of any provision of this Code shall be exclusive and no such provision shall be enforceable in any form other than one specifically designated by the NEA or its affiliates.

Principle I—Commitment to the Student

   The educator strives to help each student realize his or her potential as a worthy and effective member of society. The educator therefore works to stimulate the spirit of inquiry, the acquisition of knowledge and understanding, and the thoughtful formulation of worthy goals.

   In fulfillment of the obligation to the student, the educator—

1. Shall not unreasonably restrain the student from independent action in the pursuit of learning.
2. Shall not unreasonably deny the student access to varying points of view.
3. Shall not deliberately suppress or distort subject matter relevant to the student's progress.
4. Shall make reasonable effort to protect the student from conditions harmful to learning or to health and safety.
5. Shall not intentionally expose the student to embarrassment or disparagement.
6. Shall not on the basis of race, color, creed, sex, national origin, marital status, political or religious beliefs, family, social or cultural background, or sexual orientation unfairly:
   a. Exclude any student from participation in any program;
   b. Deny benefits to any student;
   c. Grant any advantage to any student.
7. Shall not use professional relationships with students for private advantage.
8. Shall not disclose information about students obtained in the course of professional service, unless disclosure serves a compelling professional purpose or is required by law.

Principle II—Commitment to the Profession

   The education profession is vested by the public with a trust and responsibility requiring the highest ideals of professional service.

   In the belief that the quality of the services of the education profession directly influences the nation and its citizens, the educator shall exert every effort to raise professional standards, to promote a climate that encourages the exercise of professional judgment, to achieve conditions which attract persons worthy of the trust to careers in education, and to assist in preventing the practice of the profession by unqualified persons.

   In fulfillment of the obligation to the profession, the educator—

1. Shall not in an application for a professional position deliberately make a false statement or fail to disclose a material fact related to competency and qualifications.
2. Shall not misrepresent his/her professional qualifications.
3. Shall not assist entry into the profession of a person known to be unqualified in respect to character, education, or other relevant attribute.
4. Shall not knowingly make a false statement concerning the qualifications of a candidate for a professional position.
5. Shall not assist a noneducator in the unauthorized practice of teaching.
6. Shall not disclose information about colleagues obtained in the course of professional service unless disclosure serves a compelling professional purpose or is required by law.
7. Shall not knowingly make a false or malicious statement about a colleague.
8. Shall not accept any gratuity, gift, or favor that might impair or appear to influence professional decisions or actions.

Source: From National Education Association. (1995). Code of Ethics of the Education Profession, NEA Representative Assembly. Reprinted by permission.

Let's evaluate your actions based on the information in the NEA Code of Ethics. Item 2 of Principle I, Commitment to the Student, states that a teacher "shall not unreasonably deny the student access to varying points of view." In our first example, you didn't let Eric share the editorial with the other students, so you have denied them access to a view that differs from your own. Whether or not your denial was "unreasonable" is open to interpretation, as is the case with ethical standards in any profession.

In the second example, you were desperately searching for a way to manage Greg's behavior, and by chance you found that anger (and possibly intimidation) was the only thing that seemed to work. However, Item 5 of Principle I says, a teacher "shall not intentionally expose the student to embarrassment or disparagement." This case is clear; in your desperation and frustration, you intentionally used anger and disparagement as a strategy with Greg, so you are in violation of the ethical code.

Other examples of ethical lapses sometimes seen in teaching include retaliating against students for alleged slights or offenses by grading unfairly or making unfair placement decisions, accepting fees for tutoring one's own students, and cheating on state tests by giving students more than the pre-

Professional ethics guide teachers in their interactions with students, parents and caregivers, and colleagues.
(Laura Bolesta/Merrill)

scribed time or by giving them clues and/or answers (Raths & Lynman, 2003). Ethical standards are so important to professionals that they are often written into employment contracts. These standards are also important because they can provide an important basis for your own professional decision making.

Are Teachers Professionals?

Not everyone believes that teachers are professionals. Critics' arguments include lack of rigorous training and lack of autonomy (Labaree, 2004, 2006).

Lack of Rigorous Training

The academic rigor of teachers' professional training has historically been criticized (Neville, Sherman, & Cohen, 2005). Entrance into teaching isn't as competitive as entrance into professions such as medicine or law, and many proposed reforms suggest that pedagogical content knowledge, general pedagogical knowledge, and knowledge of learners and learning be de-emphasized in favor of knowledge of content (Berry, Hoke, & Hirsch, 2004). The argument is often made, though not supported by research, that the only thing that teachers need is knowledge of the subjects they teach (Darling-Hammond & Bransford, 2005). The extended training for licensure that we discussed earlier suggests that teaching is a demanding profession that requires several forms of knowledge together with firsthand experience with students and classrooms.

Lack of Autonomy

In the last section we argued that teachers have a great deal of autonomy. Although we maintain this position, we also acknowledge that teachers have less autonomy than other professionals. For example, unlike physicians and lawyers, teachers are supervised and evaluated by their immediate school administrators, and states or districts mandate a substantial portion of the curriculum. Teachers have little to say about the standards for licensure, and many teachers even have to sign in at the beginning of the day and sign out at the end. The extent to which this detracts from them being true professionals continues to be debated.

Putting Teacher Professionalism into Perspective

The issue of whether teaching is a profession is controversial and won't be resolved in the near future. Without question, the training required for professions such as medicine and law is more extensive and rigorous than the training required for teaching, although rigor in teacher education is on the rise (Darling-Hammond & Bransford, 2005). Prospective teachers are expected to know and do more, and their professional knowledge is now more commonly assessed with tests that measure their understanding of the content they teach as well as their understanding of how to help students learn. We discuss these tests later in the chapter.

With respect to autonomy, a battle is currently being fought on both sides of the issue (Meier, 2002). Some would curtail teachers' autonomy by mandating what and how to teach and how to assess student learning. Others argue that this technical view of teaching is not feasible, because teaching requires too many split-second decisions to be reduced to mandates, and attempts to do so discourage creative people from considering teaching as a career (Kohn, 2000).

It is clear that teachers share many of the characteristics that describe members of established professions: They possess a specialized body of knowledge, they make many important decisions as they work, and they have a significant amount of autonomy. Effective teachers take time to reflect on their actions and take care to follow the ethical standards established by educational leaders. Are teachers professionals? At this time, many educational commentators seem to be saying "not quite" (Labaree, 2004, 2006; Neville et al., 2005). To truly "professionalize" teaching, researchers believe a number of reforms are necessary. We discuss these in the next section.

Making Connections:
To deepen your understanding of the topics in this section of the chapter and integrate them with topics you've already studied, go to the *Making Connections* module for Chapter 1 at **www.prenhall.com/kauchak**. Respond to questions 4–5.

Check Your Understanding

2.1   What are the essential characteristics of professionalism?

2.2   What are the primary arguments for teaching being a profession?

2.3   What are the major arguments against teaching being a profession?

2.4   How do the arguments for and against teacher professionalism balance each other?

For feedback, go to Appendix A, Check Your Understanding, *located in the back of this text.*

Diversity: The Changing Face of U.S. Classrooms

When we walk into classrooms around the United States, one fact quickly becomes clear; our students are amazingly diverse. For example, experts in California predict the following:

- By 2010, the number of Latino and white California residents will be equal, each comprising nearly 40 percent of the population.
- By 2014, half of the children in California public schools will be Hispanic, and many will have limited English language skills.
- By 2020, 43 percent of the state's residents will be Latino, 34 percent will be white, 13 percent will be Asian, and the remaining 10 percent will be African American and Native American (Coleman, 2005).

While one of the more extreme examples, California's experience is not unique; every state in our country is becoming more culturally and ethnically diverse, and in the 25 largest U.S. cities, students of color compose at least half of the student population (Ladson-Billings, 2005).

When you begin teaching, you will have students who come from a variety of cultural, ethnic, and religious backgrounds (Gray & Fleischman, 2005). Along with cultural and ethnic diversity, you will also encounter many students who speak a native language other than English. Their **socioeconomic status**—the amount of money their parents make, their parents' level of education, and the kinds of jobs their parents have—will also differ. These differences can have a powerful influence on children's learning. For example, some parents can afford annual trips to other states and even countries; other parents struggle to provide even a decent place to live and enough food to eat. Some students will have many school-related experiences such as trips to zoos and museums that make learning nearly effortless, whereas others' school-related experiences will be severely limited. These differences translate into dramatic differences when the teacher asks questions during a lesson that require students to use their background knowledge about the world.

In a single grade you will have learners who are mature for their age and others who are slower in developing. Some will be poised and self-confident; others, shy and hesitant. You will certainly have a mix of boys and girls, their preferred ways of learning will vary, and you're likely to have some students with learning problems that will require extra help. Some of these students with special needs and/or talents will be served by a team of instructors in a program formalized through an individualized education program (IEP). We discuss students with special needs in Chapter 3.

Each of these sources of diversity can strongly influence students' classroom behaviors and academic performance. How you respond to these differences will influence how much students learn, how they feel about school, and your own enjoyment of teaching. Because learner diversity is so important, we devote Chapter 3 to the topic and include a special section called "Exploring Diversity" in every chapter.

Making Connections:
To deepen your understanding of the topics in this section of the chapter and integrate them with topics you've already studied, go to the *Making Connections* module for Chapter 1 at **www.prenhall.com/kauchak**. Respond to questions 6–7.

Check Your Understanding

3.1   Identify the different dimensions of student diversity. Explain how these dimensions will influence your work as a teacher.

3.2   Why is an understanding of different teaching and learning environments important for beginning teachers?

 For feedback, go to Appendix A, Check Your Understanding, *located in the back of this text.*

The Modern Reform Movement in Education

You're considering teaching in one of the most tumultuous periods in the history of American education. Critics, both inside and outside the profession, are calling for **reforms**, suggested changes in teaching and teacher preparation intended to increase the amount students learn. To implement these reforms, teachers must be well prepared, and states and districts often hold teachers accountable for their performance in classrooms. The current reform movement has already changed teaching and will continue to do so as you enter the profession. To prepare you for these changes, we have made reform the third major theme for this text, following professionalism and learner diversity.

To place recent reform efforts into perspective, we should point out that the process of change and reform has been a part of education throughout American history (Cuban, 2005). When you study the history of American education in Chapter 5, you will see how different reforms have shaped it over the years.

Socioeconomic status. The amount of money students' parents make, their parents' level of education, and the kinds of jobs their parents have.

Reforms. Suggested changes in teaching and teacher preparation intended to increase the amount students learn.

Teaching in Rural, Suburban, and Urban Environments

Because of its powerful influence on teaching, we have made diversity a second theme of this text, along with professionalism, and every chapter includes an "Exploring Diversity" feature, which examines an issue related to diversity. In this section of the chapter, we focus on teaching in rural, suburban, and urban environments. Teaching in these three types of schools differs significantly, influenced not only by the social context, but also by the students themselves.

Teaching in Rural Schools

Researchers are engaged in an ongoing debate about the relative advantages of smaller versus larger schools (Bloomfield, 2006; Robelen, 2006). Small-school advocates need look no further than the approximately 350 remaining one-teacher schools in rural areas (Swidler, 2004). While not all rural districts have schools such as these, they are smaller in comparison to their urban and suburban counterparts. The smallest rural districts had an average of 126 students in the 2001–2002 school year, compared to 4,015 students in suburban and urban districts (U.S. Government Accounting Office, 2006). Rural schools in these smallest districts are also small, enrolling an average of 77 students, versus 560 students in nonrural schools. Small size also translates into lower numbers of students per teacher, with the smallest rural schools averaging 11 students per class versus 17 for their counterparts in larger districts (U.S. Government Accounting Office, 2006).

The students in rural districts tend to be less culturally diverse than those in urban and suburban districts, though this is slowly changing (Lichter & Johnson, 2006). Recent immigrants from Latin America and Asia are slowly finding their way into rural America, seeking jobs in construction, meat-packing, and other food-processing industries, slowing an earlier trend of general population decrease in rural areas (Macionis, 2006). Poverty is also an issue in rural districts, particularly in the South and Southwest (Hardy, 2005). For example, 42 percent of students in rural districts qualify for free or reduced lunch programs versus 36 percent in nonrural schools (U.S. Government Accounting Office, 2006).

Teaching in rural districts has both advantages and disadvantages. Because they are smaller, they have a greater sense of community, with schools often serving as the social center for the community (Brooke, 2003). Class sizes are smaller, and communication with parents is often easier. In addition, innovation and change may be easier because of rural districts' small size (Reeves & Bylund, 2005).

Teaching in Suburban Schools

The latter half of the 20th century resulted in unprecedented growth in the suburbs. At the turn of the 21st century, most of the U.S. population lived in suburbs, resulting from shifts from both urban and rural populations (Macionis, 2006). With respect to diversity, suburban schools are more culturally diverse than rural schools, with much of the diversity coming from well-educated professionals working in high-tech industries (Macionis, 2006). However, they tend to be less culturally diverse than urban schools. In addition, average household incomes tend to be higher than in rural or urban areas.

Most of the highest achieving school districts in the United States are found in suburban areas, and many suburban families select neighborhoods based on the quality of the school districts (Brimley & Garfield, 2005; Spring, 2006). The exodus to the suburbs also brought with it a growing tax base, which resulted in greater expenditures on suburban schools (Macionis & Parillo, 2007; Spring, 2006). Because of a solid tax base, suburban districts can spend more per student than either rural or urban districts, and this often shows up in smaller class sizes and greater access to resources such as science labs and technology.

New and veteran teachers alike seek jobs in suburban schools, so competition for existing jobs is the primary challenge for new teachers wanting to work in a suburban district.

Teaching in Urban Schools

With respect to jobs, urban schools are "where the action is." Consider the following statistics (Hoffman, 2003; Young, 2002):

The modern reform movement is often traced to 1983, when the National Commission on Excellence in Education published *A Nation at Risk: The Imperative for Educational Reform*. This widely read document suggested that America was "at risk" of being unable to compete in the world economic marketplace because our system of education was inadequate. The terms "at-risk students" and more recently "students placed at-risk" grew out of this book, and educators use them to refer to students who are unlikely to acquire the knowledge and skills needed for success in our modern, tech-

Urban schools provide job openings and opportunities for personal and professional growth. (Scott Cunningham/Merrill)

- The nation's 100 largest school districts represent less than 1 percent of the districts, but they are responsible for the education of nearly one-fourth of all students. For example, the New York City Public Schools and the Los Angeles Unified School District, the two largest in the nation, each have enrollments greater than the total enrollments of 27 states.
- The 100 largest districts employ more than a fifth of the nation's teachers.

Nearly 70 percent of urban students are cultural minorities, and some urban schools have enrollments that are more than 95 percent minority (Macionis & Parillo, 2007). More than half of all urban students are eligible for free or reduced-price lunch.

Unquestionably, teaching in urban schools differs from teaching in other settings. Urban schools are large, and most of their students come from culturally diverse backgrounds. Research also indicates that in urban schools, "Children are often taught by teachers who are the least prepared; children are less likely to be enrolled in academically challenging courses; they are too often treated differently in what they are expected to do and the kinds of assignments they are given and teachers often lack the resources they need to teach well" (Armour-Thomas, 2004, p. 113).

Unfortunately, a number of negative stereotypes about urban students exist, ranging from "All urban kids are in gangs" to "Urban children are mostly from poor, dysfunctional homes, homeless shelters, or foster homes and come to school 'just to grow up' and then drop out" (Goldstein, 2004, pp. 43–44). These stereotypes tend to create fear in people not familiar with the situation. This fear can then lead to actions that are damaging to everyone. One urban student reported,

When I was in high school, we had the chance to host a group of students from the suburbs. . . . So, this girl comes with her friends, and they pair us up. Later on I find that they [the students from the suburbs] were told not to wear any jewelry or nice clothes or bring any money with them so they wouldn't get robbed. . . . All they saw when they visited us were people who might rob them. (Goldstein, 2004, p. 47)

How is this information relevant to you as a prospective teacher, and how might it help you answer the question, "Do I want to be a teacher?" First, many of the stereotypes of urban students are untrue. These students want to succeed and learn and grow just as other students do. In many cases their access to educational experiences has been lacking, so they come to schools with greater needs than do more advantaged students (Armour-Thomas, 2004; Rubinson, 2004). Second, many job opportunities exist in urban environments, so your first job offer likely will be in an urban setting. Many school districts now offer special incentives, such as salary bonuses, support for housing, and moving expenses, in an effort to encourage highly qualified professionals to work in urban settings (Herszenhorn, 2006). Finally, while urban environments pose special challenges, they can also be immensely rewarding, providing opportunities for you to grow in a number of dimensions (Weiner, 2006). Now is the time to begin thinking about the opportunities that working in an urban environment might afford. We examine this topic in more detail in Chapters 3 to 6, 11, and 12.

nological society. (We discuss students placed at-risk in Chapter 4.) Since 1983 many other suggestions have been made for improving our nation's schools and the teachers who work in them.

To help you understand the scope of reforms in education, we examine two of the most prominent: *changes in teacher preparation* and *accountability and high-stakes testing*. These reforms are occurring at both the national and state levels, and we close this section with an example from Kentucky to illustrate a state-level reform.

Changes in Teacher Preparation

Increased emphasis on professionalism and criticisms suggesting that too many underqualified teachers enter the field have resulted in a number of reforms in teacher education, most enacted at the state level (Raths & Lynman, 2003). These reforms include

- Raising standards for admission into teacher training programs
- Requiring teachers to take more rigorous courses than in the past
- Requiring higher standards for licensure, including teacher-competency tests
- Expanding teacher preparation programs from 4 to 5 years
- Requiring experienced teachers to take more rigorous professional development courses (Cochran-Smith, 2005)

The emphasis on professionalism is further reinforced through the No Child Left Behind (NCLB) Act of 2001, a federal law that includes a call for improved teacher quality as a major provision. (We discuss the NCLB Act later in the chapter.) NCLB required that, by 2005–2006, all teachers were to be fully qualified, and paraprofessionals working in schools should have 2 years of college or demonstrate equivalent knowledge on a competency test (Popham, 2004b; Dillon, 2006). This provision of the law is a direct result of research indicating that teachers have a powerful effect on student learning (Milanowski & Kimball, 2005) and that many poor, minority, and urban children are frequently taught by underqualified teachers (Rhee & Levin, 2006).

Competency Testing

States and districts are increasingly assessing teacher quality through competency testing, which means it is likely that you will be required to pass a test to be admitted to the profession. Currently, most states require some type of standardized test for licensure; in addition, most colleges of education also require tests for admission into teacher-education programs (Wayne & Youngs, 2003).

Praxis: Comprehensive Teacher Testing.   The most common form of teacher testing is the Praxis Series, published by the Educational Testing Service. The Praxis Series (*praxis* refers to putting theory into practice) is currently being used in 35 states and exists at three levels (Educational Testing Service, 2006):

- Praxis I: Academic Skills Assessments. These tests are designed to measure the basic skills in reading, writing, and math that all teachers need.
- Praxis II: Subject Assessments. The subject assessments are intended to measure teachers' knowledge of the subjects they will teach. In addition to 70 content-specific tests, Praxis II also includes the Principles of Learning and Teaching (PLT) tests, which measure professional knowledge.
- Praxis III: Classroom Performance Assessments. These tests use classroom observations and work samples to assess beginning teachers' ability to plan, instruct, manage, and understand professional responsibilities. In addition, Praxis III assesses the teacher's sensitivity to learners' developmental and cultural differences.

You are most likely to encounter Praxis I before being admitted to a teacher licensure program, Praxis II after its completion, and Praxis III during your first years of teaching.

The Principles of Learning and Teaching (PLT) tests, four tests specifically designed for teachers seeking licensure in Early Childhood, or grades K–6, 5–9, and 7–12, are an important part of the Praxis Series. The topics these tests cover are outlined in the Praxis Correlation Matrix at the beginning of this text. Each of the grade-level tests has two parts (Educational Testing Service, 2006). The first consists of 24 multiple-choice questions similar to those in the self-assessment quizzes on the Companion Website (*www.prenhall.com/kauchak*) as well as the test bank that accompanies this text. The second part presents case histories that you read and analyze with short-answer questions. The PLT case histories are similar to the case studies you'll find in each chapter of this text. We have designed this text to help you pass your licensure exam, whether it is a Praxis PLT or an exam created by your state, by including case-based formats in the "Preparing for Your Licensure Exam" exercises at the end of each chapter. Suggestions on how to succeed can be found in "Keys to Success on Your Licensure Exam" at the front of the book. In addition, the Teacher Prep Website (*www.prenhall.com/teacherprep*) contains additional information that will help you prepare for these tests.

Portfolios: Individual Teacher Accountability

Testing can provide valuable information about teachers' knowledge and skills, but test content is often removed from the day-to-day challenges that teachers face (Berliner, 2006). A **professional portfolio**, or collection of materials representative of one's work, provides an alternate way to document teacher competence. Just as a portfolio of artwork is prepared by an artist, a professional portfolio is produced by a prospective teacher to document developing knowledge and skills. **Digital portfolios** allow you to compress large amounts of information onto a computer file, making it easy to edit and burn to a CD to share with prospective employers.

As you proceed through your teacher-preparation program, you will likely be required to prepare a portfolio to document your developing professional competence, and it will be a tool you can use during job interviews to demonstrate your capabilities as a teacher. We provide "Online Portfolio Activities" at the end of each chapter of this text, and "Guidelines for Beginning a Professional Portfolio" are in Appendix 1.1 at the end of this chapter.

Whether reforms such as teacher testing and the use of portfolios to document competency will result in the hoped-for improvements in education remains to be seen and will continue to be debated. One thing is certain, however; efforts to reform schools, teachers, and the way teachers are prepared will continue, and you will begin your career in the midst of these changes. One of the most significant of these changes are the INTASC standards described in the next section.

INTASC: Standards in Teacher Education

In addition to testing and portfolios, school districts are also using standards to increase the quality and rigor of teacher preparation programs. A rapidly expanding body of research consistently demonstrates that teaching now requires professionals who are highly knowledgeable and skilled (Berliner, 2006; Darling-Hammond & Bransford, 2005).

The profession is responding. Created in 1987, the Interstate New Teacher Assessment and Support Consortium (INTASC) was designed to help states develop better teachers through coordinated efforts of support and assessment. INTASC (1993) has raised the bar by setting rigorous standards for new teachers in important areas such as planning, instruction, and increasing student motivation. These standards describe what you should know and be able to do when you first walk into a classroom.

To date, INTASC has prepared general, or "core," standards organized around 10 principles (see Table 1.3) and is preparing standards for various subject-matter areas and specific student populations. INTASC is also developing a Test for Teaching Knowledge (TTK) linked to the core principles. Each of the "Online Portfolio Activities" found at the end of the chapters is linked to the INTASC core standards, and a matrix correlating INTASC standards to this text's content can be found on the inside cover.

The INTASC standards are demanding, but this is as it should be. If you expect to be treated as a professional, you should have the knowledge and skills that allow you to make the decisions expected of a professional. Being able to meet the INTASC standards is a good beginning.

Teaching in an Era of Reform

We said earlier that reform is a major theme for this book. To involve you in examining prominent reforms, we include a feature in each chapter called "Teaching in an Era of Reform." We introduce the feature in this chapter and illustrate how you can use it to increase your understanding of educational reforms in the United States.

Professional portfolio. A collection of representative work materials to document developing knowledge and skills.

Digital portfolio. A collection of materials contained in an electronic file that makes the information accessible to potential viewers.

TABLE 1.3   The INTASC Principles

Principle	Description
1. Knowledge of subject	The teacher understands the central concepts, tools of inquiry, and structures of the discipline(s) he or she teaches and can create learning experiences that make these aspects of subject matter meaningful for students.
2. Learning and human development	The teacher understands how children learn and develop, and can provide learning opportunities that support their intellectual, social and personal development.
3. Adapting instruction	The teacher understands how students differ in their approaches to learning and creates instructional opportunities that are adapted to diverse learners.
4. Strategies	The teacher understands and uses a variety of instructional strategies to encourage students' development of critical thinking, problem solving, and performance skills.
5. Motivation and management	The teacher uses an understanding of individual and group motivation and behavior to create a learning environment that encourages positive social interaction, active engagement in learning, and self-motivation.
6. Communication skills	The teacher uses knowledge of effective verbal, nonverbal, and media communication techniques to foster active inquiry, collaboration, and supportive interaction in the classroom.
7. Planning	The teacher plans instruction based upon knowledge of subject matter, students, the community, and curriculum goals.
8. Assessment	The teacher understands and uses formal and informal assessment strategies to evaluate and ensure the continuous intellectual, social and physical development of the learner.
9. Commitment	The teacher is a reflective practitioner who continually evaluates the effects of his/her choices and actions on others (students, parents, and other professionals in the learning community) and who actively seeks out opportunities to grow professionally.
10. Partnership	The teacher fosters relationships with school colleagues, parents, and agencies in the larger community to support students' learning and well-being.

Source: From Interstate New Teacher Assessment and Support Consortium (1993). *Model standards for beginning teacher licensing and development: A resource for state dialogues.* Washington, D.C.: Council of Chief State School Officers. Reprinted by permission.

Accountability. The process of requiring students to demonstrate understanding of the topics they study as measured by standardized tests, as well as holding educators at all levels responsible for students' performance.

High-stakes tests. Assessments that states and districts use to determine whether or not students will advance from one grade to another, graduate from high school, or have access to specific fields of study.

The feature includes the following elements:

- Discussion of a reform issue such as merit pay (Chapter 2) or teacher tenure (Chapter 9).
- Arguments on both sides of the issue.
- We ask you to take a position by responding to the issue.

We illustrate this process in the following section, discussing accountability and high-stakes testing as the reform issue. **Accountability** is the process of requiring students to demonstrate understanding of the topics they study as measured by standardized tests, as well as holding educators at all levels responsible for students' performance. Accountability often occurs along with **high-stakes tests**, which are assessments that states and districts use to determine whether or not students will advanced from one grade to another, graduate from high school, or have access to specific fields of study.

VIDEO PERSPECTIVES

The Test

 To view this video, go to the *Becoming a Professional* DVD included with this text, click on ABC News, and then this chapter's video: *The Test*. This ABC News video examines high-stakes testing in Florida from multiple perspectives. Interviews with students, parents, and administrators help us understand the implications of high stakes for a variety of people.

Think About This

1. What are the advantages and disadvantages of high-stakes testing?
2. What types of students are most adversely affected by high-stakes testing?
3. What can schools do to minimize the negative effects of high-stakes testing?

 To answer these questions online and receive immediate feedback, go to the Companion Website at **www.prenhall.com/kauchak**, *then to the* ABC News *Video Perspectives module for Chapter 1.*

Analyzing One Statewide Reform: The Kentucky Education Reform Act

Will reform efforts produce the hoped-for results? One of the most ambitious and well-known state reform efforts, the Kentucky Education Reform Act (KERA), was precipitated by a 1989 Kentucky Supreme Court ruling that declared that the state's system of funding public schools was unconstitutional (Flanagan & Murray, 2004). Funding disparities between rich and poor school districts had resulted in a system that was inequitable and inefficient. The state legislature responded with a comprehensive educational reform bill that attempted to address several of the issues. The major components of the effort, and the changes that resulted, are found in Table 1.4.

As you can see from Table 1.4, KERA affected every student and every teacher in the state. To fund these reforms, the Kentucky legislature approved a $1.3 billion tax increase, and public school expenditures increased 50 percent over the first 5 years of implementation ("Will KERA?", 2003).

TABLE 1.4   Major Provisions of Kentucky Education Reform Act

Reform Component	Result
Curriculum guides established	Clearly defined student learning goals for key areas such as math, reading, and social studies.
Assessment and accountability systems	Created a statewide testing system that held schools accountable for student learning.
Ungraded primary program for K–3	Eliminated grade levels and used multiage grouping to educate primary students.
Extended school services for students placed at-risk	Provided extra instruction after school and in the summer for students placed at-risk.
School-based decision making	Created school level councils consisting of parents and teachers to provide input on how schools were run.
Pre-school program for children placed at-risk	Students who were eligible for free or reduced lunches or those who were developmentally delayed received developmentally appropriate preschool programs.
Family and youth resource centers	Provided links between schools and families and offered information on other government agencies.

teaching in an era of reform

Accountability and High-Stakes Testing

In response to concerns about students graduating from high school without the skills needed to succeed either in college or the workplace, reformers have called for greater accountability for both students and teachers. Calls for accountability were prompted by evidence indicating that students were being promoted from grade to grade without mastering essential content; some students were graduating from high school without basic skills in reading, writing, and math; and even more had limited scientific literacy and a general lack of understanding of our world. For example, in a recent survey of 18- to 24-year-olds, 6 in 10 respondents couldn't find Iraq on a map of the Middle East and about half couldn't locate New York State (Manzo, 2006).

No Child Left Behind

One of the most far-reaching accountability reforms is the No Child Left Behind (NCLB) Act of 2001, which one expert called "the most significant change in federal regulation of public schools in three decades" (Hardy, 2002, p. 201). Researchers evaluating it described it as "comprehensive in its impact, affecting who teaches, what is taught, how learning is assessed and the consequences for poor performance" (Debray, McDermott, & Wohlstetter, 2005, p. 15).

Signed by President George W. Bush in 2002, NCLB officially reauthorized the Elementary and Secondary Education Act, which began in 1965 and resulted in billions of dollars be-

A major element of many current reform efforts, including No Child Left Behind, is increased emphasis on testing in schools. (Anthony/Magnacca/Merrill)

ing spent on compensatory education programs for disadvantaged students. Several key provisions of NCLB address teacher preparation, standards, accountability, and testing, and these provisions will influence teachers' professional lives in the years to come (Popham, 2004b).

Accountability is the most important provision of NCLB, and it calls for accountability at several levels. For example, NCLB requires states to create standards for what every child should know and learn for all grades. States were to develop standards for math, reading, and science by the 2005–2006 school year, and states must implement these standards in order to receive continued federal funding. Responsibility for implementing the standards and gathering information about their attainment exists at the district level. Individual schools are held accountable for ensuring that every child in that school has achieved satisfactory progress toward the standards. Schools, districts, and states must keep records of performance to document achievement of different groups of students by race, ethnicity, gender, and English proficiency.

If a school fails to make adequate yearly progress with any of these student subgroups for 2 consecutive years, students may transfer to another school. After 3 years of sub-par performance by a school, students within underachieving schools are entitled to outside tutoring at district expense. After 4 years, the state will place the school on probation and take corrective measures. States, districts, individual schools, and teachers are already feeling the pressures of accountability (Christie, 2005).

Testing is the key to NCLB accountability. Beginning in the 2005–2006 school year, districts will test each child in grades 3 through 8 every year in math and reading and will test children at least once more in grades 10–12. By 2007–2008, districts will assess students in science at least once in their academic career. States and districts will use these test scores to hold schools accountable for student achievement.

Often, accountability is accomplished through high-stakes testing. When students aren't allowed to graduate from high school because they fail a test, for example, the "stakes" are very high, thus, the term *high-stakes tests*. In a similar way, when districts and specific schools within them are singled out as failing or "leaving children behind," the stakes are also very high.

The Issue

As you might expect, accountability through high-stakes testing is very controversial. Critics argue that—faced with pressures to help students achieve in math, reading, and science—teachers will underemphasize other subjects like social studies, art, music, health, and physical education (Nichols & Berliner, 2005). This narrowing of the curriculum deprives students of a well-rounded education, critics assert, and it also stifles teacher creativity because they spend too much time teaching only test content and helping students practice for the tests.

Teachers also report that testing programs have forced them to teach in ways that contradict sound instructional practices. For example, despite knowing that computers can be an effective tool for teaching writing, teachers have abandoned technology because a state writing test is hand written (Pedulla et al., 2003).

The pressure for students to perform well on the tests can also produce unintended consequences. To avoid test-related sanctions, teachers in states with high-stakes tests frequently request transfers out of grades that are tested, and experts fear that veteran teachers will transfer out of urban schools where students often underachieve, depriving students of the expert teachers they need (Guarino et al., 2006; Lynn, 2003). In addition, research suggests that high school exit examinations, in use in 23 states in 2006, have contributed to the dropout problem, and the adverse effects are greater for low socioeconomic status and cultural minority students (Warren, Jenkins, & Kulick, 2006).

Critics also contend that current tests are not adequate for crucial decisions about students' lives (Neill, 2003; Popham, 2004) and that cutoff scores are often arbitrary. For example, when the state of Virginia lowered the cutoff score for its test by 1 point, 5,625 failing scores turned into passing scores (Bracey, 2003b). Deciding student grade promotion or graduation on the basis of one score is being increasingly criticized by a number of professional organizations, both within and outside education, including the American Educational Research Association (2006) and the American Psychological Association (2006). In addition, other experts assert that high-stakes tests can have negative side effects, including decreased motivation and higher dropout rates (Amrein & Berliner, 2003).

Finally, questions related to high-stakes testing with minority students remain unanswered. One involves test bias and whether or not existing tests can provide an accurate picture of minority achievement, and particularly the achievement of students who are not native English speakers (Abedi, Hofstetter, & Lord, 2004; Popham, 2004b).

Advocates of testing, while conceding that teacher preparation, instructional resources, and the tests themselves need to be improved, argue that these tests are the fairest and most effective means of achieving the aims of successful learning for all students (Steches, Hamilton, & Scott-Naflet, 2005). Further, they assert, evidence indicates that educational systems that require content standards and use tests that thoroughly measure the extent to which the standards are met greatly improve the achievement for all students, including those from disadvantaged backgrounds.

> *For too long, the poor achievement of our most vulnerable students has been lost in unrepresentative averages. African American, Hispanic, special education, limited English proficient, and many other students were left behind because schools were not held accountable for their individual progress. Now all students count. (U.S. Department of Education, 2004, p. 18)*

Some advocates are even promoting national standards and tests, claiming that those coming from different states vary too much and result in inequalities between states (Olson, 2005b). Hirsch (2000) summarized the testing advocates' position: "They [standards and tests that measure achievement of the standards] are the most promising educational development in half a century" (p. 64).

Polls indicate that the public and most parents support the general goals of No Child Left Behind (Olson, 2005a). Ninety-five percent of respondents in a national poll said that it is important to close the achievement gap between minority students and their peers who are not members of minorities, and 58 percent of respondents said it is the responsibility of the schools to do so (Rose & Gallup, 2005). However, more than two-thirds say that a single test cannot give a fair picture of student achievement. This suggests that, while believing that schools should do more to help all students learn, the public isn't sure about how it should be accomplished.

You Take a Position

Now it's your turn to take a position on the issue. State in writing whether you feel that accountability and high-stakes testing will improve the quality of education or harm it, and provide a two-page rationale for your position.

*For additional references and resources, go to the Companion Website at **www.prenhall.com/kauchak**, then to the Teaching in an Era of Reform module for Chapter 1. You can respond online or submit your response to your instructor.*

How successful was this "most sweeping statewide education reform plan ever enacted" (Rothman, 1997)? Evaluations range from "success beyond all expectations" to "dismal failure" (Petroska, Lindle, & Pankratz, 2000). Research suggests that this reform did improve student performance; between 1992 and 1996, 92 percent of Kentucky's schools showed improvements in achievement (Rothman, 1997). These increases were especially evident at the elementary level in math, reading, and social studies (Petroska et al., 2000). In addition, the preschool programs for students placed at-risk appeared to have long-lasting benefits for young students.

As with all reforms, however, the Kentucky plan was not without its critics. Conservatives argued that it cost too much, and as often happens with education reforms, funding for the program significantly decreased over time (D. Hoff, 2003b). In addition, teachers now question whether the emphasis on accountability narrows the curriculum and forces teachers to "teach to the test," a common complaint about accountability through testing. In many respects KERA, with its emphasis on systemic reform and accountability, was a precursor to the No Child Left Behind Act, the federal reform effort.

But the Kentucky Education Reform Act differs from No Child Left Behind in several important respects. First, it is a state versus a federal effort, which gives the people in the state more control over it. Second, it doesn't rely solely on testing and accountability to improve education. Instead, it provides extra funding for the reform, something that critics of No Child Left Behind feel hampers federal efforts to improve student performance. This extra money provides extra services to both students and their families, something experts feel is necessary for long-term change in the education of students placed at-risk (Mathis, 2005).

Making Connections:
To deepen your understanding of the topics in this section of the chapter and integrate them with topics you've already studied, go to the *Making Connections* module for Chapter 1 at **www.prenhall.com/kauchak**. Respond to questions 8 and 9.

Check Your Understanding

4.1 How is the current reform movement in education changing the teaching profession?

4.2 Describe the major changes in teacher preparation that have resulted from the reform movement in education.

4.3 What is INTASC? How has it influenced teacher preparation?

For feedback, go to Appendix A, Check Your Understanding, *located in the back of this text.*

decision making

Defining Yourself as a Professional

You are a sophomore in college taking your first education course and trying to decide whether you want to be an elementary or secondary teacher. Fortunately, your class provides clinical experiences at both levels, so you can observe teachers working with both younger and older students.

Your first experience is with a third-grade teacher. At times, the classroom seems bewildering, with small groups of students working on a number of different projects at the same time. After awhile, you start to make sense of the schedule Mrs. Ortiz puts on the board each morning, and you're beginning to learn students' names.

Then you move to a high school math classroom. The students seem really old, and they are, compared to the third graders and even you. Some are only two or three years younger than you are. At first, you're intimidated, but then after you start working with

students one-on-one, you realize they share many of the same characteristics as third graders. They come to school to learn, but having friends and being respected by others is really important to them. You also become aware that you know more math than you realized and that it's fun helping others understand how to solve problems.

At the end of the term, you find that you still haven't firmly decided on a grade level but that you know a lot more than you did before the term started. To help you decide, you reread the section "Rewards and Challenges in Teaching."

What level would you choose?

To respond to this question online and receive immediate feedback, go to the Decision Making *module of Chapter 1 on the Companion Website at* **www.prenhall.com/kauchak**.

Meeting Your Learning Objectives

1. **Describe the major rewards and challenges of teaching.**
   - Rewards in teaching include both intrinsic and extrinsic benefits. Intrinsic rewards come from within oneself and are personally satisfying for emotional or intellectual reasons. Intrinsic rewards for teaching include helping young people grow emotionally, socially, and academically. They also include opportunities for a lifetime of intellectual growth. Extrinsic rewards come from outside oneself and include desirable vacation times, convenient work schedules, occupational status, and salaries. The unique configuration of these in teaching provides attractive incentives to a number of people considering the profession.
   - Research indicates that people most commonly choose to teach because they desire to work with young people and make contributions to society. Other reasons to enter teaching include intellectual growth and interest in a content area.
   - Challenges in teaching include the complexities of classrooms as well as the multiple roles that teachers perform. Classrooms are multidimensional, and the events that occur in classrooms are simultaneous, immediate, unpredictable, and public. In terms of roles, teachers create productive learning environments, are ambassadors to the public, and work with other professionals as collaborative colleagues.

2. **Describe the different characteristics of professionalism, and explain how they relate to teaching.**
   - Characteristics of professionalism include a specialized body of knowledge, autonomy to make decisions, the ability to make decisions in ill-defined situations as well as to engage in reflection to assess one's own performance, and ethical standards that guide professional conduct.
   - Some argue that teachers are not professionals, suggesting their training isn't rigorous and they lack autonomy. Others contend that teaching is a developing profession that is still evolving.
   - Though teachers possess many of the characteristics of a profession, including a specialized body of knowledge, autonomy, decision making and reflection, and ethical standards, the future status of teaching will be largely determined by current reform efforts.

3. **Identify the different dimensions of learner diversity, and explain why understanding different teaching and learning environments is important for beginning teachers.**
   - Student diversity is a fact of life in today's classrooms and comes in various forms. Culture and ethnicity, religion, socioeconomic status, academic ability, physical and emotional maturity, gender, and learner exceptionalities are all dimensions of diversity than can influence student learning.
   - Understanding different learning and teaching environments can be significant for beginning teachers because these environments present different opportunities and challenges to beginning teachers. Rural districts tend to be smaller and more homogeneous in terms of diversity. Suburban districts are intermediate in size and funded better than other districts, but competition for teaching jobs is greater there. Urban districts are more culturally diverse and also offer the greatest number of teaching opportunities for first-year teachers. Urban environments also present unique challenges and opportunities, and school districts often offer incentives to encourage teachers to take jobs in urban classrooms.

4. **Explain how the current reform movement in education is changing the teaching profession.**
   - The current reform movement in education has resulted in a number of changes in teacher education. Prospective teachers will encounter reforms calling for higher standards, more rigorous training, and increased testing. In addition to increased use of licensure exams, beginning teachers will also be asked to demonstrate their competence through professional portfolios.

(continued)

- INTASC, the Interstate New Teacher Assessment and Support Consortium, was designed to help states develop better teachers. It outlines 10 basic principles that guide the preparation of new teachers. The "Online Portfolio Activities" at the end of each chapter are linked to these principles.
- Increasingly, students and their teachers are being held accountable for learning progress. New federal legislation in the form of the No Child Left Behind Act makes educators accountable for the learning progress of the children they teach. This accountability often occurs in the form of standardized tests designed to measure acquisition of essential content. When the test results have important consequences for either students or teachers, such as nonpromotion or sanctions, then these are termed *high-stakes tests.*
- The Kentucky Education Reform Act created a statewide system of comprehensive reform. It includes curriculum standards, accountability systems, extended school services for students placed at-risk, school-based decision making, and school-based resource centers. Because of its scope, many compare this state's act to the federal No Child Left Behind Act.

Important Concepts

accountability (p. 28)
assessment (p. 17)
autonomy (p. 16)
curriculum (p. 17)
decision making (p. 18)
digital portfolio (p. 27)
ethics (p. 19)
extrinsic rewards (p. 4)
high-stakes tests (p. 28)

intrinsic rewards (p. 4)
professionalism (p. 15)
professional portfolio (p. 27)
reflection (p. 18)
reforms (p. 23)
socioeconomic status (p. 23)
standards (p. 17)
technician (p. 18)

Developing as a Professional

Preparing for Your Licensure Exam

This exercise will provide you with practice answering questions similar to the Praxis™ Principles of Learning and Teaching exam as well as your state-specific licensure exam.

Read the following case study, and then answer the questions that follow.

Marissa Anderson enters the teacher's lounge and collapses in a large overstuffed chair.

"I'm bushed," she comments, smiling at her friend, Anthony, another third-year teacher at her school.

"Late night partying?" he asks, examining a brown paper bag for the remains of his lunch.

"Don't I wish. Those evening classes are killing me, but I almost have my ELL [English language learner] endorsement. If I weren't learning so much, I'd start to wonder."

"Anything good that I can use?" Anthony asks.

"Well, we talked last night about the importance of verbal language in learning to read and how important it is to provide lots of opportunities for kids to practice their developing English skills."

"Hmm. That makes sense, but it doesn't sound much like the reading program our district wants us to use. It has a lot of individual worksheets and stresses teacher-centered instruction."

"I know. I've been thinking about that. Our reading program probably works for students who speak English, but how can my kids do worksheets when they can't even read the directions? So I've

got a dilemma—do what the district says, or do what I know and what research shows is best for my kids. For now I'm just going to shut my door and do the right thing. Down the line I need to talk with Jan [the school principal] and see if she can help me resolve this dilemma."

Analyze this case in terms of the following dimensions of professionalism. In your analysis, identify specific parts of the case that relate to professionalism and explain the connection.

1. Specialized body of knowledge

2. Extended training for licensure

3. Decision making and reflection

4. Autonomy

5. Ethical standards of conduct

 To receive feedback on your responses to these exercises, go to the Companion Website at www.prenhall.com/kauchak, then to the Preparing for Your Licensure Exam *module for Chapter 1.*

Discussion Questions

1. Do the reasons cited in the chapter for becoming a teacher change with the grade level or content area targeted by teachers? Why?

2. Do you believe teaching is more or less rewarding than it was in the past? Is it more or less difficult? Why do you think so?

3. Which of the intrinsic and extrinsic rewards in teaching are likely to become more important in the future? Less important?

4. For which group of teachers—teachers of elementary school students (grades K–5), middle school students (grades 6–8), or secondary students (grades 9–12)—are emotional rewards likely to be the greatest? Why?

5. For which group of teachers—elementary school, middle school, or secondary school teachers—are intellectual rewards likely to be the greatest? Why?

6. Is teaching a profession? If not, what would be necessary to make it one?

7. Will the move toward teacher professionalism be beneficial for teachers? Why or why not?

Developing as a Professional: Online Activities

Going into Schools

Go to the Companion Website at *www.prenhall.com/kauchak,* and click on the *Going into Schools* module for Chapter 1. You will find a number of school-based activities that will help you link chapter content to the schools in which you work.

Virtual Field Experience: Using Teacher Prep to Explore the Profession

If you would like to participate in a Virtual Field Experience, access the Teacher Prep Website at *www.prenhall.com/teacherprep.* After logging in, complete the following steps:

1. Click on "Video Classroom" on the left panel of the screen.

2. Go to "Foundations and Introduction to Education."

3. Finally, select "Module 1: Why Become a Teacher?" This video allows you to explore the teaching profession at three different levels. Answer the questions that follow the video clip.

Online Portfolio Activities

To develop your professional portfolio, further apply your understanding of chapter content, and address the INTASC standards, go to the Companion Website, then to this chapter's *Online Portfolio Activities*. Complete the suggested activities.

Appendix 1.1   Guidelines for Beginning a Professional Portfolio

Preparing a professional portfolio involves five steps (Bullock & Hawk, 2005; Campbell et al., 2007).

Step 1. *Specify a goal.* For example, you're probably taking this course because you've either decided that you want to teach, or you're at least considering teaching. Finding a satisfying teaching job would be a likely goal.

Step 2. *Determine how both past and future experiences relate to the goal.* You might choose to tutor a student with a reading problem, for example, to get professional experience that will make you more marketable.

Step 3. *Collect items that provide evidence of your developing knowledge and skill.* In addition to your résumé, which is always included in a portfolio, you might consider the following types of entries typically found in a teaching portfolio:

- Unit and lesson plans
- Samples of your work as a student
- Philosophy of education paper
- Description of your management system, including rules and procedures
- Grading policies
- Videotapes of you interacting with students (e.g., a clip of you working with the student you are tutoring)
- Transcripts

The Online Portfolio Activities you will complete throughout this text are designed to get you thinking about several of these components. In fact, any number of the activity products would make excellent entries for your portfolio. Other suggestions for portfolio components can be found in Bullock and Hawk (2005).

As you gather and create items, you should date each potential entry. The dates will help you later when you are organizing your portfolio.

Step 4. *Decide what items among your collection best illustrate your knowledge and skills.* A prospective employer is unlikely to view a bulky collection or series of videotapes, so you need to be selective; a videotaped lesson is likely a better entry than is a clip from a tutoring session.

Although you want to be selective when initially planning your portfolio, we suggest that you err on the side of including too much in your portfolio at first. If you think you might use an item, include it now. You can always remove an item, but recovering something that's been discarded earlier is often difficult.

Step 5. *Determine how to best present the items to the person or people connected to your goal.* You may be presenting your portfolio to the principal of the school in which you want to teach, for example.

You will want to organize your portfolio to make it accessible to an evaluator. The portfolio should open with a title page, followed by a table of contents. The most impressive entries go first to highlight your accomplishments. Work samples and evidence of performance, such as video clips, should always be displayed more prominently than, say, testimonial letters, which an evaluator often disregards. A chronological arrangement would provide viewers with some idea of your progress during the program.

To help you organize, put yourself in the evaluator's shoes. Remember, the evaluator knows little about you, and your portfolio is a way of introducing yourself. You're trying to convince a prospective employer that you're knowledgeable, skilled, and committed to the profession. Let communication and ease of access be your guide for arranging the information in your portfolio. If the portfolio is well organized, it will create a positive impression; the opposite will occur if it is disorganized or if items are inaccessible.

As we move further into the information age, many preservice teachers are developing electronic portfolios (Kilbane & Milman, 2003). They include everything a paper-based portfolio includes, but they do it more efficiently. For example, one CD-ROM can hold the equivalent of 300,000 text pages. Typed documents can be scanned into word processing files and stored on floppy disks or CD-ROMs, and video can be digitized and also stored on CD-ROMs. This saves both time and energy. Evaluators who want to view a video episode in a paper-based portfolio must find a VCR, review the tape, and put it back into the correct portfolio container. In contrast, video footage in an electronic portfolio can be augmented with text and graphics, which reviewers can access with the click of a mouse.

To create an electronic portfolio, you'll need to have the proper computer equipment and software and be skilled in their use. If these are obstacles for you, you can certainly create a traditional portfolio. However, you will also want to hone your computer skills and educate yourself about electronic portfolios. With the expansion of technology into more and more areas of teaching, it is likely that paper-based portfolios will eventually become obsolete.

Regardless of whether your portfolio is paper-based or electronic, it should provide your prospective employer with an overview of your experience and qualifications and offer an inviting snapshot of you as a developing professional in the field of teaching. For a detailed discussion of professional portfolios, see Bullock and Hawk (2005) and Campbell, Cignetti, Melenyzer, Nettles, and Wyman (2007).

Developing as a Professional

Chapter Outline	**Learning Objectives**
	After you have completed your study of this chapter, you should be able to:
Beliefs of Preservice and Beginning Teachers	1. Describe the beliefs of beginning teachers.

Entering the Profession
   Traditional and Alternative Licensure
   Developing a Professional Reputation
   Making Yourself Marketable
   Finding a Job
	2. Explain differences between traditional and alternative licensure and the essential factors involved in finding a desirable job.

Your First Year of Teaching
   Survival Skills for the First Year
   Induction and Mentoring Programs
   Teacher Evaluation
	3. Identify factors that contribute to a successful first year of teaching.

Career-Long Professional Development
   Membership in Professional Organizations
   Becoming a Teacher-Leader
   Attaining Certification: The National Board for
     Professional Teaching Standards
	4. Describe career-long professional development opportunities available to teachers.

Case Studies

 Elementary
 Middle
 Secondary

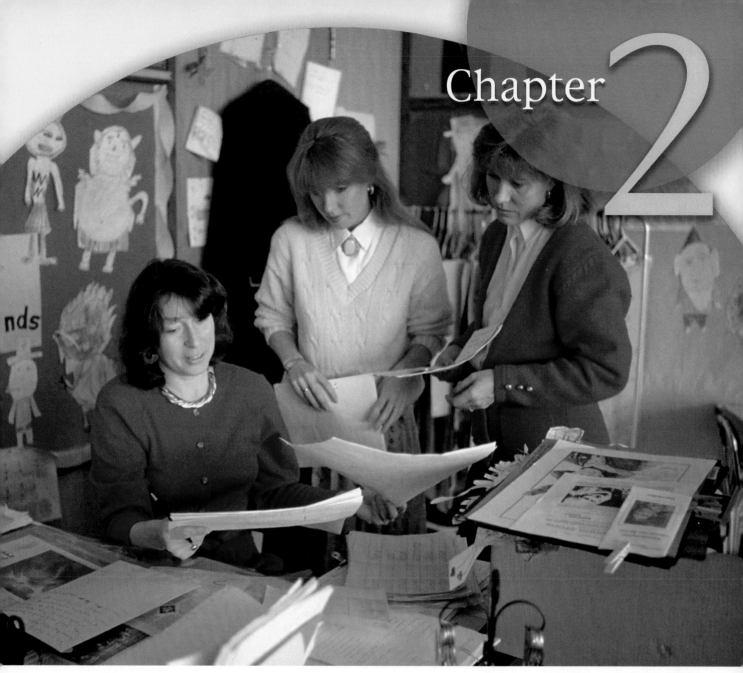

Chapter 1 was designed to help you begin the process of deciding whether you want to be a teacher. In this chapter we continue this process by examining the beliefs of beginning teachers as well as the processes involved in developing as a professional and finding your first job. Let's begin by looking at one beginning teacher's experience as she recalls her first faculty meeting.

My first faculty meeting. Very interesting. Mrs. Zellner [the principal] seems really nice. She went on and on about what a great job the teachers did last year and how test scores were way up compared to the year before. She also extended a special welcome to those of us who are new.

Speaking of new teachers, there sure are a lot of us. I wonder if they're all as scared as I am. I'm not sure what I would have done if Mrs. Landsdorp [the teacher in the room next door] hadn't taken me under her wing. She made me feel much better about starting in an urban school. So many of the kids come from low-income homes, and English isn't the first language for several of them. She said that some of the teachers tend to "write them off" and assume that they can't learn, but that isn't true at all. In fact, many of them are quite bright. They just need a lot of help and support. She's wonderful. She's sort of gruff, but Andrea [a new friend and second-year teacher] say's she's a softy underneath, and she really loves the kids.

I can't believe how much there is to do—IEPs, progress reports, CPR training, being responsible for spotting signs of abuse. When do I teach? I hope I can cut it. (Shelley, a new third-grade teacher, reflecting on her first faculty meeting)

When you finish your program, and if you choose to teach, you'll be joining people like Shelley. To see how the Shelleys of the world view themselves and teaching, please respond to the following survey. We examine each of these items below as the chapter unfolds.

---

professional knowledge: test yourself!

For each item, circle the number that best represents your thinking. Use the following scale as a guide.

1 = Strongly disagree
2 = Disagree
3 = Uncertain
4 = Agree
5 = Strongly agree

1. When I begin teaching, I will be a better teacher than most of the teachers now in the field.

    1   2   3   4   5

2. As I gain experience in teaching, I expect to become more confident in my ability to help children learn.

    1   2   3   4   5

3. The most effective teachers are those best able to clearly explain the content they teach their students.

    1   2   3   4   5

4. I will learn about most of the important aspects of teaching when I get into a classroom.

    1   2   3   4   5

5. If I thoroughly understand the content I'm teaching, I'll be able to figure out a way of getting it across to students.

    1   2   3   4   5

This is available in a downloadable format on the Companion Website for personal portfolio use.

Beliefs of Preservice and Beginning Teachers

The course for which this book is used is likely one of the first you'll take in your teacher preparation program. One of the goals of the course is to help you begin the process of learning to teach.

Teachers' beliefs have a strong influence on their teaching and the process of learning to teach (Richardson, 2003). Our goal in this section is to help you examine your own beliefs and the impact they can have on your professional growth.

Let's begin by returning to the survey you just completed. If you either agreed or strongly agreed with each of the statements, your beliefs are consistent with those commonly held by other students in teacher preparation programs. Let's see what research tells us about these beliefs.

Item 1: When I begin teaching, I will be a better teacher than most of the teachers now in the field. Preservice teachers are optimistic and idealistic: "Prospective teachers report being confident and self-assured in their teaching ability," but they "may be unrealistically optimistic about their future teaching performance" (Borko & Putnam, 1996, p. 678). The danger occurs when the realities of classrooms shock beginning teachers, who then feel as though "nobody prepared me for this" (Feiman-Nemser, 2001). Optimism wanes, and they may question their career choice; about 1 in 4 quits after the second year, and 4 in 10 leave the profession within the first 5 years (Grant, 2006).

Item 2: As I gain experience in teaching, I expect to become more confident in my ability to help children learn. As with Item 1, most preservice teachers expect to become increasingly confident in their ability to help children learn. However, the opposite often occurs. During the first few years of teaching, many tend to become less democratic in their work with students and less confident in their ability to overcome the limitations of home environments and family background (Bransford, Darling-Hammond, & LePage, 2005). We emphasize this point so that you might avoid this trap that ensnares many beginning teachers.

Item 3: The most effective teachers are those best able to clearly explain the content they teach their students. Many preservice teachers believe that teaching is essentially a process of "telling" or explaining content to students, probably because most of their own teachers simply lectured to them (van den Berg, 2002; J. Wang & Odell, 2002). However, research suggests that lecturing to students, especially young or unmotivated ones, is quite ineffective (Eggen & Kauchak, 2007).

Let's look at one intern's experience.

My first lesson with the kids. Chris [her supervising teacher] said I was on my own, sink or swim. I hardly slept last night, but today I feel like celebrating. The kids were so into it. I brought my Styrofoam ball and had the kids compare the latitude and longitude lines I had drawn on it and then look at the globe. I thought the first period was supposed to be Chris's lowest, but they did the best. He was impressed.

Now I understand the stuff Dr. Martinez [one of her professors] stressed so much when he was always after us to use concrete examples and question, question, question. I know I have a lot to learn. I thought I could just explain everything to them, but they got confused and drifted off so fast I couldn't believe it. As soon as I started asking questions about the lines on the Styrofoam ball, though, they perked right up. I think I can do this. It was actually a heady experience. (Gabriel, an intern in a seventh-grade geography class)

As Gabriel quickly discovered, teaching is much more complex than simply explaining (Donovan & Bransford, 2005). Research indicates that explaining, by itself, is often ineffective for helping students understand topics in depth.

Item 4: I will learn about most of the important aspects of teaching when I get into a classroom. This is another common preservice teacher belief. Many preservice teachers believe that experience is the only way they can learn to teach, and they also believe that their teacher education classes are little more than hoops they must jump through before getting into their own classrooms (Fajet, Bello, & Leftwich, 2005).

Experience in classrooms is essential in learning to teach, but it isn't sufficient by itself. Unfortunately, in many cases, experience results in using the same procedures and techniques year after year, even when they're ineffective. Research also consistently indicates that students who go through traditional teacher preparation programs (such as the one you're in) are more successful and satisfied in their work than those who just jump into classrooms without prior classes (Darling-Hammond, 2000). Research and theory, combined

Making Connections:
To deepen your understanding of the topics in this section of the chapter and integrate them with topics you've already studied, go to the *Making Connections* module for Chapter 2 at **www.prenhall.com/kauchak.** Respond to questions 1 and 2.

with experience, help beginning teachers make sense of the often bewildering classrooms and students they'll encounter. This is one of the reasons you're studying this text.

Item 5: If I thoroughly understand the content I'm teaching, I'll be able to figure out a way of getting it across to students. One of the most pervasive myths in teaching is that knowledge of subject matter is all that is necessary to teach it effectively. Knowledge of content is essential, of course, but learning to teach requires a great deal of additional knowledge—knowledge you'll acquire in your teacher-preparation program (Darling-Hammond & Baratz-Snowdon, 2005).

Check Your Understanding

1.1   How effective do beginning teachers believe they will be compared to teachers already in the field?

1.2   Describe beginning teachers' beliefs about what makes a teacher effective.

1.3   Describe how beginning teachers' confidence in their ability to help students learn changes as they gain experience.

For feedback, go to Appendix A, Check Your Understanding, *located in the back of this text.*

Entering the Profession

Having examined the beliefs of preservice and beginning teachers, let's look now at the processes involved in entering the teaching profession.

Traditional and Alternative Licensure

All professionals—physicians, lawyers, and psychologists, for example—must be "licensed" in order to work in their occupations, and this applies to teachers as well. This process of licensure is designed to protect the public and ensure competence in each profession. In this section, we examine the processes involved in earning a license and what you can do to make yourself marketable.

Traditional Licensure

All K–12 teachers are required by law (in all 50 states plus the District of Columbia) to be licensed by a state department of education before they can teach in public schools. **Licensure** is the process by which a state evaluates the credentials of prospective teachers. By awarding a license, the state certifies that a teacher is competent in subject-area content, teaching skills, and classroom management, and is morally fit to work with youth.

You're likely taking this course in a traditional licensure program through which you'll earn a bachelor's degree. The program consists of a general education component that includes courses in history, English, math, and science, as well as education courses designed to help you develop your professional knowledge—the pedagogical content knowledge, general pedagogical knowledge, and knowledge of learners and learning discussed in Chapter 1. If you're planning to become a high school teacher, you are also required to accumulate a specified number of course hours in the subject area (e.g., math) in which you plan to teach (36 states have this requirement) (McCabe, 2006).

Increasingly, as you learned in Chapter 1, teachers are also being asked to pass competency tests that measure their basic skills in reading, writing, and mathematics (37 states had this requirement in 2006); high school teachers' background in an academic area such as

Licensure. The process by which a state evaluates the credentials of prospective teachers to ensure that they have achieved satisfactory levels of teaching competence and are morally fit to work with youth.

chemistry or English (43 states require this); and their understanding of learning and teaching (25 states require this)
(McCabe, 2006). The Praxis™ Series, which consists of all
three of these types of components, is currently being used
in 35 states (Educational Testing Service, 2005).

The specific requirements for licensure vary from state
to state, and the student advising office in your college or
university can help you access them. If you're planning to
move to another state, your education library may have
books that describe the licensure requirements for all the
states. If it doesn't, you can write or call the state certification office directly. The addresses and phone numbers of
these offices can be found on this text's Companion Website
at *www.prenhall.com/kauchak*.

Alternative Licensure

To meet the demand for more teachers, many states are developing alternative routes to licensure, and some of you
taking this course may be involved in one of these pro-

*During the process of licensure, teachers are increasingly being asked
to demonstrate their competence through portfolios, interviews, tests,
and on-the-job performance.* (Will Hart/PhotoEdit Inc.)

grams. Currently, 45 states have alternative-route programs, and more than 75 percent of college or university teacher-education programs run one or collaborate with them. About a
third of the teachers hired each year are licensed in this way (Blair, 2003; McCabe, 2006).

A person seeking alternative licensure must hold a bachelor's degree in the content area
to be taught, such as math or English; pass a licensure test; complete a brief, intensive teacher
training experience; and complete a supervised teaching internship.

Alternative licensure is controversial. Proponents make several arguments supporting
this teacher-preparation route. Most alternative licensure candidates are older than students
in undergraduate education programs, so they've had more life experiences; they have already earned bachelor's degrees, so they are more focused on learning to teach than are undergraduates who must combine classes in their content areas with courses in professional
education (Dill & Stafford-Johnson, 2002). Also, alternative programs are shorter and tend
to attract members of cultural minorities and talented and experienced people in areas of critical need, such as math and science (Blair, 2003). Proponents also argue that students in these
programs are more academically talented than those in traditional programs.

Critics, however, point to the limited training in pedagogy that alternative licensure candidates receive (e.g., acquiring the pedagogical content knowledge, general pedagogical
knowledge, and knowledge of learners and learning that we discussed in Chapter 1). Critics
argue that this limited training results in instruction that is not responsive to students' needs
(Darling-Hammond, Chung, & Frelow, 2002). Further, the intensive mentoring and supervision during the first few months of full-time teaching that is supposed to compensate for
the new teachers' lack of formal course work often doesn't exist (Ansell & McCabe, 2003).
Consequently, the first year of teaching becomes a sink-or-swim situation, with many teachers (and their students) failing (Darling-Hammond et al., 2002).

Finally, critics cite statistics indicating that the 2-year dropout rate for alternative licensure candidates is more than three times greater than the national average for new teachers
(Darling-Hammond, 2000), though other research suggests the opposite (Guarino et al.,
2006). This negative statistic may be skewed, however, because alternative licensure teachers are disproportionately assigned to the most demanding teaching situations, such as urban schools with high numbers of cultural minorities from low-income households (Blair,
2003). It is paradoxical that the students who need experienced teachers the most are often
least likely to have them (Archer, 2003; Blair, 2003).

Conclusive assessments of alternative licensure are difficult to make because so much
variation exists among programs (Johnson & Birkeland, 2006). High-quality alternative

Developing a professional reputation begins with the college courses you are currently taking. [Michael Newman/PhotoEdit Inc.]

licensure programs are both time-consuming and costly. Research examining the performance of students taught by teachers from alternative licensure programs is also mixed. Some data suggest students fare as well as those taught by traditionally prepared teachers; however, most data do not (Darling-Hammond et al., 2001; Laczko-Kerr & Berliner, 2003).

Developing a Professional Reputation

Since you're at the beginning of your teacher-preparation program, it might appear that preparing for a job is well into the future. This isn't true. The time to begin developing a professional reputation is now. Let's look at one student's experience.

I really wish someone had reminded me of these things sooner. When I started, like a lot of others, I didn't take it all too seriously. I'd blow class off now and then, and I didn't always get there on time. I actually did study, but I guess not as hard as I should have.

When I asked Dr. Laslow for a letter of recommendation, he refused. Actually, he said he didn't know me well enough to write a good one. I couldn't believe it. He was nice about it, but he wouldn't write one, advising me to find someone who knew me better and was more familiar with my work. And a couple others were sort of lukewarm, especially in my major. I guess the classes were just too large for them to get to know me. Now it's too late. My record is a little spotty and I feel bad about it now, but I can't go back. I used to wonder why Brad and Kelly always seemed to get all the breaks. Now I get it. (Jeremy, a recent graduate without a job)

Do you know people who seem to get a lot of breaks? Do you get your share? Do your instructors know you, and do they respect and value your work? Students who get breaks do so for a reason. They attend all their classes, turn their work in on time, and attempt to learn as much as possible from their experiences. The quality of their work is consistently high. In other words, they behave professionally. Just as teachers in the field demonstrate professional behaviors, students are expected to as well. Professors value conscientiousness, and students like Jeremy trouble them. It's easy to understand why Brad and Kelly got breaks while Jeremy didn't.

What can you do to develop a professional reputation? Here are some suggestions:

- Attend all classes, and be on time. If you must miss, see your professor in advance or explain afterward.
- Turn in required assignments on time, and follow the established guidelines or criteria.
- Study conscientiously, and try to learn as much as possible in all your classes.
- Participate in class. Offer comments and ask questions. You will enjoy your classes more and also learn more from them.
- Extend your classroom behavior to your life. Take every opportunity to learn something new. For example, travel, especially to other countries, provides opportunities to learn about other cultures and the ways they approach education. Trips like these also make valuable entries on your résumé (which we'll discuss shortly).
- Read and try to be well informed. Learn for its own sake.
- Set yourself the goal to be the best student you can.

If you sincerely attempt to learn and grow, your professional reputation will take care of itself. But you must begin now.

TABLE 2.1   Making Yourself Marketable

Suggested Experience	Example	Professional Benefits
Develop a minor area of study in a high-need area.	If you're a French major, consider a minor in Spanish. If you're a biology major, consider a minor in chemistry.	You'll have more versatility in the jobs you apply for.
Join professional organizations.	Join your university's chapter of the National Education Association or a student chapter of another professional organization. (Professional organizations are listed on the Companion Website and in Table 2.3.)	You'll stay up-to-date on issues in your field and expand your network of professional contacts.
Tutor a child.	Become a reading tutor at a local school. Most schools welcome volunteer tutors and may also share your name with parents interested in a private tutor.	You'll gain direct experience working with children and may earn some extra money.
Seek leadership positions.	Run for a student government office.	Leadership experience on a résumé tells potential employers that you have effective human relations skills and the desire to be a lifelong learner.
Do volunteer work.	Spend a few hours each weekend helping out at the local food pantry.	Volunteer work can be enriching, and it indicates your desire to contribute to society.
Become an aide.	Ask your local school district about job openings for part-time classroom aides.	Working as an aide will give you valuable classroom experience and a part-time job.

Making Yourself Marketable

The most effective way to make yourself marketable is to acquire as much professional knowledge and experience as possible. The knowledge component will be addressed in the courses you'll take in your program; your professional experiences will complement this knowledge by applying it in varied contexts. Some suggestions for potential professional experiences are included in Table 2.1. If you pursue any of these experiences, you can write about them in your portfolio and include them in the résumé you construct to summarize your qualifications.

Building a Portfolio and Résumé

The interview was going okay, but I was uneasy. The principal I was interviewing with was cordial, but she certainly wasn't enthusiastic. "I've had it," I thought to myself. She even quit asking me questions after about 20 minutes. I really wanted the job, too.

As I was about to leave, I happened to mention, "Would you like to see my portfolio?" She looked at it for a couple minutes, and then she started asking some probing questions. When she stuck my DVD in her computer and saw me teaching, she really lit up. I got the job! (Shelley, the new teacher at the beginning of the chapter)

You were introduced to portfolios in Chapter 1, and activities are suggested at the end of each chapter to help you develop your professional portfolio. Specific guidelines for creating your portfolio are found in Appendix 1.1, at the end of Chapter 1.

The first item that appears in your portfolio should be a résumé summarizing your strengths and accomplishments as a teacher. A **résumé** is a document that provides an overview of an individual's job qualifications and work experience. It typically is the first thing a prospective employer sees and should make a clear and persuasive statement about your qualifications.

Résumé. A document that provides an overview of an individual's job qualifications and work experience.

When constructing your résumé, clarity and simplicity should be guiding principles. People reading your résumé want to be able to easily find personal information, such as your address and phone number, as well as information about your education, work experience, and interests. They'll expect you to list references or be willing to provide them later. An effective résumé has the following components:

- Personal data
- Professional objectives
- Education
- Teaching experience
- Work experience
- Extracurricular activities
- Honors and awards
- References

The office of career planning and placement at your college or university will be able to help you in preparing your own résumé. A sample résumé containing these components is shown in Figure 2.1.

Creating a Credentials File

Your college or university will have a placement center designed to help graduates find jobs. An essential service of this center, in addition to providing information about job openings, is to serve as a repository for your credentials file. A **credentials file** is a collection of important documents teachers submit when they apply for teaching positions. It typically includes background information about you, your résumé, type of position sought, courses taken, performance evaluations by your internship-cooperating teacher and college or university supervisor, and letters of recommendation (usually three or more). When you apply for a job, you notify the placement center, which then sends your credentials file to the prospective employer. If, after reviewing this file, the district feels there is a potential match, you'll be contacted for an interview.

Writing a Successful Letter of Application

You have written a résumé and constructed a portfolio showcasing your skills and experiences. Now it is time to actually apply for a teaching position. School districts typically have a number of positions open before the start of the school year, so your letter of application, which will serve as a cover letter for your résumé, should clearly state the kind of position for which you are applying. In addition, it should highlight key elements of your résumé that you'd like to emphasize to a potential employer. And, finally, it should close with a statement detailing your availability for an interview, the topic of the next section. (See Figure 2.2 for a sample letter of application.)

Finding a Job

To this point we have discussed factors that will make you more effective once you get a teaching position. But when and how do you get started in the process of finding a job? The answer to *when* is now. We address the question of how in this section.

Where Are the Jobs?

Your ultimate goal is to locate a teaching position that will allow you to utilize your skills and develop as a professional, but such a position may not be easy to find. Several factors influence teacher supply and demand.

Geography is one factor. Student growth patterns vary by geographic area and grade level, mirroring demographic trends in the country. The greatest student enrollment increases are

Credentials file. A collection of important documents teachers need to submit when they apply for teaching positions.

Figure 2.1   A Sample Résumé

Melinda Garcia

Personal Data
Address:
2647 Bay Meadows Road
Jacksonville, FL 32224

Home phone: 904-267-5943
Work phone: 904-620-6743
E-mail: mgarcia@msn.com

Professional Objectives:
Elementary Teaching Position, K–6
Elementary Title I Reading Teacher, K–6

Education:
B.A. Elementary Education, University of North Florida, June 2007
Major Area: Elementary Education, K–8
Endorsements: Reading, K–8

Teaching Experience:
Student Teaching: Paxon Elementary, Duval County School District.
    Cooperating Teacher: Mrs. Nola Wright.
    Worked in a first-grade urban classroom with seven students who were English Language Learners; assumed
    full control of classroom for one eight-week grading period. Also worked with Mrs. Althea Walkman,
    First Grade Title I Coordinator. Administered reading diagnostic tests and developed specialized reading
    programs for groups of students.

Math and Reading Clinical Experience: Mathew Gilbert Elementary, Duval County School District.
    Cooperating Teacher: Ms. Linda Gonzalez
    Served as a teacher aide in a fifth-grade, self-contained classroom. Taught both small-group and whole-class
    lessons in reading and math.

Elementary Tutoring: Sandalwood Elementary, Duval County School District.
    Cooperating Teacher: Mrs. Alice Watkins
    Observed and tutored third-grade students in all subject matter areas. Tutored students in reading and math
    one-on-one and in small groups.

Work Experience:
Counselor and Tutor: YWCA After-school Activities Program. June 2006 to present. Worked with elementary students
in both academic and recreation areas.

Lifeguard, Duval County Recreation Program. Summers, 2006, 2007. Full-time summer lifeguard; also provided
swimming lessons for young students (4–6 years old).

Extracurricular Activities and Interests:
Vice President, University of North Florida, Student International Reading Association.
Senator, University of North Florida, Student Government Association.
Member, University of North Florida Swim Team.

Honors and Awards:
B. A. with Honors, University of North Florida.
Florida UTEACH Scholarship Recipient, 2005–2007.

References:
References and credentials file available upon request.

Figure 2.2   Letter of Application

Melinda Garcia
2647 Bay Meadows Road
Jacksonville, FL 32224

June 20, 2007

Dr. Robert Allington
Personnel Director
Duval County School District
2341 Prudential Drive
Jacksonville, FL 32215

Dear Dr. Allington,

I am writing this letter to apply for an elementary teaching position in your district beginning this fall. I recently graduated with honors from the University of North Florida, with a degree in elementary education and an endorsement in reading.

As my enclosed résumé indicates, I have had a number of rewarding experiences working with students in your district. Early in my elementary education program, I observed and tutored students in a third-grade classroom at Sandalwood Elementary School. I then did extensive clinical experiences in fifth-grade math and reading classes at Matthew Gilbert Elementary. During my internship at Paxon Elementary School, I was assigned to a first-grade classroom with significant numbers of Title I students and English Language Learners. During this experience, I learned a great deal about helping culturally diverse first-graders become skilled readers.

As I worked toward my degree, I focused on reading as my major area of endorsement. Reading is the key to success in all other subjects, and I believe I have the knowledge and skills to help young children become successful readers. Through my extensive experiences in classrooms at different levels, I have seen how effective reading programs build on the background knowledge and skills of developing readers. Please note that I have had formal course work in reading diagnosis as well as hands-on experiences implementing different diagnostic tests. I would like to utilize this expertise in a teaching position in your district.

I have arranged for my credentials file to be sent to you from the Placement Office at the University of North Florida. Please feel free to contact me at the telephone numbers listed on my résumé for any additional information. I am available for an interview at any time this summer.

Thank you for considering my application.

Sincerely,

Melinda Garcia

Melinda Garcia

occurring in the South and West and where general population growths are also occurring. These regions will have the greatest demand for teachers (Kober, 2006).

Within geographic areas, specific locations also influence teacher supply and demand. Job opportunities are much greater in rural and urban schools than they are in the suburbs, and these districts employ a number of recruiting strategies to attract competent new teachers, such as offering signing bonuses, financial help for professional development courses, and even housing incentives (Archer, 2003). For example, New York City recently offered housing subsidies of up to $14,600 to attract math, science, and special education teachers (Herszenhorn, 2006). Shelley, our new teacher at the beginning of the chapter, experienced these patterns:

At first I looked for jobs in two suburban schools, but there were no openings. However, I received offers from three different urban schools. I was a little hesitant at first because I had read about the challenges of working in urban settings, especially for first-year teachers. But one of the assistant principals was great. She talked to me about the job, what it entailed, and the kind of help I'd receive in an induction program at that school. I was paired with a wonderful mentor (Mrs. Landsdorp), and I'm having a challenging but great year. I love these kids and think I'm going to make it.

The specific teaching position you seek will also affect your chances of finding a job. Areas such as special education, English language learning (including bilingual education and English as a second language), foreign languages (especially Spanish), technology, math, physics, and chemistry need teachers more than others such as English, history, or physical education (Murphy, DeArmond, & Guin, 2003).

What implications do these job patterns have for you? First, if you haven't already decided on a major, don't select one based on job availability alone. To be effective, you must want to teach in the area you select. Don't major in chemistry, for example, if you dislike chemistry. However, if you want to teach chemistry, you now know that there is a high probability of getting a job in the area. Second, try to become knowledgeable about where teaching jobs exist. The career placement center at your college or university can help you. You'll increase your chances of finding a job if you're flexible about where you'll teach. Your first teaching position may not be in an ideal location, but you can use it to gain experience and as a stepping stone to other positions.

Interviewing Effectively

As you saw in Chapter 1, professionalism is a theme for this book, and professional behavior in an interview is essential. This is the setting that almost certainly will determine whether or not you get a job. Some guidelines for interviewing effectively are outlined in Table 2.2.

What are some things schools look for in new teachers during an interview? Research suggests the following:

- Knowledge of a content area(s) as well as knowledge of how to help students learn (see Chapter 12)
- An understanding of how to organize and manage a classroom (see Chapter 11)
- A sincere interest in making a difference in students' lives
- A variety of life experiences that can contribute to your classroom
- The ability to work with others
- Adaptability and flexibility

Interviews provide opportunities for teaching candidates to explain their qualifications as well as find out about the positions they're applying for. (Michael Newman/PhotoEdit, Inc.)

TABLE 2.2   Guidelines for Interviewing Effectively

Guideline	Rationale
Be on time.	Nothing creates a worse impression than being late for an interview.
Dress appropriately.	Wear an outfit appropriate for an interview, and be well-groomed. Shorts, jeans, and T-shirts are inappropriate, as is an eyebrow ring. You have the right to dress and groom yourself in any way you choose, but if you are serious about getting' a job, you won't demonstrate your freedom of expression during a job interview.
Speak clearly, and use standard English and grammar.	Clear language is correlated with effective teaching, and your verbal ability creates an impression of professional ability.
Sit comfortably and calmly.	Fidgeting—or worse, glancing at your watch—suggests that you're either nervous or you'd rather be somewhere else.
Communicate empathy for children and a desire to work with them.	Communicating an understanding of learning, learner development, and instruction demonstrates that you have a professional knowledge base.

If you are genuinely interested in working with young people, and if you've been conscientious in your teacher-preparation program, the interview will largely take care of itself. Nothing communicates more effectively than a sincere desire to do the job for which you're interviewing.

Additional preparation can increase the positive impression you make, however. For example, how would you respond to the following questions, all of which are frequently asked in teacher interviews?

- Why do you want to teach?
- Why do you want to work in this school?
- What is your philosophy of education?
- How would you motivate unmotivated learners?
- How would you plan for classroom management?
- How would you handle an incident of misbehavior?
- How would you organize a unit on a topic in your area?
- How would you involve parents or caregivers in their children's education?

The more specific and concrete your response to each of the questions, the more positive an impression you will make. We suggest that you keep these questions in mind and begin to form answers to them as you go through your teacher-preparation program. If you are prepared, you will also be more at ease during the interview.

For instance, here is a specific response to the question about teaching philosophy:

"I believe that all children can learn, and I would try my best to make that happen by ensuring that all students are involved in the lessons I teach. Research suggests that active involvement is essential for learning. I would get them involved by calling on each of them as often as possible and using group work to develop content knowledge as well as develop social skills."

The answer communicates that you're clear about what you would try to do and why. Also, citing research suggests that you are knowledgeable, something all school districts value (Strong & Hindman, 2003). In contrast, a vague response, such as "I am a humanistic and learner-centered teacher," leaves the interviewer with the impression that you're just saying abstract words you learned in a class, which is much less persuasive.

Assessing Prospective Schools

The interview process is a two-way street. Not only are you being interviewed, but you are also interviewing the school. You want a job, but you also want to determine if the school is the kind of place in which you want to work. Research suggests that the upkeep and condition of the school as well as its culture have a powerful influence on teachers' satisfaction on the job (Buckley, Schneider, & Shang, 2005). When you interview, you should ask questions of the principal and other people you would work with. Doing so helps you learn about the position and communicates that you are thoughtful and serious about the job.

Some factors to consider when evaluating a school as a potential workplace include:

- *Commitment and leadership of the principal.* The principal's leadership sets the tone for the school (S. Johnson & Birkeland, 2003; Ubben, Hughes, & Norris, 2004). When teachers leave a school because of adverse conditions, dissatisfaction with support from administrators was the number one reason (Luekens, Lyter, & Fox, 2004). Does the principal demonstrate caring for students and support for teachers? The answers to these questions are highly inferential, but you can look for evidence in the principal's manner and comments.
- *School mission.* Does the principal communicate a clear mission for the school? If you have a chance to talk to other teachers, ask them if the teachers feel as if they're a team, all working for the benefit of students. The collective beliefs of teachers in a school that they can positively influence students' lives have a powerful influence on teacher morale and even student achievement (Goddard, Hoy, & Hoy, 2004).
- *School climate.* Does the emotional climate of the school seem positive? How do office personnel treat students? Does the support staff, such as custodians and cafeteria workers, feel like part of the team? Do school employees communicate a positive and upbeat attitude? Workplace conditions, both emotional and physical, are major factors influencing whether teachers leave or remain in a school (Luekens et al., 2004).
- *The physical plant.* Are student work products such as art and woodshop projects displayed in cases and on the walls? Do signs and notices suggest that the school is a positive environment for learning? Are the classrooms, halls, and restrooms generally clean and free of debris and graffiti?
- *The behavior of students.* Are students generally orderly and polite to one another and to the teachers? Do they seem happy to be at school?
- *Community support.* Do people in the community value education and support the school? How does the school involve parents in their children's education, and do they support school functions?
- *An induction program for teachers.* Does the school have a mentoring program for first-year teachers? First-year teachers who participate in mentoring programs are more likely to succeed and stay in teaching than those who don't (Darling-Hammond & Baratz-Snowdon, 2005). (We examine induction and mentoring programs in more detail later in the chapter.)

These questions are difficult to answer in one visit to a school, but they are important for your future development and satisfaction with the job. Working conditions in schools vary dramatically, and they can make the difference between a rewarding first year of teaching and one that makes you reconsider your decision to teach (S. Johnson & Birkeland, 2003). In addition, the support of parents and the community is important because it makes a huge difference in the attitudes, behaviors, and work habits of students (Marzano, 2003).

Private School Employment

You might also consider teaching in a private school; approximately 12 percent of all students attend private schools (Kober, 2006). There were 29,273 private K–12 schools in the United States in 2001, an increase of 7 percent over 1999 (National Center for Education Statistics, 2004). Most (76 percent) are religiously oriented, with Catholic schools being the most common (37 percent) of private schools. You are most likely to find private school employment in the South and in urban areas or large towns.

Average starting salaries for private school teachers are about 30 percent lower than those in public schools, however, and the difference increases to more than 40 percent for maximum salaries. In addition, private schools typically don't provide the same insurance benefits offered in public schools. Because of these adverse financial conditions, private school teachers in 2000–2001 were almost twice as likely to leave teaching as their public school counterparts (Luekens et al., 2004). When they left private schools, more than half (53 percent) transferred to public schools.

exploring diversity

The Competition for Minority Teachers

Nearly a third of school-age children in the United States are members of cultural minorities, and in two states, California and Texas, less than 50 percent of the school population is White. In the 25 largest cities, students of color compose at least half of the student population (Ladson-Billings, 2005; National Education Association, 2003). At the same time, the percentage of teachers who are members of minority groups remains fixed at about 12 percent, and in some areas is as low as 1 percent (Ladson-Billings, 2005). Projections indicate that before the mid 21st century, more than half of the nation's students will be members of cultural minorities (U.S. Bureau of Census, 2003).

Concern over these changing demographics has resulted in greater efforts to recruit minority teachers. Although no evidence suggests that nonminority teachers cannot work effectively with minority students, many educators believe that minority teachers bring valuable and unique perspectives to the classroom. Students need role models who share their cultural backgrounds, and minority role models may more effectively motivate students, because students can identify more closely with them (Pintrich & Schunk, 2002). Minority teachers can also provide more culturally relevant instruction by helping bridge differences between minority students' homes and cultures and schools. In addition, they can enrich a school's faculty by providing alternate perspectives on effective teaching and learning practices for minority students (Ladson-Billings, 2005; Yan & Gong, 2003).

To attract minority candidates to teaching, recruiters in many states have developed scholarships and loan-forgiveness programs. Alternative licensure programs often interest older people interested in a career change and are promising avenues for bringing minorities into the profession.

However, difficulties with these programs exist. For example, the recruitment strategies sometimes conflict with current reforms attempting to raise academic standards for teachers. Recruiters are attempting to attract teachers, whereas reformers are calling for more rigid academic standards, usually measured by standardized tests. This practice has a history of negatively and disproportionately affecting minorities (Guarino, Santibañez, & Daley, 2006).

School districts have also used alternative licensure to attract minorities to teaching; for example, nearly half of the candidates who went through California's alternative program in

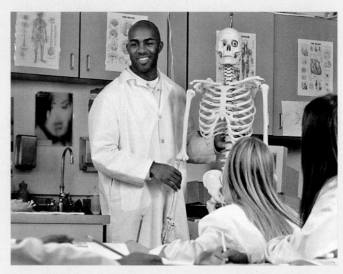

Minority teachers act as role models for minority students and help bridge gaps between homes and schools. (Getty Images, Inc—Image 100 Royalty Free)

1998–1999 were members of minority groups, as were 41 percent of those who went through the Texas program in 1998 (National Center for Education Information, 2000). However, as we saw earlier in the chapter, a much higher percentage of teachers who go through alternative licensure programs leave teaching than do those who complete traditional programs.

There is some room for optimism. The enrollment of African-American students in colleges of education increased from 6 percent to 9 percent in the 1990s, suggesting that the downward trend in the number of African-American teachers might be reversing (Archer, 2000a). Surveys indicate that African-American, Native American, and Hispanic college graduates are more likely to become teachers than are White graduates. However, the current bottleneck in K–12 schools limits the number of minority teachers who go on to college and become teachers; students in these groups are less likely to succeed in and ultimately graduate from high school (Barton, 2006; Swanson, 2004). Leaders suggest that a nation wanting the teaching force to more nearly reflect the composition of society must first focus its educational efforts on today's K–12 students.

Teachers often choose to work in private schools because these schools often waive the licensing requirements that public school teachers are required by law to meet. In addition, teachers sometimes choose private school employment because the school is dedicated to religious or intellectual principles consistent with the teacher's beliefs, communication between administrators and teachers is easier because these schools are often smaller, and parents whose children attend private schools tend to be more involved in school activities than those in public schools. Deciding to teach in a public or private school is ultimately an individual decision, influenced by your values and needs.

Making Connections:
To deepen your understanding of the topics in this section of the chapter and integrate them with topics you've already studied, go to the *Making Connections* module for Chapter 2 at **www.prenhall.com/kauchak.** Respond to questions 3–5.

Check Your Understanding

2.1   What are two differences between traditional and alternative licensure?

2.2   What are the two most essential factors involved in finding a desirable job?

2.3   In which areas are teaching jobs most plentiful?

For feedback, go to Appendix A, Check Your Understanding, *located in the back of this text.*

Your First Year of Teaching

What will your first year of teaching be like? Unfortunately, a significant number of beginning teachers drop out in the first few years on the job. About 6 percent of all public school teachers leave the profession each year, but the number of new teachers who leave after their first year is much higher—about 15 percent. In addition, another 15 percent leave after their second year, and still another 10 percent after their third (Ingersoll & Smith, 2004). After the fifth year of teaching, a discouraging 46 percent of new teachers have left the profession (Kober, 2006).

The following comments help explain why some beginning teachers leave the profession:

Wow! Was I naive. I was tired of sitting in classes, and I wanted so badly to be finished and get out into the "real world." What I never realized was just how cushy being a student was. If I was a little tired or didn't study enough, I would just coast through class. Now, no coasting. You have to be ready every minute of every day. I've never been so tired in my life. You're in front of kids all day, and then you go home and work late into the night to get ready for the next day. They have us filling out reports, doing surveys, and everything other than teaching, so I don't get a chance to plan during the day. I can't even make a phone call unless it's during my lunch break or planning period.

And then there's my fourth period. They come in from lunch just wired. It takes me half the period to get them settled down, and that's on a good day.

Sometimes I just need someone to talk to, but we're all so busy. Everybody thinks they're an expert on teaching, because they've been a student. They don't have a clue. Let them try it for 2 days, and they'd be singing a different tune. (Antonio, a first-year middle school math teacher)

New teachers face the following problems:

- Working conditions that require teachers to spend too much time on nonteaching duties and offer them too little time for planning and no time for themselves
- Unruly students and a disorderly teaching environment
- Loneliness and alienation (S. Johnson & Birkeland, 2003)

The stress of the first year is reduced, however, when teachers have someone to turn to for help, as Shelley did ("I'm not sure what I would have done if Mrs. Landsdorp hadn't taken me under her wing"). Beginning teachers without mentors and support are nearly twice as likely to leave as those with programs designed to help them make the transition from the university to the K–12 classroom (Horn, 2005).

The first year can also be rewarding. Let's look at another of Antonio's experiences:

Wow, what a day. We've been working so hard on solving equations, and all of a sudden Jeremy [one of Antonio's weaker students] bursts out right in the middle of our discussion, "Hey, I get this. It ain't all that bad." What a rush. When you see the light bulb finally come on in a kid's head, it keeps you going for another month. And, yesterday, Natalia [another struggling student] came up and said, "Mr. Martinez, I used to really, really hate math, but now I actually look forward to coming to algebra." I didn't drive home after school yesterday; I flew.

In Chapter 1 we talked about rewards in teaching, and Antonio experienced some of those rewards. It is, indeed, a heady experience to see students understand something new and know that you helped make it happen.

Survival Skills for the First Year

You can also prepare for your first year of teaching by developing what we call "survival skills." They include

- Organization
- Classroom management
- Teaching effectively
- Knowing your students

Let's look at these skills.

Organization

Organization can help teachers maximize the time they have for the numerous professional roles they perform. (Anthony Magnacca/Merrill)

One of the first experiences you'll have as a beginning teacher will be lack of time. You'll feel as though you don't have a second to yourself. As Antonio said earlier, "I've never been so tired in my life. You're in front of kids all day, and then you go home and work late into the night to get ready for the next day." And at the beginning of the chapter, Shelley commented, "I can't believe how much there is to do—IEPs, progress reports, CPR training, responsibility to look for signs of abuse. When do I teach?"

Although a simple solution to this problem doesn't exist, careful organization is essential (Mandel, 2006). A large body of research, dating back to the 1970s, indicates that effective teachers are better organized (S. Bennett, 1978; Rutter et al., 1979). A student in one of our classes made the following observation of a first-year teacher he had visited: "His desk was a mess. Books and papers piled everywhere. He couldn't find anything, and he was always shuffling through papers looking for something." If he couldn't find "anything," you can bet that he wasted time looking for lesson plans and student papers. If you frequently or even occasionally lament that "I must get organized," now is a good time to start changing your habits. Having your instructional materials stored and readily accessible, creating procedures for routine tasks (e.g., turning in, scoring, and returning papers), and establishing policies for absences and making up missed work are all essential for using time effectively. For expert teachers, these organizational skills have become automatic; for beginning teachers, they must be learned (Weinstein, 2007). (We examine organization in more detail in Chapters 11 and 12.)

Classroom Management

Classroom management has historically been the primary concern of beginning teachers, and disruptive students are an important source of stress for beginners and veterans alike (Bohn, Roehrig, & Pressley, 2004; Public Agenda, 2004). It is a major reason that teachers leave the profession during their first 3 years (L. Weiner, 2002). New teachers often feel ill-equipped to deal with management, and this dimension of effective teaching is one of the most important skills you'll learn in your teacher education program.

Because it is so important to beginning teachers, we devote Chapter 11 to creating productive learning environments and explain how classroom management contributes to an environment that is orderly and focused on learning.

Teaching Effectively

Even though classroom management is the primary concern of beginning teachers, it is virtually impossible to maintain an orderly classroom without effective teaching strategies (Good & Brophy, 2003). If instruction is boring or if students don't understand what they're supposed to be learning and why, the likelihood of having classroom management problems increases dramatically. Because effective instruction is so important for both promoting student learning and maintaining an orderly classroom, we devote all of Chapter 12 to the topic.

Knowing Your Students

Knowing your students is an essential survival skill. It communicates that you care about them as people, which is crucial both for effective teaching and for classroom management. Commit yourself to knowing all your students' first names within the first week of school.

Again, watch your professors and teachers out in the field. See how they use students' names in their instruction. You will notice a striking difference between teachers who know and address students by name and those who do not.

Knowing students' names is important, but it's only a first step. Knowing them as people provides you with insights into their needs and interests as well as the kinds of experiences they bring into your classroom. Experienced teachers often begin the school year by having students fill out a questionnaire. The following are some examples of questions that might be included:

- What do you want to learn from this class?
- What are your favorite topics?
- How do you like to learn?
- What kinds of learning activities do you enjoy?
- Describe three important things about yourself as a person.

More important than the actual questions is the fact that the teacher cares enough to ask them. It makes students feel as if they and the teacher are "in this together," which is important for maximizing student learning.

Being well organized, developing an effective classroom management system, teaching effectively, and knowing your students are essential for a successful first year. This is why we call them survival skills. But what other actions can beginning teachers take to make their first year of teaching productive? We discuss induction and mentoring programs in the next section.

Induction and Mentoring Programs

Mrs. Landsdorp is wonderful. She is so supportive, and she is the person I always go to when I want a straight answer about what's really going on in the school and the district. She's also been very helpful in giving suggestions about how to deal with difficult parents and how I should handle myself in situations where I'm uncertain. She hasn't helped me a whole lot with nitty-gritty stuff, like planning lessons or watching me teach, but that's not her fault. She has a full teaching load too, so she really doesn't have time. I guess what it really amounts to is that she's been a real source of emotional support, and this year is going better than I could have hoped for. (Shelley, a first-year third-grade teacher talking about her mentor)

Effective induction and mentoring programs can help ease the transition into the teaching profession. (Jonathan Nourok/ PhotoEdit Inc.)

The transition to teaching is rarely as smooth as Shelley experienced. Teachers are sometimes hired at the last moment, left isolated in their classrooms, and given little help—examples of the sink-or-swim experience of many beginning teachers. As you saw at the beginning of this section, nearly a third of new teachers leave the profession within the first 2 years (Ingersoll & Smith, 2004), and isolation and lack of support are reasons why.

To address this problem, schools are increasing emphasis on induction and mentoring programs. **Induction programs** are professional experiences for beginning teachers that provide systematic and sustained assistance to ease the transition into teaching. These programs may include structured staff-development activities (e.g., workshops focusing on problems commonly experienced by first-year teachers), procedures for providing new teachers with crucial information, and mentors. **Mentors** are experienced teachers who provide guidance and support for beginning teachers (Bartell, 2005). Ideally, mentors provide not only emotional support, as Shelley reported, but also technical support in planning and conducting lessons and assessing student learning. Induction and mentoring programs can reduce first-year attrition by almost one third (Ingersoll & Smith, 2004).

Successful induction programs have the following elements (Gilbert, 2005; Wayne, Youngs, & Fleischman, 2005; Wong, Britton, & Ganser, 2005):

- A systematic attempt to help beginning teachers with both classes and opportunities to observe and dialogue with experienced teachers.
- Special help in the beginning years of their career to help them link their instruction to state and district standards.
- Professional development activities designed to increase mentors' effectiveness and compensation for mentors.
- Mentor support with everyday problems and encouragement for developing a reflective professional attitude.
- Feedback to new teachers based on classroom observation.

Actual classroom observations with feedback are essential; beginning teachers provided with this help significantly improved in organizing and managing instruction, and their students were better behaved and more engaged during lessons (Evertson & Smithey, 2000).

Many beginning teachers, however, do not participate in anything more than perfunctory school orientations, and many of the mentoring programs that do exist are like the one Shelley described; they provide emotional support but little specific help in the process of learning to teach (Olson, 2003). As we said earlier, the existence of an effective mentoring program is one of the factors you should consider when looking for your first job. Ask the principal and talk to teachers—and especially those who are new—about the availability of induction and mentoring programs.

Induction programs. Professional experiences for beginning teachers that provide systematic and sustained assistance to ease the transition into teaching.

Mentors. Experienced teachers who provide guidance and support for beginning teachers.

Teacher Evaluation

As you saw in Chapter 1, teacher testing and accountability have become facts of professional life, and you likely will be required to pass competency tests before you're licensed. You will also be evaluated during your first years of teaching. Teacher evaluation has two primary purposes: **formative**, which is the process of gathering information and providing feedback that teachers can use to improve their practice, and **summative**, which is the process of gathering information about a teacher's competence, usually for the purpose of making decisions about retention and promotion (Ubben et al., 2004). You will likely encounter both in your first years of teaching.

Evaluation processes vary, so you should check to see how they are handled in your state and district. Typically, however, they are based on research about learning and teaching, and combine theory and research studies that examine the relationships between teacher actions and student learning (Borman & Kimball, 2005; Odden, Borman, & Fermanich, 2004). Research from a variety of sources is gathered and compiled, and observation instruments are created based on the literature (Pecheone & Chung, 2006). For example, research indicates that effective teachers have well-established classroom routines, use instructional strategies that produce high levels of student involvement, and quickly identify and eliminate sources of disruption (Emmer et al., 2006; Evertson et al., 2006).

Observation instruments used to evaluate teachers' effectiveness skills then ask the observer to

- Assess whether or not routines are in place and used effectively.
- Evaluate the extent to which students are attentive and involved in the lesson.
- Decide whether the teacher correctly identifies sources of misbehavior and deals with them quickly.

Observers use the same process to evaluate skills in other domains.

Before being observed, you should ask to see the instrument that will be used. If any of the categories are unclear, ask either the principal or an experienced teacher to explain. It always helps to know how you'll be evaluated, and knowing this also helps reduce the stress and anxiety that are always there when someone observes your teaching.

Some states (e.g., North Carolina) use existing standards, such as the INTASC principles you saw in Chapter 1 (see Table 1.3), as frameworks for designing evaluation systems. Teachers compile portfolios of lesson plans, videotapes, student artifacts, and reflections that address each of these principles, and trained experts then evaluate these portfolios (Lashley, 2001). Portfolio-based teacher evaluation systems are likely to become more prominent in the future, which is another reason for you to learn how to develop an effective portfolio as early in your program as possible.

> **Making Connections:**
> To deepen your understanding of the topics in this section of the chapter and integrate them with topics you've already studied, go to the *Making Connections* module for Chapter 2 at **www.prenhall.com/kauchak**. Respond to questions 6–8.

> **Formative evaluation.** The process of gathering information and providing feedback that teachers can use to improve their practice.
>
> **Summative evaluation.** The process of gathering information about a teacher's competence, often for the purpose of making administrative decisions about retention and promotion.

IN TODAY'S CLASSROOMS: VIDEO

Succeeding in Your First Year of Teaching

In this video episode, a middle school teacher, near the end of the first year of teaching, describes her experiences, including the rewards and challenges that she experienced during that year.

To view this video, go to the *Becoming a Professional* DVD included with this text, click on *In Today's Classrooms*, and then this chapter's video: *Succeeding in Your First Year of Teaching*.

*To answer the questions about the video online and receive immediate feedback, go to the Companion Website at **www.prenhall.com/kauchak**, then the* In Today's Classrooms *module for Chapter 2.*

teaching in an era of reform

Merit Pay

One of the first questions you'll want to know as a beginning teacher is how much you'll be paid and what you'll need to do to receive pay increases over the years. Currently, most teacher salary increases are based on the number of years of experience and the number of graduate and in-service credit hours that teachers have earned. However, one aspect of the teaching profession that is receiving increased attention is the issue of merit pay, a supplement to a teacher's base salary intended to reward superior performance or work in a high-need area such as special education or teaching in urban schools.

Merit pay takes several forms. Some merit systems reward individual teachers based on their students' performance on tests. Others reward teachers based on principals' observations or teaching artifacts such as exemplary lessons or student work. A third type of merit pay rewards entire schools for student test performance, and a fourth provides teachers with extra salary for teaching in high-need areas such as math and science or at challenging sites such as high-poverty, low-performing urban schools (Keller, 2002; Odden, 2003). Some advocates suggest complex systems that include elements of each of the forms of payment (Koppich, 2005).

Because many policy makers want some form of pay-for-performance for teachers, and many school districts are considering merit pay, it is likely that you will encounter the issue early in your career (Drevitch, 2006). In 2006, at least 30 states were offering incentives, such as housing benefits or loan forgiveness, to address teacher shortages in certain subjects and geographical areas (Jacobson, 2006).

The Issue

Merit pay is highly controversial. Proponents argue that exemplary teaching performance should be rewarded and that money can provide incentives for teacher excellence (Odden, 2003). The superintendent of the Houston, Texas, district, the largest one to experiment with merit pay, comments, "It simply doesn't make sense any more. The system that pays the worst teacher the same that it pays the best teacher is not working" (Cook, 2006, p. 4). Others assert that simple economics suggest teachers in certain areas, such as math and science, should receive higher salaries, because they enjoy better job prospects outside education than do those in fields such as history or English. They further argue that higher salaries are essential for attracting skilled professionals willing to work in underperforming, urban schools (Ritter & Lucas, 2005).

The majority (more than 60 percent) of teachers are in favor of higher pay for teachers who work in tough neighborhoods with low-performing students, or for those who work harder and put in longer hours, or for those who consistently receive high evaluations by their principals (Public Agenda, 2003). But teachers' support for merit pay drops to 42 percent for paying teachers in high-demand areas, and 38 percent when the system is based on student test scores.

Critics contend that merit pay is divisive, damages morale, and make teachers less likely to cooperate with each other (Ramirez, 2001). Other critics argue that the systems are often too complex and fail to address the need for higher base salaries for all teachers (Cook, 2006).

Critics also contend that merit pay systems are often put into place without establishing agreed-upon and objective measures of teacher performance, without creating effective processes for identifying high-performing teachers, or without designing mechanisms for evaluating the effectiveness of the systems (Guthrie & Springer, 2006).

Tying merit pay to student performance on high-stakes tests is one way to simplify merit systems, and a number of states are considering this approach, but research indicates that these systems are generally ineffective because of a number of problems, including the students being taught (Gratz, 2005). Students in high socioeconomic status (SES) schools are more likely to score higher and have higher achievement gains than low-SES students. Consequently, teachers who work in low-SES schools would have less opportunity to receive merit increases. This would then discourage teachers from working in these schools, the exact opposite of what some proponents of merit pay intend.

You Take a Position

Now it's your turn to take a position on the issue. State in writing whether you favor or oppose merit pay, and provide a two-page rationale for your position.

For additional references and resources, go to the Companion Website at www.prenhall.com/kauchak, then to the Teaching in an Era of Reform module for Chapter 2. You can respond online or submit your response to your instructor.

Check Your Understanding

3.1 What are four factors that will determine whether or not your first year of teaching will be successful?

3.2 Describe the characteristics of successful induction programs.

3.3 How are teacher-evaluation systems created and used?

 For feedback, go to Appendix A, Check Your Understanding, *located in the back of this text.*

Career-Long Professional Development

To this point, we have discussed finding your first job and how to succeed in your first year of teaching. Now is also the time to begin thinking about your career 3 to 5 or more years down the road, because long-term professional goals can guide you during your teacher-preparation program. In this section, we examine three aspects of career-long professional development:

- Membership in professional organizations
- Becoming a teacher-leader
- Attaining certification through the National Board for Professional Teaching Standards

Membership in Professional Organizations

One of the first steps in your professional growth should be involvement in the professional organizations in education. These organizations support a variety of activities designed to improve teaching and schools, such as the following:

- Disseminating professional publications that provide up-to-date research and information on trends in the profession
- Providing professional development activities for teachers
- Holding yearly conferences that present research about recent professional advances
- Providing resources where teachers can find answers to questions about professional issues and problems
- Providing politicians and policy makers with information about important issues facing education

Table 2.3 includes a list of prominent professional organizations, their Website addresses, and descriptions of their missions or goals. We recommend that you join at least one professional organization as an integral part of your professional growth. Many organizations have student memberships that allow you to become involved while still in school.

Two of the largest professional organizations are the National Education Association (NEA) and the American Federation of Teachers (AFT). Founded in 1857, the NEA is the largest professional organization, enrolling approximately two thirds of the teachers in this country (National Education Association, 2006a). Most (78 percent) of the members are teachers, but NEA also includes guidance counselors, librarians, and administrators. AFT was founded in 1916 and has over 1.3 million members who primarily teach in urban areas (American Federation of Teachers, 2006). AFT does not allow administrators to join and has gained notoriety for its emphasis on better pay and better working conditions. You are likely to encounter representatives from at least one, if not both, of these organizations in your first year on the job. Talk with experienced teachers in your school about the pros and cons of each.

> **Merit pay.** A supplement to a teacher's base salary intended to reward superior performance or work in a high-need area.

TABLE 2.3 Professional Organizations for Educators

Organization and Web Address	Organization Mission or Goal
American Council on the Teaching of Foreign Languages *http://www.actfl.org*	To promote and foster the study of languages and cultures as an integral component of American education and society
American Federation of Teachers *http://www.aft.org*	To improve the lives of our members and their families, to give voice to their legitimate professional, economic, and social aspirations
Association for Supervision and Curriculum Development *http://www.ascd.org*	To enhance all aspects of effective teaching and learning, including professional development, educational leadership, and capacity building
Council for Exceptional Children *http://www.cec.sped.org*	To improve educational outcomes for individuals with exceptionalities, students with disabilities, and/or the gifted
International Reading Association *http://www.reading.org*	To promote high levels of literacy for all by improving reading instruction, disseminating research and information about reading, and encouraging the lifetime reading habit
Music Teachers National Association *http://www.mtna.org/flash.html*	To advance the value of music study and music making to society and to support the professionalism of music teachers
National Art Education Association *http://www.naea-reston.org*	To promote art education through professional development, service, advancement of knowledge, and leadership
National Education Association *http://www.nea.org*	To fulfill the promise of a democratic society, NEA shall promote the cause of quality public education and advance the profession of education
National Science Teachers Association *http://www.nsta.org*	To promote excellence and innovation in science teaching and learning for all
National Council for the Social Studies *http://www.ncss.org*	To provide leadership, service, and support for all social studies educators
National Council of Teachers of English *http://www.ncte.org*	To promote the development of literacy, the use of language to construct personal and public worlds and to achieve full participation in society, through the learning and teaching of English and the related arts and sciences of language.
National Council of Teachers of Mathematics *http://www.nctm.org*	To provide broad national leadership in matters related to mathematics education
National Association for Bilingual Education *http://www.nabe.org*	To recognize, promote, and publicize bilingual education
Phi Delta Kappa *http://www.pdkintl.org*	To promote quality education as essential to the development and maintenance of a democratic way of life by providing innovative programs, relevant research, visionary leadership, and dedicated service
Teachers of English to Speakers of Other Languages *http://www.tesol.org*	To improve the teaching of English as a second language by promoting research, disseminating information, developing guidelines and promoting certification, and serving as a clearinghouse for the field

Becoming a Teacher-Leader

At this point in your career, you may react to becoming a teacher-leader with, "Teacher-leader! I'm just trying to become a *teacher* first." Expectations for teachers have risen significantly since the beginning of the 1990s, and teachers' roles are also changing. For example, teachers now have much more input into decisions about teacher preparation, certification, and staff development than they had in the past. This has thrust teachers into new leadership roles, and the term *teacher-leader* has become part of the language of educational reform. Becoming a teacher-leader also creates a tangible goal for your growth as a professional educator.

Teachers can develop leadership skills in a number of ways:

- Serving on school-level or districtwide curriculum committees
- Helping establish school-level or districtwide policies on issues such as grading, dress codes, and attendance policies
- Writing grant proposals for student- or teacher-development projects
- Proposing and facilitating staff-development projects
- Arranging school–business partnerships
- Initiating and facilitating school-to-work activities
- Conducting action research

Because of its emphasis on research and the development of professional knowledge and its potential for developing teachers as professionals, we examine action research in more detail next.

Designing and Conducting Action Research

Understanding and critically examining others' research is one way for teachers to increase their professional knowledge. Another is for teachers to conduct research in their own classrooms. **Action research** is a form of applied research designed to answer a specific school- or classroom-related question (Gall, Gall, & Borg, 2003; Wiersma & Jurs, 2005). Teachers, school administrators, or other education professionals can conduct action research, using a variety of methods. The primary intent in action research is to improve practice within a specific classroom or school (McMillan, 2004).

Four steps guide teachers as they plan and conduct action research studies (B. Johnson & Christensen, 2004):

1. Identify a problem.
2. Plan and conduct a research study.
3. Implement the findings.
4. Use the results to generate additional research.

Let's see how Tyra Forcine, an eighth-grade English teacher, attempted to implement these steps in her classroom.

Action research provides opportunities for teachers to build upon their professional knowledge by dialoguing with other teachers about important issues. (Robin Sachs/PhotoEdit Inc.)

Tyra and a group of her colleagues are discussing the problems they are having with homework. Kim Brown complains that her students often "blow off assignments," and Bill McClendon reports he has so much trouble getting his students to do homework that he has stopped assigning it.

"I've heard teachers say that homework doesn't help that much in terms of learning, anyway," Selena Cross adds.

"That doesn't make sense to me," Tyra counters, shaking her head. "It has to help. The more kids work on something, the better they have to get at it."

Tyra consistently gives her students homework and checks to see if they have done it, but because of the conversation, she decides to take a more systematic look at its effects. She can't find a satisfactory answer on the Internet or in any of her college textbooks, so she decides to find out for herself.

Tyra begins her study at the start of the third grading period. She collects homework every day and gives the students 2 points for having done it fully, 1 point for partial completion, and 0 points

> **Action research.** A form of applied research designed to answer a specific school- or classroom-related question.

for minimal effort or not turning it in. Each day she discusses some of the most troublesome items on the homework. On Fridays she quizzes students on the content covered Monday through Thursday, and she also gives a midterm test and a final exam. She then tries to see if a relationship exists between students' homework averages and their performance on the quizzes and tests.

At the end of the grading period, each student has a homework score, a quiz average, and an average on the two tests. Tyra calls the district office to ask for help in summarizing the information, and together they find a positive but fairly low correlation between homework and test averages.

"Why isn't the correlation higher?" she wonders in another lounge conversation.

"Well," Kim responds. "You're only giving the kids a 2, 1, or 0 on the homework—you're still not actually grading it. So I suspect that some of the kids are simply doing the work to finish it, and they aren't really thinking about it."

"On the other hand," Bill acknowledges, "homework and tests are correlated, so maybe I'd better rethink my stand on no homework. . . . Maybe I'll change what I do next grading period."

"Good points," Tyra responds. "I'm going to keep on giving homework, but I think I need to change what I'm doing, too. . . . It's going to be a ton of work, but I'm going to do two things. . . . I'm going to repeat my study next grading period to see if I get similar results, and then, starting in the fall, I'm going to redesign my homework, so it's easier to grade. I'll grade every assignment, and we'll see if the correlation goes up."

"Great idea," Kim replies. "If the kids see how important it is for their learning, maybe they'll take their homework more seriously, and some of the not-doing-it problem will also get better. . . . I'm going to look at that in the fall." (Adapted from Eggen & Kauchak, 2007)

Let's see how Tyra attempted to apply the four steps for action research in her classroom. First, she identified a problem: To what extent does homework contribute to my students' performance on quizzes and tests? This personalized approach increases teachers' motivation to do action research, because it answers questions that are important to them (Mills, 2002; Quiocho & Ulanoff, 2002).

Second, she systematically designed and conducted her study, and third, Tyra and her colleagues implemented the results of her project immediately. Bill, for example, planned to give homework during the next grading period. Action research is rewarding because it can address issues and problems that teachers really care about.

Finally, like most research, her project led to further studies (Hyland & Noffke, 2005). Tyra planned another study to see if scoring the homework more carefully would increase the correlation between homework and tests, and Kim planned to investigate the question of whether or not more careful scoring would lead to students' more conscientiously doing their homework.

In addition to answering questions about real classroom issues, conducting action research increases teachers' feelings of professionalism. Contributing to a body of knowledge and making decisions based on reflection helps teachers grow both personally and professionally (Darling-Hammond & Hammerness, 2005). Engaging in action research projects also contributes to teachers' perceptions of their own autonomy. These factors are outlined in Figure 2.3.

The results of well-designed studies can often be presented at professional conferences and published in professional journals. This allows the knowledge gained to be made public and integrated with other research, two important steps in the development of a professional body of knowledge (J. Hiebert, Gallimore, & Stigler, 2002).

Attaining Certification: The National Board for Professional Teaching Standards

> **Certification.** Special recognition by a professional organization indicating that an individual has met certain requirements specified by the organization.

Earlier, we saw that licensure is the process states use to ensure that teachers meet professional standards. In comparison, **certification** is special recognition by a professional organization indicating that an individual has met certain requirements specified by the organization.

Figure 2.3   Conducting Action Research Enhances Professionalism

One important form of certification is offered by the National Board for Professional Teaching Standards (NBPTS). Created in 1987 as an outgrowth of the Carnegie Forum report, *A Nation Prepared: Teachers for the 21st Century* (Carnegie Forum on Education and the Economy, 1986), the board is composed mostly of K–12 teachers but also includes union and business leaders and university faculty (NBPTS, 2006). NBPTS seeks to strengthen teaching as a profession and raise the quality of education by recognizing the contributions of exemplary teachers, compensating them financially, giving them increased responsibility, and increasing their role in decision making.

National Board certification is based on standards that grew out of the board's policy statement *What Teachers Should Know and Be Able to Do*. The NBPTS summarized the professional standards contained in this report into five core propositions about what professional educators should know and be able to do. These propositions and descriptions of how they play out in practice are outlined in Table 2.4.

National Board certification has five important features:

- It is designed for experienced teachers. Applicants must have graduated from an accredited college or university and must have taught at least 3 years.
- Applying for National Board certification is strictly voluntary and independent of any state's licensure. It is intended to indicate a high level of skill and professionalism.
- Acquiring National Board certification requires that teachers pass a set of exams in their area of specialty, such as math, science, early childhood, or physical education and health.
- Additional evidence, such as videotapes of teaching and a personal portfolio, are used in the assessment process.
- The primary control of the NBPTS is in the hands of practicing teachers, which increases the professionalism of teaching.

Certification by the NBPTS is for veterans, so you may be wondering why we are providing information about it to preservice teachers early in their programs. There are three reasons. First, professionalism is a major theme of this book, and the NBPTS is a national effort to professionalize teaching. The propositions in Table 2.4 emphasize the pedagogical content knowledge, general pedagogical knowledge, and knowledge of

TABLE 2.4   Propositions of the National Board for Professional Teaching Standards

Proposition	Description
1. Teachers are committed to to students and their learning.	• Accomplished teachers believe that all students can learn, and they treat students equitably. • Accomplished teachers understand how students develop, and they use accepted learning theory as the basis for their teaching. • Accomplished teachers are aware of the influence of context and culture on behavior, and they foster students' self-esteem, motivation, and character.
2. Teachers know the subjects they teach and how to teach those subjects to students.	• Accomplished teachers have a rich understanding of the subject(s) they teach, and they appreciate how knowledge in their subject is linked to other disciplines and applied to real-world settings. • Accomplished teachers know how to make subject matter understandable to students, and they are able to modify their instruction when difficulties arise. • Accomplished teachers demonstrate critical and analytic capacities in their teaching, and they develop those capacities in their students.
3. Teachers are responsible for managing and monitoring student learning.	• Accomplished teachers capture and sustain the interest of their students and use their time effectively. • Accomplished teachers are able to use a variety of effective instructional techniques, and they use the techniques appropriately. • Accomplished teachers can use multiple methods to assess the progress of students, and they effectively communicate this progress to parents.
4. Teachers think systematically about their practice and learn from experience.	• Accomplished teachers are models for intellectual curiosity, and they display virtues—honestly, fairness, and respect for diversity—that they seek to inspire in their students. • Accomplished teachers use their understanding of students, learning, and instruction to make principled judgments about sound practice, and they are lifelong learners. • Accomplished teachers critically examine their practice, and they seek continual professional growth.
5. Teachers are members of learning communities.	• Accomplished teachers contribute to the effectiveness of the school, and they work collaboratively with their colleagues. • Accomplished teachers evaluate school progress, and they utilize community resources. • Accomplished teachers work collaboratively with parents, and they involve parents in school activities.

learners and learning discussed in Chapter 1. The NBPTS recognizes that increasing professionalism requires teachers who are both highly knowledgeable and skilled in their areas of specialization.

Second, National Board certification can be a long-term career goal for which there is also a financial incentive. As of 2003, an estimated $316 million had been spent on this venture at the national level, and 39 states and nearly 200 school districts had spent millions of additional dollars to reward teachers who successfully completed the process (Lustick, 2002; Thirunarayanan, 2004). For example, the state of Florida appropriated $69 million during 2003–2004 to provide board-certified teachers and mentors for future board-certified teachers with a 10 percent salary raise (Thirunarayanan, 2004). In addition, in 2003–2004 the state of Washington rewarded board-certified teachers with a $3,500 bonus (Margolis, 2004). As of 2005, there were 47,356 board-certified teachers nationwide, and this number is likely to increase (McCabe, 2006).

Finally, some evidence indicates that National Board certification makes a difference in teacher quality. In a study comparing teachers who had successfully completed the process to those who had attempted but failed to achieve certification, the nationally certified teachers scored higher on nearly all measures of teaching expertise. The study involved at least 75 hours of observation of each teacher, along with interviews and samples of student work (Blair, 2000). However, a more recent study found no achievement gains for students taught by National Board–certified teachers (Keller, 2006). And another study found that the certification process encouraged teachers to become more reflective about their work and their relationships with other professionals (Lustick, 2002). National Board certification is well worth pursuing, and we encourage you to keep it in mind as you begin your career.

Making Connections:
To deepen your understanding of the topics in this section of the chapter and integrate them with topics you've already studied, go to the *Making Connections* module for Chapter 2 at **www.prenhall.com/kauchak.** Respond to questions 9 and 10.

Check Your Understanding

4.1   What are three career-long professional development opportunities that are available to you as a teacher?

4.2   What are five different activities designed to improve teaching and schools that professional organizations support?

4.3   What are the two primary assessment processes involved in attaining National Board certification?

For feedback, go to Appendix A, Check Your Understanding, *located in the back of this text.*

decision making

Defining Yourself as a Professional

You're interviewing for a position in a large, urban middle school. The leadership team of the school is composed of the school principal, a vice principal, and two assistant principals. Both the principal and vice principal are involved in the interview, which is scheduled for 1 hour.

You've been asked a number of probing questions, such as, "What is the biggest problem you faced in your internship?" "How would you motivate a class of unmotivated learners?" and "How would you enforce rules with students who are disruptive in your class?"

As you respond, the vice principal appears to listen attentively, but the principal appears distracted. He nods and responds in general terms to your answers but doesn't follow up on any of the questions.

After 45 minutes have passed, the interview seems to be winding down, so you attempt to ask some questions about the school. The principal cuts you off, saying he has a meeting he

must attend. He cordially thanks you for coming and quickly leaves the office, 10 minutes before the scheduled end of the interview. The vice principal, on the other hand, asks you to come into his office and says he is willing to try to answer any questions you have. You spend another half hour with him, and he takes you on a tour of the school, during which the discussion of the school and students continues. The principal's name doesn't come up in the discussion, but the physical plant is clean and attractive, the students are orderly as they move between classes, and one who accidentally bumps you says, "Oh, excuse me."

If it was offered, would you take a job at this school? Explain why you would or would not.

To respond to this question online and receive immediate feedback, go to the Decision Making module for Chapter 2 on the Companion Website at www.prenhall.com/kauchak.

Meeting Your Learning Objectives

1. **Describe the beliefs of beginning teachers.**
    *   Beginning teachers are idealistic and optimistic. They generally believe that they will be effective, and they often believe that they will be more effective than teachers now in the field.
    *   Beginning teachers expect to become more confident about their ability to promote learning as they acquire experience. Unfortunately, the opposite often occurs.
    *   Beginning teachers believe that effective teachers are those who are best able to clearly explain content to students, and if they understand their content, they will be able to teach it effectively.
    *   Beginning teachers tend to believe that they will learn most of what they need to know to be an effective teacher from their experiences in classrooms.

2. **Explain differences between traditional and alternative licensure and the essential factors involved in finding a desirable job.**
    *   Traditional licensure consists of a general education component, as well as education courses designed to help teachers develop professional knowledge. Secondary majors are also required to take a specified number of course hours in the subject area (e.g., math) in which they plan to teach.
    *   In alternative licensure programs, people who have bachelor's degrees in areas other than education complete a short, intensive training program with a clinical component.
    *   Finding a desirable job requires developing a professional reputation, building a portfolio and résumé, and creating a credentials file. The more quickly students in preservice programs begin to develop a professional portfolio, gathering experiences that make them marketable and building their professional reputation, the better equipped they will be to find a job when they graduate.

3. **Identify factors that contribute to a successful first year of teaching.**
    *   Lack of time and classroom management are the most common problems beginning teachers face. Getting organized, becoming well-informed, getting to know their students, and developing effective instructional strategies are teachers' most effective ways to prepare for both their internship and their first year of teaching.
    *   Induction and mentoring programs help beginning teachers make the transition from being students to being effective teachers. The best mentoring programs provide systematic help for beginning teachers, help teachers link their instruction to state and district standards, provide teachers with support in dealing with everyday problems, encourage teachers to develop a reflective professional attitude, and provide feedback based on classroom observation.
    *   Evaluation is also a part of a beginning teacher's experience. Formative evaluation is designed to provide helpful feedback to teachers; summative evaluation is designed to ensure adequate performance by teachers. Teacher evaluation based on research and standards-based evaluation are two approaches that schools commonly use throughout the United States.

4. **Describe career-long professional development opportunities available to teachers.**
    *   Professional organizations provide a variety of services for teachers throughout their careers. These include publications with current research, professional development activities, annual conferences, and resources for teachers' questions and concerns.
    *   Teachers can develop professionally by becoming teacher-leaders, such as by serving on district- and state-level committees; writing grants; designing and facilitating staff development activities; and conducting action research, research designed to address an immediate school-level problem.
    *   The National Board for Professional Teaching Standards (NBPTS), in an attempt to professionalize teaching, has established rigorous standards and assessments for teachers who have completed at least 3 years of successful service. Substantive financial rewards exist in most states for teachers who have successfully completed National Board certification.

Important Concepts

action research (p. 61)

certification (p. 62)

credentials file (p. 46)

formative evaluation (p. 57)

induction programs (p. 56)

licensure (p. 42)

mentors (p. 56)

merit pay (p. 59)

résumé (p. 45)

summative evaluation (p. 57)

Developing as a Professional

Preparing for Your Licensure Exam

This exercise will provide you with practice answering questions similar to the Praxis™ Principles of Learning and Teaching exam as well as your state-specific licensure exam.

In this chapter, we discussed use of time, classroom management, knowing your students, and teaching effectively as factors that will help you succeed in your first year of teaching. Keep these factors in mind as you read the case study below, and then answer the questions that follow.

Kaycee Vess is a first-year geography teacher in a large, urban middle school. With 29 students, her classroom is crowded. This morning, in homeroom, Shiana comes through the classroom doorway just as the tardy bell rings.

"Take your seat quickly, Shiana," Kaycee directs. "You're just about late. All right. Listen up, everyone," she continues. "Ali?"

"Here."

"Gaelen?"

"Here."

"Chu?"

"Here."

Kaycee finishes taking the roll and then walks around the room, handing back a set of papers.

"You did quite well on the assignment," she comments. "Let's keep up the good work. . . . Howard and Manny, please stop talking while I'm returning papers. Can't you just sit quietly for 1 minute?"

The boys, who were whispering, turn back to the front of the room.

"Now," Kaycee continues, returning to the front of the room, "we've been studying the Middle East, so let's review for a moment. . . . Look at the map, and identify the longitude and latitude of Cairo. Take a minute and figure it out right now."

The students begin as Kaycee goes to her file cabinet to get out some transparencies.

"Stop it, Damon," she hears Leila blurt out behind her.

"Leila," Kaycee responds sternly, "we don't talk out like that in class."

"He's poking me, Miss Vess."

"Are you poking her, Damon?"

"Uhh . . . ."

"Well?"

"Not really."

"You did, too," Leila complains.

"Both of you stop it," Kaycee warns. "Another outburst like that, Leila, and your name goes on the board."

As the students are finishing the problem, Kaycee looks up from the materials on her desk to check an example on the overhead. She hears Howard and Manny talking and laughing at the back of the room.

"Are you boys finished?"

"Yes," Manny answers.

"Well, be quiet then until everyone is done," Kaycee directs and goes back to rearranging her materials.

"Quiet, everyone," she again directs, looking up in response to a hum of voices around the room. "Is everyone finished? . . . Good. Pass your papers forward. . . . Remember, put your paper on the top of the stack. . . . Roberto, wait until the papers come from behind you before you pass yours forward."

Kaycee collects the papers, puts them on her desk, and then begins, "We've talked about the ge-ography of the Middle East, and now we want to look at the climate a bit more. It varies somewhat. For example, Syria is extremely hot in the summer but is actually quite cool in the winter. In fact, it snows in some parts.

"Now, what did we find for the latitude of Cairo?"

"Thirty," Miguel volunteers.

"North or south, Miguel? . . . Wait a minute. Howard? . . . Manny? . . . This is the third time this period that I've had to say something to you about your talking, and the period isn't even 20 minutes old yet. Get out your rules and read me the rule about talking without permission. . . . Howard?"

"Uhh . . . ."

"It's supposed to be in the front of your notebook."

"Uhh . . . ."

"Manny?"

"'No speaking without permission of the teacher,'" Manny reads from the front page of his notebook.

"Howard, where are your rules?"

"I don't know."

"Move up here," Kaycee directs, pointing to an empty desk at the front of the room. "You've been bothering me all week. If you can't learn to be quiet, you will be up here for the rest of the year."

Howard gets up and slowly moves to the desk Kaycee has pointed out. After Howard is seated, Kaycee begins again, "Where were we before we were rudely interrupted? . . . Oh yes. What did you get for the latitude of Cairo?"

"Thirty north," Miguel responds.

"Okay, good. . . . Now, Egypt also has a hot climate in the summer—in fact, very hot. The sum-mer temperatures often go over 100 Fahrenheit. Egypt is also mostly desert, so the people have trou-ble making a living. Their primary source of subsistence is the Nile River, which floods frequently. Most of the agriculture of the country is near the river."

Kaycee continues presenting information to the students for the next several minutes.

"Andrew, are you listening to this?" Kaycee interjects when she sees Andrew poke Jacinta with a ruler.

"Yes," he responds, turning to the front.

"I get frustrated when I see people not paying attention. When you don't pay attention, you can't learn, and that frustrates me because I'm here to help you learn."

Kaycee continues with her presentation.

1. How effective was Kaycee's organization? Provide evidence from the case study to support your assessment.

2. Did Kaycee know her students? How do you know?

3. How effective was Kaycee's classroom management? Provide evidence from the case study to support your analysis.

4. How effective was Kaycee's teaching? Again, provide evidence from the case study to support your evaluation.

To receive feedback on your responses to these exercises, go to the Companion Website at www.prenhall.com/kauchak, then to the Preparing for Your Licensure Exam *module for Chapter 2.*

Discussion Questions

1. What can preservice teachers do to decrease the likelihood that they will leave the profession? What can school leaders do?

2. The National Board for Professional Teaching Standards is attempting to increase the professionalism of teaching. How successful is it likely to be? Explain your thinking.

3. Some critics suggest that teaching isn't a profession, because it doesn't have a body of knowledge on which to base its decisions. How would you respond to these critics?

4. In this chapter, we suggested that you attempt to establish a professional reputation by being conscientious in your classes. What are some other ways students can develop a professional reputation?

5. We offered several suggestions for making yourself marketable in this chapter. Is it reasonable to expect that preservice teachers involve themselves in these activities? Explain your thinking.

6. What are some professional qualities beginning teachers should look for in a mentor? What are some personal qualities?

Developing as a Professional: Online Activities

Going Into Schools

Go to the Companion Website at *www.prenhall.com/kauchak*, and click on the *Going Into Schools* module for Chapter 2. You will find a number of school-based activities that will help you link chapter content to the schools in which you work.

Virtual Field Experience: Using the Internet to Explore the Profession

If you would like to participate in a Virtual Field Experience, access the following website: *http://www.rnt.org*. This site contains a number of different perspectives on recruiting and retaining new teachers as well as information on areas of high teacher demand.

Online Portfolio Activities

To develop your professional portfolio, further apply your understanding of chapter content, and address the INTASC standards, go the Companion Website at *www.prenhall.com/kauchak*, then to the *Online Portfolio Activities* for Chapter 2. Complete the suggested activities.

Part II

STUDENTS

Helping Diverse Learners Succeed in Today's Classrooms

Chapter Outline

Cultural Diversity
Urban Schools and Diversity
Cultural Attitudes and Values
Cultural Interaction Patterns
Educational Responses to Cultural Diversity

Language Diversity
Language Diversity: The Government's
Response
Language Diversity: Schools' Responses

Gender
Gender and Society
Gender and Schooling

Ability Differences
What Is Intelligence?
Ability Grouping and Tracking: Schools'
Responses to Differences in Ability
Learning Styles

Students With Exceptionalities
Federal Laws Change the Way Schools and
Teachers Help Students With Exceptionalities
Categories of Special Education Students
Students With Exceptionalities: Implications for
Teachers

Learning Objectives

*After you have completed your study of this chapter,
you should be able to*

1. Explain how cultural diversity influences
   learning and how effective teachers
   respond to this diversity.

2. Describe the major approaches to dealing
   with language diversity.

3. Explain how gender differences influence
   school success and how effective teachers
   respond to these differences.

4. Explain different views of ability
   differences, and describe how schools
   respond to ability differences.

5. Explain how schools have changed the
   ways they deal with exceptionalities, and
   describe the major categories of
   exceptionalities found in classrooms.

Case Studies

 Elementary

 Middle

 Secondary

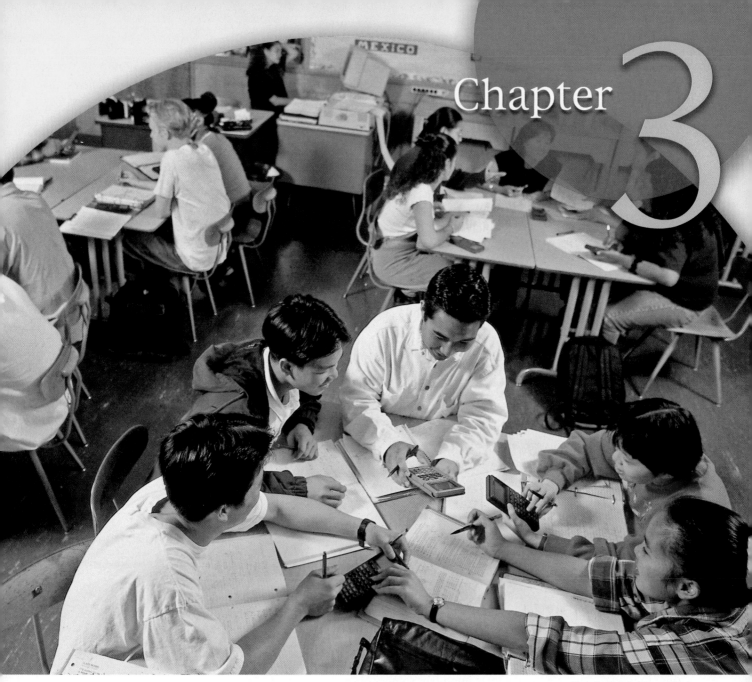

Chapter 3

Teachers begin their careers expecting to find classrooms like the ones they experienced when they were students, and in some ways they are the same. Students go to school to study and learn, but they also want to have fun and be with their friends. They expect to work but often need encouragement from their teachers. They're typical kids.

Classrooms are changing, however; an increasing number of students now come from different cultures and speak different languages at home. And other types of diversity, including differences between boys and girls, are receiving increased attention. As you read the following case study, think about these differences and how they will influence your life as a teacher.

Carla Jackson, a first-grade teacher in an urban elementary school, watches as her students stream into her room on the first day of school. Though she has read the class rolls, she can't believe the different shapes, colors, and sizes before her eyes. Some are tall and well developed—looking almost like second graders—whereas others look like they should be in preschool. She also notices differences in the way they learn and behave. Some are bright and eager, while others look sleep deprived. Several know how to print and read their names, but books appear almost strange to a few. Some use their fingers to add or even count, and others suck their thumbs when they become tired or discouraged. And the names—she hopes she'll be able to remember and pronounce them all correctly. There is Jones and Lee and Wong and Hassad and Trang and Jamal. Because she is in a large, urban school, Carla knew in advance that her students would be diverse, but she wasn't prepared for this—eleven different cultures and six different languages. She jokingly refers to her class as her "Little United Nations."

A field trip to a local zoo gives Carla a chance to see her students in a different setting. She can't believe how differently they act on the field trip. Some are active and lead the way in exploring while others hang back, clinging to her for emotional support. Some eagerly ask questions while others listen shyly. She knows that this diversity can make learning experiences richer for the students, but she hasn't quite figured out how.

When you begin teaching, the students in your classes are likely to come from a variety of backgrounds, primarily because the diversity in today's schools is rapidly increasing and also because new teachers are likely to find jobs in schools that serve diverse populations (Olson, 2003). This diversity has several dimensions (Figure 3.1), and it presents both challenges and opportunities for you as a beginning teacher.

Figure 3.1   Dimensions of Diversity

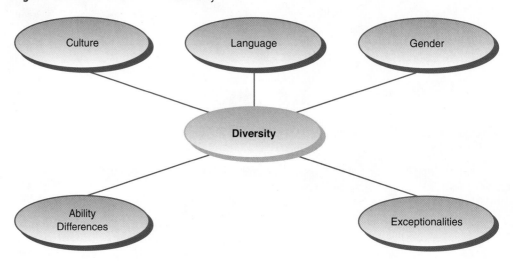

To meet these challenges, teachers need a deep understanding of diversity and teaching strategies that address the learning needs of students from varying backgrounds. Before continuing, take a few minutes to complete the questionnaire on page 75 designed to assess your thinking about different aspects of diversity in our schools.

We address each of the questions as the chapter unfolds. Let's turn now to *culture*, one of the most important sources of learner diversity.

Cultural Diversity

Think about the clothes you wear, the kind of music you like, and even the food you eat. Your clothing, music, and foods, along with other dimensions such as religion and family structure are all part of your **culture**, the knowledge, attitudes, values, customs, and behavior patterns that characterize a social group (Banks, 2006b). **Cultural diversity** refers to the different cultures that you'll encounter in classrooms and how these cultural differences influence learning. As shown in Figure 3.2, culture is one of the most important dimensions of diversity in classrooms.

Culture influences many important dimensions of our lives. For instance, take eating. Culture influences when we eat; when do you typically eat dinner? In some cultures, dinner occurs after 8:00 in the evening, while in others 6:00 is the standard dinner time. Culture also influences who we eat with. Again, does your whole family sit down together, or does everyone "eat on the run"? It also influences how we eat; do you eat with a knife and fork or chopsticks, and when you cut a piece of meat, do you then transfer the fork back to your right hand or leave it in your left hand? And, of course, culture influences what we eat, as evidenced by the growing number of ethnic restaurants around the country.

Culture. The knowledge, attitudes, values, customs, and behavior patterns that characterize a social group.

Cultural diversity. The different cultures that you'll encounter in classrooms and how these cultural differences influence learning.

professional knowledge: test yourself!

For each item, circle the number that best represents your thinking. Use the following scale as a guide:

1 = Strongly disagree
2 = Disagree
3 = Uncertain
4 = Agree
5 = Strongly agree

1. While students from different cultures have varying attitudes and values, these variations have little impact on the amount they learn.

   1   2   3   4   5

2. Students who are not native English speakers learn English most effectively if they are required to speak only English in school.

   1   2   3   4   5

3. Boys generally get better grades in school than girls.

   1   2   3   4   5

4. Students who are talented in one area of school are generally talented in all the others.

   1   2   3   4   5

5. Most students with exceptionalities require help and assistance in special classrooms designed to meet their needs.

   1   2   3   4   5

 This is available in a downloadable format on the Companion Website for personal portfolio use.

Figure 3.2 Culture and Diversity

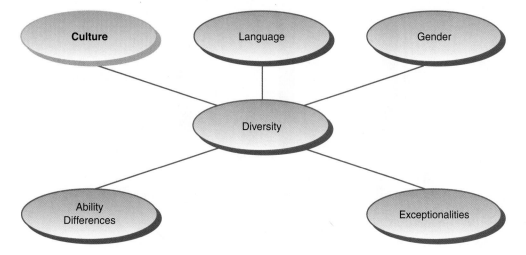

Ethnicity, which refers to a person's ancestry—the way individuals identify themselves with the nation from which they or their ancestors came—is an important part of culture (Gollnick & Chinn, 2006). Members of an ethnic group share a common identity defined by their history, language (although sometimes not spoken), customs, and traditions. Experts estimate that nearly 300 distinct ethnic groups currently reside in the United States (Gollnick & Chinn, 2006).

Immigration and other demographic shifts have resulted in dramatic changes in our country's school population. Congress passed the Immigration Act of 1965, which ended quotas based on national origin. This law resulted in more immigrants coming to the United States and also in changes in their point of origin. While most immigrants during the early 1900s came from Europe, more recent immigrants come from Central America (37%), Asia (25%), and the Caribbean (10%), with only 14 percent of recent immigrants having Europe as their point of origin (U.S. Census Bureau, 2004). This has resulted in a dramatic increase in the proportion of students who are members of cultural minorities (U.S. Department of Education, 2005b), and it helps us understand why the backgrounds of Carla's students are so diverse.

By the year 2020, the U.S. school-age population will see many more changes (see Figure 3.3). Experts predict considerable increases in the percentages of all groups of students except White, non-Hispanic. During this span of time, the percentage of White students will decrease from over 63 percent to a little more than half of the total school population (U.S. Census Bureau, 2003). By 2050, no one group will be a majority among adults.

Urban Schools and Diversity

The term *cultural minority* is often used to refer to various non-White cultural groups. Based on sheer numbers, this term may soon be obsolete and is already a misnomer in many parts of the country, especially in urban areas. For example, Hispanics, African-Americans, and Asians—when combined—now make up the majority of the population in 48 of the 100 largest U.S. cities (Macionis, 2006). In addition, children of color make up the majority of public school enrollments in six states and over 90 percent of the students in Detroit, the District of Columbia, Chicago, Houston, and Los Angeles (Kober, 2006).

The growth of minority student populations in urban areas is the result of immigration coupled with higher birth rates. For example, between 1990 and 2000, Hispanic populations increased 43 percent and Asian populations surged 40 percent in urban areas (Lichter & Johnson, 2006). Experts estimate that almost one in five students is a child of immigrants

Figure 3.3   Changes in School-Age Population, 2000–2020

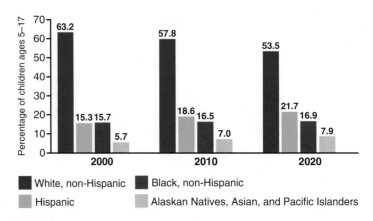

> **Ethnicity.** A person's ancestry; the way individuals identify themselves with the nation from which they or their ancestors came.

Source: U.S. Bureau of Census (2003).

(Kober, 2006). Urban centers are often called "gateway cities" for recently arriving immigrants (Lichter & Johnson, 2006), and these population increases are reflected in urban schools. In Adlai Stevenson High School in New York City, for example, African-Americans and Hispanics make up 97 percent of the student population; only five tenths of 1 percent of students are White (Kozol, 2005). Many of these recent immigrants do not speak English as their first language, which poses challenges for schools and teachers. Teachers skilled in helping students simultaneously learn English and the content of their classes are sorely needed.

Knowledge of the cultural attitudes and values these students bring to school is also essential. This is the topic of the next section.

The cultural diversity in urban schools provides teachers with both opportunities and challenges. [Mary Kate Denny/PhotoEdit Inc.]

Cultural Attitudes and Values

Our students come to school with a long learning history. Cultural influences exist in their dress, family configurations, interactions with parents and peers, and attitudes and values. When they enter our classrooms, they bring these attitudes and values with them. Some complement school learning; others do not. This suggests that the first statement in our beginning-of-chapter survey, "While students from different cultures have varying attitudes and values, these variations have little impact on the amount they learn," is not true. Let's see why.

Language is an example. Students are sometimes hesitant to drop the use of nonstandard English dialects in favor of "school English" because doing so might alienate their peers (Ogbu, 1999). The same problem occurs in classrooms where students are asked to learn English and quit using the languages of their homes. Programs encouraging students to drop their native languages can also distance students from their parents, many of whom cannot speak English.

Even school success can be an issue. Succeeding in school is sometimes interpreted by members of minorities as rejecting their native culture; to become a good student is to become "White"—to embrace and uphold only White cultural values. Members of minorities who study and succeed academically risk losing the friendship of their peers. John Ogbu, an anthropologist who studied the achievement of minority students, believes that in many schools peer values either don't support school learning or actually oppose it; students form what he called "resistance cultures" (Ogbu & Simons, 1998). Low grades, management and motivation problems, truancy, and high dropout rates are symptoms of this conflict.

Cultural attitudes and values can also complement learning. For instance, researchers studying the amazing academic success of Vietnamese and other Asian-American students found that hard work, perseverance, and pride were heavily emphasized in the home (Kristoff, 2006). In 2005, Asian-American students scored highest (1091) on the Math–Verbal parts of the SAT test, outscoring Whites by 23 points and other cultural minorities by an average of 168 points. Willingness to take challenging courses was also a factor in academic success; research showed that 40 percent of Asian-American students took calculus in high school versus 28 percent of the general population. One Vietnamese student who became the valedictorian at her high school after only 7 years in the United States commented, "Anybody can be smart, can do great on standardized tests. But unless you work hard, you're not going to do well" (Kristoff, 2006, p. 13).

Research on Indian students' success in U.S. national spelling bees found a similar emphasis on hard work and study (Bracey, 2005b). Children of Indian descent consistently place high in these academic contests, winning much more often than other ethnic groups.

Cultural Interaction Patterns

Because our students learn to interact with others at home, cultural conflict can occur when they enter our classrooms. Let's look at an example:

A second-grade class in Albuquerque, New Mexico, was reading The Boxcar Children *and was about to start a new chapter. The teacher said, "Look at the illustration at the beginning of the chapter and tell me what you think is going to happen." A few students raised their hands. The teacher called on a boy in the back row.*

He said, "I think the boy is going to meet his grandfather."

The teacher asked, "Based on what you know, how does the boy feel about meeting his grandfather?"

Trying to involve the whole class, the teacher called on another student—one of four Native Americans in the group—even though she had not raised her hand. When she didn't answer, the teacher tried rephrasing the question, but again the student sat in silence.

Feeling exasperated, the teacher wondered if there was something in the way the lesson was being conducted that made it difficult for the student to respond. She sensed that the student she had called on understood the story and was enjoying it. Why, then, wouldn't she answer what appeared to be a simple question?

The teacher recalled that this was not the first time this had happened, and that, in fact, the other Native American students in the class rarely answered questions in class discussions. She wanted to involve them, wanted them to participate in class, but could not think of ways to get them to talk. (Villegas, 1991, p. 3)

Why do you think this problem occurred? One explanation suggests that Native American children are not used to the fast-paced, give-and-take patterns that characterize many American classrooms (Starnes, 2006). When involved in discussions such as the one just described, they are uncomfortable and, as a result, reluctant to participate (Banks, 2006b).

Studies comparing the interaction patterns of White and African-American students have also found cultural differences (Heath, 1989, 1982). For instance, researchers looked at students' responses to teacher directives such as "Let's put the scissors away now." Accustomed to this indirect way of speaking, White students interpreted it as a command; African-Americans, used to more direct statements such as "Put your scissors away now," did not (Heath, 1982). Teachers viewed a student's failure to comply as either a management or a motivation problem when instead, a mismatch between home and school cultures existed.

Made aware of these differences, teachers worded their requests more directly, "Begin your homework now" (Heath, 1982). They also encouraged all students to actively participate in learning activities and liberally praised their efforts to do so. In this way, the teacher built bridges between the students' and the school's cultural learning styles.

Educational Responses to Cultural Diversity

Historically, social commentators have used different metaphors to describe the relationships among the diverse cultures in the United States. A "melting pot" was one of the first. Those who saw the United States as a melting pot emphasized **assimilation**, a process of socializing people so that they adopt dominant social norms and patterns of behavior. Assimilation attempted to make members of minority cultural groups "similar" to those belonging to the dominant cultural group, typically Whites of northern European descent.

The melting pot metaphor was especially popular in the early 1900s, when large numbers of immigrants from southern and eastern Europe came to the United States. Society assigned schools the task of teaching immigrants how "Americans" were supposed to think, talk, and behave. Immigrants, eager to become "American" and share in this country's economic wealth, generally accepted efforts to assimilate them.

About the middle of the 20th century, a shift in thinking occurred. People realized that assimilation had never totally worked and that there was no "melting pot," as indicated by

Assimilation. A process of socializing people so that they adopt dominant social norms and patterns of behavior.

neighborhoods and groups that continued to speak their home languages, celebrate their unique cultural holidays, and maintain their cultural habits, such as eating ethnic foods. The contributions of different cultural and ethnic groups were increasingly recognized, and leaders began to realize that some educational practices aimed at assimilation were actually counterproductive. For example, in an effort to encourage English language acquisition, schools in the Southwest didn't allow students to speak Spanish, even on playgrounds. Schools became hostile places where students had to choose between family and friends, and school. The policy probably did as much to alienate Hispanic youth as it did to encourage English language development (Spring, 2006).

Multicultural Education

To remedy these problems, educators began developing new approaches to addressing cultural diversity. **Multicultural education** is a general term that describes a variety of strategies schools use to accommodate cultural differences in teaching and learning. We discuss some of these strategies in the following section "Culturally Responsive Teaching." Instead of trying to create a melting pot, these approaches align with new metaphors that describe America as a "mosaic" or "tossed salad" in which society recognizes and values each culture's unique contributions.

Multicultural education is highly controversial. Critics contend that it is divisive because it places too much emphasis on differences between cultural groups and not enough on our commonalities (Schlesinger, 1992). Textbooks have been scrutinized; in 2000, a spokesperson for the *American Textbook Council* criticized modern history textbooks as emphasizing multicultural themes at the expense of basic information about U.S. history (Sewall, 2000). Recently, a major controversy erupted over singing the national anthem in Spanish (Goldstein, 2006). Critics claimed that the national anthem is a symbol of unity for a diverse people united by common values and our country's Constitution. Criticism became so widespread that bills were submitted in Congress mandating that the anthem never be recited or sung in a foreign language (despite the fact that the national anthem has historically been translated and sung in a number of different languages, including French, Polish, and Italian).

Proponents of multicultural education assert that building on students' cultures is nothing more than sound teaching; by recognizing, valuing, and utilizing students' cultures and languages in their instruction, teachers help students link the topics they're studying to what they already know, a process consistent with effective teaching (Eggen & Kauchak, 2007; Ormrod, 2006). In addition, proponents of multicultural education point out that the United States has always been a nation of immigrants and this diversity has long been recognized. For example, our society embraces the music, holidays (e.g., St. Patrick's Day, Cinco De Mayo, Hanukkah, and the Chinese New Year), and foods of many cultures. Good multicultural education continues this tradition by recognizing and building on students' cultural heritages, proponents argue.

Like all approaches, multicultural education will undoubtedly evolve as educators decide what works and what doesn't. One promising approach to working with diverse student populations is called culturally responsive teaching.

Culturally Responsive Teaching

Shannon Wilson, a fifth-grade teacher in a large urban elementary school, walks around her classroom, helping students as they work on a social studies project. A number of hands are raised, and she feels relieved that she has Maria Arguelas, her special education resource teacher, to help her. Shannon has 27 students, seven of whom are not native English speakers. Five are Hispanic, and fortunately, Maria can help them with language-related problems. Shannon often spends extra time with Kwan and Abdul, the other two non-English speakers. Maria also assists Shannon by working with four of her students who have learning disabilities.

Multicultural education. A general term that describes a variety of strategies schools use to accommodate cultural differences in teaching and learning.

Culturally responsive teaching builds on students' cultural backgrounds, accepting and valuing differences and accommodating different cultural learning styles. [Bob Daemmrich/The Image Works]

Shannon's class is preparing for Parents' Day, an afternoon when parents and other caregivers join the class in celebrating the students' ancestral countries. The students present information about the countries' history, geography, and cultures in their projects. The class has already prepared a large world map with pins marking the students' countries of origin. While several of the pins are clustered in Mexico and Central and South America, the map shows that students also come from many other parts of the world. Each student is encouraged to invite a family member to come and share a part of the family's native culture. The parents can bring food, music, and native dress from their different homelands.

Culturally responsive teaching is instruction that acknowledges and accommodates cultural diversity (Gay, 2000, 2005). It attempts to accomplish this goal in three ways:

- Accepting and valuing cultural differences
- Accommodating different cultural interaction patterns
- Building on students' cultural backgrounds

Accepting and Valuing Cultural Differences. By recognizing and accepting student diversity, teachers communicate that all students are welcome and valued. This is particularly important for members of cultural minorities, who sometimes feel alienated from school. As a simple example, Shannon had her students identify their ethnic homelands on the map. This showed an interest in each student and helped them feel accepted and valued.

Genuine caring is an essential element in making students feel part of the classroom. Teachers communicate caring in several ways, including the following:

- Devote time to students—for example, be available before and after school to help with schoolwork and discuss students' personal concerns.
- Demonstrate interest in students' lives—for example, ask about Jewish, Muslim, Latin-American, and African-American festivals.
- Involve all students in learning activities—for example, call on all students as equally as possible.

Each of these suggestions communicates that the teacher welcomes and values all students.

Accommodating Cultural Interaction Patterns. Teachers who are sensitive to possible differences between home and school interaction patterns adapt their instruction to best meet their students' needs. For example, we saw earlier that the communication patterns of Native Americans may clash with typical classroom practices (Starnes, 2006). Recognizing that these students may not be comfortable in teacher-centered question-and-answer activities, teachers can use additional strategies, such as cooperative learning, to complement teacher-centered approaches. (We discuss cooperative learning in Chapter 12, along with other effective teaching strategies.) Similarly, knowing that White and African-American students sometimes have different communication patterns, teachers can word instructions more directly, such as, "Open your books to page 53 now."

As another example, when a teacher learned that her Asian-American students were overwhelmed by the bustle of American schools, she tried to keep her classroom quiet and orderly and encouraged shy students to participate with open-ended questioning, giving

Culturally responsive teaching. Instruction that acknowledges and accommodates cultural diversity.

them extra time to respond, and gently reminding them to speak a bit louder (C. Park, 1997). Another teacher noticed this about her Vietnamese students:

> *I traditionally end every day with the students lining up and receiving a hug before they leave. My Vietnamese kids were always the stiff huggers until October. Through my understanding of their cultures, I now give all students the choice of a hug, handshake, or high five. This simple act may make children feel more comfortable interacting with me. (McAllister & Irvine, 2002, p. 440)*

Through increased sensitivity to each cultural group's learning needs, teachers can make their classrooms safe and inviting learning environments for all students. (We discuss different strategies to create productive learning environments in Chapter 11.)

Accommodating different cultural interaction patterns can result in minority students' adapting to the dominant culture (including that of schools) without losing their cultural identities, a process called "accommodation without assimilation" (Ogbu, 1992, 1999, 2003). Accommodation without assimilation helps students function comfortably in both cultures, including using different language patterns in school compared to the home or other social environments (DeMeulenaere, 2001). The challenge for teachers is to help students learn about the "culture of schooling," the norms, procedures, and expectations necessary for success in school, while honoring and valuing students' home cultures.

Building on Students' Backgrounds. Effective teachers also learn about their students' cultures and use this information to promote personal pride and motivation, as we saw in Shannon's class and as we see in the following example:

> *Jack Seltzer, a high school biology teacher on the Navajo Nation Reservation, uses his students' background experiences to illustrate hard-to-understand science concepts. He uses Churro sheep, a local breed that Navajos use for food and wool, to illustrate genetic principles. When they study plants, he focuses on local varieties of squash and corn that have been grown by students' ancestors for centuries. He uses geologic formations in nearby* Monument Valley *to illustrate igneous, sedimentary and metamorphic rocks.(Baker, 2006).*

> **Making Connections:**
> To deepen your understanding of the topics in this section of the chapter and integrate them with topics you've already studied, go to the *Making Connections* module for Chapter 3 at **www.prenhall.com/kauchak.** Respond to questions 1–5.

Both students and their parents benefit from building on students' cultural backgrounds. Student achievement increases, and parents become more positive about school, both of which enhance student motivation. Shannon recognized this when she invited parents and other caregivers to share their cultural heritages with her class. Jack also capitalized on this idea by providing examples with which the students could personally identify.

IN TODAY'S CLASSROOMS: VIDEO

Culturally Responsive Teaching

In this video episode, a teacher describes the adjustments she made to accommodate the religious beliefs of a fourth-grade Muslim girl and make her feel welcome in school. We also see how willingly the other students support the teacher's efforts.

To view this video, go to the *Becoming a Professional* DVD, included with this text, click on *In Today's Classrooms*, and then this chapter's video: *Culturally Responsive Teaching*.

*To answer the questions online and receive immediate feedback, go to the Companion Website at **www.prenhall.com/kauchak,** then to the* In Today's Classroom *module for Chapter 3.*

Check Your Understanding

1.1   How do cultural attitudes, values, and interaction patterns influence learning?

1.2   What are three ways in which effective teachers respond to cultural diversity in their classrooms?

1.3   What is the relationship between urban schools and cultural diversity?

 For feedback, go to Appendix A, Check Your Understanding, *located in the back of this text.*

Language Diversity

Ellie Barton, a language arts teacher at Northeast Middle School, is the school's English Language Learner (ELL) Coordinator. She teaches ELL classes, and she is also in charge of the school's testing and placement program.

Her job is challenging, as her students vary considerably in their knowledge of English. For instance, one group of Somali-Bantu children just arrived from a refugee camp in Kenya. They cannot read or write, because there is no written language for their native tongue, Mai-Mai. Language isn't their only challenge; many had never been in a building with more than one floor, and others found urinals and other aspects of indoor plumbing a mystery. At the other end of the continuum is a young girl from India who can read and write in four languages: Hindi, the national language of India; Urdu, the language of her Persian ancestors; Telegu, a regional language in India; and Arabic.

To sort out this language diversity, the district uses a placement test that categorizes students into three levels: newcomer classrooms for students who have little or no expertise with English; self-contained ELL classrooms, where a primary emphasis is on learning to read and write English; and sheltered English, where students receive structured help in learning academic subjects such as science and social studies. However, the placement process is not foolproof, since English skills are sometimes nonexistent, and some parents don't know the exact ages of their children. Ellie's principal deals with this information void in creative ways; he recently asked a dentist friend to look at a student's teeth to estimate the child's age (adapted from Romboy & Kinkead, 2005).

Imagine trying to help someone understand something if they don't understand the words you are saying. Further, imagine trying to help them when you can't understand what they are saying to you. This is the daunting task many teachers in today's schools face.

Language is one of the most important parts of any culture. Because language diversity has such a powerful influence on learning (see Figure 3.4), and responses to this diversity are so controversial, we devote this section of the chapter to the topic.

As we saw earlier, immigration has brought increasing numbers of students with limited backgrounds in English to our country's classrooms. The number of English language learners (ELLs) in the United States increased by 95 percent between 1991 and 2002 (Gollnick & Chinn, 2006).

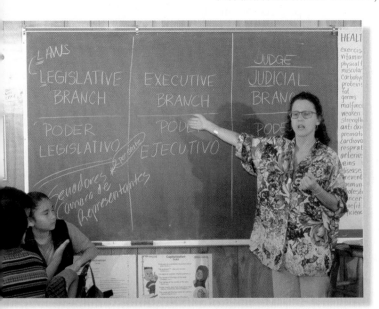

Educational responses to language diversity differ in the degree to which they build upon and attempt to maintain students' first language. [Bob Daemmrich/The Image Works]

Figure 3.4   Language and Diversity

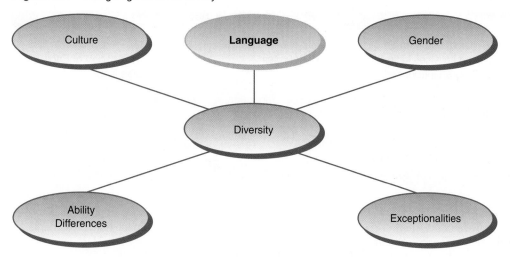

English language learners (ELLs) are students whose first language is not English and who need help in learning to speak, read, and write in English. In the 2003–2004 school year, 10 percent of U.S. students' first language was not English, and in many cities and states, these students now make up a significant proportion of the student body (Kober, 2006). Currently, 329 different languages are spoken in the United States, with the most common language groups being Spanish, Vietnamese, Hmong, Chinese, and Korean (OELA, 2004).

Language Diversity: The Government's Response

The federal government, through legislation and court rulings, initially attempted to address the needs of ELL students through bilingual approaches, approaches that attempt to maintain the first language while students learn English. For example, in 1968 Congress passed the Bilingual Education Act, which provided federal funds for educating non-native English speakers. In 1974 the Supreme Court ruled unanimously, in the controversial *Lau v. Nichols* case, that the San Francisco School District unlawfully discriminated by failing to address children's language problems (Bennett, 2007). More recently, the English Acquisition component of the No Child Left Behind (NCLB) Act of 2001 mandated that the primary objective of U.S. schools should be the teaching of English without any attempt to preserve minority languages (No Child Left Behind Act, 2001). Accordingly, the previous Office of Bilingual Education became the Office of English Language Acquisition (OELA). In 2006, during a debate on immigration reform, the U.S. Senate voted to designate English as the national language (Hulse, 2006). Each of these government actions has changed our schools, as we'll see in the next section.

Language Diversity: Schools' Responses

Schools across the country have responded to the challenge of language diversity in very different ways, outlined in Table 3.1. Although all of the programs are designed to ultimately teach English, they differ in how fast English is introduced and to what extent the first language is used and maintained.

 Maintenance language programs place the greatest emphasis on using and sustaining the first language. For example, in one bilingual program in Houston, students initially received 90 percent of instruction in Spanish and 10 percent in English (Zehr, 2002a). The emphasis on English then increased in each grade. The future of maintenance programs is uncertain given the English Acquisition component of the NCLB Act, which discourages such programs.

 At the opposite end of the continuum, **immersion** and **English as a second language (ESL) programs** emphasize rapid transition to English. Halfway between the two ends of the continuum, **transition programs** maintain the first language until students acquire sufficient English to proceed in that language.

English language learners (ELLs). Students whose first language is not English and who need help in learning to speak, read, and write in English.

Maintenance language programs. Language programs that place the greatest emphasis on using and sustaining the first language.

Immersion program. Language program that emphasizes rapid transition to English.

English as a second language (ESL) program. Language program that teaches English along with content.

Transition programs. Language programs that maintain the first language until students acquire sufficient English.

TABLE 3.1   Different Programs for ELL Students

Type of Program	Description	Advantages	Disadvantages
Maintenance	First language maintained through reading and writing activities in first language while English introduced.	Students become literate in two languages.	Requires teachers trained in first language. Acquisition of English may not be as fast.
Transition	Students learn to read in first language and are given supplementary instruction in English as a Second Language. Once English is mastered, students are placed in regular classrooms and first language discontinued.	Maintains first language. Transition to English is eased by gradual approach.	Requires teachers trained in first language. Acquisition of English may not be as fast. First language is dropped.
Immersion	Students learn English by being "immersed" in classrooms where English is the only language spoken.	When effective, quick transition to English. Does not require teachers trained in second language.	Loss of native language. Sink-or-swim approach hard on students.
English as a Second Language (ESL) Programs	Pull-out programs where students are provided with supplementary English instruction or modified instruction in content areas (also called Sheltered English programs).	Easier to administer when dealing with diverse language backgrounds.	Students may not be ready to benefit from content instruction in English. Pull-out programs segregate students.

Logistics are often a factor when schools consider which type of program to use. For example, transition programs can be effective when classes are composed of large numbers of ELL students who speak the same language (such as Spanish-speaking students in Los Angeles), because one teacher who speaks the students' native language can be hired. This isn't possible when several different first languages exist. For example, in 2001, 79 percent of the U.S. ELL population spoke Spanish, but the remaining 21 percent spoke a wide variety of other languages, making it virtually impossible to find a teacher who spoke all the different languages in one classroom (Girard, 2005). This happened at Northeast Middle School and is a major reason why Ellie Barton teaches in an ELL program that places minimal emphasis on students' first language.

teaching in an era of reform

Bilingual Education

Bilingual education has been the focus of several reform efforts. Through the Bilingual Education Act of 1968 and guidelines drafted as a result of *Lau v. Nichols* in 1974, the federal government signalled its commitment to providing services for non-native English speakers.

A counter reform occurred in California in 1998, when voters passed Proposition 227, a ballot initiative that sharply reduced bilingual education programs, replacing them with English-only immersion programs for ELL students. Similar measures were passed in Arizona and 25 other states (Garcia, 2006). These initiatives have sharply curtailed the use of bilingual education in these states. For example, before the initiatives occurred in Arizona and California, about one third of ELL students were taking bilingual education classes; after the initiatives, the numbers plummeted to 11 percent in both states (Zehr, 2002b). In addition, 26 states have passed laws making English the official language (U.S. English, Inc., 2006). (See Figure 3.5.) Although these laws are mostly symbolic, they are influencing state government publications,

Figure 3.5   States with Official Language Legislation

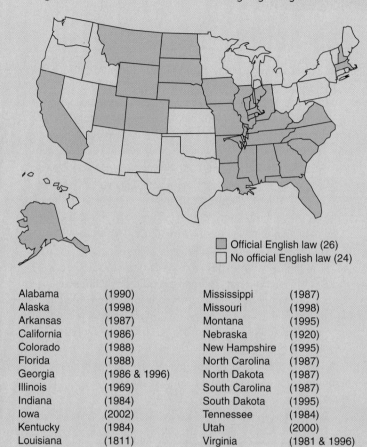

☐ Official English law (26)
☐ No official English law (24)

Alabama	(1990)	Mississippi	(1987)
Alaska	(1998)	Missouri	(1998)
Arkansas	(1987)	Montana	(1995)
California	(1986)	Nebraska	(1920)
Colorado	(1988)	New Hampshire	(1995)
Florida	(1988)	North Carolina	(1987)
Georgia	(1986 & 1996)	North Dakota	(1987)
Illinois	(1969)	South Carolina	(1987)
Indiana	(1984)	South Dakota	(1995)
Iowa	(2002)	Tennessee	(1984)
Kentucky	(1984)	Utah	(2000)
Louisiana	(1811)	Virginia	(1981 & 1996)
Massachusetts	(1975)	Wyoming	(1996)

Source: U.S. English, Inc. (2002). Washington, DC.

and they illustrate growing public sentiment in favor of English and fears about losing English as a common cultural bond.

In addition, in 2002 Congress failed to renew the Bilingual Education Act, instead packaging funds for English language learners into the NCLB Act, which requires students to attain "English fluency" in 3 years and requires schools to teach students in English after that time period.

The Issue

The essence of bilingual programs is an attempt to maintain and build on students' native languages while they learn English. Proponents make several arguments in support of bilingual education. First, they contend that the programs make sense with respect to learning because they provide a smooth and humane transition to English by building on students' first languages. They also argue that being able to speak two languages has practical benefits; a bilingual person can live and communicate in two worlds, which can increase economic and career opportunities. They also cite research. One review concluded that exist-

ing evidence favors bilingual approaches versus English immersion approaches in terms of helping students learn to read (Slavin & Cheung, 2005). Further research indicates that knowledge and skills acquired in a native language—literacy in particular—are "transferable" to the second language, providing students with a better understanding of the role of language in communication and how language works (K. Gutiérrez et al., 2002; Krashen, 1996).

Proponents of bilingual education also contend that immersion programs place unrealistic language demands on learners. They note that conversational English, such as that spoken on the playground, is learned quite quickly, but the cognitively demanding language needed for academic success is learned much more slowly (Peregoy & Boyle, 2005).

Critics of bilingual education attack it on several grounds. They contend that it is

- Divisive, encouraging groups of non-native English speakers to remain separate from mainstream American culture

- Ineffective, slowing the process of acquiring English for ELL students

- Inefficient, requiring expenditures for the training of bilingual teachers and materials that could be better spent on quality monolingual programs (English Only, 2006; Schlesinger, 1992).

Critics also cite their own research. For instance, one California school district reported that standardized test scores for students in the early grades—those most affected by the move from bilingual to immersion programs—improved from the 35th to the 45th percentile after students spent just 1 year in an immersion program, and additional research found similar positive results across California (Barone, 2000).

This issue addresses the second statement in our beginning-of-chapter survey, "Students who are not native English speakers learn English most effectively if they are required to speak only English in school." As you see from our discussion of this issue, the truth of the statement depends on whom you ask. Proponents of bilingual education would argue that the statement is false, whereas critics take the opposite position.

You Take a Position

Now it's your turn to take a position on the issue. State in writing whether you feel that schools should make efforts to retain students' native languages or whether it makes more sense to move students into English as quickly as possible, and provide a two-page rationale for your position.

For additional references and resources, go to the Companion Website at www.prenhall.com/kauchak, then to the Teaching in an Era of Reform module for Chapter 3. You can respond online or submit your response to your instructor.

Language Diversity in the Classroom

How will language diversity affect you as a teacher? First, although bilingual programs have been reduced, the need for teachers with ELL expertise will only increase. Experts estimate that U.S. schools will need an additional 290,000 teachers with ELL certification to meet the demands of these students (Zhao, 2002). In addition, 73 percent of urban school districts identified bilingual teachers as an immediate hiring need (Recruiting New Teachers, 2006). Teaching candidates who speak two languages, especially Spanish, are in high demand across the country.

Second, you will almost certainly have non-native English speakers in your classroom, and your ability to make informed professional decisions will be essential to help them learn. In working with students from diverse language backgrounds, your professional knowledge will be tested perhaps more than in any other area of your work.

Research offers the following suggestions for working with these students:

- Attempt to create a warm and inviting classroom environment by taking a personal interest in all students and involving everyone in learning activities.

- Avoid situations that draw attention to students' lack of English skills. One student commented:
  I think it is a bad strategy to make [ELLs] read aloud in front of other kids when they really can't. Teachers should give them time and make them more welcome by talking to them in Spanish first and later in English. They shouldn't expect them right away to do everything in English. (Thompson, 2000, p. 85)

- Mix teacher-centered instruction with learner-centered approaches, such as group work and cooperative learning, to allow students to interact informally and practice their developing language skills with the topics they study.

- Use concrete examples to provide reference points for new ideas and vocabulary (Echevarria & Graves, 2007; Peregoy & Boyle, 2005). For example, a middle school science teacher who was teaching the concept *bilateral symmetry* had a student come up to the front of the room and hold out his hands and feet to illustrate how both sides of his body were mirror images of each other.

These strategies represent good instructional practice for all students; for ELL students, they are essential.

Check Your Understanding

Making Connections:
To deepen your
 understanding of the topics
in this section of the chapter
and integrate them with topics
you've already studied, go to
the *Making Connections* module
for Chapter 3 at
www.prenhall.com/kauchak.
Respond to Question 6.

2.1   What has been the government's response to language diversity in our nation's schools?

2.2   What are the primary differences in the two major approaches schools use in working with English Language Learners?

2.3   What are the major ways that teachers can adapt their instruction to meet the needs of students with varying language backgrounds?

For feedback, go to Appendix A, Check Your Understanding, *located in the back of this text.*

Gender

What Geri Peterson saw on her first day of teaching advanced-placement calculus was both surprising and disturbing. Of the 26 students watching her, only 4 were girls, and they sat quietly in class, responding only when she asked them direct questions. One reason that Geri had gone into teaching was to share her interest in math with other females, but this situation gave her little chance to do so.

Lori Anderson, the school counselor at an urban middle school, looked up from the desk where she was working on her annual report to the faculty. From her course work at the university and her internship, she knew that boys traditionally outnumber girls with respect to behavioral problems, but the numbers she was seeing were disturbing. In every category—referrals by teachers, absenteeism, tardies, and fights—boys out-numbered girls by a more than 2 to 1 margin. In addition, the number of boys referred to her for special education testing far exceeded referrals for girls.

Gender and Society

The fact that males and females are different is so obvious that we often don't think about it, but research has uncovered some important differences. Researchers have found, for example, that females generally are more extroverted, anxious, and trusting; they're less assertive and have slightly lower self-esteem than males of the same age and background; and their verbal and motor skills tend to develop faster than do boys' (Berk, 2005, 2007; Gurian & Stevens, 2005). In addition, the play habits of boys and girls differ, with boys typically preferring more "rough and tumble" play. Gender differences make a significant contribution to diversity in the classroom (Figure 3.6).

Why do these gender differences exist? As with most other student differences, research suggests the causes are a combination of genetics and environment (Berk, 2005, 2007). Genetics result in physical differences such as size and growth rate and may also influence temperament, aggressiveness, and early verbal and exploratory behaviors. And some researchers now believe that boys' and girls' brains are wired differently for learning. For example, components of the brain that build word centers and fine motor skills are developmentally a year ahead in girls, which gives them an advantage in reading, use of pencils, cursive writing, and other small-motor tasks. Emotive centers in the brain are also more advanced for girls, making them calmer and more able to sit still for the long periods that classrooms often require. These researchers argue that schools, as they currently exist, may be more compatible with girls' innate genetic makeup (Gurian & Stevens, 2005).

Environment also plays an important role in shaping gender differences. From the day they're born, boys and girls are treated differently (Berk, 2005, 2007; McDevitt & Ormrod, 2007). Girls are given pink blankets, are called cute and pretty, and are handled delicately. Boys are dressed in blue, are regarded as handsome, and are seen as tougher, better coordinated, and hardier. Fathers are rougher with their sons and involve them in more physical stimulation and play; they tend to be gentler with their daughters and offer more sex-stereotyped toys, such as dolls and stuffed animals. Not surprisingly, boys and girls grow up looking and acting differently.

Figure 3.6   Gender and Diversity

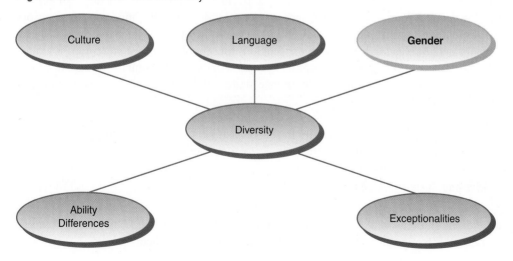

Gender and Schooling

Differences between boys and girls should generally be celebrated, but they become problems when societal or school forces limit the growth and academic potential of students—either male or female, as occurred in Geri Peterson's AP calculus class. For example, in high school, girls score lower than boys on the math sections of the SAT and ACT, two tests that are essential for college admission, and women score lower on all sections of the Graduate Record Exam, the Medical College Admissions Test, and admissions tests for law, dental, and optometry schools (Alperstein, 2005; Coley, 2001). These tests are important because they serve as gatekeepers to prestigious and high-paying professions.

Boys have their own problems. They outnumber girls in remedial English and math classes, are held back in grade more often, and are more than twice as likely to be placed in special education classes. Boys receive not only lower grades but also the majority of failing grades, and they drop out of school 4 times more often than girls. They are also cited for disciplinary infractions as much as ten times more frequently than girls (Gurian & Stevens, 2005; Hunsader, 2002).

So, what we have is an uneven picture of male and female strengths and weaknesses. But historically, concerns about girls received the most attention. For instance, in 1992's *How Schools Shortchange Girls,* the American Association of University Women (AAUW) argued that different treatment of boys and girls by both teachers and society seriously hampered the educational progress, self-esteem, and career choices of girls, with girls lagging well behind boys, particularly in math and science. In the 1998 *Gender Gaps: Where Schools Still Fail Our Children,* the AAUW reiterated many of its earlier claims.

These assertions have been controversial. For example, Christina Sommers (2000), author of *The War Against Boys: How Misguided Feminism Is Harming Our Young Men,* outlined many of the problems boys encounter in school that we described here. Yet it's the myth of the fragile girl that continues to receive the lion's share of attention, Sommers argued.

More recently, male problems in school have been receiving increased attention. For example, the January 30, 2006, issue of *Newsweek* focused on "The Trouble With Boys" as their lead story, and male educational problems extend into college. A *New York Times* article on the subject proclaimed, "At college women are leaving men in the dust" (Lewin, 2006, p. A1). As evidence, the article noted that women are more likely to attend college, earn a degree, get higher grades, and earn a master's degree.

As with gender differences in general, a combination of genetics and the environment probably explains the relative strengths and weaknesses of boys and girls in school. Because little can be done about genetics, more attention has been given to the environment, particularly **gender-role identity** differences, expectations and beliefs about appropriate roles and behaviors of the two sexes. Society as a whole treats boys and girls differently and expects them to develop fundamentally different gender-role identities. It's important to point out that these identity differences aren't a problem unless they perpetuate stereotypes or negatively influence behavior, learning, or expectations for school success. A **stereotype** is a rigid, simplistic caricature of a particular group of people. For example, women aren't good at math and men don't make good nurses are both inaccurate and damaging stereotypes because they limit career choices.

The preceding discussion addresses the third statement in our introductory questionnaire, "Boys generally get better grades in school than girls." As it turns out, quite the opposite is true; girls outperform boys on the majority of academic measures.

Gender and Career Choices

Look around your classroom for this course. If it's a typical education course, the large majority of the students in it are women. The same would be true in classes in nursing, but you would find the opposite in math, science, and computer-related fields.

Gender-role identity. Differences in expectations and beliefs about appropriate roles and behaviors of the two sexes.

Stereotype. A rigid, simplistic caricature of a particular group of people.

Where do stereotypes of "appropriate" careers for boys and girls originate? Society and the media perpetuate stereotypes, but ironically, parents—and particularly mothers—are often the most powerful sources. For instance, one study found that mothers who held negative gender-stereotyped attitudes about girls' ability in math adversely influenced their daughters' achievement in, and their attitudes toward, math (J. Campbell & Beaudry, 1998). When mothers believed that math was a male domain, their daughters took fewer math classes, got lower grades in them, and were less likely to pursue math-related fields such as computer science and statistics.

Parents can also have powerful positive influences on their children. One female software developer reported:

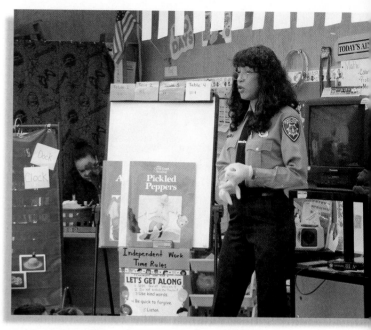

Role models are effective in preventing students from forming gender-stereotypic views about appropriate careers. [Geri Engberg/Geri Engberg Photography]

My mother always engendered in me the attitude that I could do absolutely anything I ever want to do. So she really gave me the confidence that is a big part of success in academics and maybe in other things—sometimes you get to a point where you don't have that much either skill or knowledge, and you have to just go on your guts or your confidence. You have to just kind of push your way through something until you have the time to accumulate the knowledge. And I think that that's something she engendered in me just by always being herself so confident of my abilities, rightly or wrongly. And my father certainly never detracted from that. He always portrayed her as being the smarter of the two. So I was raised in an environment where women were not only capable but were even potentially very well and highly regarded. (Zeldin & Pajares, 2000, p. 229)

Gender-stereotypic views can also negatively influence career decisions (Francis & Skelton, 2005; Wessel, 2005). Girls are less than half as likely as boys to pursue careers in engineering and physical and computer sciences (AAUW, 1998). At the high school level, only 11 percent of students taking the College Board advanced placement test in computer science in 2001 were women (Stabiner, 2003). The percentages of female physicians (26 percent), lawyers (27 percent), and engineers (8 percent), as well as new doctorates in science-related fields (38 percent), remain low as well (Wessel, 2005). The problem of gender-stereotypic views of math, science, and computer science careers is especially acute for minority females (Dance, 2002; Ginsberg, Shapiro, & Brown, 2004).

Similar problems exist for men. Go to any elementary or middle school, and you'll see that the faculties are overwhelmingly female, and, while more men are choosing nursing as a career, they remain in a distinct minority.

Single-Gender Classrooms and Schools

One response to gender-related problems has been the creation of **single-gender classes and schools**, where boys and girls are segregated for part or all of the day (Vail, 2002; Weaver-Hightower, 2005). The number of single-gender classrooms in the United States has increased ten-fold, from less than a dozen in 2000 to 211 in 2006 (Thiers, 2006).

Some research indicates that both girls and boys benefit in single-gender schools. Girls in these schools are more apt to assume leadership roles, take more math and science courses, have higher self-esteem, and have firmer beliefs that they are in control of their destinies (Datnow, Hubbard, & Conchas, 2001). Advocates of all-male schools claim that they promote male character development and are especially effective with males from low-income and minority families.

Single-gender classes and schools. Classes and schools where boys and girls are segregated for part or all of the day.

Effective teachers are sensitive to gender differences in the classroom and make a conscious effort to involve all students.
[David Young-Wolff/PhotoEdit Inc.]

This research raises other issues, however (Datnow et al., 2001; Vail, 2002). For example, because boys and girls are isolated from one another, single-gender schools and classes can exacerbate stereotypic views of the opposite sex and fail to prepare students for the "real world" in which males and females must work together (Datnow et al., 2001). In addition, some critics question the legality of single-gender schools and classrooms based on Title IX, the federal law that prohibits discrimination on the basis of gender (Fischer, Schimmel, & Stellman, 2006; Thiers, 2006). More research is needed to determine whether or not these experiments are effective for helping students learn and develop.

Gender and Schooling: Implications for Teachers

What can you do to prevent gender inequities in your classroom? To begin, you should be aware that you may have stereotypical attitudes of your own that can influence the way you interact with boys and girls. Research indicates that teachers interact with boys more often, ask them more questions, and those questions are more conceptual and abstract. In addition, boys are more likely to ask questions and volunteer comments about ideas being discussed in class (Good & Brophy, 2003). These differences increase as students move through school. In the extreme, these patterns can result in girls becoming less involved in learning activities and ultimately lowered achievement.

The following suggestions can help make your classroom more gender friendly for all students:

- Communicate openly with students about gender issues and concerns. Simply telling your students that teachers often treat boys and girls differently and that you're going to try to treat them equally is a positive first step.
- Encourage equal participation in all classes. One demanding but extremely effective technique is to call on everyone in your classes individually and by name, regardless of whether or not their hands are raised (Kauchak & Eggen, 2007).
- Make an effort to present cases of men and women in nonstereotypical roles, such as women who are engineers and men who are first-grade teachers.
- Encourage girls to pursue science-related careers and boys to consider careers in nontraditional male fields such as nursing or teaching (Francis & Skelton, 2005; Ginsberg et al., 2004).

The powerful influence that teachers can have on students is captured in the following remembrance from a 42-year-old female math professor:

It was the first time I had algebra, and I loved it. And then, all of a sudden, I excelled in it. And the teacher said, "Oh no, you should be in the honors course," or something like that. So, there's somebody who definitely influenced me because I don't think I ever even noticed. I mean, I didn't care one way or the other about mathematics. It was just something you had to do. I remember she used to run up and down the aisle. She was real excited. . . . She said, "Oh, you gotta go in this other class. You gotta." And she kind of pushed a little bit, and I was willing to be pushed. (Zeldin & Pajares, 2000, p. 232)

Making Connections:
To deepen your understanding of the topics in this section of the chapter and integrate them with topics you've already studied, go to the *Making Connections* module for Chapter 3 at **www.prenhall.com/kauchak**. Respond to questions 7 and 8.

The student ended up majoring in math and ultimately became a math professor. When teachers believe in their students, students start believing in themselves. No one is suggesting that boys and girls are, or should be, the same. Teachers should, however, attempt to provide the same academic opportunities and encouragement for all students.

Check Your Understanding

3.1   Explain how society influences gender differences in our students.

3.2   How should teachers respond to gender differences?

 For feedback, go to Appendix A, Check Your Understanding, *located in the back of this text.*

Ability Differences

 Melanie Parker, an intern from a nearby university, is ready to teach her first lesson in Mrs. Jenkins's middle school math class. The topic is the decimal system, including a review of place value, such as identifying 3,154 as composed of 3 "thousands," 1 "hundred," 5 "tens," and 4 "ones." Though nervous at the beginning, everything goes smoothly as she explains the concept and uses concrete materials to illustrate it. As she passes out practice worksheets, Mrs. Jenkins walks over to Melanie and whispers, "You're doing great. I need to run down to the office. I'll be right back." The students quickly begin to work, and Melanie's nervousness calms as she circulates among the students, periodically making comments. She notices that some are galloping through the assignment, others need minor help, and a few are totally confused. As she works with students, she notices that the quiet of the classroom is turning into a low buzz.

"Joel, why aren't you working?" Melanie asks as she turns to a student near her.

"I'm done."

"Hmm?" she thinks as she looks around the room.

"Beth, finish your assignment and stop talking," Melanie says, turning to another student visiting with her neighbor.

"I can't do this stuff!"

Melanie looks at the clock and sees that there are still 10 minutes to the bell, and, from the fidgeting and talking, it appears that several of the students have completed their assignment, while others have barely begun. Now what? (Adapted from Kauchak & Eggen, 2007.)

As experienced teachers know, and Melanie discovered, some students simply learn faster than others (Marzano, 2003), and this fact of classroom life makes instruction much more demanding. (Figure 3.7). In this section, we examine ability differences and describe how schools attempt to deal with these differences.

What Is Intelligence?

To begin this section, try to answer the following questions, and then decide what they have in common.

1. On what continent is Brazil?
2. A coat priced $45 is marked 1/3 off. When it still doesn't sell, the sale price is reduced by half. What is the price after the second discount?
3. Who was Albert Einstein?
4. In terms of size, what are the largest and smallest states in the United States?
5. How are a mountain and a plateau alike?

Figure 3.7 Ability Differences and Diversity

The common feature of these questions may surprise you. Each is similar to an item found on the Wechsler Intelligence Scale for Children—Third Edition (Wechsler, 2003), one of the most widely used intelligence tests in the United States. In other words, experts believe that the ability to answer questions such as these is an indicator of a person's intelligence, or ability to learn new information.

We all have intuitive notions of intelligence; it's how "sharp" people are, how much they know, how quickly and easily they learn, and how perceptive and sensitive they are. Researchers, however, more precisely define **intelligence** as the capacity to acquire knowledge, the ability to think and reason in the abstract, and the ability to solve problems (Louis et al., 2000; Sattler, 2001). It is these three dimensions that intelligence tests attempt to measure. These three dimensions also play a powerful role in determining learning ability and school success.

Changes in Views of Intelligence

Historically, researchers believed that intelligence was a unitary trait and that all people could be classified along a single continuum of "general" intelligence. Thinking has changed, however, and some researchers now believe that intelligence is composed of several distinct dimensions that may occur alone or in various combinations in different individuals.

Howard Gardner (1983, 1999), a Harvard psychologist who did groundbreaking work in this area, is one of the most well-known proponents of this idea. He proposed a theory of **multiple intelligences**, which suggests that overall intelligence is composed of eight relatively independent dimensions (Table 3.2).

Gardner's theory makes intuitive sense. For example, we all know people who don't seem particularly "sharp" analytically but who excel in getting along with others. This ability serves them well in a number of jobs requiring "people" skills such as sales and even teaching, and in some instances they're more successful than their "brighter" peers. Other people seem very self-aware and can capitalize on their personal strengths and minimize their weaknesses. Gardner would describe these people as high in *interpersonal* and *intrapersonal* intelligence, respectively.

While popular with educators, Gardner's theory also has its critics. Some caution that the theory and its applications have not been validated by research (Corno et al., 2002). Others disagree with the assertion that abilities in specific domains, such as naturalist or musical, qualify as separate forms of intelligence (McMahon et al., 2004; Sattler, 2001).

Despite the theory's popularity with teachers, most classrooms focus heavily on the linguistic and logical-mathematical dimensions and virtually ignore the others (Viadero, 2003b). If the other dimensions are to develop, however, students need experiences with them. For example, cooperative learning activities can help students develop interpersonal intelligence, participation in sports or dance can improve bodily-kinesthetic abilities, and playing in a band or singing in choral groups can improve musical intelligence.

Intelligence. The capacity to acquire knowledge, the ability to think and reason in the abstract, and the ability to solve problems.

Multiple intelligences. A theory that suggests that overall intelligence is composed of eight relatively independent dimensions.

TABLE 3.2   Gardner's Eight Intelligences

Dimension	Description	Example of an Individual Who Might Be High in This Dimension
Linguistic intelligence	Sensitivity to the meaning and order of words and the varied uses of language	Poet, journalist
Logical-mathematical intelligence	The ability to handle long chains of reasoning and to recognize patterns and order in the world	Scientist, mathematician
Musical intelligence	Sensitivity to pitch, melody, and tone	Composer, violinist
Spatial intelligence	The ability to perceive the visual world accurately and to re-create, transform, or modify aspects of the world on the basis of one's perceptions	Sculptor, navigator
Bodily-kinesthetic intelligence	A fine-tuned ability to use the body and to handle objects	Dancer, athlete
Interpersonal intelligence	An understanding of interpersonal relations and the ability to make distinctions among others	Therapist, salesperson
Intrapersonal intelligence	Access to one's own "feeling life"	Self-aware individual
Naturalist intelligence	The ability to recognize similarities and differences in the physical world	Biologist, anthropologist

Source: Adapted from H. Gardner and Hatch (1989) and Chekles (1997).

This section provides one perspective related to the fourth statement in our introductory questionnaire, "Students who are talented in one area of school are generally talented in all the others." A unitary view of intelligence would agree with the statement, but Gardner's theory of multiple intelligences suggests that intelligence is multifaceted and that students can excel in different ways in different areas.

Now, let's see how schools respond to differences in students' abilities to learn.

Ability Grouping and Tracking: Schools' Responses to Differences in Ability

The most common way schools respond to differences in students' abilities is by **ability grouping**, the practice of placing students of similar aptitude and achievement histories together in an attempt to match instruction to the needs of different groups (Holloway, 2001; Lou, Abrami, & Spence, 2000).

Ability grouping is popular in elementary schools and typically exists in two forms. **Between-class ability grouping** divides all students in a given grade into groups, such as high, medium, and low, whereas **within-class ability grouping** divides students within one classroom into ability groups. Most elementary teachers endorse ability grouping, particularly in reading and math.

In middle, junior high, and high schools, ability grouping goes further, with high-ability students studying advanced and college preparatory courses and lower-ability classmates receiving vocational or work-related instruction. In some schools, students are grouped only in certain areas, such as English or math. In others, the grouping exists across all content areas, a practice called **tracking**, which places students in a series of different classes or curricula on the basis of ability and career goals. Some form of tracking exists in most middle, junior high, and high schools (Oakes, 2005).

Why is ability grouping so common? Advocates claim that it increases learning because it allows teachers to adjust methods, materials, and instructional pace to better meet students' needs (Gladden, 2003). Because lesson components and assessments are similar for students in a particular group, instruction is also easier for the teacher, they argue.

Ability grouping. The practice of placing students of similar aptitude and achievement histories together in an attempt to match instruction to the needs of different groups.

Between-class ability grouping. Grouping that divides all students in a given grade into high, medium, and low groups.

Within-class ability grouping. Grouping that divides students within one classroom into ability groups.

Tracking. The practice of ability grouping that places students in a series of different classes or curricula on the basis of ability and career goals.

However, research has uncovered several serious problems with tracking:

- Homogeneously grouped low-ability students achieve less than heterogeneously grouped students of similar ability (Good & Brophy, 2003).
- Within-class grouping creates logistical problems for teachers, because different lessons and assignments are required, and monitoring students in different tasks is difficult (Good & Brophy, 2003).
- Improper placements occur, and placement tends to become permanent. Cultural minorities are underrepresented in high-ability classes and overrepresented in those with lower-ability students (Oakes, 2005).
- Low groups are stigmatized, and the self-esteem and motivation of students in these groups decrease (Stipek, 2002).

In addition, absentee rates, delinquency, truancy, and dropping out of school are much higher for students in low groups than for students in general (Slavin, 2006). Tracking also often results in racial or cultural segregation of students, which impedes social development and the ability to form friendships across cultural groups (Oakes & Wells, 2002).

Teachers can avoid many of the problems associated with ability grouping and tracking by having appropriately high expectations for all students and working with them in heterogeneous groups whenever possible. Instructional adaptations will be needed, however, to ensure the success of students of varying abilities. Some effective strategies include the following:

- Break long assignments into shorter ones, and provide additional scaffolding and support for those who need it.
- Give students who need it more time to complete assignments.
- Provide peer tutors for students requiring extra help.
- Use small-group work in which students help each other learn.
- Provide options on some assignments, such as giving students the choice of presenting a report orally or in writing (Tomlinson, 2003; Tomlinson & Callahan, 2001).

Effective teachers accommodate ability differences in a number of ways including group work, peer tutoring, and assignment options. [Scott Cunningham/Merrill]

Effective teachers adapt instruction to meet the needs of all students; these adaptations are essential for low-ability students.

Learning Styles

One thing Chris Burnette remembers from his methods classes is the need for variety. He has been primarily using large-group discussions in his middle school social studies classes, and most of the students seem to respond okay. But others seem disinterested, and their attention often drifts.

Today, Chris decides to try a small-group activity involving problem solving. The class has been studying the growth of American cities, and he wants the students to think about solutions to some of the problems of big cities. As he watches the groups interact, he is surprised at what he sees. Some of the students who are most withdrawn in whole-class discussions are leaders in the groups.

"Great!" he thinks. But at the same time, he notes that some of his more active students are sitting back and not getting involved.

How do you like to study? Do you learn most effectively with others or alone? Do you prefer teacher presentations or reading a textbook? Your answers to these questions reflect your unique **learning style**, or your preferred way of learning, problem solving, or processing information (Denig, 2003).

One approach to learning styles distinguishes between deep and surface approaches to processing information (Evans, Kirby, & Fabrigar, 2003). For instance, when you study a new idea, do you ask yourself how it relates to other ideas, what examples of the idea exist, and how it might apply in a different context? If so, you were using a deep-processing approach. On the other hand, if you simply memorized the definition, you were using a surface approach.

As you might expect, deep-processing approaches result in higher achievement if tests focus on understanding and application, but surface approaches can be successful if tests emphasize fact learning and memorization. Students who use deep-processing approaches also tend to be more intrinsically motivated, whereas those who use surface approaches tend to be more motivated by high grades and their performance compared to others (Pintrich & Schunk, 2002).

Learning Styles: Research Results

The idea of *learning styles* is popular in education, and many consultants use this label when they conduct in-service workshops for teachers. These practices are controversial, however. Advocates claim matching learning environments to learner preference results in increased achievement and improved attitudes (Carbo, 1997; Farkas, 2003). Critics counter by questioning the validity of the tests used to measure learning styles (Stahl, 1999), and they also cite research indicating that attempts to match learning environments to learning preferences have resulted in no increases and, in some cases, even decreases in learning (Brophy, 2004; Klein, 2003).

Learning Styles: Implications for Teachers

The concept of *learning style* has three implications for teachers. First, it reminds us of the need to vary instruction, since no instructional approach will be preferred by all students (Brophy, 2004). Chris Burnette discovered this when he tried to implement a one-size-fits-all approach to his teaching. As you'll see in Chapter 12, effective teachers use a variety of instructional strategies. Second, awareness of learning styles can increase our sensitivity to differences in our students, making it more likely that we will respond to our students as individuals. Third, it suggests that teachers should encourage students to think about their own learning, that is, to develop their metacognition.

Metacognition refers to students' awareness of the ways they learn most effectively and their ability to control these factors. For example, a student who realizes that studying with a stereo on reduces her ability to concentrate, and then turns the stereo off, is demonstrating metacognition. Students who are metacognitive can adjust strategies to match learning tasks better than their less metacognitive peers can and, as a result, their achievement is higher (Eggen & Kauchak, 2007). By encouraging students to think about how they learn best, teachers provide students with a powerful learning tool they can use throughout their lives.

> **Making Connections:**
> To deepen your understanding of the topics in this section of the chapter and integrate them with topics you've already studied, go to the *Making Connections* module for Chapter 3 at **www.prenhall.com/kauchak**. Respond to questions 9–13.

Check Your Understanding

4.1 Explain the differences in current definitions of intelligence.

4.2 How do schools respond to differences in ability? What does research suggest about its application in classrooms?

4.3 What are learning styles? What are the implications of learning styles for teachers?

 For feedback, go to Appendix A, Check Your Understanding, *located in the back of this text.*

> **Learning styles.** Students' personal approaches to learning, problem solving, and processing information.
>
> **Metacognition.** Students' awareness of the ways they learn most effectively and their ability to control these factors.

Students With Exceptionalities

Celina Curtis, a beginning first-grade teacher in a large urban elementary school, has survived her hectic first weeks. She is beginning to feel comfortable, but at the same time, some things are bothering her.

"It's kind of frustrating," she admits, as she shares her half-hour lunch break with Clarisse, a "veteran" of 3 years who has become her friend and confidant. "I think I'm teaching, but some of the kids just don't seem to get it."

"Maybe you're being too hard on yourself," Clarisse responds. "Students are different. Remember some of the stuff you studied in college? One thing the professors emphasized was that we should be trying our best to treat students as individuals."

"Well, . . . yes, I understand that, but that seems too simple. I still have this feeling. For instance, there's Rodney. You've seen him on the playground. He's cute, but his engine is stuck on fast. I can barely get him to sit in his seat, much less work.

"When he sits down to do a reading assignment, he really struggles. In math and science he's just fine, except when he has to read something. And he seems like a bright kid.

"Then there's Amelia; she's so sweet, but she simply doesn't get it. I've tried everything under the sun with her. I explain it, and the next time, it's as if it's all brand new. I feel sorry for her, because I know she gets frustrated when she can't keep up with the other kids. When I work with her one-on-one, it seems to help, but I don't have enough time to spend with her. She's falling farther and farther behind."

"Maybe it's not your fault. You're supposed to be bright and energetic and do your best, but you're going to burn yourself out if you keep this up," Clarisse cautions. "Check with the Teacher Assistance Team. Maybe these students need some extra help."

As Celina discovered, students differ in several important ways, and effective teachers consider these differences when they plan and teach (see Figure 3.8). **Students with exceptionalities** are learners who need special help and resources to reach their full potential. Exceptionalities include **disabilities**, functional limitations or an inability to perform a certain act, such as hear or walk, as well as **giftedness**, abilities at the upper end of the continuum that require support beyond regular classroom instruction to reach full potential. Extra help and resources can include special educators, special schools, self-contained classrooms designed especially for these students, resource rooms where students can go to receive supplemental instruction, and inclusion in regular classrooms with the support of specially trained professionals.

Students with exceptionalities. Learners who need special help and resources to reach their full potential.

Disabilities. Functional limitations or an inability to perform a certain act, such as hear or walk.

Giftedness. Abilities at the upper end of the continuum that require support beyond regular classroom instruction to reach full potential.

Figure 3.8   Exceptionalities and Diversity

Culture

Language

Gender

Diversity

Ability Differences

Exceptionalities

Special education refers to instruction designed to meet the unique needs of students with exceptionalities. The terms *children with exceptionalities, students with special needs*, and *individuals with disabilities* have all been used to describe students needing additional help to reach their full potential. Note that in all of these terms, *children, students*, and *individuals* come first. This "people-first" practice emphasizes that, foremost, these individuals are people like you and other students, and they deserve to be treated with the same care and respect.

Federal Laws Change the Way Schools and Teachers Help Students With Exceptionalities

In the past, students with exceptionalities were separated from their peers and placed in segregated classrooms or schools. However, instruction in these settings was often inferior, achievement was no better than in regular education classrooms, and students didn't learn the social and life skills they needed to function well in the real world (Karten, 2005; T. Smith et al., 2004). Educators and lawmakers looked for other ways to help these students.

In 1975 the U.S. Congress passed Public Law 94-142, the Individuals with Disabilities Education Act (IDEA). A central component of IDEA was the Free and Public Education (FAPE) provision, which guarantees a free public education for all students with exceptionalities. This law helped ensure consistency in how different states addressed the needs of these students. IDEA, combined with recent amendments, provides the following guidelines for working with students having exceptionalities. Schools should

- Guarantee an appropriate education for all students with exceptionalities.
- Identify the needs of students with exceptionalities through nondiscriminatory assessment.
- Involve parents in developing each child's educational program.
- Create an environment that is the least restrictive possible for promoting learning.
- Develop an individualized education program (IEP) of study for each student.
- Guarantee the opportunity for schools and families to hold each other accountable for a students' education.

Since 1975, Congress has amended IDEA five times in attempts to ensure that all children with disabilities are protected and provided with a free and appropriate public education (Heward, 2006). For example, amendments in 1986 extended the rights and protections of IDEA to children aged 3 through 5 and held states accountable for locating young children who need special education services. That provision is sometimes called Child Find.

Amendment 1997, known as IDEA 97, clarified and extended the quality of services to students with disabilities. This amendment helped ensure protection against discrimination in testing, and it provided due process and an IEP to meet the specific learning needs of each student. This amendment also requires districts to keep confidential records of each child and share them with parents on request.

More recently, Congress enacted another change called IDEA 2004 that has the following elements (Council for Exceptional Children, 2005):

- Methods will be established to reduce the number of students from culturally and linguistically diverse backgrounds who are inappropriately placed in special education.
- Discipline procedures will be put in place that allow districts to remove students from the classroom who "inflict serious bodily injury" on others.
- Students with disabilities will be included in accountability systems, but districts will be provided with more flexibility in meeting the highly qualified teacher requirements of the NCLB legislation of 2001.
- The special education paperwork burden will be reduced by deleting short-term objectives and benchmarks from IEPs (except for students who take alternative assessments).

The effectiveness of these legislative changes will be determined over the next few years.

Special education. Instruction designed to meet the unique needs of students with exceptionalities.

Inclusion attempts to integrate students with special needs into the regular classroom through instructional adaptations that meet their special needs. [Scott Cunningham/Merrill]

The Evolution Toward Inclusion

As educators realized that segregated classes and services were not meeting the needs of students with exceptionalities, they searched for alternatives. The first was **mainstreaming**, the practice of moving students with exceptionalities from segregated settings into regular education classrooms, often for selected activities only. Popular in the 1970s, mainstreaming began the move away from segregated services. Mainstreaming had problems, however, as one student's experience documents:

When I got to sixth grade, they put me in regular ed. classes. The work was way too hard, and the teachers did not try to help me. They went way too fast, and I got confused. I got scared and angry. I needed the help, but none of the teachers seemed to care. They didn't pay attention to me. No one ever noticed that I couldn't keep up with the work they were giving me. They were too busy teaching. (Schrimpf, 2006, p. 87)

Students with exceptionalities were often mainstreamed into regular classrooms without adequate support and services, and the results were unsatisfactory (Hardman et al., 2005).

In attempting to solve these problems, educators developed the concept of the **least restrictive environment (LRE,)** one that places students in as normal an educational setting as possible while still meeting their special academic, social, and physical needs. Broader than the concept of mainstreaming, the LRE allows a greater range of placement options, from full-time placement in the regular classroom to placement in a separate facility, if parents and educators decide that this environment best meets the child's needs (see Figure 3.9).

As educators considered mainstreaming and the LRE, they gradually developed the concept of **inclusion**, a comprehensive approach to educating students with exceptionalities that includes a total, systematic, and coordinated web of services. Inclusion has three components:

- Include students with special needs in a regular school campus.
- Place students with special needs in age- and grade-appropriate classrooms.
- Provide special education support within the regular classroom.

Mainstreaming. The practice of moving students with exceptionalities from segregated settings into regular education classrooms.

Least restrictive environment (LRE). The placement of students in as normal an educational setting as possible while still meeting their special academic, social, and physical needs.

Inclusion. A comprehensive approach to educating students with exceptionalities that advocates a total, systematic, and coordinated web of services.

Figure 3.9   Educational Service Options for Implementing the LRE

Source: U.S. Department of Education, 2007.

Individualized Education Program

To ensure that inclusion works and learners with exceptionalities don't get lost in the regular classroom, a team of educators prepares an **individualized education program (IEP)**. Special education and general education teachers, resource professionals, parents, and sometimes the student collaborate to devise this individually prescribed instructional plan. The IEP specifies the following:

- An assessment of the student's current level of performance
- Long- and short-term objectives
- Services or strategies to be used to ensure the student's academic progress
- Schedules for implementing the plan
- Criteria to be used in evaluating the plan's success

A sample IEP is illustrated in Figure 3.10. It has three important features. First, the initials of all participants indicate that its development is a cooperative effort. Second, the information in Sections 3–7 is specific enough to guide the classroom teacher and special education personnel as they implement the plan. Classroom teachers play an integral role in helping to create and implement IEPs. Third, the mother's signature indicates that a parent was involved in developing the plan and agrees with its provisions.

Inclusion and No Child Left Behind

As we saw in Chapter 1, No Child Left Behind (NCLB) has had a major influence on education. It also is affecting the education of students with exceptionalities. In an attempt to clarify how the NCLB Act would influence these students, the U.S. Department of Education issued regulations requiring students with exceptionalities to be tested as part of NCLB's comprehensive testing program (U.S. Department of Education, 2003b). Although states are allowed to create alternative tests and standards for these students, the test scores are used in determining whether a school has made adequate yearly progress.

> **Individualized education program (IEP)** An individually prescribed instructional plan devised by special education and general education teachers, resource professionals, and parents (and sometimes the student).

Figure 3.10   Individualized Education Program (IEP)

INDIVIDUALIZED EDUCATION PROGRAM

Date _____3-1-07_____

(1) Student

Name: Joe S.
School: Adams
Grade: 5
Current Placement: Regular Class/Resource Room

Date of Birth: 10-1-95   Age: 11-5

(2) Committee

		Initial
Mrs. Wrens	Principal	D.a.W.
Mrs. Snow	Regular Teacher	AS
Mr. LaJoie	Counselor	SLJ
Mr. Thomas	Resource Teacher	M.T.
Mr. Ryan	School Psychologist	H.R.R.
Mrs. S.	Parent	J.S.
Joe S.	Student	Joe S.

EP from _3-15-07_ to _3-15-08_

(3) Present Level of Educational Functioning	(4) Annual Goal Statements	(5) Instructional Objectives	(6) Objective Criteria and Evaluation
MATH Strengths 1. Can successfully compute addition and subtraction problems to two places with regrouping and zeros. 2. Knows 100 basic multiplication facts. Weaknesses 1. Frequently makes computational errors on problems with which he has had experience. 2. Does not complete seatwork. Key Math total score of 2.1 Grade Equivalent.	Joe will apply knowledge of regrouping in addition and renaming in subtraction to four-digit numbers.	1. When presented with 20 addition problems of 3-digit numbers requiring two renamings, the student will compute answers at a rate of one problem per minute and an accuracy of 90%. 2. When presented with 20 subtraction problems of 3-digit numbers requiring two renamings, the student will compute answers at the rate of one problem per minute with 90% accuracy. 3. When presented with 20 addition problems of 4-digit numbers requiring three renamings, the student will compute answers at a rate of one problem per minute and an accuracy of 90%. 4. When presented with 20 subtraction problems of 4-digit numbers requiring three renamings, the student will compute answers at a rate of one problem per minute with 90% accuracy.	Teacher-made tests (weekly) Teacher-made tests (weekly) Teacher-made tests (weekly)

(7) Educational Services to be provided

Services Required	Date initiated	Duration of Service	Individual Responsible for the Service
Regular reading-adapted	3-15-07	3-15-08	Reading Improvement Specialist and Special Education Teacher
Resource room	3-15-07	3-15-08	Special Education Teacher
Counselor consultant	3-15-07	3-15-08	Counselor
Monitoring diet and general health	3-15-07	3-15-08	School Health Nurse

Extent of time in the regular education program: 60% increasing to 80%
Justification of the educational placement:

It is felt that the structure of the resource room can best meet the goals stated for Joe, especially when coordinated with the regular classroom.

It is also felt that Joe could profit enormously from talking with a counselor. He needs someone with whom to talk and with whom he can share his feelings.

(8) I have had the opportunity to participate in the development of the Individualized Education Program.
    I agree with the Individualized Education Program   (✓)
    I disagree with the Individualized Education Program ( )

Parent's Signature _____Mrs S._____

Source: Adapted from *Developing and Implementing Individualized Education Programs* (3rd ed., pp. 308, 316) by B. B. Strickland and A. P. Tumbull, 1990, Upper Soddle River, NJ: Merrill/Prentice Hall.

Advocates of this testing requirement claim that teachers will expect more of students and work harder at teaching students with exceptionalities if they know these students will be tested (Samuels, 2006a). The logistics of how to implement these new guidelines are still being worked out.

Categories of Special Education Students

About 6 million students in the United States are enrolled in special education programs, two thirds of them for relatively minor problems (Heward, 2006). Approximately 14 percent of students in a typical school receive special education services; 78 percent are in a regular classroom for a significant portion of the school day (Kober, 2006).

Federal legislation has created categories to identify students eligible for special education services, and educators use these categories in developing programs to meet students' specific needs. The use of categories is controversial, however. Advocates argue that categories provide a common language for professionals and encourage specialized instruction that meets the specific needs of students (Heward, 2006). Opponents claim that categories are arbitrary, many differences exist within them, and categorizing encourages educators to treat students as labels rather than as people. Despite the controversy, these categories are widely used, so they should be part of your professional knowledge base.

The federal law describing the educational rights of students with disabilities, the IDEA, discussed earlier in this chapter, lists 13 categories of disability. These are listed by order of frequency in Table 3.3.

TABLE 3.3   Number of Students Ages 6–21 Who Received Special Education Services Under the Federal Government's Disability Categories (2003–2004 School Year)

Disability Category	Number	Percentage of Total
Specific learning disabilities	2,816,361	47.2
Speech or language impairments	1,118,543	18.8
Mental retardation	570,643	9.6
Emotional disturbance	482,597	8.1
Other health impairments	449,093	7.5
Autism	140,473	2.3
Multiple disabilities	131,225	2.2
Hearing impairments	71,188	1.2
Orthopedic impairments	67,772	1.1
Developmental delay	65,878	1.1
Visual impairments	25,294	0.4
Traumatic brain injury	22,459	0.4
Deaf-blindness	1,603	<0.1
All disabilities	5,963,129	100.0

Source: U.S. Department of Education. (2004b). Individuals with Disabilities Education Act (IDEA) data (Table AA3). Washington, DC: Author. Available at *http://www.ideadata.org/PartBdata.asp.*

Note that the top four categories in Table 3.3 make up more than three fourths of the exceptional student population. They are

- Students who have specific learning disabilities (47 percent)
- Students with communication disorders (19 percent)
- Students with mental retardation (10 percent)
- Student with emotional disturbance or behavior disorders (8 percent)

We focus on these four main categories in the sections that follow.

Learning Disabilities

Students with **learning disabilities** have exceptionalities that involve difficulties in acquiring and using listening, speaking, reading, writing, reasoning, or mathematical abilities (National Joint Committee on Learning Disabilities, 1994). Problems with reading, writing, and listening are most common. Rodney, in the case study that began this section, probably had a learning disability; he did fine in subjects that didn't require a lot of reading but struggled in those that did.

Students with learning disabilities make up the largest group of students with exceptionalities—almost half of the special education population and 4.4 percent of the total school population (U.S. Department of Education, 2004b). The category first became widely used in the early 1960s, and the number of school-age children diagnosed as learning disabled has continually increased since then.

Students with learning disabilities have the following problems:

- Uneven performance (e.g., capabilities in one area, extreme weaknesses in others)
- Hyperactivity and difficulty in concentrating
- Lack of follow-through in completion of assignments
- Disorganization and tendency toward distraction

Students with learning disabilities don't necessarily have all of these problems, and some are typical of general learning problems or immaturity. Unlike developmental lags, however, problems associated with learning disabilities, instead of disappearing, tend to increase over time. Students fall further behind in achievement, behavior problems increase, and self-esteem declines (Hardman et al., 2005; Heward, 2006). Lowered achievement and reduced self-esteem interact, and significant learning problems often result.

Identification is the first and perhaps the most important step in dealing with a learning disability. Classroom teachers are crucial in this process, because they collect work samples and keep records of the specific areas where students are experiencing problems with classroom work. This information is also valuable in preparing an IEP for the student.

Traditionally, educators used a discrepancy model to identify learning disabilities (Turnbull et al., 2007). For example, if differences between students' scores on intelligence tests and their performance on specific areas of the curriculum, like math or reading, exist, then educators suspect a learning disability (Shaywitz & Shaywitz, 2004). However, experts caution that language-intensive intelligence tests may not adequately identify learning disabilities in students who are ELLs (Gunderson & Siegel, 2001). This is where the classroom teacher's input and documentation are so essential.

Communication Disorders

Communication disorders are exceptionalities that interfere with students' abilities to receive and understand information from others and express their own ideas. They exist in two forms: speech and language disorders (Bernstein & Tiegerman-Farber, 2002). **Speech disorders** (sometimes called *expressive disorders*) involve problems in forming and sequencing sounds. Stuttering and mispronouncing words, such as saying, "I taw it" for "I saw it," are examples.

Learning disabilities. Exceptionalities that involve difficulties in acquiring and using listening, speaking, reading, writing, reasoning, or mathematical abilities.

Communication disorders. Exceptionalities that interfere with students' abilities to receive and understand information from others and to express their own ideas or questions.

Speech disorders (or *expressive disorders*). Problems in forming and sequencing sounds.

TABLE 3.4   Kinds of Speech Disorders

Disorder	Description	Example
Articulation disorders	Difficulty in producing certain sounds, including substituting, distorting, and omitting	"Wabbit" for *rabbit* "Thit" for *sit* "Only" for *lonely*
Fluency disorders	Repetition of the first sound of a word (stuttering) and other problems in producing "smooth" speech	"Y, Y, Y, Yes"
Voice disorders	Problems with the larynx or air passageways in the nose or throat	High-pitched or nasal voice

As shown in Table 3.4, there are three kinds of speech disorders: articulation, fluency, and voice. If they are chronic, a therapist is usually required, but sensitive teachers can help students cope with the emotional and social problems that are often associated with them.

Language disorders (also called *receptive disorders*) include problems with understanding language or using language to express ideas. Language disorders are often connected to other problems, such as a hearing impairment, learning disabilities, or mental retardation (Turnbull et al., 2007). Symptoms of a language disorder include

- Seldom speaking, even during play
- Using few words or very short sentences
- Overrelying on gestures to communicate

Because they affect learning, language disorders are more serious. The vast majority of students learn to communicate quite well by the time they start school, but a small percentage (less than 1 percent) continue to experience problems expressing themselves verbally (Hardman et al., 2005; Heward, 2006).

If teachers suspect a speech or language disorder, they should keep cultural diversity in mind. As you saw earlier in the chapter, English is not the primary language for many students. The difficulties these students encounter in learning both content and a second language should not be confused with communication disorders. English language learners will respond to an enriched language environment and teacher patience and understanding. Students with communication disorders require the help of a speech and language specialist who not only works individually with the student but also assists the classroom teacher in adapting instruction.

Mental Retardation

Students with **mental retardation** have an exceptionality that includes limitations in intellectual functioning, as indicated by difficulties in learning, and problems with adaptive skills, such as communication, self-care, and social ability (Turnbull et al., 2007). Before the 1960s, definitions of mental retardation were based primarily on below-average scores on intelligence tests, but this approach had three problems. First, errors in testing sometimes resulted in misdiagnoses, and second, disproportionate numbers of minorities and non-English-speaking students were identified as mentally retarded (Hallahan & Kauffman, 2003; Hardman, Drew, & Egan, 2005). Third, individuals with the same intelligence test scores varied widely in their ability to cope with the real world, and these differences couldn't be explained based on the tests alone (Heward, 2006). Because of these limitations, adaptive functioning was added to the definition.

Language disorders (or *receptive disorders*). Problems with understanding language or using language to express ideas.

Mental retardation. An exceptionality that includes limitations in intellectual functioning, as indicated by difficulties in learning, and problems with adaptive skills, such as communication, self-care, and social ability.

Adaptive functioning is important because it determines how the student will be integrated into the regular classroom. Only about 10 percent of students with mental retardation are served in separate facilities, which means that the other 90 percent have some type of access to regular classrooms (Turnbull et al., 2007). The key to successful classroom interventions is increased instructional supports that make learning possible and prevent the frustrations of failure. These include shorter assignments, modified assignments, help from other students, as well as assistance from the resource teacher.

Behavior Disorders

Students with **behavior disorders** have exceptionalities involving the display of serious and persistent age-inappropriate behaviors that result in social conflict, personal unhappiness, and school failure. The IDEA uses the term *emotional disturbance,* but educators more commonly use the term *behavior disorder.* In the definition, the words *serious* and *persistent* are important. Many children occasionally fight with their peers, and all children go through periods when they want to be alone. When these patterns are chronic and interfere with normal development and school performance, however, a behavior disorder may exist.

Estimates of the frequency of behavior disorders vary (Hardman et al., 2005). Some suggest that about 1 percent of the total school population and about 9 percent of the special education population have these disorders (U.S. Department of Education, 2004b), whereas others suggest that the percentage is closer to 6 to 10 percent of the total population (Hallahan & Kauffman, 2003). Identification is a problem because the characteristics are elusive, making diagnosis difficult (Turnbull et al., 2007).

Because the line between typical school-age behavioral problems and a behavior disorder is a fine one, the teacher plays a crucial role in identifying this problem. Experts suggest that the following problems may be key indicators:

- Inability to build and maintain satisfactory interpersonal relationships
- Aggressive behaviors
- Pervasive presence of unhappiness or depression (Turnbull et al., 2007)

Teacher observations are important for both identifying a problem and suggesting productive ways for dealing with it. Behavioral approaches that use systematic applications of reinforcement combined with modeling are often effective. For example, if a first grader has difficulties making friends on the playground, the teacher might model how to approach a playmate with a toy and ask to play. Praise and feedback after a successful attempt reinforces this newly learned behavior.

Students Who Are Gifted and Talented

Although we don't typically think of gifted and talented students as having exceptionalities, they often have learning needs not met by the regular education curriculum. **Gifted and talented** is a designation given to students at the upper end of the ability continuum who need special services to reach their full potential. At one time, the term *gifted* was used to identify these students, but the category has been enlarged to include both students who do well on intelligence tests and those who demonstrate above-average talents in a variety of areas such as math, creative writing, and music (G. Davis & Rimm, 2004).

The first step in meeting the needs of students who are gifted and talented is early identification. Experts recommend using a variety of methods for identification, including standardized test scores, teacher nominations, creativity measures, and peer and parent nominations (Cross, 2005; G. Davis & Rimm, 2004). Because teacher nomination is one of the methods used for identification, you will play an important role in this process. Although the majority of states require that schools identify students who are gifted and talented, in 2003 only 27 had laws requiring that schools provide services for them (Shaunessy, 2003). Nine states, however, require that schools prepare an IEP, such as that used for students in special education, detailing specific goals for meeting a gifted student's educational needs.

Behavior disorders. Exceptionalities involving the display of serious and persistent age-inappropriate behaviors that result in social conflict, personal unhappiness, and school failure.

Gifted and talented. A designation given to students at the upper end of the ability continuum who need special services to reach their full potential.

TABLE 3.5   Acceleration and Enrichment Options for Students Who Are Gifted and Talented

Enrichment Options	Acceleration Options
1. Independent study and independent projects	1. Early admission to kindergarten and first grade
2. Learning centers	2. Grade skipping
3. Field trips	3. Subject skipping
4. Saturday and summer programs	4. Credit by exam
5. Simulations and games	5. College courses in high school
6. Small-group inquiry and investigations	6. Correspondence courses
7. Academic competitions	7. Early admission to college

The regular classroom teacher may be responsible for adapting instruction for students who are gifted and talented, or students may attend special programs. These programs are typically based on either **acceleration**, which keeps the curriculum the same but allows students to move through it more quickly, or **enrichment**, which provides richer and varied content through strategies that supplement usual grade-level work (Schiever & Maker, 2003). Table 3.5 lists some acceleration and enrichment options. Failure to address the needs of these students can result in gifted underachievers, with social and emotional problems linked to boredom and lack of motivation (Cross, 2005).

Students With Exceptionalities: Implications for Teachers

Initially, inclusion meant additional services to help students with exceptionalities function in regular school settings (Turnbull et al., 2007). Gradually, the concept of collaboration replaced this additive approach. **Collaboration** involves joint communication and decision making among educational professionals to create an optimal learning environment for students with exceptionalities. In collaboration, special and regular education teachers work closely to ensure that learning experiences are integrated into the regular classroom curriculum. For example, rather than pulling a student with special needs out of the classroom for supplementary instruction in math, a special education teacher coordinates instruction with the classroom teacher and then works with the student in the regular classroom on tasks linked to the standard math curriculum, as the following example illustrates:

Sharon Snow noticed that Joey Sanchez was having difficulties with 3-digit addition problems. After checking the IEP she had helped design in collaboration with the special education team (see Figure 3.10), she found that mastering these math problems was one of Joey's goals. She met with Ken Thomas, the resource teacher, after school, and examined some recent work samples from Joey's math homework and quizzes. They discovered he was having trouble with problems that involved carrying values over to the next column like the following problem:

$$345$$
$$+296$$

During the next week when Sharon's class was working on similar problems, Ken stopped by Joey's desk to help him. At first, they went to the back of the room, and Ken reviewed place values for him. When Ken thought Joey understood how place value affected the addition problems, he sent him back to his seat to work on the next few problems. Both Sharon and Ken monitored Joey's progress

Acceleration. A program for gifted and talented students that keeps the regular curriculum but allows students to move through it more quickly.

Enrichment. A program for gifted and talented students that provides richer and varied content through strategies that supplement usual grade-level work.

Collaboration. Joint communication and decision making among educational professionals to create an optimal learning environment for students with exceptionalities.

carefully so he wouldn't get discouraged. When the number of problems seemed overwhelming to Joey, Ken broke them down into smaller blocks of five, providing feedback and encouragement after each block. Slowly, Joey started to catch on and gained confidence. Collaboration had worked.

How does collaboration change your role as a classroom teacher? You are virtually certain to have students with exceptionalities in your classroom, and you will be expected to do the following:

- Aid in the process of identifying students with exceptionalities.
- Collaborate in the creation of IEPs that will help students with exceptionalities succeed in the classroom.
- Adapt your instruction to meet the needs of students with exceptionalities, actively seeking out the help of special educators in the process.
- Maintain communication with parents, school administrators, and special educators about the progress of students in your classroom who have special needs.

Making Connections:
To deepen your understanding of the topics in this section of the chapter and integrate them with topics you've already studied, go to the *Making Connections* module for Chapter 3 at **www.prenhall.com/kauchak**. Respond to questions 14–16.

This section suggests that the fifth statement in our beginning-of-chapter survey, which said, "Most students with exceptionalities require help and assistance in special classrooms designed to meet their needs," is not true. Inclusion suggests that most students with exceptionalities are best served in regular schools and classrooms. Instruction in these classrooms is individually adapted to meet the needs of each student.

Check Your Understanding

5.1   How have schools changed the ways they deal with exceptionalities?

5.2   What are the major categories of exceptionalities found in classrooms?

 For feedback, go to Appendix A, Check Your Understanding, *located in the back of this text.*

decision making

Defining Yourself as a Professional

You've been invited to a community awards ceremony at a local church of Pacific Island immigrants that is to honor students from your school. (This invitation and the events that followed actually happened to one educator.) You gladly accept, arrive a few minutes early, and are ushered to a seat of honor on the stage. After an uncomfortable (to you) wait of over an hour, the ceremony begins, and the students proudly file to the stage to receive their awards. Each is acknowledged, given an award, and applauded. After this part of the ceremony, you have an eye-opening experience.

The children all go back and sit down in the audience again, and the meeting continues with several more items on the agenda. The kids are fine for a while, but get bored and start to fidget. Fidgeting and whispering turn into poking, prodding, and open chatting. You become a little anxious at the disruption, but none of the other adults appear to even notice, so you ignore it, too. Soon, several of the children are up and out of their seats, strolling

about the back and sides of the auditorium. All adult faces continue looking serenely up at the speaker on the stage. Then the kids start playing tag, running circles around the seating area, and yelling gleefully. No adult response—you are amazed, and struggle to resist the urge to quiet the children. Then some of the kids get up onto the stage, run around the speaker, flick the lights on and off, and open and close the curtain! Still nothing from the Islander parents who seem either unaware or unconcerned about the children's behavior! You are caught in the middle of a conflict of cultures—yours and the Pacific Islanders'. You don't know what to do. (Adapted from Winitzky, 1994.)

What would you do in this situation?

To respond to this question online and receive immediate feedback, go to the Decision Making *module for Chapter 3* on the Companion Website at **www.prenhall.com/kauchak**.

Meeting Your Learning Objectives

1. **Explain how cultural diversity influences learning and how effective teachers respond to this diversity.**
   - As students from diverse cultural backgrounds enter our classrooms, they bring with them unique attitudes and values. Sometimes these cultural attitudes and values complement school learning; other times they don't.
   - Diversity also results in differences in the cultural interaction patterns students bring to our classrooms. Often the interaction patterns of the classroom conflict with those of the home. Teachers who recognize this problem can adapt their instruction to meet the needs of students and also teach students how to adapt to the interaction patterns of the classroom.
   - Urban areas are often called "gateway cities," as many of the immigrants to the United States first settle there. Consequently, the numbers of cultural minorities attending urban schools is large. In addition, many of these recent immigrants do not speak English as their first language.
   - Educational responses to cultural diversity have changed over time. Initially, the emphasis was on assimilation, or socializing students to adopt the dominant social norms and patterns of behavior. Multicultural education, and especially culturally responsive teaching, recognizes, accommodates, and builds on student cultural differences.

2. **Describe the major approaches to dealing with language diversity.**
   - Language diversity is increasing in U.S. classrooms. During the 1960s and 1970s, the federal response to this diversity was to encourage bilingual programs. Currently, the federal emphasis is on the rapid acquisition of English with little or no emphasis on preserving students' home languages.
   - Educational responses to language diversity range from recognizing and building on the home language to attempting to teach English as quickly as possible. Currently, despite research that suggests advantages for maintaining the first language, political sentiment favors teaching English as quickly as possible.
   - Teachers who have ELL students in the classroom can do several important things to help them learn. In addition to creating a warm and inviting classroom, they can also provide multiple opportunities for students to practice their developing language skills with their peers. In addition, teachers should use a variety of concrete examples and illustrations to illustrate abstract ideas and concepts.

3. **Explain how gender differences influence school success and how effective teachers respond to these differences.**
   - Males and females are different, and these differences reflect genetic influences as well as differences in the way society treats boys and girls. Parents also exert powerful influences on gender differences.
   - Evidence suggests that both boys and girls encounter problems in today's schools. For girls these problems focus more on achievement and career choices, especially in math, science, and computer science, whereas for boys the problems are more behavioral and connected to learning problems. Suspected causes of these problems range from societal and parental expectations to differential treatment in classrooms. Teachers play a major role in ensuring that gender differences don't become gender inequalities.

4. **Explain different views of ability differences, and describe how schools respond to ability differences.**
   - Ability grouping is one of the most common responses to this dimension of diversity. Despite its popularity, ability grouping is associated with a number of problems, ranging from inappropriate and rigid placements to substandard instruction in some low-ability classrooms. An alternative is heterogeneous classrooms in which teachers adapt their instruction to the learning needs of all students.
   - Learning styles emphasize differences in the ways students process information and prefer to learn in the classroom. The concept of learning styles reminds us that all students learn differently; effective teachers are sensitive to these differences and adapt their teaching accordingly.

(continued)

5. Explain how schools have changed the way they deal with exceptionalities, and describe the major categories of exceptionalities found in classrooms.

- Initially, students with exceptionalities were segregated in special classrooms or schools. Mainstreaming did integrate students into regular classrooms but often failed to provide the necessary help and support for either the teacher or students. Inclusion is changing the way schools assist students with exceptionalities, providing them with a comprehensive, supporting network of services.
- Students with exceptionalities require extra help to reach their full potential. The majority of students with exceptionalities fall into four major categories: students with mental retardation, learning disabilities, communication disorders, and behavior disorders. A substantial number of students with exceptionalities are also gifted and talented.
- Regular classroom teachers collaborate with other professionals to provide individualized educational services to students with exceptionalities. This collaboration begins with helping to identify students with exceptionalities, continues during the creation of IEPs, and extends into the classroom, where teachers adapt their instruction to meet the learning needs of these students. Throughout this process, the teacher maintains continual communication with parents, school administrators, and other school professionals.

Important Concepts

ability grouping (p. 95)
acceleration (p. 107)
assimilation (p. 80)
behavior disorders (p. 106)
between-class ability grouping (p. 95)
collaboration (p. 107)
communication disorders (p. 104)
cultural diversity (p. 76)
culturally responsive teaching (p. 82)
culture (p. 76)
disabilities (p. 98)
English as a second language (ESLs) programs (p. 85)
English language learners (ELLs) (p. 85)
enrichment (p. 107)
ethnicity (p. 78)
gender-role identity (p. 90)
gifted and talented (p. 106)
giftedness (p. 98)
immersion programs (p. 85)
inclusion (p. 100)

individualized education program (IEP) (p. 101)
intelligence (p. 94)
language disorders (p. 105)
learning disabilities (p. 106)
learning styles (p. 97)
least restrictive environment (LRE) (p. 100)
mainstreaming (p. 100)
maintenance language programs (p. 85)
mental retardation (p. 105)
metacognition (p. 97)
multicultural education (p. 79)
multiple intelligences (p. 94)
single-gender classes and schools (p. 91)
special education (p. 99)
speech disorders (p. 104)
stereotype (p. 90)
students with exceptionalities (p. 98)
tracking (p. 95)
transition programs (p. 85)
within-class ability grouping (p. 95)

Developing as a Professional

Preparing for Your Licensure Exam

This exercise provides you with practice answering questions similar to the Praxis™ Principles of Learning and Teaching exam as well as your state-specific licensure exam. Read the case study, and answer the questions that follow:

Diane Henderson, a fifth-grade teacher at Martin Luther King Elementary School, be-gins her language arts class by saying, "Class, look up at the overhead. What do you notice about the two sentences?"

He gave the gift to her.
John sent him the letter.

She calls on Naitia.

"The second one has a proper noun."

"Okay. What else?" Diane says, smiling . . . "Sheila?"

"Both verbs are past tense."

"Indeed they are!" Diane nods and smiles again. "What else, Kelvin?" she asks quickly.

"The first has a pronoun for the subject."

"That's true," Diane confirms. "Does everyone see that?" she asks energetically.

"Now, let's look more closely at the first sentence. What is the direct object in that sentence? . . . Kwan?" Diane asks as she walks down the aisle.

"Her?" Kwan responds.

"Hmm. What do you think, Luciano?"

"Gift?" answers Luciano, hesitating.

"Class, what do you think? Is the direct object in sentence one her *or* gift? *I want everyone to think about this in your head. Okay, Todd, do you want to try?"*

"Uh, I think it's gift."

"That's correct. But why is gift *the direct object, Theresa?"*

"Because that's what he gave," Theresa replies.

"Good answer, Theresa. The direct object takes the action from the verb. But now, what about her? *What is* her?*" Diane asks, looking around the room. "Well, that's what we are going to learn about today.* Her *is an indirect object. An indirect object receives the action. So, in the first sentence,* gift *is the direct object and* her *is the indirect object. Every language has direct and indirect objects, so what we are learning today will help you with both English and all other languages.*

"Now let's look at the second sentence. It has both a direct object and an indirect object. Who can tell us which is which? Mireya?"

"The direct object in the second sentence is letter," *Mireya responds hesitantly.*

"Yes, good," Diane says and smiles reassuringly.

"So what is the indirect object? Rashad?" Diane continues.

"It must be him."

"Very good, Rashad! And why is letter *the direct object? . . . Laura?"*

"Because that's what John sent."

"And how about him? *Why is it the indirect object? . . . Jacinta?"*

"'Cause that's who received the letter."

"Good! Now look at this sentence, and tell me which is the direct and indirect object."

The batter hit the shortstop a line drive.

"Katya?"

"Umm. . . ."

"Oh, I know," Tom blurts out.

"That's great, Tom, but remember what we said about giving everyone in the class a chance to answer? Go ahead, Katya."

"I think line drive *is the direct object."*

"Good, Katya. That's right. Now who can tell us why it's the direct object? . . . Angie?"

"Because that's what the batter hit."

"And what's the indirect object, Kareem, and why?"

"I think it's shortstop *because that's who the batter hit the line drive to."*

"Yes, good answer." Diane nods and then continues.

"I think we're starting to understand the difference between direct and indirect objects. Now we need to practice to make sure. I want you to get into your learning groups, and I want each of you to complete the exercise that asks you to label the direct and indirect objects in the sentences

BEFORE you discuss it as a group. Then, I want you to take turns explaining your answers to each other. Quickly now, into your groups, and today's group leaders should come up and pick up the exercise sheets."

Diane watches as her students quickly get into their groups and start working. A list on the bulletin board ensures that everyone in the group will have an opportunity to be a "Group Leader." In addition, she has strategically composed the groups so they are heterogeneous in terms of ability, gender, and culture. She also has paired students with limited English proficiency with other students with similar language backgrounds to provide assistance.

As the students begin working on their sentences, Diane walks up and down the rows, monitoring each student's progress. After 15 minutes, Diane discusses the exercises with the whole class, focusing on sentences students had difficulties with.

Then, Diane continues, "That's excellent. Now I want each of you to write a sentence that has in it one example of an indirect and a direct object. Underline them in each case and label them. If you are having problems getting started, raise your hand and I'll be by in a minute."

While the students write their sentences, Diane circulates among them, periodically stopping to comment on students' work and to offer suggestions. Todd, a student who receives extra help from a resource teacher, sits with his head on his desk.

"What's the problem, Todd?"

"I can't do this," Todd replies with a shrug.

"Well, getting started is often the hardest part. Why don't you write down a sentence and then raise your hand, and I'll help you with the next step."

After 5 minutes, Diane announces, "All right, everyone. Please switch your paper with the person in the next row, and let's see how you did."

1. To what extent did Diane display culturally responsive teaching in her lesson?

2. To what extent did Diane's teaching reflect sensitivity to gender issues?

3. What did Diane do to accommodate differences in learning ability and learning styles?

To receive feedback on your responses to these exercises, go to the Companion Website at www.prenhall.com/kauchak, then to the Preparing for Your Licensure Exam *module for Chapter 3.*

Discussion Questions

1. Is multicultural education more important at some grade levels than in others? Why? Is multicultural education more important in some content areas than in others? Why?

2. Experts debate whether teachers should adjust instruction to match student learning styles or teach students to broaden their learning repertoires. Which approach is more desirable? Why?

3. Which approach to teaching English to ELL students makes the most sense in the teaching setting in which you hope to find yourself in your first job? Why?

4. Are single-gender classrooms a good idea? Why or why not?

5. What are the advantages and disadvantages of full-time inclusion in the regular education classroom? Should it be used with all students with exceptionalities?

6. What implications does Gardner's theory of multiple intelligences have for you as a teacher? In answering this question, be sure to relate your answer to the grade level and content area(s) in which you plan to teach.

Developing as a Professional: Online Activities

Going Into Schools

Go to the Companion Website at *www.prenhall.com/kauchak*, and click on the *Going Into Schools* module for Chapter 3. You will find a number of school-based activities that will help you link chapter content to the schools in which you work.

Virtual Field Experience: Using Teacher Prep to Explore the Profession

If you would like to participate in a Virtual Field Experience, access the Teacher Prep Website at *www.prenhall.com/teacherprep*. After logging in, complete the following steps.

1. Click on "Video Classroom" on the left panel of the screen.

2. Then go to "Foundations and Introduction to Education."

3. Finally, select the following five modules:
   - "Module 1: Ethnic Identity"
   - "Module 2: What Is Diversity?"
   - "Module 3: The Multicultural Curriculum"
   - "Module 4: What Are Our Assumptions?" and
   - "Module 5: Multicultural Assumptions in Curriculum."

   Each of these videos explores a different dimension of multicultural education. Answer the questions that follow each video clip.

Online Portfolio Activities

To develop your professional portfolio, further apply your understanding of chapter content, and address the INTASC standards, go the Companion Website at *www.prenhall.com/kauchak*, then to the *Online Portfolio Activities* for Chapter 3. Complete the suggested activities.

Changes in American Society: Their Influences on Today's Schools

Chapter Outline

Learning Objectives

After you have completed your study of this chapter you should be able to

1. Describe the changes that have occurred in the American family over the last 50 years.

2. Define socioeconomic status, and explain how different socioeconomic patterns influence school success.

3. Describe how teenage sexuality, use of alcohol and other drugs, obesity, and crime and violence in schools have changed over time and the implications of each for education.

4. Describe the characteristics of students placed at-risk, and explain how schools and teachers can assist these students in achieving success.

Case Studies

 Elementary

 Middle

 Secondary

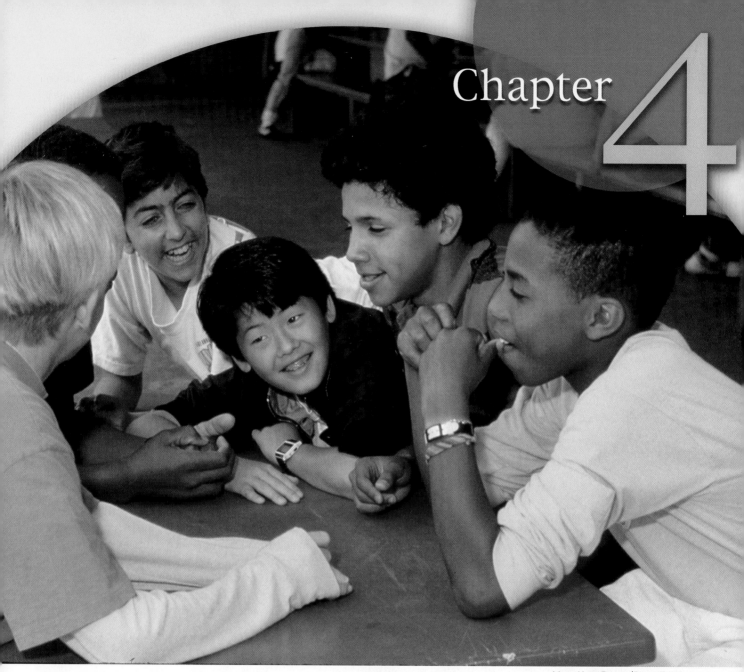

Teaching today is more challenging than at any point in our history. In addition to the increasing diversity of our students that we discussed in Chapter 3, changes in our society are also providing challenges. As you read the following case study, think about how our society is changing and how these changes might affect our students.

It is the end of August. Carla Torres, a second-year teacher, is excited about the new school year. Relocating to the Midwest because of her husband's job, she has been assigned a first-grade classroom in a large city. She spent the summer constructing units in the different content areas and is eager to get started.

Two weeks into the school year, Carla shuffles into the faculty lounge on her lunch break.

"You look tired. Been getting enough sleep?" her hallmate, 20-year veteran Rae Anne Johnson, asks.

"No, I'm not tired," Carla responds, collapsing in a chair. "Just discouraged."

"Anything you want to talk about?" Rae Anne asks.

"It's my class," Carla replies. "I had such high hopes. . . . I had my room all set up with learning centers and neat stuff. I knew what I was going to teach, and I was really looking forward to it. But these kids . . . I don't know. I'm really struggling, and now I'm beginning to wonder if it's me."

Rae Anne shrugs. "Maybe, but you're so conscientious. . . . I doubt it. What's got you so down?"

"I can't quite figure it out. Some of the kids are really squirrelly. It's hard to get them to sit down at all. Others literally fall asleep in the middle of lessons. I've got four thumb-suckers and, frankly, some of them just don't seem ready for first-grade work. I hand out a worksheet, and they look at it like I wrote it in Greek or something."

"You might be right. . . . I know it's tough. I have some of the same problems. One of my kids was all upset yesterday, so I sat her down at recess, and she told me that her parents had had a big fight the night before. And then there's Johnny . . . he's always so droopy, so I asked him if he'd had breakfast this morning. He said he never eats it, so I called his home and told his mother about the school's free breakfast program. I had to call three times to get her—I didn't want to just leave a message on the machine. She was all apologetic about sending him to school without it, but she works weird hours, and she's a single mom, so I know it's tough for her too. It's hard for a lot of kids."

"I guess you're right, but they didn't prepare me for this. I was so eager, and, I guess, idealistic about making a difference. Now, I'm not so sure."

Carla's situation is not unique. Consider another teacher's lament:

I just don't know what I'm going to do. Every year, my first grade class has more and more of these kids. They don't seem to care about right or wrong, they don't care about adult approval, they are disruptive, they can't read and they arrive at school absolutely unprepared to learn. Who are these kids? Where do they come from? Why are there more and more of them? I used to think that I was a good teacher. I really prided myself on doing an outstanding job. But I find I'm working harder and harder, and being less and less effective. A good teacher? Today I really don't know. I do know that my classroom is being overwhelmed by society's problems and I don't understand it. What's happening to our schools? What's happening to society? I don't understand all of this and I sure don't know what we're going to do about it. (Barr & Parrett, 2001, p. 1)

Today's students are indeed different from those that came to school in the years past. Fewer come from homes where the father is the breadwinner and the mother is the primary caregiver; more come to school hungry, tired, or emotionally drained because of conditions in their homes and communities; they are more sexually active; and they use alcohol and other drugs more often than students did in the past. In this chapter we examine these and other societal changes that are impacting our students and the implications of these changes for you as a teacher.

Before continuing, take a few minutes to complete the survey on page 115. We address each of the items as the chapter unfolds.

Changes in American Families

As teachers, we want to provide a quality education for all our students, and for many this is possible. They come from stable, supportive families, and they have experiences that prepare them to learn. Unfortunately, for other students, this isn't the case. Problems in their families sometimes limit their chances for success.

With head resting on his hands, Brad looks puzzled when he is asked how many brothers and sisters he has—a seemingly simple question, but not so easy for Brad to answer. He scrunches his face, pauses, pushes back in his chair, purses his lips, rolls his dark eyes, and begins counting on his fingers slowly, deliberately, then says, "Let's see, hmmm, six." *"Six?" "Wait, seven." "Seven?" "Wait, eight." "That's a hard question."* It wasn't meant to be. Brad explains: *"I didn't count my sister Mary or my sister Kerrie." "Oh?" "My dad was married to four different ladies and has had quite a few kids."* Brad has a hard time remembering when he last saw two of his siblings, who are older and live in other states. Even with his best effort, he is off one child. *(Bullough, 1999, p. 10)*

professional knowledge: test yourself!

For each item, circle the number that best represents your thinking. Use the following scale as a guide.

1 = Strongly disagree
2 = Disagree
3 = Agree/disagree
4 = Agree
5 = Strongly agree

1. Parents, in general, spend less time with their children than did the parents of the previous generation..

    1   2   3   4   5

2. The level of education attained by parents strongly influences the achievement of their children.

    1   2   3   4   5

3. Most parents want schools to avoid providing sex education, preferring to provide this education themselves.

    1   2   3   4   5

4. In recent years student use of drugs and alcohol has declined.

    1   2   3   4   5

5. Teachers are required by law to report instances of child abuse.

    1   2   3   4   5

 This is available in a downloadable format on the Companion Website for personal portfolio use.

Brad's story, while extreme, illustrates some of the ways in which the American family has changed. The "traditional" family—a husband who is the primary breadwinner, a mother who doesn't work outside the home, and two school-age children—made up only 6 percent of the total households in the United States in 2000. Census data from that year also reveal some additional facts about families and households with children:

- Families headed by married couples made up 68 percent of all households, compared to 77 percent in 1980.
- Seven of 10 women with children were in the workforce.
- The divorce rate quadrupled from 1978 to 2000.
- Twenty-three percent of children live only with their mothers, 5 percent live only with their fathers, and 4 percent live with neither.
- The incidence of poverty among single-parent families was between 7 and 8 times higher than in families headed by married couples. (Federal Interagency Forum on Child and Family Statistics, 2005; U.S. Census Bureau, 2005).

Poverty, divorce, families where both parents work, and single parents pose challenges to parents, their children, and teachers. These factors suggest that the first item on our survey, "Parents, in general, spend less time with their children than did the parents of the previous generation," is true. And even when they have time, many parents are uncertain about how to help their children with schoolwork. The combination of less time and less support means that children often come to school less prepared to learn.

What does this information imply for teachers? First, you need to be sensitive to changing family patterns. When you talk about families, make a special effort to communicate that different family configurations occur and are accepted. Also, being flexible with meeting times for parent–teacher conferences is an important way teachers can accommodate working and single parents. It communicates that you care about their children, you're committed to their education, and you're aware of the pressures that work schedules impose on parents.

Child Care

Quality child care is an important problem for the more than 60 percent of working mothers with a child under the age of 2 (U.S. Bureau of Census, 2003). When a parent is single or both parents work outside the home, young children commonly spend a considerable amount of time in child care. People have long raised questions about the effects of child care on the emotional and intellectual development of children. Critics contend that young children need the presence of a mother in the home, and child care is not an adequate substitute. Supporters counter that children can adapt to different care patterns and are not jeopardized by being in child care.

Researchers examining this issue have focused on the quality of the child care instead of the larger issue of parents working. They have found that high-quality child-care facilities contribute to children's long-term cognitive and emotional development, resulting in lower levels of delinquency, teenage pregnancy, and drug use, reduced school dropout rates, higher earnings later in life, and greater marital stability (Berk, 2005, 2006; Jacobson, 2004; Lewis, 2005).

While quality child care is important for all children, it is essential for the children of poverty. Unfortunately, research suggests that children from low-income families are the least likely to have early childhood education programs such as nursery school and prekindergarten available to them (Bracey, 2005b; National Center for Education Statistics, 2005d). In 2005, 60 percent of middle class families participated in preschool activities compared to 47 percent of poor families. And the rate of participation for poor families has decreased since 1999. Whether this is due to cost or availability is uncertain, but the United States is clearly losing a valuable opportunity to invest in its children. Experts estimate that an economic return of 13 dollars results from every dollar spent on quality child care (Jacobson, 2004).

Latchkey Children

Ana Rosa opens the door to her apartment quickly, remembering what her mother said about strangers. Once inside, she locks the door and drops her school pack on the sofa. She'll do her homework later. The house is quiet, too quiet. She turns on the television and surfs through the afternoon menu: talk shows, cartoons, and soap operas. She goes into the kitchen and checks out snacks. A soft drink and chips look good. She returns to the TV with her snacks and settles in. Only three more hours until her mom returns from work.

Latchkey children. Children who go home to empty houses after school and who are left alone until parents arrive home from work.

Latchkey children, children who return to empty houses after school and who are left alone until parents arrive home from work, represent another work-related problem that many parents face. Experts estimate that between 4 and 5 million children return to an empty house or apartment after school (Hofferth & Januniene, 2001). This presents an array of issues, ranging from concerns about children's safety to questions of supervision, excessive time spent watching television, and lack of help with homework. Teachers can address the last issue by ensuring as much as possible that students understand exactly what is expected of them on their homework assignments before sending children home.

Some schools respond with after-hours programs, but a more common solution is for schools to cooperate with community agencies, such as YMCAs or youth clubs, to offer after-school programs. In addition to providing safe, supervised environments, these programs teach children how to respond to home emergencies, use the phone to seek help, make healthful snacks, and spend time wisely.

Making Connections:
To deepen your understanding of the topics in this section of the chapter and integrate them with topics you've already studied, go to the *Making Connections* module for Chapter 4 at **www.prenhall.com/kauchak.** Respond to questions 1 and 2.

Check Your Understanding

1.1   What changes have occurred in the American family over the last 50 years?

1.2   Describe the implications of the changes in American families for child care in this country.

1.3   Who are latchkey children? What problems do they encounter in their homes?

 For feedback, go to Appendix A, Check Your Understanding, *located in the back of this text.*

Changes in Socioeconomic Patterns

Compared to the amount of time students spend in their neighborhoods and homes with family and friends, the amount of time they are with you is small. Experts estimate that school-age children spend five times as much time in their homes and neighborhoods as they do in school (Berliner, 2005a). During this out-of-school time, students learn an enormous amount about the world, and they develop attitudes and values that they bring into your classroom.

Interest in the powerful influences that families, neighborhoods, and peers can have on student learning peaked in 1966 with the publication of the famous *Coleman Report* (Coleman et al., 1966). This controversial piece of research examined student achievement scores and concluded that family background exerted a powerful and pervasive influence on student learning (Viadero, 2006b). One way to describe differences in family background is to use the concept of **socioeconomic status** (SES), which is the combination of family income, parents' occupations, and the level of parental education.

Socioeconomic status is commonly described using four classes—upper, middle, working, and lower class—with finer distinctions within each (Macionis, 2006). Table 4.1. outlines characteristics of these different socioeconomic classes. Before we continue, look at Table 4.1, and see where you are. How did your family background influence your school success and where you are today? We'll share with you our SES backgrounds later in this section.

At the top of the SES pyramid is the **upper class**, composed of highly educated (usually a college degree), highly paid (usually above $170,000) professionals who make up about 5 percent of the population. Though only a small part of the total population, the upper class controls a disproportionate amount of the wealth (some estimate that the top 5 percent own almost 60 percent of the wealth in this country), and the gap between the upper and other classes is growing (Macionis, 2006; Mishel, Berstein, & Allegretto, 2006).

The **middle class** is composed of managers, administrators, and white-collar workers who perform nonmanual work. Teachers are in this category; they hold bachelors or higher degrees, work in a professional organization, and, as you saw in Chapter 1, earn an average of $46,597 per year (American Federation of Teachers, 2004). Middle-class incomes typically

Socioeconomic status (SES). The combination of family income, parents' occupations, and the level of parental education.

Upper class. The socioeconomic class composed of highly educated (usually a college degree), highly paid (usually above $170,000) professionals who make up about 5 percent of the population.

Middle class. Socioeconomic level composed of managers, administrators, and white-collar workers who perform nonmanual work.

TABLE 4.1   Characteristics of Different Socioeconomic Classes

	Upper Class	Middle Class	Working Class	Lower Class
Income	$170,000+	$80,000–$170,000 (½) $40,000–$80,000 (½)	$25,000–$40,000	Below $25,000
Occupation	Corporate or professional (e.g., doctor, lawyer).	White collar, skilled blue collar.	Blue collar.	Minimum-wage unskilled labor.
Education	Attended college and professional schools and expect children to do the same.	High school, college or professional schools. Strive to help their children do the same or higher.	High school; may or may not encourage college.	High school or less; cost a major factor in education.
Housing	Own home in prestigious neighborhood.	Usually own home.	About half own a home.	Rent.

Source: Macionis, 2006; U.S. Census Bureau, 2001.

range between $40,000 and $170,000, and about 40 to 45 percent of the population falls into this category (Macionis, 2006).

Working class families, also called lower middle class, earn between $25,000 and $40,000 per year and compose about one third of the U.S. population. Most have a high school education and hold steady blue-collar jobs emphasizing manual labor, such as construction or factory work. About half of this group owns a home. College is a reality for only about one third of working class children.

Families in the **lower class** typically make less than $25,000 per year, have a high school education or less, and work in low-paying, entry-level jobs. About 20 percent of the U.S. population is in this category, and this percentage is increasing. Only half manage to complete high school, and only one in four reaches college. People in the lowest-earning segment of this category often depend on public assistance to supplement their incomes and are often the third or fourth generation to live in poverty.

An important factor helping people to rise out of the lower class is the federal minimum wage, which has remained at $5.15 per hour since last raised by Congress in 1997 (Herbert, 2006). During that same time period, Congress raised its own pay by $31,600. At the current rate, a single mother with two children who works 40 hours a week, 52 weeks a year, earns $10,700, almost $6,000 below the federal poverty level for a family of three. Equally troubling is the fact that the minimum wage has not kept up with increases in other wages. In the 1950s and 1960s, the minimum wage was approximately 50 percent of the average wage of nonsupervisory workers; currently, it has fallen to 31 percent of this average.

The term **underclass** is often used to describe people with low incomes who continually struggle with economic problems. Research indicates that escaping this situation is very difficult, and that poverty poses special challenges to these families and their children, a topic we examine in the next section (Macionis, 2006).

Working class. Socioeconomic level composed of blue-collar workers who perform manual labor.

Lower class. Socioeconomic level composed of people who typically make less than $25,000 per year, have a high school education or less, and work in blue-collar jobs.

Underclass. People with low incomes who continually struggle with economic problems.

Poverty

When Sally gets a spare moment (and there are precious few of them), she loves to draw, mostly fantasy creatures. "What is your favorite thing to draw?" "A mermaid thing, cuz it's not real—there's no such thing as a mermaid—but I like to draw things that aren't real. Fairy tales. Fairies, monsters." She lights up talking about her creations. But Sally's life is not a fairy tale. With her brother she hurries home from school, immediately does her homework, and "I mean right after my homework I have to clean up my room and do the dishes for dinner and cook dinner." "You cook dinner? Every day?" Staring straight across the table separating us, and without blinking her blue eyes, Sally responded slightly defensively, "I'm

a good cook." For all the talk about food, Sally's greatest fear, she said, was that she will not get enough to eat and will get sick. Who would take care of the family, then? "I worry . . . I [will] end up getting too skinny and die cuz I'm really skinny." (Bullough, 1999, p. 13)

Sally has to do all this work because her mother, who has severe diabetes, works 10 hours a day as a waitress. When her mother returns home from work, she collapses on the sofa exhausted. When Sally gets home from school, this is how she usually finds her. Life is not easy for Sally.

The lowest end of the SES continuum is characterized by pervasive poverty. The federal government establishes **poverty thresholds**, household income levels that represent the lowest earnings needed to meet basic living needs. In 2004, the poverty level for a family of four was $18,850 (U.S. Bureau of Census, 2005).

Some disturbing patterns exist in our country with respect to poverty. The number of children living in poverty is increasing, with minorities and single-parent families overrepresented (U.S. Bureau of Census, 2006). The rate of childhood poverty has risen every year since 2000, and the percentage of U.S. families below the poverty level in 2004 was five times greater than in other industrialized countries (Education Vital Signs, 2005). In that same year, 16 percent of U.S. students lived in poverty, and 36 percent of students were eligible for free or reduced federal lunch programs (Kober, 2006). What are the implications of these statistics for education?

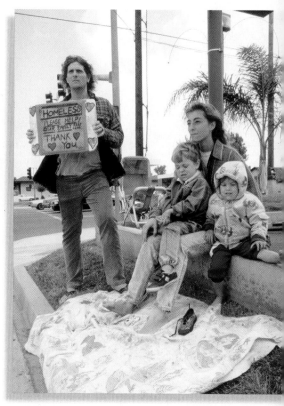

Poverty can exert a powerful negative influence on school success. (Tony Freeman/PhotoEdit Inc.)

> *What this means is that at least one-fifth of all children who come through the schoolhouse door in America today are likely to be experiencing poverty-associated problems such as substandard housing, an inadequate diet, threadbare or hand-me-down clothes, lack of health insurance, chronic dental or health problems, deprivation and violence in their communities, little or no funds for school supplies, and whose overburdened parents subsist on welfare or work long hours at miserably paid jobs. These facts pose enormous problems for America's schools. (Biddle, 2001, p. 5)*

The important effect that poverty can have on learning is reflected in integration-by-income programs implemented by a number of districts in the country, including Rochester, New York; Cambridge, Massachusetts; and San Francisco, California (Kahlenberg, 2006). These programs use a variety of ways to integrate students from different SES levels, including magnet schools, vouchers, and even busing. All are based on the belief that high concentrations of students from impoverished backgrounds detract from a school's ability to successfully meet students' learning needs. Initial results of these integration programs are promising; in North Carolina, 64 percent of integrated-by-income students passed state mandated end-of-course exams versus only 48 percent in comparable surrounding areas (Kahlenberg, 2006).

Socioeconomic Status and School Success

How does SES influence school success? Let's look at the experiences of a struggling fifth grader named Socorro. When a researcher went to her house to find out why she struggled, here is what he found:

> *When interviewing Socorro's mother, Nick passed through the apartment apparently returning to work after taking a brief break. The phone rang. Socorro's 5-year-old stepbrother curled up in his mother's lap and began talking into her ear. The television was on. There is a television in every room; one is Socorro's. The apartment is spotlessly clean. Life is busy, very busy. Once off the phone, the mother exclaims, proudly, "I let her do whatever she wants . . . she does whatever she wants." Working two jobs, one in housekeeping at a nearby hospital and another, an evening job as a parking lot attendant to obtain money*

Poverty thresholds.
Household income levels that represent the lowest earnings needed to meet basic living needs.

Inadequate medical care for low-SES students can pose a serious barrier to school success. (Roy Ramsey/PH College)

for a promised trip to Disneyland, leaves her no option: She is not home often. Socorro's father pays regular child support. While not at work, her mother's brother, who lives with the family and spends much of his day watching television, tends the children when they are home. Irritated, Socorro said that her uncle expects to be waited on, and she doesn't like it. "I want to support my kids," the mother says, and this requires that she is "never home for them." She works very hard.

Socorro's problem in school, her mother asserts, is that "her mind wanders." Her teachers tell another tale: Socorro cannot read and is struggling. Her mother seems unconcerned that Socorro frequently misses school. As her teacher said: "She is out of school more than she is in it." Attending school irregularly, Socorro is slipping further and further behind her classmates. Concerned, teachers made arrangements to place Socorro for part of the day with the special education teacher. They didn't know what else to do, having failed to gain the mother's help in getting Socorro to school regularly. (Bullough, 2001, p. 33)

Socioeconomic status influences school success in a number of ways but has its most important influence at the lower-income levels (Macionis, 2006). For example, low-SES elementary students are more than twice as likely as their higher-SES peers to fall below basic levels of reading, and are only one third as likely to achieve at a proficient level, and dropout rates for the poorest families exceed 50 percent (Allington & McGill-Franzen, 2003). About 25 percent of high school graduates from the lower SES classes go to college and earn a degree, compared to nearly 80 percent of the graduates from the highest SES classes (Macionis, 2006).

What might cause these dramatic differences in school success? Several factors related to SES influence the success of the students you'll teach. They include

- Fulfillment of basic needs
- Family stability
- School-related experiences
- Interaction patterns in the home
- Parental attitudes and values

Fulfillment of basic needs like food, shelter, and medical care is something that most families in the United States take for granted. However, many low-SES families lack adequate medical care, and an increasing number of children are coming to school without proper nourishment (Rothstein, 2004a, 2004b). In high-poverty schools, the school nurse often serves as a substitute for the family doctor because families in poverty don't have medical insurance or can't afford to see doctors (Smith, 2005). One school nurse reported,

Mondays we are hit hard. It's not like in the suburbs, where families call the pediatrician. When our kids get sick on the weekends, they go to the emergency room, or they wait. Monday morning, they are lined up, and they have to see the nurse. (Smith, 2005, p. 49)

It is hard to learn when you're sick or hurting. In addition, research has found that poor nutrition can also affect attention and memory and even lead to lower intelligence test scores (Berk, 2006).

Family stability also influences student learning and success in school. In some low-SES families, daily struggles and economic problems lead to parental frustration, anger, and depression. These pressures can also lead to marital conflicts that result in unstable home environments (Rainwater & Smeeding, 2003). Children then come to school without a sense of safety and security, and consequently are less equipped to tackle school-related challenges.

Students from poor families also have a greater incidence of depression and other emotional problems than do their more advantaged peers (Evans & English, 2002).

School-related experiences in the home influence students' learning as well (Orr, 2003; Popham, 2004a). For example, high-SES parents are more likely than their low-SES counterparts to provide their children with educational activities outside school (e.g., visits to museums, concerts, bookstores, and libraries), to have materials at home that support learning (e.g., computers with access to the Internet, newspapers, encyclopedias, and almanacs), and to arrange for formal out-of-school learning experiences (e.g., music or dance lessons, participation in tennis and soccer camps, and computer classes) (Economic Policy Institute, 2002). These experiences provide a foundation that helps students succeed in school activities. Low-SES students are also less likely to participate in enriching activities in the community as well as in extracurricular activities provided by schools, often because of parents' work demands, transportation problems, or a simple lack of awareness that the opportunities exist.

Interaction patterns in the home can also help or hinder learning. In general, high-SES parents talk with their children more than do lower-SES caregivers, and this verbal give and take provides students with practice in developing their language skills. These discussions prepare children for the kind of verbal interaction found in the schools. Sometimes called "the curriculum of the home," these rich interaction patterns, together with the enrichment experiences described in the previous paragraph, provide a foundation for reading and vocabulary development (Bardige, 2005; Holloway, 2004).

Experts estimate that by the age of 3, children with professional parents have heard 30 million words, children with working-class parents have heard 20 million, and children with parents on welfare have heard 10 million (Chance, 1997). High-SES parents are also more likely to treat their children as conversational partners, explain ideas and the causes of events, encourage independent thinking, and emphasize individual responsibility (Berk, 2005, 2006). Low-SES parents are more likely to "tell" rather than explain, their language is less elaborate, their directions are less clear, and they are less likely to encourage problem solving.

Finally, parental attitudes and values shape the way students think about schools and learning. As we said earlier, reading materials are more likely to be found in high-SES homes. Parents who enjoy books, newspapers, and magazines communicate that the information they contain is valuable and that reading is a useful activity for its own sake. When children see their parents read, they imitate the behavior, which influences their learning at school (Tompkins, 2006b).

Parents also communicate their attitudes about education through the expectations they hold for their children and through their involvement in children's activities. High-SES parents are more likely to encourage their children to graduate from high school and attend college (Brown et al., 2004). They also support their children's education by attending curricular and extracurricular activities. One mother commented, "When she sees me at her games, when she sees me going to open house, when I attend her Interscholastic League contests, she knows I am interested in her activities. Plus, we have more to talk about" (Young & Scribner, 1997, p. 12).

This section addresses the second statement in our introductory survey, "The level of education attained by parents strongly influences the achievement of their children." A large body of evidence consistently indicates that this statement is true, and the influence occurs in ways ranging from providing and talking about education-related experiences, to basic attitudes about education and learning.

SES: Some Cautions and Implications for Teachers

It's important to remember that the research findings reported in this section describe group differences, and individuals within the groups will vary widely. For example, many low-SES parents read and talk to their children, encourage their involvement in extracurricular activities, and attend school events. Both of your authors come from low-SES families, and we were given many of the enriching experiences we've discussed in reference to high-SES parents. Conversely, belonging to a high-SES family does not guarantee that a child will have enriching experiences and caring, involved parents. When you work with your students, be careful to avoid stereotypes; remember that your students are individuals and treat them as such. Keep your expectations appropriately high for all students.

A second, related, caution: We know that certain home conditions make it more difficult for students to succeed in school (Rothstein, 2004a), but we also know that schools and teachers can do much to overcome these problems (Barton, 2004; Darling-Hammond & Bransford, 2005). As you'll see later in the chapter, schools that are safe, nurturing, and demanding, and teachers with high expectations and effective instruction *can* make a significant difference in all students' lives.

Homelessness

One direct result of poverty is an increase in homelessness. A direct count of homelessness does not exist, but experts estimate that between one half to one million children are homeless sometime during any given year; in 2005 families with children accounted for 40 percent of the homeless population (National Law Center on Homelessness and Poverty, 2006). Homeless children often come from unstable families, suffer from inadequate diets, and lack medical care. At least one fifth of homeless children fail to regularly attend school (U.S. Department of Education, 2005a). Homeless children are three times more likely to repeat a grade and four times more likely to drop out of school than other children (Macionis & Parillo, 2007).

Schools attempt to respond to the problem of homelessness in several ways. Recognizing that students' home situations are difficult, they remove barriers by making school admission, attendance, and course requirements flexible. They also provide outreach services such as counselors, after-school programs, and financial aid for transportation. School officials coordinate their efforts with other community agencies to ensure that basic needs, such as food and shelter, are met.

One elementary school in Phoenix, Arizona, targets homeless children as its primary clients (Sandham, 2000). It sends school buses around the city to pick up these children and maintains a room that students can visit to get clean underwear and changes of clothes. Volunteer pediatricians staff an on-site clinic that provides free medical care and immunizations. The school even hands out alarm clocks (old-fashioned windups because many of the children don't have access to electricity) to help them get to school on time. Teacher dedication and effort make the school work. One teacher commented, "There's something about watching the buses roll out of here, with all the kids' faces pressed against the windows. I get this feeling it's what I should be doing" (Sandham, 2000, p. 29).

As a teacher, what can you do about homeless children? One important strategy is to talk with experienced teachers about available community resources for these students and their families and then pass this information on to parents. Then, being caring and flexible is a second essential response. Demonstrating that you genuinely care about students and their learning is important for all children; for those that are homeless, it's essential.

Making Connections:
To deepen your understanding of the topics in this section of the chapter and integrate them with topics you've already studied, go to the *Making Connections* module for Chapter 4 at **www.prenhall.com/kauchak**. Respond to questions 3–5.

Check Your Understanding

2.1 Define socioeconomic status.

2.2 How do different socioeconomic patterns influence school success?

2.3 How does the government define poverty? How does poverty influence learning?

2.4 How does homelessness influence learning?

For feedback, go to Appendix A, Check Your Understanding, *located in the back of this text.*

Changes in Our Students

We've seen that families and socioeconomic patterns among them have changed over time. As a result of these changes and other societal influences, our students have also changed, and they present special challenges to teachers. Consider these statistics from a survey of high school students (Grunbaum et al., 2002):

- Forty-seven percent consumed alcohol within 30 days before the survey, 13 percent drove after drinking, and 31 percent rode in a car when a driver had been drinking.
- Twenty-four percent used marijuana during the previous month; 10 percent had tried marijuana before age 13.
- Twenty-nine percent of males and 6 percent of females reported carrying a weapon to school on one or more days during the preceding month; 33 percent were in physical fights on school property during the same time period.
- Nine percent attempted suicide within the last 12 months; 19 percent had seriously contemplated it.

In this section, we examine factors related to these survey results as we look at students' sexuality, their use of alcohol and other drugs, obesity, school violence, suicide, and child abuse. These factors are outlined in Figure 4.1 and discussed in the sections that follow.

Sexuality

In the past, we tacitly thought of our teenagers as either asexual or restrained. We knew they were going through puberty but assumed that they weren't sexually active (or we chose not to think about it).

The facts suggest otherwise. In 2001 nearly one half of teens reported being sexually active by the end of high school, and nearly 1 in 10 said they had sex before age 13. Almost 13 percent of tenth graders said they had four or more sex partners (Grunbaum et al., 2002). In addition, the average age of first intercourse dropped from 19 to 15 between 1943 and 1999 (Tonn, 2005b). This level of sexual activity poses a number of risks, including teenage pregnancy and sexually transmitted diseases.

Teenage Pregnancy

Although the annual teenage birthrate has been declining steadily (from a high of 89 births per 1,000 students in 1960 to 42 per 1,000 in 2003), the United States still has the highest

Figure 4.1 Changes in Our Students

Teen pregnancies force children to mature too rapidly, diverting attention from their own personal development. (Amy Etra/PhotoEdit Inc.)

rate of teenage pregnancy and births in the Western industrialized world (National Campaign to Prevent Teen Pregnancy, 2006). Experts attribute the decline to both decreased sexual activity and increased use of contraceptives. Eighty percent of teenage pregnancies are to unmarried teens, and most (57 percent) teenage mothers keep their babies (Alan Guttmacher Institute, 2004). These pregnancies take a terrible toll on both the mother and the child.

Becoming a teenage parent forces students to mature too quickly, diverting energy from their own development to the care of a baby. Economics is also a problem; more than half of the households headed by teen mothers live in poverty (Macionis, 2006). Juggling children with work and school, teenage mothers are more likely to drop out, develop poor work skills, and have limited employment opportunities. Their babies also fare poorly; because of inadequate prenatal care, they are often born prematurely or with health problems.

Efforts to deal with the problem of teenage pregnancy focus on programs that encourage mothers to complete their educations through home instruction, or programs in which mothers bring their babies to school and attend child-care and regular classes. Despite these efforts, the majority of teen mothers drop out of school.

Sexually Transmitted Diseases

Unfortunately, many teens have sex without protecting themselves from sexually transmitted diseases such as herpes, genital warts, syphilis, and gonorrhea. AIDS (acquired immune deficiency syndrome), which can be transmitted through sexual activity, has made the problem more urgent and deadly (U.S. Department of Health and Human Services, 2006). While it was first believed that the AIDS virus was transmitted primarily through sexual contact between male homosexuals and through intravenous drug use, it is now well-known that HIV can also be spread through heterosexual sex.

Although, as you saw earlier, almost half of teenagers report being sexually active, and 1 in 7 have had four or more sex partners, only about half of sexually active teenage females and about two thirds of sexually active teenage males reported using condoms, the only reliable defense—other than abstinence—against sexually transmitted diseases (Grunbaum et al., 2002).

Sex Education

In response to teenagers' increasing sexual activity, many school districts have implemented some form of sex education. The form and content of instruction vary from state to state and community to community. Controversy over sex education usually centers on two important questions: (1) What is the proper role of the family versus the schools in sex education? and (2) what content should go into these programs?

Polls have indicated that the majority of parents favor some type of sex education (Mulrine, 2002), and courts have upheld school districts' rights to offer sex education courses (Fischer, Schimmel, & Stellman, 2006). Parents who object are free to take their children out of the programs.

This information indicates that the third statement in our introductory survey, "Most parents want schools to avoid providing sex education, preferring to provide this education themselves," is not true. Polls indicate that the majority of parents want schools to deal with sex education, not avoid it in the curriculum. You'll read more about different curricular approaches to sex education in Chapter 10.

Homosexuality

Experts estimate that between 3 and 10 percent of U.S. students are homosexual (Berk, 2006; McDevitt & Ormrod, 2004), but accurate figures are hard to obtain because of the social stigma involved. Gay and lesbian students commonly face rejection from their peers and society, which leads to feelings of alienation and depression. As a result, drug use and suicide rates among homosexual youth are considerably higher than in the heterosexual population (Berk, 2006; Macionis, 2006).

The causes of homosexuality are both controversial and complex, with some believing that it is genetic and others attributing it to learning and choice (Gollnick & Chinn, 2006). Research suggests that there is a definite genetic component; if one member of identical twins is homosexual, for example, the other member is much more likely to also be homosexual than is the case with fraternal twins (Berk, 2005, 2006).

Research also suggests that homosexuals go through a three-phase sequence in their attempts to understand who they are sexually. The first is feeling different, a slowly developing awareness that they aren't like other children. One gay student described his experience:

> As long as I can remember, I always felt a little different when it came to having crushes on other people. When I was in elementary school I never had crushes on girls, and when I look back on that time now, I was probably most attracted to my male friends. I participated in some of the typical "boy" activities, like trading baseball cards and playing video games, but I was never very interested in rough sports. (McDevitt & Ormrod, 2004, p. 403)

The second phase is a feeling of confusion, which occurs during adolescence. In this phase homosexuals attempt to understand their developing sexuality, looking for both social support and role models. The same gay male described his feelings during this phase:

> To my dismay, middle school and the onset of puberty only brought more attention to my lack of interest in girls. The first time I thought about being gay was when I was in the 6th grade, so I was probably 11 or 12 years old at the time. But in my mind, being gay was not an option and I began to expend an incredible amount of energy repressing my developing homosexual urges. (McDevitt & Ormrod, 2004, p. 403)

Finally, in the third phase, the majority of gay and lesbian teenagers reach a point where they accept their homosexuality and share it with those who are close to them. Unfortunately, rather than understanding, homosexual students are often subjected to harassment. Let's look at this topic in more detail.

Sexual Harassment

Hey, babe. Lookin' good in that sweater!
Hey, sugar. Want to make me happy tonight?

Comments like these, heard in many classrooms and hallways in our nation's schools, may constitute sexual harassment. A problem that affects both males and females, **sexual harassment** is "unwanted and unwelcome sexual behavior that interferes with your life" (American Association of University Women, 2001, p. 2). It can also interfere with a student's learning and development. In one survey, 4 out of 5 teenagers (grades 8–11) reported some type of sexual harassment in schools (American Association of University Women, 2001). Sexual comments, gestures, and looks, as well as touching and grabbing, were most commonly cited. Figure 4.2 shows the percentages of boys and girls who were subjected to various forms of sexual harassment. Equally disturbing is a recent college survey indicating that two thirds of college students experience sexual harassment at some point, including nearly one third of first year students (American Association of University Women, 2006).

The incidents of sexual harassment are similar for urban, suburban, and rural schools. However, there has been a sea change in awareness of school policies toward sexual harassment.

> **Sexual harassment.** Unwanted and/or unwelcome sexual behavior that interferes with a student's sense of well-being.

Figure 4.2   Sexual Harassment in U.S. Schools

Source: American Association of University Women Educational Foundation. (2001). *Hostile hallways: Bullying, teasing, and sexual harassment in school.* New York: Harris Interactive. Reprinted by permission.

In contrast to a 1992 study where awareness of sexual harassment policies was quite low (26 percent), a 2001 study by the American Association of University Women found that 69 percent of students were aware that school policies on sexual harassment existed. This is a positive trend, but more needs to be done to make schools safe for all students.

Harassment is an even greater problem for homosexual students (Gay, Lesbian, & Straight Education Network, 2005). One national survey found that 39 percent of teenagers were harassed because of the way they looked, and 33 percent said students are targeted for abuse because peers think they are bisexual, lesbian, or gay (Gay, Lesbian, & Straight Education Network, 2005). Comments such as "faggot" or "dyke" are common in schools, respondents reported. Sometimes the abuse goes beyond the verbal:

When I was changing classes, I had all the books in my hands. . . . I'd hear someone mutter "faggot" and have my books knocked down. People are walking over me as I'm trying to gather my books. I don't have time to turn around to see who said it. (Sears, 1993, p. 129)

Students report that this type of harassment makes them feel "sad and worthless" and "powerless" (Shakeshaft et al., 1997). This harassment contributes to higher rates of depression, substance abuse, and suicide for gay students (Berk, 2006). Unfortunately, many school counselors feel unprepared to deal with these issues (Wood, 2005).

Schools and teachers need to do a better job of making classrooms and hallways safe for all students. A U.S. Supreme Court ruling that makes school districts legally responsible in cases where sexual harassment is reported but not corrected is likely to make both teachers and administrators more sensitive to this issue (Fischer et al., 2006).

All students—boys and girls, heterosexual and homosexual—have a right to harassment-free schools, and teachers play an essential role in ensuring that this happens. Talk with your students about the problem, and emphasize that no form of sexual harassment will be tolerated.

Use of Alcohol and Other Drugs

While student use of alcohol and other drugs has declined in recent years, substance abuse still poses a serious problem for our teenagers. Consider these statistics from a 2005 national survey (Monitoring the Future, 2006):

- Over half of all students tried an illicit drug by the time they finished high school.
- Seventy-five percent of high school seniors reported drinking alcohol, with 47 percent drinking in the last 30 days.

- Forty-five percent of seniors experimented with marijuana or hashish.
- Fifty percent of high school seniors, 39 percent of 10th graders, and 26 percent of eighth graders reported smoking cigarettes.

This pattern of drug use starts early; 21 percent of eighth graders and 33 percent of tenth graders reported drug or alcohol use in the past year (L. Johnson, Bachman, & O'Malley, 2001). Schools, which ought to be drug-free havens for students, also are part of the problem. Sixty percent of high school students and 30 percent of middle schoolers reported that drugs are kept, used, or sold in their schools (Center on Addiction and Substance Abuse, 2001).

What leads teenagers to alcohol and other drug use? Some people blame the mixed messages teens receive in the media. In 2001, the tobacco industry spent $11.2 billion on advertising, and one study found that students who were exposed to smoking in movies were over two and a half times more likely to smoke than their peers who hadn't seen them (Bowman, 2004; Honawar, 2005). Although educators and parents talk about the dangers of these substances, the media, and particularly teenage pop culture, often glorify alcohol, tobacco, and other drugs, implying that they are not just acceptable but are the preferred ways of dealing with problems such as stress, loneliness, or depression.

Unfortunately, as teenagers become drug dependent, they place themselves at risk for other problems such as suicide, poor health, and automobile accidents, and they also fail to develop healthy mechanisms for coping with life's problems (Berk, 2005, 2006). Dependence on drugs can also reinforce feelings of alienation and encourage students to drop out of school. As is intuitively sensible, students who have little attachment to school and devalue its importance are those most likely to use drugs during school hours (K. Finn, Willert, & Marable, 2003).

Efforts to curtail drug use include programs that teach students facts about drugs while helping them learn to make their own decisions and understand and avoid peer pressure. They also work to develop students' self-esteem. Probably best known is the Drug Abuse Resistance Education (DARE) program, which started in California and spread across the country. In 2005, the federal government distributed $346 million to states to combat student drug use, but President Bush recommended that these funds be eliminated in 2006, calling the drug-free grants ineffective (Davis, 2006). Research on these programs is mixed, and experts agree that delivering the "Just Say No" message without further intervention efforts is almost always ineffective (Viadero, 2005b). More recent efforts to revise DARE and focus on middle schoolers' ability to understand and refuse drugs appear promising (Bowman, 2002).

This section addressed the fourth statement in our introductory survey, "In recent years, student use of drugs and alcohol had declined." The use of alcohol and other drugs by students *has* declined in recent years, but it still poses a major problem for them.

Drug and alcohol education programs attempt to help students avoid harmful and addictive substances. (David Young-Wolff/Getty Images Inc.—Stone Allstock)

Obesity

A health-care worker at the Obesity Center of Children's Hospital, Los Angeles encountered the following:

One of my patients, 16-year-old Max, who weighed close to 300 pounds, told me that he drank a six-pack of sweetened soda every day. I was appalled: he was consuming more than a thousand empty calories every day just in soda. And I was puzzled, too. Max was on his high school's junior varsity football team, which meant he arrived at school early in the morning and left late in the afternoon, after practice. How, I asked did he manage to drink six cans of soda in the remaining hours of the day?

The answer floored me: Max explained that he bought five cans of sugared soda from school vending machines every day, one each before his first class, his second class, and lunch. Before football practice he downed a fourth can, and he topped it off with a fifth can of soda when practice was over. That left one for home. I asked why he didn't drink water. He told me the water that came out of the fountains was brown and smelly and the vending machines didn't sell it. The rest of his diet was equally bad. In the mid-morning he bought a candy bar at the student store, at lunch he had high-calorie, high-fat burrito and fries or cheese nachos, and after football practice there were boxes of doughnuts. I asked about fruits and vegetables. Max told me they were usually soft and brown, or covered in butter or sauce. There was literally nothing in his daily environment that was both nutritious and appealing. (Kaufman, 2005, p. 243)

In recent years, student obesity has emerged as a major health issue facing our youth. Nationwide, 16 percent of children ages 6 to 19—more than 9 million students—were overweight in 2002, triple the proportion in 1980 (Education Vital Signs, 2006b; Schibsted, 2006). In addition to immediate health risks such as high blood pressure and joint problems, overweight youth also face rejection from their peers and the risk of developing into heavy adults with potential problems of heart disease and Type II diabetes (DeAngelis, 2004). The problem is especially acute for low-SES and Mexican-American and African-American children, whose obesity rates are often 50 percent greater than for the general student population (Education Vital Signs, 2006b).

The causes of this epidemic are multifaceted and range from lack of exercise to just plain unhealthy diets. One poll found that the average 8- to 18-year-old spends more than 44 hours a week in front of either a television or computer screen and spends less than 2 hours a day in outdoor play (Education Vital Signs, 2005; Lafee, 2005). Schools also contribute to the problem. Elementary school recess has largely been eliminated, and the number of high school students taking P.E. declined from 41 to 28 percent between 1991 and 2003 (Greifner, 2006; Schibsted, 2006). Sugar-laden soft drinks sold in schools also contribute to the problem. (An average can of non-diet soda has 10 teaspoons of sugar and 150 calories; students drinking 3 or 4 cans a day can add 5 or 6 pounds to their weight in a month.) A number of school districts, strapped for cash, signed lucrative contracts with corporations to place soft-drink machines in school hallways (Lafee, 2005).

State legislatures have responded with both stricter nutritional guidelines for school lunches and bans on soft-drink sales during school hours (Christie, 2005; Schibsted, 2006). In addition, major beverage companies such as Coca-Cola and PepsiCo, under pressure from a number of advocacy groups, agreed to limit sales of sugar-laden soft drinks in schools (Samuels, 2006b). Under the agreement, the companies will sell only water, unsweetened juice, and low-fat milk to elementary and middle schools, and only diet sodas to high schools. This is a start, but other dimensions of the problem such as exercise and healthy diets still need to be addressed.

Crime and Violence

For the past few months, Juan and his mother have been in hiding, the entire time he has attended Lafayette Elementary. His 29-year-old mother has been in gangs since she was twelve, and her sons, including Juan, grew up believing that at some point they would gain membership for themselves, and in gaining membership would enjoy status and achieve a measure of safety for themselves and their families. One bloody evening, however, crushed her and Juan's world-view, leaving behind a fearful, small boy and a mother overwhelmed with regret. (Bullough, 1999, p. 22)

Juan's uncle was shot and killed in a drive-by shooting; his uncle's girlfriend still wears a metal brace on her leg from the incident. Juan not only witnessed the shooting but had the presence of mind to pull the uncle's two children to the ground to protect them from danger. Juan's school principal, unaware of this and similar incidents, wonders why Juan is so angry in school.

Safety is a basic need for all individuals, but unfortunately, crime and violence sometimes enter school doors. The problem of school violence came to national attention in 1999 with the Columbine, Colorado, tragedy in which two students went on a rampage, gunning down 13 students before killing themselves. Then, it was amplified in 2005 when a student at Red

Lake High School in Red Lake, Minnesota, killed seven people including a teacher and a security guard, and wounded seven others.

Consider these statistics from the 2002–2003 school year:

- Thirty-three percent of high school students reported being in a fight in the previous 12 months, with 13 percent reporting that the fight was on school property.
- Twenty-three students died in schools, 15 from homicides and 8 from suicide.
- Students aged 12–18 were victims of 1.9 million nonfatal crimes, including 1.2 million thefts and 740,000 violent crimes.
- At the high school level, both males (12 percent) and females (6 percent) reported being threatened or injured with a weapon on school property (National Center for Education Statistics, 2005d).

Despite these disturbing statistics, two trends are clear. First, the incidence of violence in schools is on the decline, and students are safer in schools than on the streets where they live (National Center for Education Statistics, 2005b).

Other patterns related to school violence exist. Student concerns about safety and violence are highest at the middle school level and decline as students get older. Urban students are more likely to report serious problems with violence than suburban or rural students, and concerns about violence are greatest in high-poverty areas. School violence is often associated with gangs, and 21 percent of secondary students reported that street gangs were present at their school (National Center for Education Statistics, 2005d).

School Uniforms

Largely in response to students' wearing gang colors, a growing number of public schools are requiring students to wear uniforms. Proponents of uniforms claim that gang clothing and designer sports clothes contribute to violence, fights, and overall delinquency. Initial experiments in Baltimore and the Long Beach, California, school district were promising, and a number of districts, including those in New York, Chicago, Miami, and Phoenix, allow individual schools to require uniforms (Konheim-Kalkstein, 2006).

Proponents of school uniforms argue that they contribute to improved discipline and classroom behavior, increased school attendance and respect for teachers, better school performance, lower clothing costs, reduced social stratification, and lower rates of crime and violence (Konheim-Kalkstein, 2006). Although popular with parents and administrators, critics counter that requiring uniforms violates students' rights, students will find other ways to compete, and uniforms have minimal effect on either violence or achievement. Instead, they argue, the positive effects are due to greater parental involvement in the school and a visible and public symbol of commitment to school improvement and reform (Viadero, 2005c).

Currently, half the states have districts that require school uniforms, and the figure is likely to increase in the future (LaMorte, 2005). In general, the courts have supported the use of mandatory school uniforms, concluding that they serve a function in reducing discipline problems (Fischer et al., 2006).

Bullying

How would you react to the following incidents?

You are monitoring students on the playground when you overhear one student say to another, "No, way. Absolutely not! I already told you that you can't play with us." The student leaves and is isolated, playing alone for the remaining time with tears in her eyes. This is not the first time this individual has kept someone from joining her group of playmates.

You have assigned the students in your class to work in groups of 4 on their projects. While the students are getting in their groups you see one student push another with enough force that he falls to the ground. The push was clearly intentional and was not provoked. The child that fell yells, "Stop pushing me around! You always do this, just leave me alone." (Adapted from Bauman & Del Rio, 2006).

Bullying, a more subtle form of school violence, is receiving increased attention, as educators are realizing its damaging effects on students and its possible links to suicide and school shootings.

All of us remember teasing and taunting in the halls and school playgrounds, and many parents and educators considered this to be a normal rite of passage. Research, however, links bullying to a number of antisocial and aggressive behaviors that can have negative consequences for both bullies and victims. One U.S. Secret Service study found bullying to be a factor in two thirds of school shooting incidents (Viadero, 2003c). Another study found that both bullies and victims were more likely to carry a weapon, bring it to school, and become involved in serious fights (Viadero, 2003d).

People who bully take advantage of imbalances in power, such as greater size or physical strength, higher status, or the support of a peer group. The bullying itself can be a face-to-face attack, threats, teasing about perceived sexual orientation, or telling someone in a mean way that he or she can't participate or play. It can also include behind-the-back behaviors, such as starting or spreading malicious rumors, writing harmful graffiti, or encouraging others to exclude a particular child (D. Cooper & Snell, 2003; Siris & Osterman, 2004).

Bullying is more common than many adults realize. Surveys indicate that 74 percent of 8- to 11-year-olds and 86 percent of 12- to 15-year-olds reported bullying in their schools (Roberts, 2006). In other studies, nearly one-third of students reported that they had either bullied, been a victim of bullying, or both within the last month (Viadero, 2003d). Experts think that the incidence of bullying is actually higher than reported because it most commonly occurs in areas where students interact informally, with little adult supervision, such as playgrounds, hallways, cafeterias, and school buses (Siris & Osterman, 2004).

Teachers often fail to take steps to address the problem because they perceive bullying incidents as normal rough-and-tumble give-and-take (D. Cooper & Snell, 2003). Researchers have found that beginning teachers were less likely than veterans to respond to the first bullying incident at the beginning of this section, thinking that relational bullying was either acceptable or not worthy of a teacher intervention (Bauman & Del Rio, 2006).

VIDEO PERSPECTIVES

The In Crowd and Social Cruelty

To view this video, go to the *Becoming a Professional* DVD included with this text, click on ABC News, and then this chapter's video *The In Crowd and Social Cruelty*. This ABC News video examines social cruelty, a more subtle but pernicious form of bullying. The video analyzes popularity in schools and how it influences friendships and peer relationships. Psychologist Michael Thompson, author of *Best Friends, Worst Enemies*, explains some of the mechanisms behind social cruelty and bullying. The video also visits schools with successful anti-bullying programs.

Think About This

1. How do social cruelty and bullying affect the students involved?
2. Where are social cruelty and bullying most likely to be found in schools?
3. What can teachers do about the problems of social cruelty and bullying?

*To answer these questions online and receive immediate feedback, go to the Companion Website at **www.prenhall.com/kauchak**, then to the Video Perspectives module for Chapter 4.*

Attempts to prevent bullying focus on both individuals and the school. Bullying behaviors are often learned, with modeling and reinforcement by parents and peers playing major roles (Roberts, 2006). For example, bullies often come from homes where parents are authoritarian, hostile, and rejecting. Their parents often have poor problem-solving skills and use fighting as a solution to conflicts, with their children imitating these behaviors (Ma, 2001). In addition, bullying is also related to underdeveloped emotional self-regulation and moral reasoning and students' inability to understand or empathize with others' perspectives (Berk, 2005, 2006). Efforts to eliminate bullying at the individual level attempt to help students understand the consequences of their negative behaviors and also attempt to teach alternative prosocial behaviors (Roberts, 2006).

Schoolwide Safety Programs

Schoolwide safety programs are designed to make schools safe havens for teaching and learning through comprehensive anti-violence and anti-bullying programs (Colgan, 2005; Conoley & Goldstein, 2004). Successful programs require commitment from parents, administrators, and teachers to take a proactive stance against bullying and to monitor playgrounds, lunchrooms, and hallways, the areas where bullying is most common.

Schoolwide security programs attempt to make schools safe places to learn. (Michael Newman/PhotoEdit Inc.)

In other attempts to increase school safety, many schools are adopting comprehensive security measures, such as having visitors sign in, closing campuses during lunch, and controlling access to school buildings (Colgan, 2005; Conoley & Goldstein, 2004). Schools are also adding prevention policies that include use of hallway police, student photo ID badges, transparent book bags, hand-held metal detectors, and breathalyzers to check for alcohol consumption. In many districts, visitors are screened through an electronic system that matches drivers' licenses to a database of convicted sex offenders (Maxwell, 2006b). Students are being warned to avoid jokes about violence and given hotline numbers to anonymously report any indications that a classmate could turn violent. Schools are also creating peer buddy systems and adult mentorship programs, and are teaching conflict-resolution skills as alternatives to violence (Conoley & Goldstein, 2004; Johnson & Johnson, 2006).

The enormous publicity generated by school shooting incidents has led many schools around the country to experiment with new approaches to making our schools safer places to learn and work. One of the most controversial approaches involves the issue of zero tolerance. **Zero-tolerance policies** call for students to receive automatic suspensions or expulsions as punishment for certain offenses, primarily those involving weapons, threats, or drugs. Such policies have become increasingly popular across the nation (Ayers, Dohrn, & Ahers, 2001). We examine controversies surrounding zero-tolerance policies in *Teaching in an Era of Reform.*

Suicide

The suicide rate among adolescents has quadrupled in the last 50 years; suicide is now the third leading cause of teen death, surpassed only by accidents and homicide (Kids Health for Parents, 2006). Each year about 500,000 young people attempt suicide, and 5,000 actually succeed (Fisher, 2006). Although girls are twice as likely as boys to attempt suicide, boys are 4 times more likely to succeed. Boys tend to employ more lethal means, such as shooting themselves, whereas girls choose more survivable methods, such as overdosing on drugs.

Causes of teen suicide vary, but most are related to the stresses of adolescence. They include family conflicts, parental unemployment and divorce, drug use, failed peer relationships, and peer harassment (especially for homosexual youngsters) (Berk, 2005, 2006).

Zero-tolerance policies.
Policies that call for students to receive automatic suspensions or expulsions as punishment for certain offenses, primarily those involving weapons, threats, or drugs.

teaching in an era of reform

Zero Tolerance

The era of zero tolerance began in 1994 when Congress passed the Gun-Free Schools Act, which required states receiving federal funds to expel for 1 year any student who brought a firearm to school. Subsequent amendments broadened the focus of the act from firearms to all weapons and also included expelling students for possessing drugs or drug paraphernalia. More than three quarters of all schools report having zero-tolerance policies, and these policies are more common in school districts with large minority populations (Holloway, 2001/2002).

The Issue

The need for safe schools is obvious, and the premise behind zero-tolerance policies—students who seriously endanger or disrupt the learning environment for the majority of the school population should be removed—also is intuitively sensible. Students can't learn when they're worried about either their physical or emotional well-being. Both parents and other taxpayers rank school safety and drug use as critical problems facing U.S. schools (Rose & Gallup, 2005), and zero-tolerance policies are popular. Both teachers (70 percent) and parents (68 percent) judged zero-tolerance policies to be effective deterrents to serious infractions in schools (Public Agenda, 2004).

On the other hand, critics have identified several problems with these policies (Ayers et al., 2001). First, largely because of zero-tolerance policies, the annual U.S. suspension rate has increased dramatically (Ayers et al., 2001). A Florida study found a 14 percent increase in school suspensions between 2000 and 2004, almost twice as high as the student population growth (Gewertz, 2006a). Second, when expulsions occur, only 56 percent of students are sent to an alternative placement; the rest are sent home to fend for themselves, making the likelihood of truancy and crime even greater. One student described the problem in this way:

When they suspend you, you get in more trouble, 'cause you're out in the street. . . . And that's what happened to me once. I got into trouble one day 'cause there was a party, and they arrested everybody in that party. . . . I got in trouble more than I get in trouble at school, because I got arrested and everything. (Skiba & Peterson, 1999, p. 376)

Expelled students typically fall further behind academically, experience increased social difficulties, and sometimes never return to complete school (Barr & Parrett, 2001).

Third, the implementation of the policies is not uniform. For example, one middle school in Dade County, Florida, had an expulsion rate of 34 percent, whereas another—serving essentially the same student population—had a rate of only 2.8 percent (Ver-

gon, 2001). To minimize expulsions, students at the second school who were involved in fights, for example, were given alternative punishments (e.g., in-school suspensions) or work assignments (e.g., cleaning the cafeteria), instead of suspensions.

Fourth, because these policies don't discriminate between major and minor disruptions, schools sometimes punish students for trivial and innocent transgressions. For example, one fifth grader was suspended for bringing a miniature plastic gun to school with his G.I. Joe action figure, and in another case, a 6-year-old was suspended for kissing one of his classmates (Cornelius, 2002).

Finally, critics of zero-tolerance policies point to their disproportionate effect on members of cultural minorities. For example, in one study, African-American students in San Francisco made up 18 percent of all students but accounted for 56 percent of students suspended (Gordon, Della Piana, & Keleher, 2001). A Florida study found a similar pattern; while African-American students made up 23 percent of the student population, they received 46 percent of out-of-school suspensions (Gewertz, 2006a). Other studies found that Native American and Hispanic males were more likely to be suspended than White males, and students with disabilities were suspended at twice the rate of those without disabilities (Holloway, 2001/2002; Vergon, 2001). Explanations for these uneven rates range from higher rates of poverty and misbehavior, to inexperienced teachers, crowded classrooms, and academically sterile learning environments.

You Take a Position

As with all reforms, efforts to increase school safety are neither totally positive nor negative. Unquestionably, schools must be safe. How this should be accomplished remains controversial. As a professional, you need to be knowledgeable about these issues so you can make informed contributions to the decisions and implementation of policies in your school that will benefit all your students.

Now it's your turn to take a position on the issue. State in writing whether you feel that zero-tolerance programs make schools safer and better places to learn, and provide a two-page rationale for your position.

*For additional references and resources, go to the Companion Website at **www.prenhall.com/kauchak**, then to the* Teaching in an Era of Reform *module for Chapter 4. You can respond online or submit your response to your instructor.*

VIDEO PERSPECTIVES

Action, Reaction, and Zero Tolerance

To view this video, go to the *Becoming a Professional* DVD included with this text, click on ABC News, and then this chapter's video *Action, Reaction, and Zero Tolerance*. This ABC News video examines the effects of zero-tolerance policies on schools and students. It first visits an elementary school in Irvington, New Jersey, where an eight-year-old boy was expelled for playing cowboys and Indians with a paper gun. Next the video focuses on a high school in Virginia where the school mascot, a Spartan, is not allowed to wear a cardboard sword.

Think About This

1. What are the major goals of zero-tolerance policies?
2. What are the advantages and disadvantages of zero-tolerance policies?
3. What could schools do to minimize the negative effects of zero-tolerance policies?

To answer these questions online and receive immediate feedback, go to the Companion Website at **www.prenhall.com/kauchak**, *then to the* Video Perspectives *module for Chapter 4.*

Potential suicide indicators include

-   An abrupt decline in the quality of schoolwork
-   Withdrawal from friends or classroom and school activities
-   Neglect of personal appearance or radical changes in personality
-   Changes in eating or sleeping habits
-   Depression, as evidenced by persistent boredom or lack of interest in school activities
-   Student comments about suicide as a solution to problems (Fisher, 2006; Kids Health for Parents, 2006).

Teachers observing these signs should contact a school counselor or psychologist immediately; early intervention is essential.

Child Abuse

Child abuse is another serious problem facing today's youth. In 2003 child protective services agencies received 2.9 million reports of child abuse; investigation of these cases confirmed that more than 906,000 children had been victims of abuse or mistreatment (U.S. Department of Health and Human Services, 2006). Because abuse and neglect are often hidden or not reported, reliable figures are difficult to obtain. Almost half of abuse victims suffer from neglect, about one third experience physical abuse, and about one tenth are sexually abused (Berk, 2005, 2006). When sexual abuse occurs, it most commonly involves a family member or friend. Although child abuse can occur at any level of society, it tends to be associated with poverty and is often linked to parental substance abuse.

Teachers are in a unique position to identify child abuse because they work with children every day. Symptoms of abuse include

-   Neglected appearance
-   Sudden changes in either academic or social behavior
-   Disruptive or overly compliant behavior
-   Repeated injuries such as bruises, welts, or burns

Making Connections:
To deepen your understanding of the topics in this section of the chapter and integrate them with topics you've already studied, go to the *Making Connections* module for Chapter 4 at **www.prenhall.com/kauchak**. Respond to questions 6–13.

Teachers in all 50 states are legally bound to report suspicions of child abuse (Fischer et al., 2006). This statement clearly indicates that the fifth item in our beginning-of-chapter survey—"Teachers are required by law to report instances of child abuse"—is, indeed, true. Teachers have a clear legal responsibility to report all instances of suspected child abuse. Teachers and schools are protected from civil and criminal liability if the report is made honestly and includes behavioral data, such as observations of the symptoms just listed.

Check Your Understanding

3.1   What changes have occurred in student sexuality over time? What are the implications of these changes for education?

3.2   Explain the trends in student use of alcohol and other drugs over the last several years, and describe the implications of these changes for education.

3.3   How has the rate of student obesity changed over the years? How are schools responding to this problem?

3.4   How have crime and violence changed in U.S. schools? What are the implications for education?

For feedback, go to Appendix A, Check Your Understanding, *located in the back of this text.*

Students Placed At-Risk

The trends we've described in this chapter—changing families, poverty, violence, substance abuse, and suicide—are serious problems. In many instances, two or more of these problems occur together, placing students at-risk for academic failure. **Students placed at-risk** are those in danger of failing to complete their education with the skills necessary to survive in modern society (Slavin, Karweit, & Madden, 1989). The term *at-risk* is borrowed from medicine, where it is used to describe individuals who have conditions or habits that make them likely to develop a specific disease; for example, an overweight person with high blood pressure is described as being at-risk for a heart attack. The term became widely used after 1983, when the National Commission on Excellence in Education proclaimed the United States a "nation at risk," emphasizing the growing link between education and economic well-being in today's technological society (National Commission on Excellence in Education, 1983).

In recent years, researchers have focused considerable attention on problems and issues involving students placed at-risk. Table 4.2 outlines some of the academic, social, and emotional problems these students experience. Almost certainly, you will have some of these students in your classes.

Before continuing, we want to offer a note of caution. Some critics contend that using the term *at-risk* is ill-advised (Benard, 1994; Franklin, 1997), arguing that the term encourages teachers to develop low expectations for labeled students, which contributes to underachievement. As teachers, we need to be sensitive to the possibility of negative stereotyping

Students placed at-risk. Students in danger of failing to complete their education with the skills necessary to survive in modern society.

TABLE 4.2　Characteristics of Students Placed At-Risk

Background Factors	Educational Problems
Low SES	High dropout rates
Inner city	Low grades
Transient	Retention in grade
Minority	Low achievement
Non-native English speaker	Low participation in extracurricular activities
Divorced families	Low motivation
Retention in grade	Poor attendance
	High rate of drug use
	Misbehavior in classes
	Low self-esteem
	High criminal activity rates
	Low standardized test scores
	Lack of interest in school
	High suspension rates

and continually ask ourselves, "Am I demanding as much as possible from these students, and am I providing every opportunity for their success?"

The Dropout Problem

Because of the enormous effect it has on subsequent employment and income, dropping out of school is one of the most pernicious results of being at-risk. In 2003, high school graduates earned 34 percent more than high school dropouts; over a lifetime, a high school dropout earns $260,000 less than an individual with a high school diploma (Economic Policy Institute, 2005). In addition, dropping out of high school also closes the door to college; experts estimate a high school graduate will earn $21,992 per year versus $48,719 for a college graduate with a bachelor's degree (Sykes, 2006).

Experts disagree about the number of students who drop out of school (Bracey, 2005a; Mishel, 2006), but they agree that dropout rates vary dramatically by ethnicity. For example, in one study conducted in 2003, 70 percent of students graduated from high school, but Hispanic (56 percent), African-American (52 percent), and Native American (47 percent) students had much lower rates (see Figure 4.3) (Swanson, 2004). Think about this: nearly one third of the students who enter ninth grade won't graduate in four years, and the dropout rate increases to about half for cultural minorities!

Dropout rates are also strongly affected by poverty; students from low-income families are six times more likely to drop out than those from high-income families (Olson, 2006). Other factors contributing to high dropout rates include unstable families, high rates of student mobility, previous retention in a grade, as well as higher graduation standards and high school exit exams (Barton, 2006).

What can schools do to address this problem? Research suggests that motivation is a major factor in dropping out. In one study, 69 percent of dropouts said they weren't motivated

exploring diversity

Urban Schools and Students Placed At-Risk

Students placed at-risk face special challenges in urban schools, which tend to be large and exist in high-poverty areas. As a result, they are funded less well than their suburban counterparts. Further, because teachers perceive working in urban schools to be challenging, many veteran teachers opt for suburban schools, so urban students are typically taught by the least experienced teachers in the workforce.

Because urban schools are large, they tend to be impersonal (Kincheloe, 2004; Schutz, 2004). In smaller schools, it is easier to get to know the teachers as well as other students. Urban high schools can be "tough, confusing places where students can easily get lost" (Ilg & Massucci, 2003, p. 69).

The problem of establishing meaningful interpersonal relationships with students is compounded by diverse urban neighborhoods and the distances students often must travel over public transportation (Kincheloe, 2004). Extracurricular activities, which can serve as a meeting point for students, are often inaccessible (Brown & Evans, 2002).

The obstacles to forming meaningful teacher–student relationships are compounded by the fact that teachers in urban schools typically don't live in the same neighborhoods as do their students, making it more difficult for teachers to connect with students and empathize with their lives outside school (Charner-Laird et al., 2004). One study found that only 20 percent of urban African-American males and 28 percent of African-American female students felt that their teachers supported

Meaningful relationships with students make urban schools and classrooms more inviting places to learn. (David Young-Wolff/ PhotoEdit Inc.)

them and cared about their success (Noguera, 2003b). It is difficult for teachers to influence their students' personal, social, and moral development when the essential bonds of mutual trust and caring are absent.

Figure 4.3 Public School Graduation Rates in the United States (2003)

Source: As first appeared from Olson, L. (2006). The down staircase. *Education Week's Diplomas Count, 25* (41S), 7. Reprinted with permission from Editorial Projects in Education.

Modest Improvements in Graduation Rates

The percent of high school students graduating with a diploma stagnated during much of the 1990s, hovering around 66 percent. Since then, graduation rates have slowly but steadily improved. Although most groups show improvement, large racial and ethnic gaps in graduation rates persist.

SOURCE: EPE Research Center, 2006

As you saw earlier, poverty often has an adverse effect on student achievement, and research indicates that urban environments have higher rates of poverty (17.5 percent) than areas outside central cities (9.1 percent) (U.S. Bureau of Census, 2004). In addition, median incomes inside urban areas ($34,174) are about two thirds of those in the suburbs ($51,737) (U.S. Bureau of Census, 2005). As you'll see in Chapter 8, lower incomes and the lower residential property values that go with them mean less money for schools. Less money often means that class sizes will be larger and the schools will have fewer resources, such as computers (Archer, 2003; Blair, 2003).

Finally, as we just saw, because teachers often view working in urban areas as very challenging with too few rewards, veteran teachers opt for jobs in suburbs instead of urban settings. As a result, urban students are often taught by teachers with less experience than students in the suburbs. This is a paradox; students who need experienced and effective teachers the most are the least likely to get them. On the other hand, if you're willing to work in an urban environment, the likelihood of getting a job is high.

The challenge for urban educators is to create contexts in which urban students can interact in meaningful ways with both teachers and other students. One proposed solution is to create smaller schools, or schools within a school, that allow for the creation of more personal learning communities. Students in smaller schools "behave better, are more likely to be involved in extracurricular activities, . . . fight less, feel safe, and feel more attached to their schools" (Ilg & Massucci, 2003, p. 69).

While teachers alone can't create smaller schools, urban teachers can make a special effort to create learning communities within their classrooms that nurture both the social and cognitive development of their students. Teachers who clearly communicate caring are essential (Alder, 2002; Wilder, 2000). Caring means making the special effort to get to know students as persons and also being willing to spend extra time after school not only to listen but also to help with classroom-related tasks (Wilson & Corbett, 2001). Caring also means having high expectations and providing additional instructional structure to help ensure student success. One urban seventh grader had this to say about one of her teachers:

She's probably the strictest teacher I've ever had because she doesn't let you slide by if you've made a mistake. . . . If you've made a mistake she's going to let you know it. And if you're getting bad marks, she's going to let you know it. She's one of my strictest teachers and that's what makes me think she cares about us the most. (Alder, 2002, pp. 251–252)

Effective urban teachers combine high expectations for academic success with clear messages about the need for student effort and responsibility.

or inspired to work hard, nearly half said their classes weren't interesting, and two thirds identified a lack of challenge as a major factor in dropping out (Gewertz, 2006c). Each of these issues can be addressed with effective instruction, a topic we discuss in Chapter 12. Additional research suggests that the human factor is crucial; students at risk for dropping out need to feel that they belong in school and that someone cares about their success (Barton, 2006). Teachers are essential to making this human factor work; often they are the only people in the school who interact with students on a daily basis (Doll, Zucher, & Brehm, 2004). Effective teachers interact frequently with their students, learn about their families, and share their own lives.

It Takes a Village: The Community-Based Approach to Working With Children Placed At-Risk

Though schools can have a powerful influence on at-risk students' success, they can't do it all without outside help. Effective schools actively involve parents and other members of the community in redesigning schools to better meet the needs of children placed at-risk.

Full-service schools serve as family resource centers to provide a range of social and health services. Recognizing that many of the problems students encounter occur outside school walls, and that supporting families also strengthens children, full-service schools

> **Full-service schools.** Schools that serve as a family resource center to provide a range of social and health services.

TABLE 4.3   Services Provided by Full-Service Schools

Child care
Medical and dental screening
Immunizations
Nutrition/weight management
Employment and housing assistance
Legal and immigration advice
Individual counseling/mental health services
Substance abuse treatment
Recreation, sports, and culture
Parent education
After-school teacher assistance with homework

attempt to create a safety net of services to students and their families. Some of these services are listed in Table 4.3.

One example of a full-service model is the School Development Program, created by Yale psychiatrist James Comer (Comer, Joyner, & Ben-Avie, 2004). It integrates schools and the community by bringing principals, teachers, and parents together in school planning and management teams. School services, such as counseling and support for students with learning problems, are coordinated through teams of psychologists, counselors, and special educators. This coordination is important because services for students are often fragmented. For example, one depressed, pregnant, drug-using teenager saw three different counselors each week: a suicide prevention counselor, a parenting counselor, and a drug abuse counselor. None of them talked to each other (Tyson, 1999). Comprehensive school programs address this problem by coordinating services and by focusing on the whole child's physical, social, emotional, and academic growth in integrated efforts.

From its start in New Haven, Connecticut, the School Development Program has spread to more than 500 schools across the country. Evaluations indicate that the program is effective; achievement has increased significantly, student self-concepts have improved, and absences, suspensions, and management problems have declined in schools where the program is fully implemented (Comer et al., 2004). Research on other comprehensive school programs shows similar positive effects (Whalen, 2002).

The teacher's role in a full-service school changes from one of instructor to partner with the community. If you work in one of these schools, you'll be asked to serve on community councils that attempt to link schools with their surrounding communities. You'll also be asked to be proactive in making contacts with parents and other caregivers. While probably more work, the rewards that come from seeing your students succeed because of your outreach efforts will be substantial.

Promoting Student Resilience

Despite the societal problems presented in this chapter, many students succeed against the odds and graduate from school with the skills necessary to succeed in life. **Resilient students**

Resilient students. Students placed at-risk who have been able to rise above adverse conditions to succeed in school and in other aspects of life.

are students placed at-risk who have been able to rise above adverse conditions to succeed in school and in other aspects of life (Borman & Overman, 2004; Doll et al., 2004).

Resilient children have well-developed "self systems," including high self-esteem and feelings that they are in control of their destinies. They set personal goals, possess good interpersonal skills, and have positive expectations for success. They are motivated to learn and satisfied with school (Borman & Overman, 2004; Doll et al., 2004).

How do these adaptive skills develop? First, resilient children have relationships with caring adults who hold high moral and academic expectations for them (Reis, Colbert, & Hébert, 2005). Second, they come from schools that are both demanding and supportive; in many instances, schools serve as homes away from home. Let's look more closely at how schools and teachers help develop resilience in students.

Effective Schools for Students Placed At-Risk

Effective schools for students placed at-risk focus on personal responsibility, cooperation, and mutual respect between teachers and students (Barr & Parrett, 2001; Griffith, 2002). Effective schools emphasize

- A safe, orderly school climate in which students understand the meaning behind and the purpose of school and classroom rules
- Academic objectives focusing on mastery of content
- Caring and demanding teachers and high expectations for all students
- Cooperation, a sense of community, and prosocial values
- Student responsibility and self-regulation; decreased emphasis on external controls
- Strong parental involvement (Ilg & Massucci, 2003; Pressley et al., 2004).

These same strategies appear to work in other countries and cultures; a study of students placed at-risk in Israel arrived at essentially the same conclusions about effective schools in that country (Gaziel, 1997).

Effective Teachers for Students Placed At-Risk

Well-run and academically focused schools are important, but they aren't sufficient in themselves. Professional teachers who are highly skilled and sensitive are essential (Doll et al., 2004). In Chapter 1 we said that professionals are skilled in making decisions in ill-defined situations. This ability is crucial in working with students placed at-risk because their needs and personal sensitivities make them particularly vulnerable to failure, personal slights, hints of favoritism, and questions about the relevance of school.

How can teachers help students develop resilience? Teacher understanding and commitment to student success is one essential element. One high school teacher reported the following:

> A graduate whom I had not seen for many years stopped by after school when he saw me working late. His eyes were thick with tears as he spoke: "You never gave up on me. You never ignored me. You always encouraged me to get my work in and pass all of my classes, even when I wasn't nice to you. Thank you." (Barnoski, 2005, p. 37)

Effective teachers go the extra mile to ensure student success.

Less-effective teachers are more authoritarian and less accessible. They distance themselves from students and place

Caring teachers with high expectations for success help students placed at-risk achieve in school. (Michael Newman/PhotoEdit Inc.)

primary responsibility for learning on them. They view instructional support as "babying students" or "holding students' hands." Lecture is a common teaching strategy, and motivation is the students' responsibility. Students perceive these teachers as adversaries, to be avoided if possible, tolerated if not. They also resent teachers' lack of high expectations and standards:

> *There's this teacher [over at the regular school] . . . you can put anything down and he'll give you a check mark for it. He doesn't check it. He just gives you a mark and says, 'OK, you did your work.' How you gonna learn from that? You ain't gonna learn nothing.*
>
> *Student, JFK Academy*
> *Boston, Massachusetts*
> *(Dynarski & Gleason, 1999, p. 13)*

Alienation from school is a problem for students placed at-risk (Barr & Parrett, 2001). Boredom, lack of involvement, and feelings that they are unwelcome keep them on the fringe, prevent them from participating in school experiences, and lower their motivation to learn. When bright spots appear, they are usually the result of teachers who care about these students as people and learners (Drajem, 2002; Jordan, 2001). But beyond the human element, what else can teachers do?

Effective Instruction and Support

Teachers of students placed at-risk don't need to teach in fundamentally different ways; instead, they need to systematically apply the strategies that are effective with all students (Eggen & Kauchak, 2007). They need to provide enough instructional support to ensure success while at the same time teaching students active learning strategies that allow them to take control of their own learning. Effective practices for teaching students placed at-risk include

- Communicating high expectations for student success
- Emphasizing student responsibility
- Using interactive teaching with frequent questions
- Increasing structure and support through use of clear teacher explanations and modeling
- Giving frequent feedback and ensuring high success rates (Brophy, 2004; Haycock, 2001)

Let's see how one teacher does this.

 When students enter Dena Hine's second-grade classroom after recess, they see a review assignment on the chalkboard. As Dena takes roll, students get out their books and start on the assignment. Five minutes later, Dena begins with a brief review of the previous day's lesson. Because the students can answer her questions quickly and correctly, she feels that her class knows the content and is ready to move on.

As she introduces two-column subtraction, she comments that this is an important skill that everyone will be able to learn. Then she presents the following problem and discusses how two-column subtraction will help them solve it:

> Teresa was saving her money to buy a toy for her little sister. The toy cost $.99, and she has already saved $.67. How much more money did she need to buy the toy?

Next she gives each student bundles of 10 Popsicle sticks bound together with rubber bands. She guides students through the subtraction steps by having them take apart the bundles to illustrate the process, asking many questions as she proceeds. She also uses questioning to help them link the manipulatives—the Popsicle sticks—to the numbers she writes on the board. Then she has students solve problems on their own mini-chalkboards and hold them up to allow her to check their solutions. Whenever mistakes occur, she stops, explains the errors, and helps students correct them.

When 90 percent of the class is correctly solving the problems, Dena starts the students on additional practice problems, which they check in pairs when they are done. As they work, she helps those still having difficulty, moving around the room to respond to pairs who disagreed with each other or have questions.

Effective teachers involve their students in learning activities; they question frequently and provide opportunities to practice new skills; and they provide instruction that is challenging, motivating, and connected to students' lives (Eggen & Kauchak, 2007). High expectations and helping students meet them are the foundation for all other skills.

> **Making Connections:**
> To deepen your understanding of the topics in this section of the chapter and integrate them with topics you've already studied, go to the *Making Connections* module for Chapter 4 at **www.prenhall.com/kauchak.** Respond to questions 14 and 15.

Check Your Understanding

4.1 What are the characteristics of students placed at-risk?

4.2 What unique challenges do urban schools present to students placed at-risk?

4.3 What can schools and teachers do to help at-risk students achieve success?

 For feedback, go to Appendix A, Check Your Understanding, *located in the back of this text.*

decision making

Defining Yourself as a Professional

You're a middle school teacher in a rural district, and you meet with your homeroom students every day. You use homeroom to take care of daily routines and get to know your students as individuals. Janine has always been a bright, happy student who gets along well with her classmates. Lately she seems withdrawn, and her personal appearance is disheveled. As you periodically look at her, you see that she seems hesitant to make eye contact. You ask her to come in after school to talk. She says she has to go right home to help care for her younger brothers and sisters, so you suggest her lunch break instead. She reluctantly agrees.

When she comes in she appears nervous, fidgeting with her hands and refusing to look at you. You ask her how she feels, and she replies, "Fine." You mention that she seems to be different lately, preoccupied. She only shrugs. You ask if there is anything bothering her, and she shakes her head no. You reaffirm your availability if she ever wants to talk, and she smiles briefly. As she gathers her book to get up and leave, her sweater slides off her shoulder, revealing bruises.

"Janine, what happened to your arm?"

"Oh, I fell the other day."

"But how did you hurt the inside of your arm?"

Janine's pained and embarrassed expression suggests that a fall wasn't the cause.

"Did someone try to hurt you, Janine? You can tell me."

"Only if you promise not to tell," she blurts out.

Without thinking, you agree. She then proceeds to tearfully tell you about an angry father who has been out of work for months and who becomes violent when he drinks. As she leaves, she makes you promise that you won't tell anyone.

What would you do in this situation?

To respond to this question online and receive immediate feedback, go to the Decision Making *module for Chapter 4 on the Companion Website at* **www.prenhall.com/kauchak.**

Meeting Your Learning Objectives

1. Describe the changes that have occurred in the American family over the last 50 years.
   - The traditional family, which historically has been described as a father who is the breadwinner and a mother who works in the home and cares for two children, has become a minority in this country.
   - The majority of mothers now work outside the home, raising concerns about child care. Quality child care can provide an environment where children learn both cognitive and interpersonal skills. These skills then provide a foundation when students enter school. In addition, the benefits of quality early child care extend into adulthood.
   - Latchkey children pose another problem for working parents. Unsupervised children not only pose safety risks to themselves but also spend large amounts of unsupervised time in front of televisions and computers.

2. Define socioeconomic status, and explain how different socioeconomic patterns influence school success.
   - Socioeconomic status (SES) describes the combination of the effects of income, occupation, and educational level on people's attitudes, values, and behaviors. SES can also have powerful influences on the ways children respond to schools.
   - Poverty presents a number of challenges, ranging from lack of basic needs to unstable home environment. Recently, the rate of childhood poverty has increased, presenting challenges to both teachers and students.
   - SES influences educational success in several ways, including whether students' basic needs, such as nutrition and medical care, are met. It also influences the language skills and school-related experiences students bring to the classroom. Finally, SES shapes parents' and students' attitudes and values about the importance of education and school.
   - Homelessness affects large numbers of children, influencing their ability to succeed in school. Large percentages of homeless children don't attend school on a regular basis, and when they do, they suffer from inadequate diets and substandard medical care as well as unstable families.

3. Describe how teenage sexuality, use of alcohol and other drugs, obesity, and crime and violence in schools have changed over time and the implications of each for education.
   - Students are becoming sexually active at an earlier age, placing themselves at-risk for pregnancy and sexually transmitted disease. Schools attempt to deal with these problems through sex education programs. Other aspects of student sexuality include homosexuality and sexual harassment. Teachers play an essential role in communicating that sexual harassment is something that won't be tolerated in schools or classrooms.
   - The use of alcohol and other drugs, violence, suicide, and child abuse all present challenges to youth as well as the teachers who work with them. While the use of alcohol and drugs is declining, significant numbers of students experiment with and use these at an early age.
   - Obesity has become another health issue threatening students. While increasingly common in all students, its negative effects are seen more often in low-SES and some cultural minority youths.
   - Crime and violence are on the decline in schools as well as society as a whole but still pose a problem to educators. School uniforms have been one response to gang presence in schools. Bullying has also been identified as a major school safety issue because of its potential to not only damage individuals but also lead to more serious forms of violence. In response to these issues, schools have implemented schoolwide safety programs.
   - A major response to crime and violence in the schools has been the implementation of zero-tolerance policies that expel students from school for any infraction involving drugs or weapons. Although adopted by a number of school districts, zero-tolerance

policies have some problems, ranging from increased student dropout rates to punishing students for minor offenses and differential treatment of minority students.

4. Describe the characteristics of students placed at-risk, and explain how schools and teachers can assist these student in achieving success.

- Students placed at-risk face a number of challenges to school success, ranging from poverty to transiency to unstable families. These conditions result in several educational problems that create barriers to school success.
- Urban schools present many challenges to students placed at-risk. Urban schools are often in high-poverty areas and have less experienced teachers. They are also funded less well than their suburban counterparts and tend to be larger and more impersonal.
- Community-based approaches to working with students placed at-risk actively involve parents and the community in designing and implementing comprehensive educational programs. Community-based programs attempt to integrate the various services available to students by linking various support agencies.
- Effective schools for students placed at-risk create a safe, orderly learning environment that emphasizes academic goals. Studies of successful or resilient children suggest that caring home and school environments with supportive, understanding adults can help these students withstand societal challenges (Reis et al., 2005). Effective teachers for students placed at-risk combine supportive interpersonal contacts with instructional structure and support.

Important Concepts

full-service schools (p. 137)
latchkey children (p. 116)
lower class (p. 118)
middle class (p. 117)
poverty thresholds (p. 119)
resilient students (p. 138)
sexual harassment (p. 125)

socioeconomic status (SES) (p. 117)
students placed at-risk (p. 134)
underclass (p. 118)
upper class (p. 117)
working class (p. 118)
zero-tolerance policies (p. 131)

Developing as a Professional

Preparing for Your Licensure Exam

This exercise will provide you with practice answering questions similar to the Praxis™ Principles of Learning and Teaching Exam as well as your state-specific licensure exam. Read the following case study, and answer the questions that follow.

Kari Statler sits, taking notes, alongside the seven other new teachers hired at John F. Kennedy Middle School, a large urban school serving a diverse and often at-risk student population. The assistant principal is going over schoolwide procedures to follow as students enter the school after the morning bell and transition from class. She explains that the school's tradition of having teachers at the door to greet students not only makes the hallways safer and more orderly but also helps to make students feel more welcome. Next, she transitions into the student advisor program. The program is designed to provide middle schoolers with a place where they feel connected—both to their homeroom teacher and to their classmates. The homeroom meets for 20 minutes every day and provides teachers with an opportunity to get to know their students on a human level. The meeting concludes with a discussion of the new parental involvement program, which asks students to accompany their parents to parent–teacher conferences in order to explain their portfolios and sometimes translate for their parents.

Back in her room, Kari looks at the stack of books on her desk. "Whew, this is going to be a busy year," she thinks to herself. "All I keep hearing is tests, tests, tests. First the district, then the state, and maybe even a new one by the English department. Hmm, I had all these great ideas about teaching creative writing to students, but now it looks like all they want me to teach is grammar and punctuation. I can't just do that. My kids deserve more than that. They'll learn punctuation and grammar, but they'll also learn to write—and maybe even to enjoy it. I know they can do both, and that's my goal for the year—everyone writing clearly, with correct punctuation and grammar—and liking it besides!" A smile crosses her face.

The first week is a whirlwind of students, bells, and forms to fill out. By the second week, Kari has settled into an instructional routine. Every day begins with a short assignment to assess the content discussed the day before. Students grade their own papers, and Kari stresses the need for student honesty and responsibility. When the grading is complete, Kari asks for a show of hands to see how well everyone did. She also collects the papers so she can analyze them for any individual or group patterns or trends and so that she can adjust her instruction if need be.

To begin her unit on writing, she passes out two paragraphs, one clearly written and the other not. She asks students to pair up and analyze the two, looking for similarities and differences. In the whole-class discussion that follows, Kari uses interactive questioning to establish the need for a topic sentence, supporting sentences that relate to the topic, and a summarizing sentence that pulls together all the related ideas in the paragraph.

Next, Kari has each student write a paragraph on their favorite subject in school. Students write these on clear transparencies, which Kari will collect and display anonymously for the class to evaluate. "So far, so good," Kari thinks as she circulates among her working students.

1. What characteristics of an effective school for students placed at-risk did Kari encounter?

2. What characteristics of an effective teacher for students placed at-risk did Kari display?

3. What aspects of Kari's instruction were effective for students placed at-risk?

To receive feedback on your responses to these exercises, go to the Companion Website at www.prenhall.com/kauchak, then to the Preparing for Your Licensure Exam *for Chapter 4.*

Discussion Questions

1. How would your role as a teacher change if you worked in an upper-SES suburb? In a lower-SES part of a city?

2. How would your actual instruction change if you worked in an upper-SES suburb? In a lower-SES part of a city?

3. What role should schools play in dealing with teenage sexuality? What specifically could teachers do in this area?

4. What role should schools play in dealing with drug and alcohol abuse? What specifically could teachers do to assist in dealing with this problem?

5. What strengths do students placed at-risk bring to the classroom? How can teachers take advantage of these strengths?

6. What will be your biggest challenges in working with the parents of students placed at-risk?

Developing as a Professional: Online Activities

Going Into Schools

Go to the Companion Website at *www.prenhall.com/kauchak*, and click on the *Going Into Schools* module for Chapter 4. You will find a number of school-based activities that will help you link chapter content to the schools in which you work.

Virtual Field Experience: Using the Internet to Explore the Profession

If you would like to participate in a Virtual Field Experience, access the following website: *www.childrensdefense.org/*. Then click on "Research." This site contains a number of interesting articles on the state of children's health in the United States.

Online Portfolio Activities

To develop your professional portfolio, further apply your understanding of chapter content, and address the INTASC standards, go the Companion Website at *www.prenhall.com/kauchak*, then to the *Online Portfolio Activities* for Chapter 4. Complete the suggested activities.

Chapter 5

Courtesy of the Library of Congress

Education in the United States is unique. The organization of the schools, the content we teach, and our methods differ from those in other countries around the world. History has been a major cause of these differences. As you read the following case study, think about the ways that history affects our current educational system.

"Phew, I think I've had it," Dave Carlisle, a first-year teacher, says as he plops into an overstuffed chair in the teachers' lounge.

"Having a bad day?" Monica Henderson, one of Dave's colleagues at Westmont Middle School, asks.

"Bad day. You could say that," Dave replies. "We had lunch money missing again today. And I'm pretty sure there was cheating on the test I gave last week. It's like these kids have no moral compass. I think they could use a dose of religion."

"We already tried that," Monica replies, looking up from the papers she was grading.

"When? Before I got here?" Dave asks.

"No," Monica replies. "Back in our country's history, and often since then."

"Oh, no. Not more of that history of ed stuff you're learning in that class you're taking."

"Hey, can I help it if I'm learning some interesting stuff that makes me think about what we're trying to do?" Monica replies with a smile.

"Yeah, I know, 'Those that don't know history are destined to repeat it,'" Dave says, rolling his eyes, "but how can history help me with my cheating and stealing problems?"

Studying the history of our country's educational system may not give teachers direct answers to these questions, but it can provide you with a broader perspective on what you're doing and help you become more effective in your professional decision making. Understanding the role of religion in education, for example, can help teachers make professional decisions about the extent to which they can or should share deeply held religious beliefs with their students.

Before continuing, take a few minutes to respond to the following survey. We address each of the items as the chapter unfolds.

Each of the historical periods in our nation's history has influenced education and people's beliefs about what our children should learn and how they should be taught. And many of these influences, to a greater or lesser extent, remain with us today.

Dave and Monica's conversation is an example. The topic of students' moral development and the role of religion in promoting that development goes all the way back to the colonial period in our history. Let's take a look.

professional knowledge: test yourself!

For each item, circle the number that best represents your thinking. Use the following scale as a guide.

1 = Strongly disagree
2 = Disagree
3 = Agree/disagree
4 = Agree
5 = Strongly agree

1. The Constitution of the United States requires that religion and public schooling be kept separate from each other.

    1   2   3   4   5

2. A free public education for all students has historically been a cornerstone of education in the United States.

    1   2   3   4   5

3. The American high school has historically attempted to meet the needs of all students.

    1   2   3   4   5

4. As soon as slavery ended in this country, cultural and ethnic minorities were welcomed into U.S. schools.

    1   2   3   4   5

5. In recent times, the federal government has viewed the schools as an instrument to achieve national goals.

    1   2   3   4   5

This is available in a downloadable format on the Companion Website for personal portfolio use.

The Colonial Period (1607–1775)

Character education, seen as a way to provide moral guidance in a confusing world filled with drugs, sex, and violence, is receiving increased attention in schools (DeRoche & Williams, 2001; Viadero, 2003a). Educators generally agree that some form of moral education is needed in schools, but they disagree about the form and shape it should take. Some advocate linking character education closely to religious values that are normally taught in homes and churches. Others argue that this religious foundation is neither desirable nor possible, given the religious diversity in the United States (Wynne, 1997). The roots of character education, as well as controversies about the shape it should take, can be found in the colonial period of education in America.

Parents who believe schools should teach values and emphasize student discipline often send their children to private, church-supported schools. Should these schools receive federal assistance—money supported by general tax revenue? Proponents claim that parochial schools have as much right to federal education monies as do any other schools. Opponents claim that federal support of parochial schools violates our nation's Constitution. The controversy about the proper place of religious schools in the United States is also rooted in the colonial period.

Religion and schools are closely linked in many states. Some public schools, for example, allow prayers in classrooms, hold religious assemblies, and distribute Bibles to students (Fischer et al., 2006; LaMorte, 2005). Critics claim these practices also violate the Constitution. Proponents counter that schools should teach family, spiritual, and moral values and that religion promotes these values. The issue, repeatedly debated in court, reflects a continual tension in U.S. schools over the proper role of religion in public education (Fischer et al., 2006). This tension has its beginnings in the colonial period.

These controversies illustrate the important role of religion in American education. Why is it so important? The answers go back to the colonial period, when our country was first being shaped.

The beginnings of the relationship between religion and education in America extend back to the founding of Jamestown in 1607. Before that time, New World explorers were primarily interested in "gold and glory"—conquering the New World for riches and adventure. The Jamestown settlers, in contrast, brought families and wanted to start new lives. Like parents today, they believed that the family was central to helping children grow up straight and strong, but they realized they also needed help from schools. Colonial schools were formed in response to this felt need, and they laid the foundation for many of the controversies and structures in place today.

Although settlers came to the colonies for different reasons—in search of political independence, religious freedom, or simply a better life, for example—they all brought with them values and beliefs derived from their European roots. As a result, schooling in colonial America had the same class and gender distinctions common in Europe at the time. Formal education was usually reserved for wealthy White males and ignored females and those less wealthy. As in Europe, religion was an integral part of education, but the role of religion in the classroom differed by region.

Differences in Colonies

Education in America has always been a process of people adapting and creating schools to meet their unique needs. Although the original 13 colonies shared some similarities, such as their cultural links with Europe and people's desire for better lives, regional differences emerged, influenced by geography, economics, and the reasons the colonists came to America. Let's look at them.

The Southern Colonies

Life in the Southern colonies—Maryland, Virginia, the Carolinas, and Georgia—centered around agriculture, much of which existed on large plantations where African slaves and indentured servants worked land owned by wealthy landlords. Poor White settlers worked small farms on the margins, barely scratching out an existence.

Life for most people in the colonial South was hard, and formal education was a luxury reserved for the wealthy (Pulliam & Van Patten, 2007). Private tutors often lived on plantations, or parents pooled their resources to hire a tutor to teach the children of several families. Private schools sponsored by the Church of England and boarding schools for the wealthy were in the larger Southern cities, such as Charleston and Williamsburg. The English tradition of education for the wealthy few made an easy leap over the Atlantic to the Southern colonies.

The Middle Colonies

The middle colonies—New York, New Jersey, Delaware, and Pennsylvania—were more diverse than the colonies in the South. Although English-speaking people were the majority, substantial pockets of Dutch in New York, Swedes in Delaware, and Germans in Pennsylvania also existed. Also, whereas most of the Southern colonists were members of the Church of England, middle colonists belonged to a number of different religious groups. They were Dutch Reformists, Quakers, Lutherans, Baptists, Roman Catholics, and Jews (Pulliam & Van Patten, 2007). Because religious freedom was a major reason for coming to America, and religion played such a central role in people's daily lives, it was difficult to create public schools that satisfied everyone.

In response to this diversity, families in the middle colonies created parochial schools. Students learned in their native languages, and local religious beliefs were an integral part of the curriculum.

The New England Colonies

The New England colonies—Massachusetts, Connecticut, and New Hampshire—differed from the other colonies in two important ways. First, they were culturally and religiously homogeneous, which made consensus about school goals easier to achieve. Second, industry and commerce encouraged the clustering of people into towns, which allowed the formation of common schools.

As an example, let's look at Massachusetts. Puritans, the followers of John Calvin, settled in Massachusetts. As with colonists in the other regions, religion played a major role in the Puritans' lives. They came to America because of conflicts resulting from their attempts to reform the Church of England. Puritans believed that humans are inherently evil, having fallen when Adam and Eve committed original sin. Education helped people follow God's commandments and resist the devil's temptations. By learning to read and write, people gained access to God's word through the Bible. In addition, religious education contributed to a person's general character by promoting industry, resourcefulness, punctuality, and thrift. Puritans believed education was important because it made people more righteous.

The Puritans' views shaped the schools they created. They saw children as savage and primitive, requiring education (religion) to become civilized and God-fearing. Puritans viewed play as idleness, considered children's talk as prattle, and commonly used corporal punishment to ensure conformity. Puritan teachers beat students with switches, forced them to kneel on hard pebbles, and made them wear heavy wooden yolks as punishments for unacceptable behavior. It's easy to see why "Idle minds are the Devil's workshop" and "Spare the rod and spoil the child" were principles of Puritan education.

Religion was a major reason the Pilgrims came to America and a major force in shaping early schools. (Library of Congress)

Religion also influenced curriculum and instruction. Reading, writing, arithmetic, and religion ("the four Rs") made up the curriculum. *The New England Primer* taught children the alphabet through religious rhymes such as the following:

> *A—In Adam's Fall*
> *We Sinned all.*
> *B—Thy Life to Mend*
> *This Book Attend.*

Instruction focused on memorization and recitation; teacher expected children to sit quietly for long periods of time, and discouraged them from expressing opinions and asking questions. Teachers had no formal preparation about how or what to teach, and curriculum materials were scarce, if not nonexistent.

Paradoxically, a landmark piece of legislation, the Massachusetts Act of 1647, arose from this grim educational landscape. Also known as the **Old Deluder Satan Act**, the law was designed to create scripture-literate citizens who would thwart Satan's trickery. It required every town of 50 or more households to hire a teacher of reading and writing. The historical significance of this act is enormous, because it provided the legal foundation for public support of education. It gave birth to the idea that the public good was enhanced by government-sponsored efforts at public education, and it became a cornerstone of American education.

European Crosscurrents

As you saw in the preceding section, American colonists brought many ideas from Europe, such as the view that education should be reserved for wealthy White males. Also, because schooling existed for religious purposes or for preparing the wealthy to be leaders, educators made few attempts to relate the curriculum to the average person's practical needs or the long-term needs of a growing nation. And teaching methods emphasized passive learning in the form of memorization and recitation.

Forces of change were altering education in Europe, however, and slowly making their way across the Atlantic. Some prominent European philosophers and their ideas are outlined in Table 5.1.

As Table 5.1 shows, though the ideas came from different places, all involved a more practical, humane, and child-centered view of education. These philosophers are important because they planted the seeds of educational change that would fundamentally alter the education of students in the United States.

TABLE 5.1   Changes in Educational Thought in Europe

Thinker	Educational Views
John Amos Comenius (1592–1670) Czech philosopher	Questioned the effectiveness of memorization and recitation, emphasizing instead the need to base teaching on children's interests and needs
John Locke (1632–1704) English philosopher	Emphasized the importance of firsthand experiences in helping children learn about the world
Jean Jacques Rousseau (1712–1778) French philosopher	Viewed children as innately good and argued that teachers should provide children with opportunities for exploration and experimentation
Johann Pestalozzi (1746–1827) Swiss philosopher	Criticized authoritarian educational practices that stifled students' playfulness and natural curiosity and recommended that teachers use concrete experiences to help students learn

Old Deluder Satan Act. Early colonial law designed to create scripture-literate citizens who would thwart Satan's trickery.

The Legacy of the Colonial Period

The colonial period shaped American education in three important ways. First, with few exceptions, poor Whites, females, and minorities such as Native Americans and African-Americans were excluded from schools (Spring, 2005). William Berkeley, the aristocratic governor of Virginia, supported this exclusion and in 1671 railed against both free public education and access to books: "I thank God, *there are no free schools nor printing*, and I hope we shall not have them these hundred years, for *learning* has brought disobedience, and heresy, and sects into the world, and *printing* has divulged them, and libels against the best government" (Pulliam & Van Patten, 2003, p. 86). European ideas of class structures and privilege did not die easily in the New World. Given attitudes such as these, it's easy to see why equality of educational opportunity wasn't a legal reality until the mid-20th century. Some present-day critics argue that today's schools are still racist and sexist (Spring, 2005).

Second, the colonial period shaped our current system of education through actions that planted the seeds for public support of education (the Old Deluder Satan Act) and local control of schools. These two ideas have become important foundations of our present educational system.

Third, and perhaps most significantly, the relationship between religion and schooling prevalent in the colonial period influenced attitudes about education for many years. Examining that history helps us understand why religion continues to be an important issue in education. Let's take a closer look at religion in schools.

Religion in Schools

The U.S. Constitution, the oldest written constitution in the world that is still in force, was written in 1787 and was officially adopted in 1789. It has had 27 amendments, the first 10 of which are known as our Bill of Rights. In response to the religious diversity that existed in the colonies, the "establishment clause" of the First Amendment prohibited the government from passing legislation to establish any one official religion over another. This created the principle widely known as *separation of church and state*, and it addresses the first statement in our beginning-of-chapter survey, "The Constitution of the United States requires that religion and public schooling be kept separate from each other." Although interpretations vary, the establishment clause suggests that the statement is true.

Considering the colonial legacy and the courts' evolving interpretation of the principle of separation of church and state, it is easy to see why controversies about religion in schools exist today. Some commonly raised questions include the following:

- Should prayer be allowed in schools?
- Should federal money be used to provide instruction in religious schools?
- What role should religion play in character education?

Let's look at these questions.

Should prayer be allowed in schools? In colonial times, prayer was an integral part of the curriculum. Today, this question has become so controversial that the issue has been thrown to the courts, and their answer has usually been no. A federal court in Alabama, for example, ruled that praying in schools, holding religious assemblies, and giving students Bibles all violate separation of church and state (Fischer et al., 2006; LaMorte, 2005). However, in a case involving graduation speeches, prayers were ruled legal, because they were voluntary and given by students. Further, some members of the House of Representatives sponsored a bill in 1998 that would have allowed organized voluntary prayers in the schools, but it fell 61 votes short of the 224 necessary for a two thirds majority (Walsh, 1998). This attempted legislation revealed that prayer in U.S. schools was not a dead issue. More recently, the U.S. Supreme Court ruled 6–3 that student-led prayers at Texas football games were unconstitutional, this time concluding that the prayers did violate separation of church and state (Walsh, 2000a).

Should federal dollars be used to provide instruction in religious schools? This wasn't an issue in the colonial period, because most schools were private and religion was an integral part of the curriculum. Today, however, the role of government funding for religious instruction is more controversial and less clear. For example, courts have generally ruled in favor of using federal monies to provide supplementary instruction for poor students or students with special needs who attend religious schools (Fischer et al., 2006). The Supreme Court also ruled that religious schools could receive federal aid in the form of computers and library books (Walsh, 2000a).

Funding vouchers for religious schools is another legally contentious matter, however. **Vouchers**, checks or written documents that parents can use to purchase educational services, have been promoted as one way to increase parental choice and involvement. Parents in Cleveland and Milwaukee, sites of two well-known voucher experiments, wanted to use vouchers (public monies) to send their children to religious schools. Opponents contended this violates separation of church and state, but the U.S. Supreme Court, in a 5–4 vote, approved the use of public school funds for vouchers to religious and private schools (Walsh, 2002b). The states will be the next battlefield for this issue, because 37 state constitutions currently forbid state aid to religious schools (Gehring, 2002b).

The proper role of religion in schools continues to be a controversial issue. (Rob Crandall/The Stock Connection)

What role should religion play in character education? **Character education** is an approach to developing morality that suggests moral values and positive character traits, such as honesty and citizenship, should be emphasized, taught, and rewarded. In colonial times, religion and character education were synonymous, and in some cases religious training was the primary purpose of education. The link between the two is controversial today, however, and religious diversity is one reason why. Although most Americans consider themselves Christian, significant numbers of Muslims, Hindus, Buddhists, and Jews as well as other smaller religious groups exist in the United States. Further, considerable religious diversity, ranging from liberal to ultraconservative denominations, exists within Christian ranks. Given these differences, it is hard to come to any consensus about the role of religion in the development of students' character.

Making Connections:
To deepen your understanding of the topics in this section of the chapter and integrate them with topics you've already studied, go to the *Making Connections* module for Chapter 5 at **www.prenhall.com/kauchak**. Respond to questions 1 and 2.

Check Your Understanding

1.1 How did the diversity of the original colonies shape the educational system in the United States?

1.2 What role did religion play in colonial schools? What are the implications of this role for contemporary schools?

1.3 Explain why the Old Deluder Satan Act of Massachusetts was important for the development of our American educational system.

For feedback, go to Appendix A, Check Your Understanding, *located in the back of this text.*

Vouchers. Checks or written documents that parents can use to purchase educational services.

Character education. An approach to developing morality that suggests moral values and positive character traits, such as honesty and citizenship, should be emphasized, taught, and rewarded.

The Early National Period (1775–1820)

Teresa Sanchez has moved with her family from a large urban center in the Northeast to a sprawling city in the South. Although the teenager encounters changes in climate and lifestyle, she finds her new high school surprisingly similar to the one she had previously attended. The buildings and their physical layout are similar, with long hallways lined with lockers and interspersed with classrooms. Even the central office seems the same, and the guidance counselor who works with her assures her that she won't lose credits because of the move.

But there are differences. Teresa rides a district school bus instead of using public transportation. The students, while friendly, talk differently and their interests differ from those of her friends back home. And the textbooks she receives, while covering the same basic material, do so in different ways.

Her mother, an elementary teacher, also notices both similarities and differences. She gets a new position almost immediately but is told that her teaching certificate is only temporary and that she will have to take additional coursework for it to become permanent. The textbooks she is given are different from the ones she had previously used, but the principal's emphasis on testing at the end of the year isn't. Some things never change.

The United States, at first glance, appears homogeneous. A McDonald's in California appears much like one in Ohio, for example, and television programs across the country are very similar. However, many regional and state differences exist.

The same paradox occurs in education. Although schools across the country appear similar, a closer look reveals important regional and state differences. For example, students in Texas study Texas state history and take specially constructed tests to determine grade advancement, and students in other states study their own history and take their own state-specific graduation tests (Feller, 2006). Education to assist English language learners (ELLs) exists in most states, but the form of this assistance varies considerably among them (Hinkel, 2005). Why do these differences exist? Some answers can be found in the early national period of our country.

Before 1775 the United States was a loose collection of separate colonies that looked mostly to Europe for trade and ideas. During the 45 years of the early national period (1775–1820), however, the separate colonies became the United States of America, and this country shaped its future through the Constitution and the Bill of Rights. In the previous section, you saw how the First Amendment to the Constitution established the principle of separation of church and state. Next we'll show how other laws and amendments also shaped the future of American education.

Educational Governance: Whose Responsibility?

Severing the governmental ties between religion and education raised an important question: Who would be responsible for organizing and managing education in our new country? Establishing a national education system was one suggestion (Pulliam & Van Patten, 2007). Proponents argued that, in addition to developing an enlightened citizenry, a national system would best meet the country's agricultural, industrial, and commercial needs. Opponents, in their arguments against a national system, cited the monolithic and unresponsive systems in Europe. They also argued that the beginnings of viable local and state systems, such as those in Massachusetts, already existed. Why create another level of bureaucracy and control when it wasn't needed? The Constitution's framers sidestepped the issue with the Tenth Amendment, which said that areas not explicitly assigned to the federal government would be the responsibility of each state.

The Tenth Amendment was important for two reasons. First, it implicitly removed the federal government from a central role in running and operating schools, and second, it passed this responsibility on to the individual states. To support the educational efforts of the states, Congress passed the Land Ordinance of 1785 and the Northwest Ordinance of 1787. The goal of these acts was to promote settlement of the present-day Midwest, which was then an undeveloped area of the country (K. Alexander & Alexander, 2001). These ordinances divided the land into townships, each 6 miles square and consisting of 36 sections; in each township, the income from one section was reserved for support of public education. The rationale for this financial support was contained in the text of the Northwest Ordinance: "Religion, morality, and knowledge being necessary to good government and the happiness of mankind, schools and the means of education shall forever be encouraged." This encouragement came in the form of federal land that states could use to support education. Although not directly involved in governing or operating schools, the federal government provided material support for schools and education, a tradition that persists to this day. With respect to education, the lines of responsibility between state and federal governments were already being blurred.

The Legacy of the Early National Period

The early national period shaped the schools of the future and planted the seeds of controversies to come. In addition to establishing the principle of separation of church and state, legislators established two other far-reaching effects on our educational system: (1) Lawmakers removed control of education from the federal government and gave it to the states, and (2) the federal government expressed the view that education was essential for improving the quality of people's lives and helping the nation grow.

The influence of these actions is still felt in the policies and views of education today. For example, courts have repeatedly upheld the principle of separation of church and state, and decisions about school and classroom policies are primarily made by individual states and local school districts (although public schools must adhere to federal laws and do receive federal funding).

Also, although education remains in the hands of the states, the federal government views it as a means of achieving national goals, just as it was in the early national period (Tyack & Cuban, 1995). When the economy sputters, for example, or when significant portions of the school-age population underachieve, the federal government steps in. The No Child Left Behind Act of 2001 is an example. The law requires each state to develop a comprehensive accountability plan to ensure that all students acquire basic skills in reading, math, and science. One mandated feature of each state's plan must be a comprehensive testing system tied to state standards. The testing aspects of the No Child Left Behind Act are controversial; the state of Connecticut, for example, unsuccessfully challenged the law in court, and other states considered similar actions. The high cost of testing, which they called "an unfunded federal mandate" was Connecticut's primary complaint (Archer, 2005).

> **Making Connections:**
> To deepen your understanding of the topics in this section of the chapter and integrate them with topics you've already studied, go to the *Making Connections* module for Chapter 5 at **www.prenhall.com/kauchak.** Respond to questions 3 and 4.

Check Your Understanding

2.1   What is the Tenth Amendment to the Constitution? Why is it important for education today?

2.2   Describe the role that was established for the federal government during the early national period.

2.3   What was the historical significance of the Ordinances of 1785 and 1787?

   For feedback, go to Appendix A, Check Your Understanding, *located in the back of this text.*

The Common School Movement: The Rise of State Support for Public Education (1820–1865)

Many of you reading this text will become teachers of elementary students and will work in public schools. Let's think for a moment about these schools. First, the children you'll teach will be required by law to be there; virtually all states require students to attend school until they are 16. Second, your salary and the salaries of other teachers and administrators, the building itself, your materials and supplies, the buses that will take kids to and from school, and even some of your students' lunches will be publicly supported, meaning a portion of federal, state, and local taxes will pay for these items.

Typically, your school will be organized into grade levels. At the elementary level, 5-year-olds will be in kindergarten, and 6-year-olds will be in the first grade; at the middle and high school levels, classes target different levels of expertise, such as freshman English or senior literature. You will have a designated grade or level to teach.

To get a teaching job, you'll be required to be licensed. You'll have to complete a specified set of university courses (which is one reason you're in this class), and you'll complete some clinical experiences in schools, including an internship. You'll probably also have to take a standardized test (the content of which will vary from state to state) to assess your competency as a teacher.

What are the origins of these policies, and what are the historical roots that shaped a free public education for all students in the United States?

Although developing a literate citizenry was a goal during the early national period, American education in the early 1800s remained a patchwork of schools designed primarily for the wealthy; the vast majority of children received little or no formal education. The common school movement changed that.

Historians commonly describe the period from 1820 to 1865 as the "Age of the Common Man." Andrew Jackson, a popular and down-to-earth person who gained fame as a general in the War of 1812, was elected president in 1828. Westward expansion provided opportunities for people and changed the social landscape; the poor and landless could start over by pulling up stakes and heading west. The land area of the United States nearly doubled between 1830 and 1865, and the population increased from 13 to 32 million, 4 million of whom were new immigrants (U.S. Government Printing Office, 1975).

This expansion presented both opportunities and challenges. Industrialization created jobs and contributed to the growth of cities such as New York and Boston, but it also resulted in pollution, crime, and the development of urban slums. Many new immigrants didn't speak English and were unaccustomed to American ways of living. The country needed a citizenry that could participate in political decisions and contribute to the nation's economy, but most people were functionally illiterate. America turned to its schools for help.

The Common School Movement: Making Education Available to All

As we showed in the previous section, the American educational system at the beginning of the 19th century was a patchwork of private and quasi-public schools. Those defined as "public" often charged partial tuition, discouraging all but the wealthiest from attending. States didn't coordinate their efforts, and the quality of education was uneven at best (Pulliam & Van Patten, 2007).

Around 1820, educational changes began to occur (Pulliam & Van Patten, 2007). These changes marked the beginning of the **common school movement**, a historical attempt to make education available to all children in the United States. The following are some of the events that occurred during this period:

- States and local governments taxed citizens directly to support public schools. Educators attempted to increase the attendance of underrepresented groups such as the urban poor and freed slaves.

Common school movement. A historical attempt to make education available to all children in the United States.

- States created state education departments and appointed state superintendents of instruction.
- Educators organized schools by grade level and standardized the curriculum.
- States improved teacher preparation.

The Contributions of Horace Mann

Horace Mann, a lawyer turned educator, was a key figure in the common school movement. Secretary of the Massachusetts State Board of Education from 1837 to 1848, he was an outspoken advocate for public education, believing that it was the key to developing the country and improving the quality of life for all people.

Under Mann's influence, Massachusetts moved to the cutting edge of education in America. During the common school period, Massachusetts doubled state appropriations for education, built 50 new secondary schools, increased teacher salaries by 50 percent, and passed the nation's first compulsory school attendance law in 1852. (By 1900, 32 other states had passed similar laws.) Perhaps Mann's biggest legacy, however, was the idea that public education, in the form of tax-supported elementary schools (common schools), should be a right of all citizens.

The common school movement made education accessible to the common person. (Courtesy of the Library of Congress)

Expansion of the Common School Movement

Despite some obstacles—such as business interests that feared a loss of cheap child labor, citizens who objected to increased taxes and having to pay to educate other people's children, and competition from private and parochial schools—the common school movement prospered. Reasons for its success include the following:

- Parents began viewing education as a way of improving their children's lives.
- National and local leaders saw education as the vehicle for assimilation of immigrants and improvement of national productivity.
- The growth of industry and commerce required an increasingly educated populace.

Fifty percent of U.S. children were enrolled in public schools by the beginning of the Civil War, and by 1865, 28 of 35 states had established state boards of education. During the common school movement, tax-supported public elementary schools were firmly established as a cornerstone of the U.S. educational system. (New Jersey eliminated the need for parents to pay for an elementary education in 1871; it was the last state to do so.)

This section addresses the second statement in our beginning-of-chapter survey, "A free public education for all students has historically been a cornerstone of education in the United States." In fact, early in our country's history, education was available only to a wealthy few. Later, largely because of the efforts of Horace Mann, universal free public elementary school slowly became available to all. And access to free public secondary school for all students didn't become fully available until the 1900s.

Issues of Quality and Quantity in Teacher Education

Although the common school movement dramatically increased access to education, quality was a problem. During the early to mid-1800s,

teachers' workloads were heavy, and only the fundamentals were taught. For the most part, school buildings and equipment were very poor, even in the private schools and academies. Textbooks, blackboards, and all working materials were in extremely short supply. Buildings were not kept up, lighting was not adequate, and quite often one poorly trained teacher was in charge not only of one school but also of an entire district. Teachers who possessed only an elementary school education were frequently hired. (Pulliam & Van Patten, 2003, pp. 133–134)

Then, as now, teachers were seen as keys to improving our schools. The creation of **normal schools**, 2-year institutions developed in the early 1800s to prepare prospective elementary teachers, was the most significant attempt to solve this problem. Before the existence of normal schools, the typical teacher was a man, either preparing for or waiting for a position in the ministry. Because these teachers had no training in education, they used primitive methods, such as memorization and recitation, and they maintained order with stern disciplinary measures, including corporal punishment. Normal schools, in contrast, targeted women as potential teachers and attempted to provide both content background and pedagogical training beyond the high school level.

School quality also increased when larger elementary schools began separating students into grade levels, which eliminated congested conditions and the overlapping curricula often found in one-room schools. Grade differentiation also resulted in more age-appropriate instruction and allowed content to be taught in greater depth for older students. Finally, as paper and printing presses became more common, more textbooks became available, and educational materials improved.

The Legacy of the Common School Movement

The common school movement was a turning point in American education. The idea of universal access to a tax-supported education was planted and took root. Although not all children attended elementary schools, the number who did increased steadily during this time, and public support for the idea grew. State governance and control of education was institutionalized with the creation of state departments of education, and teacher training and quality improved with the development of normal schools.

Despite these advances, the common school movement left at least two controversial issues that remain today. One involves the inequitable funding of education from state to state and district to district, both of which affect quality. In *Savage Inequalities* (1991), Jonathon Kozol addresses this issue:

Americans abhor the notion of a social order in which economic privilege and political power are determined by hereditary class. Officially, we have a more enlightened goal in sight: namely, a society in which a family's wealth has no relation to the probability of future educational attainment and the wealth and station it affords. By this standard, education offered to poor children should be at least as good as that which is provided to the children of the upper-middle class. (p. 207)

This often doesn't occur, however (Berliner, 2005; Gill, McLean, & Courville, 2004). Wide differences in funding exist between states and among districts within states. Nationally, wealthy districts spend an average of 23 percent more on their students than do poorer districts. In Alaska wealthier districts spend more than double the amount per pupil ($16,546 versus $7,379) than poorer districts in the state (Biddle & Berliner, 2002). (You will study more about issues related to school funding in Chapter 8.)

Teacher quality is the second contentious issue that remains from the common school movement, and the question of what constitutes a well-educated and qualified teacher continues to be debated, as evidenced in two contradictory movements in education today. The first, as you will recall from your study of Chapter 2, is the increasing popularity of alternative licensure in an effort to open up entrance to the teaching profession. In contrast, the second movement is an effort to increase teacher professionalism, a theme of this text, by making entry into teaching more rigorous and demanding through increased course work and testing (Darling-Hammond & Bransford, 2005). How the issue will be resolved in the future is unclear.

Table 5.2 provides a summary of the important events in our country's early history that have shaped education, the periods during which they occurred, and the issues that remain today.

Making Connections:
To deepen your understanding of the topics in this section of the chapter and integrate them with topics you've already studied, go to the *Making Connections* module for Chapter 5 at **www.prenhall.com/kauchak**. Respond to questions 5 and 6.

Normal schools. Two-year institutions developed in the early 1800s to prepare prospective elementary teachers.

TABLE 5.2   A Summary of Historical Periods in American Education

Period	Significant Features	Issues That Remain Today
Colonial period, 1607–1775	• Education reserved for wealthy White males • Seeds planted for public support of education • Religion at the core of education	• Whether prayer should be allowed in schools and in what circumstances • Tax support for religious schools • The relationship between religion and character education
Early national period, 1775–1820	• The principle of separation of church and state established • Control of education given to the states, rather than the federal government • Education viewed as crucial for furthering the national interest	• The role of the federal government in education • National testing of students • A national curriculum
Common school movement, 1820–1865	• Access to tax-supported education for all established • Grade levels introduced in elementary schools • Normal schools created to prepare teachers	• Inequities in funding among states and school districts • Teacher quality and alternative routes to teacher certification

Check Your Understanding

3.1   How was the common school movement linked to the growing number of immigrants coming to the United States?

3.2   Who was Horace Mann, and what was his contribution to education in the United States?

3.3   What were normal schools, and why are they important today?

 For feedback, go to Appendix A, Check Your Understanding, *located in the back of this text.*

The Evolution of the American High School

Kareem and Antonio walk to high school together, have lockers that are side by side, and even have the same homeroom period. But that is where their contact ends. Kareem is in a college-preparation track, along with about a third of the other students in his school. As he goes from class to class, he sees many of the same students. Antonio is in a vocational track, and many of his classes are designed to introduce him to specific career options. A technology class focuses on business applications of computers and introduces him to jobs in the computer field. A metalworking class includes welding and even allows him to work on his family's car as a class project. Once Kareem and Antonio leave homeroom, they often don't see each other until football practice at the end of the day.

Think about your own experience in high school. Most of you probably attended a unique American invention, the **comprehensive high school**, a secondary school that attempts to meet the needs of all students by housing them together and providing curricular options (e.g., vocational or college-preparatory programs) geared toward a variety of student ability levels and interests (Hammack, 2004). For example, some of you took honors classes in English, history, chemistry, or biology. Others were in "standard" classes, designed for students of average ability.

> **Comprehensive high school.** A secondary school that attempts to meet the needs of all students by housing them together and providing curricular options (e.g., vocational or college-preparatory programs) geared toward a variety of student ability levels and interests.

Figure 5.1 The Evolution of the American High School

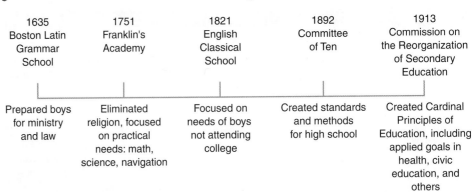

1635 Boston Latin Grammar School	1751 Franklin's Academy	1821 English Classical School	1892 Committee of Ten	1913 Commission on the Reorganization of Secondary Education
Prepared boys for ministry and law	Eliminated religion, focused on practical needs: math, science, navigation	Focused on needs of boys not attending college	Created standards and methods for high school	Created Cardinal Principles of Education, including applied goals in health, civic education, and others

Today's modern comprehensive high school can be traced back to academies, such as Franklin's Academy of Philadelphia, and English classical schools, such as the English High School in Boston. (Bohden Hrynewych/Stock Boston Inc./Jupiter Images)

Perhaps you enrolled in some vocational courses, such as word processing or woodworking, designed to provide you with immediately marketable skills. You may have even taken driver's training or other "life management" courses. All of these are part of a comprehensive American high school. How did the modern, comprehensive high school evolve?

Today, a high school education is seen as essential to success in life, because it prepares students for a job or entrance to college. This wasn't always the case. Before the turn of the 20th century, less than 10 percent of the population went beyond elementary school (U.S. Department of Education, 1995). By contrast, in the year 2000, 96 percent of all teenagers attended high school (National Center for Education Statistics, 2005b). A high school education has evolved from a luxury, to a right, to a necessity.

Historical Roots of the Comprehensive High School

The American high school as it exists today is the result of a long evolutionary history. A time line illustrating this development appears in Figure 5.1 and is discussed in this section.

The first American high school was a decidedly European institution aimed at the colonial elite. The Boston Latin School, established in 1635, was a **Latin grammar school**, a college-preparatory school originally designed to help boys prepare for the ministry or, later, for a career in law. Women didn't attend, because they could be neither ministers nor lawyers. The narrow curriculum and high cost made Latin grammar schools largely unattainable and irrelevant for the vast majority of Americans.

In reaction to this narrow academic orientation, Benjamin Franklin opened the Academy of Philadelphia, in 1751. Free of religious orientation and uniquely American, an **academy** was a secondary school that focused on the practical needs of colonial America as a growing nation. Math, navigation, astronomy, bookkeeping, logic, and rhetoric were all taught, and both boys and girls attended. The students selected courses from this menu, which set the precedent for electives and alternative programs at the secondary level that exist today.

Merchants and craftsmen, who had questioned the emphasis on Latin and Greek in the Latin grammar schools, enthusiastically supported this broader, more applied curriculum. By 1860 a quarter of a million students were enrolled in 6,000 tuition-charging academies, and they were the most common type of high school that existed until about 1890 (Butts & Cremin, 1953).

The academies were a significant addition to American education for three reasons. First, they emphasized a practical curriculum, suggesting that schools should continuously adapt to changes in society. Second, they eliminated religion from the curriculum, further widening the division between church and state, and third, they were partially supported by public funds, which estab-

Latin grammar school. A college-preparatory school originally designed to help boys prepare for the ministry or, later, for a career in law.

Academy. A secondary school that focused on the practical needs of colonial America as a growing nation.

lished a trend that flourished in the common school movement. These characteristics—practical, secular, and public—were themes that would be revisited again and again in American education.

In addition to the academies, another uniquely American educational institution appeared. In 1821 Boston established the first **English classical school**, a free secondary school designed to meet the needs of boys not planning to attend college. The English Classical School offered studies in English, math, history, science, geography, bookkeeping, and surveying and, to reflect this practical emphasis, changed its name to the English High School in 1824.

Schools modeled after the English High School spread slowly because of competition from the academies and public opposition to taxes needed to support the schools. Taxpayers did not think secondary schools should be free, natural extensions of elementary education. In addition, the schools were uncertain about their role. Unable to decide whether their mission was practical or college preparatory, the schools responded by offering both types of classes. This uncertainty also affected students; in 1900 only one tenth of the students said they expected to attend college, but the majority took a college-preparatory curriculum. As we'll see in the next section, this confusion about the American high school's role and mission continued into the 20th century and persists even today.

This section answers the third statement in our beginning-of-chapter survey, "The American high school has historically attempted to meet the needs of all students." This statement isn't true; originally, high schools were oriented toward preparing students for ministry or law careers. As we'll see in the next section, it wasn't until the 1900s that educators developed comprehensive high schools to meet the needs of all students.

Redefining the High School

The American high school near the end of the 19th century was an institution in search of an identity. Begun as an elitist, college-preparatory institution, its curriculum evolved into a disorganized mix of college-preparatory, terminal, and vocational courses. Educational leaders recognized that something needed to be done.

In 1892, in response to this need, the National Education Association (NEA) appointed a group called The Committee of Ten to examine the high school curriculum and make recommendations about standards, programs, and methods. The committee concluded that students who planned to go no further than high school needed content and teaching methods that were the same as those who were college bound, an idea that has lost favor today.

Three factors contributed to the committee's conclusions (Spring, 2005). First, no high school teachers or parents were included on the committee. It was composed of college professors and administrators only, so the bias toward a college-preparatory curriculum wasn't surprising. Second, the committee members believed in *faculty psychology*, the view that exercising the powers of the mind promoted learning. Proponents of this view held that everyone, regardless of where they were heading in life, could practice mental discipline to achieve a "stronger" mind.

A third factor influencing the committee was the large number of non-English-speaking immigrants and a growing lower class that threatened to create divisions in American society. The committee felt that a different curriculum for college and non–college-bound students might create a class-based system of education and damage national unity.

The committee recognized, however, that the college-preparatory curriculum wasn't providing prospective workers with the occupational skills needed for increasingly complex jobs. In an attempt to resolve this dilemma, the NEA appointed a second committee, called The Commission on the Reorganization of Secondary Education (Pulliam & Van Patten, 2007). In 1918 this commission issued a report, *The Cardinal Principles of Secondary Education*, which included goals in basic skills such as reading and math, vocational education, personal health, worthy home membership, civic education, effective use of leisure time, and ethical character. To accommodate these more applied goals, the commission proposed the idea of comprehensive high schools with different tracks for different students. The hope was

English classical school. A free secondary school designed to meet the needs of boys not planning to attend college.

that the diverse student body, separated into different tracks, would be integrated by sports and other extracurricular activities (Spring, 2005).

Efforts to solve the problems of intellectual and other forms of diversity persist today. Although the practice of tracking was designed to provide a customized education for all students, it has had some unintended negative consequences. As you saw in Chapter 3, the curriculum in the non–college-bound tracks often offers little intellectual challenge; teachers tend to have low expectations for students; and they often use primitive and ineffective teaching methods, such as lecture and seat work (Good & Brophy, 2003).

The Challenge of Teaching in Large Urban High Schools

The move to make high schools comprehensive also had large size as an additional negative side effect. As the size of urban high schools increases, students find it harder to identify with their school, and teachers have difficulty establishing personal relationships with students (Kincheloe, 2004; Schutz, 2004). More than 70 percent of U.S. high schools have 1,000 students or more, and a number of urban districts have high schools of over 5,000 students. Historically, the largest high school on record, DeWitt Clinton High School in the Bronx, had 12,000 students in 1934 (Allen, 2002). (Can you imagine what it must have been like to be a freshman walking into that school on the first day of the school year?)

How can teachers respond to this problem? One way is to create the feeling that students and the teacher are "in this together" and "we'll work together to adapt to the size of the school." Effective urban teachers in large high schools make a special effort to get to know students as people by quickly learning their names, learning about their hopes and fears, and spending out-of-class time with them (Wilson & Corbett, 2001). They model courtesy and respect for all students and expect similar courtesy in return. And they create clear standards for behavior that require students to treat each other the same way. This creates a sense of safety and attachment to their classrooms that can help assuage the impersonal feel of large high schools.

In addition, effective urban teachers make personal and inviting statements to their students that motivate and communicate understanding (Manouchehri, 2004). For instance, a comment such as, "This has been hard for me, too. I often try to do it this way," is a personal statement; "I know this is hard, and I can feel that you're frustrated," communicates that the teacher understands students' experiences and feelings; and statements like, "*We're* going to be working on fractions this week," is more motivating than "*You're* going to be working on. . . ." These seemingly minor differences help create a classroom community and the feeling "we're all in this together" that we described earlier (Honora, 2003). Chapter 11 discusses additional strategies to make urban classrooms productive learning environments.

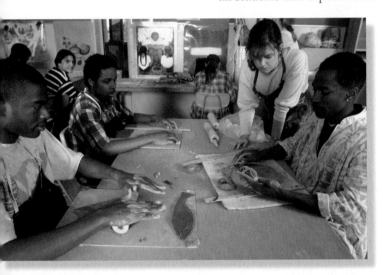

Effective urban teachers create warm, caring learning communities in their classrooms. (Michael Newman/PhotoEdit Inc.)

Junior High and Middle Schools

While groups such as the Committee of Ten and The Commission on the Reorganization of Secondary Education wrestled with curricular issues, other educators questioned the effectiveness of the 8–4 organizational pattern (8 years of elementary, 4 of high school). Critics of the pattern argued that too much emphasis was being placed on basic skills in the upper elementary grades, a time that could be better spent learning content such as science and social studies in depth. Developmental psychologists pointed out that early adolescence is a time of intellectual, emotional, and physical transition, and students undergoing these transitions require a different kind of school. In response to these arguments, educators created

junior high schools, which provide a unique academic curriculum for early adolescent youth. The first junior high, which encompassed grades 7, 8, and 9, opened in Columbus, Ohio, in 1909. The concept spread quickly, and by 1926, junior highs had been set up in 800 school systems (Gruhn & Douglass, 1971).

The 6–3–3 organizational pattern (6 years of elementary school, 3 of junior high, and 3 of high school) was more a change in form than substance, however. Most "junior" highs were exactly that—imitations of high schools with a fragmented curriculum, emphasis on academic disciplines, and little attention to the developing needs of adolescents.

In spite of these weaknesses, junior highs remained popular until the 1970s, when continued criticisms caused fundamental change. The creation of **middle schools**, schools typically for grades 6–8 and specifically designed to help students through the rapid social, emotional, and intellectual changes characteristic of early adolescence, was the response to these criticisms (Manning, 2000). Middle schools provided opportunities for teachers to get to know students by creating student and teacher teams. Working together on teams, teachers could share information about learner progress and problems as well as design interdisciplinary units that explored connections between different content areas. The curriculum became more applied and more focused on adolescents' emotional development. In addition, educational psychologists encouraged teachers to move away from the lecture-dominated instruction so common in high schools and toward more student-centered instruction, such as guided discovery and cooperative learning. (We discuss these strategies in Chapter 12.)

The middle school philosophy has grown in popularity. The number of junior highs decreased from 7,200 in 1968 to 1,000 in 1996 (Viadero, 1996), with an accompanying increase in middle schools. (You will study junior highs and middle schools in more detail in Chapter 7.)

American Secondary Schools: Future Directions

The history of American secondary schools helps us understand some of the questions facing educators today. Begun as college-preparatory institutions, high schools became comprehensive in an effort to meet the needs of a diverse student body. To help adolescents make the transition from elementary to high school, junior highs were created; when those schools failed to fulfill that mission, educators created middle schools. The academic pendulum has now swung back, however, and some leaders are calling for a redesign of middle schools to make them more academic and rigorous (Yecke, 2006).

Have American secondary schools been too trendy and overly responsive to changing conditions in society, first zigging one way and then zagging another? Or have they been too traditional and conservative, hanging onto outmoded academics in the face of dramatic changes in society? These questions are reexamined later when we discuss the modern era in American education.

Check Your Understanding

4.1 What is a comprehensive high school, and why is it important for a democratic society such as ours?

4.2 How have the goals of high school education changed over time?

4.3 How are junior highs and middle schools different?

 For feedback, go to Appendix A, Check Your Understanding, *located in the back of this text.*

Making Connections:
To deepen your understanding of the topics in this section of the chapter and integrate them with topics you've already studied, go to the *Making Connections* module for Chapter 5 at **www.prenhall.com/kauchak**. Respond to questions 7 and 8.

Junior high schools. Schools that were originally designed in the early 1900s to provide a unique academic curriculum for early adolescent youth.

Middle schools. Schools, typically for grades 6–8, specifically designed to help students through the rapid social, emotional, and intellectual changes characteristic of early adolescence.

Searching for Equality: The Education of Cultural Minorities

The first thing to do was to clean them [Native Americans] thoroughly and to dress them in their new [military] attire. . . . [Then] everything except swallowing, walking, and sleeping had to be taught; the care of person, clothing, furniture, the usages of the table, the carriage of the body, civility, all those things which white children usually learn from their childhood by mere imitation, had to be painfully in-culcated and strenuously insisted on. In addition to this, they were to be taught the rudiments of an En-glish school course and the practical use of tools. (U.S. Bureau of Indian Affairs, 1974, p. 1749)

To this point our history of American education has been generally positive. Despite lurches and false starts, education improved in quality and became more accessible to our nation's young people. The story isn't so positive for cultural minorities, however. In this section, we outline the evolution of education for cultural minorities as we consider the experiences of Native Americans, African-Americans, Hispanic Americans, and Asian-Americans.

Two themes have been pervasive in the education of cultural minorities: the concept of assimilation and the policy "separate but equal." In our discussion of multicultural education in Chapter 3, we defined **assimilation** as a process of socializing people to adopt dominant social norms and patterns of behavior. For much of history, educators sought to bring minorities into the mainstream of American life—to assimilate them—by teaching basic skills and instilling White, middle-class values. In promoting assimilation, educators also asked minorities to reject important aspects of their own histories and cultures; this rejection is apparent in the quote about Native Americans that introduces this section.

The second theme, **separate but equal**, was a policy of segregating minorities in education, transportation, housing, and other areas of public life if opportunities and facilities were considered equal to those of nonminorities. In education, the policy was implemented by creating separate schools with different curricula, teaching methods, teachers, and resources. The policy was particularly applied to the education of African-American students. Some historians believe that these efforts were well intentioned but misguided, whereas others argue that they were inherently racist (Spring, 2005).

Let's look now at the history of education of specific minority groups.

Education of Native Americans

The history of Native American education is a story of generally unsuccessful attempts to assimilate different tribes into the American mainstream. To achieve assimilation, Native Americans were expected to exchange their tribal customs and values for mainstream American values. The process left Native American students asking the question, "Who am I?" It was a difficult question to answer.

Like American education in general, the education of Native Americans began with a religious orientation. During the 1700s and 1800s, mission schools run by various religious groups provided a common school curriculum that focused on basic skills, agriculture, vocational education, and religion. Although they provided instruction in the native language, mission schools attempted to help Native Americans bridge the gap between tribal, communal life and one in which individuals owned land, had jobs, and followed the dominant culture's way of life (Spring, 2005).

From 1890 to 1930, the federal government became involved in Native American education through boarding schools run by the Bureau of Indian Affairs. Children were forced to live at the schools, English was spoken and taught, and native languages and customs were forbidden. The best way to "Americanize" the children, leaders thought, was to remove them from tribal settings and provide them with a strict program of cultural transformation (Adams, 1995).

The failure of the boarding schools was evidenced by low participation rates (only 300 of a possible 4,000 to 5,000 eligible Navajo children attended these schools in 1901), high dropout rates (many children ran away), and a tendency for students to return to the reservation after graduation because the curriculum wasn't applicable to Native American culture or interests (Button & Provenzo, 1989).

Assimilation. A process of socializing people so that they adopt dominant social norms and patterns of behavior.

Separate but equal. A policy of segregating minorities in education, transportation, housing, and other areas of public life if opportunities and facilities were considered equal to those of nonminorities. In education, the policy was evidenced by separate schools with different curricula, teaching methods, teachers, and resources.

Despite the failure of boarding schools, federal control of Native American education continued through the 1960s. Tribal schools, which included Native American culture in the curriculum, opened in 1965, but financial dependence on the federal government, limited instructional materials, and poorly paid teachers were difficult problems to overcome.

More recently, the federal government shifted responsibility for Native American education from the Bureau of Indian Affairs and tribal schools to public schools. In the 1990s, 91 percent of Native Americans attended public schools (National Center for Education Statistics, 1997). Despite this shift, and increased involvement by tribal governments, the problems in Native American education persist. Underachievement, high dropout rates, low rates of college attendance and completion, as well as high rates of poverty indicate that current educational practices remain unsuccessful (Flanagan & Park, 2005).

Education of African-Americans: Up From Slavery to . . .

The first African-Americans arrived in the United States in the early 1600s, shortly after the founding of Jamestown. Brought as slaves, they had few educational opportunities before the

Civil War. In 1850 fewer than 2 percent of African-Americans attended schools (about 4,000 in slave states and 23,000 in free states), and the literacy rate was low, ranging between 5 and 10 percent (U.S. Government Printing Office, 1975; West, 1972).

Educational accessibility improved after the Civil War. As a result of religious, philanthropic, and governmental efforts, school participation rates increased from 2 percent of the African-American population in 1850 to 10 percent in 1870 and 35 percent in 1890 (U.S. Government Printing Office, 1975). Literacy rates increased from the 5 to 10 percent at the time of the Civil War to 40 percent by 1890 and 70 percent by 1910 (U.S. Bureau of the Census, 1990).

Near the end of the 1870s, events took a negative turn, however. After the Reconstruction period following the Civil War, the federal government shifted the responsibility for educating African-Americans back to state and local governments, par-

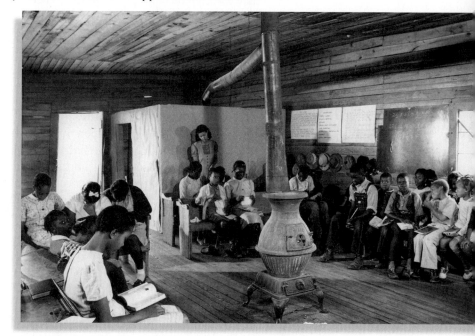

Early efforts at educating African-Americans were often substandard due to inadequate funding and resources. (Courtesy of the Library of Congress)

ticularly in the South, where the vast majority still lived. Segregated and substandard schools were predominant, and funding for African-American schools was consistently lower than for White schools. In 1877, for example, expenditures for African-American students in the South were less than half those for Whites; by the 1940s they had dropped to a fifth (J. Anderson, 1988). In 1907 White teachers in Alabama were paid five times more than African-American ones. In Georgia in the late 1920s, 99 percent of the money budgeted for teaching equipment went to White schools, even though African-Americans made up 34 percent of the state's student population (Bond, 1934). In 1952 Arkansas spent $102 to educate each White child but only $67 for each African-American child (Pulliam & Van Patten, 2007). Schools for African-Americans were clearly not separate but equal, more accurately described as *separate and unequal.*

Proposed Solutions to the Problem

The education of African-Americans was clearly inferior to that of Whites, but a clear solution to the problem remained elusive. Finally, two leaders, with sharply different perspectives, emerged.

Booker T. Washington (1856–1915) was born a slave and taught himself to read. Educated at Hampton Institute, a vocational school for African-Americans, he gained prominence for successfully establishing the Tuskegee Institute in 1881. Short of supplies and resources, he had his students build the school themselves. This hands-on approach to learning exemplified his strategy for bettering the education and lives of African-Americans in the South. He believed that hard work, practical training, and economic cooperation with Whites were the keys to success. His philosophy became popular, and he was often invited to address White audiences on the topic of African-American education. At one of these appearances, he summarized his philosophy in this way: "In all things that are purely social we can be as separate as the finger, yet one as the hand in all things essential to mutual progress" (Washington, 1932). Washington encouraged his students to become teachers; he felt that attempting to enter other professions or politics was premature and would lead to conflict with the White power structure in the South.

Although Washington was accepted by many African-Americans and popular with Whites, his policy of accommodating segregation angered other African-American leaders. W. E. B. Dubois (1868–1963) was an important opponent whose resistance to Washington's stance was predictable, given the differences in their backgrounds. Dubois was born in Massachusetts and educated in integrated schools. He attended colleges and universities in the United States and Europe and was the first African-American to receive a Ph.D. in the United States (Spring, 2005; Watkins, 2001).

Dubois was committed to changing the status of African-Americans and advocated a determined stand against segregation and racism. He focused his educational energies on students' achieving in the top 10 percent, believing that these students would provide leadership and create opportunities for the rest of the African-American population. He also felt that this group could take their place among the business, professional, and intellectual leaders of the White population. Dubois believed that Washington's separatist approach implied inferiority and, while expedient in the short term, would retard the educational progress of African-Americans in the long run. He advocated social activism and was a leader in helping establish the National Association for the Advancement of Colored People (NAACP). This organization played a major role in the advancement of African-Americans in the 20th century.

The Courts Examine "Separate But Equal"

Before the Civil War, African-Americans lived apart from the White majority because of slavery, legal restrictions, or de facto (not stipulated by law) segregation. Segregation continued after the Civil War because of the policy of "separate but equal." The policy justified segregation by claiming that African-Americans were receiving different but equal treatment under the law. The principle was first legally challenged in Massachusetts in 1850 when an African-American student wasn't allowed to attend a White school. At that time, the state court ruled that having separate but equal facilities was legal (Spring, 2005).

A federal challenge to the policy of "separate but equal" came in Louisiana in 1896 in a court case involving segregated railroads. In *Plessy v. Ferguson*, the U.S. Supreme Court ruled that separate but equal railroad facilities did not violate the Constitution (Spring, 2005). This decision was also applied to education, and "separate but equal" stood for almost 50 years. (We examine the federal government's response to the "separate but equal" policy in education in the Exploring Diversity section later in the chapter.)

Education of Hispanic Americans

Hispanic is a label that refers to a diverse group of people who are of Latin American or Caribbean heritage or who speak Spanish (Banks, 2006b; Nieto, 2004). Mexican-Americans in the Southwest, Puerto Rican Americans in the Northeast, and Cuban Americans in Florida are all included in this group. The term *Hispanic* is more popular in the Northeast, with groups in the Southwest preferring *Latino* (*Latina*, female). The term *Chicano* (*Chicana*, female) refers to Hispanics of Mexican-American heritage.

Hispanics are the fastest growing minority group in the United States. At the turn of the 21st century, they made up more than 15 percent of the nation's school-age children and are the largest minority group in California, Texas, and Florida (U.S. Bureau of Census, 2003). By the year 2025, 1 in 4 children in U.S. elementary schools is predicted to be of Hispanic origin.

Hispanic education in America began with Catholic mission schools in the Southwest, but it shifted to public schools after the Mexican–American War in 1848. Unlike African-American segregation, segregation of Hispanics was not mandated by law, but it occurred nevertheless. Hispanic students were often taught in separate schools or classes, with poorer facilities, fewer well-trained teachers, and smaller budgets. Migrant work, where farm laborers followed the crops, also contributed to educational problems, and attendance at school often suffered because of family work demands that led to transience.

Initially, the education of Hispanics focused on assimilation. Classes were taught in English, Spanish was forbidden, and students' own Hispanic heritage was ignored (Banks, 2006b; Spring, 2005). Apathy and resistance to school, as occurred with Native Americans, were pervasive, and dropping out was common. In 2003, 44 percent of the Hispanic school-age population left school before graduation, compared to 24 percent of White students (Olson, 2006a). Also, only 12 percent of 22-year-old Hispanics have a bachelor's degree, compared to 30 percent of Whites and 15 percent of African-Americans (Bowman, 2000c). When Hispanics go to college, they are much more likely to attend a 2-year institution than other groups (Pew Hispanic Foundation, 2003).

Language differences have been the source of many problems in the education of Hispanics. Language symbolizes differences between Hispanics and the dominant culture, and instruction in English interferes with students' learning. Some experts argue that language barriers explain why Hispanic students have historically scored lower on both intelligence and achievement tests, which are usually language based (Abedi, Hofstetter, & Lord, 2004; Popham, 2004b).

Education of Asian-Americans

Like Hispanics, Asian-Americans are a diverse group of people with varied histories (Banks, 2006b). The first Asian-Americans were Chinese who came to the United States to work in the California gold mines and on the first transcontinental railroad. Japanese immigrants came to California and Hawaii in the late 1800s as agricultural workers. More recently, Korean and Southeast Asian immigrants came to the United States seeking a better life and an escape from the Korean and Vietnam Wars.

Asian immigrants were initially welcomed because they relieved an acute labor shortage in the West. However, competition for jobs, together with racism, resulted in a series of changes in immigration laws that prevented further Chinese immigration in 1882 and then Japanese immigration in 1924 (Spring, 2005). A dark page in Asian-American history came during World War II, when more than 100,000 Japanese Americans were forced out of their homes near the Pacific coast and into internment camps in barren areas of the West.

Like other minority groups, Asian-Americans experienced discrimination. For example, in 1906 San Francisco established segregated schools for Asian-Americans. Instruction was in English, which resulted in problems similar to those that Native Americans and Hispanics encountered. A federal court ruled in 1974 (*Lau v. Nichols*) that the San Francisco school system had violated the rights of Chinese American students and that students who find their educational experience "wholly incomprehensible" must be taught in the first language if that language is not English.

As a group, Asian-Americans have fared better than other cultural minority groups in the American educational system. For example, Asian-Americans typically score higher on achievement tests and have higher rates of college attendance and completion than other groups, including White students (National Center for Education Statistics, 2005d), and the proportion of Asian-Americans in colleges and universities is higher than the proportion in the general population. This success has led some educators to label this group "the model minority," a stereotypic term that some Asian-Americans reject (Asian-Nation, 2005). Stereotyping, which often results in lowered expectations for members of cultural minorities, can also work in the opposite direction, blinding us to problems that our students encounter (Steele, Spencer, & Aronson, 2002). For example, many Asian-American students have problems in school, and language and poverty remain obstacles for them (Lei, 2003; Lew, 2004). We need to remember that exclusive focus on group differences can result in inappropriate expectations for and unjust treatment of individual members of those groups.

The Search for Equality: Where Are We Now?

As you saw earlier, two themes—assimilation and "separate but equal"—have been central to the education of minorities in the United States. The policy of "separate but equal" has been banned by the courts, but where does assimilation now stand?

Assimilation has always required that ethnic groups sacrifice a portion of their cultural identity to become "American." At the extreme, success meant creating a "melting pot" in which the diverse cultures of America blended into a uniform and homogeneous society. This uniform society has never been achieved, as indicated, for example, in the present-day diversity of religions in America and holidays such as Kwanzaa, St. Patrick's Day, and the Jewish and Muslim religious holidays.

In educational circles, a "tossed salad" metaphor has replaced the melting pot; in this "salad," different ethnic and cultural groups contribute unique tastes and perspectives. The extent to which Americans should share common values and beliefs is still controversial, with some arguing for greater uniformity (Schlesinger, 1992) and others advocating an America built around diversity and shared values (Spring, 2005).

VIDEO PERSPECTIVES

The Reunion

To view this video, go to the *Becoming a Professional* DVD included with this text, click on ABC News, and then this chapter's video: *The Reunion*. This ABC News documentary examines the lasting effects of school integration during the civil rights struggle in the 1960s by doing something that has never been done before— gathering together the first wave of students who went through it themselves in Shaker Heights, Ohio. This group was at the center of the storm when their parents, at the height of the civil rights movement, carried out a bold and controversial social experiment in one of America's wealthiest suburbs. Now these 1960 kindergarten classmates reunite to see where the years and education have taken them from their then-new frontier—an integrated American suburb.

Think About This

1. How does school integration relate to the idea of "separate but equal"?
2. What were the goals of integration? Why was it necessary to bus students to achieve integration?
3. In Chapter 4, you read about economic integration. How is it similar to and different from racial integration?

*To answer these questions online and receive immediate feedback, go to the Companion Website at **www.prenhall.com/kauchak**, then to the* Video Perspectives *module for Chapter 5.*

The federal government's role in the education of cultural minorities remains poorly defined. In the past, federal courts have played a major role in desegregation, but in recent times, they have been increasingly reluctant to impose busing and other legal mechanisms to achieve integration (Caldas & Bankston, 2005). During the 1960s, the commendable goal of integration, which sought to provide opportunities for cultural minorities and White majority students to attend school together and learn about each other, often became synonymous with forced busing (Pulliam & Van Patten, 2007). Busing was especially resisted by parents wanting their children to walk to and attend neighborhood schools. Public support for integration waned, and the result has been increased segregation of cultural minorities in inner-city schools (Caldas & Bankston, 2005; Kozol, 2005).

The same is true in the legislative branch; senators and members of the House of Representatives can't decide what role the federal government should play in the quest for equity and equality. Once an advocate for cultural diversity, the U.S. Senate in 2006 voted 63 to 34 to designate English as the national language (Hulse, 2006). We examine this changing federal role in education in the next section.

This section clearly indicates that the fourth item on our beginning-of-chapter survey—"As soon as slavery ended in this country, cultural and ethnic minorities were welcomed into U.S. schools"—is not true. Historically, our schools did not welcome minorities, and U.S. schools were inhospitable places for them. In fact, many minorities didn't attend U.S. schools, and when they did, their dropout rates were high. Only in the 1900s did this condition begin to change.

> **Making Connections:**
> To deepen your understanding of the topics in this section of the chapter and integrate them with topics you've already studied, go to the *Making Connections* module for Chapter 5 at **www.prenhall.com/kauchak.** Respond to questions 9 and 10.

Check Your Understanding

5.1   How does the concept of assimilation relate to Native American boarding schools?

5.2   How does "separate but equal" relate to African-Americans' educational experience in the United States?

5.3   How did the process of assimilation relate to Hispanic Americans and their native languages?

 For feedback, go to Appendix A, Check Your Understanding, *located in the back of this text.*

The Modern Era: Schools as Instruments for National Purpose and Social Change

The modern era in education began after World War II and continues to the present. It is characterized by an increased emphasis on education, which is now viewed as the key to both individual success and the progress of the nation. Given this perspective, it isn't surprising to see the federal government more actively involved in education than it was in the past. This increased involvement occurred in three areas:

- The government's response to the Cold War
- The government's War on Poverty and search for the "Great Society"
- The government's role in equity issues

Next, we look at these areas.

The Cold War: Enlisting America's Schools

After World War II, the United States became involved in a Cold War with communist countries, particularly the Soviet Union, with ever more powerful weapons being stockpiled on both sides.

It was called a Cold War because no shots were actually fired, but a struggle for world leadership evolved, nevertheless. This Cold War also significantly affected education in the United States.

The Russian launching of the satellite *Sputnik* in 1957 was a key event of the period. Believing the United States was losing the technology war, our government responded by authorizing a fivefold increase in the funding of the National Science Foundation, which had been created in 1950 to support research and improve science education. Congress also passed the National Defense Education Act (NDEA) in 1958, which was designed to enhance "the security of the nation" by improving instruction in math, science, and foreign languages. The NDEA provided funds for teacher training, new equipment, and the establishment of centers for research and dissemination of new teaching methods. During this period, Admiral Rickover, the father of the American nuclear navy, called education, "our first line of defense."

The War on Poverty and the Great Society

During the 1960s, leaders began to realize that despite the economic boom following World War II, many Americans were living in poverty. America was becoming a nation of "haves" and "have nots," and the problem was exacerbated by an economy that required ever-increasing skills from its workers.

For the unfortunate, a cycle of poverty began with inadequate education, which decreased employment opportunities, leading to a poorer quality of life that resulted in lowered achievement in the next generation (Macionis, 2006). To break this cycle and create a "Great Society" in which all could participate and benefit, President Lyndon Johnson, in his 1964 State of the Union address, stated that "this administration today, here and now, declares unconditional war on poverty in America."

Emphasis on education was a major thrust in the **War on Poverty**, a general term for federal programs designed to eradicate poverty during the 1960s. During this period, the federal government's involvement increased significantly. Initiatives included

- *Increased federal funding.* Federal funds for K–12 education went from $900 million and about 4.4 percent of the total spent on education in 1964 (before Johnson's initiatives) to $3 billion and 8.8 percent of the total educational budget by 1968.
- *The development of the Job Corps.* Modeled after the Civilian Conservation Corps of the 1930s, the Job Corps created rural and urban vocational training centers, which helped young people learn marketable skills while working in government projects.
- *The creation of the Department of Education in 1979.* Originally part of the Department of Health, Education and Welfare, education was considered so important that it was elevated to its own cabinet-level position during President Carter's administration.
- *Support for learners with exceptionalities.* In Chapter 3, you learned that the federal government passed Public Law 94-142, the Individuals with Disabilities Education Act (IDEA), in 1975. In 1976–1977, just after the law's passage, the nation educated about 3.3 million children with exceptionalities; presently the schools serve more than 6 million, an increase of nearly 82 percent (Heward, 2006).
- *The creation of national compensatory education programs.*

Let's look at compensatory programs in more detail.

Compensatory Education Programs

Compensatory education programs are government attempts to create more equal educational opportunities for disadvantaged youth. These programs provide supplementary instruction and attempt to prevent learning problems before they occur. The two best known are Head Start and Title I.

Head Start. Part of the Economic Opportunity Act of 1964, **Head Start** is a federal compensatory education program designed to help 3- to 5-year-old disadvantaged children enter school ready to learn. It has two goals: (1) to stimulate the development and academic achievement of low-income preschoolers and (2) to educate and involve parents in the edu-

War on Poverty. A general term for federal programs designed to eradicate poverty during the 1960s.

Compensatory education programs. Government attempts to create more equal educational opportunities for disadvantaged youth.

Head Start. A federal compensatory education program designed to help 3- to 5-year-old disadvantaged children enter school ready to learn.

cation of their children. In 2003, for example, 909,608 children were served in the program, which had a budget of $6.7 billion (Henry, Gordon, & Rickman, 2006). Head Start has served almost 17 million children since its inception.

The Head Start curriculum focuses on basic skills such as counting, naming colors, and prereading skills, as well as social skills such as turn-taking and following directions. Parenting goals include helping parents develop their children's literacy skills by encouraging parents to read and talk to their children and provide experiences that increase their readiness for school, such as trips to zoos, libraries, and museums.

In general, Head Start 4-year-olds perform better than comparable 4-year-olds who haven't participated in the program. In the more effective Head Start programs, such as the Perry Preschool Program in Ypsilanti, Michigan, researchers have found long-term positive effects ranging from fewer special education placements to higher numbers of high school graduates and lower crime and teen pregnancy rates (Jacobson, 2004; Lewis, 2005).

Not all Head Start programs are effective, however, and some programs have had little impact on children's readiness to learn. Poor program quality and inadequate budgets are the most commonly cited reasons (Merrow, 2002).

Title I. Title I is a federal compensatory education program that funds supplemental education services for low-income students in elementary and secondary schools. Between 1965 and 2000, more than $185 billion was spent on Title I, and these funds reached almost all of our nation's school districts. Presently funded at $14 billion per year, Title I serves 15 million low-income children in 47,600 schools (U.S. Department of Education, 2006a). Two thirds of the money goes to elementary schools, and 15 percent of the highest poverty schools receive 46 percent of Title I funds. Title I currently serves 100,000 homeless and 2.5 million English language learners. Approximately 35 percent of the recipients are White, 31 percent are Hispanic American, and 27 percent African-American.

As with Head Start, the outcomes of Title I programs have been uneven. Part of Title I's ineffectiveness resulted from initial design problems (Borman, 2002/2003). Because the funds were initially restricted to only low-income students, "pull-out" programs—where students were taken out of their regular classrooms for supplementary instruction—prevailed. During the late 1990s, 60 percent of the instruction in these pull-out programs was conducted by unlicensed aides, or paraprofessionals, and more than 40 percent of these Title I aides spent half or more of their time without the supervision of a licensed teacher (U.S. Department of Education, 1999a). The recent No Child Left Behind Act attempts to address this problem by specifying qualifications for Title I paraprofessionals. By 2005–2006, current paraprofessionals were to have finished 2 years of college or demonstrated competence through passing a rigorous test; newly hired paraprofessionals must meet this standard at the time of hire (Honawar, 2006).

Pull-out Title I programs have had other problems as well. Removing students from their classrooms causes logistical problems; the students who are pulled out miss regular instruction, and teachers have trouble helping them catch up. Also, pull-out instruction often focuses on low-level skills with few links to the regular curriculum.

In response to these criticisms, Title I programs have been redesigned to focus on total school improvement, rather than instruction in pull-out programs (Borman, 2002/2003). Newer programs attempt to achieve schoolwide improvement in a variety of ways. For example, James Comer's School Development Program (see Chapter 4) focuses on involving parents and providing improved family services such as counseling and social services (Comer et al., 2004). Another program, Success for All, attempts to prevent school failure by emphasizing family involvement and by laying a strong foundation in reading, writing, and math during the early grades (Slavin & Cheung, 2004).

Putting Compensatory Education Programs Into Perspective. Critics hope to do away with compensatory education programs and point to their uneven quality. This criticism underscores the general dilemma of federal aid to education. This aid is usually given with only broad guidelines that allow schools and districts to spend the money essentially as they see fit. This necessary flexibility also results in uneven quality.

Title I. A federal compensatory education program that funds supplemental education services for low-income students in elementary and secondary schools.

The Federal Government's Role in Pursuing Equality

Consider the following statistics. The average 12th-grade low-income student of color reads at the same level as the average eighth-grade middle-class White student (Kahlenberg, 2000). As a group, African-Americans have the lowest achievement test scores of any minority, and they are over-represented in special education classes (National Center for Education Statistics, 2006b). Close to 30 percent of Hispanics live at or below the poverty line, and college attendance and graduation rates are substantially below the general population (U.S. Bureau of Census, 2000).

The struggle for equality in education is an important area in which the federal government's role has increased. Civil rights and equity for women are two areas where the federal role has made an important difference.

The Civil Rights Movement

Linda Brown was an 8-year-old African-American student in Topeka, Kansas, in 1951. Instead of walking 5 blocks to an all-White elementary school, she was forced to cross unguarded and potentially dangerous railroad tracks to catch a bus to a school for African-Americans 21 blocks away. In addition to objecting to the distance, her father believed that the African-American school had substandard resources and programs. With the help of the NAACP, he went to court to change this.

We mentioned earlier in the chapter that the policy "separate but equal" was put into place after the Civil War. It remained a guiding principle in education until 1954, when Thurgood Marshall, who later became the first African-American on the U.S. Supreme Court, represented the NAACP in arguing against the "separate but equal" doctrine that forced Linda Brown to attend a segregated school. In a unanimous decision, the Supreme Court ruled in the famous watershed case, *Brown v. Board of Education of Topeka* (1954), that separate educational facilities are inherently unequal and that racially segregated schools generated "a feeling of inferiority." The days of segregated education for African-American students were supposed to be over.

In some school districts, however, Whites so strongly resisted integration that it had to be forced. For example, in 1957 President Eisenhower sent federal troops to an all-White high school in Little Rock, Arkansas, to enforce the Supreme Court's antisegregation decision and allow nine African-American students to attend the school in safety. In spite of these efforts, discrimination remained widespread because the responsibility for desegregation was left to individual school districts, many of which resisted change.

Congress responded with the Civil Rights Act of 1964, which prohibited discrimination against students on the basis of race, color, or national origin in all institutions receiving federal funds. The federal government now had a mechanism to both encourage and enforce integration efforts.

Equity for Women

As we mentioned at the beginning of the chapter, in the early periods of U.S. history, women were generally excluded from education, and historically, they have been underserved by our nation's schools. The federal government became involved in gender-equity issues by enacting Title IX of the Education Amendments of 1972. The purpose of this legislation was to eliminate gender bias in the schools and states:

No person in the United States shall, on the basis of sex, be excluded from participation in, be denied benefits of, or be subjected to discrimination under any education program or activity receiving federal financial assistance.

Federal efforts through legislation such as Title IX have increased funding and participation in girls' athletics. (Sean Justice/Getty Images Inc.–Image Bank)

The law has had its largest impact on physical education and sports: The number of girls participating in high school athletics increased from 294,000 in 1971 to more than 2.7 million in 2001 (U.S. Department of Education, 2002). Participation is still well below that of boys (3.8 million in 1998–1999), however, and in most schools, women's teams still do not receive comparable funding, facilities, equipment, publicity, travel budgets, or practice opportunities.

Title IX has become controversial at the college and university level. Critics of Title IX argue that in order to achieve an equal number of male and female athletes, schools have had to eliminate many of the "minor" men's sports, such as wrestling, swimming, gymnastics, and tennis (M. Davis, 2003). Supporters of Title IX argue that the extraordinary cost of college football skews the issue, and a modest cut in football expenditures would allow for a greater investment in women's sports with no cuts to other men's sports.

Putting Federal Efforts Into Perspective

So, how has federal intervention affected the struggle for equality in education? With respect to integration, progress is uncertain. For example, in the South in 1988, nearly 44 percent of African-American students attended integrated schools, up from virtually none in 1954. However, by 1996 the figure had shrunk to about 35 percent (Hendrie, 1999). In the North, segregated housing patterns led to de facto segregated schools. This problem has been exacerbated in urban areas by "White flight" to the suburbs. Consider these statistics:

In Chicago, by the academic year 2000–2001, 87 percent of public school enrollment was black or Hispanic; less than 10 percent of children in the schools were white. In Washington, D.C., 94 percent of children were black or Hispanic; less than 5 percent were white. In St. Louis, 82 percent of the student population was black or Hispanic by this point, in Philadelphia and Cleveland 78 percent, in Los Angeles 84 percent, in Detroit 95 percent, in Baltimore 88 percent. In New York City, nearly three quarters of the students were black or Hispanic in 2001. (Kozol, 2005, p. 8)

Currently, more than three fourths of Hispanic students attend schools populated predominantly by members of cultural minorities, and nearly 4 in 10 attend schools that are 90 to 100 percent minority (Borman, 2002/2003).

Various strategies have been proposed to achieve greater racial diversity in schools. Compensatory education, school boundary realignments, and mandatory busing are some. In the 1970s, **magnet schools**, public schools that provide innovative or specialized programs and accept enrollment from students in all parts of a district, were developed to aid in the integration of White and minority students. Magnet schools organize their curricula around high-interest or high-need areas such as math, science, and computers, or around general, high-quality programs designed to prepare students for college. Magnet schools are most common in large cities and today number about 4,000 schools, serving more than 2 million students, or about 3 percent of the K–12 student population (Kober, 2006). The federal government encouraged magnet schools' growth by allocating $108 million in fiscal year 2005 to encourage growth in more than 100 school districts (Magnet Schools of America, 2006; U.S. Department of Education, 2006b).

In spite of strong governmental support ($739 million for experimentation with magnet programs), magnet schools haven't always met their original goals. For instance, they tend to attract the highest-achieving minority students, which robs other students of role models. When they succeed in attracting bright students from cultural minority groups, they sometimes cannot attract high-performing White students into the same schools. Social class differences between wealthier and poorer students and cultural differences within magnet schools also work to minimize true integration and the development of cohesive learning communities (Dickinson, Holifield, Holifield, & Creer, 2000).

Civil rights and women's equity efforts also continue to be highly controversial. Some minority leaders and women's groups assert that progress for cultural minorities and women has been too slow, and the government should do more. On the other hand, conservative leaders contend that civil rights efforts have gone too far. They charge that women and minorities are receiving inappropriately preferential treatment, which amounts to reverse discrimination. These debates are likely to continue in the future as critics on various sides become increasingly vocal and polar in their positions.

> **Magnet schools.** Public schools that provide innovative or specialized programs that attempt to attract students from all parts of a district.

teaching in an era of reform

Federal Government Reform

Reforms result from various sources, such as professional organizations, states, local districts, and the federal government, with the federal government being one of the most powerful. As you saw earlier in the chapter, the federal government expanded its role in influencing education during the 20th century in three primary ways:

- Setting standards
- Creating testing programs
- Offering financial incentives

The issue in this debate about educational reform is whether reform should originate at the federal level or whether it is best done at the state or even local levels (DeBray, McDermott, & Wohlstetter, 2005).

Setting Standards

One way for the federal government to influence education is to encourage states to set standards, which provide common goals for educational efforts. The No Child Left Behind (NCLB) Act of 2001, introduced in Chapter 1, requires each state to establish its own standards and create tests to assess the extent to which its students meet those standards. An important component of this act is the requirement that each state guarantee that 100 percent of its students are proficient in reading, math, and science by the year 2014.

Testing Programs

Begun in 1969, the National Assessment of Educational Progress (NAEP) testing program, also known as "the Nation's Report Card," was designed to provide an objective, external measure of how students in the United States are performing (Popham, 2005). The program conducts periodic assessments of students in fourth, eighth, and twelfth grades in math, science, reading, writing, and the arts, and in the social studies areas of civics, geography, and U.S. history. Because of concerns about undue federal influence and the confidentiality of scores, testing is voluntary, and only group scores are reported. In 2003, all 50 states participated in some aspect of the program. In addition to providing a nationwide snapshot of the competence of U.S. students, NAEP also provides state profiles and comparisons of test scores.

Financial Incentives

If national goals are worth pursuing, and tests can measure progress toward these goals, rewarding districts that make significant progress and punishing those that don't are logical next steps. This is exactly what President George W. Bush recommended during his presidential campaign and what Congress enacted in NCLB (DeBray et al., 2005). Low-performing schools that receive federal funds can be put on a 5-year schedule of remediation, and if scores don't improve, the schools could be taken over by the state or reconstituted. In addition, states that fail to comply with NCLB provisions could lose federal educational funds.

The Issue

Setting standards seems sensible. For instance, who would oppose the idea of every student in the nation reaching proficiency in reading and math by 2014? Also, supporters of nationwide testing argue that knowing how our students are doing and how states compare to one another is sensible, and they ask, "How can we improve our education systems if we don't know what our students are learning or how much they are learning" (Ravitch, 2006)?

Financial incentives also make sense intuitively. Why shouldn't teachers and schools be rewarded for increasing the amount their students learn (or punished when learning doesn't occur)?

However, national standards have been criticized by both political conservatives and liberals, although for different reasons (Gordon, 2006). As Chester Finn, former Assistant Secretary of Education under President Reagan, observed, "Republicans oppose any proposal with the word 'national' in it; Democrats oppose anything with the word 'standards' in it" (quoted in D. Doyle, 1999, p. 56). NCLB partially dodges this issue by making individual states responsible for setting proficiency levels in different content areas.

National testing is also controversial. Critics contend it creates a national curriculum and that it causes teachers to "teach to the test," which narrows the curriculum and detracts from an overall education (Nichols & Berliner, 2005).

Critics also charge that financial incentives will further encourage teachers to teach to tests, and states and districts will align their curricula with the content being tested—in essence, creating a de facto national curriculum (Newman, 2006).

You Take a Position

Now it's your turn to take a position on the issue. State in writing whether you favor an increased federal role in school reform that includes requiring states to set standards, creating testing programs, and offering financial incentives, and provide a two-page rationale for your position.

For additional references and resources, go to the Companion Website at www.prenhall.com/kauchak, then to the Teaching in an Era of Reform module for Chapter 5. You can respond online or submit your response to your instructor.

Critics also argue that the programs have failed to eliminate achievement differences between participants and other students. This criticism is more debatable. Expecting schools, alone, to solve the social problems associated with poverty, such as drug use, violence, unstable families, and unhealthy neighborhoods, is unrealistic (Berliner, 2005). And a long history of research consistently demonstrates that these factors adversely affect learning (Macionis, 2006).

As this section has demonstrated, the fifth item from our survey—"In recent times, the federal government has viewed the schools as an instrument to achieve national goals"—is true. As the link between an educated workforce and national prosperity became clearer, the federal government increasingly viewed the schools as essential for achieving national goals. This emphasis was most pronounced in 1983 with the publication of *A Nation at Risk* (U.S. Department of Education, 1983), and more recently with No Child Left Behind legislation.

> **Making Connections:**
> To deepen your understanding of the topics in this section of the chapter and integrate them with topics you've already studied, go to the *Making Connections* module for Chapter 5 at **www.prenhall.com/kauchak.** Respond to questions 11–13.

Check Your Understanding

6.1   How was the federal government's educational response to the Cold War similar to its actions in the War on Poverty and the Great Society?

6.2   What are magnet schools, and how do they relate to attempts to achieve equality in our schools?

6.3   What is Title IX, and how is it related to the concept of equality?

For feedback, go to Appendix A, Check Your Understanding, *located in the back of this text.*

decision making

Defining Yourself as a Professional

You're a first-year teacher in a large suburban district in the Midwest. When you interviewed for the job, the principal explained that the district was experiencing demographic changes, and parents were concerned about declining test scores. The fourth grade, where you have a self-contained classroom, is particularly important, because your students take the Stanford Achievement Test, a standardized test widely used to gauge individual student progress. In addition, they participate in the NAEP, the national test designed to assess the progress of students across the country.

During the weeks before school, the principal met with teams of teachers at each grade level, going over the district curriculum and explaining how it has been aligned to cover content measured on the standardized tests. You design your unit and lesson plans around these goals and feel fairly confident as the school year begins.

After 2 or 3 weeks, you see that something is wrong. You have some classroom management problems, and a number of your students don't seem motivated. In addition, many of your students can't

do the work you assign. Some have transferred from other districts where the curriculum was different, some are struggling with English as a second language, and others just don't seem to get it.

After a number of troubled evenings, you approach one of your colleagues, an experienced teacher next door, and explain how you're considering dumping the planned curriculum, assessing your students, and starting over.

"You really think that would work?" your colleague asks after hearing your plan.

"I'm not sure, but I know what I'm doing now isn't."

"And what are you going to tell Mr. Livingston when he comes around to evaluate your teaching?"

What would you do in this situation?

*To respond to this question online and receive immediate feedback, go to the Decision Making module for Chapter 5 on the Companion Website at **www.prenhall.com/kauchak.***

Meeting Your Learning Objectives

1. Explain how the diversity of the original colonies shaped our educational system, and describe the role of religion in colonial schools.
   - Major geographic, economic, and cultural differences existed in the original 13 colonies. These differences spilled over into religious differences, which strongly influenced the decision to separate church and state.
   - Early colonial educational practices were largely negative and repressive. Over time European philosophies that were more humane and child-centered made their way across the Atlantic.
   - The colonial period resulted in three historical legacies. First, early schools were elitist, catering to wealthy, white males. Second, the foundation of public support for education was established by the Old Deluder Satan Act. Finally, the tangled relationship between religion and education began.

2. Describe how the early national period defined state and federal roles for governing education.
   - During the early national period, the framers of the Constitution used the First Amendment to separate religion from government.
   - The Tenth Amendment to the Constitution placed the primary responsibility for funding and governing education in the hands of state and local governments.
   - During this period, the federal government separated church and government, relegated educational responsibility to the states, and established the idea that schools were essential for improving the quality of life and helping the nation grow.

3. Explain how the common school movement influenced the establishment of universal public schooling.
   - During the years leading up to the Civil War, states laid the foundations of universal access to tax-supported schools. States established state departments of education to govern schools and built normal schools to advance the idea of professional training for teachers.
   - The common school movement was a turning point in American education because it planted the idea of universal access to a tax-supported education for all. Though this ideal was not achieved in practice, establishing the principle was important. Also during this period, states addressed the central issue of teacher quality by creating normal schools.

4. Describe the historical roots of contemporary secondary schools.
   - The history of the comprehensive American high school began with the Boston Latin School, the first secondary school in the colonies. This college-preparatory institution focused on the classics. Benjamin Franklin's Academy of Philadelphia introduced the idea of a practical curriculum. The English High School targeted non–college-bound students and was supported by public funds.
   - The comprehensive American high school evolved as a compromise out of a tug-of-war between committee reports that advocated either academic or applied orientations. The comprehensive high school attempts to meet the needs of all students—general education, vocational, and college preparatory—under one roof.
   - Current middle schools began as more traditional junior highs created in the early 1900s. Junior high schools were more academically oriented and were often "mini" versions of high schools. Middle schools were created to meet the unique developmental needs of young adolescents.

5. Discuss similarities and differences in different minority groups' struggles for educational equality.
   - The education of cultural minorities in the United States, aimed at assimilation, attempted to create schools that were separate but equal but generally failed. Native American education efforts attempted to assimilate students through boarding schools.
   - The education of African-Americans in the United States had a long history of separate but unequal treatment that was finally challenged in the Supreme Court in 1954.

- Education for Hispanic Americans had a similar uneven history, with both segregation and unequal funding. Bilingual education has been a central controversy in the education of Hispanics, and its status is currently in question.
- Asian-Americans experienced educational problems similar to other cultural minorities. In attempts to assimilate them quickly, schools often ignored Asian-Americans' native languages.
- The concepts of assimilation and melting pot have been replaced with metaphors such as "mosaic" or "tossed salad," which emphasize the importance of students' retaining their home cultures. In addition, the federal government's role in achieving educational equity is still being debated.

6. **Explain how schools became instruments for national purpose during the modern era.**
   - During the modern era, the federal government took a more active role in education, using it as an instrument of national purpose. During the Cold War with the Soviet Union, the federal government spent large amounts of money improving math, science, and foreign language education.
   - During the War on Poverty and the Great Society, the federal government also used courts and federal spending to battle poverty and inequalities in the schools.
   - Currently, consensus is lacking about the federal government's role in achieving education equity. The No Child Left Behind Act is the latest federal effort in this regard.

Important Concepts

academy (p. 162)
assimilation (p. 166)
character education (p. 155)
common school movement (p. 158)
compensatory education programs (p. 172)
comprehensive high school (p. 161)
English classical school (p. 163)
Head Start (p. 172)
junior high schools (p. 165)

Latin grammar school (p. 162)
magnet schools (p. 175)
middle schools (p. 165)
normal schools (p. 160)
Old Deluder Satan Act (p. 153)
separate but equal (p. 166)
Title I (p. 173)
vouchers (p. 155)
War on Poverty (p. 172)

Developing as a Professional

Preparing for Your Licensure Exam

This exercise will provide you with practice answering questions similar to the Praxis™ Principles of Learning and Teaching Exam as well as your state-specific licensure exam.

Think about the history of American education and how the teachers' comments in the following case study reflect trends in this history. Then read the case study, and answer the questions that follow.

"Oh, my aching feet!" Dave Carlisle (the first-year middle school teacher from the opening case for this chapter) moans as he sinks onto the sofa.

"Out late dancing again?" his colleague Monica asks, looking up from the lesson plans she is working on.

"Yeah, right. Don't I wish. I've been on my feet all morning lecturing on Newton's laws of motion."

"Newton's laws of motion? Isn't that stuff they'll get in high school physics?" Monica asked.

"Yeah, but I just want to be sure that they'll be ready for it when they get there. About half of the kids in my morning class are really sharp and should go on to college. They'll need this stuff," Dave replies.

"How come you're lecturing so much? I thought we agreed we'd try more problem-based learning to get the kids involved. Lecturing is not only hard on you, it's difficult for them—especially the ones struggling in science."

"Yeah, I know that, but I'm torn. Science is really important. Especially for those going on to college. Do I aim for the average student and punish my high achievers, or teach to the college bound and hope the others come along for the ride? Any ideas?"

"Sounds like we better talk about this in our next team meeting," Monica replies with a frown.

1. Analyze Dave's comments in terms of the history of the middle school and junior high school. Where would Dave's teaching more clearly fit?

2. In which type of earlier school—Latin grammar school, academy, or English classical school—would Dave's teaching fit the best? least?

3. Which report, the report from the Committee of Ten or the Cardinal Principles of Secondary Education, would Dave agree with more? Why?

To receive feedback on your responses to these exercises, go to the Companion Website at www.prenhall.com/kauchak, then to the Preparing for Your Licensure Exam *module for Chapter 5.*

Discussion Questions

1. What is the proper relationship between education and religion? Is the connection between religion and education likely to become closer or more distant over the next 10 years? Why do you think so?

2. Will trends that emphasize choice, such as the use of school vouchers and enrollment in magnet schools, likely increase or decrease in the future? Why do you think so? Will choice positively or negatively influence education?

3. What is your position on bilingual education? Should it be generally banned as it has been in some states, or was this a mistake? Explain your position.

4. How would you attempt to solve the problems with Native American education?

5. Do you believe that racial discrimination remains a major problem for society? What could or should schools do to alleviate this problem?

6. Would our educational system be better if control were at the national level instead of the local and state levels? Why or why not?

Developing as a Professional: Online Activities

Going Into Schools

Go to the Companion Website at *www.prenhall.com/kauchak,* and click on the *Going Into Schools* module for Chapter 5. You will find a number of school-based activities that will help you link chapter content to the schools in which you work.

Virtual Field Experience: Using the Internet to Explore the Profession

If you would like to participate in a Virtual Field Experience, access the following Website: *http//:www.library.gcsu.edu/~sc/magepages/magelink.html.* This site provides a comprehensive overview of the history of education in the United States.

Online Portfolio Activities

To develop your professional portfolio, further apply your understanding of chapter content, and address the INTASC standards, go the Companion Website at *www.prenhall.com/kauchak*, then to the *Online Portfolio Activities* for Chapter 5. Complete the suggested activities.

Educational Philosophy: The Intellectual Foundations of American Education

Chapter Outline

Philosophy and Philosophy of Education
   Philosophy and Teacher Professionalism
   The Relationship Between Philosophy and Theory

Branches of Philosophy
   Epistemology
   Metaphysics
   Axiology
   Logic

Traditional Schools of Philosophy
   Idealism
   Realism
   Pragmatism
   Existentialism
   Applying the Traditional Philosophies in
     Classrooms

Philosophies of Education
   Perennialism
   Essentialism
   Progressivism
   Postmodernism

Developing Your Philosophy of Education
   The Role of Beliefs in a Philosophy of Education
   Examining Your Beliefs
   Forming a Philosophy
   Philosophy of Education in Urban Environments

Learning Objectives

After you have completed your study of this chapter, you should be able to:

1. Define philosophy, including normative philosophy, and explain the difference between philosophy and theory.

2. Describe each of the branches of philosophy, and identify examples that illustrate each.

3. Describe the traditional schools of philosophy, and identify examples that illustrate each view.

4. Describe the major philosophies of education, and identify examples that illustrate each view.

5. Explain why a personal philosophy of education is important, and describe the steps involved in forming one.

Case Studies

 Elementary

 Middle

 Secondary

Chapter 6

Will Hart/PhotoEdit Inc.

Philosophy often seems rather remote and disconnected from everyday life, but this isn't at all the case. We each have a "philosophy of life," for example, which is the set of principles we choose to live by.

As with individuals, professionals have philosophies that guide their practice. As you read the following case study, think about the philosophical differences that guide the thinking of the two teachers in the conversation.

"What's happening?" Brad Norman asks Allie Skinner as he walks into the teachers' lounge during the lunch period.

"Working on this quiz," Allie mumbles, glancing up at him.

"You sure do test the heck out of your kids, don't you? Every time I come in here, you're either writing a quiz or scoring one, or recording grades, or something."

"Well, it isn't that I love tests so much, but . . . well, you know what I think."

"Yeah, yeah, I know," Brad replies, waving his hand. "If you don't challenge them, they don't learn. . . . I guess I'm just more interested in trying to motivate them."

"Wait," Allie waves. "I'm as interested in motivation as you are; it's just that I have some different views about how you get there."

"I know you think that pushing the kids . . . ," Brad begins again.

"High expectations," Allie interrupts with a wry smile.

"Whatever," Brad shrugs. "I know you think that having high expectations is important, but I don't see how testing and all that stuff relates to motivation."

"Do you want to hear about it?" Allie asks. "Might be boring."

"Sure," Brad smiles.

"Well, this is what I believe, . . . I've given all this a lot of thought, and this is the best I've been able to come up with so far. . . . I'll change my mind when I get some evidence that I'm wrong. . . . Anyway, I think kids have changed. They don't come to school with the same sort of desire to learn as they once did. I still believe that kids want to learn, or maybe more specifically, they want to believe they did *learn* something when they're finished with a topic, or class. But they're not intrinsically motivated, and by that I mean, I don't think they're motivated to study stuff for it's own sake. They're often extrinsically motivated, motivated to study as a means to some end, like a good grade, or recognition from their parents, or something like that.

"Now, I was reading in one of my journals, and the authors were talking about the link between achievement and self-esteem, and it makes sense. I thought about what they said, and I do believe that kids feel good when they learn something, particularly if it's challenging. I also think that the more they know about a topic, the better they like it. For example, wouldn't you agree that an expert in some area, like a person who really understands literature, or poetry, or physics, is more motivated in that area than a novice or a person who doesn't know much about it?

"Look at yourself; you're really into technology; you talk about it all the time. . . . The better you've gotten at it, the more you like it, and the more you want to do it."

"Yeah, probably, . . . I guess so," Brad shrugs.

"So, my goal is to get students to learn as much as possible about the topics I'm teaching. The more they learn, the more intrinsically motivated they're going to be, and they're going to be motivated because they're getting good at the topic.

"Now, there's real, practical stuff out there that they need to know, and there's only one way they're going to learn it. . . . That's practice and experience. So, I've got to get them to study and practice. One way of doing that is to quiz frequently. They study for the quizzes, they get specific feedback, and they tell me they learn a lot. Ultimately they like it, and further, their self-esteem improves, and it improves because they're learning. That's the way the world works. It's a win–win. I'm getting paid to help kids learn. If I don't do my best to make that happen, I'm not earning my salary."

"Some of what you're saying makes sense," Brad acknowledges. "However, your view is a little narrow. First, much of what I read suggests that kids would be intrinsically motivated if school wasn't so boring. How motivated would you be if you had to sit and listen to teachers drone on all day, every day?

"I like the idea of kids knowing stuff too, but school involves more than that. Where in your scheme do kids learn to solve problems and make choices and wise decisions? A head full of facts may be great if your goal in life is to be good at quiz shows, but the person who really succeeds is the one who continues to learn and can adapt to changes in the world by solving the problems they encounter. So, . . . the only way they're going to get good at making decisions is to be put in situations where they're forced to make decisions. They need lots of experience in making decisions and solving problems. That's how I think the world works.

"Plus, thinking about doing my job, it would be a heck of a lot easier to just make the kids cram some stuff in their heads, but I would be doing them a disservice if I didn't try to prepare them for life outside school.

"And as long as I'm at it," Brad continues, "exactly what is real? You said, 'There's real, practical stuff out there that they need to know.' For instance, let's say that, based on this conversation, you conclude that I'm naive and idealistic. On the other hand, I conclude that I'm actually more practical than you are, because I think schooling should help kids learn to make wise decisions and be adaptable, which requires learning activities that force them to make decisions. What is the reality? Am I naive, or am I practical? Who's to say? Reality is in fact this: To you, I'm naive, and you will operate based on that belief. To me, I'm not. So, reality is what we perceive it to be, and there's no objective source out there to decide which view is the 'right one.'"

"Aw, c'mon," Allie counters. "Sure I acknowledge your point, but look at that oak tree outside the window. You can perceive it to be anything you want, but it's still an oak. And it doesn't matter what anybody thinks; two plus two is four—not three, not five, not anything else.

"Plus, I'm not talking about a 'head full of facts.' Knowing stuff means that they understand it well enough so they can apply it to different situations when they occur. For instance, you want them to make wise decisions. They can't make a wise decision if they don't know anything."

Just then the bell rings, signaling the transition to the next class. Allie and Brad leave, agreeing to disagree and promising to continue the discussion later.

To begin your study of this chapter, respond to the following survey. We address each of these survey items in this chapter.

---

professional knowledge: test yourself!

For each item, circle the number that best represents your thinking. Use the following scale as a guide.

1 = Strongly disagree
2 = Disagree
3 = Uncertain
4 = Agree
5 = Strongly agree

1. The primary function of philosophy is to help prospective teachers understand how past experts have thought about teaching.

| 1 | 2 | 3 | 4 | 5 |

2. Philosophy is important for teachers, but it isn't a part of other professions.

| 1 | 2 | 3 | 4 | 5 |

3. Understanding philosophy is an important part of professional knowledge, but it doesn't suggest how we should teach.

| 1 | 2 | 3 | 4 | 5 |

4. Philosophy and theory are closely related, but not identical.

| 1 | 2 | 3 | 4 | 5 |

5. Teachers' primary goals should be to help students master essential content rather than to help students develop emotionally and socially.

| 1 | 2 | 3 | 4 | 5 |

This is available in a downloadable format on the Companion Website for personal portfolio use.

Philosophy and Philosophy of Education

What is philosophy, and what does "philosophy of education" mean? At its most basic level, **philosophy** is described as a search for wisdom (Ozmon & Craver, 2007), but in a more formal sense, it is a study of theories of knowledge, truth, existence, and morality, or matters of right and wrong (Gutek, 2005; Murphy, 2006).

Philosophy. The study of theories of knowledge, truth, existence, and morality.

We see evidence of this study in Allie's and Brad's discussions in the opening case. Allie, for example, said, "I've given all this a lot of thought, and this is the best I've been able to come up with so far. . . . I'll change my mind when I get some evidence that I'm wrong." She was describing knowledge, truth, and what she believed was right in her statements. Although his beliefs and conclusions were different, Brad was pursuing the same goal. This is why philosophy is important for teachers, and it addresses the first item in our survey. **A philosophy of education** goes well beyond helping prospective teachers understand how past experts have thought about teaching; it provides a framework for thinking about current educational issues and can guide professional practice. How is this framework acquired?

Philosophy and Teacher Professionalism

Item 2 in our survey said, "Philosophy is important for teachers, but it isn't a part of other professions." This statement isn't true. All professions have philosophies that help guide practitioners in their thinking and actions. For example, the famous architect Frank Lloyd Wright came from the organic school of architecture. According to this view, homes and other structures should be a part of the environment; they shouldn't exist apart from their surroundings. In the photo below on the left, we see that the Frank Lloyd Wright house blends into its background so well that it almost appears to be a part of the natural setting. A contrasting architectural philosophy holds that "form follows function." This view suggests that structures must first be functional, and the way they're built then depends on that function. The photo below on the right reflects this belief.

Other professions have their own philosophies—systems of beliefs that guide decisions about professional practice. For example, the shift in emphasis from treating illness after it's occurred to preventing illness through lifestyle changes reflects a philosophical change in medicine. Holistic medicine—whose practitioners take into account patients' beliefs and emotions, in addition to their physical symptoms, in diagnosis and treatment—represents another philosophical shift. Similar competing philosophical systems could be described for all professions.

In their conversation, Allie and Brad expressed different views, but their contrasting positions share common features, and they closely relate to teacher professionalism (see

Philosophy of education. A framework for thinking about educational issues, and a guide for professional practice.

Philosophy exerts a powerful influence on other professions, such as architecture. (left: Corbis/Stock Market; right: EMG Education Management Group)

Figure 6.1   Elements of Professionalism in Allie's and Brad's Philosophies

Figure 6.1). For example, both Allie and Brad reflected on their practice and made decisions about what topics were most important to study and how to best help students understand those topics. Allie, for example, said, "[T]here's real, practical stuff out there that they need to know, and there's only one way they're going to learn it." She decided to emphasize what she believed was essential knowledge, and she further decided to frequently assess her students to help them acquire this knowledge. Brad's reflection led him to decide that directly involving students in decision-making and problem-solving activities was more important.

Both Allie and Brad based their decisions on specialized knowledge—an aspect of professionalism that we've repeatedly emphasized. For example, Allie said, "Now, I was reading in one of my journals. . . ." She didn't base her decisions on intuition or whim; rather, they were grounded in professional knowledge. The same was true for Brad, as indicated by his comment, "First, much of what I read suggests that. . . ." He disagreed with Allie, but his decisions were also based on knowledge.

We posed the question, "How is this framework for thinking about current educational issues acquired?" at the close of the last section. It is acquired by becoming knowledgeable and reflective, and philosophy is an essential part of this professional knowledge.

This also addresses the third item on our survey: "Understanding philosophy is an important part of professional knowledge, but it doesn't suggest how we should teach." Understanding philosophy certainly is a part of professional knowledge. However, it does, indeed, suggest how we should teach; in fact, a clearly understood philosophy is essential for guiding practice.

The Relationship Between Philosophy and Theory

Philosophy and theory overlap in many ways, and the distinction between the two is often blurred (Ferrero, 2005). In fact, our definition describes philosophy as the study of theories, specifically, theories of knowledge, truth, existence, and morality (Jacobsen, 2003). A philosophy and a theory are not identical, however.

A **theory** is a set of related principles that are based on observation and are used to explain additional observations. For example, suppose we see a boy wearing a prominent sports figure's football jersey. Psychology's *social cognitive theory* tells us that "people tend to imitate behavior they observe in others" and also that "individuals are more likely to imitate someone with high status than someone with low status" (Schunk, 2004). These principles, which are based on psychologists' observations, explain why the boy is wearing the jersey by saying that he is imitating a high-status model.

Philosophies are based in part on theories. For example, Allie's emphasis on high expectations is based on theories of motivation that suggest that people are motivated to meet others' expectations. Philosophy goes beyond theory, however, not only to explain the way things are, such as why the boy wears the jersey and why students are motivated, but to also

Theory. A set of related principles that are based on observation and are used to explain additional observations.

suggest the way things *ought to be*, and to analyze theories, ideas, and beliefs. Allie, for example, suggested that schools should emphasize knowledge and understanding, whereas Brad thought they should focus on decision making and problem solving. Allie also expressed the belief that kids basically want to learn but that they're not intrinsically motivated. Brad expressed the opposite belief. In this regard, both Allie and Brad stepped beyond theory into the realm of philosophy, and this addresses the fourth item in our survey. "Philosophy and theory *are* closely related, but not identical."

Philosophies in other professions also suggest what ought to be. Using the examples cited earlier, one school of architecture suggests that structures should be a part of the environment, whereas another believes that being functional is the highest priority. In medicine, one school of thinking emphasizes prevention through healthy lifestyles, while another focuses on healing through medication and other treatments. A description of the way something ought to be—such as the way educators, architects, physicians, or other professionals ought to practice—is called a **normative philosophy** (Ferrero, 2005).

Making Connections:
 To deepen your understanding of the topics in this section of the chapter and integrate them with topics you've already studied, go to the *Making Connections* module for Chapter 6 at www.prenhall.com/kauchak. Respond to questions 1 and 2.

Check Your Understanding

1.1 Define philosophy and normative philosophy, and explain how they differ from theory.

1.2 To which part of teacher professionalism is philosophy most closely related? Explain.

1.3 What is the major difference between Allie's and Brad's normative philosophies?

For feedback, go to Appendix A, Check Your Understanding, *located in the back of this text.*

Branches of Philosophy

Just as other areas of inquiry, such as biology, geography, or literature, have different areas and topics of study, so does philosophy. In philosophy these include

- Epistemology
- Metaphysics (ontology)
- Axiology
- Logic

Let's examine them.

Epistemology

Let's look again at Allie's and Brad's discussion. Allie said, "Now, there's real, practical stuff out there that they need to know, and there's only one way they're going to learn it. . . . practice and experience. So, I've got to get them to practice." She argued that practice and experience are the ways *students come to know* the ideas they learn.

Allie was making an epistemological argument. **Epistemology** is a branch of philosophy that examines questions of how we come to know what we know. A variety of ways of knowing exist. The scientific method, in which a problem is tested by collecting facts through observation and experiment, is one. Intuition, authority, and even divine revelation are others.

Epistemology is involved in constructivism, a prominent learning theory. Constructivism suggests that the way we acquire—come to know—the understanding we possess is to "construct" it ourselves. For example, because the closer we stand to an open fire, the

Normative philosophy. A description of the way professionals ought to practice.

Epistemology. The branch of philosophy that examines questions of how we come to know what we know.

warmer we are, many people in our country have constructed the idea that we are closer to the sun in summer. (The northern hemisphere is actually farther away from the sun in summer, but the sun's rays are more direct.) The way people come to understand why summer is warmer than winter is to construct an idea—in this case faulty—that makes sense to them based on their prior experiences (Mayer, 2002).

Epistemology is important for teachers because our beliefs about how students gain knowledge and understanding affect our choices of teaching methods. Teachers who believe in constructivism, for example, provide a variety of experiences for learners and lead discussions that will help them construct understanding of the topics they're teaching. In contrast, teachers who believe that listening to an expert is the way people "come to know" are likely to lecture to students and expect them to reproduce what they've heard on tests.

Metaphysics

Whereas epistemology examines how we know, **metaphysics**—or ontology—is a branch of philosophy that considers what we know (Osborne, 1996). Metaphysics considers questions of reality and ultimately attempts to answer the question, "What is real?" (Jacobsen, 2003). With respect to metaphysics, Allie and Brad are far apart. Allie argued that "there's real, practical stuff out there that they [students] need to know," but Brad countered that "reality is what we perceive it to be, and there's no objective source out there to decide which view is the 'right one.' " Allie believes in a reality independent of our perception, but Brad believes that perception and reality are inextricably intertwined.

Our metaphysical beliefs influence both the way we teach and the goals we establish. For instance, because Allie believes in a reality independent of people's perceptions, her goal is for students to understand that reality. In contrast, because Brad believes less strongly in an objective reality, his goals more strongly emphasize students' learning to critically examine their own thinking. The teaching methods they select will be those that best help students reach these goals.

Axiology

Axiology is a branch of philosophy that considers values and ethics, and axiological issues are now prominent in American education. For example, surveys indicate that 75 percent of high school students have admitted to cheating on tests (Bracey, 2005), and cheating appears to be on the rise from elementary school through college (Goodman, 2005; Selingo, 2004).

Substantial numbers of students express concerns about bullying and their safety in schools (Schlozman, 2002). Outside schools, the corporate scandals that led to the collapse of businesses such as Enron and WorldCom, and questionable accounting practices in other companies, have sent shock waves through the business community and American society in general. Rampant greed and a sense that "if you can get away with it, it's okay," seem to be the "moral" principles of the day. The American public is increasingly looking to education for solutions to problems such as these (Rose & Gallup, 2000).

How does axiology influence teachers? Let's look again at Allie's and Brad's conversation. Allie argued, "I'm getting paid to help kids learn. If I don't do my very best to make that happen, I'm not earning my salary." Brad retorted that "it would be a heck of a lot easier to just make the kids cram some stuff in their heads, but I would be doing them, their parents, and ultimately our whole society a disservice if I didn't try to prepare them for life outside school." Both teachers argued that they wouldn't be behaving ethically if they weren't true to their beliefs about what is important in terms of values. This part of their conversation was concerned with axiology.

Logic

Some of Allie's comments to Brad demonstrate a particular thinking process. Although these are not Allie's exact words, the following statements represent her sequence of thoughts:

"The more people learn, the more intrinsically motivated they become."
"You [Brad] have learned a lot about technology."
"Because you've learned a lot about technology, you're more intrinsically motivated to learn more."

Metaphysics (ontology). The branch of philosophy that considers *what* we know.

Axiology. The branch of philosophy that considers values and ethics.

Logic is a branch of philosophy that examines the processes of deriving valid conclusions from basic principles, and Allie was illustrating a form of logic called *deductive reasoning*. Deductive reasoning begins with a proposition, called a major premise, which could be a principle or generalization such as "The more people learn, the more intrinsically motivated they are." The major premise is followed by a fact, called a minor premise, such as "You have learned a lot about technology." A deductive reasoning sequence ends with a conclusion that follows from the two premises. In Allie's case the conclusion was an explanation for why Brad was interested in technology.

Inductive reasoning is the counterpart to deductive reasoning. For instance, when students see several cases of a heavy object and a light object, such as a baseball and a paper clip, dropped simultaneously from the same height, hit the floor at the same time, they conclude that objects fall at the same rate regardless of weight (if air resistance is negligible). On the basis of the specific instances (e.g., dropping the paper clip and baseball), the students make a general conclusion about falling objects.

Logic helps both teachers and learners examine the validity of their thinking. For instance, in social studies we try to help students see that if we stereotype a specific cultural group based on the behavior or appearance of a few members of the group, we're using faulty inductive reasoning. Similarly, many controversies in education and other aspects of life exist because proponents and critics disagree on the validity of conclusions that are derived from deductive reasoning. For example, many advocates of charter schools conclude that they do a better job of educating students than our traditional public schools (Nathan, 2005). (We discuss charter schools in Chapter 8.) They base this argument on the premise that any system with a large bureaucracy is ineffective (a major premise), and our public schools, with their many layers of administration, are bureaucratic and inefficient (a minor premise). So, the critics conclude that charter schools are more effective. Supporters of public schools disagree with both the major premise and the conclusion (Colgan, 2004; Hess, 2004b). Other controversies involve similar disagreements between premises and conclusions.

Making Connections:
To deepen your
CW understanding of the
topics in this section of the
chapter and integrate them
with topics you've already
studied, go to the *Making
Connections* module for
Chapter 6 at
www.prenhall.com/kauchak.
Respond to questions 3–6.

Check Your Understanding

2.1   Describe each of the branches of philosophy.

2.2   Allie said, "I'm getting paid to help kids learn. If I don't do my best to make that happen, I'm not earning my salary." This comment best illustrates which branch of philosophy? Explain your answer.

2.3   Two teachers are in a discussion, and one says, "Everything we know depends on experience. So, the key is providing lots of experiences in the classroom. If we provide them with enough experiences, they'll learn." To which of the branches of philosophy is this person's statement most closely related? Explain your answer.

2.4   "That doesn't quite make sense," a teacher diplomatically comments to a colleague. "You said that your kids are so unmotivated, but last week you said that kids basically want to learn. . . . Those two don't fit." To which of the branches of philosophy is this person's comment most closely related? Explain your answer.

Logic. The branch of philosophy that examines the processes of deriving valid conclusions from basic principles.

For feedback, go to Appendix A, Check Your Understanding, *located in the back of this text.*

Traditional Schools of Philosophy

Throughout history, philosophers have struggled to systematically describe how the world works; that is, they've tried to answer questions about reality and what is real (metaphysics), how we know (epistemology), what is good and valuable (axiology), and whether or not our thinking is clear and accurate (logic). These efforts have resulted in four cohesive philosophies, considered by many to be the traditional philosophies that undergird most educational decisions (Jacobsen, 2003):

- Idealism
- Realism
- Pragmatism
- Existentialism

We turn to them now.

Idealism

Consider one of Brad's arguments in his conversation with Allie:

[L]et's say that, based on this conversation, you conclude that I'm naive and idealistic. On the other hand, I conclude that I'm actually more practical than you are. . . . What is the reality? Am I naive, or am I practical? . . . To you, I'm naive, and you will operate based on that belief. To me I'm not. So, reality is what we perceive it to be, and there's no objective source out there to decide which view is the "right one."

Brad was making an argument consistent with **idealism**, a traditional philosophy asserting that, because the physical world is constantly changing, ideas are the only reliable form of reality. Having originated with Plato, the great Greek philosopher, idealism is the oldest of the Western philosophies.

To idealists, ultimate reality exists in the world of ideas—hence the term *idealism*, so ideas should be the focus of teaching and learning. A curriculum based on idealism emphasizes mathematics, because of its logic, precision, and abstraction, together with great works of literature, art, and music, because of their enduring contributions. Great men and women in history are studied in order to examine their thinking and the ideas they offered.

Teachers fill an essential role for idealists. Learners are unlikely to understand many important ideas without support and guidance. Teachers provide this guidance by helping students become more precise and logical thinkers and by helping them understand the important ideas that have endured throughout history.

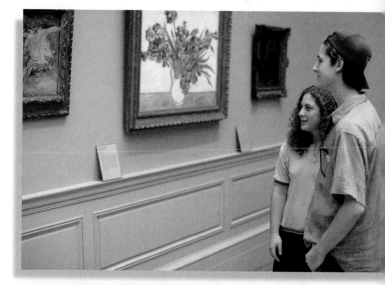

Idealism emphasizes great works of literature, music, and art, which contain powerful ideas from important contributors to our culture. (Robert Brenner/PhotoEdit Inc.)

Idealism has been criticized for being elitist and overemphasizing cold, detached topics at the expense of human emotions and intuition. It is elitist, critics argue, because the ideas chosen for analysis often come from a small, wealthy, and privileged part of the population. It is considered coldly cognitive because it emphasizes the rational and logical over other dimensions of human experience such as feelings and emotions.

Realism

In contrast with idealism, which argues that ideas are the ultimate reality, **realism** holds that the features of the universe exist whether or not a human being is there to perceive them. Realism is also an ancient philosophy, originating from the work of Aristotle and others.

Idealism. A traditional philosophy asserting that ideas are the only reliable form of reality.

Realism. A traditional philosophy suggesting that the features of the universe exist whether or not a human being is there to perceive them.

Allie's thinking in the following statements is consistent with realism: "[L]ook at that oak tree outside the window. You can perceive it to be anything you want, but it's still an oak. And it doesn't matter what anybody thinks, two plus two is four—not three, not five, not anything else." Realists argue that there are important ideas and facts that must be understood and that they can only be understood by studying the material world. Realists emphasize science and technology and strongly endorse the scientific method. They argue that ignorance of information about diet, disease, and natural disasters, for example, has caused much of the suffering in human history and that accumulation of knowledge in areas such as science and medicine has improved the quality of life for many people.

A curriculum consistent with realism emphasizes essentials, such as math, science, reading, and writing, because they are tools to help us understand our world. Critics who claim that American education is in decline because the curriculum has been "dumbed down" with too many superfluous courses and too much emphasis on self-esteem are also expressing views consistent with realism. The periodic refocus on basic skills in our schools is also consistent with this view.

Teachers working within the philosophy of realism emphasize observation, experimentation, and critical reasoning. Their goals are for learners to think clearly and understand the material world. They tend to de-emphasize formal emphasis on feelings and other personal factors, arguing that positive feelings and the improvement of self-esteem are an outgrowth of knowledge and understanding.

Critics of realism, like those who criticize idealism, argue that the philosophy is inappropriately narrow. It fails to account for the whole person—physical, emotional, and social, in addition to intellectual—in the learning process.

Pragmatism

Although it has ancient roots, pragmatism is considered a modern—even American—philosophy, with John Dewey (1902, 1906, 1923, 1938) being one of its primary proponents. **Pragmatism** is a traditional philosophy that rejects the idea of absolute, unchanging truth, instead asserting that truth is "what works." The term *pragmatism* shares a root with *pragmatic*, which means "practical" in common usage. Pragmatism shares some views with realism but is less rigid, advocating change when conditions warrant. For example, our primitive ancestors needed and ate a diet high in fat, because it might be a long time between meals, and they were very active as hunters-gatherers. Now, we have a problem. Our evolved selves still enjoy—even crave—fat, but we no longer need as much because we've become sedentary. Long ago, truth was that fat was important and healthy; today, truth is, fat is less important and too much is unhealthy. A high-fat diet no longer "works."

For pragmatists, experience is a key idea. As we've gathered experiences with respect to diet, for example, we've observed the consequences of those experiences and have adapted (or are trying to adapt) accordingly. Pragmatists contend that truth isn't an abstract idea, nor is it simply a material aspect of the world. Rather, it represents the interaction between the individual and the environment. Further, truth is personal and relative. Some people, for example, need more fat in their diets than do others.

Pragmatists attempt to connect subject matter to children's interests.
(Anthony Magnacca/Merrill)

Pragmatism. A traditional philosophy that rejects the idea of absolute, unchanging truth, instead asserting that truth is "what works."

Because truth changes, individuals need methods for dealing with these changes. As a result, teachers adhering to pragmatism place the processes involved in learning on an equal plane with content. Direct experiences and problem solving are emphasized. Information needed to solve problems comes from many sources, so studying content areas in isolation isn't effective or practical; interdisciplinary education that focuses on using various academic disciplines to analyze and solve problems is more "pragmatic." In addition, lectures focusing on abstract ideas are rejected in favor of hands-on, concrete experiences.

Critics contend that pragmatism too strongly emphasizes student interests at the expense of essential knowledge (Weiss, DeFalco, & Weiss, 2005). A conservative faction blames pragmatism, with its educational counterpart, progressivism (discussed later in the chapter), for the decline in performance by American students as compared to students in other industrialized countries. Defenders counter that pragmatism doesn't de-emphasize the importance of knowledge but instead attempts to connect it to children's interests.

Existentialism

Compared to idealism, realism, and pragmatism, existentialism is quite radical. **Existentialism** is a traditional philosophy suggesting that humanity isn't part of an orderly universe; rather, individuals create their own realities in their own unique ways. Influenced by the horrors of World War II, existentialist writers, such as Jean-Paul Sartre, hold a pessimistic view of humanity, seeing it as essentially meaningless on a small, isolated planet in an uncertain universe where nothing is determined. If nothing is determined, people have total freedom—freedom to take advantage of others, promote racial strife, or cause conflicts, for example. Conversely, we're also free to conduct ourselves morally and to promote peace and harmony. With total freedom comes total responsibility. Unwise choices can't be blamed on God's will, other people, or prior experiences.

Existentialism makes a contribution to education because it places primary emphasis on the individual, and in doing so, it reminds us that we don't teach math, science, reading, and writing; rather, we teach people, and the people we teach are at the core of learning.

Existentialists would have us change our attitudes about education. Education isn't something a student is filled with and then tested for; rather, it is an individual's search for personal understanding. Existentialist educators decry tracking, testing, and standardization, arguing that these practices detract from individuals' opportunities for growth. Schools, they suggest, should be places where students are free to engage in activities because these activities are interesting and help them define who they are.

Whereas science and technology are important for realists and pragmatists, existentialists place more emphasis on the humanities, because these studies examine the human struggle for meaning, relationships between people, and tragedy as well as triumph.

Existentialism has influenced the thinking of humanistic educators, such as Carl Rogers (1967) and Abraham Maslow (1968, 1970), who advocate a learner-centered and nondirective approach to education. Empathy is an important teacher characteristic, and teachers, they argue, should care for their students unconditionally, helping them feel like worthy individuals. In their quest for meaning, teachers should be students, and students should be teachers. Current emphases on communities of learners, in which teachers and students work together to accomplish learning goals, are consistent with this view.

Applying the Traditional Philosophies in Classrooms

How do the traditional philosophies influence teaching? To answer this question, let's listen to a conversation among a group of teachers relaxing in the workroom after school one day.

"I love this time of the year," Greg Chiesa, an English teacher, comments. "I'm going to have my kids read Moby Dick, *and then* Les Misérables. *You wouldn't think the kids would be that crazy about them, but they really get into the discussions of good and evil that Melville examines with Captain Ahab and the white whale, and they also like the whole morality issue in* Les Misérables. *I think they're attracted to dealing with these kinds of issues. Good and evil will always be with us, so they're always new."*

> **Existentialism.** A traditional philosophy suggesting that humanity isn't part of an orderly universe; rather, individuals create their own realities.

"I also have my history classes think about good and evil," Jaclyn Holt, a colleague, responds. "So, were we good or were we evil when we dropped the atomic bomb on Hiroshima and Nagasaki in World War II? Some people argue that we saved a lot of lives by dropping the bombs, but others describe it as a quantum leap forward in man's inhumanity to man. I have my kids spend a couple periods discussing that issue and the related issue of wars in general, but I don't try to impose my views on them. I want them to understand that we, as people, are ultimately responsible for what we make of life, and the same thing applies to nations. It may seem like pie in the sky, but I want the kids to grapple with the ideas and think about whether or not wars are justified and if we were right to drop the bombs."

"That sounds nice, but I want kids to examine those kinds of issues in depth, doing their own research and coming up with their own answers. That's why I put my students in teams and let them use the Internet to research important questions," Justin Bruinsma, another history teacher, adds.

"You people are too far out for me," Edna Chatman, a math and physics teacher, says, laughing. "I admit that I'm biased because I'm a math and science teacher, but I spend most of my time trying to help the kids learn important skills and develop their critical thinking so they won't be duped by propaganda and promotions when they're out in the real world. Making conclusions based on evidence is what I spend most of my time on."

As we said at the beginning of the chapter, philosophy may seem distant and abstract, since you're early in your teacher preparation program. However, in this case study, teachers' philosophical views guided their decisions about how to spend classroom time, which then influenced what and how much their students learned. Greg, for example, decided to have his students read classic literature, because it dealt with timeless issues, such as good and evil. He made this decision based on a personal philosophy grounded in idealism. Jaclyn's thinking was a bit different. She too was interested in a moral issue—whether or not the United States was justified in dropping atomic bombs in World War II—but her goal was for students to make decisions about the issues on their own. Her decision about the most appropriate way to deal with the topic was more nearly grounded in existentialism.

Justin held another view, and it also influenced his instructional decisions. Because he took a pragmatic view of knowledge, he had his students involved in problem-solving activities, and he used the Internet as a tool. Finally, Edna's focus on essential knowledge and critical thinking was grounded in realism.

These examples show that it is important to begin thinking about questions raised by the traditional philosophies. This thinking will help you begin to make decisions about what you believe is important for students to learn and how you'll help them learn it. It will also help you acquire the specialized knowledge you need to make professional decisions in your teaching. Differences among the traditional philosophies are summarized in Table 6.1.

Making Connections:
To deepen your understanding of the topics in this section of the chapter and integrate them with topics you've already studied, go to the *Making Connections* module for Chapter 6 at **www.prenhall.com/kauchak**. Respond to questions 7 and 8.

TABLE 6.1 The Traditional Schools of Philosophy

	Idealism	Realism	Pragmatism	Existentialism
Metaphysics	Reality is the world of unchanging ideas.	Reality is the physical world.	Reality is the interaction of the individual and the environment.	Reality is the subjective interpretation of the physical world.
Epistemology	Knowing is the personal rethinking of universal ideas.	Knowing is observing and understanding natural laws.	Knowing is the result of experience based on the scientific method.	Knowing is making personal choice.
Axiology	Values are absolute based on enduring ideas.	Values are absolute based on natural law.	Values are relative.	Values are chosen by the individual.
Educational implications	Curricula focus on content that emphasizes time-honored ideas.	Curricula focus on content that emphasizes natural laws.	Curricula and instruction focus on problem solving and the scientific method.	Instruction emphasizes discussion designed to increase individual self-awareness.

exploring diversity

Philosophy and Cultural Minorities

To this point in the chapter, the philosophies we've examined have been "Western," meaning their origins are European or American. Two principles undergird this Western orientation: The preeminence of the individual and the emphasis on rationale thought. The first is seen in the individual's search for truth in both idealism and realism, the interaction of the individual with the environment in pragmatism, and the individual's search for meaning in existentialism. The second is reflected in the emphasis on objectivity, science, and the scientific method. Realism and pragmatism, in particular, emphasize science as a way of knowing.

Some philosophers criticize this emphasis on science and objectivity and point to its undesirable consequences in American life. Americans are working more hours per week than they ever have in the past, technology dominates our lives, and we are chronically sleep deprived, for example. Critics of this Western orientation assert that valuable alternatives can be found in the philosophies of other cultures.

Some philosophies, such as those embedded in certain Native American cultures, use the shared folklore of elders and knowledge that comes from the heart as their sources of wisdom (Starnes, 2006). Because people in these cultures have a long history of living in harmony with the land, their philosophies emphasize ecological balance and interpersonal cooperation. This emphasis results in valuing individual achievement primarily as it contributes to a group's overall well-being. Competition and individual displays of achievement are frowned upon. Understanding these differences can help explain why Navajo students, for example, are sometimes reluctant to participate in the competitive verbal give-and-take of fast-paced questioning sessions that require individuals to demonstrate how much they know (Starnes, 2006).

Similarly, for some African cultures, feelings and personal relationships are equally or more important ways of knowing than are science and rational thought (Nieto, 2004). Further, in many African cultures, art and music are important means not only of expression but also of seeking knowledge. This philosophical view helps explain why music was such a prominent part of slaves' lives in America, why African-Americans have made such a strong contribution to modern and impressionistic art, and why African influences can be seen in much of the contemporary music in Europe and the Americas.

Many Asians also value harmony. The desire to balance nature, life, family, and society leads to reverence for elders, respect for authority, and adherence to traditions. Because cooperation is so important, being polite is highly valued, and feelings and emotions tend to be controlled in order to maintain order and proper social relationships (McDermott, 1994). Awareness of these perspectives helps teachers understand characteristics commonly attributed to Asian-American students. For instance, they are often described as being shy, reluctant to speak out in class, and restrained in their nonverbal behavior, which sometimes makes reading their nonverbal cues difficult (Park, 1997).

On the other hand, we should be cautious about drawing conclusions and making decisions on the basis of these descriptions alone. Critics argue that they are little more than stereotypes that grossly oversimplify the complexities of alternative philosophies. For example, some Americans simplistically think of Africa as a country, not realizing that it is a vast continent, more culturally and linguistically diverse than North or South America. In a similar way, the term *Asian* encompasses students from a number of diverse countries and cultures, including India, China, Japan, Vietnam, and Korea. To speak of a singular "African philosophy"—or Native American or Asian philosophy, for that matter—does an injustice to diverse groups of people and their philosophies. Further, people are people, and categorizing them on the basis of sweeping and uncertain philosophical generalizations is questionable at best and perhaps even potentially damaging (Diamond, 1999).

Rather than viewing students as Hispanic, Native American, African-American, or as representative of any other cultural or ethnic group, we should see students as individuals. Concluding that a boy named Ted Chang, for example, doesn't speak out in class solely because of the influence of his Chinese culture is unwise. Getting to know Ted as an individual will better help you understand why he is quiet and will help you find ways to involve him in learning activities, just as you would try to involve any student in your classes (Banks, 2006a).

Respecting and valuing cultural differences is a good idea; making decisions that may detract from learning, based on overgeneralizations about these differences, is not. Realizing that not all people share the same philosophical orientations will help you be more sensitive to important individual differences in your students.

Check Your Understanding

3.1 Describe each of the four traditional philosophies and the educational emphasis that each would imply.

3.2 "My job is to develop writers," an English teacher asserts. "I am an English teacher, not a counselor. . . . Students must be able to write, and it's my job to be sure that they can." To which of the traditional philosophies is the teacher's efforts most closely related? Explain.

3.3 A teacher wants her students to examine racism and injustice and involves them in a unit on nonviolent noncooperation using a study of Mohandas K. Gandhi's struggles against racism in South Africa and India as an example. She further illustrates the ideas with a study of Martin Luther King, Jr.'s, nonviolent protests against American racism. To which of the traditional philosophies is the teacher's efforts most closely related? Explain.

3.4 Because students must be able to function effectively in, and adapt to, a changing world, a teacher emphasizes the "whole person"—physical, social, emotional, and intellectual—in her students. She emphasizes and models physical fitness, involves her students in discussions to help them practice social skills and perspective taking, and involves them in problem solving about modern-day topics. To which of the traditional philosophies is the teacher's efforts most closely related? Explain.

For feedback, go to Appendix A, Check Your Understanding, *located in the back of this text.*

Philosophies of Education

The traditional philosophies presented thus far are comprehensive views of life and thought; they weren't developed as philosophies of education, even though each has implications for teaching and learning. We now examine philosophies that focus specifically on education. As you analyze these philosophies, look for relationships between them and the traditional philosophies you've studied.

In this section we examine four philosophies of education:

- Perennialism
- Essentialism
- Progressivism
- Postmodernism

Perennialism

Think about the term *perennial*. It is an adjective meaning "perpetual" or "long-lasting." **Perennialism** is an educational philosophy suggesting that nature—including human nature—is constant. In this regard, perennialism has roots in both idealism and realism (Jacobsen, 2003). Both believe in the enduring and constant nature of reality; idealists believe in enduring ideas, and realists recognize the constancy of the physical universe.

Consistent with the beliefs of idealism and realism, perennialists believe in a rigorous intellectual curriculum for all students. For them, education is preparation for future life, and the extent to which students find their studies relevant isn't essential. Math, science, and literature are important in a perennialist curriculum because they expose learners to both the

Perennialism. An educational philosophy suggesting that nature—including human nature—is constant.

rigors of logical thought as well as the great ideas that have endured throughout history. The ideal perennialist curriculum would have students study classic works ranging from Homer's *Iliad* to Darwin's *The Origin of Species* (which introduced the theory of evolution), together with a host of works in between. After reading these works, students would be engaged in discussions that encourage them to analyze and evaluate the ideas expressed (Billings & Fitzgerald, 2002).

Perennialism experienced a brief renaissance in the early 1980s with the publication of Mortimer Adler's (1982) *The Paideia Proposal: An Educational Manifesto*. Adler advocated a general curriculum for all students that included math, science, history, geography, literature, and fine arts. Understanding the content of these subject areas was a means to an end, however, and not an end in itself. The goal in studying them was to develop intellectual skills, such as writing, speaking, computing, and problem solving. The content, together with these skills, would lead to higher-level thinking, reflection, and awareness.

Adler's ideas received considerable attention from the popular press, but their application in schools has been limited. Critics argued that Adler's proposals were elitist, aimed primarily at students with the highest ability (Ozmon & Craver, 2007). They also questioned the value of distant and abstract ideas for poorly motivated and intellectually unprepared students. Adler's efforts remain alive, however, with the reissue of his book (Adler, 1998) and renewed interest in student discussion and dialogue as a vehicle for learning (Billings & Fitzgerald, 2002).

Essentialism

We've all heard of "back to the basics" movements, which occur in education on a cyclical basis. "Back to the basics" means that learning should focus on basic skills, such as reading, writing, mathematics, and to a certain extent, science and geography. (Many educational leaders now include technological literacy as a basic skill.) People who support "back to the basics" movements periodically write newspaper editorials sounding the alarm about American students' ignorance of the world around them, their inability to communicate either orally or in writing, and their lack of ability to do rudimentary math (Ravitch, 2000).

These views are consistent with **essentialism**, an educational philosophy suggesting that a critical core of knowledge and skills exists that all people should possess. They also address the fifth item on the survey at the beginning of the chapter, "Teachers' primary goals should be to help students master essential content rather than to help students develop emotionally and socially." People who adhere to an essentialist philosophy would strongly agree with this statement.

Essentialists want to ensure that the educational system produces a literate and skilled workforce able to compete in a technological society. They are concerned about a general "dumbing down" of the curriculum, they decry social promotion of students, and they are wary of student-centered instruction.

Many of the reform efforts over the last 20 or more years have arisen from essentialist views. In the 1980s, reform was spurred by *A Nation at Risk* (National Commission on Excellence in Education, 1983), the widely publicized report that recommended that all high school students master core requirements in five "basics"—English, math, science, social studies, and computer science. The federal No Child Left Behind Act of 2001 (Christie, 2005; Popham, 2004b) drives many of the changes occurring in schools today; it emphasizes the basic skills of reading and math and uses extensive testing as an accountability tool.

Essentialist philosophy is also found in teacher education programs. As a prospective teacher, you will be required to take a specified sequence of courses, and it is likely that you'll be expected to demonstrate mastery of essential teaching skills on a standardized test, either the Praxis™ Series, which we discussed in Chapter 1, or a state-specific test. This emphasis is so significant that we have included a "Preparing for Your Licensure Exam" section at the end of each chapter of this text. These requirements reflect the belief that a core of knowledge exists that all preservice teachers should master.

> **Essentialism.** An educational philosophy suggesting that a critical core of knowledge and skills exists that all people should possess.

Essentialism and perennialism share the view that knowledge and understanding are preeminent, and both are wary of educational trends, such as learner-centered education, integrated curricula, and a focus on learner self-esteem. Essentialists don't share perennialists' emphasis on universal truths through the study of classical literature, however. Instead, they emphasize knowledge and skills that are useful in today's world.

Progressivism focuses on real-world problem solving and individual student development. (Tony Freeman/PhotoEdit Inc.)

Because of its emphasis on practical, usable knowledge, the essentialist curriculum is more likely to change than is the perennialist curriculum. For instance, as our society becomes more diverse and researchers better understand how diversity affects learning, teacher preparation programs place increasing emphasis on working effectively with learners from diverse backgrounds. This means you will likely take a course in multicultural education or that topics in this area will be included in your other courses. This emphasis wouldn't have existed 20 years ago. The same is true for technology; most teacher education programs now have some type of technology component. These shifts in emphasis reflect essentialist thinking.

Progressivism

To begin our discussion of this topic, let's join a group of urban middle school teachers as they talk over lunch.

"I'm having a heck of a time motivating my students," Kelly Erhardt, *a first-year English teacher, confesses in the teachers' lounge. "I just can't get them excited about the stuff I have to teach."*

"Welcome to teaching," Dan Shafer, *a third-year "veteran," replies. "Or maybe I should say, welcome to middle school teaching. It's a real challenge. They have to see how it applies to their lives, or they have trouble getting into it. I don't know the secret, but I did have a good lesson on maps yesterday.*

"I told them we'd be working with maps all year, so understanding scale was an important idea they'd use, not only in class, but also in real life. Then, I asked how many of them have read a map on a family trip? Quite a few had. I showed them a map of our state and talked about scale. Next, I brought out a map of the United States, and we talked about the different scale. I broke students into groups, and each group had to construct a map of the room, decide on a scale, and present it to the class. Some of the groups were a little disorganized, but they're learning how to work together.

"Towards the end of the class, I had each of them begin a map of their own home that they could finish for homework. Tomorrow, if the weather cooperates, we'll go outside and make a map of our school grounds."

"That does sound like fun," Kelly *responded. "I wish we had done something like that when I studied maps. All we did was listen to the teacher talking."*

"Can't do that, or you'll lose them," Mary Burbank, *the science and health teacher, and a 10-year veteran, joins in. "Again, I don't claim to know how to motivate these kids, but I did have a decent class last week. I started with a quick trip to the cafeteria, where the staff was preparing that day's lunch.*

"When we got back to our classroom, I said, 'I know you often make jokes about cafeteria food, but I think we could all learn something important about our diets if we look at the kinds of food our cafeteria is serving and compare it to our daily diets. So, to start, I want each of you to write down everything you ate or drank yesterday, starting with breakfast. Share this with a partner and come up with one positive and one not-so-positive thing from the two lists. We'll share these with the whole

class. Then, I'm going to collect these and put them all together to analyze later. Also, later this week we'll have Mrs. Henderson, the school dietician, come in to talk about how she plans school meals. Then, we'll share with her the foods you eat and ask her to comment on your diets.' "

"You're brave," Kelly responded. "Do you really want to know what they eat? But, maybe we'd find out why they're so squirrelly."

"Squirrelly? You're starting to sound like a 10-year veteran," Mary laughed. "But really, they have to see how ideas relate to their lives. If I started out lecturing about principles of nutrition, I'd have them sleeping in their seats or dying in the aisles. Your challenge is to fund out how to make English important to them. If I knew more about English, I'd tell you myself. But you're a smart kid; you'll figure it out."

Think for a minute about the advice Kelly's colleagues gave her. None of the activities involved students' listening passively while teachers lectured; instead, the teachers played a central role in involving students in motivating learning activities. These activities reflect the emphasis placed on learner thinking and involvement that we see in many classrooms today (Bransford et al., 2005; Eggen & Kauchak, 2007).

These practices are rooted in **progressivism**, an educational philosophy emphasizing curricula that focus on real-world problem solving and individual development. People adhering to progressivism would disagree with the fifth item on our chapter's opening survey, which said, "Teachers' primary goals should be to help students master essential content rather than to help students develop emotionally and socially." They would argue that social and emotional development and learning to cooperate in groups are also important goals.

In our chapter's opening case study, Brad expressed views consistent with progressivism:

[T]he person who really succeeds is the one who continues to learn and is able to adapt to changes in the world by solving the large and small problems they encounter. . . . They need lots of experience in making decisions and solving problems. That's how I think the world works.

In our discussion of epistemology, we briefly examined the constructivist view that, instead of recording understanding, students construct it based on their experiences and prior knowledge. Constructivism is consistent with progressivism and its precursor, pragmatism. All three emphasize concrete experiences, real-world tasks, and the central role of the individual in determining reality and promoting learning. As you analyze learning in educational psychology, you will undoubtedly study constructivism in detail. As you do, remember that it's rooted in pragmatism and progressivism.

Progressivism and pragmatism are grounded in the work of John Dewey (1923, 1938), which, as you saw earlier in the chapter, continues to be debated today. Because of its influence on American education, let's briefly look at the history of the progressive movement in this country.

The Progressive Era in American History

From 1890 to 1920, the American educational system experienced dramatic growth (Pulliam & Van Patten, 2007). School enrollments, fueled by accessibility and compulsory attendance laws, increased 70 percent, and the number of teachers grew by 80 percent.

During this period of growth, educators began to reexamine schooling practices. They questioned the value of teacher-centered instruction that asked students to passively absorb information. John Dewey was at the center of this reform movement. Dewey wrote extensively on education, and his work has arguably had more impact on American education than that of any other philosopher. His ideas continue to be actively debated by educators today (e.g., Durst, 2005; Johnston, 2004; Rogers & Oaks, 2005).

Dewey first encountered progressive teaching practices through his children, who attended an experimental lab school in Chicago. He became so fascinated with student-centered teaching that in 1896 he established his own lab school connected to the University of Chicago, where he worked. The school became the birthplace of progressive education, which gained prominence during the early to mid-20th century. Progressive education advocated the learner-centered curriculum and individual problem solving that we saw illustrated at Kelly's middle school in the case study at the beginning of this section and in Brad's views in his discussion with Allie. For Dewey, classrooms became microcosms of a democratic society. Goals such as personal growth

Progressivism. An educational philosophy emphasizing curricula that focus on real-world problem solving and individual development.

and preparation for participation in a democracy were met through an activity-oriented curriculum. Content, which historically was an end in itself, now became a tool for problem solving.

Dewey's ideas created both excitement and criticism. To some, seeing learners actively involved in solving real-world problems was exciting. To others, progressive education seemed to de-emphasize content and cater to student whims.

Interest in progressive education as a general movement waned after the mid-20th century, caused by a well-intentioned but misguided attempt at fostering *life adjustment* courses such as "Developing an Effective Personality" and "Marriage and Living," which were attacked by critics who complained that they were devoid of content and lacked intellectual rigor (Norris, 2004). These criticisms, combined with the furor caused by Russia's launching of the Sputnik satellite in 1957, which, to critics, symbolized America's educational decline, resulted in the end of the progressive movement.

While the general movement declined, aspects of progressive education are alive and well today, as you saw illustrated in the activities that Dan and Mary created for their middle school students, and the emphasis on students as actively constructing their own understanding of the topics they study (Bruning, Schraw, Norby, & Ronning, 2004), which we discussed earlier in the chapter.

As in the past, teaching practices consistent with progressivism remain controversial. Critics contend that knowledge and understanding have been sacrificed because of too much emphasis placed on children's interests and self-esteem. They argue that a body of essential knowledge exists and that all students must master that knowledge in order to function effectively in society (Adler, 1998; Hirsch, 2005, 2006). The focus on standards and high-stakes testing that is so prominent in this country today is consistent with the critics' views.

Those who defend Dewey's ideas argue that the critics either misrepresent Dewey or don't understand him (Engel & Martin, 2005; Weiss, DeFalco, & Weiss, 2005).

He saw clearly that to ask, "Which is more important: the interests of the child or the knowledge of subject-matter?" was to ask a very dumb question indeed. The teacher's task, for Dewey, was to create an interaction between the child's interest and the funded knowledge of the adult world (Proefriedt, 1999, p. 28).

Dewey didn't de-emphasize knowledge and understanding in favor of student interests, his defenders assert. They argue that progressivism—when properly applied—suggests that effective education isn't a matter of process *or* content; it is a matter of process *and* content (Johnston, 2004; Weiss, DeFalco, & Weiss, 2005).

Postmodernism

During the 1960s, the United States went through major cultural upheavals. The Vietnam War was unpopular, and many Americans, even those outside the anti-war movement, grew skeptical of authority and leadership. Other trends, such as the civil rights movement, the rise of feminism, and gay and lesbian crusades, encouraged critiques of American culture, society, and education. Postmodern philosophy emerged among these critiques.

Postmodernism is an educational philosophy contending that many of the institutions in our society, including schools, are used by those in power to control and marginalize those who lack power. The powerful are typically White males, and those marginalized (lacking power) are unskilled workers, women, and cultural minorities. The curricula in elementary, secondary, and postsecondary schools, postmodernists argue, are racist, sexist, and imperialist.

As an example, postmodernists target the continued curricular emphasis on the study of Shakespeare, which is prominent in most high school literature programs. Emphasis on Shakespeare and other White male authors has resulted in little room left for literature written by women, minorities, or people from other cultures. Because White males on school

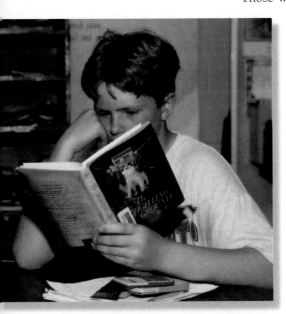

Postmodern philosophy raises questions about culture and gender bias in our schools.
(Anthony Magnacca/Merrill)

Postmodernism. An educational philosophy contending that many of the institutions in our society, including schools, are used by those in power to control and marginalize those who lack power.

boards and in district offices make curricular decisions, marginalizing those without power continues unabated.

A postmodern curriculum would reverse these trends. Literature written by women and cultural minorities would be elevated to a position as, or more, prominent than traditional literature. Further, traditional literature would be critically examined to see how it has historically shaped our notions of race, gender, and other differences among people. Issues such as the use of power, personal and group identities, cultural politics, and social criticism would enjoy prominent positions. Historical events would be examined from the perspective of power, status, and the struggles of marginalized groups in those contexts (Abowitz, 2000). For instance, Columbus's arrival in the New World has historically been presented as a critical point in the beginning of modern history in North and South America. Postmodernism recognizes that fact but emphasizes the brutalization of Native Americans by the Spaniards, the ravaging of the indigenous people by European diseases such as smallpox (for which Native Americans had no natural immunities), their enslavement, and the fact that conquering and colonization were two major goals for explorers.

Postmodernism has sparked hot debate. As postmodernists have risen to positions of power in some universities, for example, the study of Shakespeare and other time-honored American and British authors has decreased or been eliminated from the curriculum, whereas the study of female and minority authors and cultural issues has proliferated. This has caused outrage among perennialist and essentialist thinkers. They argue that postmodernism has resulted in the abandonment of schools as places for intellectual pursuits, instead using them for political purposes. They contend further that postmodernism is as control-oriented as traditional philosophies and institutions; it merely wants to establish controls more to their liking (Ozmon & Craver, 2007).

Classroom applications of the educational philosophies are summarized in Table 6.2.

Making Connections:
To deepen your understanding of the topics in this section of the chapter and integrate them with topics you've already studied, go to the *Making Connections* module for Chapter 6 at **www.prenhall.com/kauchak**. Respond to questions 9–13.

TABLE 6.2   Classroom Applications of the Educational Philosophies

	Perennialism	Essentialism	Progressivism	Postmodernism
Traditional Philosophy Most Closely Related	Idealism, realism	Idealism, realism	Pragmatism	Existentialism
Educational Goals	Train the intellect; moral development	Acquire basic skills; acquire knowledge needed to function in today's world	Acquire ability to function in the real world; develop problem-solving skills	Critically examine today's institutions; elevate the status of marginalized people (women and cultural minorities)
Curriculum	Emphasis on enduring ideas	Emphasis on basic skills	Emphasis on problem solving and skills needed in today's world	Emphasis on the works of marginalized people
Role of the Teacher	Deliver clear lectures; increase student understanding with critical questions	Deliver clear lectures; increase student understanding with critical questions	Guide learning with questioning; develop and guide practical problem-solving activities	Facilitate discussions that involve clarifying issues
Teaching Methods	Lecture; questioning; coaching in intellectual thinking	Lecture; practice and feedback; questioning	Problem-based learning; cooperative learning; guided discovery	Discussion; role play; simulation; personal research
Learning Environment	High structure; high levels of time on task	High structure; high levels of time on task	Collaborative; self-regulated; democratic	Community-oriented; self-regulated
Assessment	Frequent objective and essay tests	Frequent objective, essay, and performance tests	Continuous feedback; informal monitoring of student progress	Collaborative between teacher and student; emphasis on the exposure of hidden assumptions

teaching in an era of reform

Standards and Essential Knowledge

American students are being increasingly criticized for their lack of knowledge about the United States and the world. Editorial headlines, such as "Historical illiteracy plaguing many in high schools and colleges," are appearing with greater frequency. The facts cited are disheartening. For example, only 1 in 3 college seniors randomly chosen from 55 top-rated colleges and universities could identify George Washington as the American general at Yorktown, and only 22 percent could identify the Gettysburg address as the source of the words "Government of the people, by the people, for the people" (American Council of Trustees and Alumni, 2000). In another survey of 18- to 24-year-olds, six in ten respondents couldn't locate Iraq on a map of the Middle East, and about half couldn't locate New York on a map of the United States (Manzo, 2006b). The situation is no better in math. For example, one study revealed that only 54 percent of American fifth graders were able to solve the problem $45 \times 26 = ?$ (Stigler et al., 1999).

Research on learning indicates that prior knowledge is essential for developing understanding of new content (Bruning et al., 2004; Eggen & Kauchak, 2007). In essence, all new learning builds on what learners already know. For instance, to understand the civil unrest in the United States during the 1960s, students need to understand the relationships among people's growing distrust of government and authority, the civil rights movement, and the Vietnam War. Similarly, to understand the problems of sub-Saharan Africa, learners must also understand European colonialism, as well as the geography and climate of this vast area. New knowledge builds on prior knowledge, and when this knowledge is lacking, learning is decreased.

In response to criticisms about American students' lack of knowledge, educators have written standards (which we discussed in Chapter 1), in virtually every content area. Experts in this area call standards "essential questions: doorways to understanding" (Wiggins & McTigh, 2005, p. 105). Every state has specified stan-

dards, and to hold students and schools accountable, they have created tests to measure the extent to which the standards are being met. As you also saw in Chapter 1, the federal No Child Left Behind Act of 2001 requires all states to create standards for what every child should understand about different subjects (Christie, 2005; Popham, 2004b). Standards apply to teachers as well: 39 states now require teachers to pass exams in order to be licensed.

The Issue

Leaders who support standards believe that all people should master certain well-defined skills and bodies of knowledge, a view grounded in essentialist educational philosophy. Specifying standards and then testing students to ensure that the standards are being met is one way to ensure that students are acquiring the essential knowledge and skills, they argue. E. D. Hirsch (1987), author of the controversial but widely read book *Cultural Literacy: What Every American Needs to Know,* illustrates this position. Hirsch identified a vast list of facts, concepts, and other information that he believed all citizens should know in order to function effectively in American society. Since then, he has produced a series of edited paperbacks that he describes as *The Core Knowledge* curriculum. Hirsch has written books such as *What Your Fourth Grader Needs to Know: Fundamentals of a Good Fourth-Grade Education* (Hirsch, 2005), and similar titles for each of the grade levels K–6, and he designed these for use by both teachers and parents.

Citizens agree that knowledge is important and that our young people lack it. Hirsch's *Core Knowledge* series is popular with both parents and teachers, and many reviewers have responded positively to it.

Critics argue, however, that Hirsch's series focuses on rote memory rather than understanding, and they further assert that having students memorize more facts is an approach that has been tried and proven unsuccessful. For example, K–12 students already are exposed to a great deal of American history (they take at least one American history course during middle school and another in high school, plus smatterings during their elementary years). But, critics note, they apparently retain little of the content, as indicated by the survey results cited earlier. So the issue is more complex than simply requiring more content and courses. Students apparently aren't learning from the courses they do take.

Critics of the essential knowledge position also cite research indicating that personal motivation and the ability to use strategies to acquire knowledge are better predictors of later success than is the accumulation of facts (Berliner, 2004; Mc-Caslin & Good, 1996).

Critics also question whether increased knowledge makes people happier and more productive workers, and they cite motivational research suggesting that increasing learner readiness and eagerness to learn should be the primary goals of schools (Pintrich & Schunk, 2002). This position is more consistent with pragmatism and progressivism than with essentialism.

The essential knowledge debate raises important questions about curriculum—what is taught in schools—as well as instruction.
(Scott Cunningham/Merrill)

Finally, the question of what knowledge is "essential" is hard to determine (R. Gutiérrez, 2002). For example, is it more important to remember that Christopher Columbus "discovered America" in 1492 or that his voyage precipitated huge social and cultural changes that are still being felt today? These questions have been debated for years, and the debates will almost certainly continue. Further, the sheer amount of knowledge called for by standards is overwhelming. One testing expert commented," even if a modest number of supergeneral content standards are being used, beneath these standards there are still way too many curricular aims for teachers to successfully promote in a given year. Similarly, there are way too many curricular aims to assess in the hour or so available for the administration of any standards-based test" (Popham, 2004b, pp. 77–78).

You Take a Position

Now it's your turn to take a position on the issue. State in writing whether you favor or oppose the emphasis on essential knowledge and standards, and provide a two-page rationale for your position.

For additional references and resources, go to the Companion Website at www.prenhall.com/kauchak, then to the Teaching in an Era of Reform module for Chapter 6. You can respond online or submit your response to your instructor.

Check Your Understanding

4.1   Describe the major philosophies of education.

4.2   You walk into a classroom, and you see students working in groups on projects that they have designed and implemented. The teacher moves from group to group, making suggestions and answering questions. Which of the educational philosophies does this practice most nearly illustrate? Explain.

4.3   You visit a school, and you overhear a conversation between two teachers. One says, "I love teaching Shakespeare. His work has been studied for hundreds of years, and it's as timely now as it was then." The second retorts, "Yes, it's timely all right. It clearly demonstrates how the powerful exploited the weak simply to stay in power." The two continue an animated debate as you listen. Which educational philosophy is best illustrated by each teacher's comment? Explain.

For feedback, go to Appendix A, Check Your Understanding, *located in the back of this text.*

IN TODAY'S CLASSROOMS: VIDEO

Examining Philosophies of Teaching

Having examined both traditional and educational philosophies, you now have the opportunity to view a video of two lessons that reflect two different educational philosophies.

In the first lesson, a junior high geography teacher guides her students' analysis of a matrix containing information about different regions in the United States. In the second, a high school history teacher explores the events that led up to the Vietnam War.

To view this video, go to the *Becoming a Professional* DVD included with this text, click on *In Today's Classrooms*, and then this chapter's video: *Examining Philosophies of Teaching.* Answer the questions you'll find on the DVD.

To answer questions about the video online and receive immediate feedback, go to the Companion Website at www.prenhall.com/kauchak, then to the In Today's Classrooms *module for Chapter 6.*

Developing Your Philosophy of Education

You have now studied both the traditional and the educational philosophies. This study will help you make one of the most important decisions of your professional life: deciding what kind of teacher you want to be by forming your own philosophy of education. This decision will influence the kinds of knowledge you emphasize in your classes, the instructional decisions you make as a teacher, and the criteria you use to reflect on and analyze your teaching (see Figure 6.1).

Philosophy is also important because it will help you explain and defend your educational goals—what you will try to accomplish in your classroom. Your goals reflect the kind of teacher you want to be, and being able to explain and defend them means that you're knowledgeable and reflective.

Dialoguing with other teachers can help beginning teachers shape their own personal philosophy of education. (Getty Images–Digital Vision)

Professionals can articulate what they're doing and why. For instance, if you walk into classrooms, see students involved in basic skills activities, and ask the teachers why they selected these activities, professionals will give you clear and specific answers. They will likely answer that the activities will help the students acquire core knowledge and skills that learners need to function effectively in the world. This reflects an essentialist philosophy. Some teachers, however, do activities simply because the activities are next in the text or curriculum guide sequence or because they did the activities last year. These are inadequate and unprofessional reasons.

If teachers are clear about their philosophies, they can make systematic changes when they conclude that their instruction needs improvement. If their philosophies aren't clear, they are less likely to make needed changes, or they make changes at random. In either case, professional growth doesn't occur. This is a major reason professionals make decisions grounded in philosophy.

As you begin to form your personal philosophy, keep three ideas in mind. First, any philosophy is evolving and dynamic. This means that it will change and be refined as you learn and gather experience. So don't be concerned if your philosophy is initially uncertain; it will crystallize and become clearer as you think about and use it. Second, your personal philosophy is likely to include elements of more than one traditional or educational philosophy. Third, be willing to change your views. People have a tendency to cling to the first ideas they form; they then feel that changing their minds is a sign of weakness or fuzzy thinking. Nothing could be further from the truth. In fact, changing your views is an indicator of the open-mindedness necessary for personal and professional growth.

The Role of Beliefs in a Philosophy of Education

Early in the chapter we said that philosophy provides a framework for thinking, and it guides professional practice. To begin establishing this framework for thinking, first try to identify your own beliefs. Allie and Brad both did a good job of describing their beliefs about teaching and learning. Allie's comments, in particular, show that her beliefs were well thought out:

"They [kids] don't come to school with the same . . . desire to learn as they once did."
"[T]hey want to believe they did learn something when they're finished with a topic, or class."
"[T]hey're not intrinsically motivated."
"I do believe that kids feel good when they learn something, particularly if it's challenging."

"[T]he more they know about a topic, the better they like it."
"[T]here's real, practical stuff out there that they need to know, and there's only one way they're gonna learn it. . . . That's practice and experience."

The following questions might help you get started in the process of identifying your own beliefs.

- What is the purpose of schooling? For example, should students focus on content, or is the development of self-concept, interpersonal skills, and other personal qualities more important?
- Are students basically good and trustworthy, or do they need constant monitoring?
- Is motivating students part of my job, or should motivation come from within the students?
- Is my role as a teacher to pass knowledge on to students, or should I guide students as they learn on their own?
- How do people know things? Is intuition important and valuable? How important are feelings? Is evidence always, or often, necessary?
- How do students best learn? Should I push them, or should they be left largely on their own?

Examining Your Beliefs

Once identified, you should examine and analyze your beliefs. This is where philosophy and knowledge become important. How does Allie know that her beliefs are valid? Do they "feel" right? Do they make sense intuitively? Is feeling or intuition adequate to justify the belief, or must she have research evidence to indicate that they're valid? If Allie is an existentialist, intuition and feelings are perfectly acceptable in validating her beliefs. If she is a realist or a pragmatist, however, feelings and intuition are not adequate or trustworthy; she must have evidence.

From this discussion, we can see why *understanding* philosophy is important. For instance, if Allie describes herself as an essentialist but then accepts feelings and intuition as validation for her beliefs, her thinking is inconsistent, and she should reconsider what she really believes about knowing, learning, and teaching.

Forming a Philosophy

My job is to help these kids learn as much as they can about the topics I teach, so that's what I try to do every day. Kids basically want to learn. They may not be too crazy about it initially, and some of them might be in it mostly for grades to start with, but the more they learn about the topics, the better they like what they study. Relevance isn't as critical to the kids' motivation as understanding and success are. If the kids understand the stuff, they'll like it, and they'll feel better about themselves.

So, my goal is to get them to learn, really learn, not just memorize information. I want them to know why, how they know, and what might happen if conditions changed. If I get them to learn, really learn, motivation and self-esteem take care of themselves.

I know that I can get them to learn. We're going to have class discussions, do homework, go over it, have quizzes, and go over them. If I do my job, they'll learn.

What you've just read is a succinct description of Allie's philosophy of education. It is clear, well-articulated, and consistent with her beliefs. The relationships between her beliefs and components of her philosophy are outlined in Table 6.3.

Because Allie's philosophy is clear and well-articulated, she can use it to guide her thinking as she defines her goals and designs learning activities and assessments. It helps ensure that all three—goals, learning activities, and assessments—are consistent with one another. Although you may or may not agree with Allie's goals or the rationale for them, the fact that she's clear in her thinking increases the likelihood that her students will reach the goals, and she will be more likely to make conscious choices to change and improve her teaching when she sees evidence that change is needed.

TABLE 6.3   An Analysis of Allie's Philosophy of Education

Belief Statement	Component of Her Philosophy
"They [kids] don't come to school with the same . . . desire to learn as they once did."	"They may not be too crazy about it initially."
"[T]hey want to believe they did learn something when they're finished with a topic, or class."	"Kids basically want to learn."
"[T]hey're not intrinsically motivated."	"[S]ome of them might be in it mostly for grades to start with."
"[K]ids feel good when they learn something, particularly if it's challenging."	"If the kids understand the stuff, they'll like it, and they'll fell better about themselves." "I want them to know why, how they know, and what might happen if conditions changed."
"[T]he more they know about a topic, the better they like it."	"The more they learn about the topics, the better they like what they study. Relevance isn't as critical to the kids' motivation as understanding and success are."
"[T]here's real, practical stuff out there that they need to know, and there's only one way they're gonna learn it. . . . That's practice and experience."	"We're going to have class discussion, do homework, go over it, have quizzes, and go over them."

You now have your analysis of your beliefs, and a description of Allie's philosophy. Using this information, you should now be ready to create your own personal philosophy that can guide your thinking and actions. We said earlier that your philosophy will likely incorporate elements from more than one traditional and educational philosophy. We see this in Allie's thinking. Her view that an objective reality exists, independent of the world of ideas, is consistent with realism; from essentialism she drew the belief that a body of important information exists that all students need to know in order to function effectively in today's world; and her concerns for her students' personal needs, emotions, and self-esteem most closely relate to existentialism. In constructing your personal philosophy, you will combine traditional and educational philosophies in the same way.

Philosophy of Education in Urban Environments

Forming a coherent philosophy of education is important for all teachers; for new teachers in urban classrooms, it is essential. The philosophy of education that you develop will help you understand your role in urban classrooms and how you can best help urban students learn and develop (Szczesiul, 2004).

Examining Your Beliefs About Urban Learners

In the previous section, we emphasized the importance of understanding your own beliefs in forming your personal philosophy of education. This is particularly important when you think about working in urban environments. Answering the question, "What do I believe about urban learners and working in urban settings?" is essential, and becoming aware of your beliefs will strongly influence how you approach your work with urban students. For instance, consider the following contrasting beliefs.

- Urban students are much like all students; they want to learn, but they need some help and encouragement.

- Urban students don't want to learn, and they're only in school because they are required to be there.

- Urban students need caring and supportive teachers, as do all students.

- Working in an urban setting is much like working in any other school.

- Homework is as important a part of instruction when working with urban students as it is with all students.

- Urban students believe respecting and liking teachers is viewed as a sign of weakness.

- Working in an urban setting is dangerous, and teachers must be vigilant to prevent possible personal harm.

- There is little point in assigning homework to urban students, because they won't do it.

These are merely examples. However, you can see how these different beliefs can influence the way you approach your work with urban students. If, for example, you believe that—at a basic level—urban students want to learn, and their seeming reluctance is more a function of their life outside school than of a fundamental disinterest in learning, you will exert more effort in helping them understand the topics you teach than if you believe that they genuinely do not want to learn. Similarly, if you believe that working in an urban setting is much like working in any other school, you will interact with students in a much different way than if you believe that urban environments are dangerous, and you must constantly "watch your back."

Developing a Philosophy for Urban Settings

As with forming a philosophy of education in general, constructing a philosophy that guides your actions in urban settings begins with a careful examination of your beliefs. However, the process of identifying and articulating your beliefs with respect to urban settings requires additional study, reflection, and perhaps some soul searching, because, as you've seen in our other discussions of teaching in urban environments, many negative stereotypes about urban schools and urban students exist. If you are uninformed, it is easy to slip into accepting a stereotype as being true. When this happens, your negative beliefs will detract from your effectiveness in working with urban students.

Urban classrooms *are* challenging, and we're not suggesting a set of positive beliefs will make your work with urban students simple and easy. However, a well-formed philosophy, on which you can reflect, can serve as a powerful foundation for your thoughts and actions as you plan for instruction and interact with your urban students.

We hope that this chapter has provided you with the professional knowledge needed to begin your journey toward developing a personal philosophy and that it has encouraged you to think about teaching in a different way. At this point you won't have all the answers you need to decide what education should be and how you can help make it that way. But if you are now able to begin asking some important questions, then our goal for the chapter has been fulfilled. Good luck.

> **Making Connections:**
> To deepen your understanding of the topics in this section of the chapter and integrate them with topics you've already studied, go to the *Making Connections* module for Chapter 6 at **www.prenhall.com/kauchak**. Respond to questions 14 and 15.

Check Your Understanding

5.1   Why is a personal philosophy of education important?

5.2   What are the three essential steps involved in forming a philosophy of education?

5.3   Look again at Brad's thinking, as indicated by his conversation with Allie. Based on this information, what is his philosophy of education? Explain how the philosophy is based on his beliefs.

For feedback, go to Appendix A, Check Your Understanding, *located in the back of this text.*

decision making

Defining Yourself as a Professional

You're an American history teacher, and you want your students to do more than simply memorize their way through the information you're teaching. You want them to develop their critical-thinking skills, learn to solve problems, make informed decisions, and get involved in lessons.

This turns out to be a daunting task, however. The students seem to want you to describe every required detail in assignments, and when you call on students who don't have their hands raised, the most common response is, "I didn't have my hand up," or "I
don't know." In other cases, they say, "C'mon, just tell us what you want us to know," and "Why do we have to learn this stuff?"

How would you respond to these students?

To respond to this question online and receive immediate feedback, go to the Decision Making module for Chapter 6 on the Companion Website at www.prenhall.com/kauchak.

Meeting Your Learning Objectives

1. Define philosophy, including normative philosophy, and explain the difference between philosophy and theory.
    *   Philosophy is a search for wisdom. A normative philosophy is a description of the way something ought to be, such as the way educators ought to teach and treat their students. In forming a philosophy, a professional teacher searches for the wisdom to maximize learning for all students.
    *   Philosophy provides a framework for thinking, and it guides professional practice. Philosophy and theory overlap but are not the same. Theories are used to explain events and behavior, as they are, whereas philosophies go further to suggest the way events and behaviors ought to be.

2. Describe each of the branches of philosophy, and identify examples that illustrate each.
    *   Epistemology is the branch of philosophy that describes how we know what we know. Epistemology is important for teachers because it influences how we teach and our choice of teaching methods.
    *   Metaphysics, or ontology, considers what we know and addresses questions of reality and, ultimately, what is real. As teachers, our beliefs about reality influence our goals for our students, as we help them discover their own realities.
    *   Axiology considers values and ethics and examines questions and issues involving decisions about right and wrong. Axiology is important because the public believes that schools play an important role in shaping students' values and ultimately their moral behavior.
    *   Logic is the process of deriving valid conclusions from basic principles. Teachers help students understand the logic of different arguments and also how to think clearly about ideas.

3. Describe the traditional schools of philosophy, and identify examples that illustrate each.
    *   Idealism, realism, pragmatism, and existentialism are considered the traditional philosophies. Their views of reality, ways of knowing, and what is valuable and good often differ considerably. Each philosophy has implications for teaching and learning.

- Idealists would create a curriculum focusing on absolute and time-honored ideas. They do this by encouraging students to study the great thinkers in our history and the ideas they've produced.
- Realists would also emphasize absolutes, but in contrast with idealists, their absolutes would focus on natural laws. Realists use observation, experimentation, and critical reasoning to help students think clearly and examine the material world.
- Pragmatists see the world in relative terms and would emphasize experience and practical understanding, validated by the scientific method. Pragmatists attempt to connect subject matter to children's interests.
- Existentialists would take a more extreme position and support a curriculum emphasizing personal awareness, freedom, and responsibility. Because there is no absolute reality or truth, teachers encourage their students to create their own personal definitions of truth and good.

4. Describe the major philosophies of education, and identify examples that illustrate each view.
   - The educational philosophies perennialism, essentialism, progressivism, and postmodernism are rooted in the traditional philosophies.
   - Perennialism, as with idealism and realism, focuses on time-honored absolutes. Because truth doesn't change, a teacher's responsibility is to expose students to time-tested knowledge and truth.
   - Essentialism suggests that a critical core of information that all people should possess exists, and it suggests that schools should emphasize basic skills and academic subjects, and students should be expected to master these subjects.
   - Progressivism, rooted in pragmatism, views goals as dynamic and emphasizes that learning should be experience-based and relevant to students' lives.
   - Postmodernism sees schools and other institutions in need of restructuring, with marginalized people and their works elevated to more prominent positions in the content of schooling.

5. Explain why a personal philosophy of education is important, and describe the steps involved in forming one.
   - A personal philosophy of education is important because it guides your instructional decisions and specifies criteria you use to reflect on and analyze your teaching.
   - A personal philosophy also helps you explain and defend your educational goals.
   - Developing a personal philosophy begins with a description and analysis of your beliefs and continues with an internally consistent articulation of your philosophy.
   - Developing a personal philosophy of education increases your professionalism by providing a concrete frame of reference for reflection.

Important Concepts

axiology (p. 189)

epistemology (p. 188)

essentialism (p. 197)

existentialism (p. 193)

idealism (p. 191)

logic (p. 190)

metaphysics (ontology) (p. 189)

normative philosophy (p. 188)

perennialism (p. 196)

philosophy (p. 185)

philosophy of education (p. 186)

postmodernism (p. 200)

pragmatism (p. 192)

progressivism (p. 199)

realism (p. 191)

theory (p. 187)

Developing as a Professional

Preparing for Your Licensure Exam

This exercise will provide you with practice answering questions similar to the Praxis™ Principles of Learning and Teaching Exam as well as your state-specific licensure exam. Look again at the discussion among the teachers Greg, Jaclyn, Justin, and Edna, presented on pp. 193–194 of the chapter. We have already examined the teachers' thinking in the context of the traditional philosophies. Now, read this discussion again, and decide which educational philosophy is best illustrated in each of the teacher's comments.

1. Which educational philosophy is best reflected in Greg's comments? Explain.

2. Which educational philosophy is best reflected in Jaclyn's comments? Explain.

3. Which educational philosophy is best reflected in Justin's comments? Explain.

4. Which educational philosophy is best reflected in Edna's comments? Explain.

To receive feedback on your responses to these exercises, go to the Companion Website at www.prenhall. com/kauchak, then to the Preparing for Your Licensure Exam *module for Chapter 6.*

Discussion Questions

1. Four basic areas of philosophy are epistemology, metaphysics, axiology, and logic. Which of these is most useful for teachers? Least useful?

2. Technology is becoming increasingly important in society as well as education. Which of the four philosophies of education—perennialism, essentialism, progressivism, or postmodernism—is most compatible with applications of technology in education? Least compatible?

3. Students are becoming increasingly diverse. How well do the different philosophies of education address issues of student diversity?

4. Which philosophy of education has the most current support in the geographic area in which you plan to teach? What evidence do you have for your conclusion?

5. Of the different educational philosophies discussed in this chapter, which is most valuable in framing issues for preschool children? Middle school students? High school students? Does one particular philosophy fit with a content area that you will be teaching?

6. Teachers in elementary schools commonly emphasize reading, language arts, and math much more strongly than other parts of the curriculum such as social studies, art, and music. What does this emphasis suggest about the teachers' philosophical positions?

Developing as a Professional: Online Activities

Going Into Schools

Go to the Companion Website at *www.prenhall.com/kauchak*, and click on the *Going Into Schools* module for Chapter 6. You will find a number of school-based activities that will help you link chapter content to the schools in which you work.

Virtual Field Experience: Using the Internet to Explore the Profession

If you would like to participate in a Virtual Field Experience, access the following Website: *http://www.utm.edu/research/iep*. This site contains valuable resources that you can use to construct your own personal philosophy of education.

Online Portfolio Activities

To develop your professional portfolio, further apply your understanding of chapter content, and address the INTASC standards, go the Companion Website at *www.prenhall.com/kauchak*, then to the *Online Portfolio Activities* for Chapter 6. Complete the suggested activities.

The Organization of American Schools

Chapter Outline

What Is a School?

The Organization of Schools
- Personnel
- The Physical Plant
- Organization of the Curriculum

School Levels
- Early Childhood Programs
- Elementary Schools
- Junior High and Middle Schools
- High Schools

What Is an Effective School?
- Research on Effective Schools
- Parents' and Other Taxpayers' Perceptions of Effective Schools

Learning Objectives

After you have completed your study of this chapter, you should be able to:

1. Describe different meanings of the concept school.

2. Identify the components of a typical school organization.

3. Describe important differences among schools at different levels.

4. Identify the characteristics of an effective school.

Case Studies

 Elementary

 Middle

 Secondary

Chapter 7

Myrleen Ferguson Cate/PhotoEdit Inc.

Most of you are seriously considering becoming a teacher, but many of you haven't determined which level you want to teach. Fortunately, we've all attended schools and experienced them as students, so we're familiar with the basic ways in which they're organized. But what do schools look like from a teacher's perspective? The answer to this question could help you decide whether to become an elementary, middle school, or high school teacher. Let's take a look at one teacher's experience.

"Wow, noon. I need to get going," Chris Lucio says to his colleague April Jackson as he finishes the last bite of his lunch and jumps up from the couch in the teacher's lounge. "My kids will be chomping at the bit trying to get into the room."

Chris hurriedly leaves the lounge, stops by the main office to check his box, and then walks across the courtyard to his building.

The courtyard sits at the center of the campus of Lakeside Junior High. Created 30 years earlier as a middle school for grades 6–9, Lakeside is now one of three junior high schools housing seventh and eighth graders in Orange Park, a suburb of a large eastern city. Four main buildings surround the courtyard: one for administration and three for classrooms. The administration building houses the principal's and other administrators' offices, a cafeteria—with a stage at one end—that doubles as an auditorium, and a media center and computer lab holding 30 computers. A gymnasium and fine arts building, built 10 years ago when Lakeside became a junior high, and athletic facilities (tennis courts and baseball, softball, and soccer fields) are positioned outside the main buildings.

Chris walks briskly to the room where he teaches seventh-grade geography.

"Okay everyone, the bell is going to ring in a couple minutes. . . . Find your seats quickly," Chris calls out, unlocking the door to his room.

"Mr. Lucio, can I go to the bathroom?" Armondo asks as he heads through the open door.

"Hurry—you don't want to be tardy," Chris answers as he smiles at him.

"Are you going to come to our track meet this afternoon?" Devon, another of Chris's students asks as he enters the room. "We're going to kick butt on Ridgeview."

"Wouldn't miss it," Chris replies and thinks to himself, "Yikes, I almost forgot. . . . I promised Joe and Karen [the boys' and girls' track coaches] that I'd be a timer for the 100- and 200-meter races."

"What time does it start?" Chris asks Devon.

"Right after school—4 o'clock, I think."

As the bell signals the start of the period, Chris moves to the front of the room and starts taking roll as the students begin working on a warmup exercise that Chris has displayed on the overhead.

If you're in your mid-20 or younger, you've spent more than half of your life in school. But exactly what is a school, and what does it mean to teach and learn in one? We consider these questions in this section, but before we continue, please respond to the following survey.

---

professional knowledge: test yourself!

For each item, circle the number that best represents your thinking. Use the following scale as a guide.

1 = Strongly disagree
2 = Disagree
3 = Uncertain
4 = Agree
5 = Strongly agree

1. Teachers are the people in schools who have the ultimate responsibility for the successful operation of the school.

| 1 | 2 | 3 | 4 | 5 |

2. A major tension in the organization of elementary schools is between the dual goals of meeting the developmental needs of students and content acquisition.

| 1 | 2 | 3 | 4 | 5 |

3. Middle and junior high schools are essentially the same but are given different labels.

| 1 | 2 | 3 | 4 | 5 |

4. In general, larger schools provide students with a better-quality education, because they have better facilities and a wider variety of programs

| 1 | 2 | 3 | 4 | 5 |

5. The assessment program in a school is a major factor influencing the school's effectiveness.

| 1 | 2 | 3 | 4 | 5 |

This is available in a downloadable format on the Companion Website for personal portfolio use.

We address each of the survey items as the chapter develops.

What Is a School?

As a concept, a *school* can be described as a place where young people go to learn and develop intellectually, personally, and socially. Whether or not this is the "best" definition, however, can be debated. Churches have vacation Bible *school,* and we've all heard of students being *homeschooled.* At a simpler level, a school is a physical place—a building or set of buildings where teachers and students spend considerable amounts of time.

At a third level, school is a **social institution**, an organization with established structures and rules designed to promote certain goals. Schools are social institutions whose goals are to promote both students' growth and development and the well-being of a country and its citizens. Other social institutions include churches, religions, and governments. They all are designed to make society a better place in which to live.

We use *social institution* as the framework for our discussion in this chapter, as we examine the ways in which schools are organized and how this organization is designed to help meet their goals. Some ways of organizing schools are better than others, and these differences influence how much students learn and how they develop. These differences will also influence your life as a teacher.

Every school operates as a relatively independent unit within a **school district**, an administrative unit within a state, defined by geographical boundaries and legally responsible for the public education of children within those boundaries. A school district may encompass an entire county, or large counties may be divided into more than one district.

Districts are important because schools are embedded within them, and their rules and policies affect teachers' and students' lives. Some districts are quite bureaucratic and hierarchical, controlling major elements of curriculum and instruction. Others give more of the decisions about what and how to teach to individual schools and teachers. When you interview for a job, you will want to talk to teachers about their perceptions of the district and how its administrators treat teachers.

Let's turn now to the organization of individual schools, but before we do, check your understanding of the ideas in this section.

> **Making Connections:**
> To deepen your understanding of the topics in this section of the chapter and integrate them with topics you've already studied, go to the *Making Connections* module for Chapter 7 at **www.prenhall.com/kauchak**. Respond to questions 1 and 2.

Check Your Understanding

1.1 What are three different meanings of the concept school?

1.2 Explain how a school and a school district differ.

1.3 Is the family a social institution? Explain why it is or is not.

 For feedback, go to Appendix A, Check Your Understanding, *located in the back of this text.*

> **Social institution.** An organization with established structures and rules designed to promote certain goals.
>
> **School district.** An administrative unit within a state, defined by geographical boundaries, and legally responsible for the public education of children within those boundaries.

The Organization of Schools

Think about the schools you attended as a student. If the organization was typical of schools in the United States, you first went to an elementary school, which began with kindergarten, or even prekindergarten, followed by first grade, second grade, and so on. You then went to a middle school or junior high, and finally to a high school. As we look at how these schools are organized and why, we'll examine the following:

- Personnel
- The physical plant
- The organization of the curriculum

Personnel

No school is better than the people who work there. School personnel include all the people—the administrators, the support staff, and the teachers—who help make a school an effective social institution.

The central office is the school's nerve center; the office staff plays an important role in greeting guests and assisting both teachers and students. (Will Hart/PhotoEdit Inc.)

Administrators and Support Staff

Elementary, middle, junior high, and high schools all have **administrators**, individuals responsible for the day-to-day operation of a school. Administrators include a **principal**, the individual given ultimate administrative responsibility for the school's operation, and this definition addresses the first item on our survey at the beginning of the chapter, "Teachers are the people in schools who have the ultimate responsibility for the successful operation of the school." This ultimate responsibility lies with the principal, and, as with expert teachers, the most effective principals possess a great deal of professional knowledge (Saha & Biddle, 2006).

If the school is large, a vice principal, assistant principal, or both support the principal in his or her work and are also part of the administration. Lakeside Junior High, the school in the case study at the beginning of the chapter, has a principal, vice principal, and two assistant principals. The vice principals' responsibilities typically include scheduling, collecting student records (e.g., grade reports) from teachers, keeping master records for the school, and maintaining communication with district-level administrators and parents. One of the assistant principals manages the physical plant, arranging the distribution of lockers to students, coordinating the duties of the custodial staff, and overseeing all maintenance and construction. The other assistant principal is in charge of discipline—including referrals made by teachers and both in-school and out-of-school suspension of students, ordering and distributing textbooks to department heads, and maintaining in-service records for teachers.

Depending on the size of the school and the financial status and organization of the school district, schools may also have guidance counselors, school psychologists, and healthcare providers, such as school nurses. Lakeside Junior High also has two full-time guidance counselors and a school psychologist it shares with other schools. The guidance counselors schedule and coordinate the statewide assessment tests and provide information to students about course offerings and career options. The school psychologist administers individualized intelligence tests and other tests used in making decisions about whether students qualify for special education or programs for the gifted and talented. The school psychologist also provides individual counseling for students having emotional problems and makes recommendations for further mental health assistance.

Administrators. Individuals responsible for the day-to-day operation of a school.

Principal. The individual who has the ultimate administrative responsibility for the school's operation.

Lakeside also has a full-time licensed practical nurse; she maintains all student health records, is trained in administering CPR, supervises medical evacuations, and dispenses all medications to students. Nationally, 33 percent of schools have nurses (Kober, 2006). Students at Lakeside are not allowed to take even an over-the-counter painkiller, such as aspirin, on their own, and teachers may not give students any form of medication.

In addition, all schools have support staff, such as the following:

- Secretaries and receptionists, who greet visitors to the school
- Administrative and instructional support staff, who complete paperwork for the principal and other administrators, duplicate tests and handouts for teachers, maintain payroll records, and perform other functions
- Media center specialists, who manage books and different forms of technology
- Physical plant staff, such as custodians who clean the rooms and buildings and cafeteria workers who prepare school lunches

Schools vary in the way they assign duties to administrators, so the duties of the administrators and support staff in schools that you visit, or the school in which you take your first job, may differ from those we described here.

Why do you need to know about different school personnel and their roles? A school is a complex social institution, and all the people working in a school contribute to making it run smoothly. As a professional, your ability to work with the other personnel will influence how effective you and the school will be. For example, if you have a student who is so unruly that you can't work with him or her in your classroom, you will need the support of the assistant principal and perhaps the advice of the school psychologist to help you address the problem. Although you may be alone in your classroom when you teach, your effectiveness will depend on your ability to coordinate your efforts with many different people in your school.

A common adage suggests that you can tell a great deal about a school by observing the way a school receptionist greets students and visitors when they enter the main office. Likewise, the way you treat support staff also helps set the tone for a positive school climate. For example, requesting—instead of demanding—services, such as having a test duplicated, communicates to support staff that you value their contributions to the overall functioning of the school. The most effective schools are those in which all personnel work together for the benefit of students.

Teachers

While school principals have ultimate administrative responsibility for the school's operation, teachers are at the heart of any effective school. A huge body of literature consistently indicates that students taught by expert teachers learn more than those taught by teachers with less expertise (Bransford, Darling-Hammond, & LePage, 2005; Darling-Hammond & Baratz-Snowdon, 2005). "Supportive teachers and clear and high expectations are key to ensuring that students feel

IN TODAY'S CLASSROOMS: VIDEO

The Principal's View of Professionalism

To view this video, go to the *Becoming a Professional* DVD included with this text, click on *In Today's Classrooms*, and then this chapter's video: *The Principal's Role in Instructional Leadership*. Answer the questions you'll find on the DVD.

In this video episode, a school principal describes his role as an instructional leader.

To answer questions about the video online and receive immediate feedback, go to the Companion Website at www.prenhall.com/kauchak, then the In Today's Classrooms module for Chapter 7.

in control and confident about their ability to learn" (Lewis, 2006, p. 565). Helping you develop into an expert teacher who can support student learning is a major goal of this text.

The Physical Plant

One definition of a school that we considered was a physical place. Schools have classrooms, hallways that allow students to move from one room to another, a central administrative office, and one or more large rooms, such as auditoriums, gymnasiums, music rooms, and cafeterias. Many schools have a simple boxlike structure, with hall upon hall of separate cells, which critics argue isolates teachers and fragments the curriculum. Classrooms also offer teacher privacy and sanctuary from the hectic pace of school life. When teachers retreat into their classrooms and close their doors, no one else knows what goes on in there. Open classrooms with large movable walls have gone in and out of popularity and are usually resisted by teachers because of noise and lack of privacy (Bolkan, Roland, & Smith, 2006).

An elementary school usually includes a staff parking area, playground, and driveway used for dropping off and picking up students. Middle, junior high, and high schools also have athletic facilities, such as playing fields, stadiums, and sometimes swimming pools. In some middle schools, however, the design intentionally omitted gyms or other facilities that support competitive activities. High schools also have parking spaces available for students who drive their own cars to school.

School enrollments often increase so rapidly that physical plants can't keep up (Ortiz, 2004). As a result, many schools have "temporaries" or "modulars," individual buildings on the perimeter of school campuses that provide additional classroom space.

What will the physical arrangement of schools mean for you as a teacher? Positively, your own classroom will be your own domain where you can define yourself as a teacher. But it will also separate you from your colleagues. When you're in your classroom and you shut the door (as many teachers do), you'll be on your own. You'll be responsible for 20 to 30 second graders, for example, all day, every day. If you teach in middle or high school, you'll spend most of your workday in the confines of your classroom, where you'll be responsible for the education and safety of five or six different classes of students.

Second, although your primary responsibility will be to teach students in your classroom, you'll also be expected to carry out noninstructional activities in other areas of the school .If you teach in an elementary school, you may need to escort your students to and from the cafeteria or the media center, for example. If you're a middle or secondary teacher, you'll be expected to monitor students as they move through the corridors and attend auditorium assemblies. You may also be asked to sell tickets at football games, attend track meets, and go to band concerts. A teacher's responsibilities result, in part, from the way schools are physically organized.

Organization of the Curriculum

Schools are social institutions designed to help young people grow, develop, and prepare to function effectively in today's (and tomorrow's) world. To function effectively in today's technologically oriented and fast-changing world, students need to acquire essential knowledge and skills. Our task as educators is to organize the curriculum in a way that maximizes students' opportunities for learning and development. Theorists offer a variety of definitions of curriculum, and no single one is generally accepted (Armstrong, 2003). For our purposes in this chapter, however, we'll define **curriculum** simply as what teachers teach and what students learn. (We examine school curriculum in greater detail in Chapter 10.)

A curriculum is typically organized around learning goals, such as the following:

Curriculum. The knowledge and skills that teachers teach and students are supposed to learn.

- Students will recognize the letters of the alphabet.
- Students will write short paragraphs using correct paragraph structure.
- Students will use the correct order of operations to simplify expresions such as $9 + 4(7 - 3)/2$
- Students will understand the concepts *mass* and *inertia*.

Historically, educators have decided that the most efficient way of helping students reach goals such as these is to organize instruction according to different grade levels, ages of students, and subject areas. For instance, children in kindergarten are expected to reach the first goal, third graders the second, seventh-grade pre-algebra students the third, and eleventh-grade physics students the fourth. Learning goals for different grade levels and subject areas are part of a school's general curriculum, and these goals provide teachers with direction as they make decisions about what to teach.

School Organization and the Curriculum

How should teachers and students be grouped to help students most effectively learn the content of the curriculum? For example, does it make sense to have 6-year-olds in the same building and walking the same halls as 17- or 18-year-olds? Safety, as well as seemingly mundane concerns such as the height of drinking fountains and toilets, suggests no.

Most school systems are organized into three levels: elementary schools for younger children, middle or junior high schools for young adolescents, and high schools for later adolescents. The grades included at each level vary from place to place, however, and as a teacher you may encounter various organizational patterns. Table 7.1 outlines some of the most common.

What factors do educators consider when making decisions about organizing schools? For example, why do middle schools typically include grades 6–8 or grades 7 and 8? Two factors are most powerful: (1) the developmental characteristics of students and (2) economics and politics.

Developmental Characteristics of Students

Development refers to the physical changes in children as well as changes in the way they think and relate to their peers that result from maturation and experience. For example, fifth graders are bigger, stronger, and more coordinated than first graders; that is, they are physically more developed. Similarly, fifth graders think differently than do first graders. When shown the drawing on page 220, for example, typical first graders conclude that Block A is heavier than Block B, because their thinking tends to focus on size—the most obvious aspect of the balance and blocks. Fifth graders, on the other hand, are more likely to conclude that the blocks have the same weight, because they recognize that the beam is balanced (level). Their thinking is more developed (Eggen & Kauchak, 2007).

TABLE 7.1   Common Ways to Organize Schools

School Level	Grade Ranges
Elementary school	K–2
	K–3
	K–5
	K–6
Middle school	5–8
	6–8
	7–8
Junior high school	7–8
	7–9
	8–9
High school	9–12
	10–12

Development. The physical, intellectual, and social changes in children that occur as a result of experience.

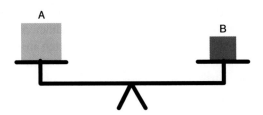

Differences in social development also exist. For example, when faced with a disagreement about who in a group gets to report on which topic, a fifth grader is more likely to step back, recognize the others' perspectives, and compromise. Socially, fifth graders are often capable of considering where a classmate is "coming from," whereas first graders tend to be more self-centered in their thinking (Berk, 2006; McDevitt & Ormrod, 2007). Advances in social development allow teachers to use instructional strategies, such as cooperative learning, that are more effective with older children than with those who are younger or less developed socially (Brophy, 2006).

Similar differences can be found between fifth graders and high school students. Many older students are physically young men and women, some think quite abstractly, and they can be socially skilled.

These developmental differences influence the ways in which schools are organized. For example, students in elementary schools are typically assigned to one teacher who monitors the cognitive, social, and emotional growth of students in that classroom. In some schools **looping,** the practice of keeping a teacher with one group of students for more than a year, is used to help individual teachers better nurture the development of individual students. Older students are more capable of learning on their own and fending for themselves, so they are assigned to a number of teachers who also serve as subject-matter specialists.

Economics and Politics

Economics and politics are also factors that influence decisions about school organization. For example, both influenced the development of Lakeside, Chris Lucio's school, first in its creation as a middle school and later in its conversion to a junior high.

At the time Lakeside was developed, the elementary schools in Orange Park had become overcrowded because of rapid population increases in the city, and the process of building additional elementary schools couldn't keep up with demand. Creating middle schools temporarily solved the problem, because sixth graders could be moved into the middle schools. This was a decision based on economics.

Also, the middle school movement was gathering momentum at this same time, and Mary Zellner, Lakeside's first principal, was an outspoken proponent of middle schools. She was a respected leader in district politics, and because of her influence, Lakeside was built according to middle school philosophy. This philosophy de-emphasized competition among students, and as a result, the school didn't have competitive athletics, which was the reason the school didn't originally have a gymnasium. Although Mary Zellner's advocacy of middle schools was grounded in research, the district-level decision to avoid competitive activities at Lakeside was a result of her political influence.

Issues then became further complicated. Coaches at Orange Park High complained that potential athletes came to them from the middle schools without the athletic experiences students attending competing schools enjoyed. (These pressures are not unusual; many middle-level schools in the United States offer organized competitive sports.) The fact that Orange Park High, the only high school in the district, had become overcrowded presented a bigger problem. District officials solved both problems by converting the middle schools into junior highs, moving ninth graders from the high school to the junior highs, and sending sixth graders back to elementary schools. By

Looping. The practice of keeping a teacher with one group of students for more than a year.

this time, the elementary schools were able to accept the additional students, because a number of new elementary schools had recently been built in the city. The decision to convert middle schools to junior highs was based on both economics and politics; it had little to do with the developmental needs of students.

Unfortunately, organizational changes such as these are not uncommon in education. Keep these factors—developmental, economic, and political—in mind as we look at schools at different levels in more depth in the next section.

Making Connections:
To deepen your understanding of the topics in this section of the chapter and integrate them with topics you've already studied, go to the *Making Connections* module for Chapter 7 at **www.prenhall.com/kauchak.** Respond to questions 3 and 4.

Check Your Understanding

2.1   What are the major components of a typical school organization?

2.2   Most school systems are organized into three levels. Describe each of the three.

2.3   What are two factors that influence the way school curriculum is organized?

For feedback, go to Appendix A, Check Your Understanding, *located in the back of this text.*

School Levels

In the previous section, we saw that schools are typically organized into elementary, middle or junior high, and high school levels. In this section, we take a closer look at how schools are organized to meet the developmental needs of students and how different organizational patterns influence the lives of teachers. Let's begin our examination of different levels of schools with a look at early childhood programs.

Early Childhood Programs

Visitors to Sharon Broderick's preschool classroom at first are struck by the seeming chaos. Students around her classroom are working on a number of different and unconnected tasks. Sharon and her aide, Carmen Sanchez, circulate among the groups, asking questions and offering suggestions.

Closer examination of the room reveals several clusters of activity organized around centers. One center has a tub of water where students measure water in different-sized cups and also determine which kinds of objects sink and float. Another has a table with an assortment of plastic geometric blocks and shapes that children are using to construct things. A third has different costumes and clothing along with two telephones that students use for pretend conversations and dialogues. A fourth contains a variety of picture books that require different amounts of expertise with letters and words. Children circulate among these different centers, and the teacher and her aide keep track of who has been to which center and completed different tasks.

Most of you reading this book probably attended kindergarten, and some of you may have even attended a prekindergarten program. However, one of your authors, educated in a small town in a rural area, attended neither, because they weren't offered there at the time. **Early childhood education** is a general term encompassing a range of educational programs for young children, including infant intervention and enrichment programs, nursery schools, public and private prekindergartens and kindergartens, and federally funded Head Start programs. Early childhood education is a mid–20th-century development in the United

Early childhood education. A general term encompassing a range of educational programs for young children, including infant intervention and enrichment programs, nursery schools, public and private prekindergartens and kindergartens, and federally funded Head Start programs.

States, although its philosophical roots go back 250 years. The French philosopher Rousseau, for example, gave this advice about educating young children:

Do not treat the child to discourses which he cannot understand. No descriptions, no eloquence, no figures of speech. . . . In general, let us never substitute the sign for the thing, except when it is impossible for us to show the thing. . . . Things! Things! I shall never tire of saying that we ascribe too much importance to words. (Rousseall, quoted in Compayre, 1888)

Rousseau was arguing that young children need to play and work with concrete objects ("Things! Things!") rather than being taught with abstract words. This idea is consistent with the need for concrete experiences that the famous developmental psychologist Jean Piaget (1952, 1970) emphasized, and it is at the core of developmentally appropriate early childhood programs.

Developmental programs accommodate differences in children's development by allowing them to acquire skills and abilities at their own pace through direct experiences. Visitors in a developmental classroom are likely to see learning centers around the room such as those in Sharon Broderick's class. Unlike traditional teacher-centered instruction, the teacher's role is to provide experiences for children and encourage exploration.

The need for learning-related experiences early in life is well recognized (Berk, 2006; McDevitt & Ormrod, 2007), and the benefits of early intervention programs are long-lasting. For example, the Perry Preschool study compared the experiences of 123 poor African-American children who either attended 3 years of preschool or did not (the program did not have room for all applicants) (Bracey, 2003a). Dramatic differences were found between the preschool students and students in the control group. By the time these students turned 27, 71 percent of the preschool group had attained a high school diploma or GED, compared to only 54 percent of the control group. Forty-two percent of the males in the preschool group reported making more than $24,000 a year, compared to only 6 percent of the males in the control group. Thirty-six percent of the preschool group, but only 13 percent of the control group, owned their own homes. Control group members had twice as many arrests as those who attended the preschool, and five times as many of the control group had been arrested five or more times. Clearly, the Perry Preschool program had long-lasting beneficial effects on the children it served.

A more ambitious program in North Carolina provided nutritional help and social services from birth, as well as parenting lessons and a language-oriented preschool program (Bracey, 2003a; Jacobsen, 2003). Follow-up studies revealed that, compared to nonparticipants, participants scored higher on intelligence and achievement tests, were twice as likely to attend postsecondary education, and delayed having children by 2 years. Early childhood education programs pay off, both in immediate school and also later in life. David Broder, a prominent *Washington Post* columnist, observed: "The evidence that high-quality education beginning at age 3 or 4 will pay lifetime dividends is overwhelming. The only question is whether we will make the needed investment" (quoted in Bracey, 2003a, p. 32).

In the early 1970s, only 23 percent of 4-year-olds were enrolled in early childhood programs; by 2001, this figure had increased to 66 percent (Magnuson, Meyers, Ruhm, & Waldfogel, 2004). Much greater emphasis is now being placed on high-quality early intervention programs in all settings. As full-time pre-K programs become increasingly common, job opportunities in these areas will continue to grow.

Elementary Schools

To begin our examination of the organization of elementary schools, let's look at the schedules of two elementary teachers. Examine the schedules in Table 7.2, and see what you notice.

Your observations might include the following:

- Both teachers are responsible for all the content areas, such as reading, language arts, math, science, and social studies.

Developmental programs. Programs that accommodate differences in children's development by allowing them to acquire skills and abilities at their own pace through direct experiences.

TABLE 7.2   Schedules for Two Elementary School Teachers

Sharon's First-Grade Schedule		Susie's Third-Grade Schedule	
8:30 AM	School begins	8:30 AM	School begins
8:30–8:45	Morning announcements	8:30–9:15	Independent work (practice previous day's language arts and math)
8:45–10:30	Language arts (including reading and writing)	9:15–10:20	Language arts (including reading and writing)
10:30–11:20	Math	10:20–10:45	Snack/independent reading
11:20–11:50	Lunch	10:45–11:15	Physical education
11:50–12:20	Read story	11:15–12:15	Language arts/social studies/science
12:20–1:15	Center time (practice on language arts and math)	12:15–12:45	Lunch
1:15–1:45	Physical education	12:45–2:00	Math
1:45–2:30	Social studies/science	2:00–2:30	Spelling/catch up on material not covered earlier
2:30–2:45	Class meeting	2:30–2:45	Read story
2:45–3:00	Call buses/dismissal	2:45–3:00	Clean up/prepare for dismissal

- The schedules are quite different. Although both teachers teach young children, Sharon begins with language arts, for example, while Susie begins by having the children practice their previous day's math and language arts.
- The amount of time the teachers allocate to each of the content areas is a personal decision. Sharon, for example, devotes 50 minutes to math, whereas Susie teaches math for 75 minutes a day.

In conversation, both teachers noted that the schedules in Table 7.2 were approximate and often changed depending on their perception of students' needs and the day of the week. For example, if students were having trouble with a math topic, they might devote more time to math on a given day (S. Mittelstadt, personal communication, August 15, 2006; S. Van Horn, personal communication, August 16, 2006).

If you observe in elementary classrooms, you're likely to see a schedule that varies from those in Table 7.2. This level of individual teacher freedom and autonomy is characteristic of elementary school organization and is a major reason that people become elementary teachers.

Why are elementary schools organized this way? In the first elementary-level schools in early America (see Chapter 5), a single teacher was typically responsible for all of the content areas. Until about the mid-1800s, elementary schools weren't even organized into grade levels. In many rural, one-room schools, a single teacher

Self-contained elementary classrooms attempt to meet young students' developmental needs. (Scott Cunningham/Merrill)

was responsible for all the grade levels and content areas. In some rural areas, one-room school houses still exist today (Swidler, 2004). So, history has influenced the way elementary schools are organized.

The developmental characteristics of students have also influenced the organization of elementary schools. We saw earlier that young children look, think, and interact with their peers in ways that are different from older students. Educators have historically believed that young children need the stability of one teacher and a single classroom to function most effectively in school. Schools can be frightening places for little children, and self-contained classrooms provide emotional security. Further, simply moving from room to room, as middle and secondary students do, can be challenging for young children. Imagine, for example, a first grader going to Room 101 for math, 108 for language arts, and so on. Rotating schedules, which are becoming increasingly popular under block scheduling, would be even more confusing.

Many educators question the idea of a single classroom and teacher. Expecting one teacher to be sufficiently knowledgeable to effectively teach reading, language arts, math, science, and social studies is asking the impossible, they say. As a result, teachers commonly de-emphasize some content areas, such as science, social studies, art, and music. Both Sharon and Susie acknowledged that they strongly emphasized reading, language arts, and math, and de-emphasized the other areas, even though these other content areas appear on their schedules (see Table 7.2).

So educators, teachers, and parents face a dilemma: Are social and emotional well-being more important than content for elementary students? Historically, the answer has been yes. This section provides us with an answer to the second item on our survey, "A major tension in the organization of elementary schools is between the dual goals of meeting the developmental needs of students and content acquisition." The answer is yes, and this tension will continue to grow as efforts to document student academic growth through testing continue to grow.

Junior High and Middle Schools

To see differences between elementary schools and middle, junior high, and high schools, we need only compare Chris's experiences (in the chapter's opening case) to Susie's and Sharon's (in Table 7.2). Elementary teachers typically teach all the content areas and set their own schedules. In contrast, as a middle school teacher, Chris teaches only one subject (geography), and he (along with all the other teachers in his school) follows a specific, predetermined schedule. The lengths of class periods are uniform for all the content areas, and the beginnings and endings are signaled by a bell. Also, Chris is not responsible for monitoring his students as they move from place to place on the Lakeside campus as elementary teachers are, but he is involved in extracurricular activities (e.g., the track meet), which are part of middle schools, junior highs, and high schools.

Why are upper-level schools organized in this way? To answer this question, think back to our description of school as a social institution designed to promote the development of children and the welfare of society. Also recall from Chapter 5 that views about educational goals have changed over time. For instance, in colonial times, people felt that society would benefit most from having students learn to read and understand the Bible. Much later (near the end of the 19th century), educators felt that having both college-bound and non-college-bound students take the same curriculum would serve the needs of society. This view was based on the belief that mental discipline was the most important function of education. Also, schools were organized to accommodate the large influx of immigrants to help them assimilate into American society.

As educational thinking evolved, leaders felt that society needed citizens well schooled in a variety of academic subjects. This emphasis on the mastery of subject matter resulted in the departmentalization found in the middle schools, junior highs, and high schools that you most likely attended. But a tension exists between this emphasis on content and meeting the development needs of students. Let's look at how this tension affected the organization of middle and junior high schools.

Historically, schools in the early 20th century were organized into eight elementary and four high school grades. This 8–4 organization changed when emphasis shifted away from basic skills, such as reading and math, and toward the more intensive study of specific content areas, such as history, literature, and science. This intensive study required teachers who were subject-matter experts. In addition, educators began to recognize the unique needs of early adolescents. The result was the development of the "junior" high school.

Most junior high schools today have a variety of offerings, although not as comprehensive as those in high schools, and they also include competitive athletics and other extracurricular activities. Although initially designed to help students make the transition between elementary and high schools, they are in every sense of the word "junior" high schools.

However, early adolescence is characterized by considerable variability in students' development. Think back to the friends you knew when you were in the sixth, seventh, or eighth grades. Some of the girls were young women, fully developed physically, whereas others were still little girls. Some boys needed to shave, but others looked like fifth graders. Boys and girls were becoming physically attracted to each other, and in many cases they didn't know why. This was the transitional period of early adolescence.

Because of these rapid physical, emotional, and intellectual changes, early adolescence is a unique period in a child's development. At no other time in a person's life, except infancy, is change so rapid or profound. As a result, many educators believe that schools for young adolescents should be organized to meet the unique needs of these students (Jackson & Davis, 2000).

This thinking, and the fact that junior highs weren't meeting early adolescents' developmental needs, led to the formation of **middle schools**. Typically for grades 6–8, middle schools are specifically designed to help students through the rapid social, emotional, and intellectual changes characteristic of early adolescence.

What is teaching in a middle school like? Let's look at one teacher's experience.

Robin West is an eighth-grade teacher in an urban middle school. She teaches physical science, and she and her team members have a common planning period. They teach the same group of students and often spend their planning period discussing the students and the topics they are teaching. Many of their students are not native English speakers, and their discussions often center on what can be done to help those who struggle with language. In addition, Robin has four students with learning disabilities in her classroom. The teachers try to integrate topics across as many of the four areas as often as possible.

"Can you help me out with anything on graphing?" Mary, the math teacher, asks the others one Monday. "The kids just see graphs as some meaningless lines. I explain the heck out of them, but it doesn't seem to help all that much."

"I know what I can do," Robin offers, after thinking for a few seconds. "I'll do some simple demonstrations and then have them link the demonstration to a graph. . . . Here, look."

She holds out her pen and drops it. She then draws a graph on a piece of paper:

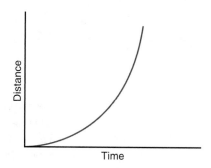

Middle schools. Schools, typically for grades 6–8, specifically designed to help students through the rapid social, emotional, and intellectual changes characteristic of early adolescence.

"The graph represents the relationship between the distance the pen falls and the time it takes to fall," she explains. "Time is on the horizontal axis, and distance is on the vertical axis. . . . I'll do

this with the kids, and you can refer to what I did when you do your work on graphs," she adds, nodding to Mary.

"Great. Thanks. . . . When will you do it?"

"We're between units now, so I can do it tomorrow. . . . Then you and I can talk about it after school for a few minutes, and I'll let you know how it went. . . . By the way, how is Lorraine Williams doing in math?"

"Not so good," Mary responds. "In fact, I was going to ask you all about her. She hasn't been turning in her homework, and she seems only 'half there' in class."

"Same thing in history," Keith, the history teacher and Lorraine's homeroom teacher, adds. "We'd better see what's going on. . . . I'll call her parents tonight."

The first middle school was created in Bay City, Michigan, in 1950, and from their inception, as this episode suggests, middle schools have tried to do things differently than junior highs (Manning, 2000). Effective middle schools make the following adaptations (Weiss & Kipnes, 2006):

- *They organize teachers and students into interdisciplinary teams.* For example, a team composed of a math, science, English, and social studies teacher instructs the same group of students and works together to coordinate topics.
- *They attempt to create and maintain long-term teacher–student relationships with attention to emotional development.* In many middle schools, a period is set aside to allow teachers to carefully track their students' academic progress and discuss nonacademic topics.
- *They use interactive teaching strategies.* Teachers are encouraged to move away from the lecture-dominated instruction so common in high schools and toward instruction based on questioning and student involvement. In addition, teachers place greater emphasis on study strategies, such as note taking and time management.
- *They eliminate activities that emphasize developmental differences, such as competitive sports.* In middle schools everyone is invited to participate in intramural sports and clubs.

When done well, the preceding adaptations have a positive influence on students (Weiss & Kipnes, 2006). For instance, interdisciplinary teams allow teachers to efficiently plan for the integration of topics across different content areas, as Robin and Mary did with math and science. Also, when teachers have the same students, they can more carefully monitor students' progress, as the team did with Lorraine. Forming relationships with students helps them adjust to an atmosphere less personal than that in their elementary schools. And eliminating competitive sports encourages greater participation in athletic activities and minimizes the advantages early-maturing students have over their later-developing classmates.

Interactive teaching strategies are particularly important in middle school. These strategies actively involve students in learning activities that can also develop their thinking and social interaction skills. Research indicates that motivation often drops during the early adolescent years, and some researchers believe that this drop is due to increased use of lecture as a teaching strategy, which places students in passive roles (Pintrich & Schunk, 2002; Stipek, 2002). We discuss interactive teaching strategies in more depth in Chapter 12.

The number of middle schools continues to increase. By the start of the 21st century, middle schools outnumbered junior highs by a ratio of 4 to 1 (National Center for Education Statistics, 2002). However, middle schools are currently being criticized from several perspectives. A comprehensive report by the Rand Corporation critical of existing middle schools contributed to the controversy (Juvonen et al., 2004). Advocates of a greater emphasis on academics question the emphasis on development and growth; instead, they recommend a return to basics, with greater attention to reading and math. One proposal receiving increased attention and actually implemented in a number of large cities, including Baltimore, Cincinnati, and Philadelphia, suggests returning to a K–8 organization model where academics are stressed (Yecke, 2006). Defenders of the middle school concept claim that the problem isn't the idea itself, but the fact that it never has been effectively implemented (Swaim, 2004). The emphasis that the No Child Left Behind (NCLB) legislation places on testing, accountability, and subject matter mastery (discussed in Chapter 1) is likely to fuel this controversy.

This section addresses the third item in our beginning-of-chapter survey, which said, "Middle and junior high schools are essentially the same but are given different labels." If middle schools are designed according to their original conceptions, the statement is false.

High Schools

Each of you attended high school, and some of you have graduated only within the last year or two. Most of you probably graduated from a **comprehensive high school**, a secondary school that attempts to meet the needs of all students (see Chapter 5 for a discussion of the history of high schools). Let's examine the comprehensive high school more closely.

The Comprehensive High School

In *The American High School*, James Conant (1959) argued persuasively that the most effective high schools are those large enough to offer diverse academic courses and facilities for all students (Hammack, 2004). In attempting to do this, most high schools organize students into tracks (Oakes, 2005). For example, students in the college-preparatory track take courses designed to prepare them for college-level work. A college-prep track might include honors or advanced placement classes in core subject areas. **Advanced placement classes** are courses taken in high school that allow students to earn college credit, making college less time-consuming and expensive. A general track composed of "standard" classes is designed for students of average ability who may or may not go on to college. Students in this track may take some vocational courses, such as word processing, designed to provide them with practical skills they can use immediately after graduating. A vocational track specifically targets students not going to college, preparing them for careers in such areas as automobile repair or technology.

Extracurricular activities provide valuable learning opportunities not typically tapped by traditional classrooms. (Scott Cunningham/Merrill).

A comprehensive high school also offers extracurricular activities (e.g., band, chorus, and theater) and athletics (e.g., football, swimming, soccer, and tennis). These options are intended to integrate students from different tracks, allowing them to mix and learn about other students, and to help all students develop personally, socially, and intellectually.

Criticisms of the Comprehensive High School.   Can a comprehensive high school be all things to all students? Critics say no and focus on four factors: tracking, size, departmentalization, and lack of academic rigor.

A paradox of the comprehensive high school is that different tracks, designed to present quality alternatives, often produce exactly the opposite. Instead of providing freedom and choice, tracking limits choices and segregates students, often leaving many with substandard educational experiences (Oakes, 2005). Lower-ability, minority, and low-socioeconomic status (SES) students are often steered into vocational or lower-level tracks, where the curriculum is less challenging and instruction is often poor. Instead of effectively preparing students for the world of work, lower tracks often segregate students from their college-bound peers and communicate that challenge and deep understanding are not for them. Some critics charge that tracking should be eliminated completely and that all students should be prepared, to the extent possible, for college work (Vander Ark, 2003).

Comprehensive high school. A secondary school that attempts to meet the needs of all students.

Advanced placement classes. Courses taken in high school that allow students to earn college credit.

A second criticism of high schools relates to school size, which exceeds 1,000 students in many U.S. high schools (Feldman, López, & Simon, 2006; Howley & Howley, 2004). As schools become larger, they also tend to become more impersonal and bureaucratic. They virtually become shopping malls in which students mill around looking for entertainment and educational bargains. Like smart shoppers, the brighter students (or their parents) know what they want and quickly find the more challenging, college-preparatory courses. Lower achievers get lost in the shuffle, spending time but not receiving a quality education (Howley & Howley, 2004). One critic remarked that because of their unwieldy size, "our high schools are the least effective part of the American education system" (Vander Ark, 2003, p. 52).

According to critics, departmentalization, or the organization of teachers and classes into separate academic areas, is a third problem of the comprehensive high school. Departmentalization fragments the curriculum and interferes with learning:

While the adults organize as separate departmental entities isolated from one another, however, their teenage students seek interconnectedness and relevancy in their school experience. What they get instead is math with no relationship to social studies, science without any connection to literature, and so forth. This relevancy-starved approach continues year in, year out with no alternatives, and any "reforms" seen in public education are invariably found at the elementary or middle school level. (Cooperman, 2003, p. 30)

To prevent such fragmentation, some educators suggest that schools cluster teachers and classes into interdisciplinary teams, as in effective middle schools, where connections between disciplines are emphasized.

A fourth criticism of comprehensive high schools relates to academic rigor; in attempting to be all things to all students, high schools fail to challenge students and provide them with the necessary job skills needed for a technologically oriented modern society (Botstein, 2006; Perkins-Gough, 2005a). Bill Gates, president of Microsoft, claimed U.S. high schools are "obsolete" and ruin the lives of millions of Americans every year because they fail to prepare students for the modern world of work (Hammack, 2005). Others decry the lack of academic challenge and the failure of high schools to engage the minds of teenage youth (Botstein, 2006). Solutions to these problems range from more rigorous graduation requirements, especially in core areas such as math, science, and English, to high school exit exams (Perkins-Gough, 2005b).

Alternatives to Comprehensive High Schools. One concrete solution to the problem of large high schools is the creation of "smaller learning communities" within large schools, allowing students to keep the same guidance counselor throughout high school, and offering specific opportunities for students and teachers to get to know one another. These ideas are discussed further in the section on school size later in the chapter.

A second alternative to large, comprehensive high schools is the creation of **career technical** schools designed to provide students with education and job skills that will enable them to get a job immediately after graduating from high school (Lynch, 2000).In more than 1,000 vocational centers nationwide, students attend part of the day or evening in specialized programs. They then attend their "home" high school for academic or general education courses during the other part of the day. In addition, about 250 career or specialty high schools in the United States focus on preparing students for work in a particular occupation or industry but also offer the academic and general courses at that school. Students attend these career technical schools full time (Lynch, 2000).

Career technical, or vocational education as it was called earlier, got its beginning in the early 1900s to better meet the need of working class children who were, for the first time, attending high schools in large numbers but were not headed for professional careers. Early vocational programs were designed to prepare students with practical skills for the nation's farms, factories, and homes. Currently, programs have evolved, with more emphasis on technology-related careers.

Career technical. A term used to identify programs designed to provide students with education and job skills that will enable them to get a job immediately after graduating from high school.

As with many other aspects of education, career technical education is going through a process of reform. Most of the reforms are aimed at increasing academic standards and related general educational knowledge together with teaching students all aspects of an industry rather than focusing on a specific job skill. The federal government currently contributes an annual $1.3 billion to these programs to encourage modernizing and focusing academic programs on essential job skills (Cavanagh, 2006a). However, interest in these programs continues to decline as more and more students opt for college-prep programs (Newman, 2006).

Making Connections:
To deepen your understanding of the topics in this section of the chapter and integrate them with topics you've already studied, go to the *Making Connections* module for Chapter 7 at **www.prenhall.com/kauchak**. Respond to questions 5–9.

teaching in an era of reform

Grade Retention

Because it makes sense to expose students to increasingly complex ideas as they develop, U.S. schools are organized so that children progress from grade to grade as they grow older. But what should happen when a student can't master course content at a specific grade level?

The United States has shown an increased interest in grade retention, the practice of having students repeat a grade if they don't meet certain criteria. An important plank in current reform efforts is the elimination of "social promotion"—that is, promoting low-achieving students to the next grade so they can be with their age-similar peers.

Grade retention is not new, but its popularity as a reform tool has grown over the years; in the 2000–2001 school year, 11 percent of Texas third graders were retained (Bali, Anagnostopoulos, & Roberts, 2005). In 2005, 7 other states linked retention to test scores, typically in grades 3, 5, and 8, and Florida even considered grade-retention policies based on test scores for all grade levels (Richard, 2005).

The Issue

Proponents of grade retention argue that retaining students in a grade until they've acquired the knowledge and skills for that level makes sense (Greene & Winters, 2006). For example, allowing students to move from the fourth to the fifth grade when they haven't mastered the content and abilities expected of typical fourth graders is counterproductive because students are less likely to succeed in the fifth grade. Spending a second year in a grade gives learners another chance to acquire the necessary understanding and skills and sends the message that schoolwork is important.

Opponents of grade retention argue that holding students back does not improve their academic performance, and they further argue that the costs don't justify any benefits that might result (Eide & Goldhaber, 2005). They also point to studies indicating that students retained in grade tend to perform lower on subsequent achievement tests than their nonretained classmates (Jimerson, Pletcher, & Graydon, 2006) and are also more likely to later drop out of school (Holmes, 2006). Opponents note

that school dropouts are five times more likely to have repeated a grade than students who complete high school and that the probability of dropping out for students who repeat two grades is nearly 100 percent. They further note that minorities and low-SES children are much more likely to be retained than are their White, wealthier counterparts (Anagnostopoulos, 2006).

Opponents also argue that grade retention causes emotional problems. In one study children rated the prospect of repeating a grade as more stressful than "wetting in class" or being caught stealing. Going blind or losing a parent were the only two life events that children said would be more stressful than being retained (Shepard & Smith, 1990). Opponents note that the psychological effects of grade retention are especially acute in adolescence, where physical size differences and peer awareness exacerbate the problem (G. Anderson, Jimerson, & Whipple, 2002).

Finally, opponents suggest, better alternatives to social promotion are available. Before- and after-school programs, summer school programs with reduced class sizes, instructional aides who work with low-achieving children, and peer tutoring are all alternatives. Each is less expensive than the thousands of dollars spent on having children repeat what they have already experienced, and students in these alternative programs are more likely to meet standards than those who have repeated grades (Jimerson, Pletcher, & Graydon, 2006).

You Take a Position

Now it's your turn to take a position on the issue. State in writing whether you do or do not believe that grade retention is beneficial and is likely to increase student learning, and provide a two-page rationale for your position.

For additional references and resources, go to the Companion Website at **www.prenhall.com/kauchak**, *then to the* Teaching in an Era of Reform *module for Chapter 7. You can respond online or submit your response to your instructor.*

Check Your Understanding

3.1   What are two ways in which teaching in an elementary school differs from teaching in a middle school, junior high, or high school?

3.2   What are four differences between effective middle schools and junior highs?

3.3   Describe a comprehensive high school. How does a comprehensive high school differ from a vocational high school?

 For feedback, go to Appendix A, Check Your Understanding, *located in the back of this text.*

What Is an Effective School?

You're either thinking about teaching or are actually planning to teach; this is the reason you're taking this course. A major factor that will influence your satisfaction in teaching will be the effectiveness of that school in promoting student learning and development. But what is an effective school, and what is it like to teach in one? We try to answer these questions in this section.

Although the public commonly refers to schools as good or not so good, as in "Woodrow Wilson is a very good elementary school," researchers use the term *effective* instead. An effective school is one in which learning for all students is maximized. But how does a school do this? Researchers attempting to answer this question identified schools that, despite challenging circumstances, produced more learning in their students than comparable ones that weren't as successful (Marzano, 2003). They also looked at poor-performing schools as counterexamples. Let's see what these researchers found.

Research on Effective Schools

Research has identified several characteristics of schools that maximize learning for all students (Bransford, Brown, & Cocking, 2000; Taylor, Pressley, & Pearson, 2002). They are outlined in Figure 7.1 and discussed in the sections that follow.

Figure 7.1   Characteristics of Effective Schools

> **Effective school.** A school in which learning for all students is maximized.

Optimal School and Class Size

This chapter focuses on school organization, and the way schools are organized has a significant effect on learning. An important dimension of this organization is size—both the size of the school and the size of classes.

School Size. Are small schools better than big ones, or is the reverse true? As it turns out, the relationship between size and quality isn't simple or direct. Schools must be large enough to provide the varied curricular offerings needed to help students learn in different content areas, but not so large that students get lost (Ready, Lee, & Welner, 2004).

How big is too big? The largest high school on record, DeWitt Clinton High School in the Bronx, boasted 12,000 students in 1934 (Allen, 2002). (Can you imagine what it must have been like to be a ninth grader walking into that school on the first day of the school year?) One-room elementary schools are at the other end of the spectrum; for example, one K–4 elementary school in Grantville, Vermont, had 18 students in 2002 (Shelley, 2003). School size also relates to level, with elementary schools being the smallest and high schools the largest. In the 2000–2001 school year, the average elementary school in the United States had 482 students, and the average secondary school had 795 students (National Center for Education Statistics, 2002). More than 70 percent of U.S. high school students, however, attend schools of 1,000 students or more, and a number of urban districts have high schools of over 5,000 students (Allen, 2002).

Research suggests the ideal size for a high school is considerably less than this, somewhere between 600 and 900 students (Lee, 2000). This research suggests that the fourth item on our beginning-of-chapter survey, which said, "In general, larger schools provide a better-quality education, because they have better facilities and a wider variety of programs," is not true. Schools must be large enough to provide adequate facilities and resources, but not so large that they lose the human, personal dimension.

School size affects low- and high-SES students differently. For example, the decrease in learning in very large or very small high schools is greater for low-SES than it is for high-SES students (Howley & Howley, 2004). The only schools not fitting this pattern are elite private schools that enroll students with similar backgrounds and provide extensive resources, such as well-equipped science and computer labs. Unfortunately, a disproportionate number of low-SES students attend either very small or very large high schools. Examples include small rural schools in sparsely populated states, such as Wyoming or Montana, and large, urban schools in major cities such as New York or Los Angeles.

How does school size influence student learning? Researchers suggest that school size, in itself, doesn't cause students to learn less than they would in an ideally sized school. Rather, size influences other factors (Feldman et al., 2006; Ready et al., 2004). As schools become larger, for example, it becomes more difficult to create learning environments that promote a sense of physical and emotional safety in students. In large schools, education is less personal, and it is harder for teachers and students to get to know one another and to work together.

Both parents and teachers want smaller schools, but the cost of building them deters taxpayers. In a national survey, parents said they felt their children received a more rigorous and personalized education in smaller schools, and teachers said that smaller schools prevented students from "falling through the cracks" (Public Agenda, 2002). Research also supports smaller schools, indicating that they have significantly higher graduation and college attendance rates and fewer discipline and safety issues than do large schools (Vander Ark, 2002).

One solution to the problem of large schools is to create schools within schools, smaller learning communities where both teachers and students feel more comfortable. For example, Kernan Middle School in Jacksonville, Florida, has over 1,200 students, more than experts recommend for any school, in particular for a middle school.

To address the issue of school size, Kernan students are placed within "houses" of approximately 400 students at the start of 6th grade. The students then stay in their houses through 8th grade, enabling them to get to know and recognize the adults in their building. They deal with a small front office managed by an assistant principal, who, for all intents and purposes, is the principal of this mini school. The students get to know all the teachers in the hallway as well as the other students who are part of their houses. The goal is for each student to be well known by at least one adult. Students are at ease in making the transition to the next grade level because of the feeling of familiarity with the house and all its components (people, rules, procedures). Typically, when asked, a student will identify himself or herself as a "house B student." At the end of the middle school experience, this student will hopefully have formed meaningful, personal relationships with more people than they would if they were in a school of 1,200 students with less of an identity (Desiree DiFabio, Personal Communication, September 11, 2006).

Class-size reduction can be an effective tool to increase achievement. [Scott Cunningham/Merrill]

Class Size. Class size also influences a school's effectiveness. Classes of 20 or fewer students are considered optimal, but many classes are much larger, especially in middle, junior high, and high schools. One of your authors recently taught a high school health teacher who had 47 students assigned to her class. If all the students showed up for class, there weren't enough desks. Although critics argue either that class size doesn't matter or that reducing class size isn't worth the cost, research consistently indicates that reducing class size does, indeed, increase learning for all students, and the effects are particularly pronounced in the lower grades and for students placed at-risk (Gilman & Kiger, 2003; Peevely, Hedges, & Nye, 2005).

Reductions in class size can have both short- and long-term positive effects (Finn, Gerber, & Boyd-Zaharias, 2005; Nye, Hedges, & Konstantopoulos, 2001). In Tennessee, where average class sizes were reduced from 25 to 15 students, researchers found immediate gains in reading and math scores. Follow-up studies revealed that the positive effects lasted through 12th grade; low-SES students who participated in the program for 4 years were twice as likely to graduate from high school as their large-class-size counterparts. Students in the smaller classes also took more challenging courses later on in school, and were more likely to attend college than their counterparts in larger classes. These positive effects were especially strong for low-SES and African-American students.

Smaller class sizes also positively affect teachers' lives; when class sizes are reduced, teachers' morale and job satisfaction increase (Muñoz & Portes, 2002). In smaller classes, teachers spend less time on discipline and more time on small-group work and diagnostic assessment. Researchers caution, however, that these positive changes don't occur automatically; teachers need to learn how to adjust their instruction to take advantage of the smaller number of students in their classrooms (Peevely, Hedges, & Nye, 2005).

Clear School Mission and Strong Leadership

In effective schools, a clearly stated mission exists, and it remains at the forefront of the thinking of the entire school staff. For example, if developing literacy is emphasized in the mission of an elementary school, evidence of this theme appears in teachers' instruction. Teachers focus on reading comprehension in all classes, not simply when they are explicitly teaching reading, and children are given extensive practice in putting their understanding of math, science, and other content into words. The same is true for other aspects of the school mission. In effective schools, teachers share an understanding of and commitment to instructional goals, priorities, and assessment procedures, and they accept responsibility for students' meeting the school's curricular goals.

Strong leadership is essential to the success of a school. In effective schools, the principal understands learning and teaching and acts as an instructional leader who can advise staff and serve as a resource to parents and students (Mosenthal et al., 2004; Sergiovanni, 2004, 2006). Faculty meetings focus on instructional issues, and learning and effective teaching are continually discussed topics.

Safe and Orderly Environment

As you saw in Chapter 4, students are concerned about school safety issues, such as fighting, bullying, and other students who are disruptive in class. Schools, which should be sheltered communities for learning, often mirror the problems of society. Marzano (2003) noted, "If teachers and students do not feel safe, they will not have the necessary psychological energy for teaching and learning" (p. 53).

The need for safe and orderly schools is supported by both research and theory. Researchers found effective schools to be places of trust, order, cooperation, and high morale (Marzano, 2003; Rutter, Maughan, Mortimore, Ouston, & Smith, 1979). Students need to feel emotionally safe in schools for learning to occur.

One essential characteristic of an effective school is hallways that are safe and orderly.
(Getty Images, Inc.–PhotoDisc)

Theories of learner development, which we briefly discussed earlier in the chapter, suggest that people are born with a desire to live in an orderly rather than chaotic world (Piaget 1952, 1970). In addition, the psychologist Abraham Maslow (1968), who described a hierarchy of human needs, argued that only the need for survival is more basic than the need for safety. Studies of classroom management also confirm the need for order; orderly classrooms promote both learning and student motivation (Emmer, Evertson, & Worsham, 2006; Evertson, Emmer, & Worsham, 2006).

Strong Parental Involvement

Schools, no matter how well they're organized, can't be effective if parents aren't involved in their children's education (Marzano, 2003). Learning is a cooperative venture, in which teachers, students, and parents are in it together.

Research indicates that students benefit from home–school cooperation in a number of ways, including the following:

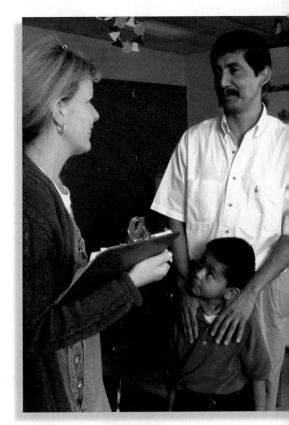

- Students achieve more, regardless of SES, ethnic/racial background, or the parents' levels of education. The more extensive the parental involvement, the higher the student achievement.
- Students earn higher grades and test scores, attend school more regularly, and complete homework more consistently.
- Students exhibit more positive attitudes and behavior.
- Student alcohol use, violence, and antisocial behaviors decrease as parental involvement increases.
- Educators hold higher expectations for students whose parents collaborate with teachers. They also hold higher opinions of those parents (U.S. Department of Education, 2001).

Effective schools develop mechanisms to allow parents and teachers to work together.
(Michael Newman/PhotoEdit Inc.)

These outcomes likely result from parents' increased participation in school activities, their more positive attitudes about schooling, and teachers' increased understanding of students' home environments. (We examine strategies for involving parents in detail in Chapter 11.)

Academic Focus

Promoting learning is the central mission of effective schools, and as we saw earlier, this mission is clear to the teachers in the school, and the tone is set by the school principal and other administrators. In academically focused schools, teachers have high expectations, and they maximize the time available for instruction. Students are directly involved in learning activities for as much of the day as possible, and instruction remains focused on essential content and skills. An array of clubs, sports, and other extracurricular offerings exist and are important, but they don't take precedence over learning. In effective schools, for example, classes are not canceled so students can attend sporting events, and class time isn't used for club meetings.

One study investigating the effects of academic focus on learning concluded, "Students learn more in schools that set high standards for academic performance, that use their instructional time wisely, and that use student learning as a criterion for making decisions" (Lee & Smith, 1999, p. 941). Schools with an academic focus are also more positive places in which to work because both students and teachers feel that learning is occurring. You will want to look for signs that academic focus is present in the schools in which you're considering working.

High Collective Efficacy

Contributing to a school's academic focus is **high collective efficacy**, the belief by teachers that their school can make a difference in students' lives (Goddard, Hoy, & Hoy, 2004). High collective efficacy begins with **personal teaching efficacy**, each teacher's belief that he or she can promote learning in all students, regardless of their backgrounds. High-efficacy teachers take responsibility for the success of their own instruction (Bruning, Schraw, Norby, & Ronning, 2004). In other words, if students aren't learning as much as they should be, rather than blaming students' lack of intelligence, poor home environments, uncooperative administrators, or some other cause, high-efficacy teachers conclude that they could be doing a better job and look for ways to increase student learning.

Three aspects of high-collective-efficacy schools are important. First, students from all socioeconomic levels—high, middle, and low—learn more in them than they do in schools where collective efficacy is lower. This, in itself, isn't surprising; it makes sense that the more teachers strive for student learning, the more students will learn. Second, and more important, low-SES students in high-collective-efficacy schools have achievement levels nearly as high as high-SES students in low-collective-efficacy schools. Third, differences in achievement levels among low-, middle-, and high-SES students in high-collective-efficacy schools are smaller than they are in low-collective-efficacy schools (Lee, 2000). In other words, high-collective-efficacy schools help reduce achievement differences between groups of students who typically benefit quite differently from schooling.

How do high-efficacy teachers and high-collective-efficacy schools accomplish these results? A number of factors contribute, but two are essential: (1) interactive instruction and (2) frequent monitoring of student progress.

High collective efficacy. The belief by teachers that their school can make a difference in students' lives.

Personal teaching efficacy. Each teacher's belief that he or she can promote learning in all students, regardless of their backgrounds.

Interactive Instruction

Cassie Jones walks through the halls of the inner-city middle school where she is the principal and listens to the sounds coming from the different classrooms. As she walks by Ben Carlson's social studies class, she hears him say, "Yesterday we talked about the stengths and weaknesses of the North and South at the outbreak of the Civil War. Who remembers one of these?"

As Cassie proceeds down the hall, she stops in front of Sarah McCarthy's science class. Sarah is at the front of the room swinging a set of keys from a piece of string. "Hmmm," Cassie thinks, "no wonder her class is so quiet—she's got them hypnotized." As she listens further, she hears Sarah ask,

"Class, this is a simple pendulum, just like the one we find in grandfather clocks. Who can tell me what factors influence the rate at which a pendulum swings?"

"Good question," thinks Cassie. "Maybe that's why her kids are so quiet."

When Cassie turns the corner, she is greeted by a steady stream of student voices arguing about something.

"I don't care what you say, stealing is wrong."

"But his family didn't have enough to eat. They were hungry—he couldn't let them starve!"

"What's Hector up to today?" Cassie thinks as she listens more closely to Hector Sanchez's English class.

"Class," Hector breaks in with a booming voice, "it's not enough just to disagree with your partners. You have to explain why. Remember, one of the reasons we read books like Sounder *is to help us understand our own lives. So, you have three more minutes in your discussion groups to explain why the father was right or wrong to steal food for his family."*

Cassie chuckles as she hears Hector's class rejoin the battle. "He's sure got them stirred up today. I guess I'm lucky to have such a talented teaching staff that has so many different strengths" (adapted from Jacobsen, Eggen, & Kauchak, 2006, pp. 194–195).

Imagine that you're walking through the hallways of a school, the doors of classrooms are open, and you glance inside. Can you determine anything about the effectiveness of the school with a simple glance? The answer is *yes*. If the prevailing pattern is one in which teachers are asking large numbers of questions and students are involved in discussions, the likelihood that the school is effective increases. In contrast, if you see teachers primarily lecturing or students spending most of their time working alone and doing seat work, the school is less likely to be effective. Evaluating schools in this way is admittedly simplistic, and many additional factors influence how much students learn. Nevertheless, interaction between teacher and students and students with one another is an essential ingredient for learning (Eggen & Kauchak, 2007).

Not only is interactive teaching essential for learning, it is also important for motivation (Pintrich & Schunk, 2002). Students at all levels prefer challenging and interactive activities to ones that require them to sit passively, listening to teacher lectures (Brophy, 2004). Effective schools provide opportunities for students to become actively involved in their learning.

Frequent Monitoring of Student Progress

The extent to which teachers frequently assess learning and provide students with feedback is another essential factor differentiating more- from less-effective schools. Experts suggest that effective learning environments are assessment centered (Bransford, Brown, & Cocking, 2000). In other words, assessment isn't tacked on at the end of an instructional period, such as teachers' giving a test once a month or at the end of a unit; rather, it is an integral part of the entire teaching–learning process. Teachers in effective schools continually collect information about students' learning progress. They regularly collect work samples and give frequent quizzes and tests, and the assessments measure more than recall of facts. Teachers return assessments, such as quizzes and assignments, shortly after they're given, and the teachers thoroughly discuss test items to provide students with feedback about their responses (Bransford et al., 2000; Marzano, 2003). The need for assessment-centered classrooms also helps us understand why interactive instruction is so essential. Teachers gather a great deal of information about students' understanding by listening to their attempts to describe their thinking.

So, now we have an answer to the fifth item on our introductory survey, "The assessment program in a school is a major factor influencing the school's effectiveness." Students, parents, and teachers all use assessment data to determine whether school learning is taking place.

Parents' and Other Taxpayers' Perceptions of Effective Schools

How do parents and taxpayers view effective schools? On what do they base their perceptions? What do they most commonly look for in judging a school? Let's take a look.

School Organization and the Achievement of Cultural Minorities

Emphasis on higher standards and increased accountability is the most prominent reform in education today. Change, however, can have unintended outcomes, and one outcome of this reform has been a widening gap between the achievement of cultural minorities—particularly African-American and Hispanic students—and the achievement of their White and Asian counterparts (Hoff, 2000). Between 1970, when the National Assessment of Educational Progress first began systematically measuring students' achievement, and 1980, African-American and Hispanic students made great progress in narrowing the achievement gap that had separated them from their White peers. This progress stopped abruptly in the late 1980s, however, and since then the gap has either remained constant or widened (Fairchild, 2006; Jencks & Phillips, 1998). Dropout rates for minority students have followed a similar pattern, either flattening out or even increasing (Olson, 2006b). Similarly, recent data on schools found lacking under NCLB rules found a preponderance of failing schools with high proportions of minority students and students of poverty (Archer, 2006a).

Researchers have cited numerous factors to explain these differences in achievement between White and minority students, including poverty, peer pressure, and parental values (Byrnes, 2003; Ogbu, 2003). These are all likely candidates, but research has also identified two aspects of school organization that are believed to influence the achievement of minority students: tracking and class size.

Cultural Minorities and Tracking

Earlier in the chapter, we mentioned that comprehensive high schools have been criticized for the practice of tracking, because evidence indicates that educational experiences on lower-level

Tracking can result in the segregation of cultural minorities into low-level classes where instruction tends to be less challenging. (AP Wide World Photos)

tracks are often substandard (Oakes, 2005). This evidence is particularly relevant for cultural minorities, because they tend to be underrepresented in higher-level tracks and overrepresented in lower-level tracks. The problem is exacerbated by the fact that minority students tend not to enroll in more demanding classes. As shown in Table 7.3, the students least likely to enroll in such classes are also least likely to graduate from college (Viadero, 2000).

Tracking and minority achievement have a form of negative synergy; that is, student achievement in low-level classes is reduced compared to the achievement of students of comparable ability in high-level classes. Because decisions about tracking are based on students' records of past achievement, minority students continue to be placed in lower-level tracks, and the negative relationship between achievement and tracking is magnified. Unfortunately, school leaders haven't identified a satisfactory solution to this problem.

Cultural Minorities and Class Size

The relationship between class size and minority achievement is more encouraging. Earlier we said that research supports the contention that student achievement is higher in smaller classes. This research is important, because the beneficial effects of reducing class size are greater for cultural minorities than for nonminorities (Gewertz, 2000; Smith, Molnar, & Zahorik, 2003).

Two studies are particularly significant. First, assessments of a major class-size-reduction project in Tennessee found the following (Finn et al., 2005; Illig, 1996):

- Children in small classes (about 15 students per class) consistently outperformed children in larger classes.
- Inner-city children (about 97 percent of whom were minorities) in small classes closed some of the achievement gap between themselves and nonminority children in large classes.
- Children in small classes outperformed children in larger classes, even when teachers in the large classes had support from aides.

In the second study, a 4-year experiment with class-size reduction in Wisconsin, researchers found that the achievement gap between minorities and nonminorities shrank by 19 percent in smaller classes, whereas in comparable regular classrooms it grew by 58 percent (Molnar, Percy, Smith, & Zahorik, 1998; Smith, Molnar, & Zahorik, 2003). In addition to narrowing the achievement gap between minority and nonminority students in first grade, the program also prevented it from widening when class-size-reduction students progressed to second- and third-grade classrooms. Researchers have found that when class sizes are reduced, teachers have more personal contacts with individual students and can design more effective learning activ-

TABLE 7.3 Percentages of Students Taking Advanced Math Courses and Graduating from Four-Year Colleges

Race/Ethnicity	1992 High School Graduates Who Completed Algebra 2 and Geometry (%)	Freshmen at Four-Year Colleges Who Graduate Within Six Years (%)
Asian-American	55.5	65
White	53.1	59
Hispanic American	41.9	46
Native American	35.7	37
African-American	35	40

Source: Data from Johnston & Viadero (2000).

ities to engage students (Blatchford, Bassett, & Brown, 2005). The results of the class-size-reduction experiment were so compelling that the Wisconsin legislature appropriated $59 million beginning in 2000 to expand the program to 400 schools (Gewertz, 2000).

If the other characteristics of an effective school don't exist, however, reducing the number of students in classes, by itself, won't increase achievement. Narrowing the achievement gap requires the systematic implementation of all the effective school characteristics.

The results of research examining parents' and other taxpayers' perceptions of effective schools are not surprising. As would be expected, people react most strongly to factors that are concrete and observable. For example, as a result of highly publicized incidents of school violence, school safety is a primary concern, and both parents and other taxpayers rank creating orderly classrooms as one of the most important problems teachers face (L. Rose & Gallup, 2004).

Parents and other taxpayers also look for qualified teachers and test results as indicators of student and school performance (Olson, 1999a). The desire for qualified teachers isn't surprising, because teachers represent schools and are the people who work most directly with parents' sons and daughters. To determine how children and schools are doing, parents also turn to standardized test scores and school report cards. Currently, under the federal NCLB, all states are required to test students annually and publish report cards on their schools; in accordance with NCLB, in 2006, all 50 states were regularly testing students and publishing annual report cards on individual schools (Archer, 2006a). Olson (1999b) summarized parents' views of effective schools: "In short, parents and taxpayers view school safety and the presence of qualified teachers as two essential ingredients of education. Once those basic conditions are met, they want results" (p. 34).

These results are consistent with the characteristics of effective schools discussed earlier. For instance, we saw school safety on both lists. Other factors, such as teaching efficacy, interactive instruction, and frequent monitoring of student progress, are more complex and harder to understand for people outside the profession.

Making Connections:
To deepen your understanding of the topics in this section of the chapter and integrate them with topics you've already studied, go to the *Making Connections* module for Chapter 7 at **www.prenhall.com/kauchak**. Respond to questions 10–13.

Check Your Understanding

4.1   Describe the characteristics of an effective school.

4.2   What is the most distinguishing characteristic of effective instruction in effective schools?

4.3   Why is frequent monitoring of student progress essential for an effective school?

   For feedback, go to Appendix A, Check Your Understanding, *located in the back of this text.*

decision making

Defining Yourself as a Professional

You're sitting in the teacher workroom about a month into a new school year, and one of your colleagues comes in and comments, "I just don't know what's wrong with these kids. I explained everything so carefully yesterday, and when they came in today it was as if they hadn't heard a word I said.

"On the other hand, these kids come from the worst backgrounds, so there isn't all that much we can do about them anyway. They won't pay attention, they don't give a rip about what we're studying, and they won't take a lick of responsibility for their own learning.

"Their parents, if they even are living with their parents, don't care either, so what's the use. If I can gut it out until the end of this year, I'm going to try for all I'm worth to get a transfer at the end the year."

What would you say to your colleague?

To respond to this question online and receive immediate *feedback, go to the* Decision Making *module for Chapter 7 on the Companion Website at* **www.prenhall.com/kauchak.**

Meeting Your Learning Objectives

1. Describe different meanings of the concept *school.*
    *   One definition describes schools as places where young people go to learn and develop intellectually, personally, and socially. And schools exist in other places such as vacation bible school or students being homeschooled. Another definition describes a school as a physical place—a building or set of buildings.
    *   This chapter describes a school as a social institution, organized to promote student growth and development, as well as the welfare of society. All societies have a number of social institutions in addition to schools, such as churches and governments.
    *   Schools are organized within districts, administrative units with the responsibility of educating children within geographic areas.

2. Identify the components of a typical school organization.
    *   Personnel make up one component of the total school organization, and personnel include the school principal and other administrators, support staff (e.g., administrative assistants, custodians, and cafeteria workers), and teachers.
    *   The physical plant, another component, includes the buildings that house classrooms, the library, computer labs, the cafeteria, and the administration. In addition, junior highs and high schools usually have gymnasiums, playing fields, sometimes swimming pools, and may even have buildings devoted to fine arts.
    *   The curriculum, what is taught in school, is a third component, and it is typically organized into grade levels, and content is intended to be taught to students of different ages.

3. Describe important differences between schools at different levels.
    *   Educators have come to realize the importance of early learning experiences—at home and in programs such as preschools and kindergartens—for long-term school success.

Developmentally appropriate programs attempt to match classroom instruction to the learning needs of young children.

- Elementary schools are organized so that a single teacher is responsible for all, or most, of the instruction in the different content areas. Elementary teachers arrange their own schedules, and the amount of time they allocate to different content areas can vary widely. Typically, elementary teachers emphasize reading, language arts, and math in their instruction, and they de-emphasize content areas such as science, social studies, and the arts.
- High schools, junior highs, and middle schools are organized very differently than elementary schools. Teachers in these schools have content specialties, they teach only in these specialty areas, and class schedules are fixed schoolwide.

4. **Identify the characteristics of an effective school.**
   - Effective schools promote learning for all students. Size is important. Effective elementary schools keep class sizes below 20 students per class, and effective high schools have enrollments in the 600–900 range.
   - Effective schools are safe and orderly, academically focused, and involve parents. Teachers in effective schools take responsibility for student learning, maintain high levels of interaction with students, and continually monitor student progress.
   - Polls indicate that parents and other taxpayers emphasize school safety and order, highly qualified teachers, and student scores on standardized tests as indicators of an effective school.

Important Concepts

administrators (p. 216)
advanced placement classes (p. 227)
career technical (p. 228)
comprehensive high school (p. 227)
curriculum (p. 218)
development (p. 219)
developmental programs (p. 222)
early childhood education (p. 221)

effective school (p. 230)
high collective efficacy (p. 234)
looping (p. 220)
middle schools (p. 225)
personal teaching efficacy (p. 234)
principal (p. 216)
school district (p. 215)
social institution (p. 215)

Developing as a Professional

Preparing for Your Licensure Exam

This exercise will provide you with practice answering questions similar to the Praxis™ Principles of Learning and Teaching Exam as well as your state-specific licensure exam. Read the following case study, and answer the questions that follow.

Donna Barber, an eighth-grade teacher at Lincoln Middle School, a school of about 1,200 students, teaches three sections of standard physical science and two sections of earth science. Donna's schedule is as follows:

Period 1 (Earth Science)	*7:45–8:40*
Period 2 (Standard)	*8:45–9:40*
Period 3 (Earth Science)	*9:45–10:40*
Period 4 (Standard)	*10:45–11:40*
Lunch	*11:45–12:40*
Period 5 (Standard)	*12:45–1:40*
Period 6 (Planning)	*1:45–2:40*

Her fifth-period class has been studying the make-up of the atom and now is moving to a discussion of static electricity.

"C'mon," Susan says to a group of students at 12:43 as they're standing outside the classroom. "The bell is going to ring, and we'll be late."

"Did you finish your homework?" Jay asks Patricia as they walk in.

"Are you kidding? You miss a homework assignment in this class, and you're a dead duck," Amy interjects.

"Yeah," Chris nods. "You don't dare come without it. You know how Mrs. Barber is constantly saying that she wants to find out how well we understand this stuff."

As he enters the classroom, Ken comments, "Boy, Mrs. Barber, you had my whole family on the ropes last night. I had both my Mom and Dad helping me find examples of the elements you assigned us."

"That's great," Donna smiles back. "I know it was a tough assignment, but it makes you think. And besides, it was designed to be practical. It will get easier the more you work at it."

Danielle, who had been standing in front of the room taking roll, hands the roll slip to Donna as the bell rings.

"Thanks, Danielle," Donna smiles, taking the slip and moving to the front of the room. "Class, just a reminder," she continues, "we're having a notebook check tomorrow, and your last test with your parents' signature on it must be in the notebook. I want to be sure your parents know what we've been studying. . . . Also, tell them to e-mail or call me if they have any questions about your score. . . . What are we in school for?"

"Learning!" the students nearly shout in unison, repeating a theme they hear from Donna on a regular basis.

"Yes," Donna smiles at their response. "And Mrs. Garnett, our principal, commented on that again in our last assembly when she emphasized that all of you can understand what you're studying and you can all be successful if you're willing to work. All the teachers in our school feel the same way."

At 12:47 Donna begins, "We've been talking about elements. Let's see what we remember. Look at the model. What element does this represent? . . . Allen?"

"Lithium," Allen responds.

"Good, and how do we know? . . . Kathleen?"

"There are three protons in there."

"All right! Very good. Now let's switch gears. We've been dealing with the nucleus of the atom, but now we're going to focus on the electrons. . . . What do we know about them? . . . Armondo?"

"They're out around the nucleus."

"Yes, good. We've said that the numbers of electrons and protons are equal, and the electrons are in orbit around the nucleus. Are they tightly or loosely attracted to the nucleus? Janice?"

"Sort of loosely, I think."

"Yes, good. We can 'scrape' electrons off," Donna continues, "so we think of them as being loosely attached. Now keep that in mind, because it's important. We can get electrons off the atoms fairly easily with heat or even by simply rubbing them, but the nucleus is very hard to break up."

"Now let's take a look," Donna says as she steps quickly over to her file cabinet and takes out an inflated balloon and a wool sweater. "Watch." She rubs the balloon vigorously with the sweater, steps over to Michelle, and holds the balloon over her hair. "What do you notice here? . . . Vicki?"

"The balloon is making Michelle's hair stick up," Vicki responds to the giggles of the class.

Donna explains that their goal for the day is to understand why the balloon makes Michelle's hair stick up. She then takes another inflated balloon, holds it against the chalkboard, and lets it go. "What happened here? Joe?"

"It just fell down," Joe shrugs.

"Let's try it again," Donna continues and rubs the balloon on the sweater and again holds it against the board.

"Now what? . . . Melody?"

"It's stuck up there now."

Donna uses a series of questions to guide the students into concluding that some of the electrons were rubbed off the sweater and collected on the balloon, so the balloon had more electrons than protons and the extra electrons attracted the protons in Michelle's hair and the board.

Donna explains to students that this is called static electricity, and she continues, "Two everyday examples of static electricity are clothes sticking together in the dryer and getting a shock after you walk across a carpet and touch a doorknob.

"For tomorrow," she says in conclusion, "I want you to write a one-paragraph explanation for each of these using the ideas we've discussed here today."

At 1:38 she says, "OK, everyone. It's time to head for your next class. Collect any paper or other scraps around your desk and get ready to go. We'll start right where we left off tomorrow."

1. Identify at least four characteristics of Lincoln Middle School that are also characteristics of an effective school. Support each of your descriptions with evidence taken directly from the case study.

2. Identify one characteristic of Lincoln Middle School that is not consistent with an effective school.

3. Identify one characteristic of an effective school for which direct evidence doesn't exist in the case study.

To receive feedback on your responses to these exercises, go to the Companion Website at www.prenhall.com/kauchak *, then to the* Preparing for Your Licensure Exam *module for Chapter 7.*

Discussion Questions

1. Based on the organization of typical elementary schools, what are the primary advantages and disadvantages of teaching in an elementary school? How could elementary schools be organized differently to improve the education of all students?

2. Based on the organization of typical middle schools, what are the primary advantages and disadvantages of teaching in a middle school? How could middle schools be organized differently to improve the education of all students?

3. Based on the organization of typical high schools, what are the primary advantages and disadvantages of teaching in a high school? How could high schools be organized differently to improve the education of all students?

4. In which kind of school—elementary, middle, junior high, or high school—do teachers have the most autonomy? The least autonomy? What implications does this have for you as a prospective teacher?

5. Consider what you know about the organization of elementary, middle, junior high, and high schools. Which type of school is best suited to your academic and personal characteristics? Why do you think so?

Developing as a Professional: Online Activities

Going Into Schools

Go to the Companion Website at *www.prenhall.com/kauchak*, and click on the *Going Into Schools* module for Chapter 7. You will find a number of school-based activities that will help you link chapter content to the schools in which you work.

Virtual Field Experience: Using the Internet to Explore the Profession

If you would like to participate in a Virtual Field Experience, access the following Website: *http://www.rand.org/pubs/monographs/2004/RANDMG138.pdf* and *http:www.Indiana.edu/~soenews/ news/news1151614366.html* . These sites contain perspectives and opinions about reform efforts in middle and high schools.

Online Portfolio Activities

To develop your professional portfolio, further apply your understanding of chapter content, and address the INTASC standards, go the Companion Website at *www.prenhall.com/kauchak*, then to the *Online Portfolio Activities* for Chapter 7. Complete the suggested activities.

Governance and Finance: Regulating and Funding Schools

Chapter Outline

Learning Objectives

After you have completed your study of this chapter, you should be able to:

1. Describe the major educational governance structures at the state and local levels.

2. Explain the different sources and targets of educational funding.

3. Describe the major current issues in school governance and finance.

Case Studies

 Elementary

 Middle

 Secondary

Jacksonville-Courier/Clayton Statler/The Image Works

Chapter 8

School governance and school finance may seem irrelevant to beginning teachers, but veterans know better. The way schools are run and school districts' use of money make big differences in the quality of teachers' professional lives. And reform efforts aimed at addressing funding inequalities, increasing decision making at the school level, and providing more educational choices to parents are changing the teaching profession today. To begin our discussion, let's look at the following case study.

Carla Buendia sits at her desk, looking at the pile of books and papers covering it. "I better get this one right, as it'll be our only chance," she thinks to herself. Carla is a member of Unified Metropolitan School District's Elementary Math Steering Committee. Unified Metropolitan is a large district in the Midwest, and the Steering Committee has been meeting regularly over the last 2 years to study the elementary math curriculum in the district. Test scores have been declining, especially in the areas of applications and problem solving, and the committee has been asked to make a recommendation to the district's school board. Tonight is the night.

"Don't be nervous," Carla tells herself, but her advice isn't working. She has been to school board meetings as a spectator when teacher salaries and contracts were being discussed, and she is clearly uneasy about being in front of the hundred or more people who will be in attendance. "Why did I ever say I'd do this?" she thinks. "Too late for that. I just better have my act together when it's my turn to speak."

It can be unsettling to go into two schools within a few miles of each other and see striking differences in how they look and feel. One is bright, cheerful, and clean, with student projects and works of art prominently displayed. The other is dark, depressing, and dirty, and the hallways are cluttered with trash. Some of these differences can be traced to the ways the schools are governed and financed.

School governance and finance also influence the resources available to teachers. As an example, drive across the state line from New Mexico, where the average spending per pupil in 2005 was $8,236, to Utah, where it was $5,245 (National Education Association, 2006b). Some politicians argue that money doesn't influence the quality of education, but evidence suggests otherwise (Biddle & Berliner, 2002; Flanagan & Grissmer, 2002). Money buys paper, supplies, and equipment, for example, and allows students to do science experiments rather than reading about them.

How do school governance and finance affect the lives of teachers and students? We try to answer these questions in this chapter, but before continuing, take a few minutes to respond to the following survey. We discuss each of the items as the chapter unfolds.

---

professional knowledge: test yourself!

For each item, circle the number that best represents your thinking. Use the following scale as a guide.

1 = Strongly disagree
2 = Disagree
3 = Agree/disagree
4 = Agree
5 = Strongly agree

1. Most states govern education in basically the same way.

    1   2   3   4   5

2. The state office of education in each state is responsible for setting rules and regulations.

    1   2   3   4   5

3. The federal government provides the largest source of educational funding.

    1   2   3   4   5

4. Most of a district's budget goes to funding instruction.

    1   2   3   4   5

5. Students across a state are provided with basically the same amount of money to fund their education.

    1   2   3   4   5

This is available in a downloadable format on the Companion Website for personal portfolio use.

Governance: How Are Schools Regulated and Run?

In a few short years, you will walk into your own classroom, look around, and think, "At last, it's all mine." That's a good feeling, and it will be all yours—sort of. Although teachers have considerable autonomy in implementing their own vision of good teaching, they also operate within a specified governance framework.

Governance: A Legal Overview

Unlike many other countries, where the federal government is responsible for schools, in the United States the Tenth Amendment to the Constitution clearly assigns legal responsibility for the education of its citizens to the 50 states.

Because the 50 states differ significantly in geography, history, economics, and politics, you might think that they would also differ in their approaches to governing education, but they don't. Each of the states has a surprisingly similar organizational structure. These structures are outlined in Figure 8.1 and described in the section that follows.

State Governance Structures

In every state a constitution outlines the roles and responsibilities of state officers with respect to education. Governors focus public attention on educational issues and attempt to solicit public support for educational funding. State legislatures meet annually to debate school finance and other issues. These legislative sessions are important to teachers because states supply almost half of a district's education budget, and legislative actions (or inactions) influence teacher salaries, class sizes, supplies, and equipment (Brimley & Garfield, 2005).

The information in this section answers the first item on our beginning-of-chapter survey, "Most states govern education in basically the same way." Despite considerable diversity with respect to views about the proper role of schools in educating children, most states govern education in much the same way.

State Board of Education

Because a governor and legislators have an entire state to run, they turn most of the responsibility for steering their state's schools to the **state board of education**, the legal governing body that exercises general control and supervision of the schools in a state. State boards are similar in purpose to district school boards and perform both regulatory and advisory functions. State boards regulate education by

- Issuing and revoking teaching licenses
- Establishing the length of the school year
- Publishing standards for approving and accrediting schools
- Developing and implementing uniform systems for gathering education data, such as standardized achievement test scores, enrollment trends, and demographics

The state board sets long- and short-term goals for its state and helps create an educational agenda for the state's governor and legislature. For example, the federal No Child Left Behind (NCLB) Act of 2001, which we have discussed at several points in this book, is a pressing issue in all states, and state boards assist governors and legislatures in shaping responses to this initiative. State board members are people outside professional education. They are usually appointed by the governor, but about a fourth of the states elect these officials who typically serve without pay (National Association of State Boards of Education, 2004).

State Office of Education

A state board of education makes policy; the **state office of education** is responsible for implementing policy on a day-to-day basis. In contrast with state boards, which are composed of lay members who meet periodically to discharge their duties, state offices of education are

State board of education. The legal governing body that exercises general control and supervision of the schools in a state.

State office of education. Office responsible for implementing a state's education policy on a day-to-day basis.

Figure 8.1   State Administrative Organizational Structure

staffed by full-time education professionals, virtually all of whom have been teachers and most of whom have advanced degrees in education.

Each state office of education is headed by a chief state officer with a title such as superintendent, commissioner, or secretary of the state board. In 2003, chief state officers were appointed by the state board of education or another board in 24 states, elected in 15 states, and appointed by the governor in 11 (Council of Chief State School Officers, 2003). The state office implements teacher and administrator licensing, supervises curriculum, approves school sites and buildings, and collects statistical data. As a new teacher, you will apply to the office of education in your state for an initial teaching license, the form and requirements of which are determined by the state board.

A state office of education influences the curriculum (what is taught) in a state in two important ways: textbook approval and state standards. Let's look at them.

Textbook Approval.   The textbooks used by individual schools must be on a state-approved list. States usually offer districts a choice of several acceptable text series for a given grade level. The textbook selection process can be highly politicized and controversial when controversial topics such as evolution in science, phonics versus whole language in reading, or problem-based versus computationally oriented approaches to math are involved. In this chapter's opening case, Carla's Elementary Math Steering Committee began its search for a math series by looking at the state-approved list. The committee then conferred with the state's math specialist to evaluate the different series.

State Standards.   A second way that state offices of education influence curricula is through state *standards,* which are statements specifying what students should know and what skills they should have upon completing an area of study. Currently, 49 of the 50 states have state-wide standards; Iowa chose to leave that decision to local school districts (Archer, 2006b).

State offices of education are also responsible for administering statewide testing programs based on standards, and initial research suggests that establishing standards and holding students and teachers responsible for reaching them have a modest effect on student achievement (Olson, 2006a).

This section addresses the second item on our beginning-of-chapter survey, "The state office of education in each state is responsible for setting rules and regulations." Although the statement is technically false—because the state *board of education* is legally responsible for general control and supervision of the schools in a state—many decisions about implementing the rules are left to the state *office of education.*

Although state boards and state offices of education influence teaching and learning, for the most part, they do so at arm's length; the day-to-day responsibility for educating students is a district responsibility. This is why Carla's experience at a district school board meeting is relevant. Let's look at districts' roles in governing education.

School Districts

As you saw in Chapter 7, a **school district** is an administrative unit within a state that is defined by geographical boundaries and is legally responsible for the public education of children within those boundaries. With respect to educational governance, it's where the action is. School districts hire and fire teachers, and they determine the content that students learn (the curriculum) and, to a certain extent, the kinds of learning experiences (instruction) students will have in schools. That's why Carla was making her presentation to the district school board. She was involved in making decisions about the district's elementary math curriculum. Decisions such as these are usually made at the district level, and school districts also determine what books will be used and make them available to students at the beginning of the school year.

School districts differ dramatically in size. For example, in 2004 there were 14,063 school districts in the United States, and if they were divided equally among states, each state would have about 280 (Kober, 2006). But states have differing views about the ideal number and size of districts. For example, the whole state of Hawaii constitutes one school district, whereas Texas has 1,040 districts. In 2004 the New York City School District had more than 1 million students, but 4,922 of U.S. school districts had 600 or fewer students. Almost half of the districts enroll fewer than 1,000 students per year. The largest 4 percent—districts enrolling more than 10,000 students each—educated more than half the students in this country (National Center for Education Statistics, 2005c).

> **School district.** An administrative unit within a state that is defined by geographical boundaries and is legally responsible for the public education of children within those boundaries.

Historically, the trend has been toward consolidating schools into fewer and larger districts. For instance, in 1930 the United States had more than 130,000 school districts; 70 years later, it had only 14,559 (Brimley & Garfield, 2005). Efficiency is the primary reason for consolidation; larger districts can offer broader services and minimize duplication of administrative staff. For example, one medium-sized district with a superintendent and district staff of 10 people is more efficient than two small districts that require a superintendent and a staff of 6 to 8 people each. On other hand, parents often resist consolidation because of loyalty to high school athletic teams and long bus rides for their children (Richard, 2004).

Small and large districts both have advantages and disadvantages. Small districts are less bureaucratic and easier to influence, but they often lack resources and instructional support staff. For example, Carla's committee functioned in a large district. As committee members did their work, they were assisted by a district math coordinator, a testing specialist, and technology experts who helped them evaluate the claims of different commercial math programs. This type of assistance doesn't exist in small districts.

Large districts also have problems. They tend to be hierarchical and bureaucratic, and getting things done takes time. Teachers sometimes feel like nameless and faceless cogs in large, impersonal organizations. Teachers can often rely on face-to-face contacts to make things happen quickly in smaller districts; in larger districts, however, decision making is placed in the hands of large and sometimes contentious committees. The ideal district has an administrative structure that is supportive and responsive to teachers but also leaves them alone to do what they love most—work with students.

Every school district has a local school board, a superintendent, and central staff. These are the people who make the district-level decisions about teaching and learning in their district's schools. Let's see how they will influence your life as a teacher.

The Local School Board

A **local school board** is a group of elected lay citizens responsible for setting policies that determine how a school district operates. With respect to governance, what kinds of rules and regulations do school boards pass? Who are the members of these boards? How are school board members selected? Because they will influence your life as a teacher, you should know the answers to these questions.

What Do School Boards Do?   The major functions of school boards occur in five areas, outlined in Figure 8.2 and discussed in the paragraphs that follow.

Working with the district budget is perhaps the most important (and contentious) school board function. School boards are responsible for raising money through taxes and disbursing funds to the schools within the district. They also make decisions about various district services, such as providing buses and maintaining lunch programs. School boards directly influence teachers by making decisions about salary increases and the benefits teachers receive. They also affect teachers indirectly by making budget decisions that impact class size and the amount of instructional materials available. Wrestling with each year's budget occupies more than a quarter of a school board's time and energy; it's a continual process that begins in the fall and ends in the spring.

Personnel responsibilities are closely aligned with financial decisions. School boards are legally responsible for hiring and firing all school personnel, including teachers, principals, custodians, and school bus drivers. Your teaching contract will be offered by a school board that has the legal authority to hire and fire teachers.

The curriculum—what teachers teach—is a third area of school board jurisdiction. School boards, assisted by district administrators, are responsible for defining the curriculum and implementing the general guidelines developed by states. In virtually all districts, teachers are consulted about the curriculum; in the better ones, teachers are directly involved in curriculum decisions. For example, in the opening case, Carla's committee helped make the decision about what math curriculum the district would adopt.

Local school board. A group of elected lay citizens responsible for setting policies that determine how a school district operates.

Figure 8.2   Functions of Local School Boards

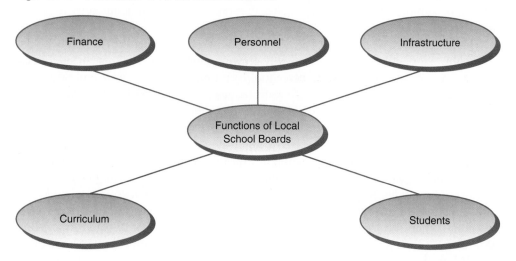

Decisions that impact students are also made by school boards. They set attendance, dress, grooming, conduct, and discipline standards for their districts. For example, the issue of school uniforms has been debated at district, state, and national levels, but the decision—sometimes after contentious debate—is ultimately made by local school boards.

School boards also determine extracurricular policies—from the mundane to the controversial. For example, some districts require students to maintain minimal grade levels to participate in sports, a policy critics contend doubly punishes struggling student athletes by failing them in the classroom and then preventing them from participating in extracurricular activities. Supporters of no-pass/no-play policies argue that they improve motivation to learn by providing incentives for academic success (Camerino, 2003). The question of whether to grant gay and lesbian clubs equal status with other school-sponsored organizations is another topic that has generated controversy at school board meetings. As you would expect, attendance at school board meetings increases when controversial issues are on their agendas, as various citizens groups attempt to influence board decisions.

Finally, school boards make decisions about district infrastructure. For example, they ensure that school buildings and school buses are maintained and safe, and they approve plans and hire contractors when new schools are built.

In recent years, given mandates such as the NCLB Act, student achievement and meeting state standards have become school board members' primary concerns, followed by issues involving budgets and decisions about curriculum and instruction (New York State School Board Association, 2006). Interestingly, student achievement wasn't even listed in school board members' top 10 concerns as recently as the late 1980s. Reform efforts and the national trend toward greater school accountability have strongly impacted the ways that school boards operate.

Members of School Boards and Their Selection.   Who serves on school boards, and how do they get there? Nearly all (about 96 percent) school boards consist of members elected for 3- or 4-year terms; the remainder have members appointed by large-city mayors or city councils (D. Land, 2002). School board elections can be controversial, for two reasons. First, the voter turnout for most school board elections is embarrassingly low; as few as 5 to 10 percent of eligible voters often decide school board membership. This fact results in boards that don't represent the citizens in the district, critics contend. The second controversy involves the question of whether school board elections should be at-large or limited to specific areas within a city. At-large elections tend to favor wealthy, White-majority candidates who have either more money to run an election campaign or benefit from White-majority voting pools (D. Land, 2002). In a limited-area election, only citizens who live in a specific part of the city are allowed to vote for candidates representing that area. Area-specific elections provide greater opportunities for minority candidates to represent local, ethnic-minority neighborhoods (Howell, 2005).

Who serves on school boards? The typical school board member is male, White, older, and wealthy, although membership is slowly growing more diverse in some areas. For example, a 2004 survey found that 61 percent of board members were male and 86 percent were White (Hess, 2004a). In addition, 59 percent make more than $75,000 per year, 38 percent have graduate degrees, and another 29 percent have 4-year degrees; only 7 percent have a high school degree or less (Carr, 2003; Hess, 2004a).

Disparities exist between the characteristics of school board members and those of the people they're elected to serve. For example, only 14 percent of board members are cultural minorities, but 33 percent of the nation's students are minorities, and that figure is projected to rise to 42 percent by the year 2010 (U.S. Department of Education, 2003a). Also, 45 percent of school board members are business people or professionals, and 85 percent make more money than the average teacher (Carr, 2003; National School Boards Association, 2000). Critics contend that wealthy school board members can't empathize with the financial hardships that teachers and community members often experience. Critics also question the ability of male-dominated school boards to effectively represent the teaching force, which is almost three-fourths female.

Alternatives to Local Control. Local control by school boards is the predominant pattern in U.S. education, but what happens when local control doesn't seem to work? Several large cities answered this question by authorizing the mayor to take over the running of the city's schools. This occurred in Boston in 1991, Chicago in 1995, New York in 2002, and currently, the mayor of Los Angeles is threatening to do the same (Maxwell, 2006a). Critics call the move in Los Angeles "undemocratic," and the effort is complicated by the fact that the Los Angeles Unified School District encompasses 26 other cities in addition to Los Angeles (Gewertz, 2006b).

A second battle to wrest control of schools from local school boards is occurring in the state of Maryland (Honawar, 2006). This battle for control of schools was precipitated by the NCLB Act, which requires low-performing schools to be restructured after 3 years of subpar performance. The Maryland legislature resisted, claiming that there is little proof that state takeovers actually improve student performance. The U.S. Department of Education threatened withholding $171 million in Title I funds if the state didn't restructure the Baltimore schools. Governance battles such as these are likely to increase as more and more schools are found lacking under NCLB guidelines.

The Superintendent

The school board makes policy, and the **superintendent**, the district's head administrative officer, along with his or her staff, implements that policy in the district's schools. The division of labor between the board and the superintendent isn't simple and well-defined, however. Because most board members have little or no background in professional education, the superintendent often plays a central role in leading the board and helping set agendas.

Superintendents are hired by school boards. Most hold an advanced degree in education (National School Boards Association, 2000), but some districts are now looking outside the field of education to find superintendents. For example, in the summer of 2000, Roy Romer, a former governor of Colorado with no experience in educational administration, was picked to lead the Los Angeles schools, the nation's second largest system with an enrollment of more than 710,000 students (Richard, 2000a). The superintendents of the three largest districts in the country—New York City, Chicago, and Los Angeles—all came from outside the field of education, as school boards tend to increasingly value management experience over professional knowledge in education. Whether this trend will continue is uncertain.

Superintendent. The school district's head administrative officer, along with his or her staff, responsible for implementing that policy in the district's schools.

As on school boards, women and minorities are underrepresented as superintendents (Carr, 2003; Gewertz, 2006d). Seventy-five percent of the teaching force and 51 percent of the general population are women, but they make up only 15 percent of superintendents. Of the 15 largest districts in the country, only one, Palm Beach County in Florida, is headed by a woman. Similarly, members of cultural minorities make up 33 percent of the student population and 13 percent of teachers, but they make up only 5 percent of superintendents.

When power and authority are shared, as is the case with school boards and superintendents, conflicts are inevitable, and when they occur, the superintendent usually loses. Nationally, the average tenure for superintendents is just under 6 years; in urban districts it is less than 3 years (Borja, 2002; Snider, 2006). Accountability, in the form of student test scores, is a major reason that superintendents' tenure is so short, especially in urban districts.

Disputes with school boards, politics, and bureaucracy are major obstacles that superintendents face. When controversy flares over issues such as student drug use, school violence, desegregation, and lagging student achievement, a community looks to the superintendent for answers. Superintendents often get caught in the crossfire of politics and public opinion and, unable to quickly solve these problems, are either terminated or feel obliged to resign.

What are superintendents paid for this frustrating and insecure job? Pay varies considerably with both location and district size; the average 2005–2006 salary was $116,244, but competition for superintendents in larger districts has resulted in salaries that are considerably higher (Swanson, 2006a). For example, superintendents in large urban districts make $172,387, and in 2005, the Miami-Dade school district in Florida paid its new superintendent $480,000 plus benefits—more than the governor of the state (Bohman, 2006; Swanson, 2006a).

The District Office

The district office assists the superintendent in translating school board policies into action (see Figure 8.1). It also coordinates the myriad curricular and instructional efforts within the district (Grove, 2002). The district office is responsible for

- Ordering textbooks and supplies
- Developing programs of study
- Ordering, distributing, and analyzing standardized tests
- Evaluating teachers and assisting those with difficulties

The district office is instrumental in translating abstract state and school board mandates into reality. The manner in which it does this can give teachers a sense of empowerment or can make them feel like hired hands.

The district office also plays an important role for new teachers (Grove, 2002). It typically provides new-teacher orientations, which may include an overview of the district's curriculum, any districtwide instructional initiatives, and district assessment programs. These policies and procedures are important because they frame the district's work expectations for new teachers. In addition, the central office coordinates mentoring and assessment programs for new teachers, helping them make the transition from university students to working professionals.

The School Principal

As you saw in Chapter 7, the **school principal**, the individual given the ultimate administrative responsibility for a school's operation, is the district administrator who has the greatest impact on teachers' lives. As you also saw in Chapter 7, many larger schools have a vice principal and two or more assistant principals as part of the administrative staff. The makeup of this staff will depend on the size and organization of the school.

> **School principal.** The individual having the ultimate administrative responsibility for a school's operation.

TABLE 8.1   Profile of School Principals

	High School Principals	Middle School Principals	Elementary School Principals
Sex			
Male	78.8%	66.8%	44.8%
Female	21.2	33.2	55.2
Ethinic Background			
White	85.9	83.0	80.8
African-American	8.4	10.5	12.0
Hispanic American	3.8	5.1	5.8
Asian-American	0.9	0.7	0.7
Native American	1.1	0.8	0.7
Other	0.7	–	0.6
Highest Degree Earned			
Bachelor's	1.4	1.8	1.8
Master's	54.8	55.5	53.9
Professioanl diploma	31.6	33.6	34.6
Doctorate	12.1	9.1	9.7
Salary (12-month) (2004–2005)	$86,938	$81,514	$76,144

Sources: Data from U.S. Department of Education (2001c); Williams (2002); and National Association of Elementary School Principals (2006).

A demographic profile of principals (see Table 8.1) mirrors that of school board members. Most are White at all levels, and males are still in the majority in secondary schools. Principals almost always have classroom experience, and most have at least a master's degree.

As the person who oversees the everyday operation of the school, the principal has wide-ranging duties; two of the most important duties are teacher selection and evaluation (Sergiovanni, 2004, 2006). His or her interview with you will be a crucial factor in whether or not you get the job, and it will give you an opportunity to learn about the person you'll be working for and the kind of school you'll be working in. During an interview, you should try to determine the principal's views about his or her role as an administrator (Cunningham & Cordeiro, 2000; Ubben et al., 2001).

The principal is also responsible for school-level curricular and instructional leadership, community relations, and the coordination of pupil services provided by school counselors, psychologists, nurses, and others. Principals also implement and monitor the school budget and ensure that the school's physical facilities are maintained.

Experienced teachers want principals who see themselves as instructional leaders and who take a hands-on ap-

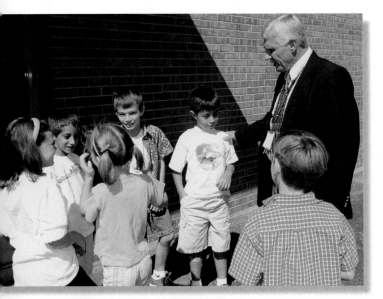

Principals are crucial in creating well-run, learning-oriented schools. (Michelle D. Bridwell/PhotoEdit Inc.)

proach to the teaching–learning process (Harris & Lowery, 2002). This leadership is especially important for beginning teachers, who need support, mentoring, and feedback. However, because of their busy schedules, many principals become managers who focus primarily on the day-to-day operation of the school and forget that their most important role is to support teaching and learning (Ginsberg & Murphy, 2002).

Principals are the most important people in the district's administrative structure because they work directly with teachers and students. Effective principals can transform a mediocre school into a positive and productive learning environment, and the opposite is also true; an ineffective principal can make a school an unpleasant place in which to work.

Making Connections:
To deepen your understanding of the topics in this section of the chapter and integrate them with topics you've already studied, go to the *Making Connections* module for Chapter 8 at **www.prenhall.com/kauchak**. Respond to questions 1–4.

Check Your Understanding

1.1 Who is legally responsible for governing education in the United States?

1.2 How does each state govern education?

1.3 What role do school districts play in governing education?

For feedback, go to Appendix A, Check Your Understanding, *located in the back of this text.*

School Finance: How Are Schools Funded?

To begin our discussion of school finance, let's return to Carla's work on her school's Elementary Math Steering Committee.

"And based on our analysis of math programs around the country, we believe this one is best for our children. . . . Any questions?" Carla asks as she concludes her presentation to the school board.

"Let me make sure that I'm clear about this," one board member responds. "In addition to the texts themselves, students will need manipulatives. . . . I'm sorry, but I'm not sure exactly what 'manipulatives' are."

"Manipulatives are concrete objects, such as cubes that could be put in a box to help kids understand the concept of volume, and plastic squares that could be used to illustrate area. The success of this program depends on students seeing math ideas in action."

"Thank you. . . . And teachers will need additional in-service training to bring them up to speed on how to use these new materials. Is that right?"

"Yes. What we've read and heard is that teacher in-service is essential to the success of this program," Carla replies, as her fellow committee members nod in agreement.

"What seems clear to me," the chair of the school board adds, "is that this program, along with our technology initiative and the changes in our language arts program, is going to need additional funding. We need to make sure that the public understands how and why taxes are going to go up next fall. We've all got a big job ahead of us—selling, no, explaining, why our schools need additional monies."

Money is important in education. It determines teachers' salaries, professional development opportunities, and access to resources, such as computers, lab supplies, maps, and a host of other supplies. It also influences the quality of schools by allowing districts to do such things as reduce class sizes and recruit and retain qualified teachers (Biddle & Berliner, 2002). For 3 consecutive years from 2003 to 2005, national polls indicated that the general public viewed lack of financial support and funding for education as the biggest problem their local school boards face; the second biggest problem was overcrowded schools, an issue closely related to financial support (Rose & Gallup, 2005). In this section, we look at where this money comes from, how it is spent, and what can be done to make school funding more equitable.

School Funding Sources

Local, state, and federal sources all provide money for education (Brimley & Garfield, 2005; Yinger, 2004). As you can see in Figure 8.3, the state share is 48.7 percent, the local share is 42.8 percent, and both are considerably greater than the federal share, which is 8.5 percent. These facts indicate that the third statement in our beginning-of-chapter survey, "The federal government provides the largest source of educational funding," is clearly false. The federal government's share is less than 10 percent.

The share of education funding coming from local, state, and federal sources has changed over time (Brimley & Garfield, 2005). For example, from 1920 to 1980 the federal share increased from virtually nothing to a peak of nearly 10 percent, declining in the 1980s to less than 7 percent before rising to its current level of 8.5 percent. The state and local shares have remained fairly steady, hovering between 42 and 49 percent for the last fifteen years. These figures are national averages, and the federal, state, and local proportions can vary significantly from state to state. For example, none of Hawaii's 2002–2003 school budget came from local sources, whereas in Florida local funds accounted for 41 percent of school funding (Brimley & Garfield, 2005).

Shifts in education funding reflect the changing views of education throughout U.S. history. In early America, education was seen as a local responsibility with virtually no involvement by the federal government. In sharp contrast, 20th-century leaders saw a direct connection between education and the country's political and economic well-being. Quality schools and a well-educated workforce became national concerns, and the federal government's role in education increased. Similarly, states began to recognize the importance of education in attracting high-tech industries and high-paying jobs. This insight, plus efforts to equalize funding within states, has led to an increasing state role in educational funding (Biddle & Berliner, 2002).

The public is undecided about the relative amounts that local, state, and federal governments should contribute to educational funding. In a 1998 Gallup poll, 21 percent fa-

Figure 8.3 Education Revenues from Local, State, and Federal Sources

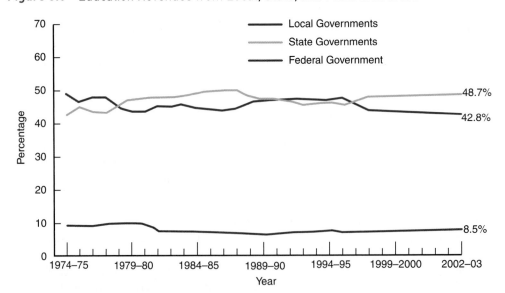

Source: Data from National Center for Education Statistics (2006).

vored local funding through property taxes, 33 percent favored state sources, and 37 percent favored federal taxes (Rose & Gallup, 1998). In a more recent poll, 49 percent said that the federal government had too much say in decisions affecting local public schools, and 43 percent said state governments also had too much control over these decisions (Rose & Gallup, 2000). The debate over the role that different levels of government should play in funding education is likely to continue.

Let's see how funds are raised at each level of government and how they make their way to classrooms.

State Revenue Sources

States are the largest source of educational funding, totaling 48.7 percent in the 2002–2003 school year (see Figure 8.3). State income taxes and sales taxes are the two largest sources of state income, each contributing about one third of all state revenues (Federation of Tax Administrators, 2006). Sales taxes are regressive, however, meaning they take proportionally more from lower-income families, who spend a larger portion of their income on necessities, such as food, clothing, and housing. Progressive states provide some relief by excluding food from items that are taxed. Personal income tax accounts for another third of state revenues. The remaining third comes from other sources such as taxes on liquor and tobacco, oil and mining revenues, and corporate income taxes.

Recently, state lotteries and gambling have also become sources of revenue, but education is often the victim of a zero-sum shell game, in which increased funding from lottery monies is balanced by decreasing monies from other sources, such as sales taxes. In 2005, 42 states had lotteries, but fewer than half allocate profits directly to education, and the percentage of income taxes going to education in these states varies considerably (Brimley & Garfield, 2005; Manzo, 2005). Also, states spend 32 cents of every lottery income dollar on expenses, and research indicates that these gambling ventures attract participants who are poor and have had little schooling (Brimley & Garfield, 2005). The long-term viability of gambling revenues for education is uncertain and highly controversial.

Local Funding

As we saw in our discussion of school governance, financing education at the local level is the responsibility of local school boards, which is why Carla made her presentation to her local board, and the need for increased funding was one of the implications of her presentation. At the local level, most funding for schools comes from **property taxes**, which are determined by the value of property in the school district (Brimley & Garfield, 2005). Other local revenue sources include income taxes, fees for building permits, traffic fines, and user fees charged to groups that hold meetings in school facilities. In collecting property taxes, local authorities first assess the value of a property and then tax the owners a small percentage of the property's value (usually less than 1 percent).

Funding education primarily through local property taxes has disadvantages, the most glaring of which is inequities between property resources in different districts

The value of property in a school district directly affects how much money schools in the district will receive from local sources.
(AP Wide World Photos)

(Brimley & Garfield, 2005). Wealthier cities or districts have a higher tax base, so they're able to collect (and spend) more money for their schools. Poorer rural and urban school districts find themselves on the opposite end of this continuum, with a lower tax base, resulting in lower revenues. Property taxes also place an unfair burden on older taxpayers, whose homes may have increased in value, while their ability to pay taxes has remained constant or decreased. In

> **Property taxes.** The major source of educational funding, determined by the assessed value of a home or property.

addition, many older taxpayers resist these charges because they no longer have children in school and don't see the immediate benefit of increased spending for schools.

The property-tax method of financing schools also has a political disadvantage (Brimley & Garfield, 2005). Unlike sales taxes, which taxpayers pay in small, continual, and almost unnoticed increments, property taxes are more visible targets for taxpayer dissatisfaction. Statements arrive once a year with a comparison to the previous year, and property-tax increases are discussed in public forums whenever school boards (e.g., Carla's in the opening case) ask their taxpayers for increased funding.

Dissatisfaction with this method of funding reached a head in California in 1978 when voters passed an initiative called Proposition 13, which limited property taxes in the state. By the 1990s, 45 other states had passed similar measures (Brimley & Garfield, 2005). The effect on educational funding has been chilling. Schools and school districts have had less to spend and have had to fight harder when requesting new funds from taxpayers.

Federal Funding for Education

The federal government is the third, smallest, and most controversial source of educational funding. As you saw earlier, federal funding for education was virtually nonexistent before 1920 but has increased over time to its present level of about 8.5 percent. Though the amount spent on education has increased in recent years to almost $67 billion in fiscal year 2005, the total still accounts for only about 2 percent of total federal expenditures (National Center for Education Statistics, 2005a). Most (46 percent) federal funds for education are channeled through the U.S. Department of Education, with the next largest proportion (20 percent) coming from the Department of Health and Human Services (Sonnenberg, 2004).

Proponents of a greater federal role in education believe that education is essential for the country's continued progress in the 21st century and that the federal government should continue to exert leadership (and provide funds) in this area. Critics warn of increased federal control over what they believe should be a local responsibility. In addition, conservatives argue against the expansion of what they consider to be an already bloated federal bureaucracy. For these critics, less is better when it comes to federal funding. Local funding, in contrast, makes schools more efficient and responsive to local needs and wishes, they say.

Although the percentage of education funds contributed by the federal government has been small, the impact has been considerable, largely because of the use of **categorical grants**, monies targeted for specific groups and designated purposes. Head Start, aimed at preschoolers, and Title I, which benefits economically disadvantaged youth, are examples of categorical aid programs targeting specific needs or populations (these programs were discussed in detail in Chapter 5). Because the funds must be used for specific purposes, categorical grants have strongly influenced local education practices.

During the 1980s, categorical funds were replaced by **block grants**, federal monies provided to states and school districts with few restrictions for use. Begun during the conservative Reagan administration, block grants purposely reduce the federal role in policy making, in essence giving states and districts control over how monies are spent. Proponents contend this makes sense—who knows local needs better than local educators? Critics contend that funds are often misspent or spent in areas where they aren't needed (Brimley & Garfield, 2005).

Educational Revenues: Where Do They Go?

In 2004–2005, the 50 states and the District of Columbia spent an average of $8,618 per pupil, but as you see in Table 8.2, spending varied considerably from state to state (National Education Association, 2006b). The District of Columbia and New Jersey spent the highest amounts ($15,073 and $13,370, respectively), while Utah spent the lowest ($5,245). The data in Table 8.2 demonstrate some regional trends. Most of the higher per-pupil expenditures are found in Northeastern and upper Midwest states, and lower expenditures are found in the South and West.

Categorical grants. Monies targeted for specific groups and designated purposes.

Block grants. Federal monies provided to states and school districts with few restrictions for use.

TABLE 8.2   State-by-State Spending per Student

State	2004–2005 ($)
Alabama	6,886
Alaska	10,042
Arizona	5,474
Arkansas	6,202
California	7,815
Colorado	8,337
Connecticut	11,893
Delaware	11,016
District of Columbia	15,073
Florida	7,035
Georgia	8,451
Hawaii	8,622
Idaho	6,743
Illinois	9,591
Indiana	8,723
Iowa	7,477
Kansas	7,558
Kentucky	7,906
Louisiana	7,589
Maine	10,723
Maryland	9,762
Massachusetts	11,681
Michigan	8,909
Minnesota	9,249
Mississippi	6,452
Missouri	7,451
Montana	8,025
Nebraska	7,608
Nevada	6,525
New Hampshire	9,624
New Jersey	13,370
New Mexico	8,236
New York	12,879
North Carolina	7,350
North Dakota	7,033
Ohio	9,557
Oklahoma	6,269
Oregon	7,842
Pennsylvania	9,638
Rhode Island	10,641
South Carolina	8,161
South Dakota	7,618
Tennessee	6,856
Texas	7,142
Utah	5,245
Vermont	11,608
Virginia	8,577
Washington	7,858
West Virginia	9,448
Wisconsin	9,619
Wyoming	10,198
U.S. and D.C. Average	8,618

Source: National Education Association (2006b). *Rankings and estimates.* Available at http://www.nea.org/index.html.

A significant portion of a district's budget goes to transportation, building maintenance, and food services. (Anthony Magnacca/Merrill)

It is tempting to conclude that a state's commitment to education can be judged by its per-pupil spending, but, in fact, some states are wealthier than others, and the number of children per taxpayer varies, so they have a greater capacity to fund education. Funding differences between states are also influenced by differences in the cost of living and the number of children that need to be educated. Utah, for example, which has the lowest per-student spending in the country ($5,245) also has the highest birth rate in the nation—approximately one and a half times the national average—so whatever funds are available must be divided among more children.

The effects of funding on excellence in education is a controversial topic, with early research concluding that the amount spent has little or no influence on achievement (Hanushek, 1996). However, more recent research in this area found that higher per-pupil expenditures resulted in higher achievement, mainly because of better-qualified teachers and smaller class sizes (Flanagan & Grissmer, 2002; Krueger & Whitmore, 2002). Increased expenditures seem to have their greatest effect on low-income and minority students.

The relationship between funding and learning isn't simple or precise, however. Achievement tests—the most commonly used measure of student learning—focus on core academic areas, such as math, science, and reading, and not every dollar spent on education goes to teaching these basic subjects. Some monies go to art and music, for example, which are valuable areas of the curriculum, but increased expenditures in these areas won't be directly reflected in higher test scores. Furthermore, as you see in Figure 8.4, only about 61 percent of

Figure 8.4   Educational Expenditures on Different District Programs

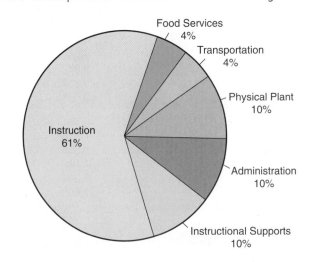

Source: Data from Odden, A., Monk, D., Nakib, Y., & Picus, L. (1995); U.S. Department of Education (2006c).

the money allocated to education is spent on instruction, most of which goes to teacher salaries (Odden et al., 1995; U.S. Department of Education, 2006). The rest is spent on areas that affect achievement only indirectly.

In addition to the 61 percent that directly supports instruction, 10 percent of school district funds goes to instructional assistance needs, such as student services, teacher professional advancement, and curriculum development (see Figure 8.4). Another 10 percent goes to administration. Approximately one third of administration funding is spent in the central district offices, and two thirds goes to schools. Maintenance of school buildings and grounds (physical plant) takes up another 10 percent of the budget. Transportation (school buses) and food services (cafeteria lunches) each account for another 4 percent.

To understand the magnitude of transportation expenditures, consider these national figures. In an average school year, 450,000 yellow school buses travel 4 billion (*billion*, not million) miles, providing 10 billion separate rides to nearly 24 million K–12 students (Brimley & Garfield, 2005). Student activities add 5 million trips. Schools provide transportation to 54 percent of the nation's student population at a cost of $493 per student.

Critics often decry the large amount of monies (39 percent) spent on areas other than academics and have initiated national efforts to mandate that 65 percent of education funds go to instruction (Hoff, 2005, 2006). However, school finance experts point out that expenditures for school nurses, school buses, and school lunches, for example, are all part of the total education process, and no research evidence links higher spending on instruction to increases in student achievement (Education Vital Signs, 2006a). In addition, experts note that the amounts schools spend on administration and maintenance of the physical plant compare favorably with those spent in industry (Bracey, 1999b; Odden et al., 1995).

This section provides an answer to the fourth item on our beginning-of-chapter survey, "Most of a district's budget goes to funding instruction." The answer is yes; the average U.S. district spends 61 percent of its budget on instruction.

> **Making Connections:**
> To deepen your understanding of the topics in this section of the chapter and integrate them with topics you've already studied, go to the *Making Connections* module for Chapter 8 at **www.prenhall.com/kauchak**. Respond to questions 5–9.

Check Your Understanding

2.1   What are the major sources of educational funding?

2.2   How are educational revenues spent?

 For feedback, go to Appendix A, Check Your Understanding, *located in the back of this text.*

Emerging Issues in School Governance and Finance

As schools confront the challenges of the 21st century, they face a number of issues in the areas of governance and finance. Some of the most important include the following:

- Equity in funding, one of the most fundamental issues facing education
- Site-based decision making, which attempts to involve teachers and parents in the running of schools
- School choice in the form of charter schools and vouchers

Let's look at these challenges.

Savage Inequalities: The Struggle for Funding Equity

Lakesha Lincoln walks into Jackson Middle School among a horde of other students. Jackson is a 72-year-old urban school in a large northeastern city. She doesn't notice that the three of the five lights down the long main hall are out, and that the hall badly needs a paint job.

She walks by the girls' bathroom, where a sign on the door says, "Bathroom out of order. Use the bathroom on the second floor." She decides she'll wait and get permission to go to the bathroom during her first-period class.

She enters her homeroom and sits down. She has barely enough room to squeeze through the rows of desks, because there are 38 students in her homeroom, and the room was built for 25. Paper is still on the floor from yesterday, and the boards haven't been cleaned from the last class of the previous day.

Students are milling around the room as the bell rings, and Mr. Jensen, her homeroom teacher, tries his best to get them to settle down. He is struggling, because he has had no professional training, and he is doing his best to feel his way through the year, since this is his first year of teaching.

Dawn Johnson walks into Forest Park Middle School, which is in the suburbs. It was built in 2001, and it is roomy, well-lit, and pleasant. Dawn walks into her homeroom, which is spotless with ample equipment and materials that support instruction. Her room is comfortable with plenty of space available for her and her 22 classmates.

The last of the students slide into their chairs as the bell rings, and Mrs. August is standing in front of the room ready to begin. She is a 10-year veteran, with a reputation for being demanding but fair. Students agree that they learn a lot from her.

As you saw earlier, research indicates that significant differences in per-pupil expenditures exist, both between and within states (Biddle & Berliner, 2002; Rothstein, 1998). Jonathan Kozol outlines this issue in his influential book, *Savage Inequalities:*

Americans abhor the notion of a social order in which economic privilege and political power are determined by hereditary class. Officially, we have a more enlightened goal in sight: namely, a society in which a family's wealth has no relation to the probability of future educational attainment and the wealth and station it affords. By this standard, education offered to poor children should be at least as good as that which is provided to the children of the upper-middle class. (1991, p. 207)

This standard of equality is not what Kozol found in his research on school funding. Instead, he found that many urban schools around the country were like Lakesha's—dirty and run down with peeling paint, broken toilets, antiquated or missing textbooks, and teachers who were uncertified or lacked experience, or both. Only miles away, suburban schools like Forest Park Middle, where Dawn goes, featured new, well-maintained buildings that were attractive and inviting learning environments. And teachers were generally seasoned, knowledgeable professionals. These stark contrasts gave Kozol's book its title.

In 1968 Demetrio Rodriguez, a sheet-metal worker in a poor suburb of San Antonio, Texas, looked at the schools his children were attending, compared them with schools in wealthier districts only 10 miles away, and found contrasts similar to those between Jackson and Forest Park middle schools. The fact that property taxes for his district produced only $37 per student compared to $412 per student for the wealthier suburb was the primary problem. These differences are not unusual. For example, in Texas during the 1980s, the 100 most affluent districts in the state spent an average of $7,233 per student, whereas the poorest 100 averaged $2,978. Faced with these inequalities, Mr. Rodriguez sued, contending that his children were being unfairly penalized by where they lived (Brimley & Garfield, 2005; Imazeki & Reschovsky, 2004).

Nationally, wealthy districts spend an average of 23 percent more on their students than do poorer districts. In Alaska, wealthier districts spend more than double the amount per pupil ($16,546 versus $7,379) than do poorer districts in the state (Biddle & Berliner, 2002). Similar patterns exist in other states (Kober, 2006).

Disparities in property tax revenues can result in dramatic differences in funding for schools that are quite close geographically. (left: Anthony Magnacca/Merrill; right: Rachel Epstein/The Image Works.

This section suggests that the fifth item in our beginning-of-chapter survey, "Students across a state are provided with basically the same amount of money to fund their education," is not true. Large disparities in the property tax base that provides funds for schools result in widely varying resources for teachers and students.

Legal challenges over funding equity have increased. The battle lines for these cases were drawn in California in 1971, when the California Supreme Court ruled in a 6–1 vote that the use of property taxes to fund education resulted in unconstitutional funding inequities in the state (*Serrano v. Priest,* 1971). In an attempt to reduce funding inequities, the state's share of education funding rose from 40 to 70 percent.

The *Serrano v. Priest* lawsuit went all the way to the U.S. Supreme Court. Many believed, based on the California decision, that the Supreme Court would find the spending patterns in Texas unconstitutional. However, in a 5–4 vote, it did just the opposite, ruling in 1973 that the U.S. Constitution does not guarantee citizens a right to an education. The Court did point out, however, that funding inequities may violate state constitutions, many of which do guarantee citizens that right.

The Supreme Court ruling on the Rodriguez case sent the issue back to state courts, and many other state suits followed. By mid-2002, courts had overturned existing systems in 21 states and upheld others in 7 states, with 10 cases still pending (Kober, 2006). Differences in state rulings are primarily the result of differences in the wording of state constitutions. Some constitutions are quite specific in guaranteeing "equal education for all," whereas others are vague in specifying that educational opportunity should be "ample" or "efficient." When rulings favored the plaintiffs, researchers found that inequities were reduced by almost 14 percent. Decreasing or eliminating reliance on the property tax was the primary reason (Flanagan & Grissmer, 2002).

The problem of funding inequalities is complicated by the fact that not all districts in a state have the same needs (Brimley & Garfield, 2005; Yinger, 2004). Some have a higher proportion of low-income children, non-native English speakers, or children who need special education services. These populations require extra resources. Reformers are calling for funding formulas that go beyond simply equalizing dollars; they want plans that meet the needs of all students (Rebell, 2004). These proposed reforms are expensive and controversial, as many parents from wealthier districts object to having their local taxes used to fund distant schools across the state. In addition, the problems involved in attempting to quantify educational needs in terms of dollars and cents is complex.

One recent change in educational funding attempts to change funding practices within districts rather than between (National Education Association, 2005). The **weighted student formula** allocates resources within a district to schools on an individual basis based on student

Weighted student formula. A means of allocating resources within a district to schools on an individual basis based on student needs.

VIDEO PERSPECTIVES

 Failing Grade

 To view this video, go to the *Becoming a Professional* DVD included with this text, click on ABC News, and then this chapter's video: *Failing Grade*.

This ABC News video examines a school district that was not only underfunded but also administratively mismanaged. The video focuses on Chester High in Pennsylvania, one of the lowest-rated schools in Pennsylvania. It has been plagued with the worst problems facing the worst schools: overcrowding, which led to a riot; a continuous turnover of staff and administrators; and even a bailout from the state just to pay the teachers' salaries.

How did it get to this stage? Chester High was part of a bold experiment in privatization in which the private sector was supposed to be able to fix all that ailed the public sector when it came to educating children. In Chester, it didn't quite work out that way. You will meet a dynamic young principal, with his own unconventional path, who tried to help these kids beat the odds. You will also meet parents who worry about their children's futures, and a school board that is at a loss.

Think About This

1. Which of Chester High's problems were due to governance? How did the multiple layers of educational governance relate to Chester High's negative situation?

2. Which of Chester High's problems were due to finance issues? How did these problems relate to Kozol's (1991) idea of "savage inequalities"?

3. Why was privatization seen as a solution to Chester High's problems? (See the *Teaching in an Era of Reform* feature in this chapter for a discussion of privatization.)

*To answer these questions online and receive immediate feedback, go to the Companion Website at **www.prenhall.com/kauchak**, then to the Video Perspectives module for Chapter 8.*

needs. Instead of every school in a district getting the same per-pupil amount, the weighted student formula provides more funds to schools that have more special education students or other students requiring additional services. Several U.S. urban school districts—Chicago, Denver, Houston, Los Angeles, and Seattle—have implemented this change. Advocates claim that it is a fairer way of distributing funds and that it decentralizes educational decision making by allowing individual schools to decide how education dollars will be spent. Comprehensive research is still needed to see if this change will work in other, smaller districts where increased funding for some schools could mean decreased, and potentially crippling, funding for others.

The role the federal government should play in reducing or eliminating funding inequities is another issue facing funding reformers. Critics of the current system point out that two thirds of funding differences occur between states rather than within states, and states receiving low levels of educational funding are clustered in the South and Southeast, areas that also have large proportions of poor and minority students. Experts estimate that it would take a minimum of $25 billion to equalize states' expenditures, a daunting figure considering current federal budget deficits (Flanagan & Grissmer, 2002).

Site-Based Decision Making

In the chapter's opening case, Carla made her proposal to her school board, which would ultimately decide which math series to use. Her recommendation came from a committee composed of other teachers in the district whose ideas and opinions were solicited and considered. Concerned parents, whose children would use the new series, were also at the meeting and had the opportunity to ask questions and influence the decision. This appears to be democracy in action, but is it? The decision would still be made at the district level, far removed from local schools.

Critics of this "top–down," district-level form of school governance contend that too many important educational decisions are made by people far removed from schools. They argue that school board members from across town may not know what is best for a particular school, for example. **Site-based decision making** is a school management reform movement that attempts to place increased responsibility for governance at the individual school level. Proponents of site-based decision making believe that the people most affected by educational decisions—teachers, parents, and even students—ought to be more directly involved in those decisions (Archer, 2006b; National Education Association, 2005). Proponents also believe that site-based decision making, in addition to being more democratic, ought to result in better-run schools. People who help make decisions about schools are more likely to support them and help them succeed.

Site-based decision making is appealing from a professional perspective. It seems sensible that professional educators should have a substantial say in how learning and teaching occur in their schools. However, in one poll, 70 percent of teachers felt they were out of the loop in their district's decision-making process (Public Agenda, 2000). Involvement in decision making creates dilemmas for teachers, however. Teachers join the profession to work with students, and the demands of extended committee work can siphon energies away from teaching (van den Berg, 2002). For example, was the effort Carla spent on the textbook selection process worth it, or would her students be better served if she had been able to devote more of her time to teaching? If decisions such as these are made at the school level, will this increase duplication of effort in the district? These questions don't have easy answers.

Site-based decision making usually exists in one of two forms. Increased community participation in advisory committees, composed of parents, teachers, community members (and sometimes students) is the most common (Archer, 2006b). School boards and building administrators maintain legal control over schools, and the advisory committees provide input in areas such as setting school goals and priorities, making curricular and extracurricular decisions, and selecting and evaluating teachers and administrators.

A more radical form of site-based decision making involves actual community control of educational decisions through an elected council. When this occurs, the district school board shares decision-making power with the council in areas such as the hiring and retention of principals and teachers, the curriculum, and budgets. Experiments in several large cities have raised thorny questions about who should serve on these community councils and whether or not decentralized decision making results in better schools for children (D. Land, 2002).

School Choice

The freedom to choose is a central American value. Americans can choose where and how they live and what occupation they work in, for example. Shouldn't they also have a choice in the kind of schools their children attend? As presently organized, public school systems are centralized and bureaucratic, and where students go to school is determined by the neighborhoods in which they live. In the name of efficiency, we've created a governance and finance system that begins in state capitals, runs through local district offices, and culminates in schools that are similar in form and function. Walk into most public schools across the country, and you'll see teachers teaching the same content in basically the same way (Cuban, 1993; Goodlad, 1984). Even the boxlike architecture of school buildings is the same.

Critics decry this uniformity and make several arguments in support of greater variety and choice. For example, we are a nation of 50 states with unique individuals and distinctive subcultures, and our schools ought to reflect this diversity. In addition, experimentation and innovation

> **Site-based decision making.** A school management reform movement that attempts to place increased responsibility for governance at the individual school level.

Proponents of school choice believe charter schools and vouchers will provide economically disadvantaged children with better schools. (Scott Cunningham/Merrill)

have been central to our nation's progress, and conformity discourages innovation. From an economic perspective, the present system represents a monopoly that forces parents to send their children to neighborhood public schools (Betts, 2005). Critics believe that alternatives would result in healthy competition, which would ultimately result in better schools. They also argue that the public school system has become bloated, bureaucratic, and unresponsive to individual citizens' needs. In response to these criticisms, reformers call for school choice.

What does choice mean? At one level, parents already have choices, because they move to neighborhoods served by particular schools. The quality of the schools is one of the major features parents consider when choosing a neighborhood (Hassel & Hassel, 2004). If parents don't like the schools in their neighborhood, they can send their children to private schools, something that 10 percent of parents currently do (U.S. Department of Education, 2000). In addition, through open enrollment programs, districts typically allow parents who believe their local schools are subpar to send their children across town to better schools. Doing so requires greater time and expense, but parents still have choices.

But choice advocates point out that many poor, minority, and inner-city parents don't have the resources to vote with their wallets or their cars. They cannot afford to move to better neighborhoods with better schools, to send their children to private schools, or even to drive across town each day to transport their children to a non-neighborhood public school. In addition, some school districts are so bad, critics contend, that other schools in the district don't really provide viable alternatives. These parents deserve the right to choose, just as much as more wealthy parents do.

But how can parents be provided with options? The concept of school choice has resulted in two educational innovations: charter schools and vouchers.

Charter Schools

Charter schools are alternative schools that are independently operated but publicly funded. In many states, parents or others dissatisfied with the local school choices have the right to create their own alternative or specialty schools. Charter schools typically begin when a group—teachers, community members, or a private corporation—develops a plan for a school, including its curriculum, staffing, and budget. This plan, or "charter," must then be accepted by the local school board or state office of education and serves as a contract with the state.

Many school districts already have alternative schools, such as magnet schools with specialized programs as well as schools designed to meet the needs of students who can't successfully function in regular schools and classrooms (e.g., young, unwed mothers or children with serious behavior or emotional problems). Charter schools are similar to other alternative schools in that they offer a different curriculum or target special populations; they differ in that they are independently administered public schools and subject to less regulatory control from a district's central administration (Carnoy, Jacobsen, Mishel, & Rothstein, 2005).

The charter school movement began in Minnesota in 1991, when the legislature approved the creation of eight teacher-created and -operated outcome-based schools. (An outcome-based school makes curricular and instructional decisions based on student performance on specified assessments.) Since that time, 39 additional states and the District of Columbia have passed charter school legislation resulting in the creation of more than 3,600 schools with more than 1 million students, or about 2 percent of the public school student population (Kober, 2006; West & Manno, 2006). The five states with the most charters in the 2005–2006 school year were California, Arizona, Florida, Ohio, and Texas, in that order (Charter Connection, 2006).

Charter schools. Alternative schools that are independently operated but publicly funded.

The focus of different charter schools varies dramatically, although most attract parents seeking smaller schools and class sizes, better quality instruction, and alternatives to public school curricula and environments (Carpenter & Finn, 2006; Casey, Andreson, Yelverton, & Wedeen, 2002). Many (about one third of all charter schools) are designed by urban community leaders to meet the needs of inner-city youth (West & Manno, 2006), and, nationally, 58 percent of charter students are members of racial or ethnic minorities, compared with 41 percent for regular public schools (Viadero, 2005a). Some, for example, focus on developing students' African heritage through language instruction, literature, and the arts. Others attract parents who want a return to the basics, while still others focus on technology and the arts.

Initial research on charter school teachers has revealed greater teacher involvement in school governance issues (Gresham, Hess, Maranto, & Milliman, 2000). As Figure 8.5 shows, 62 percent of teachers in charter elementary schools reported having high levels of influence over curriculum decisions at their schools, whereas only 25 percent of teachers at regular schools reported such influence. Similar differences occurred in teachers' beliefs about their influence over selection of instructional materials and scheduling.

School philosophy, smaller size, and characteristics of the teachers themselves are all possible reasons for teachers' greater role in decision making. The best charter schools begin with the view that teachers are central to a quality education and actively attempt to involve teachers in school planning. Charter schools also tend to be smaller, which allows change to occur more rapidly. Finally, teachers who choose to work in charter schools are likely to be more adventurous and willing to experiment with their teaching. One charter school teacher commented, "Everyone who came was one of the best in the program from wherever they came from. There were no slackers in the group" (Brouillette, 2000, p. 31).

Issues of Quality in Charter Schools. Considerable variation exists in the quality of charter schools, and this uneven quality is having a negative effect on the charter school movement (Hutton, 2005). For example, in Texas—a leader in establishing charter schools—a panel of state lawmakers recommended a moratorium on new charter schools, citing poor student performance,

Figure 8.5   Perceptions of Governance Issues by Charter and Non-Charter Arizona Teachers

Source: Data from Gresham, A., Hess, F., Maranto, R., & Milliman, S. (2000).

financial troubles, and unexpected closures (Associated Press, 2000). In 1999, Texas had 193 charter schools, and the state spent $218 million on them. However, only 59 percent of charter school students passed a state skills exam in the 1998–1999 school year, compared with the state average of 78.4 percent. In reviewing existing charter schools, the state education agency gave an "unacceptable" rating to nearly one fourth of the 103 charter schools it evaluated. In 2002 Texas revoked the charters of five schools for chronically poor performance on state tests; two charter schools serving 2,000 students were at the bottom of the state's accountability rankings for 3 years in a row (Hendrie, 2002). Nationally, in 2005, about 65 charter schools closed their doors in 17 states, about 2 percent of charters in these states (Robelen, 2006b).

California, another leader in the charter school movement, has encountered similar problems. In 2004, California's Charter School Academy, which operated more than 50 schools, abruptly closed all of its schools, leaving families, teachers, and school officials scrambling (Hutton, 2005). A subsequent state audit found the charter organization had misused state and federal funds and sought the return of $23 million from the for-profit management company (Hendrie, 2005b).

The problem of quality is partially linked to the large numbers of unlicensed teachers in charter schools. One national study found that 43 percent of charter school teachers lacked appropriate licenses, compared to 9 percent in regular public schools, and this figure increased to nearly 60 percent in predominantly African-American charters (H. Brown, 2003). In a time when teacher quality is seen as central to school-improvement efforts, these figures are troubling. A major advantage of charter schools—freedom from bureaucratic oversight— also seems to be a major weakness of this reform.

Inadequate resources and facilities are also persistent problems in charter schools (Casey, Andreson, Yelverton, & Wedeen, 2002). Many lack libraries and laboratories and sometimes even basic supplies such as paper and pencils (Carnoy et al., 2005). The arrival of for-profit corporations into the charter school arena, which you'll read about in a later section, has exacerbated the problem (Hendrie, 2003a).

Charters were proposed as a more effective alternative to existing schools; however, early research failed to demonstrate a clear relationship between charter schools and increased student achievement (Bracey, 2004; Carnoy et al., 2005). More recent research has even found that charter schools actually trailed regular public schools in both reading and math achievement (Robelen, 2006d).

The charter school movement is controversial and highly politicized. Charter advocates generally adhere to a political ideology suggesting that the private sector, such as the business world in our country, is superior to the public sector—our public school system, for example. Adherents to this ideology argue that charter schools are superior to regular public schools, because they reduce the size of the existing educational bureaucracy and are more consistent with existing business models. Research data, however, don't support this contention. These data indicate that, with a few exceptions, charters are no better, and are often inferior, to our existing public schools.

Vouchers

Vouchers are a second approach to school choice. A **voucher** is a check or written document that parents can use to purchase educational services. The voucher approach is grounded in the belief that parents know what their children need and should be free to purchase the best education wherever they can find it. Some voucher plans give parents the choice of either a public or private school, whereas others limit the choice to public schools.

Vouchers are often promoted by political conservatives who argue that public schools are a monopoly, and that opening up schools to parental choice allows market forces to improve education. All schools (not just those in immediate neighborhoods) become viable alternatives. Over time, the best schools would attract more students and flourish, whereas poorer schools would be shut down by informed consumers and market forces.

Because of possible disruptive influences on public schools and issues with religious instruction, the voucher movement is highly controversial. Critics, including the National Ed-

Voucher. A check or written document that parents can use to purchase educational services.

ucation Association and the American Federation of Teachers, the two largest professional organizations in education, argue that vouchers increase segregation, split the public along socioeconomic lines, and drain students and resources from already struggling inner-city schools (American Federation of Teachers, 2003a; National Education Association, 2002a).

Some voucher advocates would also like to use them for religious schools; critics contend that this violates the principle of separation of church and state. In Cleveland and Milwaukee, two cities that have led the country in the voucher movement, religious schools have been the major beneficiaries. For example, in Cleveland, 82 percent of participating schools in a voucher program were religiously affiliated, and 96 percent of participating students attended religious schools (National Association of Elementary School Principals, 2002). Nationally, almost 80 percent of private schools have a religious affiliation (Brimley & Garfield, 2005). Supporters of voucher programs ask why parents should have to pay for a quality education twice—once when they pay public school taxes and again when they pay tuition at private schools.

In 2002 the U.S. Supreme Court, in a narrow 5–4 decision, ruled that the voucher program in Cleveland did not violate separation of church and state (Flanigan, 2003; Walsh, 2002b). The idea that voucher funds went to parents rather than directly to religious schools was central to the decision. Since the Supreme Court made its decision, the number of applicants for the Cleveland voucher program has risen 29 percent, suggesting that more parents are taking advantage of this educational option (Hendrie, 2002). However, a research study conducted by a Cleveland-based nonprofit organization, Policy Matters Ohio, concluded that Cleveland vouchers served more as a subsidy for students already attending private schools than as an "escape hatch" for students eager to leave the public schools.

Since 1990 three state legislatures have enacted voucher systems: Wisconsin, Ohio, and Florida. However, the Wisconsin and Ohio plans apply only to Milwaukee and Cleveland, respectively, and in January of 2006, the Florida Supreme Court, in a 5–2 ruling, struck down Florida's voucher system. The court ruled that "the diversion of money not only reduced public funds for a public education but also used public funds to provide an alternative education in private schools that are not subject to the 'uniformity' requirements for public schools" (Romano, 2006, p. A05). Legal battles are likely to occur in other states and may be difficult for voucher advocates because 37 state constitutions currently have language that prohibits state aid to religious schools (Gehring, 2002b).

As with charter schools, the academic benefits of vouchers are unclear. Some research suggests that voucher programs can lead to small achievement gains (Bowman, 2000a, 2000b; Goldhaber, 1999), but other research indicates no achievement gains (Robelen, 2006c) or gains in some populations (e.g., African-American) but not others (Gewertz, 2003b; National Education Association, 2002a). A curriculum emphasizing academics, more effective instruction, and greater parental involvement are explanations offered for any gains that exist. In addition, parents provided with choice are generally more satisfied with the schools their children attend (Goldhaber, 1999). However, questions about the effects of choice on school diversity are continually raised, as we'll see later in the chapter.

In general, support for vouchers comes from dissatisfaction with existing public schools, and if public schools improve, public interest in vouchers is likely to wane. In the 2000 election, voters in California and Michigan overwhelmingly (70 percent in California and 69 percent in Michigan) voted against voucher initiatives, which opponents contend sounds a death knell for the movement (Walsh, 2000b). However, Republican legislatures in Texas, Colorado, and Louisiana are considering statewide voucher plans, primarily aimed at low-income students in poor-performing schools (Richard, 2003).

State tuition tax-credit plans are a variation on school voucher programs in which parents are given tax credits for money they spend on private-school tuition. Tuition tax credits have emerged in some states as a more politically viable alternative to publicly financed school vouchers. However, research suggests that tuition tax credits primarily benefit wealthy families who are already sending their children to private schools. In Illinois, for example, tax credits cost the state more than $61 million in lost revenues in 2000 (Gehring, 2002a). Taxpayers earning more than $80,000 claimed 46 percent of that amount, whereas less than 3 percent went to households making less

State tuition tax-credit plans. A variation on school voucher programs in which parents are given tax credits for money they spend on private-school tuition.

than $20,000. A similar problem occurred in Arizona (Bracey, 2002). Households earning more than $50,000 received 81 percent of the tax credits as well as 84 percent of the $109 million state revenues spent on tuition tax credits. More equitable ways of distributing the benefits of this form of school choice need to be designed if this reform effort is to grow.

Homeschooling provides parents with the opportunity to customize a child's education to a family's specific educational goals. (Buccina Studios/Getty Images, Inc.—Photodisc)

Making Connections:
To deepen your understanding of the topics in this section of the chapter and integrate them with topics you've already studied, go to the *Making Connections* module for Chapter 8 at **www.prenhall.com/kauchak**. Respond to questions 10 and 11.

Homeschooling. An educational option in which parents educate their children at home.

Homeschooling

Homeschooling, an educational option in which parents educate their children at home, may be the ultimate form of school choice. Homeschooling has become increasingly popular in recent years, with 2003 estimates of the number of children participating at 1.1 million students, accounting for 2.2 percent of the school-age population, up almost 30 percent from 1999 (Princiotta, Bielick, & Chapman, 2004; Zehr, 2006).

Parents choose to homeschool their children for a wide variety of reasons. Most (49 percent) do so because of concerns about the moral climate of existing schools or because of religious objections to the curriculum. Others want a more positive social climate (15 percent), or seek academic excellence (14 percent), or want to design a program that meets the specific needs of their child (12 percent) (Home School Legal Defense Association, 2004). All are seeking an alternative to existing public schools.

State laws regulating homeschooling vary greatly (Fischer et al., 2006). In most states, parents must demonstrate that their instruction is equivalent to that offered in public schools. Forty-one states don't have any minimum educational qualifications for parents who homeschool their children; eight of the remaining nine states require at least a high school diploma (Zehr, 2004). Approximately half the states require homeschooled students to participate in regular standardized testing. Homeschooled students who take these tests typically do well, scoring, on average, between the 65th and 90th percentiles on various tests (Mathews, 1999).

Despite its growing popularity, homeschooling has its critics. Some wonder whether children schooled at home will learn important social interaction skills (Galley, 2003). Other critics question whether narrow courses of study will expose children to alternative views and perspectives (Reich, 2002). One troubling trend is the tendency of some homeschool learning materials to criticize specific religious beliefs or entire religions. One study found that some of the more popular religiously oriented homeschool texts describe Islam as "a false religion," blame Hinduism for India's problems, and attribute Africa's problems to the absence of non-Christian religions (Patterson, 2001/2002). These types of messages are troubling in a pluralistic society such as ours.

teaching in an era of reform

Privatization

The move toward school choice has taken an interesting turn, with one option being privately run, for-profit schools. Modeled after HMOs (health maintenance organizations), EMOs (education maintenance organizations) propose to run and manage either whole districts or specific schools within a district.

Aspects of school privatization are not new. Schools have been outsourcing contracts for support services, such as school lunches and transportation, for years. More recently, districts have hired

companies such as IBM and Hewlett-Packard to provide technology support (Trotter, 2002a). What is new is the idea of handing over control of a whole school or district to a private corporation.

Estimates indicate that 70 percent of school districts currently engage in some type of business partnership (L. Alexander & Riley, 2002). At one time, school–business partnerships often consisted of corporations buying a football scoreboard or placing an ad in the school newspaper. More recently, Channel

One, a privately run school news/advertising company, offered 10 minutes of news to schools in return for 2 minutes of advertising. Incentives include free satellite disks, a schoolwide cable system, and free televisions in all classrooms. In 2001 Channel One reached 12,000 schools and 8 million students, 40 percent of the nation's 12- to 18-year-olds (Molnar & Reeves, 2001; Trotter, 2001). This is a huge advertising market.

Corporations such as Edison Schools, Inc., and Sylvan Learning Incorporated are leaders in the school privatization movement. Edison began in 1992 and made its stock public in 1998 with an initial Wall Street offering of $18 per share; optimism soon propelled share prices to $38 (Woodward, 2002). Chris Whittle, its founder, predicted that by 2020 Edison would run one in every 10 schools in America, but so far the company has grown slowly, and its stock sank to $2 in 2001. In 2005, Edison ran 136 schools across the country, serving 53,500 students (Reid, 2005). Edison's most visible challenge came when the school district of Philadelphia, a floundering system suffering from perennial low student achievement, offered Edison a 5-year, $60 million contract to manage 20 of its schools.

Nationwide, the privatization movement has received a big boost from the trend toward school choice, and the number of privately run schools grew from 285 in 2001 to 417 in 2003 (Walsh, 2003b); of these, 74 percent were charter schools. The number of for-profit companies in the educational arena also grew from 21 in 2001 to 47 in 2003.

Technology also plays a key role in the school privatization movement. William Bennett, former Secretary of Education, founded K12, a virtual school that serves both homeschoolers and charter schools embedded within public school districts (Bracey, 2004). Despite the use of technology, both its curriculum and instruction appear to be traditional, emphasizing the memorization of facts.

The Issue

As would be expected, private, for-profit schools are highly controversial. Should corporations, whose primary objective is making a profit, be entrusted with the education of children?

Critics make a number of arguments against privatization (Belfield & Bevin, 2005; Saltman, 2005). They question the ability of a corporate efficiency model to work in education and assert that corporate strategies will adversely affect both teachers and students. Further, they contend, privatized schools have a dual mission—improving test scores and making a profit—and corporate profits and education don't mix. Attention to the bottom line means that student welfare may be sacrificed in an effort to make money. Critics also claim that a narrow focus on the basics as well as neglect of non-native English speakers and students with special needs are additional problems. Teachers are treated as workers, not professionals, and are expected to implement a regimented, top–down curriculum.

Support for the critics' position can be found in Edison's efforts in Philadelphia, where controversy has existed from the beginning. Apparently, the district's call for outside help was based on an evaluation conducted by Edison itself and not sent out for competitive bids (Gewertz, 2002). In essence, the state of Pennsylvania hired Edison to conduct a study, completed in 2

months, for $2.7 million (Bracey, 2002). Not surprisingly, the Edison report concluded that external help should be sought, and the district authorized the creation of 20 Edison charter schools. After less than 1 year of operation, the Philadelphia School District, citing budget considerations, decided to shift $10 million of the next year's $20 million contract from Edison and other private companies to other reform projects (Gewertz, 2003b). One disillusioned parent commented, "I don't consider putting 15,000 students with a company that can't guarantee operations next year reform. It's not just a stock game, this is my child's life" (Saltman, 2005, p. 154).

Teacher morale and lagging student performance in Edison schools are persistent problems. For example, in an Edison-contracted San Francisco elementary school, approximately half of the teachers left in each of Edison's 2 years of operation, citing problems with long work hours, a regimented curriculum, and overemphasis on test preparation. There were also claims that students with academic or behavioral difficulties were "counseled out" of the school in hopes of raising test scores (Woodward, 2002). San Francisco cancelled its contract with Edison; under a renewed charter contract with the state of California, the Edison school's test scores remained low, ranking last among scores from San Francisco's 75 elementary schools.

Privatization advocates argue that these problems are exceptions, that Edison works in some of the most challenging schools in the country, and that the public shouldn't expect miracles overnight. They also assert that competition from the corporate sector is good because it encourages public schools to reexamine unproductive practices. In addition, advocates claim, the same business efficiencies that have made America a world leader can also work in schools, and a focus on performance (as measured by standardized tests) can provide schools with a clear mission to increase student achievement. They also claim that privatization can inject a breath of fresh air into the educational bureaucracy.

Research has found some benefits of privatized schools. They are cleaner and more efficiently run than public schools (Reid, 2005). Technology is typically emphasized, and more attention is given to individualized instruction. However, companies have not provided clear evidence that students learn more in privately run schools, a core assertion of privatization advocates. Some research shows improved achievement, but other research shows either no gain or declines (Shay & Gomez, 2002; Walsh, 2003c). Unfortunately, the research on achievement gains in privatized schools is murky, clouded by the sponsors—either privatization backers or critics—who seem to produce results that bolster their position.

You Take a Position

Now it's your turn to take a position on the issue. State in writing whether you do or do not favor the operation of schools by for-profit corporations, and provide a two-page rationale for your position.

For additional references and resources, go to the Companion Website at www.prenhall.com/kauchak, then to the Teaching in an Era of Reform module for Chapter 8. You can respond online or submit your response to your instructor.

School Choice and Cultural Minorities

School choice is often framed in terms of parental empowerment, or providing parents with educational alternatives. But can the process of school choice result in such unintended negative consequences as increased social and racial segregation, as some critics claim (Gill, 2005; Ross, 2005)?

Research from New Zealand, which began experimenting with school choice via a quasi voucher system in 1989, raises some cautionary flags (Fiske & Ladd, 2000). Under new choice rules, schools with more student applicants than openings could essentially choose whom they admitted and served. The better schools chose academically motivated students from affluent families, leaving less popular schools with poorer-achieving students. Researchers concluded that in New Zealand, "[c]hoice and competition are likely to polarize enrollment patterns by race, ethnicity, socioeconomic status, and students' performance" (Fiske & Ladd, 2000, p. 38). These same researchers cautioned against unregulated choice systems that could result in "polarization of enrollment patterns and exacerbation of the problems of noncompetitive schools" (Fiske & Ladd, 2000, p. 38). In other words, choice systems have the potential of encouraging social segregation and further damaging already weak inner-city schools.

The same concerns have been raised in the United States; critics contend that voucher programs and charter schools entice the best students away from poor-performing schools, leaving urban schools, in particular, in even worse shape than they are now (Ferguson, 2002). Further, offering school choice leads to segregation of students, either by income or race. One recent study supports critics' claims. Researchers found that 70 percent of African-American charter school students attend intensely segregated schools, compared with 34 percent of African-American students in regular public schools (Frankenberg & Lee, 2003). In virtually every state studied, the average African-American charter school student attended a school with a higher percentage of African-American students and a lower percentage of White students. However, a more recent study found that private, voucher-funded schools in Washington, D.C., were less racially homogeneous than their public school counterparts (Robelen, 2006a).

Problems of social and cultural polarization were also found in Arizona, a leader in the charter school movement (Schnaiberg, 2000). In 1996 two charter schools opened in the small rural school district of Safford, which had approximately 60 percent Anglo and 40 percent Hispanic students. In its first year of enrollment, the Triumphant Learning Center, a back-to-basics school with Christian overtones, enrolled 95 percent An-

glo students. Los Milagros, a charter school with Catholic ties, enrolled 75 percent Hispanic students. Although neither school consciously chose to exclude certain types of students, "subtle signals" sent messages to parents. For example, the Triumphant Learning Center emphasized increased parental involvement by encouraging parents to volunteer in the school and by closing their doors every Friday to allow more family time. Poor Hispanic families, in which both parents worked—some holding more than one job—were not able to participate. As recently as 2000, 53 percent of Los Milagros' students were Hispanic and 90 percent of the students in the Triumphant Learning Center were Anglo, but both schools are making efforts to balance their enrollments.

Another area of concern connected with school choice has to do with equal opportunities for students with special needs and how those needs should be funded. In most voucher plans, the voucher amount is equal to the average per-pupil expenditure in the district or state, but the cost for educating children with special needs can be more than twice that amount (National Education Association, 2005; Odden et al., 1995). Consequently, students with exceptionalities could find themselves underfunded or even refused admittance by certain schools. This very problem occurred in Massachusetts when for-profit charter schools openly discouraged students with exceptionalities from attending (Zollars, 2000). Only 17 percent of private schools provide special education services (Ferguson, 2002), so the problem of access to choice schools may be particularly acute for students with special needs.

Supporters of school-choice programs counter that public schools are already segregated, especially in inner cities, and that choice can actually promote integration. For example, in 1999, 55 percent of all public-school twelfth graders attended classes that had either more than 90 percent or fewer than 10 percent minorities (Greene, 2000). In contrast, only 41 percent of students in choice-driven private schools were in similarly segregated classrooms. As we saw with magnet schools in Chapter 5, school choice, when designed strategically, can actually be an integration tool.

The effects of school choice on students from minority groups will remain controversial and is likely to significantly affect education in the future. Whether these effects will be positive or negative is unclear at this time (Goldhaber & Hyde, 2002; Ross, 2005). Ideally, school choice should encourage experimentation and innovation. As with all experiments, mistakes will occur. Whether these mistakes will adversely affect students and the teachers who work with them are important questions.

Check Your Understanding

3.1 What are the major causes of funding inequities in education? What are some proposed solutions to the problem?

3.2 What are the two major forms of school choice? How are they similar and different?

3.3 What is school privatization, and what are its pros and cons?

 For feedback, go to Appendix A, Check Your Understanding, *located in the back of this text.*

decision making

Defining Yourself as a Professional

You've just graduated from a local university with a bachelor's degree, and you're certified in special education. Jobs are plentiful, you've interviewed with three different districts, and each has offered you a position.

The first was in a large urban district in the city where you grew up. The interview in the central office went well, and they asked you to interview with a school principal. When you arrived at the school, you were surprised at how run-down the school and the surrounding neighborhoods were. The principal was dedicated and enthusiastic, and when she showed you around the school, you could tell she loved what she did. Her last words to you were, "Think about us. This is a school that needs you, and you can really make a difference here."

Your second interview was in a small rural district near the university you attended. The central office was small, the interview went well, and the assistant superintendent and head of personnel concluded the interview by walking you down the street to meet the principal you'd be working for. The school was a small traditional brick building with well-lit halls and high ceilings. Though the pay was not

as good as in the urban school, the principal emphasized the opportunities for growth and leadership in a small district like this one. There were only two other full-time special education teachers in the district, and the head of the program would be retiring in a few years.

Your third interview was with a growing suburban district on the edge of a major metropolitan area in your state. The district office was modern and bustling. The head of personnel explained how the district would be hiring 50 new teachers that year and each would be assigned to a mentor. The school district had the highest tax base in the state, and this was evident in the school you visited. Computers and other forms of technology were everywhere. The pay scale was also the highest in the state.

What would you do in this situation?

*To respond to this question online and receive immediate feedback, go to the Decision Making module for Chapter 8 on the Companion Website at **www.prenhall.com/kauchak**.*

Meeting Your Learning Objectives

1. Describe the major educational governance structures at the state and local levels.
   - The responsibility for governing schools in the United States is given to the states by the Tenth Amendment to the U.S. Constitution. Despite geographical, historical, economic, and political differences between the states, the educational governance structure in each is surprisingly similar.

(continued)

- Within each state, the governor and state legislature are aided by the state board of education, a lay group of people that establishes educational policy for the state. This policy is implemented by the state office of education, an organization of education professionals. The state office of education is responsible for teacher licensing, curriculum supervision, approval of school sites and buildings, and collection of statistical data.
- Local control of education, a uniquely American idea, occurs through individual school districts. Each district is governed by a local school board, containing lay people from the community, and administered by a district superintendent. The superintendent is responsible for running the district office as well as overseeing the operations of the individual schools within the district. Principals play a major role in shaping the instructional agendas at the individual school level.

2. Explain the different sources and targets of educational funding.
- Schools are funded from three different sources. Almost one half (49 percent) of school funds come from the states, which typically gather funds using use state income taxes and special taxes. Local sources provide another 43 percent of funding and typically do this through property taxes. The third and smallest source of school funding (8.5 percent) is the federal government. (See Figure 8.3.)
- Most education monies (61 percent) go to instructional services, primarily to pay for teacher salaries. Ten percent also goes to instructional assistance needs such as student services, teacher professional development, and curriculum development. Another 10 percent goes to administration, both at the district and school level. Maintenance of school buildings and grounds takes up another 10 percent. Finally, transportation (school buses) and food services (cafeterias) each account for another 4 percent. (See Figure 8.4.)

3. Describe the major current issues in school governance and finance.
- Controversies over inequities in school finance have focused on differences within, rather than between, states. The large number of court cases involving funding inequities has caused states to reexamine funding formulas and has resulted in increased state and decreased local funding. Current approaches to funding equity go beyond absolute dollar amounts to include student and district needs.
- Site-based decision making has emerged as a major trend in governance reform. In site-based decision making, both parents and teachers have greater input into curricular and instructional decisions.
- School choice in the form of charter schools and vouchers provides parents with greater control over their children's education. Charter schools, publicly funded by independent entities, target their efforts on specific educational goals or patrons. Vouchers, essentially tickets for educational services, allow parents to shop around for schools that fit their needs. Privatization, in which corporations contract for specific services within districts, is a growing but controversial practice. The impact of school-choice programs on cultural minorities and integration efforts is still unclear.

Important Concepts

block grants (p. 256)
categorical grants (p. 256)
charter schools (p. 264)
homeschooling (p. 268)
local school board (p. 248)
property taxes (p. 255)
school district (p. 247)
school principal (p. 251)

site-based decision making (p. 262)
state board of education (p. 245)
state office of education (p. 245)
state tuition tax-credit plans (p. 267)
superintendent (p. 250)
voucher (p. 266)
weighted student formula (p. 261)

Developing as a Professional

Preparing for Your Licensure Exam

This exercise will provide you with practice answering questions similar to the Praxis™ Principles of Learning and Teaching Exam as well as your state-specific licensure exam. Read the following case study, and answer the questions that follow.

"Hi, Tom. How's the world treating you?" Andrea Martinez asks, as she drops a load of books on the desk in the teachers' lounge.

"I think I'm in the wrong job," Tom replies, looking down at the newspaper he was reading. "We got a lousy 2 percent pay increase this year. That, combined with the 1 1/2 percent last year, puts us behind even inflation. Maybe I'll need to get a third job to make ends meet."

"I know what you mean. We're struggling, too, but the economy is tight—a lot of people are unemployed. I don't know what to do myself."

"Maybe I should run for the state legislature," Tom says. "I could tell those people what it's really like to live on a teacher's salary."

"Why the legislature? Why not our school board? They're the ones who actually decide our pay raises."

"Aw, I'm probably not cut out to be a politician anyways. I'm too honest," Tom replies with a cynical grin. "I have actually thought about going back to school and becoming a principal. Their salaries beat ours."

"But so do their headaches," Andrea counters. "If big bucks are what you're after, why stop there? Why not become a superintendent? Ours makes over $150,000."

"Yeah, I heard that. But I also heard he's looking for a new job. They can't seem to keep people in that job. This one's been with us 2 years. The other one lasted 3. Maybe my job isn't so bad after all. At least I know there'll be a job waiting for me next year."

1. How would you respond to Tom and Andrea's comments about who actually determines teachers' salaries?

2. How accurate was Tom's comment that principals' salaries "beat" teachers' salaries? (You may wish to refer to Table 1.2 in Chapter 1, which lists teachers' salaries across the nation.)

3. Is the experience of Tom and Andrea's superintendent unusual? What factors lead to superintendents' short tenures?

To receive feedback on your responses to these exercises, go to the Companion Website at www.prenhall.com/kauchak, then to the Preparing for Your Licensure Exam *module for Chapter 8.*

Discussion Questions

1. Should legislation be passed to make local school boards mirror the populations they serve? For example, if 25 percent of the population is Hispanic, should one fourth of the school board be Hispanic? What advantages and disadvantages are there to this approach to equitable representation? What other alternatives might be better?

2. Ordinarily, teachers cannot be school board members in their own districts because of potential conflicts of interest. Would teachers make good school board members in districts in which they live but don't teach? Should a certain number or percentage of school board positions be reserved for teachers? Why or why not?

3. Should the percentages of male and female principals reflect the gender composition of the teachers at the school level in which the principals work? Why or why not?

4. Should school districts in a state be funded equally? What are the advantages and disadvantages to this approach? Should every school district in the nation receive equal funds? What are the advantages and disadvantages to this approach?

5. Will school choice be a positive or negative development in education? Why?

6. Should vouchers be made available to private religious schools? Why or why not?

Developing as a Professional: Online Activities

Going Into Schools

Go to the Companion Website at *www.prenhall.com/kauchak*, and click on the *Going Into Schools* module for Chapter 8. You will find a number of school-based activities that will help you link chapter content to the schools in which you work.

Virtual Field Experience: Using the Internet to Explore the Profession

If you would like to participate in a Virtual Field Experience, access the following Website: *http://www.nea.org/issues/vouchers/index/html*. This site contains data and opinions about vouchers from the perspective of the National Education Association, the largest professional organization in education.

Online Portfolio Activities

To develop your professional portfolio, further apply your understanding of chapter content, and address the INTASC standards, go the Companion Website at *www.prenhall.com/kauchak*, then to the *Online Portfolio Activities* for Chapter 8. Complete the suggested activities.

School Law: Ethical and Legal Influences on Teaching

Chapter Outline

Law, Ethics, and Teacher Professionalism
    Limitations of Laws
    Ethical Dimensions of Teaching

The U.S. Legal System
    Federal Influences
    State and Local Influences
    The Overlapping Legal System

Teachers' Rights and Responsibilities
    Teacher Employment and the Law
    Academic Freedom
    Copyright Laws
    Teacher Liability
    Child Abuse
    Teachers' Private Lives

Religion and the Law
    Prayer in Schools
    Religious Clubs and Organizations
    Religion in the Curriculum
    Teaching About Religion in the Schools

Students' Rights and Responsibilities
    Students' Freedom of Speech
    Permissible Search and Seizure
    Student Records and Privacy
    Corporal Punishment
    Students' Rights in Disciplinary Actions
    Students With AIDS

Learning Objectives

After you have completed your study of this chapter you should be able to:

1. Explain the differences between legal and ethical influences on the teaching profession.

2. Describe the U.S. legal system in terms of federal, state, and local influences on teaching.

3. Describe teachers' legal rights and responsibilities.

4. Discuss the legal implications of religion in the schools.

5. Explain students' legal rights and responsibilities.

Case Studies

 Elementary

 Middle

 Secondary

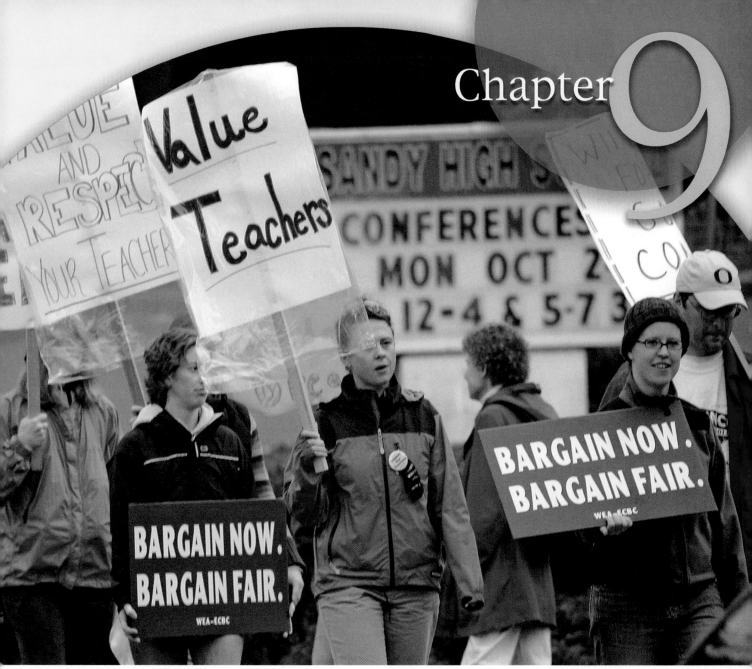

Chapter 9

Don Ryan/AP Wide World Photos

At this point in your teacher-preparation program, legal issues may seem distant, unrelated to your life as a beginning teacher, and perhaps not very interesting. Imagine, however, that you're an elementary teacher and are called to the main office to talk with a parent. Can you leave your class unsupervised? Or you're a high school teacher and you find a poem that strikes you as a powerful and moving commentary on love. Do you dare share it with your students without their parents' approval? Perhaps you're a science teacher, and you've discovered a program on the Internet that you would like to use in your classes. Can you legally download and duplicate the information? As you read the following case studies, think about the different ways that legal issues influence the lives of teachers.

Jason Taylor is a science teacher in a suburban school in the Pacific Northwest. The town in which he teaches is considering an open-space initiative that will limit urban growth. Environmentalists support the law because they believe it will help to preserve local farms and wildlife habitat in the area; business concerns in the town oppose it because of its potential to curtail economic growth. Jason talks about the initiative in class, explaining how it will help the environment. At the end of his presentation, he mentions that he is head of a local action committee and that interested students can receive extra credit for passing out fliers after school.

Some parents complain to the principal, claiming that school time shouldn't be devoted to political activity. When the principal calls in Jason to talk about the problem, Jason is adamant about his right to involve students in local politics, claiming that a part of every course ought to be devoted to civic awareness and action. The principal, unconvinced, points out that Jason was hired to teach science, not social studies, and warns that persisting on this path could cause Jason to lose his job.

Sasha Brown looks at the two folders in front of her and frowns. Her job is to recommend one of two students from her school for a prestigious science and math scholarship to the state university. Although the decision will ultimately be made by a committee she'll be on, she knows that her recommendation will carry a lot of weight because she is chair of the math department.

One of the candidates, Brandon, is a bright, conscientious student who always scores at the top of his class. The son of a local engineer, he has a good grasp of mathematical concepts. The other candidate, Sonia, is probably not as strong conceptually but often solves problems in creative and innovative ways. She's also a female—and a female hasn't won this award in its 6-year history. In addition, Sasha knows that Sonia comes from a single-parent family and really needs the scholarship.

What would you do in Jason's position? How about Sasha's? What external guidelines exist to guide you, and how do these dilemmas relate to teacher professionalism? We address these and other questions in this chapter.

Before continuing with your study of the chapter, take a few minutes to respond to the following survey. We address each of the items as the chapter unfolds.

professional knowledge: test yourself!

For each item, circle the number that best represents your thinking. Use the following scale as a guide.

1 = Strongly disagree
2 = Disagree
3 = Agree/disagree
4 = Agree
5 = Strongly agree

1. Teachers have the legal right to determine what is taught in their classroom.

1   2   3   4   5

2. Teachers are responsible for the safety of the students in their classroom.

1   2   3   4   5

3. Teachers are held to the same moral standards as other citizens.

1   2   3   4   5

4. The law prohibits any form of prayer in the schools.

1   2   3   4   5

5. Corporal punishment in schools is prohibited by law.

1   2   3   4   5

This is available in a downloadable format on the Companion Website for personal portfolio use.

Law, Ethics, and Teacher Professionalism

As you've learned from other chapters, professionals are responsible for making decisions in ill-defined situations, they have the autonomy to do so, and they use their professional knowledge as a basis for making the decisions. Understanding the legal and ethical aspects of their profession and their professional rights and responsibilities is an important part of this professional knowledge. However, research indicates that teachers' knowledge in this area is often weak, and as a result, they are ill-equipped to deal with the legal issues involving their roles in schools (Mayes & Ferrin, 2001; Stefkovich & O'Brien, 2001). Not surprisingly, students are also unaware of their constitutional rights and responsibilities (Tonn, 2005a). This chapter examines the law and how it can influence your professional decision making. We begin by putting the legal aspects of teaching into a larger perspective.

Limitations of Laws

You're working in a middle school, and you see a fight between two students on the playground. Does the law address a teacher's responsibilities in a situation like this? The answer is yes. You can't ignore the fight, because you're responsible for the safety of the children; in fact, parents have the right to sue a teacher if they can demonstrate that the teacher failed to protect students from injury, a problem labeled negligence. Should you physically break up the fight, or can you simply report it to the administration? As with many other situations, the law is vague and does not specify a particular correct response.

Laws regulate the rights and responsibilities of teachers, but two limitations of laws affect the extent to which they guide our professional decisions. The first limitation is that laws are purposely general, so they can apply to a variety of specific situations. For example, in terms of protecting their students from injury, teachers not only have to break up fights on a playground, they also need to supervise chemistry experiments, maintain order at school assemblies, and stop horseplay in locker rooms.

Jason's dilemma is another case. The law generally protects a teacher's freedom of speech, but does it allow him to campaign politically in the classroom and present issues that may not be part of the assigned curriculum? The answers to these questions are not explicitly described in laws, so professional decision making is necessary.

A second limitation of laws is that they were created in response to problems that existed in the past, so they don't provide specific guidelines for future decisions. New situations often raise new legal questions. For example, what are the rights of students and teachers who have AIDS? (We answer this question later in the chapter.) The use of technology (the subject of Chapter 13) raises additional questions, such as, What kinds of materials can we legally borrow from the Internet? What are the legal limitations to software use in schools? What can be legally copied? Experts are wrestling with these issues, and preliminary guidelines have appeared, but educators must often make decisions based on their knowledge of the law and their own professional judgment. This again illustrates why professional knowledge is so important.

Ethical Dimensions of Teaching

The law tells teachers what they can do (their rights) and what they must do (their responsibilities). However, laws don't tell teachers what they should do. For information on appropriate conduct, teachers must turn to ethics. Ethics is the discipline that examines values and offers principles that can be used to decide whether or not acts are right or wrong (Gladding, 2007).

Professional ethics provide broad guidelines for teachers as they make decisions in complex situations. [© Ellen B. Senesi/Ellen Senesi]

Professional ethics are a set of moral standards for acceptable professional behavior. For example, the Hippocratic Oath is a code of ethics that guides the medical profession. In taking the oath, physicians pledge to do their best to benefit their patients (with both curative methods and kindness), to tell the truth, and to maintain patients' confidences. Other professions have similar ethical codes, which are designed to both guide practitioners and protect clients.

You were first introduced to the National Education Association's (NEA) code of ethics in Chapter 1 when you studied teacher professionalism (see Figure 1.6). The NEA code provides guidance to teachers in ambiguous professional situations such as those described at the beginning of the chapter.

As with the law, codes of ethics are limited; they provide only general guidelines for professional behavior. Let's look again at Jason's dilemma to see why this is so. Under Principle I of the NEA Code of Ethics, Item 2 states that "the educator . . . shall not unreasonably deny the student access to varying points of view." Has Jason been balanced and fair in presenting both sides of the environmental and political issue? A code of ethics isn't, and never can be, specific enough to provide a definitive answer. Jason must answer the question for himself based on his personal philosophy of education and, within it, his personal code of ethics.

The limitations of the NEA code are also apparent in Sasha's case. Item 6 of Principle I cautions teachers not to discriminate "on the basis of race, color, creed, [or] sex," but it doesn't tell Sasha which student to choose. Judged strictly on academics, Brandon appears to be the better candidate. If Sasha believes that Sonia is less talented than Brandon, choosing her because she is female would be granting her an unfair advantage. On the other hand, Sasha may believe that Sonia's math talents are equal to (even if different from) Brandon's and that it is ethically valid to consider her financial need and the good that might result from giving recognition to a female in a male-dominated area of the curriculum.

In response to these complexities, teachers are often encouraged to "treat all students equally." However, even this edict isn't as simple as it appears on the surface. Effective teachers purposefully call on shy students to involve them in lessons, sometimes avoid calling on assertive students who tend to dominate discussions, and give students who have difficulty with English more time to answer questions and finish tests. Teachers treat students differently depending on their individual needs; professional ethics help teachers treat all students equitably, but not always equally.

These examples illustrate why developing your personal philosophy of education is so important. We saw in Chapter 6 that a philosophy of education provides a framework for thinking about educational issues and guides professional practice. Your personal philosophy will guide you as you make decisions about what is important and what is fair. Because the law and professional codes of ethics can provide only general guidelines, a personal philosophy is essential in helping you make specific decisions each day.

Making Connections:
 To deepen your understanding of the topics in this section of the chapter and integrate them with topics you've already studied, go to the *Making Connections* module for Chapter 9 at **www.prenhall.com/kauchak**. Respond to questions 1 and 2.

Check Your Understanding

1.1 What are two limitations of using existing laws as the basis for professional decision making?

1.2 How are laws different from ethics in terms of teacher decision making?

For feedback, go to Appendix A, Check Your Understanding, *located in the back of this text.*

Professional ethics. A set of moral standards for acceptable professional behavior.

The U.S. Legal System

Having briefly examined the law, ethics, and their limitations, we now look more closely at the legal system in the United States. Laws regulating schools and teachers are part of a larger, complex legal system, which exists at three interconnected levels: federal, state, and local (Underwood & Webb, 2006). This system attempts to use peoples' rights and responsibilities to each other as the basis for defining fairness.

Federal Influences

Through amendments to the Constitution and specific laws enacted by Congress, the federal government plays a central role in defining the rights and responsibilities of teachers and students.

Constitutional Amendments

Think about the following questions:

- As a teacher, how much freedom do you have in selecting topics to teach? Are you limited in what books and articles you can ask your students to read?
- Can you publicly criticize the administrators and school boards for whom you work?
- How much freedom do students have in running their school newspapers and yearbooks?

The First Amendment to the Constitution guarantees freedom of speech to all citizens of the United States (and as you saw in Chapter 5, the Constitution also established the principle of separation of church and state), but where do we draw the line with respect to the preceding questions? You certainly can't have your students read *Playboy* magazine, but how about *Catcher in the Rye,* a classic coming-of-age novel with explicit sexual references? Considering the second and third questions leaves similar uncertainties.

The Fourth Amendment protects citizens from unreasonable searches and seizures. To what extent does this amendment protect teachers and students? For instance:

- Can school officials search students' backpacks and purses when they're on school property?
- Are students' lockers considered to be personal property, or can they be searched if school officials suspect drugs or weapons are in them?

The Fourth Amendment provides general guidelines about search and seizure but doesn't specifically answer these two questions.

The Fourteenth Amendment states, "nor shall any State deprive any person of life, liberty, or property without due process of law." What does "due process" mean in the context of schools? For example:

- Can teachers be fired without a formal hearing?
- Can students be expelled from class without formal proceedings?
- How long can a student be suspended from school, and what kinds of deliberations need to precede such a suspension?

Again, the Constitution provides general guidelines about due process, but specific decisions are left to teachers and other educators. These examples further illustrate why an understanding of legal issues is so important for beginning teachers.

Federal Laws

The federal laws passed in Congress also influence education. For example, the Civil Rights Act of 1964 states, "No person in the United States shall on the grounds of race, color, or national origin, be excluded from participation in or be denied the benefits of, or be subjected to discrimination under any program or activity receiving federal financial assistance." This law was influential in ending segregation in schools in this country. Similarly, Title IX, passed in 1972, prohibits discrimination on the basis of gender and has been instrumental in helping equalize the amount of money spent on boys' and girls' sports.

State and Local Influences

States influence education by passing laws regulating teachers' qualifications, working conditions, and legal rights. For example, most states require a bachelor's degree to teach, and many are now requiring a major in an academic area.

States also create departments of education with a variety of responsibilities, such as determining the length of the school year and approving textbooks. They also pass laws creating local school districts, which are then legally responsible for the day-to-day functioning of schools.

This section addresses the first item on our beginning-of-chapter survey, "Teachers have the legal right to determine what is taught in their classroom." They *do* have the legal right to determine what is taught, but within limits; their rights and responsibilities are influenced by both federal and state laws. This has two implications for you as a beginning teacher. First, you should be familiar with constitutional amendments and laws that apply to all 50 states. Second, you need to know the laws that operate in the specific state where you work. For example, as you'll see in the next section, teacher strikes are illegal in about half of the states. Knowing the law that applies in your state can help you make a decision if collective bargaining between a district and professional organization reaches a stalemate.

The Overlapping Legal System

Overlapping levels of the legal system have been created to correspond to different levels of responsibility, but conflicts sometimes occur. When they do, the legal system attempts to solve problems and disputes at a lower level before sending them to a higher one. Let's look at two examples.

 Brenda Taylor has been hired to teach American history at a rural high school. Three days before the school year begins, her principal informs her that she will be the debate team sponsor. She objects, saying she knows nothing about debate. When the principal insists, she looks into her contract and finds that a description of her duties includes the phrase "and related extracurricular activities." It doesn't mention the debate team. She complains again to the principal, but he is adamant. She writes a letter to the school board, which appoints a grievance committee. The committee rules in the district's favor. Brenda, not willing to back down, hires a lawyer, and her case goes to a state court.

 Henry Ipsinger likes his job in a suburban middle school but disagrees with the school's priorities. In college he had learned that middle schools are supposed to be for all kids, not just the academically and athletically talented. He especially objects to his school's participation in Academic Olympics, an interschool academic competition, and the school's emphasis on competitive football and basketball.

Henry isn't afraid to express his opinions, and he does so frequently at faculty meetings, to the consternation of his principal. When his concerns aren't addressed, he takes his complaints to school board meetings. His complaints fall on deaf ears, though they do raise a number of eyebrows. He then tries politics, openly backing opposition candidates to the school board. Finally he goes too far; at the end of the school year, he is cited for insubordination, and his contract isn't renewed.

Henry is livid. He hires a lawyer, claiming his First Amendment right to freedom of speech has been violated. The case works its way through the court system all the way to the U.S. Supreme Court.

Can teachers be asked to perform duties in addition to their teaching responsibilities? Can their professional opinions cause them to be fired from their jobs? Both of these questions fall into a gray area called school law and are addressed by different court systems.

Because Brenda's and Henry's issues were different, the school and legal system dealt with their cases in different ways and at different levels. Both cases started at the local level. Brenda's complaint involved conditions of employment, so her case moved to state courts because employment issues are state responsibilities. Henry's case went to federal courts because freedom of speech is a right guaranteed by the U.S. Constitution.

In the next section, we examine teachers' rights and responsibilities, probably the most important dimensions of school law for teachers.

Making Connections:
To deepen your understanding of the topics in this section CW of the chapter and integrate them with topics you've already studied, go to the *Making Connections* module for Chapter 9 at **www.prenhall.com/kauchak**. Respond to questions 3 and 4.

Check Your Understanding

2.1   How do federal laws influence education?

2.2   How do state laws influence education policies and practices?

2.3   What is the educational significance of the overlapping legal system in the United States?

 For feedback, go to Appendix A, Check Your Understanding, *located in the back of this text.*

Teachers' Rights and Responsibilities

As citizens, teachers enjoy the same legal safeguards as all Americans, including freedom of speech and the right to due process. But because they are professionals entrusted with the care of children, they have responsibilities beyond those of other citizens, such as protecting their students from physical and emotional harm. In this section, we examine five areas in which the law influences teachers' rights and responsibilities. They're outlined in Figure 9.1. Let's look at them.

Teacher Employment and the Law

One of the first things you will think about as you join the teaching profession is how to get and keep a job. Legal guidelines influence the process.

Figure 9.1   Teachers' Rights and Responsibilities

Licensure

Licensure is the process by which a state evaluates the credentials of prospective teachers to ensure that they have achieved satisfactory levels of teaching competence and are morally fit to work with youth. Every state has licensure requirements, which typically include a bachelor's degree from an accredited college or university with a minimum number of credit hours in specified areas (e.g., those required for a teaching major or minor). In addition, prospective teachers are screened for felony arrests or a history of abusing or molesting children. Applicants who fail these screens usually have the right to petition before a state professional practices board that considers each case individually.

As you saw in Chapter 1, teachers are increasingly being asked to pass competency tests that measure their ability to perform basic skills (reading, writing, and mathematics), their background in an academic area (e.g., biology, history, or English), and their understanding of learning and teaching. As you also saw in Chapter 1, these tests are controversial, but when properly developed and validated, they have been upheld in courts (Fischer et al., 2006; Underwood & Webb, 2006). Individuals who meet these requirements receive a teaching license that makes them eligible to teach but doesn't ensure employment.

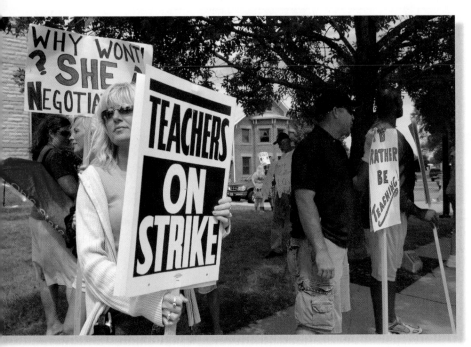

Collective bargaining between professional organizations and school districts determines teachers' salaries and working conditions. [Abigail Bobrow/AP Wide World Photos]

Contracts

A **teaching contract** is a legal employment agreement between a teacher and a local school board. In issuing contracts, school boards must comply with laws that prohibit discrimination on the basis of sex, race, religion, or age. Contracts are legally binding for both parties. School boards can be sued for breaking one without due cause, and teachers must honor contracts they have signed. Many states permit a teacher's certificate to be revoked for breach of contract, a practice growing more common as the competition for teachers increases (Archer, 2000b).

Teachers should carefully read their contracts and any district policies and procedures manuals covered by the contract. Extracurricular assignments, such as sponsoring school clubs or monitoring sports events, may not be specified in detail in an initial contract but can be required later. This is what happened to Brenda Taylor when her contract said "and related extracurricular activities." Courts have generally upheld districts' rights to require these additional responsibilities but have also said that a reasonable connection must exist between additional assignments and a teacher's regular classroom duties. So, for example, a speech or English teacher may be required to sponsor a debate club but might not have to coach an athletic team if the teacher has no corresponding background experience.

Collective Bargaining

Many of the details of the contract that you'll sign—such as working conditions, class size, salaries and benefits, and transfer policies—will be determined by collective bargaining agreements between your school district and the local professional organization. Most teachers either belong to the National Education Association or the American Federation of Teachers, and the power of collective bargaining is a major reason they do.

Licensure. The process by which a state evaluates the credentials of prospective teachers to ensure that they have achieved satisfactory levels of teaching competence and are morally fit to work with youth.

Teaching contract. A legal employment agreement between a teacher and a local school board.

Collective bargaining occurs when a local chapter of a professional organization negotiates with a school district over the rights of the teachers and the conditions of employment. Legally, teachers have a constitutional right to join a professional organization but cannot be forced to do so (Essex, 2006; Fischer et al., 2006). In most states, the law requires the local school board to negotiate with whatever professional organization represents the largest number of teachers in that district. The final agreement applies to all teachers in that district.

If teachers believe that a school district is not meeting the terms of the contract they signed or believe that they are given unreasonable responsibilities or work conditions, they can file a grievance (Imber & van Geel, 2005). A **grievance** is a formal complaint against an employer alleging unsatisfactory working conditions. When a teacher files a grievance, he or she is usually arguing that a working condition, such as class size or a teaching assignment, is in violation of the teacher's contract. A teacher cannot be dismissed for filing a grievance, and the professional organization that negotiated the contract with the district will usually provide legal counsel.

Teachers also have a limited right to strike in about half of the states. In the others, legislators group teachers with other employees such as police officers and firefighters, believing that the public welfare would suffer from a strike. Because of the variability between states in terms of issues such as strikes and items covered by collective bargaining, beginning teachers should become familiar with the educational laws governing these issues. Professional organizations in your area can be very helpful in this regard.

Tenure

Tenure is a legal safeguard that provides job security by preventing teacher dismissal without cause. Tenure is designed to protect teachers from political or personal abuses and to ensure the stability of the teaching force. It is grounded in the principle that teachers should be hired and fired on their professional merits and not because of personal connections or political views. Tenured teachers can be dismissed only for causes such as incompetence, immoral behavior, insubordination, or unprofessional conduct.

When any of these charges are filed, due process must be observed. The teacher must be provided with the following:

- Notification of the list of charges
- Adequate time to prepare a rebuttal to the charges
- Access to evidence and the names of witnesses
- A hearing, which must be conducted before an impartial decision maker
- The right to representation by legal counsel
- Opportunities to introduce evidence and cross-examine witnesses
- A school board decision based on evidence and findings of the hearing
- A transcript or record of the hearing
- The right to appeal an adverse decision

These safeguards, guaranteed by the Fourteenth Amendment, provide teachers with the same constitutional protections enjoyed by the population at large.

Dismissal

You'll work hard to become licensed and perhaps even harder to get a teaching position. Obviously, you won't want to lose your job; therefore, it's important to understand your rights so you'll be prepared should this possibility occur.

Most districts require a probationary period before tenure is granted (commonly 3 years). During this time, teachers have a yearly contract and can be dismissed for a variety of reasons, such as believed incompetence, overstaffing, or reduced school enrollments. Although some states require districts to provide a formal hearing on demand when a nontenured teacher is dismissed, this isn't common. Teachers uncertain about their rights during this period should check with their district, state office of education, or professional organization.

Collective bargaining. Process that occurs when a local chapter of a professional organization negotiates with a school district over the rights of the teachers and the conditions of employment.

Grievance. A formal complaint against an employer alleging unsatisfactory working conditions.

Tenure. A legal safeguard that provides job security by preventing teacher dismissal without cause.

Dishonesty on the initial job application can also cause a new teacher to be dismissed. Students close to obtaining their degrees are sometimes offered positions during their internships. They agree but, due to unforeseen circumstances, are then unable to graduate or obtain a license. When districts discover the problem, they can either dismiss the teacher or lower his or her status to substitute teacher, resulting in lower pay and loss of benefits.

Reduction in Force. Because of declining student numbers, budget cuts, or course or program cancellations, districts are sometimes forced to dismiss teachers. **Reduction in force** (or "riffing" as it's called in industry) is the elimination of teaching positions because of declining student enrollment or school funds. Typically, the district dismisses teachers with the least seniority—in other words, the last in are first out. Fortunately, "riffing" occurs infrequently and, as increasing numbers of students enter the educational system, should be even less common in the future.

Reduction in force can involve both tenured and nontenured teachers and is regulated either by state law or by collective bargaining agreements between districts and professional organizations (Fischer et al., 2006). Teachers faced with this possibility should consult representatives from their local professional organization.

Academic Freedom

Academic freedom refers to the right of teachers to choose both content and teaching methods based on their professional judgment. Although freedom of speech is protected by the First Amendment, professional academic freedom has limits. What are they? Consider these actual cases:

 In an attempt to motivate his students, a teacher organized his classroom around a sports-competition theme called "Learnball." Dividing his students into teams, the teacher instituted a system of rewards that included playing the radio and shooting foam basketballs. His principal objected, and when the teacher refused to change his methods, he was fired. He sued to get his job back, claiming his freedom of speech had been violated. (Bradley v. Pittsburgh Board of Education, 1990)

 An eleventh-grade English teacher was leading a discussion on taboo words. To illustrate his point, he wrote the four-letter slang word for sexual intercourse on the board. Parents complained and the teacher was dismissed. He sued to get his job back, claiming his freedom of speech had been curtailed. (Mailloux v. Kiley, 1971)

Academic freedom protects teachers' rights to choose both content and teaching methods. [Spencer Grant/PhotoEdit Inc.]

Reduction in force. The elimination of teaching positions because of declining student enrollment or school funds. Also known as "riffing."

Academic freedom. The right of teachers to choose both content and teaching methods based on their professional judgment.

Teachers are hired to teach a specific curriculum, such as first-grade math, middle school life science, or high school English. State and district curriculum frameworks exist to guide teachers, and they often identify required textbooks. Within this general framework, teachers are free to teach topics as they see fit. Sometimes these topics and methods are controversial and may result in a teacher being disciplined or dismissed, as in the cases just mentioned.

In resolving disputes about academic freedom, the courts consider the following:

- The teacher's goal in discussing a topic or using a method
- The age of the students involved
- The relevance of the materials to the course
- The quality or general acceptance of the questioned material or methods
- The existence of policies related to the issue

In the case of the teacher using the Learnball format, the courts upheld the district's dismissal. The court based its decision on the fact that this teaching strategy was not widely accepted and the teacher had been warned repeatedly by the administration to stop using it.

The case of the high school English teacher resulted in the opposite outcome. The teacher's job was reinstated because the court upheld the importance of two kinds of academic freedom: (1) the "substantive" right to use a teaching method that serves a "demonstrated" purpose and (2) the procedural right not to be discharged for the use of a teaching method not prohibited by clear regulations. The teacher's goal was for his students to understand taboo words and how they influenced literature, a topic that fell under the broad umbrella of the English curriculum. Had this not been the case, or if the teacher had been clearly warned against using this strategy, the outcome probably would have been different.

When considering the discussion of controversial topics or the use of controversial methods, teachers should try to decide if they fall within the scope of the assigned curriculum. If teachers choose to move forward, they should have clear educational goals in mind and be able to defend them if objections arise. Academic freedom protects knowledgeable, well-intentioned teachers working within their assigned responsibilities. If, as a beginning teacher, you're uncertain about an issue that could involve academic freedom, you should check with your principal or other school administrator.

Copyright laws provide guidelines for teachers when they use technology in their teaching. [Anthony Magnacca/Merrill]

Copyright Laws

As teachers, we want to share the most up-to-date information with our students. This can involve copying information from newspapers, magazines, books, and even television programs. Sometimes, however, our desire to bring this information into the classroom can violate copyright laws (Underwood & Webb, 2006).

Copyright laws are federal laws designed to protect the intellectual property of authors, which includes printed matter, videos, computer software, and various other types of original work. Just as patents protect the intellectual work of inventors, copyright laws protect the work of print writers, filmmakers, software creators, songwriters, graphic artists, and

Copyright laws. Federal laws designed to protect the intellectual property of authors, including printed matter, videos, computer software, and various other types of original work.

many others. To balance the rights of authors with the legitimate needs of teachers and learners, federal guidelines have been developed.

Fair-use guidelines are policies that specify limitations in the use of copyrighted materials for educational purposes. For example, teachers may make a single copy of a book chapter, newspaper or magazine article, short story, essay, or poem for planning purposes, and they may copy short works (poems that are less than 250 words or prose that is less than 2,500 words) for one-time use in the classroom. However, they may not create class anthologies by copying material from several sources or charge students more than it cost them to copy the materials. In addition, pages from workbooks or other consumable materials may not be copied.

Videotapes and computer software pose unique challenges. They too were created by and belong to someone, and fair-use guidelines also apply to them. For example, teachers may tape a television program, but they must use it within 10 days of taping. They may show it again for reinforcement but must erase the tape after 45 days. One copy, and no more, of software may be made as a "backup." Materials on the Internet may not be copied unless specific permission is given or unless the document is published by the federal government.

These guidelines restrict teachers, but the restrictions are not usually a major handicap. Teachers should share the principle of fair use with students to help them understand its purpose and the ways that copyright laws help protect people.

Teacher Liability

An elementary teacher on playground duty was mingling with students, watching them as they ran around. After the teacher passed one group of students, a boy picked up and threw a rock that hit another boy in the eye, causing serious injury. The injured boy's parents sued the teacher for negligence. (Fagen v. Summers, 1972)

A teacher was taking a group of first graders on a school-sponsored field trip to the Oregon coast. While some of the students were wading in the water, a big wave rolled in, bringing a big log with it, and one of the children was seriously injured. The parents sued the teacher for negligence. (Morris v. Douglas County School District, 1965)

We don't often think of schools as dangerous places, but the combination of large numbers of children, small places, and youthful exuberance and energy can result in falls, scrapes, and accidents. In addition, field trips, science laboratories, woodworking shops, and physical education classes pose special risks.

Teachers are legally responsible for the safety of children under their supervision. The courts employ the idea of *in loco parentis,* which means "in place of the parents," in gauging the limits of teacher responsibility. *In loco parentis* is a principle that requires teachers to use the same judgment and care as parents in protecting the children under their supervision. **Negligence** is a teacher's or other school employee's failure to exercise sufficient care in protecting students from injury. If negligence occurs, parents may bring a liability suit against a teacher or school district. Liability suits are a major concern of experienced teachers, influencing their day-to-day professional decision making (Public Agenda, 2004).

In attempting to define the limits of teachers' responsibilities in liability cases, the courts consider whether teachers:

- Make a reasonable attempt to anticipate dangerous conditions.
- Take proper precautions and establish rules and procedures to prevent injuries.
- Warn students of possible dangerous situations.
- Provide proper supervision.

In applying these principles to the rock-throwing incident, the courts found no direct connection between the teacher's actions and the child's injury. The teacher was

---

Fair-use guidelines. Policies that specify limitations in the use of copyrighted materials for educational purposes.

In loco parentis. A principle meaning "in place of the parents" that requires teachers to use the same judgment and care as parents in protecting the children under their supervision.

Negligence. A teacher's or other school employee's failure to exercise sufficient care in protecting students from injury.

properly supervising the children, and events happened so quickly that she was unable to prevent the accident. Had she witnessed, and failed to stop, a similar incident, or had she left the playground for personal reasons, the court's decision would probably have been different.

Field trips pose special safety and legal challenges because of the dangers of transportation and the increased possibility of injury in unfamiliar surroundings. Many school districts ask parents to sign a consent form to inform them of the trip and release school personnel from liability in case of injury. These forms don't do the latter, however; even with signed forms, teachers are still responsible for the safety of the children in their care. The courts ruled in favor of the parents in the Oregon case, because this type of accident is fairly common on beaches along the Oregon coast. The teacher, they ruled, should have anticipated the accident and acted accordingly.

As they supervise, teachers need to consider the ages and developmental levels of students, as well as the type of classroom activity. Young children need more direction and supervision, for example, as do some students with special needs. Science labs, cooking classes, use of certain equipment, and physical education classes pose special safety hazards. Professional organizations, such as the National Science Teachers Association, provide guidelines to help teachers avoid liability-causing situations in their classroom (D. Hoff, 2003b), and beginning teachers should be familiar with their guidelines. In addition, teachers should carefully plan ahead, anticipate potential dangers, and teach safety rules and procedures to all students.

In spite of conscientious planning, accidents can and do happen. Beginning teachers should consider the liability insurance offered by professional organizations. These organizations also often provide legal assistance to members who are sued. In addition, for a small amount per year, teachers can purchase a personal liability policy good for $1 million in damages (Portner, 2000).

This section addresses the second item on our beginning-of-chapter survey, "Teachers are responsible for the safety of the students in their classroom." According to the legal principle of *in loco parentis,* teachers are indeed legally responsible for the students in their care. Factors such as the age and intelligence of the students, as well as dangers inherent in a particular situation, should guide your actions as you attempt to protect the welfare of your students.

Child Abuse

Jimmy is a quiet, shy fourth-grader. He rarely volunteers in class and seems to withdraw from interactions with the rest of the children. He is skinny, and efforts to sign him up for federally financed lunches have been rebuffed by his parents, who assert they don't need help from anyone.

One day you notice a bruise on Jimmy's face. When you talk to him at lunch break, he says he fell while playing, but there aren't any scrapes or abrasions typically associated with a fall. You ask him how things are at home, and his eyes fill with tears. You ask him if he wants to talk about it; he just shakes his head no. When you ask him if someone hit him, he blurts out, "Please don't say anything, or I'll get in trouble."

What are your responsibilities in this situation? The student begged you to say nothing. Do you honor his request? The answer is no. All 50 states and the District of Columbia have laws requiring educators to report suspected child abuse (Fischer et al., 2006). In addition, teachers are protected from legal action if they act in "good faith" and "without malice." Teachers suspecting child abuse should immediately report the matter to school counselors or administrators. Schools generally have an established process for dealing with suspected child abuse cases, and these guidelines help new teachers understand their role in the process.

Teachers' Private Lives

Gary Hansen had lived with the same male roommate for several years. They were often seen shopping together in the local community, and they even went to social events together. Students and other faculty "talked," but Gary ignored the hints that he was homosexual until the principal called him into his office, confronted him with the charge, and threatened dismissal.

Mary Evans had taught in Chicago for more than 8 years and didn't mind the long commute from the suburbs because it gave her an opportunity to "clear her head." She had been living with her boyfriend for several years, and everything seemed fine until one day she found she was pregnant. After lengthy discussions with her partner, she decided to keep the baby but not get married. When her pregnancy became noticeable, her principal called her in. She affirmed that she wasn't married and didn't intend to be. He asked for her resignation, suggesting she was a poor role model for her students.

Teachers have a right to their own private lives but must meet community standards of acceptable conduct. [Michael Newman/PhotoEdit Inc.]

An individual's right to "life, liberty, and the pursuit of happiness" is one of our country's founding principles. What happens, however, when teachers' lifestyles conflict with those of the community in which they work? Are teachers' private lives really "private," or can teachers be dismissed for what they do in their free time?

In answering these questions, the courts have relied on a definition of teaching that is broader than classroom instruction. Teachers do more than help students understand English and history, for example; they also serve as role models. As a result, teachers are scrutinized more closely than are people in general. Other professionals, such as attorneys or physicians, might be able to lead lifestyles at odds with community values, but teachers might not. What are teachers' rights with respect to their private lives?

Clear answers in this area don't exist. Morality and what constitutes a good role model are contextual. For example, in the 1800s, women's teaching contracts required them to

- Abstain from marriage
- Be home between the hours of 8:00 PM and 6:00 AM unless attending school functions
- Wear dresses no more than 2 inches above the ankle

More recently, pregnant teachers were required (even if married) to take a leave of absence once their condition became noticeable. Obviously, views of morality change. As the California Supreme Court noted, "Today's morals may be tomorrow's ancient and absurd customs" (Fischer et al., 2003, p. 265).

Moral standards also vary among communities. What is acceptable in large cities may not be in the suburbs or rural areas. Cities also provide a measure of anonymity, and *notoriety* is one criterion courts use to decide if a teacher's private activities damage their credibility as role models. **Notoriety** is the extent to which a teacher's behavior becomes known and is controversial. For example, many young people are choosing to live together as an alternative to marriage, and this lifestyle is obviously less noticeable in a large city than in smaller communities.

Notoriety. The extent to which a teacher's behavior becomes known and controversial.

Where does this leave teachers? Generalizations such as "Consider the community in which you live and teach" provide some guidance, as do representative court cases. However, the law isn't clear and specific with respect to teachers' private behavior.

The issue of homosexuality illustrates how schools can become legal battlegrounds for people's differing beliefs. Some people believe that homosexuality is morally wrong and that people who are homosexual shouldn't be allowed to work with young people. Others believe that whether or not a person is homosexual is irrelevant to schools and teaching. When the issue has gone to courts, they have generally ruled in favor of homosexual teachers.

In a landmark California case, a teacher's homosexual relationship was reported to the state board of education, which revoked his license. The board argued that state law required teachers to be models of good conduct, and that homosexual behavior is inconsistent with the moral standards of the people of California (*Morrison v. State Board of Education*, 1969). The California Supreme Court disagreed, concluding that "immoral" was broad enough to be interpreted in a number of ways and stating that no evidence existed indicating that Morrison's behavior adversely affected his teaching effectiveness.

In other cases involving criminal or public sexual behavior (e.g., soliciting sex in a park), courts have ruled against teachers (Fischer et al., 2006). Notoriety was a key element in these cases.

The case involving the unwed mother further illustrates the murkiness of school law. A case in Nebraska in 1976 resulted in the dismissal of an unwed mother because the school board claimed there was "a rational connection between the plaintiff's pregnancy out of wedlock and the school board's interest in conserving marital values" (*Brown v. Bathhe,* 1976). In other cases, however, courts have ruled in favor of pregnant unwed teachers, including one in Ohio who became pregnant through artificial insemination (Fischer et al., 2006).

Although the law is ambiguous with respect to teachers' private sexual lives, it is clear regarding sexual relations with students (Hendrie, 2003b). Teachers are in a position of authority and trust, and any breach of this trust will result in dismissal. When teachers take sexual advantage of their students, they violate both legal and ethical standards.

Other teacher behaviors can also jeopardize their jobs. Drug offenses, excessive drinking, driving under the influence of alcohol, felony arrests, and even a misdemeanor, such as shoplifting, can result in dismissal (Fischer et al., 2006). The message is clear: Teachers are legally and ethically required to be good role models for their students.

This section also addresses the third item on our beginning-of-chapter survey, "Teachers are held to the same moral standards as other citizens." In fact, they are held to higher moral standards because they serve as role models for their students.

Teachers With AIDS

In determining the rights of teachers with AIDS (acquired immune deficiency syndrome) or HIV (human immunodeficiency virus) infection, the courts have generally used nondiscrimination as the legal principle guiding their decisions. The legal foundation for this principle was established in 1987 in a case involving a Florida teacher with tuberculosis (*School Board of Nassau County, Florida v. Arline*, 1987). The courts' dilemma involved weighing the rights of the individual against the public's concern about the possible spread of disease. The U.S. Supreme Court ruled in favor of the teacher, considering the disease a handicap and protecting the teacher from discrimination because of it.

The Florida decision set a precedent for a California case involving a teacher with AIDS who had been removed from the classroom and reassigned to administrative duties (*Chalk v. U.S. District Court Cent. Dist. of California*, 1988). The court ruled in favor of the teacher, using medical opinion to argue that the teacher's right to employment outweighed the minor risk of communicating the AIDS virus to children.

Making Connections:
To deepen your understanding of the topics in this section of the chapter and integrate them with topics you've already studied, go to the *Making Connections* module for Chapter 9 at **www.prenhall.com/kauchak**. Respond to questions 5–8.

Teacher Tenure

As you saw earlier in our discussion of teachers' rights and responsibilities, tenure is designed to protect teachers from political or personal abuses and to ensure the stability of the teaching force. Recently, however, tenure has been under fire by some educational reformers, who believe it is holding back the progress of the teaching profession (M. Bernstein, 2006). In 1997 lawmakers in Oregon eliminated tenure for teachers, replacing it with 2-year contracts (A. Bradley, 1999). Georgia followed suit in 2000 by eliminating tenure for new teachers, and attempted to pass legislation that would shorten the amount of time it takes to fire incompetent teachers (J. Reeves, 2004). Talk of similar measures has been heard in other states and districts across the country.

The Issue

Critics of tenure contend that it is outdated and unfair, providing teachers with protections that other professionals don't have. Further, they argue, it is unnecessary, because the existing system provides legal recourse to teachers who feel they have been wrongly dismissed (J. Johnson, 2004).

Most importantly, critics assert, it is virtually impossible to remove a tenured teacher, regardless of ability, which means that tenure protects incompetent teachers. For example, one study of 30 school districts found that only slightly more than one tenth of 1 percent of teachers believed to be incompetent were either dismissed or persuaded to resign (A. Bradley, 1999). Another study, focusing on five urban districts, found that during 1 year only four teachers out of a total of 70,000 tenured teachers were formally terminated (Rhee & Levin, 2006). Districts typically respond to the issue by moving incompetent teachers from school to school instead of taking them out of classrooms.

On the other hand, supporters of tenure argue that it was created to protect teachers from political or personal pressure and that it continues to serve that function (Fischer et al., 2003). Teachers who have tenure are more likely to address controversial issues in class without fear of retribution. In addition, tenured teachers are more likely to become politically active, especially in school-related issues such as school board elections and bond issues.

Supporters also contend that teachers need protection from the potential abuse of power that can exist if a principal or other district leader conducts a personal vendetta against a teacher for unprofessional reasons. In addition, during times of teacher shortages, the job security that tenure provides is an incentive for teachers to go into or remain in teaching.

Not surprisingly, administrators and teachers differ dramatically on the issue in some polls (J. Johnson, 2004). Both superintendents (80 percent) and principals (65 percent) believe that good teachers don't have to worry about tenure and think it is hard to justify. Fifty-eight percent of teachers, by contrast, believe that tenure is an important safeguard, protecting teachers from politics, favoritism, and losing their jobs to newcomers who could work for less.

You Take a Position

Now it's your turn to take a position on the issue. State in writing whether or not you feel that teacher tenure should be abolished, and provide a two-page rationale for your position.

*For additional references and resources, go to the Companion Website at **www.prenhall.com/kauchak**, then to the Teaching in an Era of Reform module for Chapter 9. You can respond online or submit your response to your instructor.*

Check Your Understanding

3.1 How are teacher employment issues influenced by the law?

3.2 What is academic freedom, and why is it important to teachers?

3.3 How do copyright laws influence teachers' practices?

3.4 What is teacher liability, and how does it influence teachers?

3.5 How are teachers' rights in terms of their own private lives similar to and different from those of the general public?

For feedback, go to Appendix A, Check Your Understanding, located in the back of this text.

Religion and the Law

Religion provides fertile ground for helping us understand how conflicting views of education can result in legal challenges. The role of religion in U.S. schools is and always has been controversial, and teachers are often caught in the crossfire.

You know from your study of Chapter 5 that the First Amendment to the Constitution provides for the principle of separation of church and state. The amendment reads:

Congress shall make no law respecting an establishment of religion, or prohibiting the free exercise thereof; or abridging the freedom of speech, or of the press; or the right of the people peaceably to assemble, and to petition the Government for a redress of grievances.

Each of the six clauses, or sections, of the amendment presents an important legal principle. The amendment begins with the **establishment clause**, the clause that prohibits the establishment of a national religion. The words "or prohibiting the free exercise thereof" is the **free exercise clause**, the clause that prohibits the government from interfering with individuals' rights to hold religious beliefs and freely practice religion.

Because religion plays an important role in many people's lives, the issue of religion in schools has become legally contentious, and teachers and administrators are often caught in the crossfire. Some of the questions that have arisen include the following:

- Are students and teachers allowed to pray in schools?
- Can religion be included in the school curriculum?
- Are religious clubs allowed access to public school facilities?

We answer these questions in the sections that follow.

Although the Constitution forbids the establishment of any particular religion in schools, a number of complex issues make this a controversial topic. [©Jim Young/Corbis; All Rights Reserved]

Prayer in Schools

In the past, prayer and scripture reading were common in many, if not most, schools. In fact, they were required by law in some states. For example, Pennsylvania passed legislation in 1959 that required daily Bible reading in the schools (but exempted children whose parents did not want them to participate). The law was challenged, and the U.S. Supreme Court ruled that it violated the First Amendment's establishment clause (*Abington School District v. Schempp*, 1963). Nondenominational or generic prayers designed to skirt the issue of promoting a specific religion have also been outlawed. In a New York case, the Supreme Court held that generic prayers violated the establishment clause as well (*Engle v. Vitale*, 1962). Neither schools nor teachers can officially encourage student prayer; however, prayer is permissible when student initiated and when it doesn't interfere with other students or the functioning of the school (Underwood & Webb, 2006).

The law also forbids the official use of religious symbols in schools. For example, the courts ruled that a 2-by-3-foot portrait of Jesus Christ displayed in the hallway next to the principal's office was unconstitutional (Fischer et al., 2006). Also, the U.S. Supreme Court

Establishment clause. The clause of the First Amendment that prohibits the establishment of a national religion.

Free exercise clause. The clause of the First Amendment that prohibits the government from interfering with individuals' rights to hold religious beliefs and freely practice religion.

struck down a Kentucky law requiring that the Ten Commandments be posted in school classrooms (*Stone v. Graham,* 1981).

These cases illustrate a legal trend: Officially sanctioned prayer and religious symbols—whether they come from school boards, principals, or teachers—are not allowed in public schools. They violate the principle of separation of church and state, which acknowledges religious diversity. Students may be Christians, Jews, Muslims, Buddhists, Hindus, or members of other religions. Imposing a particular form of prayer or religion on children in a school can be both illegal and unethical, because it can exclude children on the basis of religion.

Although the courts have been clear about denying prayer as a regular part of schools' opening ceremonies, the issue of prayer at graduation and other school activities is less clear. In a landmark case, a high school principal asked a clergyman to provide the graduation invocation and also suggested the content of the prayer. This was ruled a violation of separation of church and state by the U.S. Supreme Court (*Lee v. Weismann,* 1992). The school's involvement in the prayer was the key point; whether or not the Court would have banned the prayer if it had been initiated by students or parents is uncertain. In a more recent decision, the Supreme Court voted 6–3 against student-led prayers at football games in Texas (Walsh, 2000a). The Court concluded that students would perceive the pregame prayer as "stamped with the school's seal of approval," thus violating separation of church and state.

This section addresses the fourth item on our beginning-of-chapter survey, "The law prohibits any form of prayer in the schools." The law does not prohibit prayer in the school per se. Students can legally pray in school, but neither school officials nor teachers can lead or sanction organized prayer in schools.

Religious Clubs and Organizations

Organized prayer in schools is illegal, but it may be legal for extracurricular religious clubs to meet on school grounds. In one instance, a student in Omaha, Nebraska, requested permission to meet with her Bible study group before school. Officials refused, concerned about the possibility of undesirable groups, such as the Ku Klux Klan, using the case as precedent. The U.S. Supreme Court ruled in the student's favor, stating that schools must allow religious, philosophical, and political groups to use school facilities in the same ways as other extracurricular organizations (*Board of Education of the Westside Community School v. Mergens,* 1990). The fact that the club was not school sponsored or initiated was central to the Court's argument.

A link between church and state may also be permissible in some situations involving religious organization: For instance, the Supreme Court recently approved the use of federally funded computers and library books for Catholic schools in Louisiana (Walsh, 2000a). The principle of separation of church and state will likely be revisited in future educational court cases.

Religion in the Curriculum

A high school biology teacher prefaces his presentation on evolution with a warning, stating that it is only a "theory" and that many theories have been proven wrong in the past. He encourages students to keep an open mind and offers creationism, or the Biblical version of the origin of the world, as an alternate theory. As part of his presentation, he holds up a pamphlet, published by a religious organization; the pamphlet refutes evolution and argues that creationism provides a more valid explanation. He offers the pamphlets to interested students.

Where does religion fit in the school curriculum? Can a well-intentioned teacher use the classroom to promote his or her religious views? Given court decisions on school prayer, simplistic answers might be "no" or "never." But considering the enormous influence that religion has had on human history—as evidenced in art and literature—the issue becomes more complex.

Evolution is one point of tension. Concern over this issue dates back to the famous 1925 "Scopes Monkey Trial," in which a high school teacher (John Scopes) was prosecuted for violating a Tennessee state law that made it illegal to teach "any theory which denies the story of the Divine Creation of man as taught in the Bible and to teach instead that man is descended from a lower order of animals." Scopes argued that the law violated his academic freedom, contending that the theory of evolution had scientific merit and should be shared with his high school biology students. Scopes was found guilty of violating the state law and fined $100, but the decision was later reversed on a technicality.

Several states have since attempted to use legislation to resolve the evolution issue. In the 1960s, the Arkansas legislature passed a law banning the teaching of evolution in that state. The U.S. Supreme Court declared the law unconstitutional, because it violated the establishment clause of the First Amendment. In 1982 the Louisiana legislature, trying to create a middle ground, passed a "Balanced Treatment Act," requiring that evolution and creationism be given equal treatment in the curriculum. The U.S. Supreme Court threw this law out, arguing that, instead of being balanced, it was designed to promote a particular religious viewpoint.

In a more recent case involving religion in the public schools, a federal judge in Pennsylvania ruled that intelligent design did not qualify as a scientific theory (Cavanagh, 2006b; Whitson, 2006). Intelligent design is the belief that the complexity we see in living things, including humans, is the result of some unnamed guiding force. The Dover, Pennsylvania, school board voted to require that intelligent design be taught as an alternative to evolution. Parents in the district sued, claiming that intelligent design was an attempt to interject religion into the public schools. The judge agreed, concluding, "The overwhelming evidence at trial established that ID [intelligent design] is a religious view, a mere relabeling of creationism, and not a scientific theory" (Cavanagh, 2006b, p. 10). While the court's ruling only has legal standing in the U.S. District Court for the Middle District of Pennsylvania, legal experts predict that this ruling will carry considerable weight in any future cases involving intelligent design. (We examine issues related to intelligent design in the curriculum in more detail in Chapter 10.)

The broader issue of religion in the curriculum has also surfaced in several other court cases. In Tennessee, fundamentalist parents objected to including literature such as *The Wizard of Oz, Rumpelstiltskin,* and *Macbeth* in the curriculum, arguing that these works exposed children to feminism, witchcraft, pacifism, and vegetarianism. A lower court supported the parents, but a higher federal court reversed the decision, asserting that accommodating every parent's religious claims would "leave public education goals in shreds." It supported the right of districts to use religiously controversial materials if they were useful in achieving important educational goals (*Mozert v. Hawkins County Public Schools,* 1987, 1988). Comparable cases in Alabama (*Smith v. Board of School Commissioners of Mobile County,* 1987) and Illinois (*Fleischfresser v. Directors of School District No. 200,* 1994) resulted in similar outcomes. When schools can show that learning materials have a clear purpose, such as exposing students to time-honored literature, parental objections are usually overridden.

Teaching About Religion in the Schools

Legal controversies have had a dampening effect on teaching about religion in the schools. Here we emphasize the difference between teaching *about* different religions and *advocating* a particular one. Religion has had an enormous impact on history (e.g., the Crusades, New World exploration) as well as art and literature. Avoiding the study of religion leaves students in a cultural vacuum that is both inaccurate and potentially dangerous (Kunzman, 2006).

But how can schools teach about religion without provoking religious controversies? The U.S. Department of Education wrestled with this problem and developed the following guidelines (U.S. Department of Education, 1999b):

- Teachers and administrators in public schools should not advocate any religion.
- Public schools should not interfere with or intrude on a student's religious beliefs.
- Public schools may teach about the history of religion, comparative religions, the Bible as literature, and the role of religion in the history of the United States and other countries.

VIDEO PERSPECTIVES

A Battle Between Faith and Science

To view this video, go to the *Becoming a Professional* DVD included with this text, click on ABC News, and then this chapter's video: *A Battle Between Faith and Science.*

This ABC News video examines the controversies surrounding the teaching of evolution and intelligent design in Dover, Pennsylvania. In this small town in central Pennsylvania, the debate turned into a kind of war, a war of words between people with deeply held convictions on both sides of the argument—those who believe in creationism and those who fight for evolution. And there is no middle ground, no compromise. A lawsuit against the school board focused on the board's introduction of a book into the curriculum called *Of Pandas and People*. The book argues that Darwin's treatise on the origin of life is only a theory, while introducing readers to the study of intelligent design, a different theory that argues an "intelligent designer" created humankind. The textbook doesn't mention God, but the theory is supported by many Christians in the Dover community, and to them, creationism is a fact.

Think About This

1. What are some reasons that religion is such a hotly debated topic in American education?
2. What areas of the curriculum are most likely to encounter problems with religious issues?
3. What are the advantages and disadvantages of including religion in our schools?

To answer these questions online and receive immediate feedback, go to the Companion Website at www.prenhall.com/kauchak, then to the Video Perspectives *module for Chapter 9.*

Making Connections:
To deepen your understanding of the topics in this section of the chapter and integrate them with topics you've already studied, go to the *Making Connections* module for Chapter 9 at **www.prenhall.com/kauchak.** Respond to questions 9 and 10.

Critics caution that the Bible should not be used as a history textbook, should not be framed and taught strictly from a Christian perspective, and should not be used to promote the Christian faith or religious values (Gehring, 2000). The First Amendment Center (1999), a national organization promoting free speech, published the guidelines, *The Bible and Public Schools: A First Amendment Guide,* to address this issue. The guidelines, endorsed by the National Education Association, the American Federation of Teachers, and the National School Boards Association, recommend using secondary sources to provide additional scholarly perspectives with respect to the Bible as a historical document (Gehring, 1999b). These guidelines seem straightforward, but future legal battles over this emotion-laden issue are likely.

Check Your Understanding

4.1   What federal law influences the discussion of religion in the schools?

4.2   What is the legal status of prayer in schools?

4.3   Can a school allow religious clubs or organizations to meet on school grounds?

4.4   What is the legal status of religion in the curriculum?

For feedback, go to Appendix A, Check Your Understanding, *located in the back of this text.*

Students' Rights and Responsibilities

As it does for teachers, the law also helps define students' rights and responsibilities. Understanding these rights and responsibilities can guide teachers and others in their treatment of students. Sharing this understanding with students allows teachers to teach them about the legal system and their rights and responsibilities as future adult citizens.

Students' rights and responsibilities fall into several general areas, which we outline in Figure 9.2 and discuss in the sections that follow.

Students' Freedom of Speech

Many parents in an urban middle school are advocating mandatory school uniforms. They believe that having students wear uniforms would reduce classroom management problems, discourage the display of gang colors, and minimize social comparisons between wealthy and less wealthy students. The school administration has voiced support for the proposal.

The student editors of the school newspaper hear of this proposal and conduct an informal poll of students, which indicates that a majority of students are opposed to uniforms. The editors want to publish these results along with an editorial arguing for student choice in what to wear. The principal refuses to let them print the article. What are students' rights in this matter?

As you've seen at several points in this chapter, the First Amendment guarantees U.S. citizens freedom of speech, and we want our students to understand and appreciate this right as they prepare to be responsible citizens. Do they retain this right when they enter our schools? The answer is yes, but within limits. They do have the right to express themselves in schools, provided doing so doesn't interfere with learning.

The landmark case in this area occurred in the late 1960s during the peak of the Vietnam War. As a protest against the war, three high school students wore black arm bands to school, despite the school's ban on such protests (*Tinker v. Des Moines Community School District,* 1969). When the students were suspended, they sued the school district, arguing that the suspensions violated their freedom of speech. The case went all the way to the U.S. Supreme Court, which ruled in favor of the students. The Court ruled that freedom of speech is an essential right for all citizens and that students' freedom of expression should not be curtailed if it isn't disruptive and doesn't interfere with the educational mission of the schools (Zirkel, 2001/2002).

Students' freedom of speech was tested again in 1986. During a high school assembly to nominate student government leaders, a student made a speech that contained a graphic and explicit metaphor comparing a candidate to a male sex organ. Not surprisingly, students in

Figure 9.2 Students' Rights and Responsibilities

the audience hooted, made sexual gestures, and became disruptive. The student was reprimanded, and he sued, claiming his freedom of speech had been curtailed. This case also went to the U.S. Supreme Court, which ruled that "schools . . . may determine that the essential lessons of civil, mature conduct cannot be conveyed in a school that tolerates lewd, indecent or offensive speech" (*Bethel School District No. 403 v. Fraser,* 1986). In this instance, freedom of speech *did* interfere with learning and could therefore be limited.

With respect to freedom of speech, school newspapers pose a special problem. Court rulings have reflected the idea that a school newspaper is an integral part of a school's extracurricular activities and should reflect a school's goals (Zirkel, 2001/2002). In a pivotal case, students working on a newspaper wanted to print two articles, one detailing the personal stories of three anonymous, pregnant teenage students, and the other dealing with the effects of divorce on children. The principal objected, arguing that the students in the first story might be identified because of the details in the articles. The newspaper authors sued, but the U.S. Supreme Court decided that school newspapers could be regulated in cases of "legitimate pedagogical concerns" (*Hazelwood School District v. Kuhlmeier,* 1988).

More recently, the issue of students' freedom of speech has resurfaced over the issue of messages and images on T-shirts (Hendrie, 2005c). In one case, a Virginia middle school banned a T-shirt with a National Rifle Association Shooting Sports Camp logo on the back containing 3 figures holding or shooting guns. The parents of the student objected, and the courts agreed, saying there was no link between the T-shirt and the district's ability to run safe and manageable schools (Galley, 2004). In a second case, schools banned a student from wearing a T-shirt with the message "Homosexuality is shameful." A federal court upheld the ban, saying that schools can limit a student's right to free speech when the content of that speech is injurious to other students (Trotter, 2006b). Courts and schools have a responsibility to protect students' freedom of speech but must weigh this right against the rights of others and the efficient operation of the schools.

What should teachers communicate to students about freedom of speech? Whether publishing a newspaper, writing an essay, or giving a speech, students should be encouraged to express their views and opinions, both because ownership of ideas promotes learning and because it prepares them to take stands and express personal opinions later in life. However, students also need to learn that individual freedoms have limits; for example, these freedoms may not impinge on the rights of others. By encouraging the open exchange of ideas, while reminding students of their responsibilities to one another, teachers can create classrooms that become democratic models. This is a worthwhile ideal.

Permissible Search and Seizure

The Fourth Amendment to the Constitution protects U.S. citizens from unlawful searches and seizures, and warrants are normally required before a person or that person's property can be searched. How do these protections apply to students? Again, educators face dilemmas. We don't want to run our schools like prisons or teach students that personal privacy is not a right. However, as drug and alcohol use and violence on school campuses remain persistent problems, many school leaders feel compelled to conduct searches of students and their property or even use entryway metal detectors to maintain the safety of the schools. Where do the courts draw the line on the issue?

Student freedom from unlawful search and seizure became an issue when a teacher discovered two girls smoking cigarettes in a restroom in a high school in New Jersey in the

School officials may search student lockers if they have probable cause to believe they contain something illegal or dangerous.
[David Young-Wolff/PhotoEdit Inc.]

1980s. When questioned by the vice principal, one student admitted smoking and the other (T.L.O.) denied the charge. The vice principal opened T.L.O.'s purse and found rolling papers in addition to cigarettes, which prompted him to empty the purse. Inside were marijuana, a pipe, empty plastic bags, a number of dollar bills, and a list titled "People who owe me money" (*New Jersey v. T.L.O.*, 1985). T.L.O. confessed that she had been selling marijuana at school and was sentenced to a year's probation by the juvenile court.

T.L.O. appealed the ruling, claiming that she was the victim of an illegal search. The U.S. Supreme Court reviewed the evidence and upheld both the verdict and the legality of the search, concluding that school searches are legal if they are targeted at a problem. Schools must have probable cause to conduct the search; that is, they must have a reasonable suspicion that the student being searched deserves the treatment (Zirkel, 2001/2002).

In addition to probable cause, the nature of the search is important. Does it involve passing through a metal detector or opening a school bag, or is it more intrusive? The courts have consistently upheld the legality of metal detectors at school entrances, asserting that such searches are nonintrusive (Zirkel, 1999). However, more intrusive strip searches are generally considered illegal. In one case, a high school student was strip-searched for drugs after a police dog mistakenly identified her as carrying drugs. (Authorities later found that the dog was drawn to the young girl because she had been playing earlier that day with her dog, which was in heat.) The school district was required to pay damages to the girl's family (*Doe v. Renfrow*, 1980). In a more recent case, high school students were required to strip to their underwear in an attempt to recover missing money ($364) (Hendrie, 2005a). A federal circuit court found the search unconstitutional, concluding that the missing money did not justify the intrusiveness of the search. While condoning searches for probable cause, the courts remain sensitive to the rights of students (Ehlenberger, 2001/2002). School lockers, however, are considered school property and may be searched if reasonable cause (e.g., suspicion of drug or weapon possession) exists.

The use of urine tests to detect drug use illustrates how legal issues can become convoluted. In one case, the Supreme Court held that random drug testing for student athletes was legal, arguing that the safety of students and the importance of a drug-free school environment outweighed the privacy rights of student athletes who were participating voluntarily (*Board of Education of Independent School District No. 92 of Pottawatomie County v. Earls*, 2002). Another case involved an Indiana youth suspended for fighting (Zirkel, 1999). The school required the student to undergo a urine test for drugs before being readmitted after a 5-day suspension. In this case, the courts ruled in favor of the student, defending the boy's right to privacy and the lack of solid reasons for the urine tests. The courts have been unanimous in prohibiting school-wide drug testing (Underwood & Webb, 2006).

Student Records and Privacy

Students' records—grades, standardized test scores, teacher comments, and letters of recommendation—can determine whether or not students are admitted to special programs or colleges of their choice. They also influence students' abilities to get jobs. What legal safeguards guide the creation and use of these potentially life- and career-influencing records?

In 1974 Congress passed the Family Educational Rights and Privacy Act (FERPA) as an amendment to the Elementary and Secondary Education Act of 1965. Also called the **Buckley Amendment**, FERPA is a federal act that makes school records open and accessible to students and their parents. Under this act, schools must do the following:

1. Inform parents of their rights regarding their child's records.
2. Provide parents access to their child's records.
3. Maintain procedures that allow parents to challenge and possibly amend information that they believe is inaccurate.
4. Protect parents from disclosure of confidential information to third parties without their consent.

Buckley Amendment. A federal act that makes school records open and accessible to students and their parents.

The law doesn't guarantee access to all student records, however. Teachers may jot down notes during a busy school day, such as reminders about a student's behavior that will help the teacher decide whether to refer the child for special education testing. These notes cannot be made public without the teacher's consent. Also, a teacher's letter of recommendation may remain confidential if students waive their rights to access. To protect teachers in these situations, the Buckley Amendment excludes teachers' private notes, grade books, or correspondence with administrators.

A recent court case further defined the types of information protected by the Buckley Amendment (Walsh, 2002c). A mother in Oklahoma objected to the practice of having her children's papers graded by other students and the results called out in class. She claimed this violated her children's rights to privacy, and a federal circuit court agreed. However, in a unanimous decision, the U.S. Supreme Court overturned the lower court's decision. The Supreme Court concluded that the term *education records* did not cover student homework or classroom work.

Administrators and teachers have mixed feelings about the Buckley Amendment because of the extra effort and paperwork required to put these procedural safeguards into place and because of potential encroachments into teachers' private records. However, the law has improved parents' access to information as they try to make sound decisions about their children, and it has made school officials more sensitive to the importance of confidentiality for students' and parents' needs for information.

Corporal Punishment

In one Pennsylvania elementary school, a 36-year-old, 6-foot-tall, 210-pound school principal paddled a 45-pound first-grade boy four different times during one school day for a total of 60 to 70 swats. After the incident, the boy needed psychological counseling, cried frequently, and had nightmares and trouble sleeping (Commonwealth of Pennsylvania v. Douglass, 1991).

The Fayette County Board of Education in Tennessee specified in 1994 that any paddles used to discipline students must be

- *Not less than ⅜ inch or more than ½ inch thick*
- *Free of splinters*
- *Constructed of quality white ash*
- *Three inches wide (except the handle) and not more than 15 inches long for grades K–5*
- *Three and a half inches wide (except the handle) and not more than 18 inches long for grades 6–12*

Students can receive a maximum of three swats with these district-approved paddles (R. Johnston, 1994).

Corporal punishment—the use of physical, punitive disciplinary actions to correct student misbehavior—is highly controversial, both because of the legal issues involved and because using physical punishment as a disciplinary tool is questionable. In a 1977 landmark case, the U.S. Supreme Court ruled that corporal punishment in schools is not a violation of the Eighth Amendment to the Constitution (which prohibits cruel and unusual punishment). The Court further ruled that states may authorize corporal punishment without prior hearing and without the prior permission of parents (*Ingraham v. Wright*, 1977). In the 2002–2003 school year, more than 300,000 students were disciplined with corporal punishment, and corporal punishment is much more common in the rural south and the lower midwest (Lyman, 2006). As of 2004, it was prohibited in 28 states and the District of Columbia, which means the door is left open for the use of corporal punishment in the remaining 22 states. So where does that leave prospective teachers?

In states where corporal punishment is permitted, legal guidelines suggest teachers may use corporal punishment under the following conditions:

- The punishment is intended to correct misbehavior.
- Administering the punishment doesn't involve anger or malice.
- The punishment is neither cruel nor excessive and doesn't result in lasting injury.

Corporal punishment. The use of physical, punitive disciplinary actions to correct student misbehavior.

Teachers considering this disciplinary option should also ask themselves several questions:

- Is this the best way to teach students about inappropriate behavior?
- Would other options be more effective in encouraging students to consider their behaviors and the effects of those behaviors on others?
- What does corporal punishment teach children about the use of force to solve problems?

Psychologists generally disapprove of the use of corporal punishment, not only because of the possibilities that negative side effects can occur, such as modeled aggression, but also because more effective alternatives exist (Berk, 2005). Because of both legal and psychological issues, corporal punishment should be avoided in all but the most extreme conditions.

This section addresses the last item on our beginning-of-chapter survey, "Corporal punishment in schools is prohibited by law." As you saw above, the majority of states (28) prohibit the use of corporal punishment, but it is legal in 22 others. Despite its legality, experts suggest that corporal punishment should be avoided in all but the most extreme circumstances.

Students' Rights in Disciplinary Actions

 Jessie Tynes, a sixth-grade teacher, turns around just in time to see Billy punch Jared. "Billy, what did I tell you about keeping your hands to yourself?" the teacher demands. "This school and my classroom have no room for this kind of nonsense! You're out of this class until I meet with your parents. Come with me to the principal's office where you'll sit until we can solve this problem of keeping your hands to yourself."

Sean, a high school junior, is walking to his locker when someone reaches in from behind to knock his books on the floor. When he turns around, he sees Dave standing behind him with a smirk on his face. Losing his temper, Sean pushes Dave. A scuffle begins, but it is broken up by Mr. Higgins, the vice principal. Both students receive 10-day suspensions from school.

How are the problems similar? How are they different? What legal guidelines assist educators as they try to deal fairly and effectively with school discipline problems? Both incidents involve infractions of school rules, but they differ in the severity of the problem and resulting actions. These differences are important when the courts consider due process, a central issue with respect to students' rights.

Students have a right to an education, and the courts specify that limiting this right can occur only when due process is followed. However, the courts also acknowledge the rights of schools to discipline students in the day-to-day running of schools.

Suspending Billy from class, for example, would be considered an internal affair best resolved by his teacher, parents, and himself. Unless a suspension lasts longer than 10 days or results in expulsion from school, teachers and administrators are generally free to discipline as they see fit, assuming the punishment is fair and administered equitably.

Actions that lead to out-of-school expulsion, such as the incident between Sean and Dave, entry on a student's record, or permanent expulsion require more formalized safeguards, especially if they last longer than 10 days. These include the following:

1. A written notice specifying charges and the time and place of a fair, impartial hearing
2. A description of the procedures to be used, including the nature of evidence and names of witnesses
3. The right of students to legal counsel and to cross-examine and present their own evidence
4. A written or taped record of the proceedings as well as the findings and recommendations
5. The right of appeal

As this list shows, the procedures involved in long-term (longer than 10 days) suspensions and expulsions are quite detailed and formal. Whether due process means that students have a right to a lawyer during suspension proceedings remains unclear, however. A current court case in North Carolina involving this issue could set a national precedent (Bowman, 2003). Due process rights exist to safeguard students' rights to an education, an economic necessity in today's modern world. Since long-term suspensions or expulsion consume considerable amounts of time and energy, schools generally use them only as a last resort.

Disciplinary Actions and Students With Exceptionalities

Students with exceptionalities are provided with additional legal safeguards under the Individuals with Disabilities Education Acts (IDEA) of 1997 and 2004. These laws were passed to ensure students with exceptionalities access to an education while still safeguarding the rights of other students (Hardman, Drew, & Egan, 2006; Heward, 2006). IDEA 1997 enabled school administrators to discipline students with disabilities in the same way as students without disabilities but required them to review a change of placement, suspension, or expulsion in excess of 10 days. The purpose of this special review was to determine if the student's behavior was related to a disability, such as a behavior disorder. If the review determined that the student's behavior was not related to the disability, the same disciplinary procedures used with other students could be imposed, but the school must still continue to provide educational services in the alternative placement.

The Individuals with Disabilities Education Act of 2004 revised these discipline procedures to make it easier to remove a student with disabilities under special circumstances (e.g., the student brings a weapon to school; possesses, uses, or sells illegal drugs at school; or inflicts serious injury to someone at school). Under these circumstances, school officials can remove a student with disabilities to an interim alternative educational setting for up to 45 school days, regardless of whether the misconduct was related to the child's disability. This latter provision was designed to ensure the safety of other students and teachers.

Students With AIDS

AIDS became a major health and legal issue in the schools in the 1980s. Previously thought to be limited to sexually active gay men and drug users who shared hypodermic needles, AIDS entered the school-age population through contaminated blood transfusions.

Battle lines were quickly drawn. Concerned parents worried that the AIDS virus would be spread in school through either casual contact or the sometimes rough-and-tumble world of children on playgrounds. Parents of children with AIDS wanted their children to have access to as normal an education as possible. The courts were soon drawn into the fray.

A landmark and precedent-setting case occurred in St. Petersburg, Florida, in 1987 and involved 7-year-old Randy Ray, a hemophiliac infected with the AIDS virus through a blood transfusion. Because of his condition and fears about possible spread of the disease, school officials refused to allow Randy and his two brothers, who also were infected, to attend school. His parents first reacted by moving elsewhere, but when that failed to open school doors, they moved back to St. Petersburg and sued the school district.

A U.S. district court ruled that the boys should be allowed to attend school with special safeguards, including special attention to the potential hazards of blood spills (*Ray v. School District of DeSoto County,* 1987). Subsequent cases involving other students with HIV/AIDS have been similarly resolved, with courts holding that these children are protected by the Individuals with Disabilities Act of 1991 as well as Section 504 of the Rehabilitation Act of 1973, laws that prohibit discrimination against individuals with disabilities. Central to the courts' decisions has been the potential negative effects of exclusion on the social and emotional well-being of the child. The courts have been clear in rejecting exclusion as the automatic solution to the problem of dealing with HIV-infected students and instead have required schools to address the specific risk factors involved in each case.

Making Connections:
To deepen your CW understanding of the topics in this section of the chapter and integrate them with topics you've already studied, go to the *Making Connections* module for Chapter 9 at **www.prenhall.com/kauchak.** Respond to questions 11–14.

Affirmative Action

Affirmative action—a collection of policies and procedures designed to overcome past racial, ethnic, gender, or disability discrimination—was one outcome of the civil rights movement of the 1960s. Affirmative action was based on the belief that merely outlawing discrimination was not enough; to correct past discriminatory practices, society should take steps to ensure racial and gender equity and balance in all aspects of society, including schools. Currently, advocates of some forms of affirmative action emphasize the educational benefits of racial diversity for all students.

The legal basis for affirmative action comes from three sources. The Fourteenth Amendment to the Constitution guarantees equal protection under the law. Titles VI and VII of the Civil Rights Act of 1964 specifically prohibit discrimination in federally assisted educational programs with respect to race, color, religion, sex, or national origin. The Americans with Disabilities Act of 1990 extends similar protection to persons with disabilities.

Affirmative action affects schools in two important areas: hiring policies for teachers and admission policies for students. In an attempt to remedy past discriminatory hiring practices, courts required a number of school districts under affirmative action guidelines to hire more minority teachers. Higher courts have generally upheld this practice if affirmative action is deemed necessary to reverse past discriminatory practices (Fischer et al., 2003).

However, in cases where discrimination was not evident as a problem in past instances, courts discourage preferential hiring practices for minorities on criteria other than merit or qualifications. For example, because of declining enrollments, a school district in New Jersey was forced to reduce the teaching staff in the business department of a high school by one teacher. Two teachers, one White and one African-American, had equal seniority and were considered to be of equal quality. The school board decided to retain the African-American, using affirmative action as a rationale. The White teacher sued, claiming she was being discriminated against, and the courts agreed, arguing that minorities had not been underrepresented in the district's teaching force in the past (*Taxman v. Board of Education of Township of Piscataway*, 1996). Subsequently, higher federal courts ruled in her favor, deciding that for affirmative action to be legal, a logical basis for its use must be present (Fischer et al., 2003).

Affirmative action affects K–12 students in two ways (Walsh, 2002a). A number of

> **Affirmative action.** A collection of policies and procedures designed to overcome past racial, ethnic, gender, and disability discrimination.

districts nationwide attempt to achieve racially balanced schools through voluntary transfers across schools. In these cases, a student from a poor-performing school would have the option to transfer to a better school elsewhere in the district. In addition, magnet schools, designed to provide diversity by attracting talented students, use race as one selection criteria.

Affirmative action cases have resulted in charges of reverse discrimination, with critics alleging that minorities and women have been given unfair preferential treatment in hiring and admission decisions. One such claim was made in 1974 by Alan Bakke, a White student denied admission to medical school. Bakke sued the school because minority candidates with grades and test scores lower than his had been admitted. The case reached the U.S. Supreme Court, which ruled in a 5–4 vote that Bakke should be admitted. However, in making its decision, the Court did not rule out other forms of race-conscious admission procedures (*Regents of the University of California v. Bakke*, 1978). Recently, the Supreme Court heard an affirmative action case involving the University of Michigan. In a close 5–4 vote, the Court upheld the practice of considering race in admissions decisions (Walsh, 2003a). The benefits of a diverse student body were central to the Court's decision. Experts predict that this decision will influence not only colleges and universities but also future efforts to achieve racial balance in K–12 schools.

The issue of affirmative action is likely to remain controversial in the future. Toward the end of the 1990s, voters in California and Washington supported legislation eliminating preferential admission policies in higher education (Dworkin, 1998). In addition, court cases have raised questions about the legality of racial quotas for magnet schools (Dowling-Sendor, 1999). Legal experts in this area conclude, "In sum, the Supreme Court, like the country as a whole, is deeply divided on the question of the constitutionality and desirability of affirmative action (Fischer et al., 2003, p. 316).

A court case currently before the Supreme Court could provide some insights into the future of affirmative action. While not directly involving affirmative action, the court case, brought by parents in both Jefferson County, Kentucky, and Seattle, Washington, questions the legality of using race to assign students to schools (Trotter, 2006a). District administrators support this practice, believing that racial diversity has both educational and social benefits and is one powerful tool to battle segregation in housing that then leads to segregated schools. Parents opposing this practice believe that their children suffer because of lack of access to certain schools and having to travel long distances to help the district attain racial diversity.

Check Your Understanding

5.1   What are students' rights in terms of freedom of speech?

5.2   Can students be searched? What about their lockers and other possessions?

5.3   What is the Buckley Amendment? Why is it important to both schools and teachers?

5.4   Is corporal punishment legal in schools?

5.5   What are students' rights in terms of disciplinary actions?

5.6   What are the legal rights of students with AIDS?

 For feedback, go to Appendix A, Check Your Understanding, *located in the back of this text.*

decision making

Defining Yourself as a Professional

You are an elementary teacher in a self-contained classroom. You have a class of 29 lively sixth graders, and you've been struggling all year with classroom management. Damien, a larger than average boy, seems to resist your efforts at every turn.

You like science and have tried to provide concrete, hands-on science activities whenever you can. You've been debating about a fun activity on chemical changes where students actually test different mystery powders (e.g., sugar, salt, baking soda) with different liquids such as water and vinegar. You decide to go ahead with it and strategically place Damien up toward the front of the room where you can watch him, and have paired him with Katie, one of your more responsible female students.

Everything is going well until you go to the back of the room to answer a question and hear a student shriek, "Damien!" As you rush to the front of the room, you see Katie holding her eye, with a mixture of vinegar and baking soda dripping down her cheek. Damien is sitting there with a guilty look on his face. As you rush the crying Katie to the office, you wonder if there isn't something you should have done differently.

What would you do in this situation?

To respond to this question online and receive immediate feedback, go to the Decision Making *module for Chapter 9 on the Companion Website at* **www.prenhall.com/kauchak**.

Meeting Your Learning Objectives

1. Explain the differences between legal and ethical influences on the teaching profession.
   - Laws and ethical codes provide guidelines as teachers make professional decisions. Laws specify what teachers must and can do. Codes of ethics provide guidelines for what teachers should do as conscientious and caring professionals. Professional organizations such as the National Education Association and American Federation of Teachers publish codes of ethics for teachers.
   - Two major drawbacks to using both laws and ethical codes to guide professional decisions are (1) they are general, lacking in specificity, and (2) they are created to address problems in the past and, consequently, may not be relevant to current issues and topics.

2. Describe the U.S. legal system in terms of federal, state, and local influences on teaching.
   - The U.S. legal system is a complex web of interconnected bodies. At the federal level the U.S. Constitution provides broad guidelines for legal issues, and Congress passes laws that impact education.
   - Most of the direct legal responsibility for running schools belongs to states and local school districts. The U.S. Constitution gives states the legal rights to govern education, and many day-to-day responsibilities are passed on to districts.
   - The overlapping U.S. legal system places the legal responsibility for specific issues or cases at different levels depending on the particular issue involved.

3. Describe teachers' legal rights and responsibilities.
   - Teachers have rights and responsibilities as professional educators. Licensure provides them with the right to teach; a teaching contract specifies the legal conditions for employment. Most new teachers are hired on probationary status. Once granted tenure, teachers cannot be dismissed without due process.
   - Teachers' academic freedom is guaranteed by the First Amendment to the Constitution. However, in deciding on issues of academic freedom, the courts examine the educational relevance of the content or method involved and the age of the students.
   - Copyright laws, designed to protect the property rights of authors, provide restrictions on teachers' use of others' original materials. New questions about fair use are being raised by the increased use of videotape and DVDs and material presented on the Internet.
   - Liability poses unique challenges to teachers. The courts hold that teachers act *in loco parentis,* and when they fail to protect the children under their charge, they can be sued for negligence. When deciding on issues of liability, the courts take into account the age and developmental level of students as well as the kinds of risks involved in an activity.
   - Teachers' private lives are not as private as some would wish. Teachers are expected to be role models to students, so their activities in their hours away from school are often scrutinized and, if illegal, can result in dismissal.

4. Discuss the legal implications of religion in the schools.
   - Because of differing beliefs about the proper role of religion in education, religion provides a legal battleground in the schools. Organized or school-sponsored prayer is banned in schools, but students' rights to pray in school is protected by law.
   - Courts have approved religious clubs and organizations and private expressions of student religious beliefs. Religious clubs are provided the same legal safeguards as other extracurricular organizations.
   - Although the courts disapprove of religious advocacy, teaching about religion is legal when it can be justified educationally.

5. Explain students' legal rights and responsibilities.
   - Many of the same issues of rights involving freedom of speech and due process that affect teachers also pertain to students. Students' right to freedom of speech are protected by the courts, but the expression of free speech must not interfere with the school's or teacher's instructional agenda.
   - Students are protected from unreasonable search and seizure by the U.S. Constitution. However, lockers are considered school property, and students' and their belongings may be searched if school officials have a reasonable suspicion about the possession of drugs or dangerous weapons.
   - Students' education records are protected by federal legislation called the Buckley Amendment. The main thrust of this law is to protect the privacy rights of students' educational records.
   - Corporal punishment is legally allowed in a number of states. Those laws contain safeguards against injury and anger or malice.
   - Because the courts view attending public schools as a legal right, school officials must conduct student suspension or expulsion from school in a prescribed manner that makes the process transparent to parents or guardians.
   - The educational rights of students with AIDS are protected by law. School officials must address specific risk factors to other students when excluding children with AIDS from educational activities.

Important Concepts

academic freedom (p. 286)

affirmative action (p. 303)

Buckley Amendment (p. 299)

collective bargaining (p. 285)

copyright laws (p. 287)

corporal punishment (p. 300)

establishment clause (p. 293)

fair use guidelines (p. 288)

free exercise clause (p. 293)

grievance (p. 285)

in loco parentis (p. 288)

licensure (p. 284)

negligence (p. 288)

notoriety (p. 290)

professional ethics (p. 280)

reduction in force (p. 286)

teaching contract (p. 284)

tenure (p. 285)

Developing as a Professional

Preparing for Your Licensure Exam

This exercise will provide you with practice answering questions similar to the Praxis™ Principles of Learning and Teaching Exam as well as your state-specific licensure exam. Read the following case study, and answer the questions that follow.

"Hi, Kyle. What are you working on?" Jan Trefino asks, as she returns the borrowed overhead projector to her neighbor's high school classroom.

"Oh, just trying to plan for next week. You know, try to stay a day or two ahead of the students. How did it work?"

"Great! Thanks a lot. It was a real life-saver. I had all these transparencies and. . . . While I have you here, can I ask you a question? Since you're a veteran, you seem to know everything."

"Yeah, right. Teaching for 4 years will do that to you," Kyle says, laughing. "What's the question?"

"Well, the unit coming up is on the labor movement in the United States, and I'd like to connect it with some of the controversies we've been reading about in the local papers. I'd like to talk about the unionization of the migrant farm workers, but I'm a little nervous about getting into hot water. Any advice?"

"I'd say go for it. Students need to see how abstract ideas from the past relate to their everyday lives," Kyle responds. "Let me tell you about something that happened to me in my English class. We were reading a short story about a young runaway girl who was in trouble. The story hinted at, but didn't say explicitly, that she might be pregnant. So as we were discussing the story, I mentioned that there were agencies around like adoption agencies and Planned Parenthood to help people in that situation."

"Yikes, you're brave. Any fallout?"

"Not yet, though I may have overstepped my bounds when one student started preaching about morality and religion. I cut him off, saying, 'We can't talk about religion in school.' He gave me a funny look but didn't say anything more."

"So, you think it's okay to bring in clippings from the local newspaper about the union controversy?" Jan asks.

"Sure, if it's in the newspaper, why couldn't you?"

1. What professional legal issue were Jan and Kyle wrestling with, and what legal safeguards influence this issue?

2. How did the two teachers differ in terms of work experience, and how might this influence their curricular decisions?

3. Comment on Kyle's statement, "We can't talk about religion in school," from a legal perspective.

4. From a professional ethics perspective, what advice do you have for Jan about her discussion of local union controversies?

To receive feedback on your responses to these exercises, go to the Companion Website at www.prenhall.com/kauchak, then to the Preparing for Your Licensure Exam *module for Chapter 9.*

Discussion Questions

1. What are the advantages and disadvantages of teacher tenure? What arguments might there be for a longer period of probation before granting a teacher tenure? A shorter period? Should teachers be reviewed periodically after tenure is granted?

2. What is the proper role of religion in the schools? In what areas of the curriculum should religion enter? Should teachers reveal their religious beliefs to students? What should a teacher do if a student shares his or her religious beliefs with the class?

3. Touching can be a powerful way of expressing caring or concern. Should teachers touch their students? How and under what circumstances? How might circumstances differ depending on the age and gender of students and the age and gender of the teacher?

4. What place should corporal punishment have in schools? How might the use of corporal punishment be influenced by the following factors: age of student, type of misbehavior, and age and gender of teacher?

5. Should teachers' private lives be placed under any more public examination than the lives of other professionals, such as doctors or lawyers? Why or why not?

Developing as a Professional: Online Activities

Going Into Schools

Go to the Companion Website at *www.prenhall.com/kauchak*, and click on the *Going Into Schools* module for Chapter 9. You will find a number of school-based activities that will help you link chapter content to the schools in which you work.

Virtual Field Experience: Using the Internet to Explore the Profession

If you would like to participate in a Virtual Field Experience, access the following Website: *http://www.nea.org/he/tenure.html*. This site provides data and opinions about teacher tenure from the perspective of the National Education Association, the largest professional organization in education.

Online Portfolio Activities

To develop your professional portfolio, further apply your understanding of chapter content, and address the INTASC standards, go the Companion Website at *www.prenhall.com/kauchak*, then to the *Online Portfolio Activities* for Chapter 9. Complete the suggested activities.

Part IV

TEACHING

The Curriculum in an Era of Standards and Accountability

Chapter Outline

What Is Curriculum?
  The Relationship Between Curriculum and Instruction

Components of the Curriculum
  The Explicit Curriculum
  The Implicit Curriculum
  The Null Curriculum
  The Extracurriculum

Forces That Influence the Curriculum
  Standards and Accountability
  The Federal Government
  Textbooks
  Teacher Professionalism and Individual Teachers' Philosophies

Curriculum Controversies
  Sex Education
  Moral and Character Education
  Intelligent Design
  Censorship

Learning Objectives

After you have completed your study of this chapter, you should be able to:

1. Describe different definitions of *curriculum.*

2. Explain how the explicit, implicit, and null curriculums, and the extracurriculum differ.

3. Identify different forces that influence the curriculum, and explain how each exerts its influence.

4. Describe prominent controversial issues in our country and their impact on the curriculum.

Case Studies

 Elementary   *Middle*   *Secondary*

Chapter 10

SW Productions/Getty Images, Inc.—Photodisc

In your work as a teacher, you'll continually be faced with many questions, three of the most important being: "What am I teaching?" "Why am I teaching it?" and "How will I help my students understand it?" These questions are so fundamental that we almost forget that a great deal of thought and decision making (and sometimes controversy) go into answering them. Let's look in on one teacher involved in this decision-making process.

It's Saturday afternoon, and Suzanne Brush, a second-grade teacher, is planning for her coming week. She looks at one of her state's standards in math, which appears as follows:

Data Analysis and Probability
Standard 1:
The student understands and uses the tools of data analysis for managing information. (MA.E.1.1)
1. Displays solutions to problems by generating, collecting, organizing, and analyzing data using simple graphs and charts.
   (Florida Department of Education, Sunshine State Standards, Mathematics PreK–2, 2005, p. 2)

"Okay, . . .they need to be able to collect data and analyze it using graphs and charts," she says to herself.

She also goes online and looks at some sample test items from the state high-stakes test to look for some examples of how her students' understanding of the standard will be measured. She finds the following item:

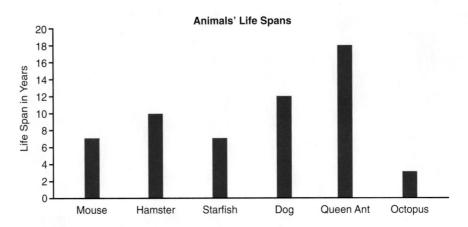

How much longer is the life of a dog than an octopus?

a. 4 years
b. 6 years
c. 9 years
d. 12 years

Source: Adapted from Florida Comprehensive Assessment Test (2007). *Mathematics Sample Test Book.* Tallahassee: Florida Department of Education.

She thinks about the standard and how her students will be assessed, and, after considering several different instructional activities, she decides to have the students sample different flavors of jelly beans, pick their favorites, and chart their preferences on a bar graph. "Yes, I think that will work, and they'll like it," she smiles to herself. "I'll do it on Monday." She then prepares the necessary materials and finishes, feeling quite satisfied about her decisions.

After getting her students settled down for math on Monday, she begins, "I'm planning a party for our class. While I was doing that, a question came to my mind that I thought maybe you could help me solve today. I need to know how I can figure out the class's favorite kind of jelly bean. How could we find out? If you can help me out, raise your hand."

After several suggestions from students, the class decides to give each student several different kinds of jelly beans and have each choose a favorite.

"It just so happens," Suzanne smiles, "that I brought in some jelly beans today, and you'll be able to taste these jelly beans and vote for your favorite flavor."

She gives each student a small plastic bag with seven different-flavored jelly beans in it, and when they finish tasting each one, she says, "Now I need your help. . . . Raise your hand if you can tell me what we can do now that we have this information. How can we organize it so that we can look at it as a whole group? . . . Jacinta?"

Students offer different ideas, and Suzanne then says, "Here's what we're going to do. We have an empty graph up in the front of the room," as she moves to the front and displays the outline of a graph that appears as follows:

Suzanne then explains that she has some colored cardboard pieces for the graph that match the colors of the jelly beans. She directs students to come to the front of the room and paste the colored piece that represents their favorite jelly bean on the graph. When the students are done, the graph appeared as follows:

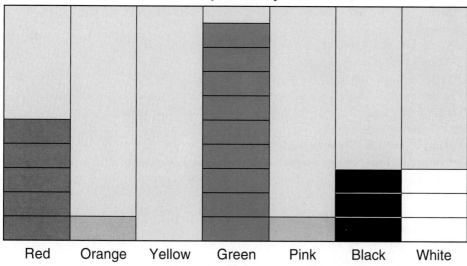

Suzanne then reassembles the class and says, "We collected the information and organized it up here on the graph. Now we need to look at it and analyze it. . . . Tell us what we know by looking at this graph. . . . Candice, what do we know?" she asks, walking toward the middle of the room.

"People like green," Candice answers.

"Candice said most people like the green jelly beans. . . . Candice, how many people like green?"

". . . Nine."

"Nine people like green. . . . And how did you find that out? Can you go up there and show us how you read the graph?"

Candice goes up to the graph and moves her hand up from the bottom, counting the green pieces as she goes and matching the top one to the nine on the vertical axis.

Suzanne has the students make several more observations of the information on the graph and then says, "Okay, now I'm going to ask you a different kind of question. . . . How many more people liked the green jelly beans than the red? Look up at the graph. Try to find the information, set up the problem, and then we'll see what you come out with. . . . I'm looking for a volunteer to share an answer with us. . . . Dominique?"

"Nine plus 5 is 14," Dominique responds.

"Dominique says 9 plus 5 is 14. Let's test it out." (She asks Dominique to go up to the graph and show the class how she arrived at her answer.) We want to know the difference. . . . How many more people liked green than red, and you say 14 people, . . . 14 more people liked green. Does that work?"

"I mean 9 take away 5," Dominique says after looking at the graph for a few seconds.

"She got up here and she changed her mind," Suzanne smiles warmly. "Tell them."

"Nine take away 5 is 4."

"Nine take away 5 is 4. So how many more people liked green than red? . . .Carlos?"

"Four."

"Four, good, four," Suzanne emphasizes, smiling. "The key was, you had to find the difference between the two numbers."

After students generate several more similar problems, she continues, "I have one more question, and then we'll switch gears a little bit. How many people participated in this voting? How many people took part or participated in this voting?"

Suzanne watches as students turn to the graph. "Matt? . . . How many people?" she asks as she sees that most students are finished and several have their hands raised.

"Twenty-two," Matt answers.

"Twenty-two," Suzanne repeats. "And how did you solve the problem? That's the most important thing."

"Nine plus 5 plus 3 plus 3 plus 1 plus 1 equals 22," he answers.

"Where'd you get all those numbers?"

"There," he said, pointing to the graph.

"He went from the highest to the lowest, added the numbers, and the answer was 22."

As lunchtime nears, Suzanne concludes by saying, "Raise your hand if you can tell me what you learned this morning in math."

"How to bar graph," Jenny responds.

"How to bar graph," Suzanne repeats. "More important, when we set up a problem, what do we have to do to solve the problem. . . . Timmy?"

"Add or subtract."

"Okay, but what do we have to decide before we add or subtract?"

"Which numbers to use."

"So, we have to collect the information, and then we have to organize it. We organized it by setting up a bar graph, something that we can look at and talk about and use to decide what we need to do with the information. Then we set up some problems, and we solved them. It's a nice way to look at information and make decisions about certain things," she says as she ends the lesson.

As you saw in the case study, Suzanne made decisions both about the general topic she planned to teach—specifically, what she wanted students to understand about the topic—and how she would help students reach that understanding. The first was a curriculum decision; the second, an instructional one. To examine your thinking about curriculum, please begin your study of this chapter by responding to the survey on page 315. We examine each of these items as the chapter unfolds.

professional knowledge: test yourself!

For each item, circle the number that best represents your thinking. Use the following scale as a guide.

1 = Strongly disagree
2 = Disagree
3 = Uncertain
4 = Agree
5 = Strongly agree

1. Teachers' attitudes and behaviors are often reflected in the curriculum.

| 1 | 2 | 3 | 4 | 5 |

2. Teachers sometimes influence the curriculum as strongly by what they choose *not to teach* as by what they choose *to teach*.

| 1 | 2 | 3 | 4 | 5 |

3. Extracurricular activities, such as clubs and sports, can provide positive outlets for students, but they aren't an essential part of the curriculum.

| 1 | 2 | 3 | 4 | 5 |

4. Because standards and accountability are so important in today's schools, the most important decisions about curriculum and instruction are now out of teachers' hands.

| 1 | 2 | 3 | 4 | 5 |

5. The major dispute about moral or character education is whether it should be taught in schools.

| 1 | 2 | 3 | 4 | 5 |

 This is available in a downloadable format on the Companion Website for personal portfolio use.

What Is Curriculum?

To begin this section, let's look again at Suzanne's lesson. She wanted her students to understand that information can be simplified and made more usable by representing it in a graph. She also had her students practice basic math skills and problem solving by asking questions such as "How many more people liked the green jelly beans than the red?" and then having students create similar problems.

Suzanne's lesson reflects decisions about both curriculum and instruction. Let's see how they relate to each other.

The Relationship Between Curriculum and Instruction

Educational theorists offer a variety of definitions of curriculum, and no single one is generally accepted (Ornstein & Hunkins, 2004; Wiles & Bondi, 2007). Some common definitions include

- The subject matter taught to students
- A course of study, or a systematic arrangement of courses
- The planned educational experiences offered by a school
- The experiences students have under the guidance of the school
- The process teachers go through in selecting and organizing learning experiences for their students

Making Connections:
To deepen your understanding of the topics in this section of the chapter and integrate them with topics you've already studied, go to the *Making Connections* module for Chapter 10 at **www.prenhall.com/kauchak**. Respond to questions 1 and 2.

Also, definitions of curriculum and instruction often overlap, and in some cases the notion of curriculum appears to subsume instruction. We will avoid these issues and, as we have in previous chapters, simply define **curriculum** as everything that teachers teach and students learn in schools and define **instruction** as the strategies teachers use to help students reach learning goals in the curriculum.

For example, Suzanne wanted her second graders to understand that graphs help us represent information; her learning goal was the result of a curriculum decision. To reach the goal, she had her students sample a variety of jelly beans, pick their favorite flavors, represent their preferences on a large graph, and play with the information mathematically; the strategy she used to help her students reach the goal reflected a decision about instruction. As an instructional alternative, she could have simply explained why graphs are valuable, given her students some information, and had them graph it. (We examine instruction in detail in Chapter 12.)

Check Your Understanding

1.1   Describe at least four definitions of curriculum.

1.2   What is one important difference between the definition of curriculum used in this text and the definitions described in item 1.1?

1.3   What is the relationship between curriculum and instruction?

For feedback, go to Appendix A, Check Your Understanding, *located in the back of this text.*

Components of the Curriculum

When we describe the curriculum as "everything that teachers teach and students learn in schools," we are not just referring to the contents of each day's lesson. We are referring more broadly to *the content, skills, values, and attitudes that students learn in school.* Experts often describe the curriculum as having four components (Eisner, 1993):

Curriculum. Everything that teachers teach and students learn in schools.

Instruction. The strategies teachers use to help students reach learning goals in the curriculum.

- The explicit curriculum
- The implicit, or "hidden," curriculum
- The null curriculum
- Extracurriculum

Next we look at each of these.

TABLE 10.1   Schedules for Two Elementary School Teachers

Sharon's First-Grade Schedule		Susie's Third-Grade Schedule	
8:30 AM	School begins	8:30 AM	School begins
8:30–8:45	Morning announcements	8:30–9:15	Independent work (practice previous day's language arts and math)
8:45–10:30	Language arts (including reading and writing)	9:15–10:20	Language arts (including reading and writing)
10:30–11:20	Math		
11:20–11:50	Lunch	10:20–10:45	Snack/independent reading
11:50–12:20	Read story	10:45–11:15	Physical education
12:20–1:15	Center time (practice on language arts and math)	11:15–12:15	Language arts/social studies/science
1:15–1:45	Physical education	12:15–12:45	Lunch
1:45–2:30	Social studies/science	12:45–2:00	Math
2:30–2:45	Class meeting	2:00–2:30	Spelling/catch up on material not covered earlier
2:45–3:00	Call buses/dismissal	2:30–2:45	Read story
		2:45–3:00	Clean up/prepare for dismissal

The Explicit Curriculum

The **explicit curriculum**, or the formal curriculum, is the stated curriculum found in textbooks, curriculum guides, and standards, as well as other planned formal educational experiences (Olivia, 2005). It includes everything teachers are expected to teach, learners are expected to learn, and what schools are held accountable for. Suzanne's lesson on graphing was part of the explicit curriculum. The explicit curriculum at the elementary level is heavily influenced by language arts and math, as you will see in the next section.

Curriculum in Elementary Schools

To begin this section, we'll look again at Sharon's and Susie's schedules, which you first saw in Chapter 7. As you may recall from that chapter, Sharon is a first-grade teacher, and Susie teaches third grade. Their schedules appear in Table 10.1.

The elementary curriculum is heavily influenced by language arts and reading. [Patrick White/Merrill]

You also saw in Chapter 7 that both teachers are responsible for all the content areas, such as language arts, math, and science, and the amount of time each teacher devotes to different content areas is a personal decision.

The way elementary schools are organized has an important influence on the curriculum. To see how, take another look at Sharon's and Susie's schedules. Remember that we're now focusing on what is taught—the curriculum. What do you notice? Some similarities include the following:

- Both teachers strongly emphasize math and, especially, language arts. In a 6-hour instructional day (subtracting the time for lunch), Sharon devotes 1 hour and 45 minutes

Explicit curriculum. The curriculum found in textbooks, curriculum guides, standards, as well as other planned formal educational experiences.

and Susie a minimum of 1 hour and 35 minutes to language arts (including spelling). Both teachers schedule additional time for reading stories.

- Science and social studies receive limited emphasis.
- Art and music don't appear in the schedules, and neither does computer instruction, in spite of today's emphasis on technology.

Both teachers reported that they have computers in their classrooms, however, and that their students take turns working with them. Art and music are handled by resource teachers who come in on a rotating basis. Both also reported that science and social studies, when taught, are usually integrated with language arts; they are seldom taught independently (S. Mittelstadt, personal communication, January 22, 2006; S. Van Horn, personal communication, January 21, 2006). This kind of curriculum emphasis is common in elementary classrooms.

If you observe in elementary classrooms, you're likely to encounter schedules that vary somewhat from those in Table 10.1. These variations are significant because they reflect personal decisions individual teachers make about the curriculum. The emphasis on language arts and math and corresponding de-emphasis on science, social studies, and the arts reflect curricular decisions that teachers make.

The curricular decisions Sharon and Susie made result largely from their children being held accountable in these areas by the statewide high-stakes assessment test. This is the reason the chapter is titled, "The Curriculum in an Era of Standards and Accountability." We address how standards and accountability influence curriculum later in the chapter.

Curriculum in Middle Schools

In Chapter 7, you saw that middle schools are specifically designed to meet the needs of early adolescents, helping them make the often difficult transition from elementary to high schools. Students must move from the security of one classroom and one teacher to a school in which they travel from classroom to classroom to learn from different teachers. The rationale for this curricular organization is greater emphasis on content; students need experts in various content areas to challenge them. Unlike in elementary schools, the content areas are each allocated the same amount of time (the length of one class period).

The middle school curriculum also attempts to focus on real-life issues that personally concern middle school students, and curriculum developers attempt to make connections among the different content areas (A. Jackson & Davis, 2000; C. Weiss & Kipnes, 2006). Let's look at several teachers attempting to help students make these connections.

Carrie Fisher is a seventh-grade social studies teacher in an urban middle school. She and her team members have a common planning period twice a week when the students go to P.E. During this planning period, they touch base on the topics they're teaching and discuss the students they share in their classes. The students are heterogeneously grouped, and major learning differences occur in all of their classes.

To begin today's meeting, Carrie announces, "I'll be starting the Civil War in about 3 weeks. At the end of the unit, each group will have to make a report on some aspect of the war. Is there any way I can connect with what you're doing in the curriculum?"

"I could have them read Crane's The Red Badge of Courage. *That's on the district's optional list and really does a good job of communicating the realities of the Civil War," Jim Heath, the language arts teacher, offers.*

"That would be great," Carrie replies. "That's just what they need—something to help them understand that history is about real people. How about you, Jacinta? Any links to math?"

"Well, we're just starting to discuss different kinds of graphs. If you can give me some different kinds of data from the Civil War, I can use them to illustrate how different kinds of data fit with different kinds of graphs. Then they can include different kinds of graphs in their final reports."

These teachers were trying to make the curriculum meaningful for students by helping connect topics across disciplines and to real-world applications. Although these connections are valuable at any level, they are particularly emphasized in elementary and middle schools.

Curriculum in Junior High and High Schools

We also saw in Chapter 7 that the organization of junior high schools is similar to that of high schools—hence the name. This organization influences the curriculum. Whereas one team of teachers in middle schools often have the same group of students, as we saw with Carrie and her colleagues, no such coordination exists in the curriculum for junior high and high schools. The curriculum in junior high and high schools focuses on separate disciplines and becomes more specialized. Some say it also becomes more fragmented.

Integrated Curriculum. The emphasis on content in junior and senior high school has implications for the learning experiences students encounter. A high school student might study algebra from 9:20 to 10:10, English from 10:15 to 11:05, and so on, through the rest of the day. Critics argue that compartmentalizing the curriculum in this way detracts from learning, because teaching and learning bear little resemblance to the world outside school. Instead, they argue, schools should offer an **integrated curriculum** (also referred to as an interdisciplinary curriculum) in which concepts and skills from various disciplines are combined and related (D. F. Brown, 2006; K. Wood, 2005). As we saw earlier, both Sharon and Susie integrated science and social studies topics with language arts, and different forms of integration occur informally in many elementary classrooms. For example, teachers might have students read about a science topic and then have them conduct an experiment or interview someone who has expertise in the area. As a culminating activity, they might have students write about the topic, thus integrating science with language arts.

Curriculum integration, which attempts to connect separate content areas, is most popular at the elementary level.
[Frank Siteman/PhotoEdit Inc.]

In middle and secondary schools, some efforts have been made to formally integrate topics within a content area. For example, in middle schools, students typically take general science in sixth grade, life science in seventh, and physical science in eighth. Some schools integrate these content areas by having students study related topics from earth, life, and physical science in each of the middle school years. For example, using energy as a focal point, students might study the sun as an energy source in earth science, food as a source of energy in life science, and nuclear power in physical science.

Proponents of integrated curriculum cite the following benefits (D. F. Brown, 2006; Drake & Burns, 2004):

- Integrating a curriculum increases the relevance of content by making connections among ideas explicit.
- Integrating a curriculum improves achievement.
- Integrating a curriculum promotes collaborative planning, which increases communication among teachers.

Even the most ardent proponents, however, acknowledge that the process of integrating curriculum is very demanding and time-consuming, and few teachers have the knowledge of content in different disciplines that is required to create effective integrated units (Nikitina, 2006). Also, in attempts to create links across content areas, teachers are often unable to help students develop a deep understanding of important concepts and bodies of knowledge in individual areas.

> **Integrated curriculum.**
> Curriculum in which concepts and skills from various disciplines are combined and related.

Curriculum integration is most popular at the elementary level, where a single teacher can relate several topics, and at the middle school level, where teams of teachers periodically meet to interconnect content areas. It is least common at the high school level, where a disciplinary approach to the curriculum is entrenched. The emphasis on standards and accountability that is so prominent in today's schools is likely to reduce the emphasis on integrating curriculum at all levels, and popular approaches to curriculum development do not emphasize it (e.g., Wiggins & McTighe, 2005).

The Implicit Curriculum

A second component of the school curriculum includes the unstated and sometimes unintended aspects of the curriculum. Also called the *hidden curriculum* (Feinberg & Soltis, 2004) or the *informal curriculum* (McCaslin & Good, 1996), the **implicit curriculum** consists of the kinds of learning children acquire from the nature and organization of the classroom and school as well as the attitudes and actions of their teachers (Olivia, 2005). It is reflected in the ways teachers present their content, the kinds of routines that are established, the general climate of the classroom, and the unstated values and priorities that shape the school day. It also suggests that the first item on our beginning-of-chapter survey, which said, "Teachers' attitudes and values are often reflected in the curriculum" is true.

A great deal of learning takes place through the implicit curriculum, and it begins when children are very young.

Students, even those of so tender an age, learn early what it takes to "do school." They learn early what a teacher does in a classroom. They learn early how they must behave in order to get on. (Eisner, 2003, p. 648)

As an example of the implicit curriculum, let's look back at some of the dialogue between Suzanne and her second graders.

Suzanne:	*How many more people liked the green jelly beans than the red? Look up at the graph. Try to find the information, set up the problem, and then we'll see what you come out with. . . . (She stops briefly to offer Carlos some help.) I'm looking for a volunteer to share an answer with us. . . . Dominique?"*
Dominique:	*Nine plus 5 is 14.*
Suzanne:	*Dominique says 9 plus 5 is 14. Let's test it out. (She asks Dominique to go up to the graph and show the class how she arrived at her answer.) We want to know the difference. . . . How many more people liked green than red, and you say 14 people, . . . 14 more people liked green. Does that work?*
Dominique:	*(Looking at the graph) I mean 9 take away 5.*
Suzanne:	*She got up here and she changed her mind (smiling). Tell them.*
Dominique:	*Nine take away 5 is 4.*
Suzanne:	*Nine take away 5 is 4. So how many more people liked green than red? . . . Carlos?*

Earlier in the chapter, we defined curriculum as "everything that teachers teach and students learn in school." What did Suzanne's students learn from this brief episode? The following are some possibilities:

- Math is supposed to be more than simply memorizing basic facts.
- Making a mistake is a normal part of learning.
- Learning is much more than sitting quietly as a teacher talks.

These are powerful messages of the implicit curriculum.

Students learn from the implicit curriculum in many ways. For instance, expert teachers create orderly classrooms in which learners accept responsibility for their own behavior (Emmer, Evertson, & Worsham, 2006; Evertson et al., 2006), and these teachers invite all students to participate in lessons (Good & Brophy, 2003; Eggen & Kauchak, 2007). In ef-

Implicit curriculum. The kinds of learning children acquire from the nature and organization of the classroom and school as well as the attitudes and actions of their teachers.

fective classrooms, students learn that the world is an orderly place and that they are responsible for keeping it so. They also learn that all students are welcome and expected to participate and learn. These messages reflect the implicit curriculum and are important parts of students' total learning experience.

Sometimes the implicit and explicit curriculum conflict. For example, research indicates that students who have independent and questioning minds, who are assertive, who challenge authority, and who insist on explanations are sometimes rejected by teachers (Kedar-Voivodas, 1983). This results in a clash between the explicit curriculum, which focuses on learning and mastery of content, and the implicit curriculum, which rewards docile students and conformity (Apple, 1995). What do students learn when they're expected to listen passively as teachers lecture, or if competition for grades is emphasized? They may learn that "playing the game" and "beating the system" are more important than hard individual work and mastery of content. These are not messages we want schools to send.

With awareness, teachers can help ensure that the implicit, or hidden, curriculum of their classrooms is consistent with the explicit curriculum. Making learning the focal point of your teaching, modeling your own interest in the topics you teach, respecting students and expecting them to respect you and each other, all communicate values and are part of the implicit curriculum. The learning that occurs through the implicit curriculum may be some of the most important that students experience in schools (Eisner, 1993, 2003).

The Null Curriculum

The decisions schools and teachers make about what they won't teach may be as important as what they do teach (Eisner, 1993, 2003). Topics left out of the course of study are referred to as the **null curriculum**. Teachers don't have time to "cover" everything, so they choose the topics they consider most important or with which they feel most comfortable. For example, social studies teachers typically cover the events of the American Civil War, but they are less likely to carefully examine factors such as slavery and racism that converged to trigger the war. These important but controversial cause-and-effect events then become part of the null curriculum.

Teachers demonstrate their professionalism when they think carefully about the topics they choose to emphasize and those they choose to leave out. As with the implicit curriculum, important messages

Extracurricular activities provide valuable learning opportunities for both students and teachers. [©Tony Freeman/PhotoEdit]

about learning are tacitly communicated through the null curriculum, and this addresses the second item on our beginning-of-chapter survey, "Teachers sometimes influence the curriculum as strongly by what they choose *not to teach* as by what they choose *to teach*." The information in this section suggests that the statement is true.

The Extracurriculum

A fourth component of the curriculum, the **extracurriculum**, consists of learning experiences that extend beyond the core of students' formal studies. The extracurriculum includes clubs, sports, school plays, and other activities that don't earn academic credit.

Although outside the explicit curriculum, extracurricular activities provide valuable learning experiences. Research indicates that a well-developed extracurricular program is an

Null curriculum. Topics left out of the course of study.

Extracurriculum. Learning experiences that extend beyond the core of students' formal studies.

integral part of an effective school, and students who participate in extracurricular activities derive the following benefits (A. Feldman & Matjasko, 2005; Fredericks & Eccles, 2006):

- Higher academic performance and attainment
- Reduced dropout rates
- Lower rates of substance abuse
- Less sexual activity among girls
- Better psychological adjustment, including higher self-esteem and reduced feelings of social isolation
- Reduced rates of delinquent behavior

Unfortunately, however, research also indicates that low-ability students, members of cultural minorities, and students placed at-risk are less likely to participate in extracurricular activities, which can lead to feelings of alienation toward the school (Guest & Schneider, 2003; San Antonio, 2006). Also, many low socioeconomic status (SES) students are forced to work during high school to make ends meet, a practice that not only competes with participation in extracurricular activities, but also can have adverse effects on school success in general (H. Marsh & Kleitman, 2005).

Sports, one form of extracurricular activity, can be an important positive influence on students, especially for members of cultural minorities. Participation in sports can reduce behavior problems and increase positive attitudes toward school (Broh, 2002; Jordan & Brooks, 2000). Studies of the effects of participation in sports on women found that girls who engaged in sports had lower teen pregnancy rates, were less likely to be sexually active, and had fewer sexual partners (A. Feldman & Matjasko, 2005; Sabo, Miller, Farrell, Barnes, & Melnick, 1998). Experts concluded, "Sports might . . . help girls cut loose from the conventional form of femininity that encourages them to establish self-worth mainly in terms of sexuality and heterosexual appeal" (Sabo et al., 1998, p. 22). All this information indicates that the third item on our beginning-of-chapter survey, "Extracurricular activities, such as clubs and sports, can provide positive outlets for students, but they aren't an essential part of the curriculum" is not true. Extracurricular activities are an essential part of students' total school experience.

Educators wanting to help students develop in healthy ways in this sometimes confusing world might look more closely at extracurricular activities for answers. Experts recommend that schools take a more proactive role in recruiting students for extracurricular activities, such as by making them aware of the activities available (Black, 2002). This is especially important for students placed at-risk, minorities, and students with exceptionalities, groups that traditionally have been underrepresented in extracurricular activities.

Extracurricular activities also offer opportunities for professional growth for beginning teachers. Sponsoring clubs and coaching teams can provide you with a salary supplement, as well as opportunities to interact with your colleagues at a personal level. In addition, working with students in these activities can be emotionally rewarding and can provide you with insights into students' personalities and lives. Both of your authors coached sports and sponsored clubs while teaching in public schools and found the experience time-consuming but rewarding. We were able to get to know students in ways not possible in the regular classroom.

Making Connections:
To deepen your CW understanding of the topics in this section of the chapter and integrate them with topics you've already studied, go to the *Making Connections* module for Chapter 10 at **www.prenhall.com/kauchak**. Respond to questions 3–6.

Check Your Understanding

2.1 What is the difference between the explicit and the implicit curriculum?

2.2 How is the null curriculum different from both the explicit and the implicit curriculum?

2.3 Compare the extracurriculum to the other forms of curriculum.

 For feedback, go to Appendix A, Check Your Understanding, *located in the back of this text.*

Forces That Influence the Curriculum

To this point, we've examined the curriculum as it currently exists in schools. But how does it come to be that way? Why do we see the considerable emphasis on language arts and math in many elementary school schedules? Why are music and art deemphasized? Answers to questions such as these can be found by examining the different forces that influence the curriculum (Hewitt, 2006). They are outlined in Figure 10.1 and discussed in this section.

Standards and Accountability

Standards are statements specifying what students should know and what skills they should have upon completing an area of study, and *accountability* is the process of requiring students to demonstrate understanding of the topics they study as measured by standardized tests, as well as holding educators at all levels responsible for students' performance. Both influence the curriculum. The "standards movement" is the result of research indicating, for example, that only 42 percent of college seniors could place the Civil War in the correct half century (Bertman, 2000); about 15 percent of 18- to 24-year-olds could locate Afghanistan, Iraq, and Israel on a map (Paxson, 2003); and, in math and science, American students lag behind many of their counterparts in other countries (Gonzales et al., 2004; Lemke et al., 2004). The result has been a move toward **standards-based education**, the process of focusing curricula and instruction on predetermined standards.

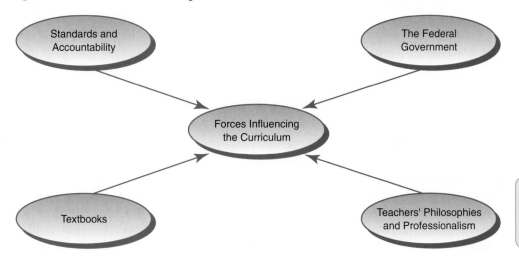

Testing, a central component of current reform efforts, exerts a powerful influence on curriculum, or what is taught. [Steve Lyne, Rex Interstock/Stock Connection/Jupiter Images]

State Standards and High-Stakes Testing

You saw the influence of standards and accountability on curriculum decisions illustrated in this chapter's opening case study. In planning her lesson, Suzanne first referred to state standards, and she even looked for a sample test item to ensure that the way she designed her lesson would be consistent with the standard and the high-stakes test her students would be required to take. You also saw the influence of state standards reflected in Sharon's and Susie's class schedules in Table 10.1. The amount of time they allocate

Figure 10.1   Forces Influencing Curriculum

Standards and Accountability → Forces Influencing the Curriculum ← The Federal Government

Textbooks → Forces Influencing the Curriculum ← Teachers' Philosophies and Professionalism

Standards-based education. The process of focusing curricula and instruction on predetermined standards.

to reading/language arts and math reflects the fact that the high-stakes test for their state focuses on these areas. "What gets tested, gets taught" is a common maxim in education (Cuban, 1996).

As a result of the No Child Left Behind (NCLB) Act of 2001, which requires states to create standards for what every child should know and learn in different subject areas and grades, state standards are arguably the most powerful force influencing the curriculum today (Marzano & Kendall, 2003; Wiggins & McTighe, 2005). And even if there is a political change after the presidential election in 2008, and the influence of NCLB is reduced, standards will remain. Regardless of the state in which you teach, they will be a part of your teaching life for the foreseeable future. Reflecting this, all states publish their standards on the Internet, and a simple Google or other search will allow you to easily access the standards for your state.

In addition to the standards themselves, states usually provide support materials to help teachers implement the standards. These include specific student performance descriptions, overviews of desired instructional practices, curriculum planning tools, and methods of assessment. In addition, in-service training is usually provided.

While state standards are the most significant force influencing the curriculum, professional organizations also publish lists of standards that influence the curriculum.

Professional Organization Standards

Professional organizations exist in virtually every teaching area. Math teachers, for example, might join the National Council of Teachers of Mathematics (NCTM), or teachers of students with exceptionalities might join the Council for Exceptional Children. Among other services, the organizations hold national conferences and produce a variety of publications. (You saw a list of professional organizations, their Website addresses, and brief mission statements in Table 2.3 in Chapter 2.)

Professional organizations also produce standards, and these standards can also influence your curriculum decisions. The following are examples from the NCTM (2000–2004). (These are only samples for pre-K–2 and grades 6–8; you can access standards for grades 3–5 and 9–12 together with complete lists online at *www.nctm.org*.)

> **Number and Operations Standard**
> Instructional programs from prekindergarten through grade 12 should enable all students to—
>   Compute fluently and make reasonable estimates.
> **Pre-K–2 Expectations**
> In prekindergarten through grade 2 all students should—
> • Develop and use strategies for whole-number computations, with a focus on addition and subtraction.
> • Develop fluency with basic number combinations for addition and subtraction.
> **Grades 6–8 Expectations**
> In grades 6–8 all students should—
> • Select appropriate methods and tools for computing with fractions and decimals from among mental computation, estimation, calculators or computers, and paper and pencil, depending on the situation, and apply the selected methods.
> • Develop and analyze algorithms for computing with fractions, decimals, and integers and develop fluency in their use.

Unfortunately, professional organizations representing content areas, such as math, science, and social studies, don't always speak with a single voice, so examining the curriculum standards generated by different groups can sometimes be confusing. Science is an example. The National Research Council (1996) published the *National Science Education Standards*, and a different professional organization, the American Association for the Advancement of Science (1989), also published a list of recommendations. The intent of both lists of standards is to achieve the goal of scientific literacy for all students by the time they leave school, but the lists differ in fundamental ways, such as emphasis on scientific literacy for all versus a deep understanding of science by a few. Teachers are often left to sort through these issues by themselves, but an increasing number of publications are now providing some support. As one example, K. P. King (2007) has authored *Integrating the National Science Education Standards Into Classroom Practice*, and support materials for teachers now exist in other areas as well.

The Federal Government

As you saw in Chapter 5, the framers of the U.S. Constitution granted control of education to the states rather than the federal government. However, the federal government has a long and rich history of involvement in education, and this role has increased rather than decreased over time. The NCLB mandate that all states publish standards and create assessments to measure the extent to which students have reached the standards is one example of this increased federal role.

The federal government's efforts to influence school curricula dramatically increased in the 1950s, when people began to view education as a major vehicle to accomplish national goals. Table 10.2 outlines some of the major pieces of federal legislation that have impacted not only the curriculum but also other aspects of school function.

As we can see from Table 10.2, federal legislation has led to significant changes in U.S. classrooms. For example, when you begin your teaching career, you will almost certainly have some students with exceptionalities in your classes; examples include students who have learning disabilities and children with behavior disorders. Their participation in your classroom is influenced by the Individuals with Disabilities Education Act (IDEA), legislation passed in 1975 requiring that all students have access to the regular curriculum. The National Defense Education Act (passed in 1958) resulted in much greater emphasis on math, science, and foreign languages,

TABLE 10.2   The Federal Government's Influence on the Curriculum

Act	Date	Impact on Curriculum
National Defense Education Act	1958	Made math, science, and foreign language high curriculum priorities.
Economic Opportunity Act	1964	Increased emphasis on vocational training and teaching marketable skills.
Civil Rights Act	1964	Prohibited discrimination on the basis of race, color, or national origin. Intended to provide all students with equal access to the curriculum.
Elementary and Secondary Education Act	1965	Created Title I, designed to help disadvantaged children acquire basic skills.
Bilingual Education Act	1968	Provided for teaching the curriculum in students' native languages as they gradually learned English.
Title IX	1972	Increased girls' participation in physical education and sports.
Individuals with Disabilities Education Act (IDEA)	1975	Increased participation of learners with exceptionalities in the regular curriculum.
Environmental Education Act	1991	Stimulated the modern environmental education movement.
Goals 2000: Educate America Act	1994	Established goals to be met by American education by the year 2000.
The No Child Left Behind Act	2001	Requires states to establish standards for what learners should know and be able to do in different subjects and holds them accountable for student performance on tests linked to these standards.

particularly in high schools. Although this emphasis has varied somewhat over the years, well-qualified math, science, and foreign language teachers continue to be in high demand.

Despite questions about quality, most teachers rely heavily on the use of textbooks. [Lynn Saville/Prentice Hall School Division]

Textbooks

You're a beginning teacher, and you're thinking about what you will teach during the next week. Where will you turn for help? If you're typical, you will reach for a textbook, the book you and your students will be using for the content area you're teaching.

For better or worse, textbooks are a fact of teaching life. Research indicates that teachers depend heavily on them; teachers use them to select content, sequence topics, and locate instructional activities (Reys, Reys, & Chávez, 2004). In the United States, districts spend more than $4 billion per year on textbooks. In some of your education classes in college, you may be encouraged to set textbooks aside or at least not depend heavily on them. If your behavior is consistent with patterns identified by research, you're unlikely to do so (Zahorik, 1991). Some experts believe that textbooks may be the most powerful influence on curriculum decisions, with teachers basing up to 90 percent of teaching on them (C. Marsh & Willis, 2007).

Textbooks can be valuable resources, however, and we don't advocate that you abandon them. Instead, we recommend that you use them strategically, deemphasizing, or even eliminating, some topics and chapters in the text while including other topics not in them. The following are reasons for using them selectively and strategically:

- *Student needs.* The topics presented in textbooks may not be consistent with the specific needs of your students, school, or district. Following a textbook too closely then fails to meet these needs effectively.
- *Scope.* To appeal to a wide market, textbook publishers include a huge number of topics, more than teachers can possibly teach in the time available. Curriculum experts conclude that texts and curriculum guides often contain twice as much material as is feasible for students to learn. They recommend that teachers select the most important concepts and skills to emphasize and concentrate on the quality of understanding rather than on the quantity of information presented (Marzano, 2003).
- *Quality.* Textbooks are sometimes poorly written, lack adequate examples, or even contain errors of fact. One study of history textbooks found "[c]ontent is thinner and thinner, and what there is, is increasingly deformed by . . . politics" (Sewall, 2000), and an analysis of middle school science texts found them to be shallow, superficial, and frequently outdated (Reys et al., 2004). Similar problems have been found in other subject areas (Hecht, 2006; Oakes & Saunders, 2004). Following textbooks too closely can lead to superficial understanding or even faulty ideas that detract from learning.

On the other hand, researchers have found that innovative textbooks and other curriculum materials can be positive catalysts for change, encouraging teachers to rethink what and how they teach (Pittman & Frykholm, 2002). In addition, because of the focus on standards, most publishers now key objectives in their textbooks to state standards.

Teacher Professionalism and Individual Teachers' Philosophies

We said earlier that the curriculum reflects learning goals and the reasons educators select the goals. Because time doesn't allow equal emphasis on all goals, teachers have to make decisions about priorities. For instance, of the following goals, which would you consider to be most important?

- To thoroughly understand traditional content, such as important concepts and ideas from literature, science, history, and advanced mathematics

- To develop basic skills, such as the ability to read fluently, write effectively, and complete mathematical tasks
- To develop workplace skills, such as the ability to work with others and solve problems
- To develop self-esteem and the motivation to be involved in learning for its own sake

Answers to this question vary. Some educators suggest that the last goal is most important, arguing that intrinsically motivated people will adapt and acquire the skills needed to function effectively in a rapidly changing world. The development of the individual is preeminent in their view. Others favor the third goal, suggesting that society needs people who can solve problems and function well in groups. Still others advocate the first or second goal, asserting that academic skills, knowledge, and understanding are the keys to expertise and the ability to solve today's complex problems.

These arguments are grounded in different philosophical positions (see Chapter 6), which reflect varying degrees of emphasis on the needs of individuals, our society, or the academic disciplines. Each of these positions has both strengths and weaknesses, as outlined in Table 10.3.

Many of today's curriculum controversies are rooted in these different philosophical positions. For example, the recent reform movement has resulted from widespread complaints about young people entering the workforce without the basic knowledge and skills needed to function effectively in today's society (Hirsch, 2001). Reformers are making an essentialist argument, and we see this essentialist position reflected in Sharon's and Susie's work with their students. Their schedules reflect an emphasis on language arts, reading, and math, which are all basic skills.

Although an emphasis on basic skills is currently prominent, the needs of individuals occupy an important place in the curriculum as well. Advocates contend that a major goal of schools should be to give students self-confidence about their ability to learn; critics contend that an emphasis on the development of self-esteem has led to lowered standards and decreased achievement (Pintrich & Schunk, 2002). But students can't learn if they dislike themselves and the content they're learning, advocates assert.

One reason you're taking this course is to better understand your essential role in promoting student learning. In Chapter 1, we said that professionals are people who use their

TABLE 10.3   Philosophical Foundations of Curricula

Basis for Curriculum	Dominant Educational Philosophy	Advantages	Disadvantages
Needs of individuals	Progressivism	• Concern for individuals is placed at the heart of curriculum development. • Learner motivation is promoted.	• Efforts to respond to the special needs of each individual are virtually impossible. • Students may not be the best judges of their long-range needs, opting for shallow learning experiences.
Needs of society	Progressivism	• Students learn to integrate information from a variety of sources. • Curriculum is relevant, contributing to learner motivation.	• Society's needs change rapidly, often making curriculum obsolete. • Learners may be steered into career choices too early, limiting long-range opportunities.
Academic disciplines	Essentialism Perennialism	• Research indicates that expertise and problem-solving ability depend on knowledge (Bruning, Shraw, Norby & Ronning, 2004). • Schools and teachers are being held accountable, and accountability depends on discipline-based tests.	• Academic disciplines tend to artificially "compartmentalize" what students learn. • Students complain that traditional subjects are irrelevant.

knowledge and understanding to make decisions in complex and ill-defined situations. Nowhere will professionalism be more important than in making curriculum decisions.

Although a number of factors influence what is taught and learned, you, the teacher, are at the center of the process, and each of the elements of professionalism we discussed in Chapter 1 comes into play (Remillard, 2005). For instance, professionals frequently make curriculum decisions on their own (autonomy), and these decisions are based on professional knowledge and reflections from their past experiences. They're also made with benefits to students as the primary goal, which is an essential aspect of professional ethics.

We see these elements of professionalism illustrated in Suzanne's, Sharon's, and Susie's work. Suzanne Brush, for example, used state standards as a guide, but the decisions about how to plan and present the content were hers and hers alone. She relied on her professional knowledge when she designed the learning activity to promote her students' involvement and interest. No substitute for this teacher knowledge and professionalism exists.

Susie and Sharon also made curriculum decisions based on their professional knowledge. Because she believes that her particular students benefit from additional experiences with language, Susie allocates 1 hour and 5 minutes to language arts in the morning and sometimes teaches additional language arts from 11:15 to 12:15. Sharon teaches math in the morning, rather than the afternoon, because she believes that her first graders tend to be less attentive and alert after lunch.

These are teacher decisions. No one told Suzanne how to plan and conduct her lesson. Also, if Susie chooses to teach science on Monday from 11:15 to 12:15 and additional language arts on Tuesday during the same time, it is her decision, based on her understanding of her students' needs, the content, and her goals. These are professional decisions that only teachers can make.

Middle and secondary teachers have only slightly less autonomy because of the influence of bells and predetermined time schedules. For example, a teacher in beginning algebra might choose to spend a great deal of time on basic skills, such as solving problems like $x + 2x + 3x = 24$, or she might choose to emphasize word problems such as the following:

> Greg has some coins in his pocket, Sally has twice as many as Greg, and Juanita has three times as many as Greg. They have 24 coins altogether. How many does each student have?

Again, these are professional decisions based on understanding and knowledge—understanding what students need and how they learn and knowing how to represent a topic so it makes sense to them. One geography teacher might focus on the influence of geography on culture, whereas another might emphasize climate and physical features, such as mountains, rivers, and plains. Teachers make similar curricular decisions in all the content areas every day.

Teachers are essentially "alone" as professionals when they shut their classroom doors. Closing the door is symbolic, representing teachers' professional control over the curriculum taught in their classrooms and how it is taught.

The information in this section also addresses the fourth item on our beginning-of-chapter survey, "Because standards and accountability are so important in today's schools, the most important decisions about curriculum and instruction are now out of teachers' hands." This statement is false. As you saw earlier in this section, standards present general frameworks for teachers, but the most important decisions about curriculum and instruction remain in their hands.

What does this information mean for you as a teacher? Nowhere in teaching is professionalism more important than in making curriculum decisions (Remillard, 2005; Thornton, 2005). This is particularly true regarding textbooks. It's easy to allow textbooks to make professional decisions for you; this is what many teachers do when they teach the next chapter simply because it's there. However, as you saw in our discussion of textbooks and how they influence curricular decisions, this is not the most professional course of action. Professional decision making with respect to the curriculum requires a great deal of knowledge, effort, and energy. However, teachers report that the process of personal curriculum construction can be one of the most creative and satisfying aspects of teaching (Clandinin & Connelly, 1996).

Making Connections:
To deepen your understanding of the topics in this section of the chapter and integrate them with topics you've already studied, go to the *Making Connections* module for Chapter 10 at **www.prenhall.com/kauchak**. Respond to questions 7–10.

IN TODAY'S CLASSROOMS: VIDEO

Curriculum, Standards, and Accountability

To view this video, go to the *Becoming a Professional* DVD included with this text, click on *In Today's Classrooms*, and then this chapter's video: *Curriculum, Standards, and Accountability.* Answer the questions you'll find on the DVD.

In this video episode, Suzanne Brush, the teacher in the chapter's opening case study, implements the state standard you saw described in her learning activity.

To answer questions about the video online and receive immediate feedback, go to the Companion Website at www.prenhall.com/kauchak, then to the In Today's Classrooms *module for Chapter 10.*

teaching in an era of reform

A National Curriculum

In your study of Chapter 5, you saw that in the late 1700s, the federal government declined to take a central role in the operation of schools, and instead passed the Tenth Amendment, placing curriculum decisions in the hands of the states. The principle of state control of curricula has been in place since that time.

Today, this principle is being questioned by some prominent voices who advocate a national curriculum with nationwide standards (Kosar, 2005). And the politics of this controversy has become blurred. Historically, political liberals have advocated a strong federal role in education, whereas conservatives have supported "states" rights and have advocated a smaller federal presence. However, the NCLB legislation was a massive federal intervention and was promoted and passed by the very conservative Bush administration (Gordon, 2006). Though it still left control of the curriculum in states' hands, NCLB exerts a powerful influence on how states implement and test for these standards. A national curriculum with mandated federal testing would be a logical next step for some.

The Issue

The idea of national standards with national standardized tests is highly controversial. Proponents make the following arguments in support of a national curriculum:

- Students in countries such as Germany and Japan, which have national standards and national exams, achieve higher than American students (Kober, 2006).

- A national curriculum would provide stability and coherence. The population in the United States is highly mobile: 20 percent of Americans relocate every year, some inner-city schools have a 50 percent turnover rate during the school year, and by the end of third grade, one in six children attends three or more schools (Hartman, 2006). Teachers working with new students from different districts or states often can't tell what they have or haven't already studied.

- Standards vary significantly from state to state; some states have much lower standards and levels of achievement than do others. A national curriculum would create

uniform standards for all and help raise achievement for low-SES and cultural minority students (Kosar, 2005).

However, opponents of a national curriculum argue that it would create a massive and unwieldy federal bureaucracy, which would also weaken local control and accountability. They also argue that a national curriculum would not be responsive to student diversity and would create more problems for disadvantaged students. Other critics assert that this "either–or" approach—either a nationalized curriculum or the complete elimination of federal intervention in the curriculum—is invalid, and they further argue that the clash of ideas from different sources makes reforms actually work (Pogrow, 2006).

One compromise that has been suggested is for the federal government to recommend, but not require, exemplary textbooks, because teachers tend to rely on textbooks in making curriculum decisions. For example, several years ago, the U.S. Department of Education published a list of promising and exemplary math texts, most based on NCTM standards (Viadero, 1999).

Even this approach has drawn criticism, however. One critic, a conservative math professor, commented, "This is an abomination. It [the math curriculum] has no business being debated by the federal government" (Viadero, 1999, p. 14). The same type of effort to influence the curriculum is also occurring in the area of reading, with similarly controversial results (Manzo, 2004, 2006a).

You Take a Position

Now it's your turn to take a position on the issue. State in writing whether you believe that our country should have a national curriculum, and provide a two-page rationale for your position.

For additional references and resources, go to the Companion Website at www.prenhall.com/kauchak, then to the Teaching in an Era of Reform *module for Chapter 10. You can respond online or submit your response to your instructor.*

Check Your Understanding

3.1   Identify four forces that influence the curriculum.

3.2   How does each of the forces in 3.1 exert its influence on the curriculum?

3.3   Why is teacher professionalism so important in making curricular decisions?

For feedback, go to Appendix A, Check Your Understanding, *located in the back of this text.*

Curriculum Controversies

Should schools teach sex education, or should this be handled in the home or church? How about the development of ethics and morals; what should be the role of schools in promoting morality? Should teachers present students with disclaimers in their science curriculum saying that the theory of evolution is only one among other explanations of our natural world? And should teachers be allowed to have students read essentially anything that their professional judgment dictates? Each issue, and its impact on the curriculum, is controversial, and we examine each.

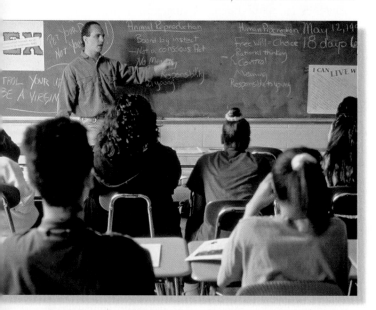

Sex education, while controversial, has become a common curriculum component in many school districts. [Schnepf/Getty Images, Inc.—Liaison]

Sex Education

Sex education is controversial for at least two reasons. First, some people insist that it shouldn't be part of the school curriculum, believing that it is the sole or primary responsibility of families or churches. They contend that sex is inextricably connected with personal, moral, and religious values, and the proper place for sex education is the home, where parents can embed it in a larger moral framework.

Proponents of sex education counter with the following statistics, which you first saw in Chapter 4 (National Campaign to Prevent Teen Pregnancy, 2004):

- In 2001 nearly one half of teens reported being sexually active by the end of high school, and nearly 1 in 10 said they had sex before age 13.
- Almost 13 percent of 10th graders said they had four or more sex partners (Grunbaum et al., 2002).
- The average age of first intercourse dropped from 19 to 15 between 1943 and 1999 (Tonn, 2005b).
- The United States has the highest rate of teenage pregnancy and births in the Western industrialized world (National Campaign to Prevent Teen Pregnancy, 2004).
- Eighty percent of teenagers who become pregnant are unmarried, and most (57 percent) teenage mothers keep their babies (Alan Guttmacher Institute, 2004). These pregnancies take an enormous toll on both the mother and the child.

If parents and churches are responsible for sex education, they're doing a poor job, proponents of sex education contend. They further argue that schools have both a right and a responsibility to ensure that all students have access to information about their developing sexuality, and courts have upheld school districts' rights to offer sex education courses (Fischer, Schimmel, & Stellman, 2006). Parents who object are free to take their children out of the programs.

Further, polls indicate that the majority of parents and the population at large favor some type of sex education. For example, in one poll 93 percent of high school parents and 95 percent of middle school parents said they favor sex education and believe that their children should be given information to protect themselves from unplanned pregnancies and sexually transmitted diseases (Kaiser Family Foundation, 2004a). In another, 94 percent of parents said they want schools to address real-life issues, such as pressure to have sex and the emotional consequences of becoming sexually active (T. Hoff, 2002).

Polls indicate that students feel the same way. In one survey, 17-year-olds indicated that the participants felt a great need for sex education, boys and girls should be taught in nonsegregated groups, men and women should cooperate in leading classes, enrollment in classes should be voluntary, and a variety of viewpoints should be presented (Michener, 2006).

The content of sex education courses is a second controversial issue, and it is highly politicized. Religious conservatives support abstinence-only programs and are strongly opposed to any other form of sex education, arguing that it encourages sexual promiscuity and is fundamentally dangerous to the well-being of our young people and society in general (Dimick & Apple, 2005). The Bush administration has been generally supportive of conservative groups and long supported abstinence-only programs. For example, the Bush 2006 budget provided over $200 million to support these programs, an 18.5 percent increase over 2005 (Rocha, 2006). Liberal groups are equally adamant, arguing that conservatives are doing a disservice to children, including their own (Roffman, 2005). A recent poll revealed that only 7 percent of parents thought that sexuality education should *not* be taught in schools, and of these, only 15 percent advocated an abstinence-only approach (Kaiser Family Foundation, 2004a).

What does research say? The best available evidence indicates that the most effective programs combine abstinence education together with information about birth control and the development of refusal skills and communication (LaChausse, 2006; Coyle, Kirby, & Robin, 2006). Further, clear and open communication between parents and their children is essential (H. Wilson & Donenberg, 2004).

Evidence supporting the effectiveness of abstinence-only programs is limited (M. Young & Penhollow, 2006). Further, researchers contend, programs that have the most positive results are the ones least likely to be embraced by the abstinence-only advocates. However, proponents of abstinence-only programs argue that more research is needed before definitive conclusions can be drawn (Buhi & Goodson, 2006).

In a review of different sex education programs, C. Everett Koop, the former U.S. Surgeon General, concluded that "given that one-half of adolescents in the United States are already sexually active and at risk of unintended pregnancy and STD/HIV infection, it also seems clear that adolescents need accurate information about contraceptive methods so that they can reduce those risks" (quoted in T. Hoff, 2002, p. 61).

Moral and Character Education

The proper place of values and moral education in the curriculum is also controversial. Although most educators agree that this type of education is needed, they disagree about the form it should take.

One position, called **character education**, suggests that moral values and positive character traits, such as honesty and citizenship, should be emphasized, taught, and rewarded. Proponents believe that right and wrong do exist and that parents and schools have a responsibility to teach students to recognize the difference (Joseph & Efron, 2005). Instruction

> **Character education.** A curriculum approach to developing student morality suggesting that moral values and positive character traits, such as honesty and citizenship, should be emphasized, taught, and rewarded.

in character education emphasizes the study of values, practicing these values both in school and elsewhere, and rewarding displays of these values when they occur.

Moral education, by contrast, is more value free, emphasizing instead the development of students' moral reasoning. Moral education uses moral dilemmas and classroom discussions to teach problem solving and to bring about changes in the way learners think about moral issues.

Critics of character education argue that it indoctrinates rather than educates (Joseph & Efron, 2005; Kohn, 1997); critics of moral education assert that it has a relativistic view of morals, with no right or wrong answers (Wynne, 1997). The strength of character education is its willingness to identify and promote core values, such as honesty, caring, and respect for others. Few would argue that these values are inappropriate. Further, research indicates that character education programs are effective for developing both students' social skills and their academic abilities (Viadero, 2003b). However, emphasizing student thinking and decision making is important as well, and this is the focus of the moral education perspective.

For either moral or character education to work, some public consensus must exist about what values are important for students to learn, and polls suggest that it does exist (Rose & Gallup, 2000). When asked whether the following values should be taught in public schools, the following percentages of a national sample replied affirmatively: honesty (97 percent), democracy (93 percent), acceptance of people of different races and ethnic backgrounds (93 percent), and caring for friends and family members (90 percent). Fewer people supported the idea of teaching acceptance of people with different sexual orientations, specifically homosexuals or bisexuals (55 percent), and acceptance of the right of a woman to choose an abortion (48 percent). Research indicates, however, that these less-popular issues receive little or no emphasis in the curriculum (Thornton, 2003).

The classroom environment and the teacher's leadership are more important than the specific approach to developing moral behavior in young people. Students must feel that they belong in school, that their teachers are supportive, and that it is safe to offer their views without fear of embarrassment or ridicule (Bryan, 2005; Cohen, 2006). And, other than parents, teachers serving as models of moral behavior is probably the most powerful factor in developing caring and responsible young people (Quick & Normore, 2004).

So, now we have an answer to the fifth item in our introductory survey, "The major dispute about moral or character education is whether it should be taught in schools." Both educators and the general public largely agree that values *should* be taught in schools. The major dispute arises over *how* values should be taught.

Service Learning

Cindy Lloyd's students at Somerset Intermediate School in Westover, Maryland, conducted a grocery drive called Harvest for the Hungry. In addition to collecting and distributing food for the poor, they studied the effects of malnutrition in science. In social studies, they learned about the economics and politics of food distribution. They read novels and poetry about poverty, wrote newspaper articles about their campaign, and toured a food bank (adapted from F. Smith, 2006).

Service learning is an approach to character education that combines service to the community with content-learning objectives. It attempts to blend civic action with academic subjects to provide students with a broader appreciation of the disciplines, while enhancing students' sense of civic responsibility (Butin, 2003). The rationale is that providing service changes both the provider and the recipient of the service.

Service-learning programs differ in terms of their relative emphasis on the service component versus growth to students, though all service-learning classes have elements of both (Butin, 2003). Examples of service-learning programs that focus on social service in-

Moral education. A curriculum approach to developing student morality that emphasizes students' decision-making and moral reasoning.

Service learning. An approach to promoting ethical and moral development that combines service to the community with content-learning objectives.

clude environmental education projects designed to encourage people to recycle, volunteer work in hospitals, and voter education projects aimed at getting people out to vote. Service-learning programs that emphasize student growth include internships and field-based programs that allow students to see academic concepts applied in real-life situations. Because of this emphasis on application, service learning also has motivational benefits. One urban high school student commented,

> Every Wednesday we go out for the entire day and do community service, and it's really made a big difference to me. In our building, we have Early Head Start, where moms drop their babies off, and I go down there and help. That's really made me want to go to school on Wednesdays, getting to loosen up and have a little bit of fun . . . (Cushman, 2006, p. 37)

Service learning attempts to teach values by actively involving students in helping projects. [Tony Freeman/PhotoEdit Inc.]

The popularity of service-learning programs is growing. Between 1984 and 2004, the number of K–12 students involved in service-learning programs rose from 900,000 to more than 10.6 million, while the proportion of high school students participating in service learning grew from 2 to 25 percent during the same time period (Fiske, 2001; F. Smith, 2006).

An important policy question is whether to make service learning voluntary or required. The state of Maryland requires 75 hours of service before high school graduation (F. Smith, 2006). A number of districts in California, Washington, Pennsylvania, and North Carolina have similar requirements (Fischer et al., 2006). Not all parents support the service-learning requirements, however, and some have legally challenged schools that have mandatory service-learning courses. Courts have upheld the legality of these courses, noting that they promote habits of good citizenship and introduce students to the idea of social responsibility.

Intelligent Design

Intelligent design is a theory suggesting that certain features of the universe and of living things are so complex that their existence is best explained by an intelligent cause, rather than an undirected process such as natural selection. Proponents of intelligent design argue that it is a scientific theory that stands on equal footing with, or is superior to, current scientific theories regarding the evolution and origin of life, and polls indicate that a significant portion (55 percent) of the public believes in intelligent design and favors intelligent design being taught in schools along with evolution (Harris Interactive, Inc., 2005).

Opponents argue that intelligent design is little more than **creationism**, a religious view suggesting that the universe was created by God as described in the Bible, framed in terms designed to make it appear scientific. And the overwhelming majority of the scientific community views intelligent design as unscientific, pseudoscience, or junk science (Attiel et al., 2006; Bergin, 2006). The U.S. National Academy of Sciences has stated that intelligent design and other claims of supernatural intervention in the origin of life are not science because they cannot be tested by experiment, do not generate any predictions, and propose no new hypotheses of their own (Steering Committee on Science and Creationism, 1999).

Intelligent design. A theory suggesting that certain features of the universe and of living things are so complex that their existence is best explained by an intelligent cause, rather than an undirected process such as natural selection.

Creationism. A religious view suggesting that the universe was created by God as described in the Bible.

Intelligent design is intensely controversial and highly politicized, so much so that "Evolution Wars: The Push to Teach 'Intelligent Design' Raises a Question: Does God Have a Place in Science Class?" was the cover feature of the August 15, 2005, issue of *Time* magazine. This topic issue periodically resurfaces; for example, President George W. Bush made a public statement in 2005 in support of teaching intelligent design in schools (P. Baker & Slevin, 2005), and its inclusion in the curriculum was hotly debated in Kansas, Ohio, and other states in 2006 (A. Hopkins, 2006).

The issue has even gone to court. In the first direct challenge to a Pennsylvania school district's requirement that science classes teach intelligent design as a viable alternative to evolution, a United States federal court ruled that the requirement was a violation of the Establishment Clause of the First Amendment to the U.S. Constitution (*Kitzmiller et al. v. Dover Area School District, 2005*).

Controversies over intelligent design are not likely to diminish in the near future, and you may encounter the issue when you begin teaching.

Censorship

What do the following books have in common?

> *Of Mice and Men* by John Steinbeck
> *The Diary of a Young Girl* by Anne Frank
> *The Adventures of Huckleberry Finn* by Mark Twain
> *To Kill a Mockingbird* by Harper Lee
> *Leaves of Grass* by Walt Whitman

All of these works have, at various times, been targeted to be banned from the public school curriculum. The language arts area has often served as a battleground for curriculum controversy due to the issue of censorship. **Censorship** is the practice of prohibiting the use of objectionable materials, such as certain books used in libraries or in academic classes.

Issues of censorship have existed throughout history and will continue to exist in the foreseeable future. These issues are probably even more prominent and more politicized now with ongoing concerns about issues such as the fight against terrorism, moral values, and the rights of gays and lesbians, together with the increased political power of religious conservatives in the United States. In 2005, Oklahoma legislators urged libraries to limit students' access to books with gay themes (Oder, 2005), and librarians in Arkansas were pressured to remove books with similar themes from school libraries (L. Weiss, 2005).

The question of what books and what kind of content students should be allowed, or required, to read in schools remains unanswered. For instance, J. K. Rowling's wildly popular Harry Potter series has raised questions, and more controversial is Phillip Pullman's (2002) *His Dark Materials* trilogy, a series of three novels that are openly anti-Christian in their orientation (Wartofsky, 2001). Defenders of both Rowling and Pullman argue that the books inspire kids to read and involve moral themes, their messages are quite harmless, and censorship is not an appropriate response to controversial literature (Glanzer, 2005). Critics argue that the books send the wrong message to young adults (Glanzer, 2004). The fact that both series are very popular with young people only fuels the controversy.

Censorship also raises questions with conflicting answers about other important issues in education. One is parents' control over their children's education. Shouldn't parents have a say in the books their children read? A second, related, question involves professional autonomy. Shouldn't teachers be free to select books that professional judgment tells them are important, if not essential, to student learning and development? In considering these opposing views, the courts have usually decided against censorship of books, ruling that schools and teachers have a right to expose students to different ideas and points of view through literature (Fischer et al., 2006).

Making Connections: To deepen your understanding of the topics in this section of the chapter and integrate them with topics you've already studied, go to the *Making Connections* module for Chapter 10 at **www.prenhall.com/kauchak**. Respond to questions 11–13.

Censorship. The practice of prohibiting the use of objectionable materials, such as certain books used in libraries or in academic classes.

Women and Minorities in the Curriculum

The curriculum in U.S. schools has been criticized because it has, according to critics, failed to adequately represent the contributions of women and cultural minorities (Sincero & Woyshner, 2003). For example, until as recently as the 1960s and 1970s, the majority of the works included in junior high and high school literature books were written by White males, such as William Shakespeare, Mark Twain, and Robert Frost, with only a few additional contributions by White women.

Recognition of the historical contributions of minorities was similarly lacking. For example, Dr. Charles Drew (1904–1950), an African-American, developed the procedure for separating plasma from whole blood. This was an enormous contribution that unquestionably saved many soldiers' lives in World War II. Dr. Charles Norman (b. 1930), another African-American, was the first person to implant an artificial heart in a human. Until recently, most history books ignored contributions such as these.

In response to critics, as well as shifts in our society, this has changed. For example, a postage stamp was issued in Drew's honor in 1981, and science fiction writer Isaac Asimov, a friend of Norman's, based his novel *Fantastic Voyage* on work done in Norman's laboratory. History texts have been expanded to include the contributions of women and minorities. Literature books, too, have changed. Many now include works written by members of various cultural minority groups, such as Maya Angelou, Sandra Cisneros, Gary Soto, and Toni Cade Bambara (Probst, Anderson, Brinnin, Leggett, & Irvin, 1997).

The issue is controversial, with critics charging that cultural minorities remain underrepresented in the curriculum (Banks, 2006b). Content focusing primarily on the contributions of men of northern European descent—often derisively described as a "Eurocentric" curriculum—is perceived as out of balance and irrelevant to minorities. For example, a recent analysis of California's social studies standards found that 77 percent of significant contributions mentioned were by Euro-Americans (Sleeter, 2005). Because more than a third of our schoolchildren are minorities and this percentage is increasing, the curriculum should be further broadened to better reflect minority members' contributions and presence in our society, critics argue. In addition, they assert, some time-honored literature, such as Mark Twain's *The Adventures of Huckleberry Finn,* portrays characters in ways that promote racial stereotypes and prejudice.

Some critics argue further that entire curricula should be oriented to specific ethnic groups. For instance, to help African-American students understand and appreciate their cultural heritage, proponents of an "Afrocentric" curriculum advocate focusing on the achievements of African cultures, particularly ancient Egypt. Students who study the contributions of people with ethnicity similar to their own will gain in self-esteem, motivation, and learning, they contend. Afrocentric curricula are currently being experimented with in a number of inner-city school districts (Gollnick & Chinn, 2006).

These positions have critics of their own, however. Some educators and social commentators question the accuracy and balance of the content and whether the emphasis on differences leads to racial and ethnic separatism (Coughlin, 1996; Ravitch, 1990). They also argue that schools have already gone too far in emphasizing cultural differences, resulting in the reduction or elimination of studies that focus on some of the great contributions of literature, such as the works of Shakespeare (Hirsch, 1987; Ravitch, 2000). Further, they maintain, we are all Americans, and an overemphasis on diversity has resulted in the failure of students to develop a common cultural heritage and shared national identity (Schlesinger, 1992).

The role of women in the curriculum is also controversial. For example, many feminist groups contend that women continue to be both underrepresented and misrepresented in the curriculum, arguing that students read too many books and materials that portray men as doctors, lawyers, and engineers, and women as nurses, teachers, and secretaries. A recent study of California's history–social science standards found that of the 96 Americans mentioned in the standards, only 18 percent were female (Sleeter, 2005). When this occurs, they assert, girls are sent messages about what are and are not appropriate roles and careers for them (American Association of University Women, 1992).

However, a strong and systematic national effort has been made to address the needs of girls and women in today's schools (Riordan, 2004). Some people contend that the emphasis on girls' needs has gone too far, the argument made in *The War Against Boys,* the provocative book by Christine Hoff Sommers (2000) discussed in Chapter 3.

The debate continues, and the controversy is likely to remain in the future.

Check Your Understanding

4.1   How do issues involving sex education and moral development differ in their influence on the school curriculum?

4.2   What is intelligent design? How could it influence curriculum decisions?

4.3   How could issues involving censorship influence teachers' curriculum decisions?

 For feedback, go to Appendix A, Check Your Understanding, *located in the back of this text.*

decision making

Defining Yourself as a Professional

You're a biology teacher, and you frequently examine topics that illustrate evolution in your classes, and your school doesn't have an official policy in place with respect to the teaching of intelligent design as an alternative to evolution. As a science teacher, your views tend to be aligned with the prevailing views of the scientific community, which is that intelligent design is not a scientific theory and as such is not an alternative to the theory of evolution. Therefore, in your view, intelligent design should not be taught in science classes.

The day after one of your topics dealt with evolutionary advances in different organisms, one of your students brings three short articles extolling the virtues of intelligent design to your biol- *ogy class. He asks to distribute the articles to his classmates and discuss the content in them, because he believes that you are expressing only one view—and a biased view—of the existence of the natural universe.*

What would you say to this student with respect to his request?

To respond to this question online and receive immediate feedback, go to the Decision Making *module for Chapter 10 on the Companion Website at **www.prenhall.com/kauchak**.*

Meeting Your Learning Objectives

1. **Describe different definitions of curriculum.**
   - Curriculum is defined in a variety of ways, such as the subject matter taught to students, a systematic arrangement of courses, the planned educational experiences offered by a school, experiences students have in school, and the process teachers go through in selecting and organizing learning experiences for their students.
   - In this chapter curriculum is simply defined as everything teachers teach and students learn in schools.

2. **Explain how the explicit, implicit, and null curriculums, and the extracurriculum differ.**
   - The explicit curriculum is the curriculum found in textbooks and other formal educational experiences.
   - The implicit, or hidden, curriculum is reflected in the climate of the school and classroom, along with their unstated values and priorities. It differs from the explicit curriculum in that it isn't specifically prescribed, and in some cases, it is out of the teachers' conscious control.
   - The null curriculum differs from the explicit and implicit curriculum in that they both reflect what *is taught*, whereas the null curriculum reflects what *is not taught*.
   - The extracurriculum includes learning experiences that extend beyond the core of students' formal studies. Participation in extracurricular activities correlates with a

number of positive outcomes, including increased achievement and more positive attitudes toward school.

3. **Identify different forces that influence the curriculum, and explain how each exerts its influence.**
   - Standards and accountability, the federal government, textbooks, and philosophical views of teaching and learning all influence the curriculum.
   - Standards and accountability influence the curriculum because standards specify what students should be learning, and what is tested often becomes what is taught.
   - The federal government influences curriculum through its legislative mandates as well as the programs it supports financially.
   - Textbooks influence the curriculum, because many teachers use textbooks as a primary source for their decisions about what to teach.
   - Teachers' philosophies influence the curriculum because philosophy is grounded in beliefs, and professionals teach what they believe is important and use approaches that they believe are most effective.

4. **Describe prominent controversial issues in our country and their impact on the curriculum.**
   - Sex education, education in morals and values, intelligent design versus evolution, censorship, and the underrepresentation of women and minorities in the curriculum remain controversial issues. These issues are likely to remain unresolved in the near future.
   - These social issues influence the curriculum because they impact what topics are, or are not, taught.

Important Concepts

censorship (p. 334)
character education (p. 331)
creationism (p. 333)
curriculum (p. 316)
explicit curriculum (p. 317)
extracurriculum (p. 321)
implicit curriculum (p. 320)

instruction (p. 316)
integrated curriculum (p. 319)
intelligent design (p. 333)
moral education (p. 332)
null curriculum (p. 321)
service learning (p. 332)
standards-based education (p. 323)

Developing as a Professional

Preparing for Your Licensure Exam

This exercise will provide you with practice answering questions similar to the Praxis™ Principles of Learning and Teaching Exam as well as your state-specific licensure exam. Read the following case study, and answer the questions that follow.

David Hendricks, an earth science teacher, is preparing a unit on the solar system. "The kids need to be able to think about this kind of stuff," he thinks to himself. He assembles a large model to illustrate the planets in their orbital planes and their relative distances from the sun. He also prepares an outline of a matrix that has room for information about the planets' sizes, forces of gravity compared to the Earth's, periods of rotation and revolution, and other physical characteristics. On Monday he introduces the unit, and has students work in groups of three to gather information about individual planets from books, computer files, and the Internet. The groups select the planet they want to study and have to negotiate if more than one group wants the same planet. The students spend the rest of the day and Tuesday gathering information about the planets and putting it into the matrix.

On Wednesday and Thursday, David leads a discussion during which he raises a number of questions, such as, "Is Pluto a planet and if it is, why is its orbit different from the orbits of the other planets? Why is Saturn's gravity about the same as the Earth's when its diameter is so much larger? Why is Mercury so hot on one side and so cold on the other?" During the discussion, he comments that learning to think about relationships such as these is the most interesting part of studying the solar system. On Friday he gives the students a quiz that covers the topics in the unit.

Steve Grant, another earth science teacher, is also working on a unit on the solar system. After checking with the text he is using, he prepares a series of lessons on important facts about the solar system. The students are told to read the next chapter in their books, and he spends the first day of the unit identifying the parts of the solar system and the names of the planets. He lists the planets on the board in order and points out that Mercury, Venus, Earth, and Mars are quite small and close to the sun, so they are called the inner planets, and that the others are called the outer planets. He also tells students that Venus is called the Earth's twin because its size is about the same as the Earth's. He then shows the students a transparency that illustrates the inner and outer planets.

On Tuesday Steve reviews the information he presented on Monday and says, "Remember when we listed the names of the planets on the board, I said that we needed to know all of them in order. This is important. Look back in your notes if you're not sure."

He then presents information about asteroids and comets, pointing out that Halley's comet is the most famous. He explains that Pluto is the smallest planet and is farthest away from the sun, and that many scientists believe that its origin is unlike that of the other planets.

Steve continues presenting information about the planets on Wednesday and Thursday. For example, he tells students that Venus is very hot because of its thick cloud cover, that Saturn is essentially a large ball of gas, and that Mercury is very hot on one side but cold on the other because it rotates very slowly on its axis. On Friday, he gives the students a quiz that covers the information he presented.

1. Describe differences in David's explicit curriculum compared to Steve's. Explain how these differences relate to teacher autonomy.

2. Describe differences in the implicit curriculum for these two teachers.

3. Describe differences between the two teachers with respect to the forces that influence teachers' curriculum decisions.

4. Explain how David's and Steve's curriculum decisions influenced their instruction.

To receive feedback on your responses to these exercises, go to the Companion Website at www.prenhall.com/kauchak, then to the Preparing for Your Licensure Exam *module for Chapter 10.*

Discussion Questions

1. Which has the greater influence on students' learning, the curriculum or instruction? Why do you think so?

2. Think back to your own experiences in schools, and then consider what you've read in this chapter. Which has changed more over time, the curriculum or instruction? Why do you think so?

3. Some critics argue that the implicit curriculum has more impact on students' overall education than does the explicit curriculum. Do you agree or disagree with this argument? Defend your position with a concrete example.

4. During financial crises, some schools have reduced their extracurricular offerings. To what extent does this detract from students' overall education? Defend your position with a concrete example.

5. Which of the factors that influence the curriculum do you believe will most influence your teaching? Why do you think so?

Developing as a Professional: Online Activities

Going Into Schools

Go the Companion Website at *www.prenhall.com/kauchak*, and click on the *Going Into Schools* module for Chapter 10. You will find a number of school-based activities that will help you link chapter content to the schools in which you work.

Virtual Field Experience: Using the Internet to Explore the Profession

If you would like to participate in a Virtual Field Experience, access the following Website for the Association for Supervision and Curriculum Development: *http://www.ascd.org*. This site represents the largest professional organization in teaching that focuses on curriculum. This organization also publishes *Educational Leadership*, an important monthly publication for educators.

Online Portfolio Activities

To develop your professional portfolio, further apply your understanding of chapter content, and address the INTASC standards, go the Companion Website at *www.prenhall.com/kauchak*, then to the *Online Portfolio Activities* module for Chapter 10. Complete the suggested activities.

Creating Productive Learning Environments

Chapter Outline

Characteristics of Productive Learning Environments
A Focus on Learning • A Focus on Learners

The Human Dimension of Productive Learning Environments
Caring: An Essential Element in Teaching • Personal Teaching Efficacy • Positive Teacher Expectations • Modeling and Enthusiasm

Classroom Management: Creating Safe and Supportive Learning Environments
Classroom Management: A National Concern • Classroom Management Goals • Preventing Problems Through Planning • Intervening Effectively • Handling Serious Management Problems: Violence and Aggression • Effective Classroom Management in Urban Schools

Creating Productive Learning Environments: Involving Parents
Benefits of Parental Involvement • Strategies for Involving Parents

Learning Objectives

After you have completed your study of this chapter, you should be able to:

1. Describe the essential characteristics of a productive learning environment.

2. Explain how teachers' personal characteristics contribute to a productive learning environment.

3. Describe how classroom management contributes to a productive learning environment.

4. Explain how involving parents contributes to a productive learning environment.

Case Studies

 Elementary

 Middle

 Secondary

© Ellen B. Senisi/Ellen Senisi

Chapter 11

Creating productive learning environments is one of teachers' most important roles. As you read the following case study, ask yourself what a productive learning environment looks like and how Shannon Brinkman, the teacher, helps create one in her classroom.

Shannon, a fifth-grade teacher, is in her third year of teaching in an urban elementary school in the Southwest. As she anticipates the new year, she spends several days preparing her room. She tapes posters and pictures on the walls and labels the clock, windows, door, and other common objects with signs in both Spanish and English.

As her students enter her classroom on the first day, she greets them at the door and tells them to find the desk with their name on it. As soon as the students are settled, she asks them to introduce themselves and say a few words about themselves, their favorite activities, and anything else they think might be interesting.

After students have introduced themselves, Shannon comments, "We are going to have a great year this year. I asked you to introduce yourselves, because we all want to get to know each other and work together to help each other learn and grow as much as possible. This classroom is like a family, and in families people help each other. So, that's what we will do throughout this year.

"So, to be sure we all can help each other and learn as much as possible, we need some guidelines that will help our classroom run as smoothly as possible," she continues and then asks the students to make suggestions that will help them all be comfortable and keep the classroom safe and orderly. They discuss the suggestions, and Shannon makes notes about rules and procedures, which she plans to post the next morning.

After the discussion, she then takes a picture of each student with her digital camera and then turns to her planned math topic. She prints the pictures that evening and has them displayed on the bulletin board under a large sign saying, "Our Class," when the students come in the next day.

During language arts that day, she divides students into pairs and has them interview each other about things like family, hobbies, and favorite foods. The next day she teaches them a standard format and has each write a paragraph about the other student that they would put on the bulletin board next to the pictures. Students take turns using the two computers in the back of the room to enter their paragraphs into the computer. When students encounter difficulties, she has several students who are more familiar with computers help out.

Think about some of your past experiences in classrooms. Why were some comfortable and inviting, whereas others seemed cold and impersonal? This question is important, because the classroom environment you create will significantly influence the amount your students learn and how much they enjoy school. In this chapter, we examine the characteristics of productive learning environments and how teachers can create them.

Before proceeding on with this chapter, take a few minutes to complete the questionnaire on page 453. We address each of the items in the chapter.

Characteristics of Productive Learning Environments

As you saw in Chapter 1, classrooms are complex places where teachers make an enormous number of decisions. One of the first, and most important, is deciding how to create a **productive learning environment**, a classroom that is orderly and focuses on learning. *Orderly* doesn't mean rigid or punitive; rather, it means safe, relaxed, and inviting. In an orderly environment, students are respectful and accept responsibility for their actions, teachers rarely raise their voices, and the focus is on helping everyone learn. How can teachers create this type of environment in their classroom? Research provides some answers.

A Focus on Learning

Learning is the central purpose of schooling. While this simple statement may seem self-evident, keeping it in mind is important because it helps simplify our decision making. For example, we try to create an environment that is comfortable and inviting because it contributes to student learning. We emphasize respect and personal responsibility because this emphasis helps students develop personally, socially, and morally. We avoid criticizing students because criticism decreases learning. We create systems of procedures and rules because students learn more in environments that are safe and predictable.

This focus on learning guides our actions as teachers and helps answer the question, Why are productive learning environments so important? They are important because they promote learning for all students.

A Focus on Learners

Productive environments are also *learner* centered. What does this mean? Learner-centered classrooms have three characteristics. They emphasize

- Classrooms as learning communities
- Personal and social development
- A positive classroom climate

Productive learning environment. A classroom that is orderly and focuses on learning.

Let's look at each of these.

professional knowledge: test yourself!

For each item, circle the number that best represents your thinking. Use the following scale as a guide.

1 = Strongly disagree
2 = Disagree
3 = Agree/disagree
4 = Agree
5 = Strongly agree

1. Teacher caring is most important in the lower elementary grades, and its importance diminishes as students grow older.

      1   2   3   4   5

2. Teachers who have the most orderly classrooms are those who can quickly and effectively respond to student misbehavior.

      1   2   3   4   5

3. The most effective way to increase the amount students learn about a content area, such as math, is to allocate more time to the study of the content area.

      1   2   3   4   5

4. Teachers are legally required to intervene if students in their classrooms become involved in a fight or a scuffle.

      1   2   3   4   5

5. Involving parents in their children's education can actually increase student achievement.

      1   2   3   4   5

 This is available in a downloadable format on the Companion Website for personal portfolio use.

Classrooms as Learning Communities

Learner-centered classrooms create **learning communities**, classrooms in which the teacher and all the students work together to help everyone learn (Haberman, 2004; LePage et al., 2005).

A learning community is characterized by the following:

- *Inclusiveness.* All students—high and low achievers, members of cultural minorities, students with and without exceptionalities, boys and girls—participate in learning activities and believe they can succeed. Each feels that they belong in the classroom. Shannon began this process by having her students interview each other so that they could get to know each other and feel part of the classroom. Teachers also make it a point to involve all students in learning activities, such as calling on them as equally as possible.

> **Learning communities.** Classrooms in which the teacher and all the students work together to help everyone learn.

- *Respect for others.* We said earlier that teachers avoid criticizing students because criticism decreases learning. Avoiding criticism doesn't mean that students are allowed to do as they please, nor does it mean that teachers lower expectations for their students. Rather, it means that teachers respond to students with courtesy and respect, and expect the same courtesy and respect in return. For example, when the teacher speaks, students show respect by listening. When a student has the floor, he or she deserves the same respect from others. When students learn to be respectful, they grow as human beings, and this growth is part of the total learning process.

- *Safety and security.* In a learning community, students must be safe, not only from physical harm but also from name-calling, bullying, and other forms of hurtful interactions. The teacher again sets the tone with the classroom rules and procedures that he or she introduces the first day of school and reinforces throughout the year. One middle school teacher has her cardinal rule, "No Put-Downs," realizing that middle schoolers sometimes forget about the feelings of others and that sarcasm and biting humor can get laughs. When this happens, students become reluctant to share ideas, and they learn less. (We examine rules and procedures in detail later in the chapter.)

- *Trust and connectedness.* In learning communities, students learn to trust and depend on each other for assistance. Shannon promoted this support when she had students who knew more about word processing help others. When students know they can depend on each other, connectedness and trust develop.

Classrooms that share these characteristics increase student learning, and they are also pleasant environments in which to teach and learn (LePage et al., 2005; Zins et al., 2004).

Personal and Social Development

A second important dimension of learner-centered classrooms is that they provide opportunities for students to learn about themselves and others. Learning involves more than understanding how to add fractions, explain the causes of the Revolutionary War, or write an effective essay. In addition to developing cognitive abilities, it also includes developing students' personal and social development. Increasing awareness of their own strengths and weaknesses, and learning to get along with others are important dimensions of learning that will influence students' happiness and success later in life (Berk, 2005, 2007; Zins et al., 2004). Educators understand the importance of this development, as evidenced by statements such as "Works and plays well with others," "Accepts responsibility," and "Is courteous and considerate," on elementary and middle school report cards.

Personal development refers to the growth of enduring personality traits that influence the way individuals interact with their physical and social environments. Students' personalities are determined in part by genetics, but peers, parents, and other adults, especially teachers, are also influential (Berk, 2005, 2007). Some important aspects of personal development include (Zins et al., 2004):

- Self-discipline and motivation to learn
- Organizational skills and goal setting
- Personal and moral responsibility
- Control of personal impulses
- Self-awareness in terms of personal strengths, needs, and values

Personal development. The growth of enduring personality traits that influence the way individuals interact with their physical and social environments.

Teachers promote personal development by discussing these traits, explaining why they're important, modeling them in their teaching, and providing opportunities for students to practice them. For example, when Shannon gave her biography writing assignment, she explained its purpose, gave students a due date, and emphasized that each student was responsible for producing a usable product for the bulletin board. When students met this goal, they not only increased their writing skills but also developed personally.

Social development refers to the advances students make in their ability to interact with and get along with others. Healthy social development affects both learning and students' satisfaction with school. In a review of research in this area, experts concluded, "there is a growing body of scientifically based research supporting the strong impact that enhanced social and emotional behaviors can have on success in school and ultimately in life" (Zins et al., 2004, p. 19). Researchers have linked healthy social development to a number of important outcomes including increased academic achievement and motivation to learn, greater satisfaction with school, and reduced dropout and substance abuse rates (LePage et al., 2005; Zins et al., 2004).

To illustrate how teachers and classrooms influence social development, let's return to Shannon's classroom, where her students are working in small groups on social studies projects.

Small-group work provides students with opportunities to develop socially and personally. (Hope Madden/Merrill)

Rolando, Katrina, Meagan, and Bill are involved in a social studies project on the American West. They've been working as a group for 3 days and are preparing a report to be delivered to the class. There is some disagreement about who gets to research which topics and present them to the class.

"So what should we do?" Katrina asks, looking at the others. "Rolando, Meagan, and Bill all want to report on the Pony Express."

"I thought of it first," Rolando argues.

"But everyone knows I like horses," Meagan counters.

"Why don't we compromise?" Katrina asks, "Rolando, didn't you say that you were kind of interested in railroads because your grandfather worked on them? Couldn't you talk to him and get some information for the report? And Meagan, I know you like horses. Couldn't you report on horses and the Plains Indians? . . . And Bill, what about you?"

"I don't care . . . whatever," Bill replies, folding his arms and peering belligerently at the group. At just that moment, Shannon approaches the group.

"How are we doing?" she asks. Seeing that they appear uneasy, she continues, "Does everyone want to report on the same topic?" At once she hears these comments,

"Nobody listens to me."

"She's always so bossy."

"Who cares?"

"Hmm," Shannon replies. "You know other groups are having similar problems. Maybe we ought to talk about this as a class."

Shannon's students were at different points in their social development. Katrina, for example, demonstrated **perspective taking**, the ability to understand the thoughts and feelings of others, when she suggested that Rolando and Meagan switch assignments because of their interest in different topics. She understood that the reason they were balking was because each was interested in the Pony Express.

Perspective taking develops slowly and with practice (Berk, 2005, 2007). Children up to about age 8 typically don't understand responses such as Bill's angry reaction or why Rolando might be happy reporting on railroads. As they develop, their ability to see the world from others' perspectives grows. Perspective taking is important because it helps people handle difficult social situations and feel empathy and compassion for others.

Students skilled in perspective taking are better liked and respected by their peers (Berk, 2005; Schult, 2002). Students who haven't developed this ability tend to be mistrusting and

Social development. The advances students make in their ability to interact with and get along with others.

Perspective taking. The ability to understand the thoughts and feelings of others.

often interpret the intentions of others as hostile, which can lead to arguing, fighting, and other antisocial acts. They also tend to feel less guilt or remorse when they make mistakes and hurt other people's feelings (Crick et al., 2002; Dodge et al., 2003).

Teachers can promote perspective taking by making students aware of others' feelings, providing opportunities to interact with one another as Shannon did with her group project, and intervening when problems arise (Berk, 2007).

Productive learning environments also help students develop **social problem-solving skills,** the ability to resolve conflicts in ways that are beneficial to all involved. Katrina demonstrated social problem-solving skills when she suggested a compromise that would satisfy everyone.

Social problem solving occurs in four sequential steps (Berk, 2005, 2007):

1. Observe and interpret social cues. ("Bill seems upset, probably because he isn't getting his first choice.")
2. Identify social goals. ("If we are going to finish this project, everyone must contribute.")
3. Generate strategies. ("Can we find different topics that will satisfy everyone?")
4. Implement and evaluate the strategies. ("This will work if everyone agrees to shift their topic slightly.")

Social problem solving is a powerful tool. Students who are good at it have more friends, fight less, and work more effectively in groups (Johnson & Johnson, 2004; Patrick et al., 2002).

Like perspective taking, social problem-solving skills develop gradually (Berk, 2007). Young children, for example, are not adept at reading social cues, and they tend to create simplistic solutions that satisfy themselves but not others. Older children realize that persuasion and compromise can benefit everyone, and they're better at adapting when initial efforts aren't successful.

As with perspective taking, teachers can promote social problem-solving skills by making students aware of their importance, modeling the skills, and giving students opportunities to practice, as Shannon did by guiding her groups.

In addition to perspective taking and social problem solving, productive learning environments also develop other social skills such as

- Respect for others
- Working cooperatively with classmates
- Empathy and compassion
- Appreciation of diversity (Zins et al., 2004)

Personal and social development also grow in classrooms where the classroom climate is positive and supportive. Let's see what this means and how it might be achieved.

Positive Classroom Climate

Classroom climate refers to the emotional and psychological environment of a classroom, and a positive classroom climate is essential to a productive learning environment (D. Brown, 2004). When classroom climate is positive, the teacher and students demonstrate mutual respect and courtesy, and everyone feels safe to express thoughts and opinions and ask questions without fear of embarrassment or ridicule. It is virtually impossible for students to develop personal traits, such as self-awareness and motivation to learn, or social skills, such as respect for others and empathy and compassion, if the classroom climate is negative or threatening.

Shannon attempted to promote a positive classroom climate in several ways. Before the school year began, she created displays and placed pictures on her classroom walls in an attempt to make her room physically attractive. Then, because she knew that a number of native Spanish-speaking students were in her class, she labeled objects around the room in both English and Spanish. As the students entered the first day, she greeted them at the door, had them introduce themselves, and displayed their pictures on the bulletin board. She immedi-

Social problem-solving skills. The ability to resolve conflicts in ways that are beneficial to all involved.

Classroom climate. The emotional and psychological environment of a classroom.

ately initiated a discussion of the procedures that they would follow to keep their classroom safe and orderly. Each of these moves was an attempt to make her classroom inviting.

What else can teachers do to promote a positive classroom climate? Let's see what Mr. Appleby, an English teacher in a rural high school in the South, says about making his classroom a place where students want to be.

 If you pay attention to these kids and do some things for them they appreciate it [Mr. Appleby explained,] . . . I think it's more important for a kid to feel he's got somebody at school—an adult—somebody he can trust or can talk to or who can cheer him up when he's feeling raunchy . . . . they need to know that when they walk into your classroom that you'll say something nice to them or that they can talk to you if things are bad 'cause there's nobody else they can go to . . . kids need to feel they can open up and share some of their feelings which they may not ever do because they may be in a family situation where they get slapped for it or put down for it . . . as they frequently are, you know. . . . (Dillon, 1989, p. 238)

How do students react to teachers' attempts to create this type of climate? Let's see what two of Mr. Appleby's students have to say.

Melinda: *I act differently in his class—I guess because of the type of teacher he is. . . . He is hisself—he acts natural—not tryin' to be what somebody wants him to be . . . he makes sure that nobody makes fun of anybody if they mess up when they read out loud.*

Bernard: *I like him just by the way he'd talk, he were good to you . . . he don't be afraid to tell you how he feels—he don't talk mean to you, he just speak right to you . . . some teachers only likes the smart people—and Coach Appleby don't do that. (Dillon, 1989, pp. 241–242).*

Shannon and Mr. Appleby both recognized that their professional commitment is first to their students and not to the content they're teaching. This doesn't imply that content isn't important or that teachers should lower their academic expectations but, rather, that students learn more when they feel cared about and the classroom climate is positive (Raider-Roth, 2005).

> **Making Connections:**
> To deepen your understanding of the topics in this section of the chapter and integrate them with topics you've already studied, go to the *Making Connections* module for Chapter 11 at **www.prenhall.com/kauchak.** Respond to questions 1 and 2.

Check Your Understanding

1.1 Describe the essential characteristics of a productive learning environment.

1.2 How do productive learning environments help promote personal and social development?

1.3 In this section, we said that learning is the primary purpose of schooling, but we also emphasized a positive classroom climate. How are the two related?

For feedback, go to Appendix A, Check Your Understanding, *located in the back of this text.*

The Human Dimension of Productive Learning Environments

Teachers are essential to creating productive learning environments; they set the emotional tone for the classroom, creating either an inviting or a threatening environment. (As a student, one of your authors entered his high school biology class and was greeted with, "My name is Isabel Wilharm, and the name means exactly what it says. Step out of line and I *will harm.*") Then, they design learning experiences that can engage, ignore, or even distance students. They interact with students during instruction in ways that motivate, interest, or possibly bore them.

Think about some of the best teachers you've had. What comes to mind? If you're typical, the first thing you remember is that you believed that they cared about you as a person, were committed to your learning, and were enthusiastic about the topics they taught. We examine the human dimension of creating productive learning environments as we discuss the following teacher characteristics:

- Caring
- Personal teaching efficacy
- Positive expectations
- Modeling and enthusiasm

Caring: An Essential Element in Teaching

Caring refers to a teacher's investment in the protection and development of the young people in his or her classes (Noddings, 2001), and a caring teacher is at the heart of a productive learning environment. The importance of caring is captured by one fourth grader's comment:

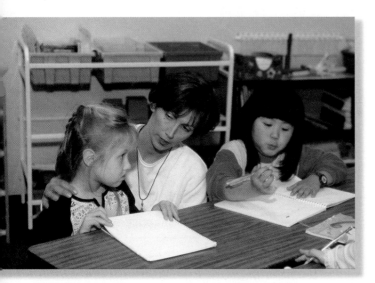

Caring, an essential component of a productive learning environment, connects teachers with students on a human level. (Anthony Magnacca/Merrill)

"If a teacher doesn't care about you, it affects your mind. You feel like you're a nobody, and it makes you want to drop out of school" (Noblit, Rogers, & McCadden, 1995, p. 683).

Students are more motivated to learn and achieve higher in classrooms where they believe their teachers like, understand, and empathize with them (Furrer & Skinner, 2003). Students who feel they are welcome and who receive personal support from their teachers also demonstrate more interest in their class work and describe it as more important than students whose teachers are distant. A supportive classroom environment, where each student is valued regardless of academic ability or performance, is essential for both learning and motivation for all students (Stipek, 2002).

This section answers the first "Professional Knowledge: Test Yourself!" item, "Teacher caring is most important in the lower elementary grades, and its importance diminishes as students grow older." Teacher caring is, in fact, essential at *all* levels, and its importance *does not* diminish as students grow older.

Communicating Caring

How do teachers communicate that they care about their students? Some ways include

- Learning students' names quickly and calling on students by their first name
- Greeting them daily and getting to know them as individuals
- Using effective nonverbal communication such as making eye contact and smiling
- Using "we" and "our" in reference to class activities and assignments
- Spending time with students
- Demonstrating respect for students as individuals

Caring. A teacher's investment in the protection and development of the young people in his or her classes.

The last two items on the list deserve special emphasis. We all have 24 hours in our days—no more, no less—and the way we choose to allocate our time is the truest measure of our priorities. Choosing to allocate time to an individual student communicates caring better than any other single factor. Helping students who have problems with an assignment or calling a parent after school hours communicates that teachers care about students and whether or not they are learning. Spending a moment to ask a question about a baby brother or compliment a new hairstyle communicates caring about a student as a human being.

Showing respect is also essential. Teachers show respect in subtle ways, such as the way they look at students and how long they wait for students to answer questions. Interestingly, maintaining high standards is one of the most powerful ways to show respect. One school motivation expert observed,

> One of the best ways to show respect for students is to hold them to high standards—by not accepting sloppy, thoughtless, or incomplete work, by pressing them to clarify vague comments, by encouraging them not to give up, and by not praising work that does not reflect genuine effort. Ironically, reactions that are often intended to protect students' self-esteem—such as accepting low quality work—convey a lack of interest, patience, or caring. (Stipek, 2002, p. 157)

This view is corroborated by research. When junior high students were asked, "How do you know when a teacher cares about you?" they responded that paying attention to them as human beings was important, but more striking was their belief that teachers who care are committed to their learning and hold them to high standards (Wilson & Corbett, 2001).

Respect, of course, is a two-way street. Teachers should model respect for students, and in turn they have the right to expect students to respect them and one another. "Treat everyone with respect" is a rule that should be universally posted and enforced. An occasional minor incident of rudeness can be overlooked, but teachers should clearly communicate that chronic disrespect for themselves or the students in their classes will not be tolerated.

Personal Teaching Efficacy

In addition to caring, teachers who create productive learning environments believe in their ability to help students learn and grow. To illustrate this important idea, let's look at a brief conversation between Shannon and Jim Fantini, one of her colleagues.

"My students didn't score as well as I would have liked on the math part of the Stanford Achievement Test last year, and I promised myself they were going to do better this year," Shannon comments as she glances through a set of math quizzes.

"But you said your students aren't as sharp this year," Jim responds.

"That doesn't matter. I need to push them harder. I think I can do a better job than I did last year. They're going to be so good at doing decimals and percentages that they'll be able to do the problems in their sleep."

"You never give up, do you?" Jim smiles, shaking his head.

Shannon's comments illustrate **personal teaching efficacy**, a teacher's belief in his or her ability to promote learning in all students regardless of their prior knowledge or experiences (Bruning et al., 2004). Shannon's comments "I think I can do a better job than I did last year" and "They're going to be so good at doing decimals and percentages . . ." reflect her belief in her ability to help all her students learn and her decision to take responsibility for the success or failure of her own instruction. This characterizes teachers with high personal teaching efficacy.

When students aren't learning, high-efficacy teachers don't blame it on lack of intelligence, poor home environments, uncooperative administrators, or some other external cause. Instead, they redouble their efforts. They emphasize praise rather than criticism, persevere with low achievers, and maximize the time available for instruction. Low-efficacy teachers, in contrast, are less student centered, spend less time on learning activities, "give up" on low achievers, and are more critical when students fail. Not surprisingly, students taught by high-efficacy teachers learn more than those taught by low-efficacy teachers (Tschannen-Moran, Woolfolk-Hoy, & Hoy, 1998).

Personal teaching efficacy. A teacher's belief in his or her ability to promote learning in all students regardless of their prior knowledge or experiences.

Positive Teacher Expectations

Teachers who create productive learning environments have faith not only in their own capabilities but also in the capabilities of their students. **Positive teacher expectations** are teachers' beliefs in students' capabilities to learn.

To illustrate the importance of teacher expectations, let's analyze two short interactions between a teacher and her students.

Mrs. Davis:	*What kind of triangle is this? . . . Lisa?*
Lisa:	*I . . . don't know.*
Mrs. Davis:	*What do you notice about the lengths of these three sides?*
Lisa:	*They're . . . equal. It's an equilateral triangle.*

Now compare what you've just read with the following:

Mrs. Davis:	*What kind of triangle is this? . . . Jessica?*
Jessica:	*I . . . I don't know.*
Mrs. Davis:	*Can you help her out, Gena?*

The difference in the way Mrs. Davis communicated with the two students is subtle but important. By prompting Lisa, she demonstrated that she expected Lisa to be able to answer, but turning the question to another student suggested that she didn't have the same expectations for Jessica. A single incident isn't significant, but if Mrs. Davis's interactions with the two girls represent a pattern, long-term and substantial differences in achievement can result (Good & Brophy, 2003; R. Weinstein, 2002).

> Teacher expectations about students' learning can have profound implications for what students actually learn. Expectations affect the content and pace of the curriculum, the organization of instruction, evaluation, instructional interactions with individual students, and many subtle and not-so-subtle behaviors that affect students' own expectations for learning and their behavior. *(Stipek, 2002, p. 210).*

Research indicates that teachers treat students for whom they have high expectations differently than those for whom they have low expectations. High-expectation students receive differential treatment in the following areas (Good & Brophy, 2003):

- *Emotional support:* Teachers interact more with perceived high achievers; their interactions are more positive; they make more eye contact, stand closer, and orient their bodies more directly toward the students; and they seat these students closer to the front of the class.
- *Teacher effort and demands:* Teachers give perceived high achievers more thorough explanations, their instruction is more enthusiastic, they ask more follow-up questions, and they require more complete and accurate student answers.
- *Questioning:* Teachers call on perceived high achievers more often, they allow the students more time to answer, and they provide more encouragement and prompt perceived high achievers more often.
- *Feedback and evaluation:* Teachers praise perceived high achievers more and criticize them less. They offer perceived high achievers more complete and lengthier feedback and more conceptual evaluations.

Students are sensitive to these differences, and even early elementary children are aware of differential treatment (Stipek, 2002). In one study, researchers concluded, "After ten seconds of seeing and/or hearing a teacher, even very young students (third grade) could detect whether the teacher talked about, or to, an excellent or a weak student and could determine the extent to which that student was loved by the teacher" (Babad, Bernieri, & Rosenthal, 1991, p. 230). This

Positive teacher expectations. Teachers' beliefs in students' capabilities to learn.

is both amazing and disquieting; it challenges teachers to communicate caring and high expectations to all students.

Expectations can be self-fulfilling; when we treat students as if they are low achievers, they don't try as hard. Reduced effort results in less learning, and a downward spiral begins (R. Weinstein, 2002). Unfortunately, teachers often aren't aware of their lowered expectations. When introduced to this research and encouraged to analyze their own classrooms with this framework, teachers can learn to treat all students as potential learners, and as a result, the learning environment becomes more productive.

Modeling and Enthusiasm

"Actions speak louder than words" is a cliché, but it is often true, and it is particularly important in productive learning environments.

Teacher modeling of enthusiasm can motivate students about the topics they are learning. (Tony Freeman/PhotoEdit Inc.)

Think about times that you have become excited about a class or topic you were studying. Often, your excitement was the result of **teacher modeling**, the tendency of people to observe and imitate others' behaviors and attitudes (Bandura, 2001, 2004). Your teacher demonstrated his or her own genuine interest in the topic, and as a result your interest also increased. Like all people, students tend to imitate behaviors and attitudes, and teachers who are enthusiastic about the topics they teach increase the likelihood that students will feel the same way.

The impact of modeling has important implications for teachers because students constantly observe their actions. For example, imagine how you would feel if one of your instructors said, "I know this stuff is boring, but we have to learn it" compared to, "Now this topic is exciting; it will help us understand how our students think." Obviously, you're more likely to be interested in the second topic.

The impact of modeling goes farther. If you want your students to be courteous and respectful to you and each other, for instance, you must treat them with courtesy and respect. If you want them to be responsible and conscientious, you must model these same characteristics in ways such as returning their papers promptly, having your instructional materials organized and ready to use, and using your instructional time effectively.

As we said at the beginning of this section, creating productive learning environments begins with the teacher, and caring, high personal teaching efficacy, positive expectations, and teacher modeling are essential elements of effective classrooms.

Making Connections:
To deepen your understanding of the topics in this section of the chapter and integrate them with topics you've already studied, go to the *Making Connections* module for Chapter 11 at **www.prenhall.com/kauchak**. Respond to questions 3 and 4.

Check Your Understanding

2.1 Why is caring important for a productive learning environment? What can teachers do to show they care?

2.2 What are personal teacher efficacy and positive teacher expectations? How are they related?

2.3 What is teacher modeling? How is it related to teacher enthusiasm?

 For feedback, go to Appendix A, Check Your Understanding, *located in the back of this text.*

Teacher modeling. The tendency of people to observe and imitate others' behaviors and attitudes.

Classroom Management: Creating Safe and Supportive Learning Environments

To begin this section, let's revisit Shannon's classroom, where she is involved in a math lesson reviewing decimals and percentages during the second marking period of the school year.

"What kind of problem is this, . . . Gabriel?" she asks as she walks down the aisle and points to a problem on the overhead.

". . . It's . . . a percentage problem," Gabriel responds after thinking for a few seconds.

As soon as Shannon walks past him, Kevin sticks his foot across the aisle, tapping Alison on the leg with his shoe while he watches Shannon's back. *"Stop it, Kevin,"* Alison mutters, swiping at him with her hand.

Shannon turns, comes back up the aisle, and continues, *"Good, Gabriel,"* and standing next to Kevin, asks, *"And how do we know it's a percentage problem, . . . Kevin?"* looking directly at him.

"Uhhh . . . "

"What words in the problem give us a clue that it's a percentage problem, Kevin?"

". . . 'Which is the better buy?'" Kevin answers, pointing at the sales numbers from the two different stores. *"We have to figure out which store sale saved us more. That's a percentage problem."*

"Good," Shannon replies, and she then moves over to the overhead and displays additional word problems involving percentages.

"Go ahead and do the first problem," Shannon directs. Be sure you're able to explain your answers."

She watches as the students work on the problem and then moves over to Sondra, who has been whispering and passing notes to Nicole across the aisle. *"Move up here,"* she says quietly, nodding to a desk at the front of the room.

"What did I do?" Sondra protests.

"When we talked about our rules at the beginning of the year, we agreed that it was important to listen when other people are talking and to be quiet when others are working," Shannon whispers.

She watches as Sondra changes seats. Then, tapping her knuckle on the overhead, Shannon says, *"Okay, let's see how we did on the problem. Explain what you did first, . . . Juanita."*

Shannon's experience illustrates why classroom management can be a vexing problem for teachers. She had carefully planned her lesson and was conducting it effectively, but she still had to respond to Kevin's and Sondra's disruptions. Incidents like these are common in many classrooms, and, if left unattended, they can seriously disrupt learning.

Classroom Management: A National Concern

From the 1960s until the present, national polls have identified classroom management as one of the most challenging problems teachers face. In 2003 and 2004, the public viewed it as the second greatest problem facing schools, and in 2005 it ranked third after lack of financial support and overcrowded schools (Rose & Gallup, 2005). It has historically been the primary concern of beginning teachers, and disruptive students are an important source of stress for beginners and veterans alike (Bohn, Roehrig, & Pressley, 2004; Public Agenda, 2004). It is a major reason that teachers leave the profession during their first 3 years; it's also a primary cause of teachers leaving urban classrooms (L. Weiner, 2002); and colleges of education are being asked to address the issue more carefully (J. Johnson, 2005).

Classroom management has become a major concern of policy makers, parents, and the public at large, particularly in the wake of highly publicized incidents of school violence such as the shootings at Columbine High School in Colorado in 1999 that left 14 students and a teacher dead, and Red Lake, Minnesota, in 2005 resulting in the deaths of 7 people including a teacher and security guard. Although incidents of school violence cause fear and concern in both parents and students, they are extremely rare (National Center for Education

Statistics, 2005); establishing and maintaining orderly, learning-focused classrooms is the major challenge teachers face.

The importance of classroom management in creating productive learning environments is well documented. One group of researchers concluded, "Effective classroom management has been shown to increase student engagement, decrease disruptive behaviors, and enhance use of instructional time, all of which result in improved student achievement" (Wang et al., 1993, p. 262).

Classroom Management Goals

Some of the earliest research on classroom management was done by a researcher named Jacob Kounin (1970), who found that the key to orderly classrooms is the teacher's ability to prevent problems from occurring in the first place, rather than handling misbehavior once it occurs. This research has been consistently corroborated over the years (Emmer, Evertson, & Worsham, 2006; Evertson, Emmer, & Worsham, 2006; Good & Brophy, 2003). Experts estimate that anticipation and prevention make up 80 percent of an effective management system (Freiberg, 1999b).

This research was important because it helped teachers understand the difference between **classroom management**, teachers' strategies that create and maintain an orderly learning environment, and **discipline**, teachers' responses to student misbehavior. Expert teachers place primary emphasis on management, which reduces their need for discipline.

We now have an answer to the second item on our introductory "Professional Knowledge" survey, "Teachers who have the most orderly classrooms are those who can quickly and effectively respond to student misbehavior." Though it is important to respond to management problems quickly, the most important aspect of effective classroom managers is that they are proactive and prevent problems before they occur through careful planning.

Effective classroom managers have three primary goals:

- Develop learner responsibility.
- Create a positive classroom climate.
- Maximize time and opportunities for learning.

Let's look at them.

Developing Learner Responsibility

Earlier in the chapter, we said that productive learning environments are learner centered, where teachers emphasize personal and social development. As conceptions of classroom management move away from discipline and toward prevention, educators place increased emphasis on helping students take responsibility for their own behaviors and their own roles in creating productive learning environments. Both contribute to personal and social development.

Student understanding is essential for developing responsibility (Emmer & Stough, 2001; Jones, 2005). Students need to understand *why* an orderly environment is necessary and their role in creating one. Students obey rules because the rules make sense, instead of obeying rules simply because they exist or because they will be punished for breaking one. Teachers promote this orientation by emphasizing the reasons for rules and procedures and explicitly teaching responsibility.

Let's see how one middle school teacher, Doug Ramsey, does this.

Allen, a rambunctious seventh grader, runs down the hall toward the lunchroom. As he rounds the corner, he bumps into Alyssia, causing her to drop her books.

"Oops," *he replies, continuing his race to the lunchroom.*

"Hold it, Allen," *Doug, who is monitoring the hall, commands.* "Go back and help her pick up her books and apologize."

"Aww."

"Go on," *Doug says firmly.*

Classroom management. Teachers' strategies that create and maintain an orderly learning environment.

Discipline. Teachers' responses to student misbehavior.

Allen walks back to Alyssia, helps her pick up her books, mumbles an apology, and then returns. As he approaches, Doug again stops him.

"Now, why did I make you do that?" Doug asks.

"Cuz we're not supposed to run."

"Sure," Doug says evenly, "but more important, if people are running in the halls, what might happen?"

"Somebody might get hurt," Allen responds sheepishly.

"Exactly, and we don't want that to happen. . . . That's why we have a rule saying, don't run in the hallways. Remember that you're responsible for your actions. Think about not wanting to hurt yourself or anybody else, and the next time you'll walk whether a teacher is here or not. . . . Now, go on to lunch."

By emphasizing the reason for the rule prohibiting running in the hallways, Doug helped Allen understand his behavior and its effect on other people. Research indicates that children who understand the effects of their actions on others become more altruistic and are more likely to take actions to make up for their misbehavior (Berk, 2007).

Developing student responsibility is both sensible and practical. Learners are more likely to obey rules when they understand the reasons for them, one of which is to protect their rights and the rights of others (Good & Brophy, 2003). This responsibility orientation can also contribute to ethical thinking and character development (Berk, 2007). For instance, in time, students may learn not to call each other insulting names, because name calling not only is unacceptable but it also hurts other people's feelings. By promoting student understanding and responsibility, teachers find that classroom management becomes easier and students develop personally. Such development takes time, but with effort it can be accomplished.

Creating a Positive Classroom Climate

We emphasized the importance of positive classroom climate earlier in the chapter, and an effective classroom management system contributes to this climate (D. Brown, 2004). Students are more likely to feel safe, secure, and welcome when their classroom environment is orderly and predictable. And students are more likely to be courteous and respectful in an orderly classroom. It is virtually impossible to create a positive classroom climate if students are disruptive or disrespectful (Certo, Cauley, & Chafen, 2002; Davis, 2003).

Maximizing Time and Opportunities for Learning

Throughout the chapter we have emphasized that learning is the central purpose of schooling. To optimize learning, teachers must use their available time efficiently. Maximizing the amount of time available for learning is the third goal of classroom management. To meet this goal, some reformers have suggested lengthening the school year, school day, and even the amount of time devoted to certain subjects. Improving learning by increasing study time isn't as simple as it appears on the surface, however, because just allocating more time to a topic may not result in significant increases in learning (C. Weinstein & Mignano, 2003).

Classroom time exists at four different levels:

- Allocated time
- Instructional time
- Engaged time
- Academic learning time

The levels can be viewed as the area of a series of concentric circles, and the correlation with learning becomes stronger as the areas of the circles get smaller. This relationship is illustrated in Figure 11.1 and discussed in the following paragraphs.

Figure 11.1 Levels of Time

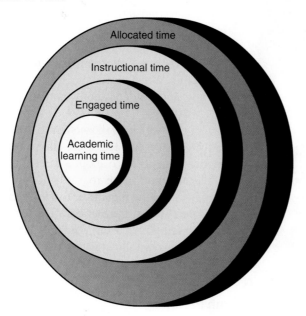

Allocated time
Instructional time
Engaged time
Academic learning time

Allocated time is the amount of time a teacher designates for a particular content area or topic. For example, teachers in elementary schools typically allocate much of their time to reading, language arts, and math, with much less allocated to science, social studies, and other subjects. Although middle, junior high, and high school teachers appear to have less control over time allocations because of their fixed schedules and bells signaling the beginning and end of class periods, all teachers have considerable flexibility. A 10th-grade English teacher, for example, could choose to emphasize writing rather than grammar or literature by simply spending more time on it.

Instructional time is the amount left for teaching after teachers have completed routine management and administrative tasks, such as taking roll, returning papers, and making announcements. Teachers also lose instructional time when they respond to student disruptions and make transitions from one activity to another. Some lost time is out of a teachers' control, but they are often unaware of time as a valuable resource, thinking of it instead as something to be filled, used up, or even "killed." For example, compare two teachers. One has a warm-up exercise on the board when students enter the classroom, and takes roll and completes routine tasks while they finish it. She then moves immediately to her lesson, and when finished, gives an assignment, and monitors the class while they work on it. A second teacher takes roll and completes routine tasks while her students sit talking. After a few minutes, she begins her lesson and finishes it with 10 minutes left in the period, during which she lets students talk quietly. If these differences represent patterns, the second teacher loses nearly 40 hours of instructional time over the course of a school year! The obvious result is less student learning.

Imagine going into a classroom to observe a teacher. Intuitively, one of the first things you would look for is whether students are paying attention and thinking about the current topic. This describes **engaged time** or time-on-task, which is the time students actually spend actively involved in learning activities. The correlation between engaged time and learning is much higher than the correlation between learning and either allocated or instructional time.

Teachers influence the engagement rates of their students with the instructional strategies they use. Interactive strategies, such as questioning and group work, which place students in active roles, result in more engaged time than strategies such as lecture, which places students in passive roles (Eggen & Kauchak, 2007).

Allocated time. The amount of time a teacher designates for a particular content area or topic.

Instructional time. The amount left for teaching after routine management and administrative tasks are completed.

Engaged time The time students actually spend actively involved in learning activities. Also called *time on task*.

Academic learning time combines student engagement with success to produce learning. (Michael Newman/PhotoEdit Inc.)

Student frustration also influences engaged time. If work is beyond students' capabilities, they become frustrated, give up, and go off task. *Success* is a key variable in these cases, which leads to the concept of **academic learning time**: the amount of time students are both engaged and successful. When academic learning time is high, both learning and student motivation increase (Brophy, 2004; Stipek, 2002).

So, now we know the answer to the third item on our introductory survey, "The most effective way to increase the amount students learn about a content area, such as math, is to allocate more time to the study of the content area." Though allocating more time to a topic can have a weak positive effect on learning, the most effective way to increase learning is by increasing academic learning time. Students who are successfully engaged in a topic learn significantly more than those who aren't.

Preventing Problems Through Planning

In productive classroom environments, management is nearly invisible. The atmosphere is calm but not rigid, movement around the classroom and interaction in lessons are comfortable, and students work quietly. Learning is taking place. Teachers give few directions that focus on behavior, they reprimand students infrequently, and reprimands rarely intrude on learning. This was the case in Shannon's lesson; she stopped Kevin's and Sondra's disruptions without interrupting the flow of the lesson.

The cornerstone of an effective management system is a clearly understood and consistently monitored set of rules and procedures that prevents management problems before they occur (Emmer et al., 2006; Evertson et al., 2006). Obviously, some classes are tougher to manage than others, but an orderly classroom is possible in most instances. It doesn't happen by accident, however. It requires careful planning, and beginning teachers often underestimate the amount of time and energy it takes.

In planning rules and procedures, effective teachers consider the developmental levels of their students. For example, first graders are usually compliant and eager to please their teachers, but they also have short attention spans and tire easily (Evertson et al., 2006). In comparison, middle schoolers often attempt to test their developing independence, and they're sometimes rebellious and capricious. They need rules that are clearly stated and administered (Emmer et al., 2006). If you're a first-grade teacher, you will make different planning decisions than if you're a middle school teacher. For first-grade students, you'll need to carefully teach rules and procedures through modeling and examples and systematically reinforce them over time. Middle schoolers understand rules and procedures but need firm and consistent application of them combined with caring and positive expectations for good behavior (C. Weinstein, 2007).

Preparing Procedures and Rules

Having considered your students' developmental characteristics, you also need to make decisions about procedures and rules you will implement in your classroom. **Procedures** are the routines students follow in their daily learning activities, such as how they turn in papers, sharpen pencils, and make transitions from one activity to another. For instance, Shannon's students turn in their papers from the ends of the rows, with each student putting his or her paper on the top of the stack as it moves forward. This allows Shannon to collect the stacks from the students in the front, and when she returns the papers, she simply gives the stacks to the first students in each row, they take their papers and pass the stacks back to the students behind them. Simple procedures such as these both create a sense of order for students and save teachers time and energy.

Academic learning time. Combining engagement and success, this is the amount of time students are successful while engaged.

Procedures. Management routines students follow in their daily learning activities.

Effective teachers create procedures for activities such as

- Entering and leaving the classroom
- Handing in and returning papers
- Accessing materials such as scissors and paper
- Sharpening pencils
- Making trips to the bathroom
- Making up work after an absence

After planning and teaching students about procedures, expert teachers have students practice until the procedures become routines that students follow virtually without thinking about them.

Rules (e.g., "Listen when someone else is talking") are guidelines that provide standards for acceptable classroom behavior, and research confirms their value in creating productive learning environments (Emmer et al., 2006; Evertson et al., 2006). When consistently enforced, clear, reasonable rules not only reduce behavior problems that interfere with learning but also promote a feeling of pride and responsibility in the classroom community. Perhaps surprisingly, students also see the enforcement of rules as evidence of caring: "Students also say that they want teachers to articulate and enforce clear standards of behavior. They view this not just as part of the teacher's job but as evidence that the teacher cares about them" (Brophy, 1998, p. 23).

Some examples of rules at different grade levels are found in Table 11.1. Note that some rules occur at all levels, such as students staying in their seats and waiting for permission to speak. Other rules are specific to a grade level and reflect the developmental characteristics of students at that level.

Deciding on rules for your classroom is the first step; actually implementing and making them work is the next. Guidelines for implementing rules include:

- State rules positively.
- Emphasize rationales for rules.
- Minimize the number of rules.
- Monitor rules throughout the school year.

Each of these guidelines is intended to help students understand rules and the reasons for them, and this understanding helps students begin to accept responsibility for their

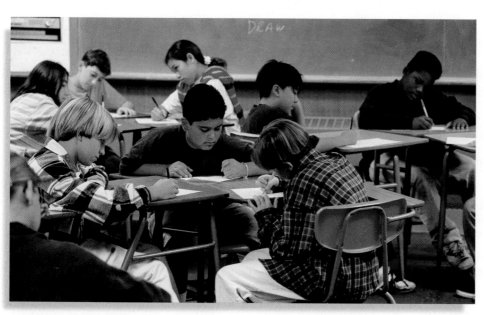

Classroom rules and procedures establish standards for behaviors that allow learning to take place.
(David Young-Wolff/PhotoEdit Inc.)

Rules. Guidelines that provide standards or norms for acceptable classroom behavior.

TABLE 11.1   **Examples of Classroom Rules**

First-Grade Teacher	Seventh-Grade Teacher	Tenth-Grade Teacher
• We raise our hands before speaking.	• Be in your seat and quiet when the bell rings.	• Do all grooming outside class.
• We leave our seats only when given permission by the teacher.	• Follow directions the first time they're given.	• Be in your seat before the bell rings.
• We stand politely in line at all times.	• Bring covered textbooks, notebook, pen, pencils, and planner to class every day.	• Stay in your seat at all times.
• We keep our hands to ourselves.	• Raise your hand for permission to speak or to leave your seat.	• Bring all materials daily. This includes your book, notebook, pen/pencil, and paper.
• We listen when someone else is talking.	• Keep hands, feet, and objects to yourself.	• Give your full attention to others in discussions, and wait your turn to speak.
	• Leave class only when dismissed by the teacher.	• Leave when I dismiss you, not when the bell rings.

Source: Eggen, P., & Kauchak, D. (2007). *Educational psychology: Windows on classrooms* (7th ed., p. 379). Upper Saddle River, NJ: Merrill/Prentice Hall.

own behavior. Stating rules positively communicates desirable expectations for students. Providing rationales for rules is perhaps the most essential guideline. Students are much more likely to accept responsibility for their own behavior and obey rules when they understand the reasons for them. Keeping the number small helps prevent students from breaking rules simply because they forget. Finally, in spite of teachers' best efforts during planning and the initial teaching of rules, students will need periodic reminders throughout the year.

Intervening Effectively

Even when teachers have planned carefully, disruptions inevitably occur, as we saw in Shannon's lesson. Dealing with off-task or potentially disruptive behavior requires immediate and

IN TODAY'S CLASSROOMS: VIDEO

Establishing Rules and Procedures at the Beginning of the School Year

Having seen how important rules and procedures are for an effective classroom management system, you now can see how one teacher implements these in her classroom.

The episode focuses on a middle school teacher who takes the time at the beginning of the school year to describe and explain the rules and procedures for the school year. As she describes each rule, she helps students understand how it contributes to a productive learning environment. In addition, she also includes a community-building exercise in which students in the class get to know each other better.

To complete this activity, go to the *Becoming a Professional* DVD, and view the video episode "Establishing Rules and Procedures at the Beginning of the School Year."

To answer questions about the video online and receive immediate feedback, go to the Companion Website at www.prenhall.com/kauchak, then to the In Today's Classroom module for Chapter 11.

judicious decision making. If a misbehavior is brief and minor, such as a student asking another student a quick question, it often can be ignored. However, if the behavior has the potential to disrupt the learning activity, you must intervene. Some guidelines to help you intervene effectively include the following:

- Intervene immediately.
- Direct the intervention at the correct student(s).
- Use the least intrusive intervention.

Let's see how Shannon implemented these guidelines. First, after concluding that Kevin's and Sondra's behaviors could distract others and detract from learning, she intervened immediately. Second, she identified the correct students. She recognized that Alison's muttering was a response to Kevin tapping her, so she said nothing to Alison; instead, she quickly moved to where Kevin was seated to address his behavior. Third, she used the least intrusive intervention possible. She stopped Kevin's misbehavior by looking him in the eye and calling on him, and she briefly whispered her direction to Sondra and reminded her of an agreed-upon classroom rule. Her actions simultaneously stopped the misbehaviors without disrupting the flow of her lesson.

During the episode, Shannon demonstrated a concept called **withitness**, a teacher's awareness of what is going on in all parts of the classroom at all times and the communication of this awareness to students both verbally and nonverbally (Kounin, 1970). Withit teachers seem to have eyes in the backs of their heads, and they use this awareness to monitor and direct student behavior. For instance, had Shannon admonished Alison for her muttering instead of Kevin, she would have "caught the wrong one," and in doing so, communicate that she didn't know what was going on in her classroom.

Keeping a lesson moving while simultaneously intervening requires sophisticated skills, but expert teachers do it virtually without thinking. In some cases, teachers may need to use a more intrusive intervention, such as reprimanding a student, talking to a student in the hallway, or even removing the student from the classroom if the disruption is severe. However, with effective instruction and careful planning, most disruptions can be handled as Shannon did.

Handling Serious Management Problems: Violence and Aggression

Tyrone, one of your students, has difficulty maintaining his attention and staying on task. He frequently makes loud and inappropriate comments in class and disrupts learning activities. You warn him, reminding him that being disruptive is unacceptable, and blurting out another comment will result in time-out.

Within a minute, Tyrone blurts out again. "Please go to the time-out area," you say evenly. "I'm not going and you can't make me," he says defiantly. He remains seated as his desk.

How do you react?

As you work with a small group of your fourth graders, a fight suddenly breaks out between Trey and Neil, who are supposed to be working on a group project together. You look up to the sounds of shouting and see Trey flailing at Neil, who is essentially attempting to fend off Trey's blows. Trey is often verbally aggressive and sometimes threatens other students.

What do you do?

We have emphasized repeatedly that productive learning environments are safe and inviting; the threat of violence obviously disrupts this feeling. Earlier we said that incidents

> **Withitness.** A teacher's awareness of what is going on in all parts of the classroom at all times and the communication of this awareness to students both verbally and nonverbally.

teaching in an era of reform

Assertive Discipline

In their work with teachers, Lee and Marlene Canter (Canter & Canter, 1976, 2001) observed many classrooms that were chaotic, with students out of control. In response they developed a classroom management system called Assertive Discipline, which was designed to address this problem.

What Is Assertive Discipline?

Assertive discipline is a comprehensive approach to classroom management that clearly specifies both teachers' and students' rights and responsibilities (Charles, 2005; Manning & Bucher, 2003). According to assertive discipline advocates, teachers have the right to teach in classrooms that are free from disruptions, and students have the right to learn in classrooms that are orderly and free from interruptions. Teachers create an orderly classroom by clearly communicating classroom rules and consistently enforcing the rules, with consequences specified in advance. For example, if talking without being given permission is against classroom rules, the first instance of talking results in a consequence, such as the student's name on the board; a second infraction results in a check by the student's name, and a third leads to detention. The specific rules and consequences depend on the teacher's judgment, but consistent enforcement is essential. In the case of chronic or severe misbehavior, the teacher may send a student to the principal or call parents.

In addition to a system of rules and consequences, the Canters advocate being assertive, rather than hostile or nonassertive, in their interactions with students. For example,

compare the following teacher responses to a student who is talking instead of beginning an in-class assignment.

Assertive: John, you need to stop talking and begin your assignment, NOW. That's a check by your name. One more and you stay in for recess.

Hostile: John, how many times do I have to tell you to stop talking and get to work? Your misbehavior is driving me crazy!

Nonassertive: John, I don't know what I'm going to do with you. Please stop talking.

The assertive response clearly identifies the misbehavior and communicates the consequences for misbehaving. The other two don't clearly address the misbehavior, nor do they describe consequences for continuing to misbehave.

The Issue

Assertive discipline is a successful but controversial approach to classroom management. Advocates laud the clear definition of teacher and student roles and responsibilities. Teachers are there to teach and students are there to learn, they argue, and the teacher has the right to establish and implement a management system that allows learning to take place.

Proponents also contend that its emphasis on the combination of positive reinforcement together with appropriate sanctions is extremely effective (Canter, 1988). One classroom management expert observes, "A great many teachers are very enthusiastic about Assertive Discipline because it helps them deal with students positively and teach with little interruption. It

of school violence are rare. As part of school wide safety programs (see Chapter 4), most schools have created prevention programs, taken security measures, and established detailed procedures to protect students and teachers from violent acts such as those that make national headlines (National Center for Education Statistics, 2005). When serious problems do arise, teachers are most likely to encounter verbal aggression or student fighting. These incidents are also quite rare, but teachers must be prepared for them. Once you know what options are available, you will feel more confident about your ability to deal with these problems.

When students are verbally aggressive, your goal is to keep the problem from escalating. Responding to Tyrone in a calm and unemotional tone of voice is a first step. Once the student has calmed down, you can arrange to talk to him after school, send him to a school counselor, or ask for additional support. In the case involving fighting, you should follow also preserves instructional time and helps relieve the annoyance of verbal confrontations" (Charles, 2005, p. 51).

Assertive discipline is especially popular with beginning teachers because it is relatively easy to understand and implement, and it has been proven effective in addressing the myriad of minor infractions that virtually "drive some teachers crazy." Even the original title, *Assertive Discipline: A Take-Charge Approach for Today's Educator* (Canter & Canter, 1976), was designed to instill confidence in teachers who are apprehensive about managing a classroom.

However, critics argue that the use of rewards and punishers to maintain an orderly classroom overemphasizes control and obedience at the expense of personal development (Freiberg, 1999c; Kohn, 1993b). By focusing on changing behavior instead of emphasizing the reasons for rules and by failing to teach students that they are responsible for their actions, assertive discipline works in the short run, critics claim, but doesn't contribute to students' long-term personal and social development.

One parent had this experience with her daughter's first week of kindergarten:

> After each of the first four days of school, the mother asked her daughter what she had learned. The child's answers were succinct: On the first day she learned "to sit still"; on the second day she learned "to walk in a straight line"; on the third day she learned "to raise her hand"; and on the fourth day she learned "to be quiet." On the fifth day, the mother decided not to ask any more questions! *(C. Weinstein & Mignano, 2003, p. 78)*

Critics argue that preoccupation with order and control can send the wrong message to students about classrooms and learning.

Critics further contend that assertive discipline treats symptoms, such as talking without permission, as the problem instead of examining possible causes, such as ineffective instruction or not understanding why it is important to give everyone a chance to speak.

Despite the controversy, the program is enormously popular and widespread. It is difficult to find a school district in the country that hasn't had at least some exposure to assertive discipline, and probably more than a million teachers have been trained in at least some aspects of the program.

You Take a Position

Now it's your turn to take a position on the issue. State in writing whether you feel that assertive discipline will contribute to a productive learning environment or detract from it, and provide a two-page rationale for your position.

*For additional references and resources, go to the Companion Website at **www.prenhall.com/kauchak**, then to the Teaching in an Era of Reform module for Chapter 11. You can respond online or submit your response to your instructor.*

three steps: (1) Stop the incident (if possible), (2) protect the victim, and (3) get help. For instance, a loud noise, such as shouting, clapping, or slamming a chair against the floor will often surprise the students enough so they'll stop. At that point, you can begin to talk to them, check to see if anyone is hurt, and then take the students to the main office, where help is available. If your interventions don't stop the scuffle, you should immediately rush an uninvolved student to the office for help. Unless you're sure that you can separate the students without danger to yourself, or them, attempting to do so is unwise.

You are legally required to intervene in the case of a fight. If you ignore a fight, even on the playground, parents can sue for negligence on the grounds that you failed to protect a student from injury (Fischer et al., 2006). However, the law doesn't say that you're required to physically break up the fight; immediately reporting it to administrators is an acceptable form of intervention.

Serious management problems require both short- and long-term strategies. (Elena Rooraid/PhotoEdit Inc.)

So, now we know the answer to the fourth item on our introductory survey, "Teachers are legally required to intervene if students in their classrooms become involved in a fight or a scuffle." Teachers *are* legally required to intervene if a fight or scuffle occurs in their classroom. To ignore would place students' safety in jeopardy and could result in a liability lawsuit.

Breaking up a scuffle is, of course, only a short-term solution. Whenever students are aggressive or violent, experts recommend involving parents and other school personnel (Burstyn et al., 2001). Parents want to be notified immediately if school problems occur. In addition, school counselors, school psychologists, social workers, and principals have all been trained to deal with these problems and can provide advice and assistance. Experienced teachers can also provide a wealth of information about how they've handled similar problems. No teacher should face serious problems of violence or aggression alone. Further, excellent programs are available to teach conflict resolution and to help troubled students (D. Johnson & Johnson, 2006). If teachers can get help when they first suspect a problem, many incidents can be prevented.

To conclude this section, we want to put violence and aggression into perspective. Although they are possibilities—and you should understand options for dealing with them—the vast majority of your management problems will involve issues of cooperation and motivation. Many problems can be prevented, others can be dealt with quickly, while some require individual attention. We have all heard about students carrying guns to school and incidents of assault on teachers. Statistically, however, considering the huge numbers of students who pass through schools each day, these incidents remain very infrequent.

Effective Classroom Management in Urban Schools

Urban schools provide unique challenges to teachers attempting to create productive learning environments. Consider the case of Mary Gregg, a first-grade teacher in an urban school in the San Francisco Bay Area.

Mary's classroom is a small portable room with a low ceiling and very loud air fans. The room has one teacher table and six rectangular student tables with six chairs at each. Mary has 32 first graders (14 girls and 18 boys). Twenty-five of the children are children of color; a majority are recent immigrants from Southeast Asia, with some African Americans and Latinos, and seven European Americans. (LePage et al., 2005)

Research on teaching in urban contexts reveals three themes. First, students in urban environments come from very diverse backgrounds (Noguera, 2003a; Macionis & Parillo, 2007). As a result of this diversity, their prior knowledge and experiences vary, and what they view as acceptable patterns of behavior also varies, sometimes dramatically. Second, urban classes are often large; Mary had 32 first graders in a room built for 25. Third, and perhaps most pernicious, negative stereotypes about urban environments create the perception that creating a productive learning environment through classroom management is difficult if not impossible. Two of the most common stereotypes are, "Students can't control themselves," and "Students don't know how to behave because the parents don't care" (Goldstein, 2004, p. 43). In response to this stereotype, urban teachers often "teach defensively," "choosing methods of presentation and evaluation that simplify content and reduce demands on students in return for classroom order and minimal student compliance on assignments" (LePage et al., 2005, p. 331). (We discuss effective instruction in urban classrooms in Chapter 12.)

This defensive approach to classroom management and instruction results in lowered expectations and decreased student motivation. Students who are not motivated to learn are more likely to be disruptive because they don't see the point in what they're being asked to do, a downward spiral of motivation and learning occurs, and management issues become increasingly troublesome.

However, it doesn't have to be this way. In spite of diversity and large numbers of students in a small classroom, effective urban teachers can create active and orderly learning environments. Let's look at Mary Gregg's classroom management during a lesson on buoyancy.

Once into the science activity, management appears to be invisible. There is, of course, some splashing and throwing things into the water, but as the lesson progresses, the teacher engages in on-the-spot logistical management decisions. For instance, everyone is supposed to get a chance to go to the table to choose objects to be placed in cups. After choosing the first one to go, Mary sets them to the task. Very quickly, it is the second person's turn and the students do not know how to choose who should get the next turn. At first she says "you choose," then foresees an "It's my turn. No it's my turn" problem and redirects them with a counterclockwise motion to go around the table. (LePage et al., 2005, pp. 328–329)

This example demonstrates that, while challenging, classroom management in an urban environment doesn't have to be overly restrictive or punitive. How is this accomplished? Research suggests four important factors:

- Caring and supportive teachers
- Clear standards for acceptable behavior
- Structure
- Effective instruction

Caring and Supportive Teachers

We have emphasized the need for caring and supportive teachers throughout this chapter. Teachers who care are important in all schools but are critical in urban environments. When students perceive their teachers as uncaring, disengagement from school life occurs, and students are much more likely to display disruptive behaviors than their more involved peers (Charles, 2005; Jones & Jones, 2004).

Clear Standards for Acceptable Behavior

Because they bring diverse experiences to class, urban students' views of acceptable behaviors often vary. As a result, being clear about what behaviors are and are not acceptable is essential in urban classrooms (D. Brown, 2004). As we saw earlier in the chapter, students see clear standards of behavior as evidence that the teacher cares about them. One urban student had this to say about clear behavioral expectations:

She's probably the strictest teacher I've ever had because she doesn't let you slide by if you've made a mistake. She going [sic] to let you know. If you've made a mistake, she's going to let you know it. And, if you're getting bad marks, she's going to let you know it. She's one of my strictest teachers, and that's what makes me think she cares about us the most. (Alder, 2002, pp. 251–252).

The line between clear standards for behavior and an overemphasis on control is not cut and dried. One major difference is that in productive urban classrooms, order is created through "the ethical use of power" (Alder, 2002, p. 245). Effective teachers are demanding but also helpful; they model and emphasize personal responsibility, respect, and cooperation;

and they are willing to take the time to ensure that students understand the reasons for rules (C. Weinstein & Mignano, 2003). Further, in responding to the inevitable incidents of students failing to bring needed materials to class, talking, or otherwise being disruptive, effective teachers in urban schools enforce rules but provide rationales for them and remind students that completing assigned tasks is essential because it helps develop the skills needed for more advanced work (D. Brown, 2004). In contrast, less-effective teachers tend to focus on negative consequences, such as, "If you don't finish this work, you won't pass the class" (Manouchehri, 2004).

Structure

Students in urban schools sometimes come from environments where stability and structure may not be a regular part of everyday life. This makes order, structure, and predictability even more important in urban classrooms. Procedures that lead to well-established routines are important, and predictable consequences for behaviors are essential. A predictable environment leads to an atmosphere of order and safety, which is crucial for developing the sense of attachment to school that is essential for learning and motivation.

Effective Instruction

If students aren't learning and aren't actively involved in classroom life, management problems are inevitable. Classroom management and instruction are interdependent, and, unfortunately, students in urban classrooms are often involved in low-level activities such as listening to lectures and doing seat work that isn't challenging. This type of instruction contributes to low motivation and feelings of disengagement, which further increases the likelihood of management problems. We discuss instructional strategies that challenge and motivate students in Chapter 12.

> **Making Connections:**
> To deepen your understanding of the topics in this section of the chapter and integrate them with topics you've already studied, go to the *Making Connections* module for Chapter 11 at **www.prenhall.com/kauchak**. Respond to questions 5 and 6.

Check Your Understanding

3.1 Why has classroom management become a national concern?

3.2 What are the major goals of classroom management? How do they contribute to a productive learning environment?

3.3 How are classroom management and discipline different? How can teachers prevent management problems through planning?

3.4 What are the characteristics of effective interventions?

3.5 What actions—both short- and long-term—should teachers take when encountering incidents of violence and aggression?

3.6 What makes urban classrooms unique in terms of classroom management?

 For feedback, go to Appendix A, Check Your Understanding, *located in the back of this text.*

Creating Productive Learning Environments: Involving Parents

Learning is a cooperative venture; teachers, students, and parents are in it together. Students must be cooperative and motivated to learn if a learning environment is to be productive, and parental support is essential for promoting this cooperation and motivation.

Benefits of Parental Involvement

Students benefit from parental involvement in several ways:

- Greater willingness to do homework
- Higher long-term achievement
- More positive attitudes and behaviors
- Better attendance and graduation rates
- Greater enrollment in postsecondary education (Garcia, 2004; Hong & Ho, 2005)

These outcomes result from parents' increased participation in school activities, higher expectations for their children's achievement, and teachers' increased understanding of learners' home environments. Deciding how to respond to a student's disruptive behavior is easier, for example, when his teacher knows that his mother or father has lost a job, his parents are going through a divorce, or a family member is ill.

Parents can also help reinforce classroom management plans. One teacher reported:

I had this boy in my class who was extremely disruptive. He wouldn't work, kept "forgetting" his homework, distracted other children, wandered about the room. You name it; he did it. The three of us—the mother, the boy and I—talked about what we could do, and we decided to try a system of home rewards. We agreed that I would send a note home each day, reporting on the boy's behavior. For every week with at least three good notes, the mother let him rent a video game. In this way, the child's access to video games was directly dependent on his behavior. This system really made a difference. (C. Weinstein & Mignano, 2003, p. 117)

Parent–teacher collaboration can have long-term benefits for teachers. For example, teachers who encourage parental involvement report more positive feelings about teaching and their school. They also have higher expectations for parents and rate them as being more helpful (Epstein, 2001).

This section answers the fifth question on our "Professional Knowledge: Test Yourself" questionnaire. Involving parents in their children's education can have a number of beneficial results, including even increased student achievement.

Strategies for Involving Parents

Virtually all schools have formal communication channels, such as open houses (usually occurring within the first 2 weeks of the year, when teachers introduce themselves and describe general guidelines); interim progress reports, which tell parents about their youngsters' achievements at the midpoint of each grading period; parent–teacher conferences; and, of course, report cards. Although these processes are schoolwide and necessary, you can do more, such as the following:

- Send a letter home to parents within the first week of school that expresses positive expectations for students and solicits parents' help (see Figure 11.2).
- Maintain communication by sending home packets of student work, descriptions of new units, and other information about academic work.
- Emphasize students' accomplishments through newsletters, e-mails, or individual notes.

It is important to note that all forms of communication with parents need to be carefully proofread to ensure that they are free of spelling, grammatical, and punctuation errors. First impressions are important and lasting. Your communications create perceptions of your competence, and errors detract from your credibility.

One of the most effective ways to involve parents is to call them. Earlier in the chapter, we said that *time* is the best indicator of caring that exists. When you allocate some of your

Figure 11.2   Letter to Parents

August 22, 2007

Dear Parents,

I am looking forward to a productive and exciting year, and I am writing this letter to encourage your involvement and support. You always have been, and still are, the most important people in your child's education. We cannot do the job without you.

For us to work together most effectively, some guidelines are necessary. With the students' help, we prepared the ones listed here. Please read this information carefully, and sign where indicated. If you have any questions, please call me at Southside Elementary School (555-5935) or at home (555-8403) in the evenings.

Sincerely,

Shannon Brinkman

Shannon Brinkman

AS A PARENT, I WILL TRY MY BEST TO DO THE FOLLOWING:

1. I will ask my child about school every day (evening meal is a good time). I will ask about what he or she is studying and try to learn about it.
2. I will provide a quiet time and place each evening for homework. I will set an example by also working at that time or reading while my child is working.
3. Instead of asking if homework is finished, I will ask to see it. I will ask my child to explain some of the information to me to check for understanding.

Parent's Signature _____

STUDENT SURVIVAL GUIDELINES

1. I will be in class and seated when the bell rings.
2. I will follow directions the first time they are given.
3. I will bring homework, notebook, paper, and a sharp pencil to class each day.
4. I will raise my hand for permission to speak or leave my seat.
5. I will keep my hands, feet, and objects to myself.

HOMEWORK GUIDELINES

1. Our motto is I WILL ALWAYS TRY. I WILL NEVER GIVE UP.
2. I will complete all assignments. If an assignment is not finished or ready when called for, I understand that I get no credit for it.
3. If I miss work because of an absence, it is my responsibility to come in before school (8:15–8:45) to make it up.
4. I know that I get one day to make up a quiz or test or turn in my work for each day I'm absent.
5. I understand that extra credit work is not given. If I do all the required work, extra credit isn't necessary.

Student's Signature _____

Home–school partnerships create effective communication channels with parents and promote higher achievement and motivation. (Michelle Bridwell/PhotoEdit Inc.)

personal time to call parents, this communicates your commitment to their child better than any other way. Also, talking to a parent allows you to be specific in describing a student's needs and gives you a chance to again solicit support. If a student is missing assignments, for example, you can alert the parent, ask for possible causes or explanations, and encourage the parents to more closely monitor their child's study habits.

When we talk to parents, we need to establish a positive, cooperative tone that lays the foundation for joint efforts. Consider the following:

> *"Hello, Mrs. Hansen? This is Connie Lichter, Jared's math teacher."*
> *"Oh, uh, is something wrong?"*
> *"Not really. I just wanted to call to share with you some information about your son. He's a bright, energetic boy, and I enjoy seeing him in class every day. But he's been having some problems handing in his homework assignments in my class."*
>
> *"I didn't know he had math homework. He never brings any home."*
>
> *"That might be part of the problem. He just might forget that he has any to do. I have a suggestion. Why don't we set up a system that will help him remember. I'll ask the class to write down their math homework in their folders every day. Please ask Jared to share that with you every night, and make sure that it's done. When it's done, why don't you initial it so I know you and he talked? I think that will help a lot. How does that sound?"*
>
> *"Sure. I'll try that."*
>
> *"Good. We don't want him to fall behind. If he has problems with the homework, have him come to my room before or after school, and I'll help him. Is there anything else I can do? . . . If not, I look forward to meeting you soon."*

This phone conversation was positive and created a partnership between home and school. In addition, it created a specific plan of action.

Making Connections:
To deepen your understanding of the topics in this section of the chapter and integrate them with topics you've already studied, go to the *Making Connections* module for Chapter 11 at **www.prenhall.com/kauchak**. Respond to questions 7 and 8.

As it continues to expand, technology provides an additional channel for improving communication. For example, as they become more accessible, both voice mail and e-mail can be used to connect with busy parents. In many schools, newsletters and other communications are offered in electronic, as well as paper, form.

Check Your Understanding

4.1   Explain how involving parents contributes to a productive learning environment.

4.2   What strategies do effective teachers use to communicate with parents?

 For feedback, go to Appendix A, Check Your Understanding, *located in the back of this text.*

---

exploring diversity

Communicating With Parents

Classrooms with large numbers of students from diverse backgrounds present unique communication challenges. Lower parent participation in school activities is often associated with families that are members of cultural minorities, are lower socioeconomic status (SES), and have a child enrolled in either special education or English-as-a-second-language programs (Tiedt & Tiedt, 2005; C. Weinstein & Mignano, 2003). Each factor makes communication between home and school more challenging, both for parents and teachers.

Economic, Cultural, and Language Barriers

Economics, culture, and language can all create barriers that limit the involvement of minority and low-SES parents in school activities (Barton et al., 2004; Gollnick & Chinn, 2006). Low-SES parents frequently lack resources—such as child care, transportation, Internet access, and even telephones—that allow them to engage in school activities. Multiple jobs often prevent parents from helping their children with homework. In addition, high rates of family mobility can create obstacles to effective parent–school communication (Nakagawa et al., 2002).

Cultural differences can sometimes be misinterpreted. Because of their respect for teachers, for example, some Asian and Latino parents hesitate to become involved in matters they believe are best handled by the school, but teachers sometimes misinterpret this deference to authority as apathy (C. Weinstein & Mignano, 2003).

Language can be another barrier. Parents of bilingual students may not speak English, which leaves the child responsible for interpreting communications sent home by teachers. Homework also poses a special problem because parents cannot interpret assignments or provide help, and schools sometimes compound the difficulty by using educational jargon when they send letters home.

Involving Minority Parents

Teachers can narrow the home–school gap by offering parents specific strategies for working with their children (Epstein, 2001). Let's see how one teacher does this:

Nancy Collins, a middle school English teacher, has students who speak five different native languages in her class. During the first 2 days of school, she prepares a letter to parents, and with the help of her students, translates it into their native languages. The letter begins by describing how pleased she was to

have students from varying backgrounds in her class, saying that they enrich all her students' educations.

She continues with a short list of procedures and encourages the parents to support their children's efforts by

1. *Asking their children about school each night*
2. *Providing a quiet place to study for at least 90 minutes a day*
3. *Limiting television until homework is finished*
4. *Asking to see samples of their children's work and grades they've received*

She tells them that the school is having an open house and the class with the highest attendance will win a contest. She concludes the letter by reemphasizing that she is pleased to have so much diversity in her class. She asks parents to sign and return the letter.

The day before the open house, Nancy has each of her students compose a handwritten letter to their parents in their native languages, asking them to attend. Nancy writes "Hoping to see you there" at the bottom of each note and signs it.

Nancy's letter was effective in three ways. First, writing it in students' native languages communicated sensitivity and caring. Second, the letter included specific suggestions; these are important because they provide parents with concrete suggestions for helping their children. Even parents who cannot read a homework assignment are more involved if they ask their children to explain their schoolwork. The suggestions also let parents know they are needed. Third, by encouraging parents to attend the school's open house, Nancy increased the likelihood that they would do so. If they did, and the experience was positive, their involvement would likely increase.

The process of involving parents begins with awareness. As we more fully realize that parents from cultural minorities and low-SES backgrounds are often reluctant to become involved in school activities, we can redouble our efforts. We can also try to be as clear and specific as possible in our suggestions for parents as they work with their youngsters.

Finally, if parents speak English, phone calls are as effective with them as they are with nonminority parents. Experts suggest calling parents at work, where they are easier to reach, and scheduling conferences around their work schedules (Lindeman, 2001). Some teachers even conduct home visits (Bullough, 2001). Although home visits are demanding and time consuming, nothing communicates a stronger commitment to a young person's education.

decision making

Defining Yourself as a Professional

You're a first-year, sixth-grade world history teacher in an urban middle school, and you're having a difficult time maintaining order in your classroom. You're beginning the study of factors leading up to World War I, and you explain that one of the factors was increased nationalism—loyalty to a country's language and culture. As you're explaining, some of the students talk openly to each other, and a few even get out of their seats and sharpen pencils in the middle of your presentation. You point to the rules on the bulletin board, but this only seems to work for a while. You threaten them with referrals and other punishments, which work briefly, but the disruptions soon recur.

Other students seem listless and make no effort to pay attention; several even put their heads down on the desk during the lesson. You try walking around the room as you talk, and you stand near the inattentive students, but neither strategy works well. So you decide to address the issue directly. You walk up to the front of the room and say in a loud voice, "Class, this content is really important. It will help you understand why we continue to have wars in eastern Europe." As you conclude, you hear a barely audible, "Who cares?" from one of the students.

What would you do in this situation, both long-term and immediately? Why?

To respond to this question online and receive immediate feedback, go to the Decision Making Module for Chapter 11 on the Companion Website at www.prenhall.com/kauchak.

Meeting Your Learning Objectives

1. **Describe the essential characteristics of a productive learning environment.**
   - A productive learning environment is a place that is learning centered. In learning-centered classrooms, the primary focus is on students acquiring essential knowledge and skills. Teacher decision making is driven by the question, "How will my actions contribute to student learning?"
   - A second characteristic of a productive learning environment is that it is learner centered—a place where students can learn about themselves and others. Productive learning environments provide opportunities for students to develop social skills such as problem solving and perspective taking. They also provide opportunities for students to learn about their own strengths and weaknesses.

2. **Explain how teachers' personal characteristics contribute to a productive learning environment.**
   - Teacher caring is a crucial element of any productive classroom learning environment. It creates a foundation of trust for teacher–student relationships.
   - *Personal teaching efficacy* refers to a teacher's belief that he or she can affect student learning. It results in better quality instruction and increased student–teacher interactions.
   - Positive teacher expectations refer to teacher beliefs about students' ability to learn. Like personal teaching efficacy, it results in improved instruction and more effective teacher–student interactions.
   - Teacher modeling is a major way that teachers influence students' attitudes and beliefs. Teachers also model enthusiasm for the topics they teach, which can influence students' attitudes toward the subject matter.

3. **Describe how classroom management contributes to a productive learning environment.**
   - Classroom management is a national concern because of two major factors. First, the public often associates school violence with ineffective classroom management. Second, the public also believes, and rightly so, that there is a link between effective classroom management and increased learning.
   - Classroom management helps develop learner responsibility, it contributes to a positive classroom climate, and it maximizes time and opportunities for learning.
   - Effective classroom management depends upon a system of rules and procedures that provide guidelines for student behavior.
   - Effective interventions are immediate, target the correct student(s), and interfere with instruction and learning as little as possible.
   - Serious management problems, while rare and infrequent, can occur in classrooms. Teachers should understand procedures for dealing with these both immediately and long term.
   - Urban schools present unique management challenges. Effective urban teachers are caring and supportive, have clear standards for behavior, provide structure in their classrooms, and use effective instruction to complement their management.

4. **Explain how involving parents contributes to a productive learning environment.**
   - Students whose parents are involved in their education have better attitudes toward school, achieve higher, and are more likely to attend postsecondary education.
   - Teachers who encourage parental involvement also feel more positive about teaching and their school, and they have higher expectations for parents.
   - Teachers can involve parents by sending samples of student work home, emphasizing student accomplishments, and calling parents when necessary.

Important Concepts

academic learning time (p. 466)

allocated time (p. 465)

caring (p. 458)

classroom climate (p. 456)

classroom management (p. 463)

discipline (p. 463)

engaged time (p. 465)

instructional time (p. 465)

learning communities (p. 453)

personal development (p. 454)

personal teaching efficacy (p. 459)

perspective taking (p. 455)

positive teacher expectations (p. 460)

procedures (p. 466)

productive learning environment (p. 452)

rules (p. 467)

social development (p. 455)

social problem-solving skills (p. 456)

teacher modeling (p. 461)

withitness (p. 469)

Developing as a Professional

Preparing for Your Licensure Exam

This exercise will provide you with practice answering questions similar to the Praxis II exam as well as your state-specific licensure exam. Read the case study, and answer the questions that follow.

Nick Giardo is excited about the beginning of his first year of teaching at Sandalwood Junior High. Student teaching was a little rocky, but he is sure that most of his problems were due to his taking over another teacher's class in mid-year. As he sits at his desk planning for the new year, he thinks, "This has got to be better than student teaching"; then with a half smile mumbles audibly, "How could it be any worse?"

As students file into his first-period class, he is in the back of the room putting the final touches on a bulletin board. After the bell rings, he walks to the front of the room and says, "Welcome to U.S. History 101. I'm Mr. Giardo, and I'll be your teacher for the year. I see you've all found seats, so why don't we begin."

At this point, two confused students straggle in, looking for their classrooms. One of these students belongs there, the other does not. Mr. Giardo directs the one to sit down while he escorts the other into the hallway to help him find his class. As he returns to the room, there is a general buzz of student talk. Beginning again, he says, "Okay, class. Let's get started. This is American History, and I'm really excited about the year. I expect all of you to learn a lot about U.S. history and to become as excited about the topic as I am. Since you've all been in school before, I'm not going to waste a lot of time with rules. You all know how to play the game. The rules are up on the board, and I expect you to follow them . . . or else," he concluded with a stern look around the room, attempting to make eye contact with each student.

"Instead, I'd like to jump right into the content. I want this course to be important to you, so I'd like to get some idea of the kinds of things you'd like to learn about in here. I'd like you to break up into groups of four or five, and make a list of the kinds of things you'd like to learn this year. Then we'll come back together and discuss our lists."

As the students begin to talk in their groups, one student raises his hand. Nick pulls up a chair and sits down to talk with the student. As he does so, students in back of him start throwing spitballs and erasers.

The year is off to a rocky start.

1. Analyze Nick's classroom based on the characteristics of a productive learning environment.

2. Assess Nick's actions based on the human dimension of productive learning environments.

3. Assess Nick's application of research that describes the role of rules and procedures in creating an orderly classroom.

To receive feedback on your responses to these exercises, go to the Companion Website at www.prenhall.com/kauchak, and then to the Preparing for Your Licensure Exam *module for Chapter 11.*

Discussion Questions

1. Almost any teacher would agree that it is important to be a good role model. Given that belief, why do you suppose some teachers don't model the behaviors they expect their students to imitate?

2. Why is assertive discipline so popular in many schools? What are the advantages and disadvantages of this approach to management?

3. How can a teacher tell if students have developed responsibility? How might the definition of responsibility change with grade level? What types of instructional and managerial strategies promote responsibility? What types discourage the development of responsibility?

4. How do the following factors influence the optimal number of procedures in a classroom?
   a. Grade level
   b. Subject matter
   c. Type of student (e.g., high versus low achiever)
   d. Type of instruction (e.g., large group versus small group)

5. What advantages are there to seeking student input on rules? Disadvantages? Is this practice more important with younger or older students? Why?

6. If you were a substitute teacher (or a student teacher) and were going to take over a class mid-year, what kinds of things would you need to know and do in terms of classroom management?

Developing as a Professional: Online Activities

Going into Schools

Go to the Companion Website at *www.prenhall.com/kauchak*, and click on the *Going into Schools* module for Chapter 11. You will find a number of school-based activities that will help you link chapter content to the schools in which you work.

Virtual Field Experience: Using Teacher Prep to Explore the Profession

If you would like to participate in a Virtual Field Experience, access the Teacher Prep Website at *www.prenhall.com/teacherprep*. After logging in, complete the following steps:

1. Click on "Video Classroom" on the left panel of the screen.
2. Go to "General Methods."

TEACHER PREP

3. Finally, select "Module 4: Classroom Management." This video focuses on low-profile management strategies that minimize interruptions to instruction. Answer the questions that follow the video clip.

Online Portfolio Activities

To develop your professional portfolio, further apply your understanding of chapter content, and address the INTASC standards, go the Companion Website at www.prenhall.com/kauchak, then to the *Online Portfolio Activities* for Chapter 11. Complete the suggested activities.

Effective Instruction in American Schools

Chapter Outline

Learning and Teaching in Today's Classrooms
  Principles of Learning
  The Relationships Between Teaching and
    Learning

Planning for Effective Teaching
  Select Topics
  Specify Learning Objectives
  Prepare and Organize Learning Activities
  Plan for Assessment
  Ensure Instructional Alignment
  Planning in a Standards-Based Environment

Implementing Instruction: Essential Teaching Skills
  Organization
  Clear Communication
  Focus: Attracting and Maintaining Attention
  Questioning
  Feedback
  Review and Closure

Models of Instruction
  Direct Instruction
  Lecture-Discussion
  Guided Discovery
  Cooperative Learning

Learning Objectives

After you have completed your study of this chapter, you should be able to:

1. Describe the principles of cognitive learning theory, and identify examples of the principles in practice.

2. Describe essential steps in planning for instruction.

3. Explain how essential teaching skills contribute to learning.

4. Explain the relationships between principles of learning and different phases of models of instruction.

Case Studies

 Elementary

 Middle

 Secondary

Chapter 12

A major reason you're taking this and other courses in your teacher-preparation program is to help you develop your professional knowledge and skills, with the ultimate goal of becoming an expert teacher. Understanding how to plan and conduct effective lessons is perhaps the most important professional knowledge you will acquire in your teacher-education program. Helping you begin the process of developing that understanding is the goal of this chapter.

Let's begin by looking at one elementary teacher's thinking as she plans for her next week's math instruction.

"What are you doing?" Jim Barton asks his wife, Shirley, a fourth-grade teacher, as he sees her hard at work on a Saturday afternoon cutting and drawing on cardboard pieces.

"Working on a unit on equivalent fractions and adding fractions with unlike denominators. . . . What do you think? . . . Do they look like pizzas and cakes?" she asks, holding up the pieces of cardboard.

"They really do," he smiles, a bit impressed.

"My students had trouble with the equivalency standard on the state test last year, so I'm going to try to use more concrete, real-world examples. I want them to thoroughly understand equivalent fractions, so they'll be able to add fractions with unlike denominators."

"Equivalency standard?"

"Yeah. . . . See here," Shirley says, pointing to a document on her desk. "It says, 'Knows that two numbers in different forms are equivalent or nonequivalent, using whole numbers, decimals, fractions, and mixed numbers.' . . . For instance, ⅓ and 2/6 are equivalent forms of the same fraction. . . . Next, I want them to be able to convert fractions with unlike denominators to have common denominators, so they can add them."

"I see," Jim says, genuinely interested.

"Well, you know how kids are," Shirley continues. "They like to take the easy way out, and they often have misconceptions. . . . Like, this problem," Shirley continues, writing ½ + ⅓ on a piece of paper. "What's the answer?"

"Five-sixths," Jim answers, after a second or two.

"Wrong. . . . It's two-fifths."

Shirley grins at Jim's puzzled look at her response of " two-fifths" and then continues, "The kids see that we're adding, so they just add the top numbers and get 2 and add the bottom numbers and get 5. . . . The real answer is, of course, five-sixths, just as you said, but initially that isn't as sensible to them as two-fifths. So, that's the kind of thing I'm working on."

"Okay," Shirley thinks to herself as Jim leaves the room, "I'll use the pizzas for review, and then I'll use the cakes to help them understand equivalent fractions."

She then prepares a worksheet with additional geometric figures that students will complete for additional practice on finding equivalent fractions. "If they do okay on the worksheet, I'll give them some problems in a quiz Friday, so I can see how well they really understand both equivalent fractions and adding fractions with unlike denominators," she mumbles out loud. "If they don't do well, I'll give them some more practice. . . . I think I'm ready."

We'll examine Shirley's planning in detail in the next section, but before we do, please respond to the survey (on page 377) that will introduce you to your study of this chapter. We examine each of these items as the chapter unfolds.

Learning and Teaching in Today's Classrooms

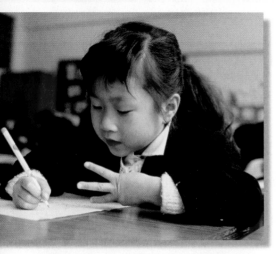

Cognitive theories of learning emphasize that students are mentally active as they attempt to understand the world. [Alan Oddie/PhotoEdit Inc.]

If we look closely at Shirley's planning, we see that her understanding of the ways that kids think and learn were important in guiding her decisions during planning. And this understanding will also guide her instruction, as we'll see later in the chapter. Let's take a closer look at several basic principles that support our understanding of the way students think and learn.

Principles of Learning

The cognitive revolution, an important change in the way educators think about learning, began about the middle of the 20th century and continues to this day. This revolution marked a major shift in educators' understanding of the way students learn and now provides the foundation on which school leaders and teachers base their approaches to instruction.

Cognitive learning theories explain learning by focusing on changes in the ways people think that result from their efforts to make sense of the world. These theories help us explain tasks as simple as remembering a phone number and as complex as solving math and chemistry problems.

professional knowledge: test yourself!

For each item, circle the number that best represents your thinking. Use the following scale as a guide.

1 = Strongly disagree
2 = Disagree
3 = Uncertain
4 = Agree
5 = Strongly agree

1. Students tend to retain ideas that make sense to them, even if the ideas are inconsistent with teachers' explanations.

| 1 | 2 | 3 | 4 | 5 |

2. Because assessing students, such as giving quizzes and tests, uses instructional time, students who are frequently assessed learn less than those who are assessed less frequently.

| 1 | 2 | 3 | 4 | 5 |

3. Effective planning primarily involves identifying the important topics students should learn.

| 1 | 2 | 3 | 4 | 5 |

4. The most effective teachers in today's schools are those who are best able to clearly explain the content they are teaching to their students.

| 1 | 2 | 3 | 4 | 5 |

5. Rather than exclusively using one particular teaching strategy, effective teachers vary their instruction.

| 1 | 2 | 3 | 4 | 5 |

 This is available in a downloadable format on the Companion Website for personal portfolio use.

Cognitive learning theories are grounded in the following principles:

- Learning depends on experiences.
- Learners *construct*—they do not record—knowledge in an attempt to make sense of their experiences.
- Knowledge that is constructed depends on and builds on knowledge that learners already possess.
- Learning is enhanced by social interaction.
- Learning requires practice and feedback.

Learning Depends on Experiences

You have learned to drive a car, but your only experience has been with cars that have automatic transmissions. Then, you take a part-time job as a delivery truck driver, but all the trucks have standard transmissions. You initially struggle, but now you're very comfortable driving vehicles with standard transmissions.

> **Cognitive learning theories.**
> Explanations for learning that focus on changes in the ways people think that result from their efforts to make sense of the world.

This simple example illustrates the importance of experience in learning. Your initial experiences with automatic transmissions helped you learn to drive, and because of additional experience, you have now learned to drive vehicles with standard transmissions.

This principle applies to schools as well. Everything that occurs in schools provides students with experiences that contribute to their learning. Shirley planned experiences intended to help her fifth graders understand equivalent fractions. This course provides you with experiences that are designed to increase your understanding of teaching and help you develop as a professional. The same is true for all learning. Experiences provide the raw material that people use to construct ideas.

Learners Construct Knowledge in an Attempt to Make Sense of Their Experiences

When our students learn, they don't behave like tape recorders, passively recording ideas in their memories in the form in which they are presented. Instead, they are cognitively active, and in an attempt to understand how the world works, they construct knowledge and understanding that makes sense to them.

Shirley's students are examples. To them, it made more sense to add both the top and bottom numbers in fractions than it did to add only the top numbers. Research has uncovered a number of misconceptions that students bring to class and that teachers must battle before more accurate understanding can occur (Crockett, 2004). For example, many students believe that people are warmer in the summer, because the earth is closer to the sun during that season. This makes intuitive sense to students who become warmer the closer they stand to a fire or heater. Unfortunately, this misconception then competes with teachers' attempts to help students see that the tilting of the earth's axis toward and away from the sun is a more accurate explanation, because it also helps us understand why the seasons in the southern hemisphere are the opposite of ours in the north. Again, it is important to remember that students' learning, both accurate and inaccurate, results from experience, and subsequent experiences are usually necessary to change students' ideas.

This section suggests that the first item on our survey, "Students tend to retain ideas that make sense to them, even if the ideas are inconsistent with teachers' explanations" is true. In fact, students' misconceptions can be difficult to dispel, and simply offering them a correct explanation is often ineffective.

Knowledge That Is Constructed Depends on and Builds on Learners' Prior Knowledge

People don't construct knowledge in a vacuum; new knowledge builds on what they already know. For instance, Shirley's students had a great deal of practice with addition. At no time in finding a sum did they add some numbers but not others. So—to them—adding both the top and bottom numbers in a fraction was sensible, more sensible than adding only the numbers on top and essentially ignoring those on the bottom.

Prior knowledge can also help us understand why students sometimes struggle with grammar rules. For example, they learn that when one boy meets another boy, we have two *boys*. The same applies to *girls*. However, when we see one body of water and then a second body of water, we don't have two *bodys* of water; we have two *bodies* of water.

Knowing that people attempt to make sense of the world and realizing that they will use what they already know in the process help us understand why students have so many misconceptions and why they sometimes have "off-the-wall" ideas. Based on their existing knowledge and experiences, the misconceptions and ideas make sense to them.

Learning Is Enhanced by Social Interaction

Social interaction helps students create and refine new ideas (Bruning et al., 2004). Experts estimate that 25 percent of what students learn in classrooms results from their interactions with fellow students (Brophy, 2006). We can see how this principle applies to Shirley's students. Without a discussion of why we add only the top numbers when finding the sums of fractions, they are likely to retain the misconception. Also, social interaction is a form of experience, and, as with experience in general, it influences all forms of learning.

Learning Requires Practice and Feedback

People learn to do well what they practice—an idea captured by the saying, "Practice makes perfect" (Schunk, 2004). This principle explains why true learning takes so much time and effort and is also supported by neurological studies (Craig, 2003). To become proficient at word processing, we practice at the computer; to become skilled writers, we practice writing; to solve problems effectively, we solve many problems. Shirley understood this principle when she prepared a worksheet designed to provide her students with additional practice in finding equivalent fractions.

For practice to be effective, we need to receive feedback about our performance. **Feedback** is information about existing understanding that we use to increase future understanding. As learners construct knowledge, they use additional information to determine the extent to which their understanding is valid. For instance, feedback on the screen provides us with immediate feedback about our word processing. In a similar way, feedback from students, fellow teachers, and principals provides teachers with information about their teaching performance. Much of our learning, in life and in the classroom, is influenced by the feedback we receive from the world (Nietfeld, Cao, & Osborne, 2004).

One of our most important roles as teachers is to provide students with feedback that can help them arrive at more accurate and sophisticated understandings of the world around them. In this regard, feedback is additional experience that students use to increase their learning.

The Relationships Between Teaching and Learning

Effective instruction builds on the principles of learning discussed in the previous section to maximize learning in the classroom. Simply, it is instruction based on principles of learning that maximizes learning for all students. Effective teachers are those who systematically apply the principles of learning in their planning and teaching.

As people have experiences, they continue to construct knowledge throughout their lifetimes, and they continue to learn and develop. However, schools as social institutions are designed to promote certain goals; they can't simple say, "Have experiences and learn and develop." Some experiences are more beneficial for learning than others. Effective teachers plan for and provide specific experiences for students, guide the social interaction that supports their knowledge construction, and design forms of practice and feedback that will help confirm or refine students' developing understanding. Effective instruction involves teachers' systematic attempts to help their students reach predetermined goals. This is particularly important now that standards and accountability are facts of teachers' lives.

Making Connections:
To deepen your understanding of the topics in this section of the chapter and integrate them with topics you've already studied, go to the *Making Connections* module for Chapter 12 at **www.prenhall.com/kauchak**. Respond to questions 1 and 2.

Check Your Understanding

1.1 Describe the principles on which cognitive learning theories are based.

1.2 You and a friend are trying to install a sound card in your computer, but you're a little uncertain about how to do it. You open the cabinet, look inside, and as you talk about how to proceed, she suggests looking to see where the speakers are attached. "Good idea," you say, and you easily install the card. Which principle of learning is best illustrated by this example?

1.3 Research indicates that properly designed homework increases learning (Kohn, 2006; H. Cooper, Robinson, & Patall, 2006). To which principle of learning is this research most closely related?

 For feedback, go to Appendix A, Check Your Understanding, *located in the back of this text.*

Feedback. Information about existing understanding that we use to enhance future understanding.

Effective instruction. Instruction that builds on principles of learning to maximize learning in the classroom.

Planning for Effective Teaching

Effective teaching doesn't just happen; it must be planned for and designed in a systematic way. Through careful planning, teachers provide students with experiences that allow them to construct new ideas and understanding. In the opening case, Shirley made decisions about the following strategies during her planning:

- Select topics that are important for students to study.
- Specify learning objectives related to the topics.
- Prepare and organize learning activities to help students reach the objectives.
- Plan assessments to measure the amount students have learned.
- Ensure that instruction and assessments are aligned with her learning objectives (L. Anderson & Krathwohl, 2001).

These planning decisions are outlined in Figure 12.1 and discussed in the sections that follow.

Select Topics

As you saw in Chapter 10, "What is important for students to learn?" is one of the most fundamental questions that teachers face as they plan (L. Anderson & Krathwohl, 2001). Standards—such as the one Shirley showed her husband, Jim—textbooks, and curriculum guides are all sources teachers commonly use to help answer this question (Reys, Reys, & Chavez, 2004). Their personal philosophies, students' interest in the topic, and real-world applications also influence the answer to this question. Teachers' knowledge of content is particularly important in helping decide which topics are important enough to allocate valuable teaching time to them, because there simply isn't time to teach everything. Effective teachers know their content well enough to identify key content ideas to target and emphasize.

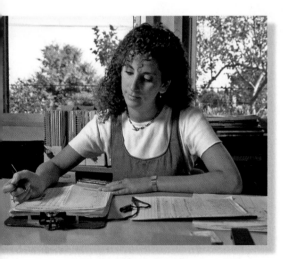

Careful planning helps teachers define their goals and make sure that instructional activities are aligned with these goals. [Mary Kate Denny/PhotoEdit Inc.]

Specify Learning Objectives

Although deciding what is important to study is an essential first step, teachers must also answer a second question: What do I want my students to know or be able to do with respect to the topic? The answer to this question is a **learning objective**. Clear learning objectives are essential because they guide the rest of the decisions teachers make during both planning and instruction. Without clear objectives, teachers won't know how to design their learning activities, nor can they create accurate assessments. Objectives also guide teachers as they implement their learning activities. When learning activities are unsuccessful, it can often be traced back to teachers' not being clear about their objectives.

Figure 12.1   Planning for Instruction

> **Learning objectives.**
> Statements that specify what students should know or be able to do with respect to a topic or course of study.

Select topics

Specify learning objectives

Prepare and organize learning activities

Plan for assessment

Ensure instructional alignment

TABLE 12.1   Objectives Using Mager's Approach

Objective	Condition	Performance	Criteria
Given 3 pairs of fractions, fourth graders wil will determine if each pair is or is not equivalent.	Given 3 pairs of fractions	Determine	Each
Given pairs of fractions with unlike denominators, fourth graders will create equivalent fractions for each pair.	Given pairs of fractions with unlike denominators	Create	Each
Given word problems involving the addition of fractions with unlike denominators, fourth graders will correctly add the fractions in each.	Given word problems with unlike denominators	Add	Each correctly

Different approaches to writing objectives exist, and we'll briefly introduce two of the most popular here. (You will study these approaches in detail later in your methods classes.) One approach was pioneered in 1962 by Robert Mager in his highly readable book *Preparing Instructional Objectives*. Mager's work strongly influenced teaching and remains widely used today (Mager, 1998). If Shirley wrote objectives using Mager's approach, they might appear as you see in Table 12.1.

Norman Gronlund (2004) offered a popular alternative to Mager's approach; he suggested that teachers state a general objective, such as *know, understand,* or *apply,* followed by specific learning outcomes that operationally define what students will be able to do. Table 12.2 includes examples of objectives written according to Gronlund's suggestions. Note that in both approaches, the emphasis is on what students are learning, not what the teacher is doing. Effective planning begins with a focus on students' learning; teacher actions follow logically afterward.

To assist teachers in planning learning activities for their students, researchers developed a classification system based on principles of learning (L. Anderson & Krathwohl, 2001). A revision of the famous "Bloom's Taxonomy," first published in 1956 (Bloom, Englehart, Furst, Hill, & Krathwohl, 1956), the new system uses a matrix with 24 cells that represent the intersection of four types of knowledge with six cognitive processes (see Figure 12.2).

Teachers use the taxonomy to think about and clarify their learning objectives. For instance, one of Shirley's objectives was for students to be able to convert unequivalent into equivalent fractions. The objective involves applying a procedure, so it would be placed in the cell where *procedural knowledge* intersects with the cognitive process *apply.* In order to convert unequivalent fractions to equivalent fractions, students first need to understand the concept *equivalent fractions.* That objective would be placed in the cell where *conceptual knowledge* intersects with the cognitive process *understand.* Using the taxonomy during planning allows teachers to see what types of knowledge and cognitive processes they are emphasizing in their teaching.

TABLE 12.2   Objectives Using Gronlund's Approach

General Objective	Specific Learning Outcome
Understands *equivalent fractions*	1. Identifies pairs of fractions that are and are not equivalent. 2. Creates equivalent fractions
Understands the addition of fractions with unlike denominators	1. Recognizes need for creating equivalent fractions 2. Performs operations 3. Solves problems

Source: Gronlund (2004).

Figure 12.2   A Taxonomy for Learning, Teaching, and Assessing

The Knowledge Dimension	The Cognitive Process Dimension					
	1. Remember	2. Understand	3. Apply	4. Analyze	5. Evaluate	6. Create
A. Factual knowledge						
B. Conceptual knowledge						
C. Procedural knowledge						
D. Metacognitive knowledge						

Source: From Lorin W. Anderson & David R. Krathwohl, *A Taxonomy for Learning, Teaching and Assessing: A Revision of Bloom's Objectives,* p. 28. Copyright 2001. Published by Allyn and Bacon, Boston, MA. Copyright © by Pearson Education. Reprinted by permission of the publisher.

The taxonomy reminds us that teaching and learning are complex processes with many possible outcomes. It also helps us remember that we want our students to do much more than just "remember" "factual knowledge," one of the cells in the taxonomy. Unfortunately, a great deal of schooling focuses as much on this most basic objective as it does on the other 23 combined. Moving to the other forms of knowledge and more advanced cognitive processes is even more important in the 21st century, as student thinking, decision making, and problem solving are increasingly emphasized (van Gelder, 2005).

Prepare and Organize Learning Activities

Once Shirley identified her learning objectives—what she wanted her students to learn and know—she then prepared and organized her learning activities. This process primarily involved finding or creating high-quality examples or problems that illustrated the topic and then sequencing them so that they would be most meaningful to her students.

High-quality examples are representations of content that ideally have all the information in them that the students need to reach teachers' learning objectives, and their importance in promoting learning is crucial. They provide the basic experiences that students need for learning; examples are what learners use to construct their knowledge (Haas, 2005; J. Freeman, McPhail, & Berndt, 2002). Examples are also important in classrooms with diverse learners, because they contain information that students need in order to reach teachers' learning objectives, accommodating differences in students' prior knowledge. High-quality examples are important to all topics at all grade levels and are especially valuable for limited-English-proficiency learners because their prior experiences may not match those of other students (Bae, 2003; Echevarria & Graves, 2007).

Shirley used cardboard "pizzas" and "cakes" as examples to provide concrete learning experiences for her students. For example, she divided her "pizzas" into eight equal parts to illustrate equivalent fractions with similar denominators. She used the cake examples to build

Effective instructional activities provide students with opportunities to construct ideas. [©Ellen B. Senisi/Ellen Senisi]

High-quality examples. Representations of content that ideally have all the information in them that students need in order to reach teachers' learning objectives.

on this knowledge and to help her students learn how to convert unequivalent into equivalent fractions. (We'll see how Shirley used them in the next section of the chapter when we discuss implementing instruction.)

Examples are also important in language arts. Teachers often use actual student writing samples to provide concrete examples of good organization, grammar, and punctuation. Middle and high school teachers often use specific examples taken from literature to teach concepts such as metaphor, simile, and irony. Elementary teachers frequently use words embedded in sentences as examples to teach the different parts of speech. All of these abstract ideas would be difficult to teach and learn without the use of examples

The importance of high-quality examples in teaching can't be overstated, and research documents their powerful role in learning in the classroom. Effective teachers use examples to illustrate topics in ways that are understandable to students, whereas less effective teachers tend to rely on verbal explanations (Cassady, 1999; Haas, 2005).

Plan for Assessment

Assessment, which is the process of gathering information about students' learning progress, is an integral part of effective teaching, and expert teachers continually think about assessment during planning. Effective assessments not only answer the question, "How can I determine if my students have reached the learning objectives?" but also, "How can I use assessment to facilitate learning?"

We saw thinking about assessment in Shirley's planning. She said to herself, "I'll give them some problems in a quiz Friday, so I can see how well they really understand both equivalent fractions and adding fractions with unlike denominators. . . . If they don't do well, I'll give them some more practice." Let's look at some of the items that Shirley used to assess her students' learning.

Part I.

Look at the drawings of pairs of fractions below. Circle the pairs that are equivalent, and explain why they are equivalent in each case.

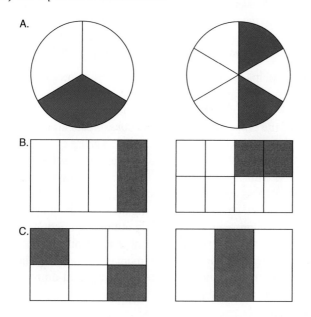

Part II.

Add the following fractions.

$$\frac{1}{5} + \frac{2}{5} = \underline{\hspace{2cm}} \qquad \frac{2}{7} + \frac{4}{7} = \underline{\hspace{2cm}}$$

$$\frac{1}{3} + \frac{1}{2} = \underline{\hspace{2cm}} \qquad \frac{3}{4} + \frac{1}{8} = \underline{\hspace{2cm}}$$

Assessment. How student understanding is measured.

Shirley designed these assessment items to provide both Shirley and her students with valuable information about their learning progress. If students succeed with these items, Shirley can proceed to other topics, building on her students' developing understanding of fractions. If students do not succeed, Shirley can use their responses to redesign her instruction to address learning problems.

Research supports the crucial role of assessment in learning:

Weekly or even more frequent classroom tests provide teachers with information useful in planning their lessons. . . . Frequent tests encourage students to be prepared for classes. Even in themselves, tests can be a powerful source of learning: Regular essays and feedback, for example, help students not only comprehend subject matter but become better writers. (Walberg, 2003, p. 42)

Research also shows that expert teachers, like Shirley, assess frequently during instruction, using both verbal questions and frequent exercises to provide students and themselves with continual information about learning progress during a lesson (Ciofalo & Wylie, 2006).

This section also indicates that the second item on our beginning-of-chapter survey, "Because assessing students, such as giving quizzes and tests, uses instructional time, students who are frequently assessed learn less than those who are assessed less frequently" is clearly not true. While the process of assessment does take time, it makes a major contribution to learning and is one of the most valuable uses of instructional time.

Assessment decisions are also essential during planning because they help teachers align their instruction with important standards and objectives. Let's see how teachers do that.

Ensure Instructional Alignment

Thinking about assessment during planning helped Shirley answer an additional question, "How do I know that my instruction and assessments are logically connected to my objectives?" **Instructional alignment** is the match between learning objectives, learning activities, and assessments, and it is an essential component of effective instruction (Bransford et al., 2000; L. Anderson & Krathwohl, 2001).

Without this alignment, it is difficult to know what is being learned. Students may be learning valuable information, but one cannot tell unless there is alignment between what they are learning and the assessment of that learning. Similarly, students may be learning things that others don't value unless curricula and assessments are aligned with . . . learning goals. (Bransford et al., 2000, pp. 51–52)

Instructional alignment helps teachers match instructional strategies and assessments to learning objectives and also helps students identify and understand what is important to learn (Morrison, Kemp, & Ross, 2007). Shirley's instruction was aligned. Her objectives were for students to understand the concept *equivalent fractions,* create equivalent fractions, and add fractions with unlike denominators. She then planned to give a quiz with "problems similar to my cake example." On the quiz, the students were asked to solve problems similar to those they practiced in class. This is the essence of instructional alignment.

Maintaining alignment isn't as easy as it appears. For instance, if a teacher's objective is for students to be able to write effectively, yet learning activities focus on isolated grammar skills, the instruction is out of alignment. It is similarly out of alignment if the objective is for students to apply math concepts to real-world problems, but learning activities have students practicing computation problems. Instructional alignment encourages teachers to ask, "What does my objective (e.g., 'apply math concepts') actually mean, and do my learning and assessment activities actually lead to the objective?"

Planning in a Standards-Based Environment

Standards influence teaching in a number of ways. For example, in Chapter 1 you saw that *standards* specify what students should know and what skills they should have after completing an area of study and were an essential part of accountability. In Chapter 10, you saw that standards also influence the curriculum; the first thing Suzanne Brush did in planning her lesson with her second graders was to refer to her state standard. Shirley did the same in her planning.

Instructional alignment. The match between learning objectives, learning activities, and assessments.

Unfortunately, standards are often written with varying degrees of specificity, so teachers have to interpret the meaning of the standard, as did both Suzanne and Shirley (Hamilton, Berends, & Stecher, 2005). Once they had made their interpretation, they were then able to make important decisions about learning activities and assessments. Careful planning ensured that they would help students meet the standards and that they had aligned their objectives, learning activities, and assessments.

This section provides us with an answer to the third statement in our introductory survey, "Effective planning primarily involves identifying the important topics students should learn." This statement is false. Though planning involves identifying topics for students to learn, it is much broader and includes other components to ensure that instructional activities result in productive student learning.

Making Connections:
To deepen your understanding of the topics in this section of the chapter and integrate them with topics you've already studied, go to the *Making Connections* module for Chapter 12 at **www.prenhall.com/kauchak**. Respond to questions 3–6.

Check Your Understanding

2.1   What are the five essential steps in planning for instruction?

2.2   Planning in a standards-based environment involves one additional step beyond the planning steps described in this section of the chapter. What is that additional step?

2.3   Classify the following objectives into one of the cells of the taxonomy table in Figure 12.2, and explain your classification: (1) Students will identify examples of figures of speech such as similes, metaphors, and personifications in written paragraphs. (2) students will write original paragraphs that include those figures of speech.

For feedback, go to Appendix A, Check Your Understanding, *located in the back of this text.*

Implementing Instruction: Essential Teaching Skills

Effective teaching is based on **essential teaching skills**, abilities that all teachers, including those in their first year of teaching, should have in order to maximize student learning. To see what these are, let's return to Shirley's work. We join her on Monday morning just before math, which she schedules each day from 10:00 to 11:00.

Shirley walks up and down the aisles, placing sheets of paper on each student's desk as students finish their writing assignment in language arts.

"Quickly turn in your writing, and get out your math books," she directs. Students stop writing and pass their papers forward, each putting his or her paper on top of the stack. Shirley places the papers into a folder and at 10:01 pulls out her cardboard pizzas. "Let's see what we remember about adding fractions. Look at these pizzas. We need to find out, What fraction of one whole pizza did we eat?"

After giving students time to think, she continues, "How many pieces of the first pizza did we eat? . . . Dean?" she asks as she displays the pizzas, which now have some pieces removed, as we see here.

Essential teaching skills. Abilities that all teachers, including those in their first year, should have in order to maximize student learning.

"Three."

"And how about this pizza? How many pieces did we eat? . . . Kathy?"

"Two."

She then writes ⅜ + ⅖ on the board and, pointing to these numbers, asks, "Why did I write ⅜ here and ⅖ there? . . . Omar?"

"You have . . . 8 pieces in each pizza . . . and you ate 3 of them," Omar responds hesitantly, pointing to the one on the left.

"Good," Shirley smiles. "And what about the second one? How many pieces of that pizza did we eat? . . . Selina?"

"Two."

"So what fraction of a total pizza did we eat altogether? . . . Gabriel?"

"Five . . . eighths of a pizza?" Gabriel responds after thinking for a few seconds.

"Good, Gabriel. . . . And, why is it ⅝ . . . Kevin?"

"Uhhh. . ."

"How many pieces altogether in each pizza?"

"Eight," Kevin answers.

"Good, . . . and how many did we eat, altogether?"

"Five."

"Yes," she smiles at Kevin, "so we ate ⅝ of one pizza."

Shirley then writes some additional problems on the board, such as 3/7 + 4/7 = ? and ⅖ + ⅕ = ? and writes ⅛ + ⅖ and reviews them as she did with her pizzas.

"Now remember," she emphasizes, "in each of these problems, the two fractions have the same denominator. . . . Be sure to keep that in mind as we continue our study of fractions.

"Now, we're going to shift gears because I've got another, different kind of problem," Shirley continues, pulling out the two cardboard cakes.

"Now, we have cakes instead of pizza, . . . and I'm still hungry, so I eat this piece," she said, pointing to a third. "Then I go sort of wild and eat this piece too," she adds, pointing to one of the halves. "How much cake have I eaten?"

"A third of one and a half of the other," Tenisha volunteers.

"Makes sense, . . .but is that more than a whole cake, a whole cake, or part of a cake?"

". . . I think less," Adam offers.

"How do you think we could find out for sure?" Shirley wonders. She pauses and then says, "To help us, take two of the sheets of paper that I put on your desks, and carefully fold them like our cakes here."

The students begin, and Shirley helps some of them who have trouble folding their papers into thirds.

"Now we have two whole cakes. Let's think about our problem again. If we eat a third of one and a half of the other one, how much have we eaten altogether? . . . How can we figure that out?"

". . . Let's lay one on top of the other," Jan suggests, after thinking for several seconds.

"Good idea. . . . Go ahead and try it."

"It's less than a whole cake," Tanya offers after peering carefully at the papers.

"How much less?"

The students offer a few uncertain suggestions, and Shirley then asks, "Let's think about the work we've been doing. What did we just review?" She points at the chalkboard.

"Adding up the pizzas," Juan offers.

"And what do we know about them?"

"They have the same-size parts, and these are different," he says, pointing to the cakes.

"Maybe we need to cut them different so they're the same," Enrico suggested.

"Good idea, Enrico. . . . Let me make a suggestion about how we can get them to be the same, using Enrico's idea. . . . Go ahead and shade one part of each of your papers, so you have a third shaded on this one and a half shaded on the other one," Shirley says, pointing to the papers.

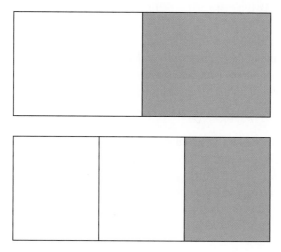

She continues, "How much cake do we have here? . . . Tim?"

"A third."

"Fine," Shirley smiles. "Now, let's all fold our cakes this way." She folds the three-piece cake in half horizontally as she watches the students. "How many pieces do I have altogether now? . . . Karen?"

". . . It looks like six."

"Yes. Good, Karen. I saw you actually counting them," Shirley notes and then counts the six squares again out loud. "So what portion is now shaded? . . . Jon?"

"Two sixths."

"Excellent, Jon!" She moves to the chalkboard and writes ⅓ = ⅔.

"Now, how do we know that the ⅓ and the ⅔ are equal?"

"It's the same amount of cake," Dan shrugs.

"Exactly," Shirley smiles.

Shirley continues by having the students divide the two-piece cake in thirds, horizontally, so it appears as follows:

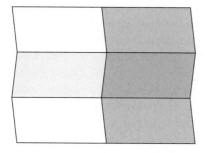

"What do we see here?"

". . . They both have the same number of pieces," Lorraine notes.

"And all the pieces are the same size," Crystal adds.

"Ooh, ooh, I know!" Adam said excitedly. "We've eaten ⅚ of the cake."

"That's an interesting thought, Adam. Would you explain that for us please?"

"It's like the pizza. We have two pieces there, and three pieces there, so it's ⅚ of the pizza, . . . uh cake."

Shirley then models a process for finding equivalent fractions by multiplying the numerator and denominator by the same number, guides the students through two more problems, and then asks, "So, what is the purpose in doing what we've done here? . . . Kelly?"

"To get fractions with the same denominators so we can add them."

"Exactly," Shirley smiles. "Now I'm going to give you the name. They're called EQUIVALENT FRACTIONS."

"Now let's see what we have. What have we been doing here? . . . Toni?"

". . . We're finding equivalent fractions."

"Good, Toni, and why do we want to find them? . . . Gary?"

". . . So we can add fractions when the denominators are not the same."

Shirley praises the class for their good work and then gives them an assignment that involves finding equivalent fractions. "Everyone, do the first one on your sheet, and tell me how much you get when you add ⅔ and ¼."

As the students work the first problem, Shirley walks up and down the rows, checking each student's progress as she goes. Periodically, she stops to point something out to an individual, then moves on.

"Let's see how we did," Shirley suggests when everyone has completed the problem. "What's the first thing you noticed? . . . Michelle?"

". . . The denominators aren't the same."

"Good! So what did we do?"

Some of the students solve the problem without difficulty, but others struggle. With Shirley's guidance they realize that multiplying the numerator and denominator of ⅔ by 4 gives them 8/12, and multiplying the numerator and denominator of ¼ by 3 gives them 3/12, so they can add the 8/12 and the 3/12 to get 11/12.

Shirley then has the students solve the second problem and guides the class through an analysis of it as she did with the first problem. She repeats the process with a third problem.

After reviewing the third problem, she has them work independently on additional fractions problems for the remainder of their time in math. As they do their seat work, she walks up and down the aisles looking over the children's shoulders, offering a few seconds of assistance to different individuals.

Finally, seeing it is 10:59, Shirley says, "It's nearly time for our break. As soon as you've cleaned up around your desks, we'll go."

Shirley demonstrated several essential teaching skills in her instruction. Understanding these essential teaching skills is important for your development as a teacher, because you'll be expected to demonstrate them when you have your own classrooms. In addition, hopefully you will see teachers demonstrating these teaching skills in their classrooms when you go into different classrooms to observe as part of your teacher education program. Grounded in the principles of learning that you saw at the beginning of the chapter, and derived from a long line of classroom research (Good & Brophy, 2003), these essential teaching skills are outlined in Figure 12.3 and discussed in the sections that follow.

Before we discuss the essential teaching skills in detail, we want to emphasize that the personal teacher characteristics essential for creating a productive learning environment that we discussed in Chapter 11—*caring, personal teaching efficacy, positive expectations,* and *modeling and enthusiasm*—also provide a foundation for effective instruction. Teachers with these characteristics create classroom climates that are positive and inviting, they also promote learning, and they use these personal characteristics as a foundation for the essential teaching skills.

Let's turn now to these essential teaching skills.

Figure 12.3 Essential Teaching Skills

Organization

To understand the role of organization in learning, let's look back at Shirley's lesson. She scheduled math from 10:00 to 11:00 and made the transition from language arts to math in 3 minutes, starting her math lesson at 10:01. She continued the lesson until 10:59; so, of a possible 60 minutes of time allocated to math, she used 58 minutes for instruction. In addition, she had her cardboard pizzas and cakes placed where she could easily access them and distributed the sheets of paper on the students' desks as they turned in their language arts papers. Further, Shirley had taught her students time-saving routines; for instance, they placed their papers on the top of the stacks as they were passed forward, without being reminded to do so.

These examples illustrate **organization**, the set of teacher actions that maximizes the amount of time available for instruction. Teacher actions that promote organization are outlined in Table 12.3.

Less-effective teachers are less well organized, and this detracts from student learning. They spend more time in transitions from one activity to another, failing to start lessons when they're scheduled; they spend valuable class time accessing materials; and their routines are not well established. The result is fewer minutes available for instruction and, ultimately, reduced student learning.

Clear Communication

Effective teaching requires clear communication. The link between effective teacher communication and student achievement is well established (Good & Brophy, 2003; I. Weiss & Pasley, 2004). In addition, the way teachers interact with students influences their motivation, their

TABLE 12.3 Teacher Actions That Promote Organization

Teacher Action	Example
Starting on time	Shirley's students had their math books out and were waiting at 10:01.
Making smooth transitions	Shirley made the transition from language arts to math in 3 minutes.
Preparing materials in advance	Shirley had her cardboard pizzas and cakes easily accessible.
Establishing routines	At Shirley's signal, the students put their paper on the top of the stack without being told specifically to do so.

Organization. The set of teacher actions that maximizes the amount of time available for instruction.

satisfaction with instruction, and their attitudes toward school (Pintrich & Schunk, 2002). Effective and less-effective teachers exhibit differences in four communication-related areas:

- Language clarity
- Thematic lessons
- Transition signals
- Emphasis

Effective teachers think about what they are trying to communicate and say it clearly. **Language clarity** eliminates vague terms (e.g., *perhaps, maybe, might, and so on,* and *usually*) in questions and explanations. When teachers use these terms in their classroom interactions, students are left uncertain about the topics they're studying, and this uncertainty detracts from learning (Shuell, 1996). For example, suppose you ask, "What do well-organized teachers do that promotes learning?" One instructor responds, "Usually, they use their time somewhat better and so on." Another responds, "They use their time well; they begin lessons on time, they have their materials ready, and they have well-established routines." The first response is muddled and uncertain, whereas the second is clear and precise.

Effective teachers also create lessons that are thematic. **Thematic lessons** lead to a specific point, and all parts of a teacher's instruction are related. If the point of the lesson isn't clear, if it is sequenced inappropriately, or if incidental information is interjected without indicating how it relates to the topic, the lesson becomes disconnected and less meaningful for students. Effective teachers keep their lessons on track, minimizing time on matters unrelated to the topic (Leinhardt, 2001).

Effective teachers also use transition signals to connect different parts of their lesson. **Transition signals** are verbal statements within a lesson that indicate to students that one idea is ending and another is beginning and that suggest connections between the two ideas. Shirley signaled a transition when she said, "Now, we're going to shift gears because I've got another, different kind of problem," as she pulled out her cardboard cakes. As another example, an American government teacher might signal a transition by saying, "We've been talking about the Senate, which is one house of Congress. Now we'll turn to the House of Representatives, the second part of Congress." Because students may be at a different place mentally, a transition signal alerts them that the lesson is making a conceptual shift—a move to a new topic—and allows them to adjust and prepare for it.

Not all information in a lesson is equally important; effective teachers use **emphasis**, verbal and vocal cues, and repetition to alert students to important information in a lesson (Jetton & Alexander, 1997). Shirley, for example, used emphasis when she said, "In each of these problems, the two fractions have the same denominator. . . . Be sure to keep that in mind as we continue our study of fractions." When teachers say, "This is very important," or "Listen carefully now," they're using verbal emphasis. Teachers can also give vocal cues— by enunciating certain words or speaking more loudly, for instance—to draw attention to important points.

Teachers' knowledge of content is an important factor in clear communication. When teachers are confident of their own understanding of the topics they teach, communication tends to be clear and precise. When they are less certain, clear communication decreases. They use more vague terms in their questions and explanations, their lessons are less thematic, and they fail to emphasize the most important points in the lesson. If you're uncertain about a topic, you should spend extra time studying, which will then be reflected in clearer language (Eggen & Kauchak, 2007).

Each of the factors in effective communication is grounded in the learning principle, "Learners construct knowledge in an attempt to make sense of their experiences." When teachers use clear language, teach thematic lessons, signal transitions, and emphasize important points, it is easier for students to make sense of lessons and remember the content in a meaningful way.

Language clarity. Teacher talk that omits vague terms in questions and explanations.

Thematic lessons. Lessons in which all parts of a teacher's instruction are related, so that the lesson leads to a specific point.

Transition signals. Verbal statements within a lesson that indicate one idea is ending and another is beginning, and suggest connections between the two ideas.

Emphasis. Verbal and vocal cues and repetition used to alert students to important information in a lesson.

Focus: Attracting and Maintaining Attention

Learning begins with attention; students can't learn lesson content if they aren't paying attention. So, effective teachers plan activities that attract and maintain students' attention.

Shirley's "pizzas," "cakes," and folded pieces of paper acted as a form of focus—concrete objects, pictures, models, materials displayed on the overhead, or even information written on the chalkboard that attract and maintain attention during learning activities. High-quality examples, such as those Shirley used in her lesson, are a very effective form of focus. Building lessons around high-quality examples provides students with experiences that they can use to construct their understanding, so, in addition to helping maintain attention, they also serve as the raw material for constructing ideas.

Questioning

In the last 20 years, a major shift in classroom instruction has occurred. In the past, teachers explained topics and students were expected to listen quietly and then work independently at their desks. However, as you saw in our discussion of learning principles, and as expert teachers know, learners are, by nature, cognitively active. To maximize learning, teachers should actively involve students in learning activities, and one of the most effective ways of doing this is through questioning.

Being able to ask effective questions is the most important ability teachers have for guiding student learning (J. Olson & Clough, 2004; Leinhardt & Steele, 2005). A teacher skilled in questioning can determine how much students already know about a topic, encourage learners to rethink their ideas, help them form relationships, involve shy or reticent students, recapture students' wandering attention, promote success, and enhance self-esteem.

With respect to questioning, effective and less-effective teachers differ in four areas:

- Frequency
- Equitable distribution
- Wait-time
- Prompting

Frequency

Questioning frequency refers to the number of questions a teacher asks during a given period of instructional time. Effective teachers ask many more questions than do less-effective teachers, and Shirley's lesson illustrates this point. Instead of relying on explaining and telling as a strategy, Shirley developed her entire lesson through questioning. Students involved in question-and-answer sessions are more attentive than those who listen passively to teacher explanations, and as a result, achievement increases (J. Finn et al., 2003; Leinhardt & Steele, 2005).

Equitable Distribution

Whom should teachers call on during a lesson? One answer might be, "whomever has a hand up." But this might not be the best answer. To begin to investigate this question, let's look again at some dialogue from Shirley's lesson.

Examples provide a focal point for the lesson and illustrate concrete characteristics of abstract ideas. [Scott Teven/The Stock Connection]

Questioning allows teachers to guide student learning while also gauging learning progress. [Richard Hutchings/PhotoEdit Inc.]

Focus. Activities or materials used to attract and maintain attention during lessons.

Questioning frequency. Refers to the number of times a teacher asks questions during a given period of instructional time.

> Shirley: Let's see what we remember about adding fractions. Look at these pizzas. What fraction of one whole pizza did we eat?" After giving students time to think, she continues, "How many pieces of the first pizza did we eat? . . . Dean? (as she displayed the cardboard pizzas).
>
> Dean: Three.
>
> Shirley: And how about this pizza? How many pieces did we eat? . . . Kathy?
>
> Kathy: Two.
>
> Shirley: Why did I write ⅜ here and ⅔ there? . . . Omar? (as she pointed to the fractions she had written on the board).
>
> Omar: You have . . . 8 pieces altogether . . . and you ate 3 of them.
>
> Shirley: Good. And what about the second one? How many pieces of that pizza did we eat? . . . Selina?
>
> Selina: Two.
>
> Shirley: So what fraction of a total pizza did we eat altogether? . . . Gabriel?

In this dialogue, we see that Shirley directed each of her questions to a different student, and in each case, she addressed the student by name. This pattern illustrates **equitable distribution**, the practice of calling on all students—both volunteers and nonvolunteers—as equally as possible (Kerman, 1979). This practice sends an important message to students. By treating students equally, the teacher is saying, "I don't care whether you're a boy or girl, minority or nonminority, high achiever or low achiever, I want you in my classroom, and I want you actively involved. I believe you're capable of learning, and I will do whatever it takes to ensure that you're successful."

When a teacher practices equitable distribution, students believe that the teacher expects them to participate and learn. Perhaps even more important, because the teacher is making this effort, students believe the teacher is genuinely committed to their learning.

Equitable distribution is a powerful tool for promoting both achievement and student motivation (Stipek, 2002). In classrooms where it is practiced, student achievement rises, classroom management problems decrease, and attendance rates go up (Good & Brophy, 2003; Kerman, 1979). Equitable distribution also works at the college level; students who expect to be called on prepare more fully for class, retain more information, and have greater confidence in what they learn (McDougall & Granby, 1996).

Less-effective teachers spend more time lecturing and explaining than do effective teachers, and when they do question, they either call on volunteers or the highest achievers in their classes (S. M. Jones & Dindia, 2004). This subtly communicates that they have lower expectations for nonparticipants and also communicates that they care less about these students (Stipek, 2002).

Wait-Time

Look again at the dialogue between Shirley and her students. In each case, after asking a question, Shirley paused briefly and gave students a few seconds to think before she called on someone. This period of silence after a question is asked and after a student responds is called **wait-time**. Giving students a few seconds to think about their answers makes sense, but in most classrooms, wait-times are very short, often one second or less (Rowe, 1986; R. Stahl et al., 2005). Increasing wait-time to about 3 to 5 seconds positively influences learning in three ways (Rowe, 1986; Tobin, 1987):

- The length and quality of student responses improve.
- Failures to respond are reduced.
- Student participation in general, as well as participation from minority students, improves.

Equitable distribution. The practice of calling on all students—both volunteers and nonvolunteers—as equally as possible.

Wait-time. The amount of time a teacher pauses after asking a question both before and after calling on a student to answer.

Prompting

Equitable distribution is fine, you may be thinking, but what do I do if a student is unable to respond? Prompting provides one alternative. To understand how prompting works, let's look at some additional dialogue from Shirley's lesson.

> Shirley: Why is it [the fraction of the pizza they ate] ⅝? . . . Kevin?
> Kevin: . . .
> Shirley: How many pieces altogether in each pizza?
> Kevin: Eight.
> Shirley: Good, . . . and how many did we eat, altogether?
> Kevin: Five.

Kevin was initially unable to answer correctly, so Shirley provided him with a **prompt**, a teacher question or directive that elicits a student response after the student has failed to answer or has given an incorrect or incomplete answer. The importance of prompting is well documented by research (Good & Brophy, 2003; Shuell, 1996). As with equitable distribution, it communicates that the teacher believes the student is capable and that he or she expects the student to answer.

Less-effective teachers, instead of prompting, tend to turn the question to another student, asking, for instance, "Can someone help Kevin out here?" This communicates that the teacher doesn't believe Kevin is capable of answering and doesn't expect him to do so. This is not a message we want to send students.

This section addresses the fourth item on our beginning-of-chapter survey, "The most effective teachers in today's schools are those who are best able to clearly explain the content they are teaching their students." In fact, quite the opposite is true. The most effective teachers are those best able to involve their students in the learning process through questioning. This doesn't imply that teachers shouldn't be good at explaining; rather, it suggests that teachers' being able to guide students' developing understanding is the essence of effective instruction.

Feedback

Feedback is an important principle of learning; it is also an essential teaching skill. Have you ever been in a class where you had to wait until the midterm exam to find out how you were doing? Have you handed in assignments and had to wait weeks before they were scored and returned? In both instances, you were left uncertain about your learning progress because of the absence of feedback. Effective feedback is immediate and specific, and provides corrective information about the extent to which students' understanding of a topic is valid.

One of the most effective ways of providing feedback is through our interactions with learners. Shirley did this in her prompting of Kevin. She used questioning—and particularly prompting—to provide feedback. This kind of interactive feedback is very effective for promoting learning. It applies the learning principles that we discussed at the beginning of the chapter because it places students in cognitively active roles and guides students' construction (or reconstruction) of understanding.

Review and Closure

Effective teachers communicate lesson themes in a number of ways. One of the most effective of these is through review. **Review** is a summary that helps students link what they have already learned to what will follow in the next learning activity. It can occur at any point in a lesson, although it is most common at the beginning and end.

Beginning reviews help students activate the prior knowledge needed to understand the content of the current lesson. Shirley, for example, reviewed adding fractions with like denominators

> **Prompt.** A teacher question or directive that elicits a student response after the student has failed to answer or has given an incorrect or incomplete answer
>
> **Review.** A summary that helps students link what they have already learned to what will follow in the next learning activity.

before she began her discussion of equivalent fractions, and this review helped ensure that everyone was on the same page cognitively. Providing students with concrete examples during review increases its effectiveness by providing additional links to what students already know.

Closure is a form of review occurring at the end of a lesson. The purpose of closure is to help students organize what they've learned into a meaningful idea; it pulls the different aspects of the topic together and signals the end of a lesson. To illustrate how Shirley brought her lesson to closure, let's look again at some of the dialogue.

Shirley:	So, what is the purpose in doing what we've done here? . . . Kelly?
Kelly:	To get fractions with the same denominators so we can add them.
Shirley:	Exactly. . . . Now I'm going to give you the name. They're called EQUIVALENT FRACTIONS. . . . Now let's see what we have. What have we been doing here? . . . Toni?
Toni:	. . . We're finding equivalent fractions.
Shirley:	Good, Toni, and why do we want to find them? . . . Gary?
Gary:	. . . So we can add fractions when the denominators are not the same.

> **Closure.** A form of review occurring at the end of a lesson.

Closure summarizes ideas and reminds students of the major goal of the lesson.

exploring diversity

Effective Instruction in Urban Classrooms

In our discussions of urban contexts in earlier chapters, several themes emerged. First, urban students are diverse, with backgrounds from a number of countries and cultures (R. A. Goldstein, 2004; Rosenshine, 2006). Second, many urban learners struggle in school, the result of a number of factors including large schools and crowded classrooms, less-experienced teachers, and inadequate funding and facilities (Armour-Thomas, 2004). These themes have several implications for effective instruction in urban classrooms.

The Need for Examples

As we saw earlier in the chapter, the need for high-quality examples is important for all learners, regardless of context. However, because of the diversity of urban students' prior experiences, high-quality examples are critical when teaching in urban classrooms. These examples help minimize differences in urban students' backgrounds by providing a concrete and common frame of reference for classroom discussions. For example, a science teacher explaining the concept of density might use the following examples:

- A clear plastic glass filled with cotton that can be compressed
- Several different pieces of screening that are the same size but have different numbers of meshes in them
- Bringing several different-sized groups of students to stand in the same area of the classroom.

By using examples such as these in the classroom, the teacher minimizes the need for background experiences and provides a common frame of reference to explore the concept of density. In addition to examples, graphs, models, visuals, and concrete objects are especially valuable for English Language Learners who struggle with both content and language (Echevarria, Powers, & Short, 2006).

Effective urban teachers also attempt to connect their examples to situations with which their students can identify. For example, a world history teacher in an urban high school was discussing the rise of nationalism as an important factor in the events leading up to World War I. The concept was defined in students' textbooks as a feeling of loyalty and devotion to one's country, language, and culture. This definition is both abstract and distant from the world in which these urban students lived. In an attempt to personalize the concept and connect it to students' lives, the teacher related nationalism to the rivalries their athletic teams had with other urban high schools in the area, emphasizing both loyalties within their school as well as competition with other schools. Students started nodding as they began to understand how nationalism could be both a uniting and divisive force. Urban students, like students in general, sometimes wonder how abstract ideas relate to their lives; making explicit links between new content and their day-to-day experiences increases not only learning but also motivation (Rosenshine, 2006).

The Need for Interactive Instruction

When working in challenging environments, teachers have a tendency to revert to instructional strategies that afford them the most control. This often results in the use of an inordinate amount of passive learning activities like lecture and seat work (Duke, 2000; Eggen, 1998). One urban high school student complained,

In my chemistry class, the teacher just keeps going and going and writing on the board. She never stops to ask the class, "Is

IN TODAY'S CLASSROOMS: VIDEO

Essential Teaching Skills in an Urban Classroom

To view this video, go to the *Becoming a Professional* DVD included with this text, click on *In Today's Classrooms*, and then this chapter's video: *Essential Teaching Skills in an Urban Classroom*. Answer the questions you'll find on the DVD.

In this video episode, Scott Sowell, a middle school teacher in an urban classroom, demonstrates essential teaching skills in a science lesson.

*To answer questions about the video online and receive immediate feedback, go to the Companion Website at **www.prenhall.com/kauchak**, then to the* In Today's Classrooms *module for Chapter 12.*   CW

---

everyone with me?" She's in her own little world. She never turns around, she just talks to the board, not to us. (Cushman, 2003, p. 8)

Exactly the opposite is needed. "A great deal of classroom research suggests that students need active instruction from their teachers, not solitary work with instructional materials, in order to make good achievement progress" (Brophy, 2004, p. 155).

In a comparison of more- and less-effective urban elementary teachers, researchers found that less-effective teachers interacted with students only 47 percent of the time versus 70 percent of the time for their more-effective counterparts (Waxman, Huang, Anderson, & Weinstein, 1997). Interactive teaching is characteristic of good instruction in general; its importance with urban students is crucial (Barr & Parrett, 2001; Rosenshine, 2006).

A common teacher lament is, "I tried calling on students but they either couldn't or wouldn't answer." This is why concrete examples and questioning skills such as prompting are so important. The examples provide a common focal point and frame of reference for all students; teacher questions help students use those examples to construct meaning. With teacher support and encouragement, urban students can learn to construct and connect ideas, and improved motivation and increased learning will result.

Equitable distribution is also essential in urban classrooms. Nothing better communicates that you expect all students to achieve and that you're holding them accountable for learning than developing lessons with questioning, calling on all students, and prompting them when necessary to ensure that all participate. Making equitable distribution the prevailing pattern in your classroom can do more than anything else to communicate that you believe that all your students can learn and you expect them to do so.

The Need for Practice and Feedback

Effective teaching also provides urban students opportunities to actively try out their developing ideas and receive feedback about them. You saw both at the beginning of the chapter and in our discussion of essential teaching skills that feedback is an essential learning principle, and, as with high-quality examples and interactive questioning, it is even more important when working with urban students. The knowledge different urban students construct is likely to vary considerably because their background experiences tend to be very diverse. This means that detailed discussions of assignments, homework, and quiz and test results are essential when working with urban students. Time spent providing detailed feedback about student work provides a tangible link between you and your students and assists them in constructing new knowledge.

Student success is critical in the process (Brophy, 2004). Because urban students may not have a history of successful school experiences, lack of success can result in frustration for them and can further detract from motivation that may already be low.

By now you might be saying to yourself, "Wait a minute. Aren't these procedures for urban students just good teaching?" If you did, you're absolutely correct. Effective instructional practices for urban students are not qualitatively different from those for "regular" students. The same principles of good teaching that work in the regular classroom also work with urban students. It is, however, all the more critical that teachers apply effective instructional practices conscientiously and thoroughly with urban students. Collectively, these practices provide an instructional safety net that minimizes the possibility for frustration and failure, two factors that are especially damaging for urban students.

Check Your Understanding

3.1   As middle schoolers walk into their geography class, they see a large matrix comparing the climate, geography, and economy of the northern and southern states before the Civil War. As soon as the bell stops ringing, the teacher says, "Write a minimum of two differences each in the geography, climate, and economy columns of the chart." The students begin, and as they're writing, the teacher takes roll. Which of the essential teaching skills does this example best illustrate? Explain.

3.2   Shirley used her cardboard pizzas in her review, and she used her cakes to introduce the topic of *equivalent fractions.* Which essential teaching skill did the use of these materials best illustrate? Explain.

3.3   Identify at least two essential teaching skills that are illustrated in each of the chapters of this book.

For feedback, go to Appendix A, Check Your Understanding, *located in the back of this text.*

Making Connections:
To deepen your understanding of the topics in this section of the chapter and integrate them with topics you've already studied, go to the *Making Connections* module for Chapter 12 at **www.prenhall.com/kauchak**. Respond to questions 7–10.

Models of Instruction

In addition to essential teaching skills, effective teachers also employ a number of alternate teaching strategies or models in their classrooms. **Models of instruction** are prescriptive approaches to teaching designed to help students acquire a deep understanding of specific forms of knowledge. They are grounded in the principles of learning you saw at the beginning of the chapter, are supported by research, and include sets of steps designed to help students reach specified learning objectives.

Research indicates that no single instructional model is most effective for all students or for helping students reach all learning objectives (Kroesbergen & van Luit, 2002; Marzano, 2003). This research indicates that the final item on our beginning-of-chapter survey, "Rather than exclusively using one particular teaching strategy, effective teachers vary their instruction" is true. Effective teachers use a variety of instructional strategies, depending on the content and students they are teaching (Eggen & Kauchak, 2006). In this section, we examine four instructional models, the first two of which are teacher directed, and the third and fourth, more learner centered. They are:

- Direct instruction
- Lecture-discussion
- Guided discovery
- Cooperative learning

Direct Instruction

Direct instruction is an instructional strategy designed to teach essential knowledge and skills that are needed for later learning (Eggen & Kauchak, 2006), and its effectiveness is well documented by research (Carnine, Silbert, Kame'enui, Tarver, & Jongjohann, 2006; Kroesbergen, van Luit, & Maas, 2004). Understanding equivalent fractions and adding fractions with both like and unlike denominators, which were the focus of Shirley's lesson, are examples of essential knowledge and skills, as are students' acquiring specific writing strategies, chemistry students' learning to balance equations, and geography students' using longitude and latitude to pinpoint locations. Direct instruction is useful when skills can be broken down into specific steps and has

Models of instruction. Prescriptive approaches to teaching designed to help students acquire a deep understanding of specific forms of knowledge.

Direct instruction. An instructional strategy designed to teach well-defined knowledge and skills that are needed for later learning.

been found to be particularly effective in working with low achievers and students with exceptionalities (Kroesbergen et al., 2004; Turnbull, Turnbull, Shank, Smith, & Leal, 2007).

Direct instruction ranges from a highly structured, nearly scripted approach (Carnine et al., 2006) to one that is more flexible in its implementation (Eggen & Kauchak, 2006). We discuss the latter here, which typically occurs in four phases, outlined in Table 12.4 and discussed in the following sections.

Shirley used direct instruction in her lesson. Let's see how she implemented each of the phases.

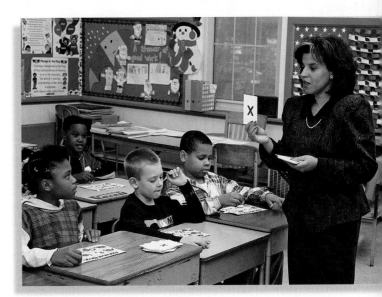

Direct instruction provides students with opportunities to practice new knowledge and skills. [Scott Cunningham/Merrill]

Introduction and Review

Shirley introduced her lesson using her cardboard pizzas as examples. The purpose in using the pizzas was to attract students' attention and pull them into the lesson. She then had students solve problems involving the addition of fractions with like denominators. This review served as the springboard for her lesson on finding equivalent fractions.

The value of introduction and review is well established by research, and although its importance seems obvious, the majority of teacher lessons begin with little or no attempt to attract attention or activate relevant prior knowledge (Brophy, 2004).

Developing Understanding

In the developing understanding phase of the direct instruction model, the teacher models and explains the skill being taught. Developing understanding is perhaps the most important phase of direct instruction, and ironically, it is the one teachers often perform least well. Instead of working to develop student understanding, they often emphasize memorization, fail to ask enough questions, or move too quickly to practice (Rittle-Johnson & Alibali, 1999).

Shirley's lesson was very effective in this phase. She began with her "cakes" and, in the process, asked a great many questions to ensure that her students engaged with and understood the new ideas she presented. She continued providing examples and modeled the

TABLE 12.4   The Phases of Direct Instruction

Phase	Purpose
Introduction and review: Teachers begin with a review of previous work.	• Attract students' attention. • Access learners' prior knowledge.
Developing understanding: Teachers describe and model the skill or guide students to an understanding of the concept. Teachers use many examples and emphasize high levels of student involvement.	• Develop students' understanding of the concept or skill.
Guided practice: Students practice the skill or identify additional examples of the concept, and the teacher provides guidance and detailed feedback.	• Increase students' expertise with the concept or skill.
Independent practice: Students practice on their own.	• Develop students' understanding to the point where they can identify examples of the concept or perform the skill with little effort.

process for finding equivalent fractions by multiplying the numerator and denominator by the same number. She didn't move to guided practice until she was confident that most of her students had a thorough understanding of the process. This is essential for the success of the next phase, guided practice (Kauchak & Eggen, 2007; Kroesbergen et al., 2004).

Guided Practice

Guided practice provides students with opportunities to try out the new skill and for teachers to provide feedback about learning progress. Once Shirley felt most students understood the concept of equivalent fractions and knew how to create them, she assigned three problems that required students to find equivalent fractions and asked them to solve the first one. As they worked, she carefully monitored their progress and then provided detailed feedback about the first problem before asking the students to solve the second one. She repeated this process with both the second and third problems. Had students struggled, she would have had them solve additional problems under her guidance until she believed they were ready to practice independently on their own.

Independent Practice

In the final phase of direct instruction, independent practice, Shirley helped students make the transition from working under her guidance to working on their own. The goal in this phase is for students' understanding to be developed to the point that they can perform the operation with little conscious effort. During independent practice, the teacher reduces the amount of support she gives and shifts responsibility to the students.

Teacher monitoring continues to be important, however. Effective teachers carefully monitor students to assess their developing understanding (Safer & Fleischman, 2005); less-effective teachers are more likely to merely check to see that students are on task (e.g., on the right page and following directions).

Homework is one type of independent practice, and when properly used, it can reinforce students' developing understanding and skills (H. Cooper et al., 2006; Kohn, 2006). *Properly used* means that teachers assign homework that is an extension of what students have studied and practiced in class; that is, it is aligned with learning objectives and learning activities (Bransford et al., 2000). Although grading homework can be time-consuming, teachers should have some mechanism for giving students credit and providing feedback if they are to take it seriously and use it as a learning tool.

Lecture-Discussion

Lecture-discussion is an instructional strategy designed to help students acquire **organized bodies of knowledge**, topics that connect facts, concepts, and principles, and make the relationships among them explicit (Eggen & Kauchak, 2006). For example, when students examine relationships among plot, character, and symbolism in a novel such as *Moby Dick* in literature; study landforms, climate, and economy in different regions of the world in geography; or compare parasitic and nonparasitic worms and how differences between them are reflected in their body structures in biology, they are acquiring organized bodies of knowledge.

Lecture-discussions are designed to overcome the weaknesses of traditional lectures, which include the following:

- Lectures place learners in passive roles. This is inconsistent with the principles of learning that you saw at the beginning of the chapter and is arguably the primary disadvantage of the strategy. Because of the large amounts of teacher talk and passive student roles, lectures are ineffective for attracting and maintaining student attention. We have all sat through mind-numbing lectures with the goal of simply getting the time to pass more quickly.
- Lectures involve one-way communication and don't allow teachers to determine whether or not students are interpreting or learning information accurately.
- Teachers often present too much information in lectures, so much of it is lost before students can make sense of it.

Lecture-discussion. An instructional model designed to help students acquire organized bodies of knowledge and understand the relationships of ideas within them.

Organized bodies of knowledge. Topics that connect facts, concepts, generalizations, and principles, and make the relationships among them explicit.

TABLE 12.5   The Phases of Lecture-Discussions

Phase	Purpose
Introduction and review: The teacher begins with a form of introductory focus and reviews previous work.	• Attract attention. • Access prior knowledge from long-term memory.
Presenting information: The teacher presents information. Presentations are kept short to prevent overloading learners' working memories.	• Acquire knowledge about the topic.
Comprehension monitoring: The teacher asks a series of questions to check learners' understanding.	• Check students' ongoing knowledge constructions. • Put students in active roles. • Begin constructing integrated ideas.
Integration: The teacher asks additional questions to help learners integrate new and prior knowledge.	• Construct integrated ideas that connect concepts, both old and new.

Lecture-discussions help overcome the weaknesses of lectures by interspersing short periods of presenting information with systematic teacher questioning.

As with direct instruction, lecture-discussions exist in four phases, which are outlined in Table 12.5 and discussed in the sections that follow.

Let's see how a 10th-grade American history teacher implements these phases with her students.

Diane Anderson is discussing the events leading up to the American Revolutionary War in her American history high school class. She begins with a review by saying, "About where are we now in our progress?" as she points to a time line above the chalkboard.

"About there," Adam responds, pointing to the middle of the 1700s.

"Yes, good," Diane smiles. "We're almost to the Revolutionary War. However, I would like for us to understand important events that lead up to that war, so we're going to back up a ways, actually, all the way to the early 1600s. When we're finished today, we'll see that the Revolutionary War didn't just happen; there were events that led up to it that made it almost inevitable. . . . That's the important part of history . . . to see how events that happen at one time affect events at other times, and all the way to today.

"For instance," Diane continues, "the conflicts between the British and the French in America became so costly for the British that they began policies in the colonies that ultimately led to the Revolution. That's what we want to begin looking at today. . . . Here we go."

She then begins, "We know that the British established Jamestown in 1607, but we haven't really looked at French expansion into the New World. Let's look again at the map. Here we see Jamestown, but at about the same time, a French explorer named Champlain came down the St. Lawrence River and formed Quebec City, here." She points again to the map. "Over the years, at least 35 of the 50 states were discovered or mapped by the French, and they founded several of our big cities, such as Detroit, St. Louis, New Orleans, and Des Moines." She continues pointing to a series of locations she had marked on the map.

"Now, what do you notice about the location of the two groups?"

After thinking a few seconds, Alfredo offers, "The French had a lot of Canada, . . . and it looks like this country, too," pointing to the north and west on the map.

"It looks like the east was . . . British, and the west was French," Troy adds.

"Yes, and remember, this was all happening at about the same time," Diane continues. "Also, the French were more friendly with the American Indians than the British were. Also, the French had what they called a seigniorial system, where the settlers were given land if they would serve in the military. So, . . . what does this suggest about the military power of the French?"

"Probably powerful," Josh suggests. "The people got land if they went in the army."

"And the American Indians probably helped, because they were friendly with the French," Tenisha adds.

"Now, what else do you notice here?" Diane asks, moving her hand back and forth across the width of the map.

"Mountains?" Danielle answers uncertainly.

"Yes, exactly," Diane smiles. "Why are they important? What do mountains do?"

". . . The British were sort of fenced in, and the French could expand and do as they pleased."

"Good. And now the plot thickens. The British needed land and wanted to expand. So they headed west over the mountains and guess who they ran into? . . . Sarah?"

"The French?" Sarah responded.

"Right! And conflict broke out. Now, when the French and British were fighting, why do you suppose the French were initially more successful than the British? . . . Dan?"

"Well, they had that sig . . . seigniorial system, so they were more eager to fight, because of the land and everything."

"Other thoughts? . . . Bette?"

"I think that the American Indians were part of it. The French got along better with them, so they helped the French."

"Okay, good thinking everyone, now let's think about the British. . . . Let's look at some of their advantages." (Adapted from Eggen & Kauchak, 2007)

Let's look now at Diane's efforts to help her students understand events leading up to the Revolutionary War, an organized body of knowledge. She introduced the lesson with a review and attempted to capture students' *attention* by explaining how events in the past influence the way we live today. Then, she *presented information* about Jamestown, Quebec, and French settlements in the present-day United States. After this brief presentation, she used questioning to involve her students in the *comprehension-monitoring* phase. To illustrate this phase, let's look at some of the dialogue from the lesson.

> Diane: Now, what do you notice about the location of the two groups?
> Alfredo: The French had a lot of Canada, . . . and it looks like this country, too (pointing to the north and west on the map).
> Troy: It looks like the east was . . . British, and the west was French.

Diane's questions were intended to actively involve students, check their level of understanding, and help them construct understanding of the body of knowledge. Satisfied with their level of understanding, she returned to presenting information when she said, "Yes, and remember, this was all happening at about the same time." She continued by briefly describing the French seignorial system and pointing out the friendly relations between the French and American Indians.

Then she again turned back to the students.

> Diane: So, . . . what does this suggest about the military power of the French?
> Josh: Probably powerful. The people got land if they went in the army.
> Tenisha: And the American Indians probably helped, because they were friendly with the French.

The two segments appear similar, but there is an important distinction. In the first, Diane was *monitoring comprehension;* students' responses to the question, "Now, what do you notice about the location of the two groups?" helped her assess their perceptions of what she had presented in the first segment. In the second, she encouraged students to *integrate* different ideas, including the seigniorial system, the relationship between the French and the American Indians, and French military power.

After completing this cycle of *presenting information, monitoring comprehension,* and *integration,* she would repeat the process, with the second integration being broader than the first. Diane's goal for the entire lesson was for her students to understand a complex body of knowledge that represented the cause–effect relationships between the French and Indian Wars and the American Revolutionary War.

The effectiveness of lecture-discussions depends on the quality of discussions during the lesson. As you saw in the discussion of learning principles at the beginning of the chapter, students construct understanding that makes sense to them, so the understanding they construct won't necessarily mirror the way the teacher has organized the body of knowledge. The question-driven discussions allow the teacher to assess the process of knowledge construction and help students reconstruct their understanding when necessary. This is the primary reason lecture-discussion is a more effective instructional model than traditional lecture.

Guided Discovery

Guided discovery is an instructional model designed to teach concepts and relationships among them (Eggen & Kauchak, 2006; Mayer, 2004). When using this strategy, teachers present students with examples, guide them as they attempt to find patterns in the examples, and come to closure when students can describe the idea that the teacher is attempting to teach (Clark & Mayer, 2003; Moreno, 2004). It is often contrasted with "pure" or unstructured discovery, where learners identify patterns and relationships without guidance from a teacher. Research indicates that unstructured discovery is less effective than guided approaches because students don't use time efficiently; without help, students often become lost and frustrated; and this confusion can lead to misconceptions (Clark & Mayer, 2003; Mayer, 2002, 2004). As a result, unstructured discovery is rarely seen in today's classrooms, except in student projects and investigations.

When done well, guided discovery's effectiveness is supported by research: "Guided discovery may take more or less time than expository instruction, depending on the task, but tends to result in better long-term retention and transfer than expository instruction" (Mayer, 2002, p. 68). When using guided discovery, teachers spend less time explaining and more time asking questions, so students tend to be more cognitively active than they are in more teacher-centered approaches (Bay, Staver, Bryan, & Hale, 1992; Moreno & Duran, 2004).

As with direct instruction and lecture-discussion, guided discovery exists in four phases, which are outlined in Table 12.6.

Essential Teaching Skills in an Urban Classroom, which is the *In Today's Classrooms* episode on the DVD that accompanies this text, illustrates a guided discovery lesson. In that episode, Scott's goal is for students to understand Bernoulli's principle, the principle that helps explain how airplanes are able to fly, why shower curtains wrap around people's legs when they're taking a shower, and why cars feel a slight tug when a large truck whisks past them. If you haven't seen the episode, we urge you to watch it before continuing with your reading here so that you'll have a concrete frame of reference for our discussion.

Let's look at Scott's lesson in more detail.

> **Guided discovery.** An instructional model designed to teach concepts and relationships among them through the use of examples.

TABLE 12.6   Phases of Guided Discovery

Phase	Learning Component
Introduction and review: The teacher begins with a review and introduction to the topic.	• Attract attention • Activate students' prior knowledge
Developing understanding: The teacher provides examples and guides the students as they identify patterns in the examples.	• Provide experiences from which knowledge will be constructed • Promote social interaction
Closure: The teacher guides the students as they describe the pattern they've identified in the examples.	• Complete construction of understanding of the topic
Application: Students identify additional examples of the concept, or they explain a real-world event on the basis of the rule or principle.	• Apply understanding to the real world

Introduction and Review

Scott began his lesson by reviewing the concept of force and the principle, "Objects move in the direction of a greater force." As with Shirley Barton in her review of adding fractions, his was very effective because in reviewing the concept *force,* he used examples to illustrate force, such as pushing on the board, tugging on the stapler, and blowing on a walkie talkie. Then, he used additional examples to illustrate the principle "Objects move in the direction of the greater force."

Developing Understanding

Scott then had students blow over pieces of paper, between the papers, and through the necks of funnels; each was an example that illustrated Bernoulli's principle. After students worked with each example, Scott asked for observations, such as, "What did you notice when we blew over the top?" The open-ended questions promoted active involvement and helped students begin to develop their understanding.

Scott then drew sketches on the board and had students restate the essential observations and conclusions. Let's look at some dialogue from the lesson that illustrates this process.

> Scott: Was I blowing on the top or the bottom? . . . Rachel? (Referring to the first sketch on the board where students blew over the top of paper)
> Rachel: The top.
> Scott: And what happened there? . . . Heather?
> Heather: The paper rose up.

He did a similar analysis with the second and third examples and then guided students as they formed conclusions.

> Scott: Let's think about the forces acting on these [turning back to the first sketch]. What forces are acting on the paper? . . . Colin?
> Colin: Gravity.
> Scott: And which direction is gravity pulling?
> Colin: Down.
> Scott: What other force is acting on the paper? . . . William?
> William: Air [pointing up].
> Scott: How do you know it's pushing up?
> William: The paper moved up.

Through questioning, teachers help students analyze patterns in the examples they encounter to form abstractions, such as concepts, generalizations, and principles. This occurs in the closure phase of the model.

Closure

Scott then moved the lesson to closure, beginning the process by saying, "Now let's look at the forces and where we blew. Study the drawings carefully, and see what kind of relationship exists between the two," and he continued to use questioning to guide students' developing understanding. Teacher questioning in this phase continues to be essential (Moreno, 2004; Moreno & Duran, 2004).

Closure is particularly important when using guided discovery because the instruction is less explicit and the direction the lesson is taking is less obvious than it is with either direct instruction or lecture-discussion. Articulating the definition of a concept or stating the principle, as was the case in Scott's lesson, helps eliminate any uncertainty that may remain in students' thinking about the specific content focus of the lesson.

Application

Applying understanding to new and real-world situations is the final phase of a guided discovery lesson. For example, Scott could ask the students to explain how Bernoulli's principle helps us understand why airplanes can fly. He would then guide them to conclude that the force the air exerts on the top of the wing is less than on the bottom, since the air is moving more rapidly over the top. This causes the wing to lift and the airplane to fly.

The application phase in guided discovery serves a function similar to independent practice in direct instruction and to integration in lecture-discussion. In all three cases, the goal is for the students to develop a deeper understanding of the topic they've studied.

Cooperative Learning

A kindergarten teacher is teaching her students basic shapes. After explaining and illustrating each with cardboard shapes, she divides the class into groups of two and asks each group to find examples of circles, squares, and triangles in their own classroom. When the class comes back together, students share their examples.

A middle school math teacher is teaching how to solve word problems involving areas of different geometric shapes. She divides the class into teams of four students and asks each team to solve the next few problems. Students in each team take turns explaining their solutions to the problems. Later, the teams take turns at the board explaining how they solved the different problems.

A senior high English teacher is reviewing literary devices such as simile, metaphor, personification, and alliteration. He assigns a scene from Shakespeare's Julius Caesar and asks students in groups of two to identify as many of these devices as they can. The whole class compares their findings after 15 minutes.

What do these lessons have in common? They are all examples of cooperative learning strategies being employed at different grade levels. **Cooperative learning** is a set of instructional strategies used to help learners meet specific learning and social interaction objectives in structured groups. As its name implies, it relies on cooperative social interaction to facilitate knowledge construction, so it is based on the learning principle "Learning is enhanced by social interaction." It has become one of the most popular instructional models in schools today; one study found that 93 percent of elementary teachers used some form of cooperative learning in their classrooms (Antil, Jenkins, Wayne, & Vadasy, 1998).

When implemented effectively, cooperative learning involves all students, which can be difficult in large groups. In whole-class discussions, less-confident students may get few chances to participate, so they often drift off.

Cooperative learning can also be effective for teaching students to collaborate in learning (Payton, Munro, O'Brien, & Weissberg, 2006). By participating in cooperative learn-

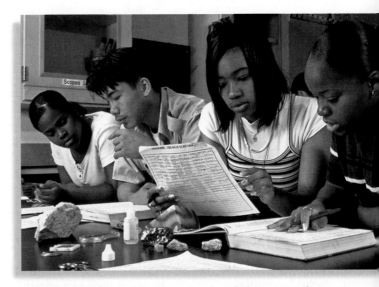

Cooperative learning activities encourage knowledge construction through social interaction. [Will Hart/PhotoEdit Inc.]

ing activities, students learn to understand the needs and feelings of others as well as how to build on the ideas of others in constructing knowledge. Advocates also argue that groups of learners co-construct more powerful understandings than individuals do alone, affirming the maxim "Two heads are better than one" (Summers, Woodruff, Tomberlin, Williams, & Svinicki, 2001). This external, co-constructed knowledge can then be internalized by individual students, facilitating learning (Brenner, 2001).

Though the specific form varies with the specific model being used, most researchers agree that cooperative learning consists of students working together in groups small enough (typically two to five) so that everyone can participate in a clearly assigned task

> **Cooperative learning.** A set of instructional strategies used to help learners meet specific learning and social interaction objectives in structured groups.

(D. Johnson & Johnson, 2006). They also agree that cooperative learning shares at least four other features:

- Learning objectives direct the groups' activities.
- Social interaction is emphasized.
- Students are held individually accountable for their understanding.
- Learners depend on one another to reach objectives.

The last characteristic is important because it emphasizes the crucial role that peer cooperation plays in learning (D. Johnson & Johnson, 2006). Accountability is also essential because it keeps students focused on the objectives and reminds them that learning is the purpose of the activity.

Unlike the first three models we discussed, cooperative learning activities don't follow a specific set of steps or phases. However, successful implementation of cooperative learning activities requires careful teacher thought and planning. We examine factors influencing its success in the following sections.

Introducing Cooperative Learning

Introducing students to cooperative learning requires careful planning (Gillies, 2000; Terwel et al., 2001). Poorly organized activities can result in less learning than whole-group lessons (Brophy, 2006).

Suggestions for initially organizing cooperative learning activities include the following:

- Seat group members together, so they can move back and forth from group work to whole-class activities with little disruption.
- Have learning materials ready for easy distribution to each group.
- Introduce students to cooperative learning with short, simple tasks, and make objectives and directions clear.
- Specify the amount of time students have to accomplish the task (and keep it relatively short).
- Monitor groups while they work.
- Require that students produce a product as a result of the cooperative learning activity (e.g., written answers to specific questions).

These characteristics maximize the time available for learning and provide a focal point for students' cooperative learning efforts.

Cooperative Learning Strategies

Different models of cooperative learning are all grounded in the learning principle "Learning is enhanced by social interaction," but each is designed to accomplish different objectives. Different models are outlined in Table 12.7. Other cooperative learning strategies exist, and although they differ in format, all are grounded in this basic principle.

As we said at the beginning of the chapter, our goal in writing it is for you to see examples of effective planning and implementation of instruction. We realize that you won't be able to implement the essential teaching skills or the teaching models described in this chapter after one reading. These are sophisticated abilities that require time and effort to learn. They are intended, instead, to introduce you to effective instruction, so you have ideals for which you can look when you observe in classrooms and toward which you can strive as you move toward becoming a true professional.

Making Connections

CW To deepen your understanding of the topics in this section of the chapter and integrate them with topics you've already studied, go to the *Making Connections* module for Chapter 12 at **www.prenhall.com/kauchak**. Respond to questions 11–13.

TABLE 12.7   Cooperative Learning Models

Model	Description	Example
Reciprocal Questioning	Pairs work together to ask and answer questions about a lesson or text	Teacher provides question stems, such as "Summarize . . ." or "Why was . . . important?" and students use the stems to create specific questions about the topic.
Scripted Cooperation	Pairs work together to elaborate on each other's thinking	*Math:* First member of a pair offers a problem solution. The second member then elaborates, and the process is repeated. *Reading:* Pairs read a passage and the first member offers a summary. The second elaborates, and the process continues.
Jigsaw II	Individuals become expert on subsections of a topic and teach it to others in their group	One student studies the geography of a region; another, the economy; a third, the climate. Each attends "expert" meetings, and the "experts" then teach their content to others in their group.
Student Teams Achievement Divisions (STADs)	Social interaction is used to help students learn facts, concepts, and skills	The independent-practice phase of direct instruction is replaced with team study, during which team members check and compare their answers. Team study is followed by quizzes, and individual improvement points lead to team awards.

teaching in an era of reform

Teacher-Centered Versus Learner-Centered Instruction

How active a role should teachers play in directing student learning? As we saw in the previous section, different instructional models suggest different roles for teachers as they guide and assist student learning. Historically, classroom instruction was *teacher centered*, which means that teachers carefully specify goals, present the content to be learned, and then direct learning activities (Shuell, 1996). Lecture is an example, as are traditional forms of direct instruction. Both define a central teacher role in presenting information and monitoring learning progress.

Criticisms of teacher-centered instruction led to a wave of reform, resulting in what is commonly called *learner-centered instruction*, in which teachers guide learners toward an understanding of the topics they study, rather than telling or lecturing. This was the approach that Scott Sowell employed in using guided discovery to teach Bernoulli's principle. Prominent professional publications emphasizing this approach to instruction include *How Students Learn: Reforming Our Schools Through Learner-Centered Education*, published by the American Psychological Association in 1998, and *The Right to Learn*, which was written by well-known Columbia University educator Linda Darling-Hammond and published in 1997.

The Issue

Critics of teacher-centered instruction argue that it is based on outdated views of learning that emphasize teacher actions rather than student understanding (S. Lee, 2006; Pogrow, 2006). The following episode, in which a teacher is attempting to help her third graders understand place value, illustrates this criticism:

The teacher, based on the directions given in the teacher's manual, begins by putting 45 tally marks on the chalkboard and circles four groups of 10.

Teacher:	*How many groups of 10 do we have there, boys and girls?*
Children:	*4.*
Teacher:	*We have 4 groups of 10, and how many left over?*
Children:	*5.*
Teacher:	*We had 4 tens and how many left over?*
Beth:	*4 tens.*
Sarah:	*5.*

(continued)

Teacher:	*5. Now, can anybody tell me what number that could be? We have 4 tens and 5 ones. What is that number? Ann?*
Ann:	*(Remains silent)*
Teacher:	*If we have 4 tens and 5 ones, what is that number?*
Ann:	*9.*
Teacher:	*Look at how many we have there (points to the 4 groups of ten) and 5 ones. If we have 4 tens and 5 ones we have? (slight pause) 45.*
Children:	*45.*
Teacher:	*Very good. (T. Wood, Cobb, & Yackel, 1992, p. 180)*

As the dialogue suggests, Ann and probably many others in the class didn't understand place value, but the teacher did little to increase their understanding. Once students gave the desired response, they were reinforced with "Very good," and the lesson moved on, despite the fact that students didn't really understand the point of the lesson. This happens all too often in teacher-centered instruction that fails to actively engage students' minds.

Critics also point to research indicating that student verbalization or overt performance at the expense of understanding occurs in many classrooms (Goodlad, 1984; Opdenakker & Van Damme, 2006). Critics contend that all too often teacher-centered approaches to instruction make learners passive observers during instruction (J. Wallace & Wildly, 2004) and that "the most effective learning takes place when students . . . play an active role in making sense of ideas" (Kohn, 1999, p. 43).

Learner-centered instruction proponents argue further that this approach focuses on learning and individual learners to a greater extent than does teacher-centered instruction (S. Lee, 2006), and they point to research indicating that a learner-centered teaching style is particularly effective with low-ability students (Opdenakker & Van Damme, 2006). In addition, learner-centered instruction not only teaches content but also develops critical thinking skills that students can use in their lives (Kuhn, 2005; I. Winn, 2005).

Critics of learner-centered instruction counter by saying that the approach is one more example of widespread "dumbing down" of the curriculum, that learning basic skills is abandoned in favor of fuzzy thinking, and self-esteem is emphasized instead of understanding (Battista, 1999; Schoen, Fey, Hirsch, & Coxford, 1999). They defend teacher-centered instruction by asserting that the lack of understanding so prominent in classrooms is not the result of teacher-centered instruction per se; it is with teachers' inability to implement it effectively. When teacher-centered instruction is done effectively, they argue, none of the criticisms is valid, and they point to research indicating that teacher-centered approaches, such as direct instruction, can be effective in a variety of situations (Carnine et al., 2006). Because of these criticisms, as well as pressures to help students meet accountability standards, a pendulum shift back in the direction of teacher-centered instruction is currently occurring (Pogrow, 2006). Whether this pendulum shift will result in increased student learning is currently unclear.

You Take a Position

Now it's your turn to take a position on the issue. State in writing whether you favor learner-centered instruction or teacher-centered instruction, and provide a two-page rationale for your position.

For additional references and resources, go to the Companion Website at **www.prenhall.com/kauchak**, *then to the* Teaching in an Era of Reform *module for Chapter 12. You can respond online or submit your response to your instructor.*

Check Your Understanding

4.1 Using the principles of learning presented at the beginning of the chapter as a basis, explain why the introduction phase is important in direct instruction, lecture-discussion, and guided discovery.

4.2 Which phase of direct instruction is most important for ensuring successful independent practice? Explain.

4.3 We said, "When guided discovery is done well, research supports its effectiveness." What is necessary in order for instruction to be "done well"? Explain.

4.4 A teacher places her third graders in groups of three and gives each group magnets and a packet including a dime, spoon, aluminum foil, rubber band, wooden pencil, paper clip, and nails. She tells the groups to experiment with the magnets and items for 10 minutes and write their observations on paper. As they work, she answers questions and makes comments. The class as a whole group discusses the results. How effectively did the teacher begin this cooperative learning activity with her students? Cite evidence from the example to support your conclusion.

 For feedback, go to Appendix A, Check Your Understanding, *located in the back of this text.*

decision making

Defining Yourself as a Professional

You're a middle school life science teacher beginning a unit on the different body systems, such as the skeletal, the circulatory, the digestive, and the muscular systems. You plan to begin with the skeletal system, and you want your students to understand the relationship between the structures and the functions of the different parts of the skeleton, such as understanding that the skull is essentially solid because it protects the brain, which is the most important organ in the body; the rib cage exists to protect other important organs, such as the heart and lungs; and the leg bones are *the size and shape they are because they support the body as we stand and move.*

What models of instruction could you use to help you reach your goals? Explain why you would use those models.

To respond to this question online and receive immediate feedback, go to the Decision Making module for Chapter 12 on the Companion Website at www.prenhall.com/kauchak.

Meeting Your Learning Objectives

1. **Describe the principles of cognitive learning theory, and identify examples of the principles in practice.**
   - Cognitive learning theory suggests that learning depends on experiences; people construct knowledge in an attempt to make sense of those experiences; knowledge that is constructed depends on and builds on what learners already know; social interaction enhances learning; and learning requires practice and feedback.
   - Teachers apply these learning principles when they use high-quality examples in their teaching, promote high levels of teacher–student and student–student interaction, give students a chance to practice their newly acquired knowledge and skills, and make assessment an integral part of the teaching–learning process.

2. **Describe essential steps in planning for instruction.**
   - Planning for instruction involves identifying topics; specifying learning objectives; preparing and organizing learning activities; designing assessments; and ensuring that instruction is aligned, that is, ensuring that learning activities and assessments are consistent with objectives.
   - Finding or creating high-quality examples or problems is the most important part of preparing and organizing learning activities, and this is a major reason that specifying clear learning objectives is so important. If objectives are clear, then teachers know what information the examples should contain, and they can then attempt to find or create them.
   - Planning in a standards-based environment often requires teachers to first interpret the standard. Once the standard is clearly understood, the teacher can construct learning objectives and design learning activities.

3. **Explain how essential teaching skills contribute to learning.**
   - Effective teachers are well organized, which means they begin their lessons on time, have their materials prepared and ready, and have well-established routines in their classrooms.
   - Effective teachers communicate clearly, use focus to attract students' attention, involve students through questioning, provide informative feedback, and use reviews to activate students' prior knowledge.

(continued)

4. Explain relationships between principles of learning and different phases of models of instruction.
   - Each of the models of instruction begins with an introduction and review. This phase activates students' prior knowledge and is based on the learning principle "Knowledge that is constructed depends and builds on knowledge that learners already possess."
   - In the *developing-understanding* phases of the models, learners acquire experiences that they use as a basis for constructing the knowledge about the topic being taught.
   - Each of the models strongly emphasizes social interaction between the teacher and students and the students with each other, which is grounded in the learning principle "Learning is enhanced by social interaction."

Important Concepts

assessment (p. 383)
closure (p. 374)
cognitive learning theories (p. 377)
cooperative learning (p. 403)
direct instruction (p. 396)
effective instruction (p. 379)
emphasis (p. 390)
equitable distribution (p. 392)
essential teaching skills (p. 385)
feedback (p. 379)
focus (p. 391)
guided discovery (p. 401)
high-quality examples (p. 382)

instructional alignment (p. 384)
language clarity (p. 390)
learning objective (p. 380)
lecture-discussion (p. 398)
models of instruction (p. 396)
organization (p. 389)
organized bodies of knowledge (p. 398)
prompt (p. 393)
questioning frequency (p. 391)
review (p. 393)
thematic lessons (p. 390)
transition signals (p. 390)
wait-time (p. 392)

Developing as a Professional

Preparing for Your Licensure Exam

This exercise will provide you with practice answering questions similar to the Praxis™ Principles of Learning and Teaching Exam as well as your state-specific licensure exam. Read the following case study, and answer the questions that follow.

Diane Smith, a fifth-grade teacher at Oneida Elementary, is beginning a language arts lesson on comparative and superlative adjectives. She wants her students to understand and to be able to use comparative and superlative adjectives correctly in their writing.

She begins by providing students with a written paragraph in which several adjectives are embedded. She has the students identify the adjectives and the nouns they modify, and then turns to her lesson for the day by having two of her students hold their pencils up, so everyone can see them.

Diane: Candice and Daniel, hold your pencils up high, so everyone can see. What do you notice about the pencils? . . . Mary?
Mary: Candice's is red and Daniel's is blue.
Diane: OK, what else? . . . Sheila?

Sheila: *You write with them.*
Diane: *Indeed you do! What else, Kevin?*
Kevin: *Candice's is longer.*
Diane: *That's true. Does everyone see that? Hold them up again.*

Candice and Daniel hold their pencils up again, and Diane moves to the chalkboard and writes:

Candice has a long pencil.   *Candice has a longer pencil than Daniel has.*

Diane: *Now, let's look at Matt and Aaron. What do you notice about their hair? . . . Maddie?*
Maddie: *Matt's is longer than Aaron's.*
Diane: *Good, Maddie. What else? What about the color? . . . Nicholas?*
Nicholas: *Aaron's is brown, and Matt's is blond.*
Diane: *Okay, good, Nicholas. So which one has darker hair?*
The Class: *Aaron!*

Diane then writes five more sentences on the board:

Candice has a long pencil.   *Candice has a longer pencil than Daniel has.*

Aaron has brown hair.   *Aaron has darker hair than Matt has.*

Matt has blond hair.

Diane: *Now let's look at the adjectives in the sentences on the left compared to the adjectives in the sentences on the right. How do they compare? Heather?*
Heather: *The adjectives in the sentences on the right have an "er" on the end of them.*

Diane guides the students to the conclusion that comparative adjectives have an "er" on the end of them and then repeats the process for superlative adjectives. Next, she gives the students an assignment in which they are to write a paragraph that includes at least two examples of comparative adjectives and two examples of superlative adjectives. The students complete their paragraphs by the end of their language arts time. Diane collects the paragraphs and discusses them with the class the next day. At the end of the week, Diane gives a quiz in which the students have to identify examples of comparative and superlative adjectives embedded in a written paragraph and also write a paragraph of their own that includes examples of each. (Adapted from Eggen & Kauchak, 2007, p. 124)

1. Was Diane's instruction aligned? Explain why it was or was not.

2. Which model of teaching is best illustrated in Diane's instruction? Explain.

3. Assess Diane's questioning. Support your assessment with information taken directly from the case study.

4. Explain how Diane applied each of the learning principles presented at the beginning of the chapter in her lesson.

To receive feedback on your responses to these exercises, go to the Companion Website at www.prenhall.com/kauchak, then to the Preparing for Your Licensure Exam *module for Chapter 12.*

Discussion Questions

1. Why is the practice of calling on volunteers to answer a question so prevalent? What are its advantages? What are its disadvantages?

2. How does the importance of the following essential teaching skills vary with grade level or content area: focus, questioning, feedback, and review and closure?

3. Many teachers lecture instead of guiding their students to their goals using questioning. Why do you think this is the case?

4. Which of the four instructional models is easiest to implement? Why? Most difficult or challenging?

5. How does the effectiveness of the four instructional models vary with grade level? Are some of these more effective or useful for certain content areas? Which and why?

Developing as a Professional: Online Activities

Going Into Schools

Go to the Companion Website at *www.prenhall.com/kauchak*, and click on the *Going Into Schools* module for Chapter 12. You will find a number of school-based activities that will help you link chapter content to the schools in which you work.

Virtual Field Experience: Using Teacher Prep to Explore the Profession

If you would like to participate in a Virtual Field Experience, access the Teacher Prep Website at *www.prenhall.com/teacherprep*. After logging in, complete the following steps:

1. Click on "Video Classroom" on the left panel of the screen.

2. Go to "General Methods."

3. Finally, select "Module 9: Cooperative Learning and the Collaborative Process." This video provides you with a concrete example of a cooperative learning model being used in an elementary math class. Answer the questions that follow the video clip.

Online Portfolio Activities

To develop your professional portfolio, further apply your understanding of chapter content, and address the INTASC standards, go to the Companion Website at *www.prenhall.com/kauchak*, then to the *Online Portfolio Activities* for Chapter 12. Complete the suggested activities.

Technology in American Schools

Chapter Outline

What Is Technology?
    Contrasting Views of Technology

Technology and Instruction
    Drill and Practice
    Tutorials
    Using Technology to Teach Problem Solving
      and Higher-Level Thinking Skills
    Word Processing: Using Technology to Teach
      Writing
    Using the Internet as an Instructional Tool

Teacher-Support Applications
    Preparing Instructional Materials
    Assessing Student Learning
    Communicating With Parents

Instructional Issues in the Use of Educational
Technology
    Quality of Available Software
    Instructional Alignment Problems
    Accountability and Time Constraints
    Access Issues in the Use of Technology
    Plagiarism and Cheating

Learning Objectives

After you have completed your study of this chapter, you should be able to:

1. Define technology, and describe the difference between hardware and process views of technology.

2. Describe different instructional uses of technology.

3. Explain how technology can assist teachers in different professional tasks.

4. Discuss how different instructional issues affect the use of educational technology in the classroom.

Case Studies

 Elementary

 Middle

 Secondary

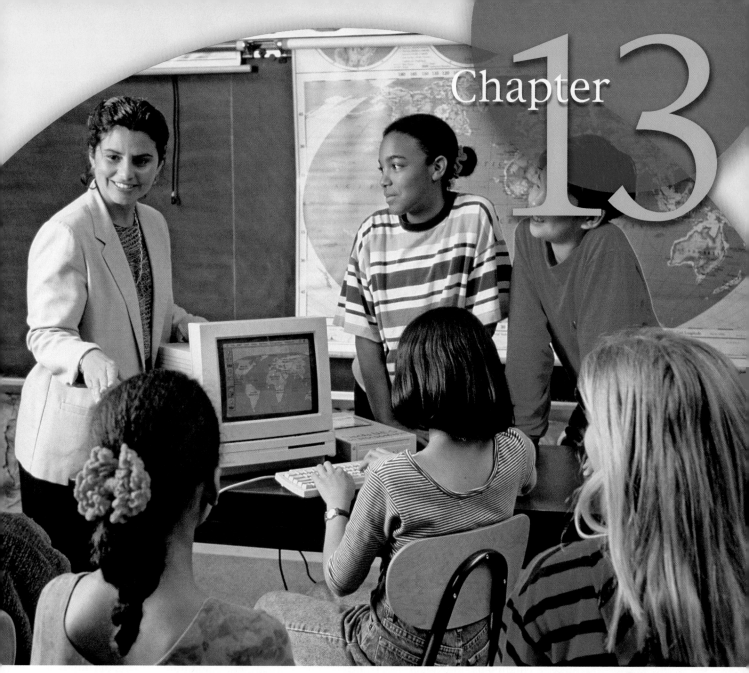

David Young-Wolff/PhotoEdit Inc.

Technology is changing education in the United States in many ways and is important to you as a beginning teacher for several reasons. How you use technology can affect how much your students learn as well as how hard you will have to work. Technology can also make you a better teacher, but only if you understand it and how it can influence learning. As you read the following case studies, think about the different ways that teachers use technology to promote learning.

Latisha Evans, a first-year teacher at Henderson Middle School, runs into one of her colleagues and friends, Carl DeGroot, in the hallway.

"You sure look excited," Carl comments with a smile. "What's happening?"

"Wow," Latisha responds, gesturing for emphasis. "They got it today; they really got it. . . . I've been trying to get my language arts classes to understand what we mean by internal conflict, and it seemed to be just too abstract for them. . . . Plus, they would only half pay attention when I would explain it. . . . So I wrote up a few little vignettes, like 'Kelly didn't know what to do. She was looking forward to the class trip, but if she went she wouldn't be able to try out for city soccer league.' Then, I put them together with a PowerPoint presentation and included some pictures of people with pensive looks on their faces and that kind of thing. . . . Neat animation tricks to make each example appear on the screen and then follow it with the pictures. . . . It was the best I've ever done. Using PowerPoint to get their attention really made a difference."

Pete Anderson, a five-year veteran at Henderson Middle School, is highly regarded by the principal, his students, and their parents. As we enter Pete's classroom, it appears chaotic, and we wonder how anyone could consider him a "good" teacher. One group of five students is working on a 4-by-8-foot sheet of heavy paper to be used in a presentation to their classmates. Two other groups of four students are working on different displays, and the seven computers in his room are all being used by pairs of students searching the Internet. The noise level is quite high, giving the impression that there is no order. As we walk around the room, we notice that each group of students is working intently. Pete explains that he had the students organize themselves into pairs—with one group of three, since he has 27 students—and each pair selected one of the original 13 colonies. Their task was to create a company like the Hudson Bay Trading Company for each colony. Pairs could team up and work on two related colonies together if they chose to do so, as indicated by the group of five and the two groups of four.

Pete explains that he wanted to try something different in this unit on American history. Instead of simply presenting information to students and discussing it, he continues, he presented students with a problem—creating a company that could use the resources of the particular colony or colonies. The students went to work searching for information that would help them solve the problem. They were using the classroom's computers to gather information, and they had to collaborate in making decisions about how to present the information to their classmates. Their presentation had to include a description of how their investors could make a profit using the resources of the colony.

In this chapter we present an overview of educational technology and its uses in schools as we try to answer the following questions:

- *What is technology?*
- *What different types of technology are available to teachers as they attempt to help students learn?*
- *How can technology assist teachers in their professional tasks?*

Before continuing with the chapter, take a few minutes to respond to the survey on page 415. You will find answers to each of the items as you read through the chapter.

What Is Technology?

We tend to think of technology as a recent innovation in American education, and we usually link technology to computers. In fact, it is much broader and has been used in teaching for as long as schools have existed. For example, teachers in our country's first schools had children use individual slate boards to practice their "letters and numbers." As the multi-age, one-room school evolved into schools organized by grade levels, the chalkboard became an essential tool for communicating with larger groups of students. These are rudimentary forms of technology.

The invention of electricity revolutionized instruction by allowing teachers to use radio, television, filmstrips, films, and overhead projectors. Technology further evolved, and now teachers routinely use videotapes and DVDs, virtually all have at least one computer in their classrooms, and some even have video projection equipment, such as Latisha used to give her PowerPoint presentation. These are all forms of technology.

But how is this increasingly powerful resource most effectively used? Will it make your job as a teacher simpler and more efficient or more complex and demanding? Before we begin answering these questions, let's consider the most basic question: What is technology?

Contrasting Views of Technology

In the past 50 years, experts have defined educational technology in two distinct ways: (1) as hardware and (2) as a process. Those holding a hardware view see technology as primarily machines and devices to deliver information (Jonassen, Howland, Moore, & Marra,

professional knowledge: test yourself!

For each item, circle the number that best represents your thinking. Use the following scale as a guide.

1 = Strongly disagree
2 = Disagree
3 = Agree/disagree
4 = Agree
5 = Strongly agree

1. Technology provides an effective way to teach problem solving and higher-level thinking skills.

    1   2   3   4   5

2. Word processing relieves teachers of having to teach most writing skills.

    1   2   3   4   5

3. Technology can be a major time-saver for teachers.

    1   2   3   4   5

4. Reinforcing facts and skills is the primary use of technology in schools.

    1   2   3   4   5

5. Plagiarism and cheating in the classroom have become more widespread because of the presence of technology.

    1   2   3   4   5

 This is available in a downloadable format on the Companion Website for personal portfolio use.

2003). A hardware view believes technology can increase learning by providing tools to replace or amplify the teacher (Ertmer, 2005). Using drill-and-practice software versus teacher-led review is an example of technology replacing the teacher; Latisha's use of a PowerPoint presentation is an example of using technology to amplify a message.

Whether their tools have been chalkboards, filmstrips, or computers, teachers throughout most of America's history have traditionally thought of technology as an accessory to instruction, something to be added on to make communication more effective or as an alternative to the teacher.

Over time, experts developed a more comprehensive, transformative view of technology, something that can fundamentally change how students learn and teachers teach (Ertmer, 2005). Instead of an accessory, technology is something to be integrated into teaching and learning. Teachers can use it to improve the effectiveness of instructional strategies and increase student motivation, and students can use it as both a communication and a learning tool. This perspective asks teachers to think broadly about how they can use technology more systematically to promote learning. Pete's incorporation of technology and other learning resources into his history instruction illustrates this more process-oriented view.

Hardware and process views of technology are grounded in different theories of learning and teaching. The hardware view is based on a transmission model of teaching that assumes the teacher presents information to students and technology enhances the "transmission" of the information to be learned. In contrast, the process view of technology is based on the cognitive learning principles that you saw in Chapter 12. This perspective views learners as active in constructing their own knowledge and using technology as aids to classroom learning (Forcier & Descy, 2005; Jonassen et al., 2003).

Experts now think of **educational technology** as "a combination of the processes and tools involved in addressing educational needs and problems" (Roblyer, 2006, p. 9). Pete emphasized the process aspects of technology by presenting his students with a problem and helping them as they tried to solve it; his students used the computers as tools as they worked toward solving the problem. Remembering that technology is a combination of tools and processes, let's turn now to some of its instructional uses.

Making Connections:

To deepen your understanding of the topics in this section of the chapter and integrate them with topics you've already studied, go to the *Making Connections* module for Chapter 13 at **www.prenhall.com/kauchak**. Respond to questions 1 and 2.

Check Your Understanding

1.1   As we look at technology in a historical sense, such as using the chalkboard, overhead, or filmstrip projector, which view of technology—hardware or process—was more prominent? Explain.

1.2   How was the definition of educational technology—"a combination of the processes and tools involved in addressing educational needs and problems"— illustrated in Pete's work with his students?

For feedback, go to Appendix A, Check Your Understanding, *located in the back of this text.*

Technology and Instruction

Teachers use educational technology to support instruction in many ways. As you read the following case studies, think about the different goals that teachers have for integrating technology into their instruction.

 Fifth-grade teacher Sandy Hutton is involved in a unit on the circulatory system and wants her students to understand how the heart works and how blood pressure influences it. On a CD-ROM accompanying the class's science textbook, Sandy finds a model that illustrates how the heart is like a bicycle pump with valves opening and closing. She shares the model with her class by using her computer to project it on a screen, and she brings in an old bicycle pump to illustrate how valves open and close to create pressure. With the help of the school nurse, she finds several sphygmomanometers (devices for measuring blood pressure), which students use to measure their pulse and blood pressure during different types of activities. She organizes students into small groups and asks each group to search for patterns in their measurements and to organize the information into charts on their computers. Finally, the groups share their results with the entire class.

Next door, Maria Delgado's students are working on a tutorial designed to improve their skills with adding and subtracting fractions. When she pretested them at the beginning of the year, she found that many didn't know that ¼ was larger than ⅛. Others had a basic grasp of fraction concepts but were a little shaky on doing computations with fractions. She knows she has her work cut out for her. Fortunately, she finds a computer tutorial that students can work on at their own pace. It pretests students, directs them to appropriate learning levels in the program, and provides instruction with immediate feedback as they proceed. As Maria circulates around the room assisting students, she can see that they are starting to understand.

Educational technology. A combination of the processes and tools involved in addressing educational needs and problems.

Figure 13.1   Classroom Applications of Technology

Drill and practice

Tutorials

Teaching problem solving and higher-level thinking skills

Using word processing to teach writing

Using the Internet as an instructional tool

Educational technology can assist teachers with their instruction in a number of ways. Some are illustrated in Figure 13.1 and described in the sections that follow.

Drill and Practice

When educators recognized that computers and other forms of technology could perform tasks quickly and systematically, they began to search for ways to use these innovations to imitate the functions of human teachers (Roblyer, 2006). For instance, students often use work sheets and flash cards to practice basic skills, such as word recognition and phonetic analysis in reading, and addition and multiplication facts in math. Educators wondered, could computers be used to provide an improved form of practice? This question led to the development of **drill-and-practice programs**, software designed to provide extensive practice with feedback (Lever-Duffy, McDonald, & Mizell, 2003).

Because students can use drill-and-practice programs on their own, teachers don't have to be directly involved. However, they don't substitute for teachers' expertise, and developers of these programs assume that students have had previous instruction related to the facts or concepts. For example, when students first learn about multiplication, effective teachers help them understand that 6 × 9 means 6 sets of 9 items, or 9 sets of 6 items, and they present several concrete examples to illustrate the concept of *multiplication*. After this initial instruction, teachers have students use drill-and-practice programs to help students practice until the skill becomes automatic—that is, until they know the facts essentially without having to think about them.

Some drill-and-practice software programs use a "game" format to increase student motivation. For example, instead of typing in the correct response to 6 × 9 = ?, students might aim a laser blaster at an alien emblazoned with 54.

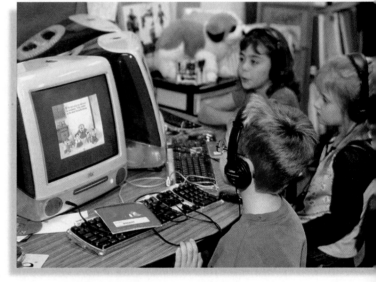

Drill-and-practice and tutorials can be used to supplement instruction in basic skills. [Anthony Magnacca/Merrill].

The best drill-and-practice programs are adaptive, matching the demands of the task to a student's ability. For example, in a program designed to improve knowledge of multiplication facts, an adaptive program begins by pretesting to determine what multiplication facts students already know. The program then strategically presents problems to ensure high success rates. When students fail to answer, or answer incorrectly, the program prompts by providing the answer and then retests that fact. The program introduces more difficult problems only when students have reached a certain skill level. Because the ultimate goal is for students to be able to recall math facts automatically, the program shortens the amount of time given to answer as students become more proficient. This also increases motivation by challenging students to become quicker in their responses.

Drill-and-practice programs. Software designed to provide extensive practice with feedback.

What are the benefits of drill-and-practice programs? First, they provide practice with effective feedback, informing students immediately of what they've mastered and where they need more work. Research supports the effectiveness of this process (Attewell, 2001). Second, they are often motivating for students turned off by paper-and-pencil exercises (Gee, 2005), and third, they save teachers' time, because they don't have to present information and score students' responses.

Researchers caution, however, that more time on computers does not necessarily equal more learning (Roblyer, 2006). More important are the quality of the learning experiences and the extent to which they are linked to the teacher's goals.

Tutorials

Lisa Hoover, a first-grade teacher, has created a number of learning centers in her classroom where her students can work independently. Students can earn "classroom money" for good behavior and finishing assignments and can use the money to purchase prizes from the class store. The students who work in the store as clerks must first complete several of the math units, with the last one focusing on giving change. Lisa's students have widely varying backgrounds, and she believes that they shouldn't complete the giving-change unit until they're ready. As a result, she has students who want to take the unit at various times during the fall semester. In the past, they often had to wait or she had to drop some other activity to teach them the rules for calculating and counting change. Recently, Lisa took a technology course in which she learned to use a software program called HyperStudio. She uses the program to design an interactive multimedia lesson—a tutorial—on giving change. The tutorial includes pictures of various coins and presents a number of scenarios that provide students with practice in giving change. Now students can complete the unit anytime they have access to one of the computers in the classroom. In addition, Lisa designs the tutorial so that it will give students virtually unlimited numbers of problems and continual help until they master the information. Lisa notices that students easily get used to the process and are happy about having immediate access to the instruction.

In contrast with drill-and-practice software, which focuses on mastery of isolated facts, a **tutorial** is a software program that delivers an entire integrated instructional sequence similar to a teacher's instruction on the topic. Tutorials attempt to create comprehensive learning systems that act like effective teachers by responding to student questions and errors with immediate help (P. Alexander, 2006). Tutorials include specific learning objectives, multiple pathways to them, and quizzes with feedback geared to the objectives.

Carnegie Learning's *Cognitive Tutor* is one example of an effective tutorial (Carnegie Learning, 2005). A series of programs pretests students and then presents instruction with frequent assessment and feedback through math problems of increasing complexity. For example, when the student responds 2.8 to the problem, $-2.3 + .5 = ?$, the program responds, "Think about the sign of the numbers." Challenge is provided with a "Skillometer," a bar graph that increases with learning progress and decreases when students ask for hints.

One of the most popular applications of tutorials are programs that teach word processing skills including printing, saving, spell-checking, and formatting text with different fonts, sizes, and styles (J. Keller, 2004). The best include motivational features such as timed tests that provide challenge and lead to automaticity, as well as charts that illustrate the progression of skill mastery.

Tutorials can fulfill several needs, including initial instruction, additional support for students whose understanding isn't fully developed, advanced study for higher achievers, or alternatives to teacher-led instruction. Tutorials can be linear, but the best are branched, which adapt to learners' responses (Roblyer, 2006). For example, when a student responds incorrectly to a multiple-choice item, the program explains why that choice isn't correct and repeats the initial instruction. Effective tutorials are carefully sequenced so that new concepts and skills are systematically developed and grounded in ideas that students already understand.

Tutorial. A software program that delivers an entire integrated instructional sequence similar to a teacher's instruction on the topic.

As with all forms of instruction, the effectiveness of tutorials depends on the quality of interactions between the technology (teacher) and the learner, and the best require users to respond frequently. As students answer, effective tutorials accept all possible variations of correct answers, and they provide corrective feedback only when necessary. They also record and report individual students' performance to allow teachers to monitor learning progress and intervene when necessary.

Multimedia and Hypermedia

Tutorials can be simple software, like the one Maria's students used to help them with addition and subtraction, or they can use **multimedia**, such as Lisa used when she combined text, graphics, pictures, audio, and video. **Hypermedia**, a linked form of multimedia, allows learners to make connections to different points in the program based on their prior knowledge and learning progress. Currently, most multimedia products are also hypermedia systems (Roblyer, 2006).

For example, a multimedia presentation on the solar system might include written material, a DVD, video, and graphics. Students view a computer screen that contains **icons**, pictures that act as symbols for some item or action. They click on a text icon, which then brings up written information about Saturn's rings, for instance. Then, they can click on a DVD icon (e.g., a small picture of a DVD), and they can view a clip that provides a telescopic image of the rings. They can also click on a video icon that will present a simulated flight to the planet and a graphic illustrating the relative size of Saturn versus the other planets in the solar system. Multimedia systems vary in complexity, but they all have some combination of the components we just described. They attempt to promote learning by presenting information in both verbal and visual forms.

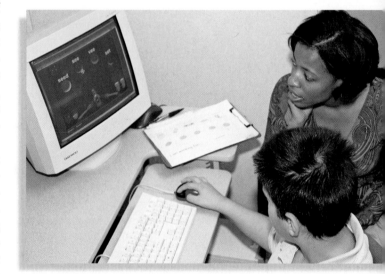

Teachers can use simulations and problem-solving software to develop students' thinking skills. [Laura Bolesta/Merrill]

Effective tutorials have several valuable features that make the instruction within them flexible, adaptive, and efficient. For example, Lisa's lesson was available anytime; students didn't have to wait until Lisa had free time to teach them. Second, it was adaptive and individualized, providing each student with the right amount of practice needed to master the content. She had previously used printed work sheets, but the instruction was inefficient because she had to interrupt what she was doing to assess and monitor the task in order to provide immediate feedback. In addition, her students found the hypermedia with pictures and video clips more motivating than work sheets.

Tutorials have been criticized for focusing too much on memorized information instead of challenging students to think and apply understanding (Newby, Stepich, Lehman, & Russell, 2006; Roblyer, 2006). Although this doesn't have to be the case, finding high-quality tutorial software and effective hypermedia materials is an obstacle facing teachers who want to integrate tutorials into their classrooms. We discuss this problem later in the chapter.

Using Technology to Teach Problem Solving and Higher-Level Thinking Skills

Knowing facts and knowing how to perform basic skills are important parts of the school curriculum, and many experts consider them to be the building blocks of learning (Bruning et al., 2004). But other important kinds of learning also exist. Students also need to learn how to find patterns in information and use these patterns to solve problems. Technology provides effective tools to help reach these goals.

> **Multimedia.** Combinations of media, including text, graphics, pictures, audio, and video that are designed to communicate information.
>
> **Hypermedia.** A linked form of multimedia that allows learners to make connections to different points in the program based on their background knowledge and learning progress.
>
> **Icons.** Pictures displayed on computer screens that act as symbols for some action or item.

Simulations

Simulations teach higher-order thinking skills by bringing the real world into the classroom. **Simulations** are programs, either in software or Web-based form, that model a real or imaginary system in order to help learners understand that system (Forcier & Descy, 2005). Let's look at an example.

Karl Evans is concluding a unit on ancient Greece in world history. Connecting his urban students with cultures that existed thousands of years ago is a constant challenge. In an attempt to increase his students' interest, he has them work on an archeological simulation. Teams of students are responsible for excavating different quadrants of the simulated archeological site. They "dig up" pottery shards, fragments of weapons, pieces of masonry, and bits of ancient texts. They try to identify each artifact and fit it into an emerging picture of the site as a whole. They also consult reference works on Greek history, art, and architecture. Some ambiguous evidence exists in the site, so some teams find data suggesting it was a temple, whereas others find artifacts indicating a home or battlefield. The teams present their findings to the class in weekly meetings, and a spirited debate follows as the amateur archeologists struggle to reconcile inconsistencies in the data. On this day, they take turns at computers, graph their findings on large wall-charts, call across the room to ask if anyone has a spearhead to compare with one just found, and argue about whose final interpretation will best explain the bulk of the evidence. (Adapted from Brunner & Tally, 1999)

As opposed to textbooks and lectures, simulations have the advantage of involving students in complex, realistic learning tasks that are usually unavailable in classrooms. Simulations become virtual field trips that allow students to see and do things impossible within the confines of their classroom walls. Simulations also provide benefits to teachers; as students are immersed in a simulation, teachers can work with different groups, asking questions and guiding learning.

Simulations also provide safety along with realism. One simulated driver's education course, for example, has students use a driving simulator to experience a near accident designed to help them learn to drive defensively (and avoid the wrath of their driving instructors) (Trotter, 2003). The simulator can provide students with risky scenarios such as driving in rain, fog, or at night. The experience is particularly effective because the simulation is both realistic and safe.

As another example, students can use computer software to simulate a frog dissection rather than cut up an actual frog. Although the simulation has the disadvantage of not allowing students the experience of working with a real frog, it has three advantages: It is less expensive, since it can be used over and over; it is more flexible, because the frog can be "reassembled"; and the simulation avoids sacrificing a frog for science (Roblyer, 2006).

One of the most popular social studies simulations, *Oregon Trail* (and subsequent versions), allows students to travel like the original Oregon Trail pioneers from Independence, Missouri, to Oregon's Willamette Valley (Forcier & Descy, 2005). Students shop for supplies with a specified budget before they start and make decisions along the way about the pace of travel, food supplies, and health problems. As students proceed, they interact with Native Americans and other settlers, gaining valuable historical information. A networked version of the program allows a number of users to interact simultaneously during their journeys.

Other simulations immerse students in World War II or allow them to develop empires similar to the Aztecs or Incas (Trotter, 2004). As the quality of software improves, simulations will become more sophisticated and more interactive, further increasing learner motivation and understanding.

Problem Solving

Computer software can also be used to teach students to solve problems. When we teach problem solving, we not only want students to get the right answer, we also want them to be-

Simulations. Programs, either in software or Web-based form, that model a system or process.

come better at figuring out how to solve future problems. Creating real-world problems that aren't cut and dried is one difficulty in teaching problem solving in traditional classroom settings. Problems in textbooks are usually well defined and routine; that is, the information needed to solve a problem (and only that information) is included, and even the procedure for finding the solution (e.g., using subtraction in a math problem) is often suggested by where the problem is presented (in a chapter on subtraction, for example) (Cognition and Technology Group at Vanderbilt, 1997).

Unlike textbook problems, the problems people typically face in the real world are often ill-defined and unlikely to have routine solutions. Technology can help learners acquire experience solving more realistic problems. For example,

Bill Sperry begins his middle school math class by showing a videodisc episode that realistically shows a young man, Jasper, encountering the following problem:

Jasper has just purchased a new boat and is planning to drive it home. The boat consumes 5 gallons of fuel per hour and travels at 8 mph. The gas tank holds 12 gallons of gas. The boat is currently located at mile marker 156. Jasper's home dock is at mile marker 132. There are two gas stations on the way home. One is at mile marker 140.3 and the other is at mile marker 133. They charge $1.19 and $1.25 per gallon, respectively. They don't take credit cards. Jasper started the day with $20. He bought 5 gallons of gas at $1.25 per gallon (not including a discount of 4 cents per gallon for paying cash) and paid $8.25 for repairs to his boat. It's 2:35. Sundown is at 7:52. Can Jasper make it home before sunset without running out of fuel? (S. Williams et al., 1996, p. 2)

After students view the episode, Bill breaks them into groups of four and says, "Okay, everyone, I'd like each group to work on solving this problem for the rest of this class. Let's see how far we get. But before we break into groups, I want to remind you. What's the first thing each group needs to do? . . . Javier?"

"Find out what the problem is asking."

"Good. . . . Did everyone hear what Javier said? . . . The first thing you need to do is decide what the problem is asking. Okay, go to it."

Students then move into their groups as Bill circulates around the room, answering questions.

The problem that Bill used is a condensed episode taken from a videodisc-based, problem-solving series called *The Adventures of Jasper Woodbury* (Cognition and Technology Group at Vanderbilt, 1997). The series consists of 12 episodes that each begin with a 15- to 20-minute realistic video with human actors. The video illustrates a challenge, like the one above, to the characters in the episode. Researchers designed these video-based episodes to be complex and open-ended in an effort to teach skills better matched to actual problems in the real world (S. Williams et al., 1996).

The problems in each episode are purposefully left ill-defined to give students practice in identifying the problem (e.g., What am I supposed to find out?) and separating relevant from irrelevant information (e.g., Is the cost of gas important?). They also get experience in breaking the problem down into subgoals, such as finding out how much money Jasper has left for the trip home. As students solve these problems, they work in teams over several class periods, ranging from a few days to more than a week. Students share their ideas, receive feedback to refine their thinking, and present their solutions to the class. These learning activities provide additional opportunities to analyze strengths and weaknesses of different solution strategies as well as opportunities to work together with other students in solving problems.

Simulations such as these provide realistic problem-solving experiences, but they require a great deal of sophisticated support from the teacher to be effective (Azevedo, 2005). Teachers must plan carefully and monitor students closely to prevent them from getting frustrated and wasting time.

Database and spreadsheet programs provide opportunities for students to learn how to analyze, organize, and present information. [GeoStock/Getty Images–Photodisc]

Databases

Databases, another form of technology, can also be used to teach problem solving and higher-level thinking skills. A **database program** is a computer program that allows users to store, organize, and manipulate information, including both text and numerical data (Forcier & Descy, 2005). The user can then sort and find both patterns and specific information in the database. Let's look at a teacher using databases to help her middle school students understand genetics.

To begin her unit, Angela divides her students into teams of 4. She has the teams gather information about the physical characteristics of their families, such as eye and hair color, gender, height, and weight. To help them find patterns and make conclusions about the genetic backgrounds of their group, they put the information into a database.

A portion of her students' database appears in Figure 13.2. Angela used a database program to help her students organize information about genetics. Earlier in the chapter, you saw how Sandy Hutton taught information about the heart; she used a database to help organize information relating exercise with pulse and blood pressure. If you have ever used a library catalog (either an old card catalog or an electronic catalog), you have used a form of database.

As another example, a teacher working on a unit involving factors that influence economic growth might have students develop a database containing information on several countries: population and population density, gross national product, defense budget, literacy rate, and personal income. Once the database is constructed, learners can compare the countries and form conclusions about their economies and potential for growth. Commercial programs such as AppleWorks or Microsoft Office are available to assist teachers as they integrate databases into their instruction.

Spreadsheets

Spreadsheet programs are computer programs used to organize and manipulate numerical data. Spreadsheets produce a two-dimensional matrix of interrelated rows and columns and

> **Database program.** A computer program that allows users to store, organize, and manipulate information, including both text and numerical data.
>
> **Spreadsheet programs.** Computer programs that are used to organize and manipulate numerical data.

Figure 13.2 Database Structure for Investigating Genetics

Record	Field 1 Student Name	Field 2 Father's Hair Color	Field 3 Father's Eye Color	Field 4 Father's Height	Field 5 Father's Weight	Field 6 Mother's Hair Color
1	Alvarez, Maria	Black	Brown	5' 11"	170	Brown
2	Battle, Ken	Blond	Blue	6' 1"	190	Brown
3	Chu, Karen	Black	Brown	5' 10"	165	Black
Etc.						

are the much-advanced cousins of calculators. They were first used for accounting purposes but have evolved into sophisticated problem-solving tools.

To illustrate how spreadsheets can support instruction, let's see how Brad Evers, a social studies teacher, used one to help his students understand research methods in history.

Brad, who teaches in a small New England town, is struggling to help his students understand where the history they are studying came from and what historians do. He decides to focus his class on the history of a local cemetery to help them gain insights into the story of their own town. Students divide into groups and gather data from tombstones in different sections of the local cemetery. They discuss questions such as, "How long did people live in different time periods?" "How does this compare to today?" "Did women live longer than men?" and "Were there periods of unusually high mortality?"

After visiting the cemetery, individuals enter the data into a spreadsheet, organizing it by gender, age, and year of death. Brad uses the spreadsheet for a class discussion about what they have learned, both about local history and about the work of historians. (Adapted from Forcier & Descy, 2005.)

Because of its ability to display and manipulate numerical information, a spreadsheet allowed Brad's students to calculate averages and make comparisons, such as the average lifespan of people in the 1700s and 1800s with lifespan today (see Figure 13.3). Teachers can also use spreadsheets to create charts and graphs that correspond to data trends. For example, Brad's class might graph the average life span of people from different periods.

Teachers typically have two goals when they use databases and spreadsheets. One is to have students learn about the capabilities of these tools, and the other is to use them in their problem solving. However, these technology tools won't work on their own. Students must be given explicit instruction, both with respect to their capabilities, and in how they can be applied in problem-solving activities (Forcier & Descy, 2005). As we saw in our discussion of other forms of technology, tools such as databases and spreadsheets don't replace teachers, and in many cases, these tools increase rather than decrease the demands on teachers. These tools do, however, have the potential to provide rich and varied learning experiences.

This section addresses the first item on our "Professional Knowledge: Test Yourself!" survey, "Technology provides an effective way to teach problem solving and higher-level thinking skills." Technology *does* provide a number of ways to teach problem solving and higher-level thinking skills; teachers can use technology to present problems and simulations and to analyze data through databases and spreadsheets.

Figure 13.3   Spreadsheet to Analyze Historical Trends

Time Period	Person	Gender	Date of Birth	Date of Death	Additional Information on Tombstone
1700–1800					
1800–1900					
1900–2000					

Word Processing: Using Technology to Teach Writing

Using word processing to teach writing is probably the most widespread use of educational technology. To see why, let's look at what writing instruction used to look like.

Your teacher emphasized that a draft copy was to be done in pencil, so you could erase your mistakes and write in corrections. When you were given approval to make a final copy, you took out a nice, clean sheet of white notebook paper and a new ballpoint pen. Using your best handwriting to copy the letter, you had the date, address, greeting, and first paragraph looking great when Bobby "accidentally" bumped your arm. Your pen slashed across the letter, ruining it. After yelling at Bobby, you pulled out another clean sheet of notebook paper and began again.

[It] looked great! Then your teacher reminded you to proofread your letter before turning it in. You thought it was a waste of time, but you did it anyway. To your dismay, you realized a complete sentence had been left out, so that the last paragraph did not make any sense. You reluctantly pulled out yet another clean sheet of notebook paper. All of the elation was gone. In fact, you were beginning to dislike writing. (Morrison & Lowther, 2002, p. 179)

Memories like these may be familiar to many of us. Fortunately, technology, in the form of word processing, is making writing and learning to write easier, more efficient, and more fun. Word processing has the potential to improve student writing in the following ways. It can

- Make text more legible.
- Increase the amount of text available for viewing at one time.
- Improve the efficiency of entering, revising, and editing text.
- Allow students to store and combine ideas.
- Facilitate the development of communities of writers by using e-mail to share drafts and provide feedback on written products (Morrison & Lowther, 2002).

Research indicates that students who use word processing write more, revise their products more thoroughly, make fewer grammatical and punctuation errors, and have more positive attitudes toward writing (Bangert-Drowns, 1993; Roblyer, 2006). However, word processing alone won't teach writing. Teachers still play an essential role in setting goals, guiding students, and providing feedback. Word processing is an effective tool for teaching writing, but it isn't a panacea.

This section addresses the second item on our beginning-of-chapter survey, "Word processing relieves teachers of having to teach most writing skills." While word processing does provide a number of advantages in teaching writing, it doesn't substitute for sound basic instruction from the teacher.

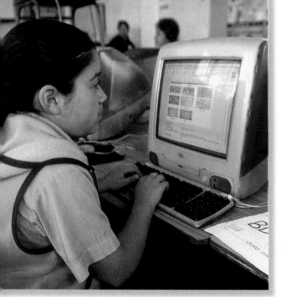

The Internet provides a number of instructional options including problem-based learning and distance education. [David Young Wolff/ PhotoEdit Inc.]

Internet. The complex web of interconnections among computers that allows people to communicate and share information worldwide.

World Wide Web. A system on the Internet that allows people to access, view, and maintain documents that include text, data, sound, and video.

Using the Internet as an Instructional Tool

Individual computers provide a number of instructional options, but students remain isolated without some mechanism for sharing information across distances. The **Internet** is a complex web of interconnections among computers that allows millions of people to communicate and share information worldwide.

The Internet was established in 1969 by the Department of Defense to facilitate communication among researchers in 30 different locations around the country (Roblyer, 2006). The **World Wide Web**, a system on the Internet, allows people to access, view, and maintain documents that include text, data, sound, and video. The advantages of the Internet became readily apparent, and its availability in schools has grown dramatically, as Figure 13.4 shows.

The Internet has literally become a part of our daily lives; we communicate with friends and colleagues on the Internet and even use it to shop for items such as clothes, music, and airplane tickets. Government agencies, businesses, schools, and many individuals have their

Figure 13.4 Percentage of Public School Classrooms with Internet Access: 1994–2003

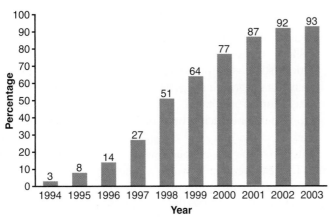

Source: National Center for Education Statistics, Internet Access in U.S. Public Schools and Classrooms, 1994–2003. Washington, DC: Author, February 2005, p. 4.

own **Websites,** locations on the World Wide Web identified with a **uniform resource locator (URL).** A URL is a series of letters and/or symbols that acts as an address for a site on the Internet. For example, some interesting Websites include *The Internet Movie Database*, which contains information about virtually every movie ever made; the *ESPN Sports Page*, which provides up-to-the-minute sports results; the *Doonesbury* comic strip; and *Sleepnet*, which provides help for insomniacs.

The Internet as a source of information is widely known; students use it to gather information for school reports and projects, and teachers use the information they find to plan lessons (R. Wallace, 2004). However, the Internet's potential to enhance communication, promote social development, and teach problem solving isn't as commonly examined. We discuss these uses in the next sections.

The Internet as a Communication Tool

Computer-mediated communication (CMC), telecommunication between people via electronic mail (e-mail), has revolutionized the way we interact with others. We can now quickly and efficiently communicate with people virtually anywhere in the world, for example, and we can also transmit pictures and other attachments, such as written text, pictures, databases, or spreadsheets.

Chat rooms provide one communication alternative. A **chat room** is a site on the Internet where many people can simultaneously communicate in real time. For example, when one user in a chat room types comments, these are immediately seen by everyone in the "room." Chat rooms are considered the most interactive of all the written communication options; in essence, they are online discussion groups. A **bulletin board** is an electronic message center for a given topic. It functions just like a physical bulletin board; it's a place where messages can be posted and stored. Students can read the comments of others and then leave their own messages.

Because the Internet efficiently connects students to others all over the world and allows them to share views and perspectives, it can promote learning as well as social growth. This kind of access is impossible to obtain in any other way.

Advantages and Disadvantages of Internet Communication. As with any educational tool, Internet communication has both advantages and disadvantages (Forcier & Descy, 2005; Morrison & Lowther, 2002; W. Winn, 2002). For example, Internet interactions can be more equitable than face-to-face communication, because extraneous factors such as attractiveness, prestige, and material possessions are eliminated. In addition,

Website. A location on the World Wide Web identified with a uniform resource locator (URL).

Uniform resource locator (URL). A series of letters and/or symbols that acts as an address for a site on the Internet.

Computer-mediated communication (CMC). Telecommunication between people via electronic mail (e-mail).

Chat room. A site on the Internet where many people can simultaneously communicate in real time.

Bulletin board. An electronic message center for a given topic.

communicating on the Internet gives students time to think, reflect, and connect ideas, so their thoughts and arguments are often more connected and complete (Marttunen & Laurinen, 2001).

Internet communication, however, uses only one medium—the written word—which doesn't help students learn to read nonverbal social cues, such as facial expressions and eye contact, or vocal signals, such as emphasis and intonation. This is a problem for two reasons. First, communications research suggests that a large part of a message's credibility is communicated through nonverbal channels (Aronson, Wilson, & Akert, 2005). It is more difficult for people to understand each others' messages in the absence of nonverbal cues. Second, because Internet communication doesn't give students experience in learning to read social cues, writers may be out of touch with their audiences and may feel a greater sense of anonymity. This can be helpful when it encourages students to disagree or to express opinions, but it can also lead students to show insensitivity and treat others like objects instead of people (Franek, 2005/2006). Cyberbullying has become an increasing problem in our schools, and, unlike in-person bullying, may be harder to detect and prevent (Willard, 2006).

In addition, some experts caution that the amount of time students spend on computers can impair social development by limiting the number of face-to-face interactions they have (Kuh & Vesper, 1999; Monke, 2005/2006). Other research, however, suggests that children who are active online are no less likely to spend time reading, playing outside, or interacting with their families (Trotter, 2000), and they are less likely to spend large amounts of time watching television (UCLA Center for Communication Policy, 2001).

Using the Internet in Problem-Based Learning

The Internet can also be a useful tool for developing students' problem-solving skills through problem-based learning. **Problem-based learning** is an instructional strategy that uses a problem and the data gathered in attempts to solve it as the focal point of a lesson (Kain, 2003). Problem-based learning is more open-ended than problem solving, which typically results in convergent answers. The Internet can facilitate problem-based learning by serving as a source of information and a way to share information across sites.

As an example of problem-based learning, a Web-based simulation project linked fifth-grade students from Missouri with similar students in Taiwan (Jonassen et al., 2003). Students collected information about the different things they did after school and created graphs from the data. Projects such as these use text, graphics, videos, and simulations as conversational props to support exchanges between students. When students use the Internet in this way, they not only develop problem-solving abilities, they also learn how to use technology to obtain and organize information, and develop their social cooperation skills.

The popularity of the Internet in problem-based learning is due to two important capabilities (Roblyer, 2006). First, students using the Internet can access large amounts of information through the millions of Websites that currently exist, and second, they can communicate with other research teams working at different sites to either share data or collaborate in problem solving. Internet linkages allow students to transcend the physical boundaries of their classroom to access resources around the world.

Distance Learning Technologies

When most people think of instruction, they imagine a teacher standing in front of a room of students. **Distance learning**, a catch-all term used to describe organized instructional pro-

Problem-based learning. An instructional strategy that uses a problem and the data gathered in attempts to solve it as the focal point of a lesson.

Distance learning. Organized instructional programs in which teachers and learners, though physically separated, are connected through technology.

grams in which teachers and learners, though physically separated, are connected through technology, is changing that view (Newby et al., 2006; Simonson, Smaldino, Albright, & Zvacek, 2006). Distance learning meets student learning needs in three ways (Picciano, 2001). First, it can offer students in rural communities courses in specialized areas, such as advanced physics or Japanese, for which a local teacher is unavailable. Second, it can provide instruction for nontraditional students, such as adults who can't attend classes during the day or those who are homebound. Third, it can deliver a class to students over a broad geographic area where driving to a central location is not possible.

The earliest efforts at distance education were correspondence courses for which students read books, answered questions, and received feedback from instructors through the mail. Currently, distance education includes a number of options:

- Videoconferencing, which allows learners and teachers from various sites to ask and answer questions over great distances.
- Computer conferencing that allows students and teachers the opportunity to interact via the Internet. Like bulletin boards and chat rooms, these interactions can provide either simultaneous or synchronous interaction.
- Web-based systems that allow learners to not only watch instructional programs on television but also access information for research. For example, in one program, students across the country viewed Gettysburg battlefields, heard profiles of individual soldiers, and were directed to Websites where they could find additional information for study (Furlan, 2000).

Research suggests that the type of distance learning employed is not as important as the quality and organization of the course and the availability of the instructor for answering questions and providing feedback (Roblyer, 2006). In addition, the most effective online courses provide students with choices in terms of when and how to work on assignments and opportunities to interact with other students (Tallent-Runnels et al., 2006).

Higher and postsecondary education have shown the greatest interest in distance education; about 60 percent of American colleges and universities presently offer some type of distance learning program, and these numbers are growing (Roblyer, 2006). Distance education has also entered the teacher education arena, offering courses and degrees at both the prelicensure and master's levels (B. Keller, 2005). Flexibility and convenience are major attractions, but experts warn that teachers should investigate thoroughly before enrolling, as the courses can be expensive and their quality varies widely (Cavanagh, 2004).

Virtual K–12 school programs are also appearing around the country, providing alternatives to standard attendance at school. In the 2005–2006 school year, 22 states had statewide virtual schools, and 16 states allowed for the creation of cyber charter schools (Swanson, 2006b). Although most common at the high school level, virtual courses are also appearing in elementary and middle schools (Galley, 2003). Most popular with homeschooled students, virtual courses also provide students in rural areas with access to education and students in all areas with courses in hard-to-teach areas such as advanced mathematics or some languages. Experts caution that students, when first introduced to online instruction, may need assistance in learning how to learn from these courses (J. Richardson & Newby, 2005). Critics warn against relying too heavily on this technology and argue that the lack of social interaction may result in less learning and decreased social development (Maeroff, 2003; Monke, 2005/2006).

Employing Technology to Support Learners With Disabilities

Julio is partially deaf, barely able to use a hearing aid to understand speech. Kerry Tanner, his seventh-grade science teacher, works closely with the special education instructor assigned to her classroom to help Julio. Seated near the front of the room to facilitate lip-reading, Julio takes notes on a laptop computer during teacher presentations. Other students take turns sharing their notes with him so he can compare and fill in gaps. He especially likes to communicate with other students on the Internet, as this levels the communication playing field. When he views video clips on his computer, he uses a special device with earphones to increase the volume.

Jaleena is partially sighted, with a visual acuity of less than 20/80, even with corrective lenses. Despite this disability, she is doing well in her fourth-grade class. Tera Banks, her teacher, has placed her in the front of the room so that she can better see the chalkboard and overhead and has assigned students to work with her on her projects. Using a magnifying device, she can read most written material, but the computer is giving her special problems. The small letters and punctuation on Website addresses and other information make it difficult for her to use the computer as an information source. Tera works with the special education consultant in her district to get a monitor that magnifies the display. She knows it is working when she sees Jaleena quietly working alone at her computer on the report due next Friday.

As we've seen, technology is changing the ways we teach and the way students learn. **Assistive technology,** a set of adaptive tools that support students with disabilities in learning activities and daily life tasks, is having a particularly important impact on students with exceptionalities. These assistive tools are required by federal law under the Individuals with Disabilities Education Act (IDEA) and include motorized chairs, remote control devices that turn machines on and off with the nod of the head or other muscle action, and machines that amplify sights and sounds (Heward, 2006; J. Hopkins, 2006).

> **Assistive technology.** A set of adaptive tools that support students with disabilities in learning activities and daily life tasks.

Probably the most widespread contribution of assistive technology is in the area of computer adaptations. Let's look at them.

Adaptations to Computer Input Devices

To use computers, students must be able to input their words and ideas. This can be difficult for those with visual or other physical disabilities that don't allow standard keyboarding. Devices that enhance the keyboard, such as making it larger and easier to see, arranging the letters alphabetically to make them easier to find, or using pictures for nonreaders are adaptations that accommodate these disabilities. *AlphaSmart*, one widely used program, helps developing writers by providing spell-check and word-prediction scaffolding (Fine, 2002). When a student hesitates to finish a word, the computer, based on the first few letters, then either completes the word or offers a menu of suggestions. Advocates claim it frees students to concentrate on ideas and text organization.

Additional adaptations bypass the keyboard altogether. For example, speech/voice-recognition software can translate speech into text on the computer screen (Silver-Pacuilla & Fleischman, 2006). These systems can be invaluable for students with physical disabilities that affect hand and finger movement. Other adaptations use switches activated by a body movement, such as a head nod, to interact with the computer. Touch screens also allow students to go directly to the monitor to indicate their responses.

Research also indicates that students with learning disabilities encounter difficulties translating ideas into written words (Hasselbring & Bausch, 2005/2006; Quinlan, 2004). Speech-recognition technology eases the cognitive bottleneck in working memory by helping to produce initial drafts that are longer, with fewer errors.

Adaptations to Output Devices

Adaptations to output devices also exist. For example, the size of the visual display is increased by using a special large-screen monitor, such as the one Jaleena used, or by using a magnification device that increases the size of the print. For students who are blind, speech synthesizers can read words and translate them into sounds. In addition, special printers can convert words into Braille and Braille into words.

These technologies are important because they prevent disabilities from becoming obstacles to learning. Their importance to students with exceptionalities is likely to increase as technology becomes a more integral part of classroom instruction.

Check Your Understanding

2.1   What is one similarity and one important difference between drill-and-practice and tutorial software?

2.2   As tools for promoting learning, what are the primary functions of simulations, databases, and spreadsheets?

2.3   What are three advantages of word processing over conventional methods of teaching writing?

2.4   What are two ways that teachers can use the Internet to increase students' learning?

2.5   What is assistive technology, and what are its major uses in the classroom?

 For feedback, go to Appendix A, Check Your Understanding, *located in the back of this text.*

> **Making Connections:**
> To deepen your understanding of the topics in this section of the chapter and integrate them with topics you've already studied, go to the *Making Connections* module for Chapter 13 at **www.prenhall.com/kauchak**. Respond to questions 3–8.

Teacher-Support Applications

So far we have emphasized technology as a tool to support student learning. It can also assist teachers by making their work in three major areas simpler and more efficient:

- Preparing instructional materials
- Assessing student learning
- Communicating with parents

Preparing Instructional Materials

Helping students learn in the 21st century is more complex than at any point in history (Eggen & Kauchak, 2007). Technology provides one tool to make abstract and complex ideas more accessible. For example, language arts teachers often use samples of student work to illustrate effective writing. Technology allows teachers to easily extract these examples and share them anonymously with the whole class. In addition, revising learning materials is simple with the support of technology but labor intensive without it.

Teachers can also create databases and spreadsheets that students can use in learning activities, such as the example involving factors that influence economic develop-

Technology provides teachers with an effective tool to plan and present lessons. [Cleve Bryant/PhotoEdit Inc.]

ment that you saw earlier. In that case, students can gather the information to include in the database, or teachers may choose to create the databases themselves and have students analyze them.

PowerPoint: Presenting Information in Dynamic Ways

Presenting new information is an important instructional role that is sometimes deemphasized with the current focus on constructivist learning theory. However, all new learning is based on students' prior knowledge, and teachers are often faced with the problem of presenting information in clear and motivating formats (Donavan & Bransford, 2005). Microsoft's PowerPoint format provides one effective alternative.

IN TODAY'S CLASSROOMS: VIDEO

Integrating Technology Into Instruction

To view this video, go to the *Becoming a Professional* DVD included with this text, click on *In Today's Classrooms*, and then this chapter's video: *Integrating Technology Into Instruction*. Answer the questions you'll find on the DVD.

This video examines two classrooms' applications of technology. In the first segment, a fifth-grade science teacher uses databases to teach basic principles of human genetics. In the second, a high school social studies teacher uses PowerPoint to structure a lesson on ancient Greece.

To answer questions about the video online and receive immediate feedback, go to the Companion Website at **www.prenhall.com/kauchak***, then to the* In Today's Classrooms *module for Chapter 13.*

Jokingly referred to as "an overhead projector on steroids" (Cuban, 2005), PowerPoint is actually a versatile presentation format. Once mastered, it allows teachers to include the following in their presentations:

- Written text
- Photographs
- Samples of student work
- Charts and graphs
- Video clips
- Voice-overs

Students can also learn to use PowerPoint in their presentations, and these options can encourage them to think more deeply about the material they are presenting and its effect on their audience (Saltpeter, 2005).

PowerPoint does not have to be a one-way presentation of information. As teachers present information, they can—and should—check whether students understand and are connecting ideas. Teachers can also use PowerPoint to present quizzes that provide both teachers and students with immediate feedback about learner progress (Finkelstein, 2005).

Assessing Student Learning

Assessing student learning is one of the most important tasks teachers face. Research confirms that frequent and thorough assessments increase learning (Bransford et al., 2000), but creating these assessments can be demanding for teachers. Technology, and particularly computers, can serve four time-saving assessment functions (Newby et al., 2006). They are summarized in Table 13.1 and discussed in the sections that follow.

Planning and Constructing Tests

The word processing capabilities of computers provide teachers with an effective tool for writing, storing, and revising individual test items and then constructing tests from these items. In addition, a number of commercially prepared software programs can assist in this process. These programs can be used to achieve the following:

- Develop a test file or item bank of multiple-choice, true–false, matching, and short-answer items that can be stored in the system.
- Organize items within a file by topic, chapter, objective, or difficulty.
- Select items from the created file bank randomly, selectively, or by categories to generate multiple versions of a test.

TABLE 13.1   Assessment Functions Supported by Computers

Function	Examples
Planning and constructing tests	Preparing objectives Writing, editing, and storing items Compiling items into tests Printing tests
Administering tests	Administering tests online Providing immediate corrective feedback Analyzing results
Scoring and interpreting tests	Scoring tests Summarizing results Analyzing items
Maintaining student records	Recording results Developing class summaries Reporting results to students Preparing grade reports

- Modify items and integrate them into the total test.
- Produce student-ready copies and an answer key.

Software test generators have three advantages over basic word processing. First, they produce a standard layout; the teacher doesn't have to worry about spacing or format. Second, they automatically produce alternate forms, which can be helpful for creating makeup tests and preventing cheating. Third, they can be used to customize commercially prepared test banks that come with textbooks.

Administering Tests

Research shows that active learning and feedback can have powerful effects on learning (Eggen & Kauchak, 2007), but logistics can be an obstacle to providing feedback; it is challenging to grade a large number of student quizzes and return them in a timely way, for example. Technology provides one solution (Trotter, 2005). In some classrooms, students take quizzes by watching a TV screen mounted at the front of the room. They respond with hand-held "clickers" that record their answers on the instructor's computer, which provides the teacher and students with immediate feedback about the number of students who got the right answer and the number who chose each incorrect answer.

Computer software also exists that allows teachers to construct tests and administer them online (Roblyer, 2006). This is useful in dealing with students who are absent on the day of the test or in individualized programs where students progress at different rates. These programs can also give students immediate feedback about right and wrong answers and can provide the teacher with updated information about individual student performance on the test and the performance of the class as a whole.

Experts believe that online testing will play a major role in states' new accountability programs (Edwards, 2003). Currently, 12 states and the District of Columbia have either a computerized exam or pilot project under way to evaluate the effectiveness of computer-based testing. The almost immediate feedback provided to both teachers and students is a major strength of these systems. These same technologies can also provide valuable practice in preparing for high-stakes tests (Borja, 2003). However, experts caution that teachers should carefully monitor students during testing, as student expertise with computer keyboards can affect test performance.

Scoring and Interpreting Tests

Technology can also assist in scoring tests and reporting results, saving time for the teacher and providing students with more immediate and informative feedback. For example, a high school teacher with five sections of 30 students and a 40-item exam faces the daunting task of grading 6,000 (5 × 30 × 40) individual items! Scoring, analyzing test data, converting scores to grades, and recording the grades can be enormously time-consuming without the help of technology.

A number of software programs are available to machine-score tests (e.g., *QuickSCORE*). These programs perform the following functions:

- Score objective tests and provide descriptive statistics, such as test mean, median, mode, range, and standard deviation.
- Generate a list of items showing difficulty level, the percentage of students who selected each response, the percentage of students who didn't respond to an item, and the correlation of each item with the total test.
- Sort student responses by score, grade/age, or gender.

Maintaining Student Records

Technology can also assist with record keeping after the test, another time-consuming teacher task. One teacher commented,

I keep my grades in an electronic gradebook. By entering my grades into an electronic gradebook as I grade papers, I always know how my students are progressing and exactly where my students stand in relation to each other. It does take a little time to enter the grades, but it makes my job easier during reporting periods. All I have to do is open my disk and record my students' grades on the grade sheet. (Morrison & Lowther, 2002, p. 348)

In addition to saving teacher time and energy, these programs are accurate (assuming the original data are accurately entered) and immediate, which allows teachers to generate grades at the end of a marking period with just a few keystrokes. In addition, records are available at any time, providing students and their parents with ongoing feedback. Some programs can even print student reports in a language other than English, such as Spanish.

Schools are also using technology to keep attendance records and keep track of lunch money (Hurst, 2004; Jennings, 2000). For example, when students come into school, they slide their identification cards into a device similar to those used by credit card machines. In addition to keeping daily attendance, the machines are effective for helping schools identify unwelcome outside visitors and students who cut classes during the day.

Communicating With Parents

As you saw in Chapter 11, involving parents in their children's education is an important teacher role. Communication is an essential step in that process, and technology can help make home–school links more effective.

Parents' and teachers' busy schedules present obstacles to home–school communication. Voice mail and e-mail can help overcome these obstacles by creating communication channels between parents who work and teachers who are busy with students all day (Jacobson, 2005). For instance, parents (and students) can e-mail teachers to monitor students' learning progress, check current grades, and get information about missed assignments. Experts caution, however, that teachers should be sensitive to the fact that not all homes have computers, a topic we'll return to later in the chapter.

A growing number of teachers use Websites to share their syllabi and their classroom rules and procedures, as well as to describe current class topics and assignments. Schools also use electronic hotlines to keep parents informed about current events, schedule changes, lunch menus, and bus schedules.

One innovation uses the Internet to provide parents with real-time images of their children at school (Kleiman, 2001). Increasing numbers of preschool and day-care programs are installing cameras and Internet systems that provide parents with secure-access Websites to visit and monitor their children during the day.

This section addresses the third item on our beginning-of-chapter survey, "Technology can be a major time-saver for teachers." If teachers have the expertise, technology can, indeed, save teachers time by assisting with professional tasks ranging from instruction to assessment to communicating with parents.

Making Connections:
To deepen your understanding of the topics in this section of the chapter and integrate them with topics you've already studied, go to the *Making Connections* module for Chapter 13 at **www.prenhall.com/kauchak.** Respond to questions 9 and 10.

Check Your Understanding

3.1   How can technology assist teachers in the preparation of learning materials?

3.2   What are the major logistical challenges teachers face in assessment, and how can technology address them?

3.3   How can technology assist teachers in their efforts to communicate with parents and other caregivers?

 For feedback, go to Appendix A, Check Your Understanding, *located in the back of this text.*

Instructional Issues in the Use of Educational Technology

Technology is changing both teaching and learning in the 21st century, and controversies exist about its application. Though virtually all U.S. schools have Internet access, and the student/computer ratio has decreased in the last two decades from 125 to the current 3.8 students per computer, technology use in schools remains spotty (National Center for Education Statistics, 2006a; Swanson, 2006b). Based on his extensive work in schools, Cuban (2005) estimates that only 10 percent of teachers seamlessly integrate technology into their classrooms at least once a week, and 40 percent don't use it at all. A poll of teachers supports his findings; 45 percent reported they didn't integrate computers into their daily curriculum (CDW Government, 2005). Technology use is most prevalent at the elementary level, where teachers have more time with students and more flexibility with the curriculum. At the high school and college levels, technology use is less common because of the heavy emphasis on specific content acquisition.

In this section, we examine the following instructional issues facing teachers as they attempt to use technology in their classrooms:

- Quality of available software
- Instructional alignment problems
- Accountability and time constraints
- Access issues in the use of technology
- Plagiarism and cheating
- Censorship

Quality of Available Software

Quality of available software is an important technology issue because it affects student learning and the integration of software into instruction. Teachers generally rate existing software as good, but two important factors influence its quality (Trotter, 1999a; Zehr, 1999). First, the market drives software production. Companies create software to make money, and quality is often less important than profit. Second, much software is based on antiquated views of learning that result in the proliferation of "drill and kill" programs that are little more than electronic flash cards. Experts estimate that 85 percent of current classroom software emphasizes the learning of basic skills (Jonassen, 2000). One study of middle and high school classrooms found that electronic presentations or word processing were the most common uses, and little emphasis was placed on problem solving or higher-level thinking (Burns, 2005/2006).

Some educational software is both creative and innovative, however. For example, teachers can use voice-recognition software to provide one-on-one tutoring to beginning readers (Watch Me! Read, 2005; Mostow, 2005). Using this software, a child can read aloud from a book that comes with the program or any other materials that are scanned into the tool. When the child skips an important word or misreads a word, the program coaches the student to try again. As more emphasis is placed on beginning reading by the No Child Left Behind Act, software such as this will be increasingly used.

This section suggests that the fourth statement on our beginning-of-chapter survey, "Reinforcing facts and skills is the primary use of technology in schools," is true; experts estimate that 85 percent of the software currently in use in schools is to reinforce basic facts and skills. However, as you've seen in this chapter, teachers can also use technology to support instruction in many other creative ways.

Instructional Alignment Problems

Effective instruction requires that learning objectives and instruction are consistent with each other (Bransford et al., 2000; Porter, 2002). For example, if a teacher wants to develop students' ability to write effectively but spends the majority of classroom time having students punctuate sentences in work sheets, her instruction is out of alignment. With respect to technology, this means that matching technology tools with learning objectives is essential (Coppola, 2004). For example, after a search of catalogues and Websites, a teacher may find an attractive (and perhaps high-quality) software program. However, if the software doesn't match state or district curriculum guides, mandated tests, or the teacher's specific learning objectives, it amounts to a waste of time and money on "bells and whistles" and shouldn't be used. In one national teacher survey, the match between software and state/district curricula was rated C or lower by over 59 percent of teachers, and the match with state/district tests received a C or lower by over 39 percent of the same teachers (Trotter, 1999b). This problem is not unique to technology; textbook series are also often out of alignment with respect to both state and district goals and standardized tests (Porter, 2002). Again, we see why teacher professional knowledge and expertise are so important.

Accountability and Time Constraints

Pressure to cover the curriculum is a related issue. Schools and classrooms are busy places, and teachers struggle to "get it all in." Teachers often feel that integrating technology with an already crowded curriculum is nearly overwhelming. Many of the better quality software programs are problem based (like the Jasper series we saw earlier in the chapter), but they *do* take more time (Cognition and Technology Group at Vanderbilt, 1997). When pressed for time, teachers often resort to simple instructional strategies, such as lectures. For example, one study of secondary social studies teachers found that they rarely used electronic historical resources for student investigations (J. Lee & Doolittle, 2003). And when they did use the resources, it was primarily to download pictures and other artifacts to illustrate lectures.

When faced with the pressures of accountability-driven tests, teachers have trouble implementing advice from learning experts suggesting that "slower and deeper is better than faster and broader" (Schunk, 2004). In this regard, Larry Cuban, a respected educational historian, concluded, "The current frenzy for testing and accountability is so extreme that the idea of squeezing something else (like technology) into the core curriculum . . . is highly unlikely" (Zehr, 2000, p. 18). Integrating technology requires preparation time, and amount of preparation needed and ease of use are two reasons teachers commonly give for not using technology more often (Trotter, 1999a).

Access Issues in the Use of Technology

The simple matter of access is one of the most important issues in the use of technology. If teachers and students don't have access to technology, they obviously can't use it to increase learning.

One survey of educational technology use across the country found that, by 2003, nearly 100 percent of public schools and 93 percent of classrooms had Internet access (Ansell & Park, 2003; National Center for Education Statistics, 2006a). In the time span from 2003 to 2005, the ratio of students per Internet-connected computer dropped from 4.4 to 3.8 (Swanson, 2006b). So, in a class of 30 students, the "average" teacher will have about seven Internet-connected computers available. This is a significant improvement from one Internet-connected computer per 12 students in 1998, but still requires instructional juggling to provide computer access to all students when they need it. When asked to identify major barriers to effective use of technology, 61 percent of teachers targeted insufficient number of computers as a major problem (Rother, 2005).

You saw in Chapter 8 that great disparities in educational funding exist between "rich" and "poor" school districts. These disparities result in differences in teachers' salaries, the kinds of buildings and classrooms teachers and students work in, and the resources available to promote learning. They also impact students' access to technology, suggesting a possible "digital divide" between different groups of students (Corporation for Public Broadcasting, 2003; Trotter, 2006c).

Considerable variation exists among different ethnic groups and families with differing levels of parents' education and income. For example, as you see in Figure 13.5, 80 percent of Caucasian households with school-age children had a computer in the home versus only 61 percent of African American and 67 percent of Hispanic households (Kaiser Family Foundation, 2004b). And while 67 percent of White students were likely to use the Internet, just 47 percent of African-American students and 44 percent of Hispanic students were likely to do so (Trotter, 2006c). Also, 82 percent of students whose parents had a college degree had access to the Internet at home versus 74 percent and 68 percent for households with some or no college, respectively.

Figure 13.5   Ethnicity, Parental Education, and Home Internet Access for Children (Ages 8–18), 2003–2004

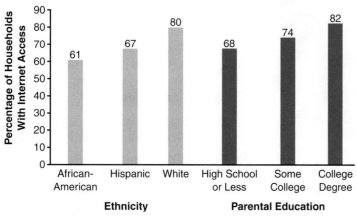

Source: Adapted from Kaiser Family Foundation (2004b). *Survey Snapshot: The Digital Divide.*

Figure 13.6   Household Income and Technology Access in 2002

Percentage

	Ownership of Computer	Online Use at Home	Access to Internet From Any Location
Low Income	65	29	55
Middle Income	85	49	62
High Income	98	66	77

◻ Low Income   ◼ Middle Income   ◻ High Income

Source: Adapted from Corporation for Public Broadcasting (2003).

Further, as you see in Figure 13.6, in 2002 65 percent of low-income families reported owning computers versus 98 percent of high-income families (Corporation for Public Broadcasting, 2003). When asked about their ability to access the Internet from any location (home, school, or library), 55 percent of low-income students reported access versus 77 percent of high-income students. The biggest difference between the groups was seen in online home use of computers; less than half as many low-income as high-income students said they used the Internet at home. The cost of buying, installing, and maintaining computers is probably the main reason for this disparity. When students are expected to work on computers at home to complete assignments, access can be a serious problem.

These differences are troubling for several reasons. Research suggests that the number and quality of computers influence teachers' use of technology. When obstacles are too great, teachers tend not to use it, which deprives their students of valuable learning opportunities (Collis, Peters, & Pals, 2001). From a student perspective, these statistics raise the question of whether all students are being provided with equal opportunities to learn. In the long term, access to computers can also influence the kinds of career options available to students. Students are less likely to pursue high-tech careers in areas such as science and engineering if they have inadequate technology backgrounds or have not been introduced to ways that technology is used in these areas. According to one estimate, "by 2010, one in every four new jobs will . . . involve the use, design, application, or maintenance of computers" (AAUW Education Foundation, 2000, p. 56). The challenge for educators is to prepare all students to compete in such an environment.

Plagiarism and Cheating

The easy access to information, and even complete papers, on the Internet has become a temptation for students and a problem for teachers. Students are downloading papers or sections of papers and handing them in as their own. In addition to ethical problems, plagiarism robs students of experiences in analyzing, organizing, and expressing their own ideas.

Teachers can prevent plagiarism and cheating by working closely with students during the writing process. [Dennis MacDonald/ PhotoEdit Inc.]

Internet Censorship

The Internet can be a powerful learning tool, but students' ability to access information from it at the click of a button also raises concerns about the kinds of materials available to children. Internet filtering via software programs can block out entire lists of Web pages based on specific, predetermined categories, or people can use certain words to limit access to sites. For example, states typically use filters to prevent students from accessing information in five broad categories: criminal skills, hate speech, drugs, gambling, and sex (Callister & Burbules, 2004).

The Issue

Several controversies surround the practice of filtering. The first is the whole issue of censorship and free speech. Free speech advocates contend that such filtering is unconstitutional, violating students' rights to free speech and access to information.

Also, censorship results in the exclusion of many interesting and educationally defensible sites (Callister & Burbules, 2004). For example, one sex screen banned information on breast cancer, a gambling screen excluded the History of Nevada Website, and a criminal skills page eliminated sites on Marxism and even the Declaration of Independence (presumably because it calls for citizens to violently overthrow their government, if necessary). Critics contend that this indiscriminate screening process not only robs students of important information but also may be politically biased, as in the case with Marxism.

Censor advocates counter that Internet filtering is no different from selecting curriculum content and textbooks for students based on fundamental principles of good teaching.

Internet filters can prevent students from accessing pornography, violent material, or games. [Michael Newman/PhotoEdit Inc.]

This comparison with school books illustrates how challenging and complex Internet filtering can be. Textbook selection is centralized and consequently much easier; school districts and schools are given lists of several textbook series that a state curriculum committee finds acceptable. Internet filtering, by contrast, is aimed at a moving target, because new Websites appear daily. For example, the Tennessee statewide system controls access to 100,000 computers used by 900,000 students. The system needs to be updated every night and has blocked access to 7 million Web pages (Furlan, 1999).

A third controversy surrounding Internet filtering is the level at which it should occur. Some argue for federal legislation, claiming this is a national problem; others argue for state or district control, pointing out that local agencies are in a better position to decide what is best for the needs of their children. When local control occurs, however, there is the possibility of duplication of effort, with thousands of local districts performing essentially the same function. This issue has no easy answers. In 2000, the U.S. Congress passed the Children's Internet Protection Act, which requires that all schools and libraries that receive federal funds for Internet connection install pornography filters in their systems (Walsh & Hendrie, 2003). These restrictions, however, only apply to pornography and don't deal with other gray areas such as violence and games that the Tennessee state filter attempts to screen. The U.S. Supreme Court, in a case questioning this law, upheld its legality, but questions still remain (Hendrie & Walsh, 2003). An important one is whether filters can effectively discriminate between developmental levels, that is, what may be inappropriate for a 7-year-old may not be for a 17-year-old.

The whole area of Internet access will, in all likelihood, continue to grow in importance as more classrooms use the Internet to access data.

You Take a Position

Now it's your turn to take a position on the issue. State in writing whether you favor or oppose the use of Internet filtering in schools, and provide a two-page rationale for your position. If you favor, at what level should this filtering take place?

For additional references and resources, go to the Companion Website at www.prenhall.com/kauchak, then to the Teaching in an Era of Reform *module for Chapter 13. You can respond online or submit your response to your instructor.*

Suggestions for addressing this problem range from instructional approaches to high-tech solutions that analyze student work and compare it to databases containing hundreds of thousands of papers. Instructionally, the place to start is the writing assignment itself (D. Johnson, 2004). For example, assignments that require students to react personally to content and think at higher levels motivate them to think on their own and also discourage plagiarism and cheating (Freedman, 2004). Teachers can also hold honest discussions about problems involved with plagiarism. Teachers can also reduce the problem by closely working with students, from the initial draft stages to the final product. If all else fails, Websites exist that can help teachers detect copying and wholesale borrowing of intact passages. Web addresses for companies that do this can be found on the Website for this book.

This section addresses the fifth item on our beginning-of-chapter survey, "Plagiarism and cheating in the classroom have become more widespread because of the presence of technology." Unfortunately, evidence indicates that the statement is true. Technology provides a number of tools that students can use to access information and insert into papers verbatim.

> **Making Connections:**
> To deepen your understanding of the topics in this section of the chapter and integrate them with topics you've already studied, go to the *Making Connections* module for Chapter 13 at **www.prenhall.com/kauchak**. Respond to questions 11–13.

Check Your Understanding

4.1   How do alignment and software quality affect classroom technology use?

4.2   How do accountability and time constraints influence teachers' use of technology?

4.3   How is the easy access of information on the Internet both an advantage and a problem for teachers?

4.4   What is the digital divide, and how does access differ for different groups of students?

 For feedback, go to Appendix A, Check Your Understanding, *located in the back of this text.*

decision making

Defining Yourself as a Professional

*Your students have almost completed a unit you created that required them to research a topic on the Internet, gather data, and organize it using databases and spreadsheets. The students have collected a considerable amount of data, and you are amazed with how well they have manipulated and analyzed the information. In fact, you are wondering if you made the "Think Sheets" too simple. The students are working together, and it appears even the slower and less-motivated students are going to earn high marks for their work. Shortly after lunch, you receive a note from the office indicating that Mrs. Karmzynsky, the mother of one of your students, would like to meet with you after school. After commenting on the great job you are doing with your reading instruc-*tion, Mrs. Karmzynsky expresses her concern about your teaching methods in other areas. She and Mr. Karmzynsky are concerned about the amount of time students spend working together and the lack of focus on the content in the textbook. Emphatically, she asks, "How can you expect these students to learn if they are not studying the chapters in the text?"

What would you do in this situation?

To respond to this question online and receive immediate feedback, go to the Decision Making *module for Chapter 13 on the Companion Website at* **www.prenhall.com/kauchak**.

Meeting Your Learning Objectives

1. **Define technology, and describe the difference between hardware and process views of technology.**
   - One view of technology looks at it in terms of hardware, such as computers, whereas another sees technology as an integrative process that completely transforms instruction.
   - Most experts see instructional technology as a combination of the processes and tools needed to address educational needs.

2. **Describe different instructional uses of technology.**
   - Technology has many different uses in the classroom. Most involve drill-and-practice software, which focuses on learning basic skills. Drill-and-practice software provides students with opportunities to practice skills and receive immediate feedback.
   - Tutorials, which provide entire instructional sequences, can also be used to teach skills. Tutorials are similar to drill-and-practice software in that they provide opportunities for practice with feedback. However, tutorials also provide initial instruction on a topic and may also include hypermedia and multimedia, which increase realism.
   - Teachers can also use technology to teach higher-level thinking skills through simulations, which bring realistic slices of the world into classrooms, and problem-solving activities, which capture aspects of real-world situations for instructional purposes.
   - Database and spreadsheet programs, which assist students in organizing and analyzing data, can also become powerful tools to teach higher-level thinking skills.
   - The word-processing capabilities of computers have revolutionized the teaching of writing by allowing students to edit and revise their works in progress. Technology also provides opportunities for students to share their writing drafts and receive feedback from peers.
   - The Internet can help both teachers and students in the teaching–learning process. It provides a ready source of information and allows students to communicate with others around the world who are involved in similar research ventures. It has also provided educational opportunities through various forms of distance learning.
   - Assistive technology provides students with exceptionalities with tools to function successfully in the classroom. Major adaptations are to input and output aspects of computers. Input adaptations make it easier to type in information to the computer; output devices make reading computer screens easier.

3. **Explain how technology can assist teachers in different professional tasks.**
   - Technology can help teachers in planning by assisting them in preparing instructional materials. It also allows teachers to share samples of student work for whole-class analysis. In addition, PowerPoint provides another instructional alternative for presenting information.
   - Technology can assist teachers in assessing student learning. It can help design and administer tests and maintain student records. A number of commercial software programs provide assistance in these areas.
   - Technology can assist teachers as they attempt to communicate with parents and other caregivers. Voice mail and e-mail provide effective communication links with busy parents. In addition, teacher Websites provide opportunities for teachers to share information about their classes.

4. **Discuss how different instructional issues affect the use of educational technology in the classroom.**
   - The quality of available software is an important issue in the use of technology. Software often focuses on low-level skills and uses drill and practice to reach these goals.
   - The extent to which software is aligned with teacher's learning objectives is a second major issue in the use of technology. Teachers often encounter difficulties integrating technology into their instruction because the technology does not align with state or district learning standards or goals.

(continued)

- Time constraints are additional issues. Teachers are required to teach essential concepts and skills, and they are held accountable for their students' learning. Time constraints often detract from using innovative forms of technology.
- Student access to technology is a major issue in education. Students can't learn from technology if they don't have access to it. While virtually all classrooms have computers and most have Internet access, student access to computers and the Internet at home varies with ethnicity, parents' education, and income.
- The wealth of information on the Internet provides challenges to teachers in terms of plagiarism and cheating. Instructionally, teachers can talk with students about the importance of doing their own work and can also provide assistance during the writing process. Websites also exist where teachers can investigate whether passages have been lifted verbatim.
- Censorship attempts to protect students from objectionable material. Technology exists that can block students' access to objectionable materials. However, educators aren't sure if this censorship should occur at the federal, state, or local levels.

Important Concepts

assistive technology (p. 428)
bulletin board (p. 425)
chat room (p. 425)
computer-mediated communication (CMC) (p. 425)
database program (p. 422)
distance learning (p. 426)
drill-and-practice programs (p. 417)
educational technology (p. 416)
hypermedia (p. 419)

icons (p. 419)
Internet (p. 424)
multimedia (p. 419)
problem-based learning (p. 426)
simulations (p. 420)
spreadsheet programs (p. 422)
tutorial (p. 418)
uniform resource locator (URL) (p. 425)
Website (p. 425)
World Wide Web (p. 424)

Developing as a Professional

Preparing for Your Licensure Exam

This exercise will provide you with practice answering questions similar to the Praxis™ Principles of Learning and Teaching Exam, as well as your state-specific licensure exam. Read the following case study, and answer the questions that follow.

Maria Villenas, a middle-school health teacher in an inner-city urban school, sits at her desk during her planning period.

"How can I make this unit on nutrition come alive for my students?" she thinks as she gazes at the mound of planning materials on her desk. "I know last year's lecture almost put them and me to sleep."

"I know," she thinks. "They love thinking about themselves and finding out how they're similar and different from their friends. I'll have them keep a food journal for a week, and then we'll see if we can organize the class's eating habits into a chart or graph. That should give them practice in using the computer to organize information as well as with working in groups. Hmm, I'll need to check the district's curriculum guidelines for nutrition to make sure I'm still covering all the bases."

With these thoughts in mind, Maria prepares the following lesson plan:

Lesson Plan

Topic: Food and Nutrition

Goals

1. Students should understand the role of calories in their diet.

2. Students should understand the Food Guide Pyramid and apply it to their diets.

3. Students should be able to analyze diets in terms of calories and the major food groups.

Procedures

1. Introduce concept of calories. Have students read section in text on calories. Students will complete work sheet in small groups. Discuss as a whole-group activity.

2. Display food pyramid transparency. Explain differences among carbohydrates, proteins, and fats. Illustrate with common foods. Place students in small groups to categorize additional foods. Check categorization in whole group.

3. Introduce journaling assignment. Take first 5 minutes of class each day to allow time for students to edit and answer questions.

Follow-up

1. Check on availability of software to do spreadsheets.

2. Explain and demonstrate how to use computer to analyze and graph data.

3. Form research groups to analyze data. Make sure equal numbers of high-ability and low-ability students and boys and girls are in each group. Assign rotating roles so boys and high-ability students don't do everything.

4. Make sure research groups have plenty of research time to complete assignments, because many students don't have computers at home to work on.

5. Plan for group presentations.

Assessment

1. Test on basic concepts (check last year's and update).

2. Group presentation.

"Whew," Maria sighs. "This is going to be a lot of work, and it'll take time, but it should be a fun learning experience—for them and me."

1. Did Maria's lesson plan reflect a hardware or process view of technology use? Explain.

2. Did Maria's lesson focus more on problem solving or problem-based learning? Explain.

3. Which of the following instructional issues did Maria wrestle with as she planned her lesson: instructional goals, quality of software, curricular alignment with instructional goals, curricular pressures, preparation time constraints, plagiarism and cheating, and Internet access?

To receive feedback on your responses to these exercises, go to the Companion Website at www.prenhall.com/kauchak, then to the Preparing for Your Licensure Exam *module for Chapter 13.*

Discussion Questions

1. Which view of technology—hardware or process—is more prevalent in the schools? Why is this the case? What could be done to improve the balance?

2. In what areas of the curriculum is it most useful to use technology for instruction? In what areas is it least useful? Why?

3. What are the relative advantages and disadvantages of using drill-and-practice software and tutorials versus teacher-led instruction? In what areas and at what levels are these forms of technology most effective?

4. Should Internet filtering occur at the national or local level? What are the advantages and disadvantages of each approach?

5. What can teachers do to overcome the digital divide in their own classrooms? What can they do at the school or district level?

6. What is the biggest obstacle to more effective technology use in schools? What can beginning teachers realistically do to address this problem?

Developing as a Professional: Online Activities

Going Into Schools

Go to the Companion Website at *www.prenhall.com/kauchak,* and click on the *Going Into Schools* module for Chapter 13. You will find a number of school-based activities that will help you link chapter content to the schools in which you work.

Virtual Field Experience: Using Teacher Prep to Explore the Profession

If you would like to participate in a Virtual Field Experience, access the Teacher Prep Website at *www.prenhall.com/teacherprep.* After logging in, complete the following steps:

1. Click on "Video Classroom" on the left panel of the screen.

2. Go to "Foundations and Introduction to Education."

3. Finally, click on "Module 7: Technology." This video focuses on different ways that teachers can integrate technology into instruction. Answer the questions that follow the video clip.

Online Portfolio Activities

To develop your professional portfolio, further apply your understanding of chapter content, and address the INTASC standards, go the Companion Website at *www.prenhall.com/kauchak*, then to the *Online Portfolio Activities* for Chapter 13. Complete the suggested activities.

Check Your Understanding

Chapter 1   Do I Want to Be a Teacher?

1.1   What are the major rewards in teaching?

The major rewards in teaching can be divided into two main categories, intrinsic and extrinsic. In terms of intrinsic benefits, emotional rewards such as getting to know students on a personal level and helping young people grow and develop are important, as well as the intellectual rewards of learning new content and playing with ideas.

Extrinsic rewards include job security, frequent vacations, convenient work schedules, and the relatively high occupational status of teaching.

1.2   What are the major challenges in teaching?

The major challenges in teaching include the complexities of classrooms, which make professional decision making so difficult, as well as the multiple roles that teachers perform.

The first challenge—the complexity of classrooms—is described by five interrelated characteristics of teaching: It is (1) multidimensional and (2) simultaneous, meaning a number of things are going on in classrooms at the same time. (3) Classroom events are also pressing, requiring immediate attention from the teacher. (4) Classroom events, being human, are unpredictable. (5) Finally, classrooms are also public, making the decisions a teacher makes visible to students, and even parents and other professionals.

A second challenge facing teachers is their performance of multiple roles. Teachers are expected to create productive learning environments, work as partners with parents and caregivers, and collaborate with colleagues.

1.3   Identify the four most often cited reasons to enter teaching.

Results from a national poll, as well as our own informal surveys, indicate that wanting to work with young people and wanting to contribute to society are the two major reasons that people go into teaching. Our results showed that opportunities for personal growth and learning more about a content area were also important.

2.1   What are the essential characteristics of professionalism?

A specialized body of knowledge that sets the professional apart from the lay public is perhaps the most important characteristic of professionalism. Autonomy, which provides the freedom to make important decisions, is a second characteristic. A specialized body of knowledge together with autonomy allow the professional to make decisions in ill-defined situations, and reflection helps professionals improve their decisions. Finally, ethical standards provide sets of principles that guide professionals as they work with students and caregivers.

2.2   What are the primary arguments for teaching being a profession?

Proponents of teaching as a profession point to the growing body of research on teaching that shows that effective teaching requires several different kinds of knowledge and requires an extended period of training for licensure. In addition, teaching professionals engage in continuous decision making in their classrooms and reflect on the effectiveness of these decisions. Teachers also have considerable autonomy in their classrooms and are guided by ethical standards for conduct.

2.3   What are the major arguments against teaching being a profession?

Critics who claim that teaching isn't a true profession base their claims on two major points. First, they point out that teaching often doesn't require rigorous training before licensure. Second, they point out that teacher autonomy is limited by curricular standards and assessment procedures.

2.4   How do the arguments for and against teacher professionalism balance each other?

Though the rigor required for teaching isn't as great as other professions, it is increasing. In addition, though their current autonomy is restricted by standards and testing, teachers still have a considerable amount of autonomy in the classroom. The future of the professionalization movement in teaching will be significantly influenced by current reform efforts.

3.1   Identify the different dimensions of student diversity. Explain how these dimensions will influence your work as a teacher.

Culture and ethnicity, language, religion, socioeconomic status, academic ability, physical and emotional maturity, gender, and learner exceptionalities are all sources of diversity. These different dimensions of diversity provide both challenges and opportunities to teachers. Diverse classrooms are more challenging to work in because they increase the number of decisions that teachers have to make. They also provide opportunities for both teacher and student growth. By working with diverse students, teachers learn about themselves and also have opportunities to enrich the lives of their students by helping them understand commonalities and differences in all people.

3.2   Why is an understanding of different teaching and learning environments important for beginning teachers?

Each of the different teaching and learning environments offers both opportunities and challenges to beginning teachers. Rural districts are smaller and tend to be more culturally homogeneous. Suburban districts are intermediate in size and tend to be better funded. Urban districts are larger and more culturally diverse. The number of jobs available in urban settings is increasing, and many urban districts target beginning teachers for job offers. They do this by offering a number of incentives to work in their classrooms.

4.1   How is the current reform movement in education changing the teaching profession?

The current reform movement in education is changing the profession in at least two ways. First, changes are occurring in teacher preparation, with teachers being held to higher academic standards and having their competency measured through state licensure exams.

Second, standards, specifying what students should know and be able to do after a course of study, and accountability, the process of holding students and their teachers responsible for demonstrating that they have met specified standards, are at the heart of the reform movement. Standards and accountability are influencing the curriculum—what teachers teach— and in some cases even how they teach, meaning that they teach in ways that maximize the likelihood of students doing well on the tests. In addition, high-stakes testing is often used to determine whether students can progress from one grade to the next or graduate.

4.2   Describe the major changes in teacher preparation that have resulted from the reform movement in education.

Major changes in teacher preparation primarily target higher standards for admission and higher academic standards within the programs themselves. Candidates are required to take more rigorous courses both before they enter and within teacher preparation programs. Prospective teachers also face higher licensure requirements for entering the profession, including teacher-competency tests. Many teacher-preparation programs are being expanded from 4 to 5 years, and experienced teachers are being asked to take more rigorous professional development courses.

4.3   What is INTASC? How has it influenced teacher preparation?

The Interstate New Teacher Assessment and Support Consortium (INTASC) was created in 1987 to help states develop better teachers through coordinated interstate cooperation. It created core standards for teacher preparation organized around 10 principles. These include knowledge of subject, knowledge of learners and human development, planning and instructional strategies as well as ways to work with parents and colleagues. These standards have improved the quality of teacher education and brought about greater uniformity in programs across states.

Chapter 2   Developing as a Professional

1.1   How effective do beginning teachers believe they will be compared to teachers already in the field?

Beginning teachers are idealistic and believe they will be very effective. They further believe that they will be more effective than teachers who are now in the field, and they believe that their confidence in their ability to promote student learning will increase as they gain experience.

1.2   Describe beginning teachers' beliefs about what makes a teacher effective.

Beginning teachers believe that the most effective teachers are those best able to clearly explain the content they teach to their students, and they also believe that if they thoroughly understand their content, they will figure out a way of helping students learn it.

1.3   Describe how beginning teachers' confidence in their ability to help students learn changes as they gain experience.

Unfortunately, as beginning teachers acquire experience in their first few years of teaching, their confidence in their ability to help students learn tends to decrease, and they often feel as if "No one prepared me for this."

2.1   What are two differences between traditional and alternative licensure?

First, students in traditional licensure programs take professional training courses in education while working toward their bachelor's degree. Alternative licensure students have already earned a bachelor's degree in some field other than education.

Second, traditional licensure people get much more professional training in education than do alternative licensure candidates. Typically, alternative licensure candidates take short intensive training in education, and they are supposed to receive extensive mentoring when they get out on the job. This mentoring is commonly missing, however.

2.2   What are the two most essential factors involved in finding a desirable job?

The two most essential factors involved in finding a desirable job are developing a positive professional reputation and interviewing effectively. If you have developed a positive professional reputation, you will earn supportive letters of recommendation, which make you more marketable.

Interviewers assess a variety of factors during an interview, such as your professional knowledge, personality characteristics, dress, use of language, and enthusiasm for teaching. How you come across in each of these areas will be significant in whether or not you're offered a job.

2.3   **In which areas are teaching jobs most plentiful?**

Two categories of plentiful jobs exist. The first is related to content area. For example, jobs are plentiful in areas such as math, science (particularly chemistry and physics), special education, and foreign languages, and particularly Spanish.

Many jobs also exist in challenging teaching situations, such as underperforming urban schools with high percentages of minority students and students whose native language is other than English.

3.1   **What are four factors that will determine whether or not your first year of teaching will be successful?**

Organization, classroom management, effective instruction, and knowing your students are four factors that will influence how successful your first year will be. For this reason, we describe them as "survival skills" for your first year of teaching. Each is important, but classroom management is one of the most essential. More beginning teachers leave the profession because of their inability to manage students than for any other reason.

3.2   **Describe the characteristics of successful induction programs.**

Effective induction programs include systematic efforts that are designed to help beginning teachers and give special attention to new teachers to help them link their instruction to state and district standards. They also include professional development activities designed to increase mentors' effectiveness and compensation for mentors, offer support with everyday problems, and encourage teachers to develop a reflective professional attitude. In addition, new teachers in effective induction programs are observed, and they're given detailed feedback and support with planning and instruction.

3.3   **How are teacher-evaluation systems created and used?**

Educators base the design of teacher-evaluation systems on research and theory that describes connections between teaching and learning. Educators gather and compile findings from a variety of sources and create observation instruments based on research. Administrators or supervising teachers then observe and evaluate teachers using the observation instruments as a guide.

4.1   **What are three career-long professional development opportunities that are available to you as a teacher?**

Involving yourself in professional organizations, becoming a teacher-leader, and attaining National Board certification are all long-term professional development opportunities.

4.2   **What are five different activities designed to improve teaching and schools that professional organizations support?**

Professional organizations attempt to improve teaching and schools by (1) producing and disseminating professional publications that provide up-to-date research and information on trends in the profession, (2) providing professional development activities for teachers, (3) holding yearly conferences that present theory and research about recent professional advances, (4) providing resources where teachers can find answers to questions about professional issues and problems, and (5) providing politicians and policy makers with information about important issues facing education.

4.3 What are the two primary assessment processes involved in attaining National Board certification?

The two primary assessment processes involved in acquiring National Board certification are passing a set of exams in an area of specialty, such as math, science, early childhood, or physical education and health, and submitting evidence of teaching ability, such as video-tapes of classroom instruction and a personal portfolio that demonstrates expertise.

Chapter 3   Helping Diverse Learners Succeed in Today's Classrooms

1.1 How do cultural attitudes, values, and interaction patterns influence learning?

Some cultural attitudes and values complement classroom learning. For example, some cultures view success in school as an essential component of upward mobility and conse-quently emphasize the value of schoolwork as well as homework. At other times, cultural values can conflict with school success. This primarily occurs when success in school threat-ens the loss of the home culture. Language is a prime example here. Sometimes learning English is interpreted as also losing the native language.

Not all cultures have the same adult–children interaction patterns. When these inter-action patterns are compatible with the question-and-answer style of most classrooms, then learning is facilitated. When the home interaction patterns differ from classroom interaction patterns, then problems can occur. Sensitive teachers are aware of this and both adapt their own interaction patterns and also help students change theirs to succeed in the classroom.

1.2 What are three ways in which effective teachers respond to cultural diversity in their classrooms?

Culturally responsive teaching has three essential components. First, effective teachers ac-cept and value cultural differences and positively communicate this to students. Second, culturally responsive teachers adapt their interaction patterns to students and also teach students about successful classroom interaction practices. Finally, effective teachers build on students' cultural backgrounds, using their neighborhood and home experiences as the foundation for classroom learning.

1.3 What is the relationship between urban schools and cultural diversity?

Urban schools tend to have greater proportions of cultural minorities than their rural or suburban counterparts. In addition, many of these students do not speak English as their first language, requiring teachers skilled in English as a second language.

2.1 What has been the government's response to language diversity in our nation's schools?

Initially, Congress supported bilingual education with the passage of the Bilingual Educa-tion Act of 1968. This was reinforced in 1974 by a U.S. Supreme Court decision requiring districts to address the learning needs of non-English speakers. More recently, both federal and state governments have reversed these trends, emphasizing English-only approaches at the expense of bilingualism.

2.2 What are the primary differences in the two major approaches schools use in working with English language learners?

There are two very different approaches to dealing with ELL students. The bilingual approach attempts to maintain the native language, using it as the foundation for learning English. A contrasting approach focuses exclusively on learning English. For political and practical rea-sons, this second approach appears to be currently dominant in the United States.

2.3 **What are the major ways that teachers can adapt their instruction to meet the needs of students with varying language backgrounds?**

First, teachers should make an effort to make their classrooms welcoming places where students feel comfortable. Then, teachers should provide opportunities for students to practice their developing language skills with other students. Cooperative learning, peer tutoring, and buddy systems are all effective. Finally, teachers should illustrate their lessons with many examples to provide concrete references for new ideas and vocabulary.

3.1 **Explain how society influences gender differences in our students.**

Gender differences influence the educational experiences of boys and girls primarily through gender-role identity. Every society influences people's perceptions of the proper roles of males and females. Ours does as well, and students come into our classrooms with preconceived notions about how males and females should act, and what careers they should select.

3.2 **How should teachers respond to gender differences?**

Teachers often treat boys and girls differently based on their own stereotypical views of gender roles. Teachers should be aware of these possibilities and attempt to treat boys and girls equally in learning activities. This means that they should call on boys and girls as equally as possible, give them similar amounts of time to answer, ask the same levels of questions, and provide feedback that is similarly detailed.

4.1 **Explain the differences in current definitions of intelligence.**

The most widely held definition of intelligence says that it has three components: the capacity to acquire knowledge, the ability to think and reason in the abstract, and the ability to solve problems. A differing view of intelligence, based upon Howard Gardner's work (1983, 1999), suggests that it is composed of eight relatively independent dimensions.

4.2 **How do schools respond to differences in ability? What does research suggest about its application in classrooms?**

Ability grouping is the process of placing students with similar academic abilities in the same learning environments. While well-intentioned, it has several potential drawbacks, including lowered teacher expectations and poorer instruction for those in lower groups. Experts (Good & Brophy, 2003; Tomlinson, 2003) recommend that teachers minimize its use in classrooms and constantly be aware of potentials for adverse effects.

4.3 **What are learning styles? What are the implications of learning styles for teachers?**

Learning styles are students' preferred way of learning, problem solving, or processing information. Learning styles have at least three implications for teachers. First, to meet students' diverse learning styles, teachers should use a variety of teaching strategies. Second, learning styles remind us that each student is a unique individual. Finally, learning styles suggest the need to make students metacognitively aware of their own learning strengths and weaknesses.

5.1 **How have schools changed the ways they deal with exceptionalities?**

In the past, students with exceptionalities were separated from their peers in segregated schools or classrooms. Then mainstreaming was adopted, which moved students with exceptionalities from segregated settings into regular classrooms. However, adequate support and services often didn't follow the students. Currently, inclusion attempts to provide a comprehensive web of services for students with exceptionalities who are placed in regular classrooms and schools.

5.2 **What are the major categories of exceptionalities found in classrooms?**

In the IDEA, the federal government specifies 13 different categories of special education students; over three fourths of these fall into four categories: learning disabilities, communication disorders, mental retardation, and behavior disorders. Learning disabilities involve

*difficulties in acquiring and using listening, speaking, reading, writing, reasoning, or math-
ematical abilities. Communication disorders interfere with students' abilities to receive and understand information from others and to express their own ideas or questions. Mental
retardation includes limitations in intellectual functioning, as indicated by difficulties in learning, and problems with adaptive skills, such as communication, self-care, and social interaction. Behavior disorders involve the display of serious and persistent age-inappropriate
behaviors that result in social conflict, personal unhappiness, and school failure.*

Chapter 4   Changes in American Society

1.1   **What changes have occurred in the American family over the last 50 years?**

*An increased number of families have parents who are or have been divorced, have single
parents, or have both parents working. In addition, an increasing number of families live
near or below the poverty level. As a result, parents and other caregivers spend much less
time with their children than they did 50 years ago.*

1.2   **Describe the implications of the changes in American families for child care in
this country.**

*In the 1950s, most families (57 percent) had a single breadwinner, and the mother stayed
home to care for the children. Currently, only about 25 percent of young children are cared
for in the home. This creates a pressing need for quality child care that not only meets children's emotional needs but also prepares them for school.*

1.3   **Who are latchkey children? What problems do they encounter in their homes?**

*Latchkey children return home after school to an empty house. They not only have less
parental supervision, they also have less access to parental help with homework.*

2.1   **Define *socioeconomic status*.**

*Socioeconomic status is a classification system that combines parents' income, occupation,
and level of education.*

2.2   **How do different socioeconomic patterns influence school success?**

*Socioeconomic status influences school success in several ways. First, it influences whether
basic needs such as food and shelter are met. It can also influence family stability; lower-
SES families are less likely to provide safe and stable home environments. It also affects the
availability of school-related experiences such as travel and going to museums and zoos.
Socioeconomic status also influences the amount and kind of adult–child interactions in the
home. Finally, SES influences parental attitudes and values about education.*

2.3   **How does the government define poverty? How does poverty influence learning?**

*The federal government establishes a poverty threshold, the household income level that
represents the lowest level of earning needed to meet basic living needs. In 2004, the poverty
level for a family of four was $18,850. Poverty influences a family's ability to meet basic
needs such as food and shelter as well as educational needs such as books, and the ability
to be home to supervise and help with homework.*

2.4   **How does homelessness influence learning?**

*Experts estimate that between one half to one million children are homeless at some time
during the year. Homeless children suffer from inadequate diets and medical care, often
come from unstable families, and often don't attend school regularly.*

*   Because their basic needs aren't met, homeless children can't take advantage of learning opportunities in school. In addition, because they don't have a stable home life to return
to, they find it difficult to do homework and read at home.*

3.1   **What changes have occurred in student sexuality over time? What are implications of these changes for education?**

Students are more likely to become sexually active earlier, leading to teenage pregnancies. These changes suggest the need for basic sex education that can help students make informed choices.

3.2   **Explain the trends in student use of alcohol and other drugs over the last several years, and describe the implications of these changes for education.**

While the use of alcohol, tobacco, marijuana, and cocaine has decreased in recent years, use among students still remains high. This suggests that students need to be educated about the legal, physical, and psychological consequences of using these drugs.

3.3   **How has the rate of student obesity changed over the years? How are schools responding to this problem?**

The rate of student obesity has tripled since 1980. Schools have attempted to combat this problem by banning the sale of calorie-laden soft drinks in schools. Other issues, such as exercise and healthy diets, still need to be addressed.

3.4   **How have crime and violence changed in U.S. schools? What are the implications for education?**

The overall rates of crime and violence in schools have decreased in recent years. However, they still are a reality in many schools and need to be dealt with on multiple levels. At the school level, administrators need to have a comprehensive plan in place for both preventing and addressing crime and violence. Teachers also need to be aware of the possibilities for crime and violence, as well as bullying, in their classrooms and need to know how to deal with them immediately.

4.1   **What are the characteristics of students placed at-risk?**

Students placed at-risk often come from unstable families and are often victims of high rates of poverty, violence, and alcohol and drug abuse as well as child abuse. They are often members of cultural minorities and English may not be spoken at home.

4.2   **What unique challenges do urban schools present to students placed at-risk?**

Urban schools present a number of challenges to students placed at-risk. They tend to exist in high poverty areas, a factor often associated with lower achievement. They are also funded less well than their suburban counterparts and have fewer experienced teachers. In addition, urban schools are often larger, making it harder for students to establish meaningful interpersonal relationships.

4.3   **What can schools and teachers do to help at-risk students achieve success?**

Effective schools for students placed at-risk emphasize a safe and orderly school climate, mastery of essential content, caring and demanding teachers, cooperation, student responsibility and self-regulation, and strong parental involvement.

Effective teachers for students placed at-risk share many of the characteristics of effective schools. They are caring, have high expectations, and emphasize student responsibility. They also provide instruction that is interactive, with increased structure, support, and feedback.

Chapter 5   Education in the United States

1.1   **How did the diversity of the original colonies shape the educational system in the United States?**

Because of cultural, geographic, economic, and religious differences in the original colonies, it was not possible to create a uniform, monolithic school system that would satisfy everyone. This led to regional or state control of education, a system that survives today.

1.2   **What role did religion play in colonial schools? What are the implications of this role for contemporary schools?**

Religion was often the reason that many colonists came to North America, and it played a central role in colonial life. The colonists therefore included religion as a central part of the school curriculum. The proper role of religion in schools is a contentious issue today because of differing views of the purposes of schools and schooling.

1.3   **Explain why the Old Deluder Satan Act of Massachusetts was important for the development of our American educational system.**

The Old Deluder Satan Act required every town of 50 or more households to hire a teacher to instruct the children in that town. This provided the legal foundation for the public support of education.

2.1   **What is the Tenth Amendment to the Constitution? Why is it important for education today?**

The Tenth Amendment to the Constitution mandated that responsibilities for education not explicitly assigned to the federal government would be the responsibility of each state. This put the responsibility for funding and governing education in the hands of the states. This system of state-controlled education exists today and is unique to the United States.

2.2   **Describe the role that was established for the federal government during the early national period.**

During the early national period, legislators established federal funding for public schools and introduced the idea that schools were instruments of national purpose.

2.3   **What was the historical significance of the Ordinances of 1785 and 1787?**

These ordinances were designed to encourage people to settle in frontier areas. Part of this legislation set aside a section of land for public education. These laws set the precedent of involving the federal government in supporting public education and established a historical framework for viewing public schools as instruments of national purpose. In other words, schools could be used to shape our country's goals and purposes.

3.1   **How was the common school movement linked to the growing number of immigrants coming to the United States?**

Immigrants brought with them different cultures and languages. Our government needed ways to make them productive citizens and assimilate them into the increasingly industrialized U.S. economy. Governmentally supported and run schools were seen as a major way to do this.

3.2   **Who was Horace Mann, and what was his contribution to education in the United States?**

Horace Mann was an outspoken advocate for universal public education. He was the Secretary of the Massachusetts State Board of Education from 1837 to 1848. Because of his influence, Massachusetts doubled state appropriations for education, built 50 new secondary schools, increased teacher salaries by 50 percent, and passed the nation's first compulsory school attendance law in 1852. He was a powerful and effective advocate for the importance of public education for everyone.

3.3   **What were normal schools, and why are they important today**

Normal schools were special schools created for the preparation of teachers. They were important because they addressed the whole issue of teacher preparation and quality, an issue that is currently being debated with fast-track and alternative certification programs.

4.1   **What is a comprehensive high school, and why is it important for a democratic society such as ours?**

A comprehensive high school attempts to educate all students—general education, vocational education, and college preparatory students—under one roof. Advocates of the comprehensive high school assert that this integration and mixing of students is important so that students of all ability levels can learn about each other.

4.2   **How have the goals of high school education changed over time?**

Initially, the predecessors of the contemporary high school were elitist and oriented primarily to preparation for college; institutions such as the Latin Grammar School were strictly college preparatory. Later, schools such as Benjamin Franklin's Academy or the English Classical School reoriented themselves to more practical subjects such as bookkeeping and surveying. Initial participation in these schools was still limited to the very wealthy or talented. The idea of a universal high school education didn't really take root until the 1900s.

4.3   **How are junior highs and middle schools different?**

Junior highs were designed to prepare students for high school. Consequently, they focused primarily on academics and, for the most part, ignored the social and emotional needs of young adolescents. Middle schools evolved out of growing recognition that the developmental needs of early adolescents were unique and were not being met by junior high schools. Middle school adaptations for developing adolescents included a more applied and integrated curriculum, more learner-centered instruction, and classes that allowed teachers and students to interact and get to know each other.

5.1   **How does the concept of assimilation relate to Native American boarding schools?**

Assimilation is the process of socializing cultural minorities so they adopt the social norms and behaviors of the dominant culture, or Whites. Boarding schools attempt to speed up the process by taking Native American youth away from their families and instructing them in residential facilities. These efforts were mainly ineffective.

5.2   **How does "separate but equal" relate to African-Americans' educational experience in the United States?**

Early attempts to educate African-Americans placed them in segregated schools that purported to be separate but equal. Unfortunately, they were separate but unequal in terms of resources and quality.

5.3   **How did the process of assimilation relate to Hispanic Americans and their native languages?**

In hopes of assimilating Hispanic Americans quickly, schools frequently taught classes in English only, and Spanish was forbidden. This practice not only caused the loss of the first language but also resulted in conflicts between home and school. Bilingual education attempted to retain and build on students' first language skills, but the status of bilingual education is currently in doubt because of restrictive legislation in a number of states.

6.1   **How was the federal government's educational response to the Cold War similar to its actions in the War on Poverty and the Great Society?**

Both federal initiatives viewed education as a tool for national progress. In the case of the Cold War, education was enlisted as a means to improve science and technology, to combat against the perceived growing threat of Communism. In the War on Poverty, education was seen as a tool to eliminate poverty and the economic disparities in our country.

6.2   **What are magnet schools, and how do they relate to attempts to achieve equality in our schools?**

Magnet schools were created as an alternative to forced busing and integration. Magnet schools attempt to achieve integration by attracting bright students from all cultural groups. The results on magnet schools are mixed. While they do achieve integration, critics charge that they tend to steal bright minority students from their home schools and that social integration within magnet schools often doesn't occur.

6.3   **What is Title IX, and how is it related to the concept of equality?**

Title IX was federal legislation enacted in 1972 to eliminate gender bias in the United States. It's most dramatic influence in education has been in the area of sports, where gender-equity advocates have used it to gain equity in facilities and expenditures.

Chapter 6   Educational Philosophy

1.1   **Define philosophy and normative philosophy, and explain how they differ from theory.**

A theory is a set of related principles that are based on observations and are used to explain additional observations. Philosophy includes theoretical studies of knowledge, truth, existence, and morality, but goes beyond these theories to examine the way the world ought to be, which is called normative philosophy.

1.2   **To which part of teacher professionalism is philosophy most closely related? Explain.**

Philosophy is most closely related to a "specialized body of knowledge." All professions have specialized knowledge, and philosophy is part of this knowledge for professional educators.

1.3   **What is the major difference between Allie's and Brad's *normative philosophies*?**

First, Allie believed that essential knowledge exists, and students must study, practice, and be assessed with respect to that essential knowledge. For her, study, practice, and assessment are the ways teaching and learning "ought to be." Brad, instead, believed that experiences with decision making and problem solving were more nearly the way teaching and learning "ought to be."

2.1   **Describe each of the branches of philosophy.**

The four branches of philosophy are epistemology, *which examines questions about how we come to know the knowledge we acquire;* metaphysics, *which analyzes reality and what is and is not real;* axiology, *which examines matters of right and wrong; and* logic, *which analyzes the process of deriving valid conclusions from basic premises.*

2.2   **Allie said, "I'm getting paid to help kids learn. If I don't do my best to make that happen, I'm not earning my salary." This comment best illustrates which branch of philosophy? Explain your answer.**

This comment most closely relates to axiology. Allie is saying that it would be unethical if she didn't do her best to help her students learn as much as possible.

2.3   **Two teachers are in a discussion, and one says, "Everything we know depends on experience. So, the key is providing lots of experiences in the classroom. If we provide them with enough experiences, they'll learn." To which of the branches of philosophy is this person's statement most closely related? Explain your answer.**

This person's comment most closely relates to epistemology. She is suggesting that the way people come to know what they know is through experiences.

2.4   "That doesn't quite make sense," a teacher diplomatically comments to a colleague. "You said that your kids are so unmotivated, but last week you said that kids basically want to learn. . . . Those two don't fit." To which of the branches of philosophy is this person's comment most closely related? Explain your answer.

This person's comment is most closely related to logic. He is saying that the conclusion, "Kids are not motivated," doesn't logically follow from the premise, "Kids basically want to learn."

3.1   Describe each of the four traditional philosophies and the educational emphasis that each would imply.

Idealism asserts that the world of ideas is the ultimate reality, because the physical world is constantly changing. Teachers practicing idealism would emphasize the study of mathematics and classic works of science, literature, art, and music, because these reflect time-honored ideas.

Realism suggests that a reality exists in the physical world. Teachers grounding their work in realism place primary emphasis on students' developing skills and subject matter knowledge, because these represent this physical reality.

Pragmatism suggests that reality changes as the world evolves. Teachers basing their work on pragmatism emphasize experience, knowledge, and skills that help students adapt to the real world.

Existentialism suggests that people create their own reality. Teachers operating within this framework emphasize student autonomy and classroom learning communities where students and teachers all learn from each other.

3.2   "My job is to develop writers," an English teacher asserts. "I am an English teacher, not a counselor. . . . Students must be able to write, and it's my job to be sure that they can." To which of the traditional philosophies is the teacher's efforts most closely related? Explain.

This teacher is grounding his work in realism. His emphasis on helping students acquire specific skills reflects this view, because skills are needed to cope with the physical reality that has always existed.

3.3   A teacher wants her students to examine racism and injustice and involves them in a unit on nonviolent noncooperation using a study of Mohandas K. Gandhi's struggles against racism in South Africa and India as an example. She further illustrates the ideas with a study of Martin Luther King, Jr.'s nonviolent protests against American racism. To which of the traditional philosophies is the teacher's efforts most closely related? Explain.

This teacher is basing her work on idealism. Issues of injustice have existed throughout history, and using Gandhi's and Martin Luther King, Jr's works as examples to study this issue reflects this orientation.

3.4   Because students must be able to function effectively in, and adapt to, a changing world, a teacher emphasizes the "whole person"—physical, social, emotional, and intellectual—in her students. She emphasizes and models physical fitness, involves her students in discussions to help them practice social skills and perspective taking, and she involves them in problem solving about modern-day topics. To which of the traditional philosophies is the teacher's efforts most closely related? Explain.

This teacher is basing his work on pragmatism. His emphasis on functioning effectively in a changing world illustrates a pragmatic approach to education.

4.1   Describe the major philosophies of education.

Perennialism is the belief that human nature is constant, and a rigorous intellectual curriculum should exist for all students. Math, science, and literature are important, because they expose students to logical thought and ideas that have endured throughout history.

Essentialism *is the belief that a critical core of information exists that all people should possess. Basic skills and academic subjects would make up a curriculum based on essentialist philosophy.*

Progressivism *is the belief that education should focus on real-world problem solving and individual development. Learner-centered curricula would be emphasized in a school grounded in progressivism.*

Postmodernism *contends that the institutions in our society are racist, sexist, and imperialist. A curriculum grounded in postmodernism would emphasize literature written by groups that have been historically marginalized and would investigate issues such as the use of power, personal and group identities, cultural politics, and social criticism.*

4.2   **You walk into a classroom, and you see students working in groups on projects that they have designed and implemented. The teacher moves from group to group, making suggestions and answering questions. Which of the educational philosophies does this practice most nearly illustrate? Explain.**

This practice most nearly illustrates progressivism. The students are involved in solving real-world problems, which is emphasized with progressivism.

4.3   **You visit a school, and you overhear a conversation between two teachers. One says, "I love teaching Shakespeare. His work has been studied for hundreds of years, and it's as timely now as it was then." The second retorts, "Yes, it's timely all right. It clearly demonstrates how the powerful exploited the weak simply to stay in power." The two continue an animated debate as you listen. Which educational philosophy is best illustrated by each teacher's comment? Explain.**

The first teacher is expressing views consistent with perennialism. Perennialism emphasizes thought that has endured throughout history, and the study of Shakespeare reflects this emphasis. The second teacher's views are consistent with postmodernism, which emphasizes issues such as the study of power and exploitation of the marginalized.

5.1   **Why is a personal philosophy of education important?**

Forming a personal philosophy of education is important because your philosophy will influence the kinds of knowledge you emphasize in your classes, the instructional decisions you make as a teacher, and the criteria you use to reflect on and analyze your teaching.

A personal philosophy is also important because it will help you explain and defend your educational goals—what you will try to accomplish in your classroom. Your goals reflect the kind of teacher you want to be, and being able to explain and defend them means that you're knowledgeable and reflective, which are essential characteristics of professionalism.

5.2   **What are the three essential steps involved in forming a philosophy of education?**

Forming a personal philosophy of education begins with a statement of beliefs about the purpose of schooling and the nature of teaching and learning. The second step then involves an examination of those beliefs to ensure that they are consistent with each other, and the third step is actually articulating your philosophy in an internally consistent statement. The statement then gives you a concrete framework that you can use to guide your actions, and because it's tangible, it can be modified when your professional knowledge expands and your beliefs change.

5.3   **Look again at Brad's thinking, as indicated by his conversation with Allie. Based on this information, what is his philosophy of education? Explain how the philosophy is based on his beliefs.**

Based on his conversation with Allie, Brad's philosophy of education is as follows: In Brad's view, school should be preparation for life after students leave the classroom, and the way they best prepare for life is to practice life skills, which are the abilities to make decisions and solve real-world problems, not learn isolated facts. For Brad, important knowledge is the knowledge people need to make decisions and solve problems.

These views are based on the belief that the only way people learn to make decisions and solve problems is to practice both. It is also based on the belief that reality is uncertain, so reality depends on the situation people are in at the time. In this regard, Brad's views are closely aligned with pragmatism.

Chapter 7   The Organization of American Schools

1.1   What are three different meanings of the concept *school*?

One definition describes a school as a place where students go to learn and develop; a second describes a school as a physical place—a building or set of buildings. A social institution, an organization with established structures and rules designed to promote certain goals is the third definition and will serve as the framework for this chapter.

1.2   Explain how a *school* and a *school district* differ.

A school is a social institution that exists with the goal of promoting students' growth and development, whereas a school district is a larger administrative unit designed to help schools reach their goals.

1.3   Is the *family* a social institution? Explain why it is or is not.

The family is widely considered to be a social institution. It has a structure that has historically been viewed as composed of a father, mother, and one or more children, with the goal of promoting the well-being of the entire family. (Some of the politics surrounding social issues, such as gay marriage, center on controversies about what the family's "established structure" should be.)

2.1   What are the major components of a typical school organization?

The components of a typical school include personnel, the physical plant, and the organization of the curriculum. The administrative staff, which includes the principal, vice principal, and one or more assistant principals in large schools; support staff, such as clerical workers, receptionists, and custodians; and teachers make up the personnel of a school.

The physical plant often includes several buildings, such as an administrative building, classroom buildings, a cafeteria, and in most middle, junior high, and high schools, sports facilities, such as a gymnasium, football and baseball fields, and perhaps a running track.

The curriculum is designed to teach content that is appropriate for students at different ages, which is the reason that schools are usually organized into elementary, middle or junior high, and high school levels.

2.2   Most school systems are organized into three levels. Describe each of the three.

As you saw in the feedback for exercise 2.1, schools are typically organized into elementary, middle or junior high, and high school levels. Elementary schools usually house students from kindergarten, or pre-K, through the fifth or sixth grade. Middle schools usually involve some combination of fifth through eighth grades, with 6–8 being the most common. Junior highs most commonly include some combination of grades 7–9, and high schools typically consist of grades 9–12 or 10–12.

2.3   What are two factors that influence the way school curriculum is organized?

The developmental characteristics of students and economics–politics are the two factors that most commonly influence the way the curriculum is organized. Since a typical first grader thinks differently than does a typical fifth grader, for example, the curriculum is organized to accommodate those developmental differences.

Economic factors, such as school overcrowding, and political factors, such as high school coaches' wanting potential athletes to be prepared for high school teams, also influence the way schools are organized.

3.1   **What are two ways in which teaching in an elementary school differs from teaching in a middle, junior high, or high school?**

Elementary teachers are responsible for teaching all the content areas, such as reading, math, science, social studies, art, and music, whereas teachers at the upper levels are responsible for teaching only one area, such as math (or sometimes two, such as a combination of math and science classes). This is one important difference.

In addition, teachers in elementary schools set their own schedule; that is, they decide how many minutes per day that they will allocate to each of the content areas. At the upper levels, the time allocated for each class period is preset by schoolwide schedules and bells.

3.2   **What are four differences between effective middle schools and junior highs?**

First, effective middle schools organize teachers and students into interdisciplinary teams, so that all the teachers on a team have the same group of students and instruction emphasizes connections between different curriculum areas. This isn't the case in junior highs. Second, middle schools more strongly emphasize long-term teacher–student relationships with greater attention to students' emotional development than do junior highs. Third, teachers in effective middle schools more strongly emphasize interactive teaching strategies than do teachers in junior highs. Finally, middle schools eliminate activities in which developmental differences among students become apparent, such as competitive athletics.

3.3   **Describe a comprehensive high school. How does a comprehensive high school differ from a vocational high school?**

A comprehensive high school is a school that attempts to meet the needs of all students. This means that it attempts to provide offerings for students who are likely to attend college, but at the same time meet the needs of students who will be entering the job market after graduating from high school.

Vocational high schools are more likely to offer a curriculum designed to provide students with education and job skills that will enable them to get a job immediately after graduating from high school.

4.1   **Describe the characteristics of an effective school.**

Research indicates that effective schools are optimal in size—neither too small nor too large; they have a clear school mission and strong leadership; their environments are safe and orderly; parental involvement is strong; and they maintain a solid academic focus.

4.2   **What is the most distinguishing characteristic of effective instruction in effective schools?**

The most distinguishing characteristic of effective instruction is interactive teaching. Instead of lecturing and giving students extensive seat work, effective teachers design learning activities that actively involve students in the content they are learning.

4.3   **Why is frequent monitoring of student progress essential for an effective school?**

Frequent monitoring of student progress performs several important functions. First, and most important, it tells students whether they are learning important ideas and skills. It also informs teachers of learning gains, allowing them to adjust instruction to meet learning gaps. Finally, it provides helpful information to administrators and parents about children's learning progress.

Chapter 8   Governance and Finance

1.1   **Who is legally responsible for governing education in the United States?**

The Tenth Amendment to the Constitution clearly assigns legal responsibility for education to the 50 states.

1.2   **How does each state govern education?**

State governance of education begins with the governor and legislature. Though they have many other responsibilities, both influence education by focusing attention on educational issues. In addition, state legislatures supply about half of a district's education budget.

The organization directly and legally responsible for governing education is the state board of education. Primarily consisting of noneducators, the state board issues and revokes teaching licenses, establishes the length of the school year, creates standards for approving and accrediting schools, and develops and implements a system for gathering educational data.

The state office of education, composed of professional educators, implements education policy on a daily basis. The state office of education is responsible for teacher licensing, curriculum supervision, approval of school sites and buildings, and collection of statistical data.

1.3   **What role do school districts play in governing education?**

School districts are responsible for the day-to-day functioning of schools. They hire teachers and ensure that students have classrooms and books. They are governed by a local school board, consisting of elected citizens from the community. The school board sets policy; the district superintendent implements that policy. The district office, consisting of educational professionals, orders textbooks and supplies, develops programs of study, administers standardized tests, and evaluates teachers. Finally, the school principal is responsible for governing at the school level. The school principal is key to the quality of education at the school level.

2.1   **What are the major sources of educational funding?**

The largest percentages (49 and 43 percent, respectively) come from state and local sources. The remaining 8.5 percent comes from the federal government.

Local funding primarily comes from property taxes. State funds for education come from a variety of sources, the two largest being state income taxes and sales taxes. Smaller percentages of state education funds also come from taxes on liquor and tobacco, oil and mining revenues, corporate income taxes, and income from state lotteries and gambling.

2.2   **How are educational revenues spent?**

The largest percentage of the educational budget (61 percent) goes to instruction, including teacher salaries. Ten percent also goes to instructional assistance needs such as student services, teacher professional development, and curriculum development. Another 10 percent goes to administration, both at the district and school level. Maintenance of school buildings and grounds takes up another 10 percent. Finally, transportation (school buses) and food services (cafeterias) each account for another 4 percent.

3.1   **What are the major causes of funding inequities in education? What are some proposed solutions to the problem?**

Funding inequities in education result largely from unequal revenue bases. Within a state, this can result from districts that have differing property values. Because significant portions of educational funding come from property taxes, inequities between districts within a state are common. Between-state differences can also result from differences in states' tax bases. One proposed solution is a greater federal role in equalizing between-state differences. Cost and the problem of possible federal controls that might go along with the funding are two obstacles to this proposal.

3.2   **What are the two major forms of school choice? How are they similar and different?**

The two major forms of school choice are charter schools and vouchers. They are similar in their philosophical underpinnings. Both come from attempts to break up the perceived monopoly that exists in education by providing more alternatives or choices to parents. They differ in how they propose to do this. Vouchers are, in one sense, less radical in that they keep existing educational options as they are and provide parents with tickets or vouchers to shop around and choose an alternative to their neighborhood schools. Charter schools, by contrast, create alternative schools, with self-contained governance and instructional systems.

3.3   **What is school privatization, and what are its pros and cons?**

Privatization involves the outsourcing of educational services to private companies or corporations. This can involve hiring companies to provide services such as school lunches or transportation, or turning a whole school over to a private business. Advocates of privatization claim that competition from the private sector is good because it will encourage public schools to perform better. They also contend that the same business efficiencies that work in the business world will produce similar efficiencies in education. Critics point to a narrowed curriculum in privatized schools because of teaching to the test. They also point to the deprofessionalization of teachers that occurs when they are treated like employees rather than knowledgeable professionals.

Chapter 9   School Law

1.1   **What are two limitations of using existing laws as the basis for professional decision making?**

One limitation is that laws are left purposefully abstract and general so they can apply to a large number of bases. This makes laws vague in terms of specific instances requiring decision making. A second limitation of using laws is that they were created in response to problems that existed in the past and may not provide specific guidelines for future professional decisions.

1.2   **How are laws different from ethics in terms of teacher decision making?**

Laws tell teachers what they can do (their rights) as well as what they must do (their responsibilities), but they don't tell teachers what they should do. This is the role of professional ethics, which attempts to provide guidelines for professional conduct.

2.1   **How do federal laws influence education?**

Federal laws primarily influence education through three amendments to the Constitution. The First Amendment to the Constitution guarantees all citizens freedom of speech. This amendment forms the basis for academic freedom in the classroom. The Fourth Amendment protects citizens from unreasonable searches and seizures. This amendment protects students from unwarranted or unreasonable searches while they are on school grounds. The Fourteenth Amendment to the Constitution guarantees due process in issues involving deprivation of life, liberty, or property. This amendment not only protects teachers from dismissal without a formal hearing, it also protects students from expulsion or suspension from school without due process.

2.2   **How do state laws influence education policies and practices?**

States are legally entrusted with the education of children. States influence education by passing laws regulating teachers' qualifications, working conditions, and legal rights. States also create departments of education, which are given responsibilities for formulating educational policies in the state.

2.3 **What is the educational significance of the overlapping legal system in the United States?**

Because different laws influencing education are created at different levels, legal issues and problems that arise from these different levels need to be resolved at the level at which the law was formed. For example, if a legal dispute involves a teacher's qualifications for being a teacher, this would go to a state court because the laws regulating teacher qualifications are formed at that level.

3.1 **How are teacher employment issues influenced by the law?**

Teacher employment issues are influenced in several ways by legal considerations. First, licensure is a state responsibility, and rules and regulations passed by each state determine licensure policies and procedures. Local school boards are given the legal responsibility for issuing contracts, which specify the legal conditions for a teacher's employment. Teacher tenure, which is a legal safeguard that provides job security for teachers, is determined at the state level and protects teachers from dismissal without cause. Because of these overlapping spheres of influence, teacher dismissal is a gray area that may be influenced both by state as well as district legal regulations.

3.2 **What is academic freedom, and why is it important to teachers?**

Academic freedom, which is based on the First Amendment to the Constitution, protects the right of teachers to choose both content and teaching methods based on their professional judgment. It protects teachers from undue external influences on their classroom instruction.

3.3 **How do copyright laws influence teachers' practices?**

Copyright laws are federal laws designed to protect the intellectual property of authors. Fair-use guidelines specify limitations on the number of copies of books that teachers can reproduce for their classrooms. They also place restrictions on the use of videotaped programs and computer software.

3.4 **What is teacher liability, and how does it influence teachers?**

Teachers are legally responsible for the safety of children under their case. The term in loco parentis *means that teachers are legally expected to act in the place of parents. Failure to do so can result in negligence and a legal suit involving liability for the teacher.*

3.5 **How are teachers' rights in terms of their own private lives similar to and different from those of the general public?**

All citizens of the United States are guaranteed the right to "life, liberty, and the pursuit of happiness." However, because teachers, as professionals, are expected to be role models for the children they teach, their rights as private individuals may be curtailed.

4.1 **What federal law influences the discussion of religion in the schools?**

The First Amendment to the Constitution states, "Congress shall make no law respecting an establishment of religion, or prohibiting the free exercise thereof." This law explicitly forbids the teaching of religion in the schools, but it also prohibits the government from interfering with individuals' rights to hold religious beliefs and freely practice religion.

4.2 **What is the legal status of prayer in schools?**

Neither schools nor teachers can officially encourage school prayer; however, prayer is permissible when student initiated and when it doesn't interfere with other students or the school. For example, an individual student or students saying grace before lunch in a cafeteria would be permissible under the law.

4.3   **Can a school allow religious clubs or organizations to meet on school grounds?**

If the school does not specifically sponsor the religious club or organization, the U.S. Supreme Court has ruled that it is legal for schools to allow religious, philosophical, and political groups to use school facilities in the same way as other extracurricular organizations.

4.4   **What is the legal status of religion in the curriculum?**

Advocacy of religion in the schools is legally forbidden. However, teachers may discuss how religion has influenced history or culture.

5.1   **What are students' rights in terms of freedom of speech?**

The First Amendment to the Constitution guarantees all U.S. citizens freedom of speech. Students in school have this same right, provided that doing so doesn't interfere with learning. So, for example, students can't get up in a social studies class and make a speech about their political beliefs. This doesn't mean they can't express their beliefs briefly if the context is appropriate, but in exercising free speech, they can't interfere with the teacher's (and the class's) academic agenda.

5.2   **Can students be searched? What about their lockers and other possessions?**

If school authorities believe there is probable cause in terms of a student possessing drugs or a dangerous weapon, the school may conduct a nonobtrusive search of the student and his or her possessions (nonobtrusive does not include a strip search). School lockers are considered school property and may be searched if reasonable cause of a drug or weapons violation exists.

5.3   **What is the Buckley Amendment? Why is it important to both schools and teachers?**

The Buckley Amendment protects a family's rights to privacy in terms of school records. It requires schools to (1) inform parents of their rights regarding their child's records, (2) provide parents access to their child's records, (3) maintain procedures that allow parents to challenge those records, and (4) protect parents from disclosure of confidential information. Since teachers are legal extensions of schools, they are legally bound by the same safeguards.

5.4   **Is corporal punishment legal in schools?**

Corporal punishment is a state-by-state legal issue. In those states that do allow corporal punishment, it must be administered to correct misbehavior, can't involve anger or malice, and can't be cruel or excessive or result in lasting injury.

5.5   **What are students' rights in terms of disciplinary actions?**

Students have a right to an education, and this right can only be abridged or changed through due process. If school administrators must suspend a student for an extended period of time, they must notify the student in writing of the reasons or charges, share the legal procedures and evidence, guarantee the student access to legal counsel, and record proceedings and findings, and the student must have a right to appeal.

5.6   **What are the legal rights of students with AIDS?**

Because they have a right to an education, students with AIDS cannot be automatically excluded from school activities. Schools must address specific risk factors to other students when they change the instructional activities or opportunities for a student with AIDS.

Chapter 10   The Curriculum in an Era of Standards and Accountability

1.1   **Describe at least four definitions of curriculum.**

Curriculum has been defined in various ways, including the subject matter taught to students; a course of study, or a systematic arrangement of courses; the planned educational experiences offered by a school; the experiences students have under the guidance of the school; and the process teachers go through in selecting and organizing learning experiences for their students.

1.2   **What is one important difference between the definition of curriculum used in this text and the definitions described in item 1.1?**

The definition used in this text is broader than those in item 1.1. It includes "everything that teachers teach and students learn in schools," which also includes attitudes and values students learn that aren't formally taught. In some cases, these attitudes and values are as important for student growth as the "planned educational experiences offered by a school," which is one of the definitions outlined in this section of the chapter.

1.3   **What is the relationship between curriculum and instruction?**

In simple terms, curriculum is what teachers teach, and it includes teachers' specific learning goals. The ways teachers attempt to help students reach the learning goals describes instruction.

2.1   **What is the difference between the explicit and the implicit curriculum?**

The explicit curriculum is what teachers intentionally teach based on textbooks, curriculum guides, standards, and other sources. In comparison, the implicit curriculum more nearly depends on classroom and school climate and organization and teachers' attitudes and values as well as their actions. As a result, some aspects of the implicit curriculum may be out of the teacher's conscious control.

2.2   **How is the null curriculum different from both the explicit and the implicit curriculum?**

The explicit and implicit curriculum describe what is taught, whereas the null curriculum describes what is not taught. In particular, the differences between the explicit and the null curriculum reflect teachers' views about what is important to study and learn.

2.3   **Compare the extracurriculum to the other forms of curriculum.**

The extracurriculum differs from the explicit curriculum in that the extracurriculum exists outside students' areas of formal study. It is similar to the implicit curriculum in that important forms of learning result from both, but they are outside the scope of the explicit curriculum. The extracurriculum differs from the null curriculum in that the extracurriculum relates to what is learned (albeit, informally), whereas the null curriculum relates to what is not learned.

3.1   **Identify four forces that influence the curriculum.**

The four most important forces that influence curricular decisions are standards and accountability, the federal government, textbooks, and philosophy.

3.2   **How does each of the forces in 3.1 exert its influence on the curriculum?**

The influence of standards and accountability is illustrated by the fact that many teachers in elementary schools strongly emphasize reading/language arts and math in their curriculum and instruction because these are the areas that are measured on high-stakes tests.

The federal government's influence is illustrated in legislation, such as the Individuals with Disabilities Education Act, which requires that all students, including those with learning issues, have access to the regular curriculum.

Textbooks influence the curriculum because many teachers tend to teach the topics presented in their textbooks essentially as presented by the textbook and in the order the textbook presents it.

A school's and teachers' philosophies influence the curriculum through their priorities. For example, Suzanne Brush chose to present her topic in a certain way because of her philosophy with respect to teaching. A teacher with a different philosophy might have chosen a very different approach.

3.3   **Why is teacher professionalism so important in making curricular decisions?**

Teacher professionalism is essential because—even though we are living in an era of reform, standards, and accountability—teachers must make most of the decisions that will influence the amount that students learn. You saw this illustrated in Suzanne's teaching. While she used the standard and the sample test item as a guide, she made all the decisions about what she would specifically teach, how to best present the topic, how to make it meaningful to the students, and what to emphasize. This is the case for all teachers. No amount of specifying standards and accountability measures or any other mandates will ever replace the professionalism of the teacher in promoting student learning.

4.1   **How do issues involving sex education and moral development differ in their influence on the school curriculum?**

Issues involving sex education influence the curriculum primarily in what content should be taught. For example, some authorities argue that students should only be exposed to curriculum that endorses abstinence from sex. Others believe that students should receive information about condoms, the prevention of sexually transmitted disease, and strategies for refusal to be pressured into having sex.

By comparison, authorities generally agree that ethics and morals should be taught in schools, but they disagree about the approach that educators should take. So, with respect to the development of morals, the issue becomes more one of the approach to instruction than of the content to be taught.

4.2   **What is intelligent design? How could it influence curriculum decisions?**

Intelligent design suggests that certain features of the universe and of living things are so complex that their existence is best explained by an intelligent cause, rather than an undirected process such as natural selection. Proponents argue that it should be taught as a viable, and alternative, theory to the theory of evolution in science classes. Critics argue that it is not a real scientific theory, and while it may have a place in a social studies class, it does not belong in the science curriculum.

4.3   **How could issues involving censorship influence teachers' curriculum decisions?**

If certain works of literature are highly controversial, you might choose to not have your students read them, even if you believe that they would contribute to your students' learning (when in doubt, check with your principal). You are probably more likely to make a noncontroversial decision when you first begin teaching, because you will be somewhat unsure of yourself. As you gain experience and confidence, you will be more likely to take a more controversial stand when you feel your students will benefit from your decision.

Chapter 11   Creating Productive Learning Environments

1.1   **Describe the essential characteristics of a productive learning environment.**

Productive learning environments are orderly and focus on learning. Orderly environments are safe and inviting rather then rigid and punitive. In them, students feel free to share their thinking without fear of embarrassment or ridicule.

Learning is the central purpose of schooling. In productive learning environments, students not only learn content, they also learn about themselves and how to get along with others.

1.2   How do productive learning environments help promote personal and social development?

Classrooms are social places that provide opportunities for students to learn both personal and social skills. In terms of personal knowledge, productive learning environments provide opportunities for students to learn to recognize their personal strengths, needs, and values, as well as to develop self-motivation and discipline, goal-setting and organizational skills, impulse control and self-management, and personal and moral responsibility. In terms of social development, productive learning environments provide opportunities for students to learn perspective taking and social problem solving along with how to work cooperatively with others, respect for others, empathy for others, and appreciation for diversity.

1.3   In this section, we said that learning is the primary purpose of schooling, but we also emphasized a positive classroom climate. How are the two related?

Promoting learning and emphasizing a positive classroom climate are related in two ways. First, learning includes the knowledge and skills that schools emphasize as well as learning about ourselves and how we relate to our peers. A positive classroom climate provides opportunities for students to learn about themselves and each other.

Second, students learn more knowledge and skills, as well as more about themselves and relating to their peers, when the emotional climate in a classroom is positive.

2.1   Why is caring important for a productive learning environment? What can teachers do to show they care?

Caring refers to teachers' investment in the protection and development of the young people in their classes. Caring provides an emotional foundation for all teacher–student interactions and meets students' basic needs for safety and belonging. Teachers communicate caring by treating students as unique individuals and giving them their time.

2.2   What are personal teacher efficacy and positive teacher expectations? How are they related?

Personal teacher efficacy is a teacher's belief that he or she can promote learning in all students regardless of their backgrounds. As opposed to personal teacher efficacy, which focuses on the teacher, the term positive teacher expectations refers to teachers' beliefs in their students' ability to learn. The focus of personal teacher efficacy is on teachers' ability to produce learning, while the focus of positive teacher expectations is on students' ability to learn. These attitudes are related in that both influence teachers' actions in the classroom.

2.3   What is teacher modeling? How is it related to teacher enthusiasm?

Teacher modeling refers to the tendency of students to observe and imitate teachers' attitudes and beliefs. Much of what teachers teach in classrooms occurs through modeling. One important dimension of teacher modeling is enthusiasm, both for learning in general as well as learning a particular subject. When teachers are enthusiastic about the topics they are teaching, this motivates students, increasing their enthusiasm for learning.

3.1   Why has classroom management become a national concern?

The public views classroom management as important for several reasons. Perhaps most prominently, the public associates failed classroom management with reports of school violence. In addition, the public correctly links orderly classrooms and schools with increased learning.

3.2   What are the major goals of classroom management? How do they contribute to a productive learning environment?

The major goals of classroom management are to teach students self-responsibility, create a safe and orderly place where students can live and learn, and maximize opportunities for learning. They each contribute to a productive learning environment in different ways. Teaching students to be responsible for their own actions is a long-term goal that, if successful, shifts focus from the teacher as enforcer to the student as a responsible citizen. Creating a safe and orderly classroom is a precondition for all other activities; students need to feel that their classroom is a place that is safe and free from external threats. Finally, maximizing opportunities for learning creates a learning-focused classroom where students are actively engaged in acquiring new knowledge and skills.

3.3   How are classroom management and discipline different? How can teachers prevent management problems through planning?

Classroom management is the process of creating a productive learning environment through strategies that create and maintain classroom order. Discipline, by contrast, focuses on teachers' responses to student misbehavior. The differences between the two are important because research shows that effective managers emphasize management over discipline. Ineffective managers, by contrast, are continually reacting to student misbehavior because they don't have a comprehensive and effective management system in place.

Major tools to prevent management problems are rules and procedures. Rules specify standards for acceptable classroom behavior. When linked to the reasons for them, they provide guidelines for ethical student behavior. For example, the rule, "Listen when someone else is speaking," not only creates an orderly classroom but it also hopefully teaches students how to treat each other outside the classroom. Courtesy in conversation requires that we take turns listening and speaking.

Procedures, by contrast, describe efficient ways of performing classroom tasks. They don't have a moral or ethical component; instead, they contribute to a smooth and orderly classroom.

3.4   What are the characteristics of effective interventions?

Effective interventions are short and unobtrusive, interfering with instruction and learning as little as possible. Effective interventions are also immediate, nipping potential problems in the bud. Finally, and perhaps most important, interventions should target the correct student(s).

3.5   What actions—both short- and long-term—should teachers take when encountering incidents of violence and aggression?

Short-term, the teacher should intervene immediately to address the problem. This might consist of a personal intervention, or, if this is not possible, the teacher should send for help immediately. Long-term, teachers should involve parents and other school personnel in addressing the problems. Parents should be notified, and the expertise and guidance of experienced school personnel should be sought.

3.6   What makes urban classrooms unique in terms of classroom management?

First, because urban classrooms tend to be diverse, teachers need to make sure that all students understand classroom rules and procedures and how they contribute to learning. Second, urban classrooms tend to be large, making classroom management more challenging. Third, negative stereotypes often exist about urban students, resulting in teachers teaching defensively rather than positively.

4.1   Explain how involving parents contributes to a productive learning environment.

Productive learning environments are orderly and focus on learning. Research indicates that when parents are involved, students are more willing to do homework, their long-term achievement is higher, their attitudes are more positive, and they behave more responsibly. In addition their attendance and graduation rates are higher. Each contributes to a safe, orderly, learning-focused environment.

4.2   **What strategies do effective teachers use to communicate with parents?**

Effective teachers use a variety of strategies to communicate with parents. In addition to open houses, interim progress reports, and report cards, effective teachers also send letters home; periodically send home packets of student work; and use newsletters, e-mails, and individual notes. In addition, phone calls and home visits are also effective.

Chapter 12   Effective Instruction in American Classrooms

1.1   **Describe the principles on which cognitive learning theories are based.**

The principles on which cognitive learning theory is based are
- *Learning depends on experiences.* This principle is evident in our everyday lives. Learning to drive is a simple example. If our experience with driving involves only vehicles with automatic transmissions, our ability to drive is less fully developed than it would be if we have experiences driving cars with both automatic and standard transmissions.
- *Learners construct—they do not record—knowledge in an attempt to make sense of those experiences.* Learners don't behave like tape recorders, keeping an exact copy of what they hear or read in their memories. Instead, they mentally modify the experiences to make sense of them.
- *Knowledge that is constructed depends on and builds on knowledge that learners already possess.* People construct understanding based on what they already know. For example, many people believe our summers (in the northern hemisphere) are warmer than our winters because we are closer to the sun in the summer. (We, in fact, are slightly farther away, but the sun's rays are more direct.) This idea is based on knowing that as we move closer to an open fire or a hot stove burner, we get warmer.
- *Learning is enhanced by social interaction.* As people discuss ideas, understanding that they wouldn't have acquired on their own is constructed. This is consistent with the old adage "Two heads are better than one."
- *Learning requires practice and feedback.* People learn to do well only what they practice doing. Learning also requires feedback that gives them information about the validity of their understanding.

1.2   **You and a friend are trying to install a sound card in your computer, but you're a little uncertain about how to do it. You open the cabinet, look inside, and as you talk about how to proceed, she suggests looking to see where the speakers are attached. "Good idea," you say, and you easily install the card. Which principle of learning is best illustrated by this example?**

This illustrates the principle "Learning is enhanced by social interaction" You have a problem, discuss it, and solve it during the course of the discussion.

1.3   **Research indicates that properly designed homework increases learning (Cooper, Robinson, & Patall, 2006; Kohn, 2006). To which principle of learning is this research most closely related?**

Homework is a form of practice, so it most closely relates to the principle "Learning requires practice and feedback." Properly designed homework means that the homework is directly related to teachers' learning objectives and learning activities.

2.1   **What are the five essential steps in planning for instruction?**

The five steps involved in planning for instruction consist of the following:
1. *Select topics.* Standards, curriculum guides, textbooks, and the teacher's professional knowledge are sources that help guide this decision.
2. *Specify learning objectives.* Though the format for preparing learning objectives varies, the important aspect of preparing learning objectives is being clear about what you want students to know, to understand, or to be able to do.

3. *Prepare and organize learning activities.* Finding or creating examples, as Shirley Barton did with her "pizzas" and "cakes," and then sequencing the examples is the primary process involved in preparing and organizing learning activities.
4. *Prepare assessments.* Assessments should be created during planning instead of after learning activities have been completed.
5. *Ensure instructional alignment.* Instructional alignment means that teachers are careful to ensure that their learning activities and assessments are consistent with their objectives.

2.2   **Planning in a standards-based environment involves one additional step beyond the planning steps described in this section of the chapter. What is that additional step?**

When teachers' planning involves standards, the first step is to interpret the standard. Descriptions of standards vary; some are very specific, whereas others are quite general. When working with a standard described in general terms, teachers must first make a decision about what the standard means, then follow the rest of the planning steps—that is, plan learning activities and assessments.

2.3   **Classify the following objectives into one of the cells of the taxonomy table in Figure 12.2, and explain your classification: (1) Students will identify examples of figures of speech such as similes, metaphors, and personifications in written paragraphs. (2) Students will write original paragraphs that include those figures of speech.**

Because figures of speech are concepts, and being able to identify examples of them indicates understanding, the first objective would be classified in the cell where conceptual knowledge *intersects with* understand.

   Writing paragraphs involves a procedure, and the fact that they must be original involves the cognitive process create, *so the second objective would be classified in the cell where* procedural knowledge *intersects with* create.

3.1   **As middle schoolers walk into their geography class, they see a large matrix comparing the climate, geography, and economy of the northern and southern states before the Civil War. As soon as the bell stops ringing, the teacher says, "Write a minimum of two differences each in the geography, climate, and economy columns of the chart." The students begin, and as they're writing, the teacher takes roll. Which of the essential teaching skills does this example best illustrate? Explain.**

Organization is the essential teaching skill best illustrated in this example. The teacher began her class right on time, and her chart was prepared and waiting when the students walked into the room.

3.2   **Shirley used her cardboard pizzas in her review, and she used her cakes to introduce the topic of *equivalent fractions*. Which essential teaching skill did the use of these materials best illustrate? Explain.**

Focus is the essential teaching skill best illustrated by Shirley's use of the pizzas and cakes. Each was an example that Shirley used to attract and maintain students' attention.

3.3   **Identify at least two essential teaching skills that are illustrated in each of the chapters of this book.**

The two essential teaching skills that are best illustrated in each chapter are feedback *and* review and closure. *For example, when you go to Appendix A, we provide you with feedback for all of the "Check Your Understanding" questions, and when you go to the book's Companion Website, you have feedback for the "Making Connections" questions and the "Preparing for Your Licensure Exam" questions that appear at the end of the chapter.*

In the "Meeting Your Learning Objectives" section of each chapter, we provide you with a review of the chapter's contents, which is aligned with the learning objectives.

We also attempt to model effective communication in our writing. We try to use clear language; emphasize important points with figures, tables, bulleted lists, and marginal definitions; and develop the chapters in thematic ways.

4.1 **Using the principles of learning presented at the beginning of the chapter as a basis, explain why the introduction phase is important in direct instruction, lecture-discussion, and guided discovery.**

One of the learning principles says, "Knowledge that is constructed depends on and builds on knowledge that learners already possess." The introduction phase activates students' prior knowledge, which then serves as a springboard for understanding the topic being taught.

4.2 **Which phase of direct instruction is most important for ensuring successful independent practice? Explain.**

The developing-understanding *phase is most important for ensuring successful independent practice, and it is in this phase that we see the most difference between effective and ineffective teachers. If the developing-understanding phase is ineffective, both guided practice and independent practice will be difficult and confusing. Remember, independent practice strengthens earlier understanding; it does not teach the skill. If teachers have to provide a great deal of explanation during independent practice, error rates increase and student achievement decreases.*

4.3 **We said, "When guided discovery is done well, research supports its effectiveness." What is necessary in order for instruction to be "done well"? Explain.**

If instruction is done well, the teacher's objectives are clear, and the learning activity is aligned with the objectives. Also, the teacher carefully monitors students' thinking throughout and intervenes early enough to prevent misconceptions, but not so soon as to reduce opportunities for constructing understanding.

4.4 **A teacher places her third graders in groups of three, gives each group magnets and a packet including a dime, spoon, aluminum foil, rubber band, wooden pencil, paper clip, and nails. She tells the groups to experiment with the magnets and items for 10 minutes and write their observations on paper. As they work, she answers questions and makes comments. The class as a whole group discusses the results. How effectively did the teacher begin this cooperative learning activity with her students? Cite evidence from the example to support your conclusion.**

She introduced cooperative learning quite effectively. Her task was short and simple, it was clear and specific (write observations on paper), the written observations provided a product, and she monitored the students' work. We have no evidence about them moving into and out of the groups or about the amount of time they had to work.

Chapter 13   Technology in American Schools

1.1 **As we look at technology in a historical sense, such as using the chalkboard, overhead, or filmstrip projector, which view of technology—hardware or process—was more prominent? Explain.**

In thinking of technology historically, the hardware view was more prominent. Teachers viewed the chalkboard, overhead, and other aids primarily as tools to augment the teacher's message.

1.2   How was the definition of educational technology—"A combination of the processes and tools involved in addressing educational needs and problems"— illustrated in Pete's work with his students?

Pete integrated technology into his teaching, using it as an instructional tool to help him accomplish his learning goals. He involved his students in constructive problem solving as they attempted to create a company like the Hudson Bay Trading Company. They used their computers and the Internet as tools to gather information to help them with their problem solving.

2.1   What is one similarity and one important difference between drill-and-practice and tutorial software?

They are similar in that both are used to teach specific skills and concepts. They differ in that drill-and-practice software is used after some other form of initial instruction, whereas tutorials are self-contained, providing both initial instruction and practice.

2.2   As tools for promoting learning, what are the primary functions of simulations, databases, and spreadsheets?

Simulations provide realistic contexts for complex learning; they are especially useful in teaching problem solving. As tools for promoting learning, the primary function of databases and spreadsheets is to assist learners in organizing and presenting data during problem-based learning.

2.3   What are three advantages of word processing over conventional methods of teaching writing?

Probably the most important advantage of word processing over conventional methods of teaching writing is that it enables writers to efficiently enter, revise, and edit text. Second, it allows writers to store and combine ideas from a variety of sources, and third, it facilitates communities of writers by allowing written products to be e-mailed to others for feedback.

2.4   What are two ways that teachers can use the Internet to increase students' learning?

One way of using the Internet to increase students' learning is by using it as an information source; it provides a vast array of resources to both teachers and students. The second is as a means of connecting teachers and students over vast distances, which increases communication and promotes a form of social interaction unavailable in any other way.

2.5   What is assistive technology, and what are its major uses in the classroom?

Assistive technology consists of an array of adaptive tools that support students with disabilities in learning activities and daily life tasks. Two major instructional adaptations focus on computer input and output devices.

3.1   How can technology assist teachers in the preparation of learning materials?

Teachers can use technology to make difficult-to-learn ideas accessible to students. They can also use it to organize information in databases and spreadsheets for student analysis.

3.2   What are the major logistical challenges teachers face in assessment, and how can technology address them?

The major logistical challenges teachers face in assessment are planning and constructing tests, administering and scoring them, and maintaining student records. Technology can assist in all of these challenges by storing information in a systematic way, making subsequent retrieval and use easier.

3.3   **How can technology assist teachers in their efforts to communicate with parents and other caregivers?**

Voice mail, Websites, and e-mail provide asynchronous means of sending and receiving messages. These allow both parents and teachers to communicate outside the strictures of time.

4.1   **How do alignment and software quality affect classroom technology use?**

Unfortunately, much of technology software available today is of low quality, primarily targeting low-level skill learning and is based on behaviorist learning principles. If the software does not match a teacher's goals, it is out of alignment and can't help meet these goals.

4.2   **How do accountability and time constraints influence teachers' use of technology?**

Not only are teachers busy professionals with little extra time to spare, they also are under accountability pressures to maximize student learning. Both of these factors work against greater technology use by teachers. They often don't have sufficient preparation time to integrate technology into their teaching, and when they do, the available software doesn't match the accountability standards they are trying to meet.

4.3   **How is the easy access of information on the Internet both an advantage and a problem for teachers?**

Easy access to information on the Internet provides teachers with a personal planning resource as well as a source of information for their students. However, this wealth of information also provides problems for teachers. Plagiarism, or the lifting of entire passages from the Internet, is a growing problem. In addition, students also have access to information that may be inappropriate for them or that doesn't match their learning objectives.

4.4   **What is the digital divide, and how does access differ for different groups of students?**

The digital divide refers to gaps in access to technology between different groups of students. Research shows that although virtually all students have access to computers in schools, home access to computers varies with income and ethnicity.

References

AAUW Education Foundation Commission on Technology, Gender, and Teacher Education. (2000). *Tech-savvy: Educating girls in the new computer age.* Washington, DC: Author.

Abedi, J., Hofstetter, C., & Lord, C. (2004). Assessment accommodations for English language learners: Implications for policy-based empirical research. *Review of Educational Research, 74*(1), 1–28.

Abington School District v. Schempp, 374 U.S. 203 (1963).

Abowitz, K. (2000). A pragmatist revisioning of resistance theory. *American Educational Research Journal, 39,* 877–907.

Adams, D. (1995). *Education for extinction: American Indians in the boarding school experience, 1875–1928.* Lawrence: University Press of Kansas.

Adler, M. (1982). *The Paideia proposal: An educational manifesto.* New York: Macmillan.

Adler, M. (1998). *The Paideia proposal: An educational manifesto.* (Reprint.) New York: Simon & Schuster.

Alan Guttmacher Institute. (2004). *Teen pregnancy: Trends and lessons learned.* Retrieved June 13, 2006, from *http://www.agi-us.org/pubs/ib_1_02.pdf*

Alder, N. (2002). Interpretations of the meaning of care: Creating caring relationship in urban middle school classrooms. *Urban Education, 37*(2), 241–266.

Alexander, K., & Alexander, M. D. (2001). *American public school law.* Belmont, CA: Wadsworth.

Alexander, L., & Riley, R. (2002). A compass in the storm. *Education Week, 22*(6), 36–37, 48.

Alexander, P. (2006). *Psychology in learning and instruction.* Upper Saddle River, NJ: Merrill/Prentice Hall.

Allen, R. (2002). Big schools: The way we are. *Educational Leadership, 59*(5), 36–41.

Allington, R. L., & McGill-Franzen, A. (2003). The impact of summer setback on the reading achievement gap. *Phi Delta Kappan, 85*(1), 68–71.

Alperstein, J. F. (2005). Commentary on girls, boys, test scores and more. *Teachers College Record.* Date Published: May 16, 2005. Retrieved June 21, 2005, from *http://tcrecord.org* ID Number: 11874

American Association for the Advancement of Science. (1989). *Project 2061: Science for all Americans.* Washington, DC: Author.

American Association of University Women. (1992). *How schools shortchange girls.* Annapolis Junction, MD: Author.

American Association of University Women. (1998). *Gender gaps: Where schools still fail our children.* Annapolis Junction, MD: Author.

American Association of University Women. (2006). *Drawing the line: Sexual harassment on campus.* New York: Harris Interactive.

American Association of University Women Educational Foundation. (2001). *Hostile hallways: Bullying, teasing, and sexual harassment in school.* New York: Harris Interactive.

American Council of Trustees and Alumni. (2000). *Losing America's memory: Historical illiteracy in the 21st century.* Washington, DC: Author.

American Educational Research Association. (2006). Retrieved September 6, 2006, from *http://www.aera.net*

American Federation of Teachers. (2003). *Voucher home page.* Retrieved February 3, 2004, from *http://www.aft.org/research/vouchers*

American Federation of Teachers. (2004). *Survey and analysis of teacher salary trends 2004.* Retrieved February 2004, from *http://www.aft.org/research/survey02/SalarySurvey02.pdf*

American Federation of Teachers. (2006). Retrieved August 16, 2006, from *http://www.aft.org*

American Psychological Association. (1998). *How students learn: Reforming our schools through learner-centered education.* Washington, DC: Author.

American Psychological Association. (2006). Retrieved September 6, 2006, from *http://www.apa.org*

Amrein, A., & Berliner, D. (2003). The effects of high-stakes testing on student motivation and learning. *Educational Leadership, 60*(5), 32–38.

Anagnostopoulos, D. (2006). "Real students" and "true demotes": Ending social promotion and the moral ordering of urban high schools. *American Educational Research Journal, 43*(1), 5–42.

Anderson, G., Jimerson, S., & Whipple, A. (2002). *Student's ratings of stressful experiences at home and school: Loss of a parent and grade retention as superlative stressors.* Manuscript prepared for publication, available from authors at the University of California, Santa Barbara, CA.

Anderson, J. (1988). *The education of Blacks in the South.* Chapel Hill: University of North Carolina Press.

Anderson, L., & Krathwohl, D. (Eds.). (2001). *A taxonomy for learning, teaching, and assessing: A revision of Bloom's taxonomy of educational objectives.* New York: Addison Wesley Longman.

Ansell, S., & McCabe, M. (2003). Off target. *Education Week, 22*(17), 57–58.

Ansell, S., & Park, J. (2003). Tracking tech trends. *Education Week, 22*(35), 43–49.

Antil, L., Jenkins, J., Wayne, S., & Vadasy, P. (1998). Cooperative learning: Prevalence, conceptualizations, and the relation between research and practice. *American Educational Research Journal, 35*(3), 419–454.

Apple, M. (1995). *Education and power* (2nd ed.). New York: Rutledge.

Archer, J. (2000a). Competition fierce for minority teachers. *Education Week, 19*(18), 32–33.

Archer, J. (2000b). Teachers warned against teaching contracts. *Education Week, 20*(15), 30.

Archer, J. (2003). Increasing the odds. *Education Week, 22*(17), 52–56.

Archer, J. (2005). Connecticut files court challenge to NCLB. *Education Week, 25*(1), 23, 27.

Archer, J. (2006a). Building capacity. *Supplement to Education Week, 26*(3), S3–S12.

Archer, J. (2006b). The road less traveled. *Education Week, 25*(17), 34–37.

Armour-Thomas, E. (2004). What is the nature of evaluation and assessment in an urban context? In S. R. Steinberg & J. L. Kincheloe (Eds.), *19 Urban questions: Teaching in the city* (pp. 109–118). New York: Peter Lang.

Armstrong, D. (2003). *Curriculum today.* Upper Saddle River, NJ: Merrill/Prentice Hall.

Aronson, E., Wilson, T., & Akert, R. (2005). *Social psychology* (5th ed.). Upper Saddle River, NJ: Pearson.

Asian-Nation. (2005). Retrieved February 17, 2005, from *http://www.asian-nation.org/model-minority.shtml*

Associated Press. (2000). Texas legislative panel calls for charter schools moratorium. *Boston Globe,* December 29, A13.

Attewell, P. (2001). The first and second digital divides. *Sociology of Education, 74*(July), 252–259.

Attiel, A., Sober, S., Numbers, R., Amasino, R., Cox, B., Berceau, B., Powell, T., & Cox, M. (2006). Defending science education against intelligent design: A call to action. *Journal of Clinical Investigation, 116,* 1134–1138.

Ayers, W., Dohrn, B. & Ayers, R. (Eds.). (2001). *Zero tolerance.* New York: New Press.

Azevedo, R. (2005). Computer environments as metacognitive tools for enhancing learning. *Educational Psychologist, 40*(4), 193–197.

Babad, E., Bernieri, F., & Rosenthal, R. (1991). Students as judges of teachers' verbal and nonverbal behavior. *American Educational Research Journal, 28*(1), 211–234.

Bae, G. (2003, April). *Rethinking constructivism in multicultural contexts: Does constructivism in education take the issue of diversity into consideration?* Paper presented at the annual meeting of the American Educational Research Association, Chicago.

Baker, D. (2006, July 3). For Navajo, science and tradition intertwine. *Salt Lake Tribune,* pp. D1, D5.

Baker, P., & Slevin, P. (2005, August 3). Bush remarks on "Intelligent Design" Theory fuel debate. *The Washington Post.* Retrieved October 1, 2006, from *http://www.washingtonpost.com/wp-dyn/content/article/2005/08/02/AR2005080201686.html*

Bali, V., Anagnostopoulos, D., & Roberts, R. (2005). Toward a political explanation of grade retention. *Educational Evaluation and Policy Analysis, 27*(2), 133–155.

Bandura, A. (2001). *Social cognitive theory. Annual Review of Psychology.* Palo Alto, CA: Annual Review.

Bandura, A. (2004, May). *Toward a psychology of human agency.* Paper presented at the meeting of the American Psychological Society, Chicago.

Bangert-Drowns, R. (1993). The word processor as an instructional tool: A meta-analysis of word processing in writing instruction. *Review of Educational Research, 63,* 69–93.

Banks, J. (2006a). *An introduction to multicultural education* (4th ed.). Boston: Allyn & Bacon.

Banks, J. (2006b). *Cultural diversity and education* (6th ed.). Boston: Allyn & Bacon.

Bardige, B. (2005). *At a loss for words: How America is failing our children and what we can do about it.* Philadelphia: Temple University Press.

Barnoski, L. (2005). My purpose. *Education Week, 25*(13), 37.

Barone, M. (2000). In plain English: Bilingual education flunks out of schools in California. *U.S. News & World Report, 128*(21), 37.

Barr, R., & Parrett, W. (2001). *Hope fulfilled for at-risk and violent youth* (2nd ed.). Boston: Allyn & Bacon.

Bartell, C. (2005). *Cultivating high-quality teaching through induction and mentoring.* Thousand Oaks, CA: Corwin Press.

Barton, A., Drake, C., Perez, J. G., St. Louis, K., & George, M. (2004). Ecologies of parental engagement in urban education. *Educational Researcher, 33*(4), 3–12.

Barton, P. (2004). Why does the gap persist? *Educational Leadership, 62*(3), 9–13.

Barton, P. (2006). The dropout problem: Losing ground. *Educational Leadership, 63*(5), 14–18.

Battista, M. (1999). The mathematical miseducation of America's youth: Ignoring research and scientific study in education. *Phi Delta Kappan, 80,* 425–433.

Bauman, S., & Del Rio, A. (2006). Preservice teachers' responses to bullying scenarios: Comparing physical, verbal, and relational bullying. *Journal of Educational Psychology, 98*(1), 219–231.

Bay, M., Staver, J., Bryan, T., & Hale, J. (1992). Science instruction for the mildly handicapped: Direct instruction versus discovery teaching. *Journal of Research in Science Teaching, 29,* 555–570.

Belfield, C., & Levin, H. (2005). *The privatization of school choice: Consequences for parents, schools, and public policy.* Boulder, CO: Paradigm Publishers.

Benard, B. (1994). *Fostering resilience in urban schools.* San Francisco: Far West Laboratory.

Bennett, C. (1999). *Comprehensive multicultural education: Theory and practice* (4th ed.). Boston: Allyn & Bacon.

Bennett, C. (2007). *Multicultural education* (6th ed.). Boston: Allyn & Bacon.

Bennett, S. (1978). Recent research on teaching: A dream, a belief, and a model. *British Journal of Educational Psychology, 48,* 27–147.

Bergin, M. (2006). Junk science. *World Magazine, 21*(8), 317–345.

Berk, L. (2005). *Infants & children* (5th ed.). Boston: Allyn & Bacon.

Berk, L. (2006). *Child development* (7th ed.). Boston: Allyn & Bacon.

Berk, L. (2007). *Development through the lifespan* (4th ed.). Boston: Allyn & Bacon.

Berliner, D. (2004). If the underlying premise for No Child Left Behind is false, how can that act solve our problems? In K. Goodman, P. Shannon, Y. Goodman, & R. Rapoport (Eds.), *Saving our schools.* Berkeley, CA: RDR Books.

Berliner, D. (2005a). *Our impoverished view of educational reform.* Paper presented at the annual meeting of the American Educational Research Association, Montreal.

Berliner, D. (2005b). The near impossibility of testing for teacher quality. *Journal of Teacher Education, 56*(3), 205–213.

Bernstein, D., & Tiegerman-Farber, E. (2002). *Language and communication disorders in children* (5th ed.). Boston: Allyn & Bacon.

Bernstein, M. (2006). Is tenure an anachronism? *Education Week, 25*(28), 34.

Berry, B., Hoke, M., & Hirsch, E. (2004). The search for highly qualified teachers. *Phi Delta Kappan, 85*(9), 684–689.

Bertman, S. (2000). *Cultural amnesia: America's future and the crisis of memory.* Westport, CT: Praeger.

Bethel School District No. 403 v. Fraser, 106 S. Ct. 3159 (1986).

Betts, J. (2005). The economic theory of school choice. In J. Betts & T. Loveless (Eds.), *Getting choice right: Ensuring equity and efficiency in education policy* (pp. 14–39). Washington, DC: Brookings Institution Press.

Biddle, B. (2001). Poverty, ethnicity, and achievement in American schools. In B. J. Biddle (Ed.), *Social class, poverty, and education* (pp. 1–30). New York: Routlege Falmer.

Biddle, B., & Berliner, D. (2002). Unequal school: Funding in the United States. *Education Leadership, 59*(8), 48–59.

Billings, L., & Fitzgerald, J. (2002). Dialogic discussion and the Paideia Seminar. *American Educational Research Journal, 39,* 907–942.

Black, S. (2002). The well-rounded student. *American School Board Journal, 189*(6), 33–35.

Blair, J. (2000). AFT urges new tests, expanded training for teachers. *Education Week, 19*(32), 11.

Blair, J. (2003). Skirting tradition. *Education Week, 22*(17), 35–38.

Blatchford, P., Bassett, P., & Brown, P. (2005). Teachers' and pupils' behavior in large and small classes: A systematic observation study of pupils aged 10 and 11 years. *Journal of Educational Psychology, 97*(3), 454–467.

Bloom, B., Englehart, M., Furst, E., Hill, W., & Krathwohl, O. (1956). *Taxonomy of educational objectives: The classification of educational goals: Handbook 1. The cognitive domain.* White Plains, NY: Longman.

Bloomfield, D. (2006). Come clean on small schools. *Education Week, 25*(20), 34, 35.

Board of Education of Independent School District No. 92 of Pottawatomie County v. Earls 536 U.S. 822, 1225. Ct. 2559 (2002).

Board of Education of the Westside Community School v. Mergens, 496 U.S. 226 (1990).

Bohman, D. (2006). *School superintendent pay*. Retrieved March 7, 2006, from *http://www.tampabays10.com/news.aspx?storyied=25049*

Bohn, C. M., Roehrig, A. D., & Pressley, M. (2004). The first days of school in the classrooms of two more effective and four less effective primary-grades teachers. *Elementary School Journal, 104*(4), 269–288.

Bolkan, J. V., Roland, J., & Smith, D. N. (2006). Designing the new school. *Learning and Leading With Technology, 33*(7), 10–14.

Bond, H. (1934). *The education of the Negro in the American social order*. New York: Prentice Hall.

Borja, R. (2002). Study: Urban school chiefs' tenure is 4.6 years. *Education Week, 21*(21), 5.

Borja, R. (2003). Prepping for the big test. *Education Week, 22*(35), 23–26.

Borko, H., & Putnam, R. (1996). Learning to teach. In D. Berliner, & R. Calfee (Eds.), *Handbook of educational psychology* (pp. 673–708). New York: Simon & Schuster Macmillan.

Borman, G. (2002/2003). How can Title I improve achievement? *Educational Leadership, 60*(4), 49, 53.

Borman, G., & Kimball, S. (2005). Teacher quality and educational inequality: Do teachers with higher standards-based evaluation ratings close student achievement gaps? *The Elementary School Journal, 106*(1), 3–20.

Borman, G., & Overman, L. (2004). Academic resilience in mathematics among poor and minority students. *Elementary School Journal, 104*(3), 177–196.

Botstein, L. (2006). The trouble with high school. *School Administrator, 63*(1), 16–19.

Bowman, D. (2000a). Arizona poised to revisit graduation exam. *Education Week, 20*(13), 16, 18.

Bowman, D. (2000b). Charters, vouchers earning mixed report card. *Education Week, 19*(34), 1, 19–21.

Bowman, D. (2000c). White House proposes goals for improving Hispanic education. *Education Week, 19*(41), 9.

Bowman, D. (2002). Researchers see promising signs in DARE's new drug ed. program. *Education Week, 22*(11), 6–7.

Bowman, D. (2003). Student drug testing gathers prominent support. *Education Week, 23*(3), 1, 16, 17.

Bowman, D. (2004). Spending on anti-smoking education slips. *Education Week, 23*(43), 18–20.

Bracey, G. (1999). Top-heavy. *Phi Delta Kappan, 80*, 472–473.

Bracey, G. (2002). The 12th Bracey report on the condition of public education. *Phi Delta Kappan, 84*, 135–150.

Bracey, G. (2003a). Investing in preschool. *American School Board Journal, 90*(1), 32–35.

Bracey, G. (2003b). Not all alike. *Phi Delta Kappan, 84*, 717–718.

Bracey, G. (2004). The 14th Bracy Report on the condition of public education. *Phi Delta Kappan, 86*(2), 149–167.

Bracey, G. (2005a). A nation of cheats. *Phi Delta Kappan, 86*(5), 412–413.

Bracey, G. (2005b). And now, the Indian spelling gene. *Phi Delta Kappan, 87*(1), 91–93.

Bracey, G. (2005c). Dropouts to the fore. *Phi Delta Kappan, 86*(8), 711–712.

Bracey, G. (2005d). Plus ca change. *Phi Delta Kappan, 86*(6), 476–478.

Bradley v. Pittsburgh Board of Education, 913 F.2d 1064 (3d Cir. 1990).

Bradley, A. (1999). Confronting a tough issue: Teacher tenure. *Education Week, 18*(17), 48–52.

Bransford, J., Brown, A., & Cocking, R. (Eds.). (2000). *How people learn: Brain, mind, experience, and school*. Washington, DC: National Academy Press.

Bransford, J., Darling-Hammond, L., & LePage, P. (2005). Introduction. In L. Darling-Hammond & J. Bransford (Eds.), *Preparing teachers for a changing world: What teachers should learn and be able to do* (pp. 1–39). San Francisco: Jossey-Bass/Wiley.

Bransford, J., Derry, S., Berliner, D., Hammerness, K. (2005). Theories of learning and their roles in teaching. In L. Darling-Hammond & J. Bransford (Eds.), *Preparing teachers for a changing world: What teachers should learn and be able to do* (pp. 40–87). San Francisco: Jossey-Bass.

Brenner, D. (2001, April). *Translating social constructivism into methodology for documenting learning*. Paper presented at the annual meeting of the American Educational Research Association, Seattle, WA.

Brimley, V., & Garfield, R. (2005). *Financing education* (9th ed.). Boston: Allyn & Bacon.

Broh, B. (2002). Linking extracurricular programming to academic achievement: Who benefits and why? *Sociology of Education, 75*, 69–91.

Brooke, R. (Ed.). (2003). *Rural voices: Place-conscious education and the teaching of writing*. New York: Teachers College Press.

Brophy, J. (1998). *Motivating students to learn*. Boston: McGraw-Hill.

Brophy, J. (2004). *Motivating students to learn* (2nd ed.). Boston: McGraw-Hill.

Brophy, J. (2006). Graham Nuthall and social constructivist teaching: Research-based cautions and qualifications. *Teaching and Teacher Education, 22,* 529–537.

Brouillette, L. (2000, April). *What is behind all that rhetoric? A case study of the creation of a charter school.* Paper presented at the annual meeting of the American Educational Research Association, New Orleans, LA.

Brown, D. (2004). Urban teachers' professed classroom management strategies: Reflections of culturally responsive teaching. *Urban Education, 39*(3), 266–289.

Brown, D. F. (2006). It's the curriculum, stupid: There's something wrong with it. *Phi Delta Kappan, 87*(10), 777–783.

Brown, H. (2003). Charter schools found lacking resources. *Education Week, 22*(31), 30.

Brown, K., Anfara, V., & Roney, K. (2004). Student achievement in high performing, suburban middle schools and low performing, urban middle schools: Plausible explanations for the differences. *Education and Urban Society, 36*(4), 428–456.

Brown, R., & Evans, W. (2002). Extracurricular activity and ethnicity: Creating greater school connections among diverse student populations. *Urban Education, 37*(1), 41–58.

Brown v. Bathhe, 416 F. Supp. 1194 (D. Neb. 1976).

Brown v. Board of Education of Topeka, 347 U.S. 483 (1954).

Bruning, R., Schraw, G., Norby, M., & Ronning, R. (2004). *Cognitive psychology and instruction* (4th ed.). Upper Saddle River, NJ: Prentice Hall.

Brunner, C., & Tally, W. (1999). *The new media literacy handbook: An educator's guide to bringing new media into the classroom.* New York: Anchor Books.

Bryan, L. (2005). Once upon a time: A Grimm approach to character education. *Journal of Social Studies Research, 29*(1), 3–6.

Buckley, J., Schneider, M., & Shang, Y. (2005). Fix it and they might stay: School facility quality and teacher retention in Washington, D.C. *Teachers College Record, 107*(5), 1107–1123.

Buhi, E., & Goodson, P. (2006). Abstinence education: Research and practice—a reaction to Young and Penhollow. *American Journal of Health Education, 37*(4), 253–254.

Bullock, A., & Hawk, P. (2005). *Developing a teaching portfolio: A guide for preservice and practicing teachers* (2nd ed.). Upper Saddle River, NJ: Merrill/Prentice Hall.

Bullough, R., Jr. (1989). *First-year teacher: A case study.* New York: Teachers College Press.

Bullough, R., Jr. (1999, April). *In praise of children at-risk: Life on the other side of the teacher's desk.* Paper presented at the annual meeting of the American Educational Research, Association, Montreal.

Bullough, R., Jr. (2001). *Uncertain lives: Children of promise, teachers of hope.* New York: Teachers College Press.

Burns, M. (2005/2006). Tools for the mind. *Educational Leadership, 63*(4), 48–53.

Burstyn, J., Bender, G., Casalla, R., Gordon, H., Guerra, D., Luschen, K., Steven, R., & William, K. (2001). *Preventing violence in schools: A challenge to American democracy.* Mahwah, NJ: Lawrence Erlbaum.

Butin, D. (2003). Of what use is it? Multiple conceptualizations of service learning within education. *Teachers College Record, 105*(9), 1674–1692. Retrieved June 2, 2005, from *http://www.tcrecord.org* ID Number 11561

Button, H., & Provenzo, E. (1989). *History of education in American culture.* New York: Holt, Rinehart & Winston.

Butts, R., & Cremin, L. (1953). *A history of education in America.* New York: Holt, Rinehart & Winston.

Byrnes, J. (2003). Factors predictive of mathematics achievement in White, Black, and Hispanic 12th graders. *Journal of Educational Psychology, 95,* 316–326.

Caldas, S., & Bankston, C. (2005). *Forced to fail: The paradox of school desegregation.* Westport, CT: Praeger.

Callister, T., & Burbules, N. (2004). Just give it to me straight: A case against filtering the Internet. *Phi Delta Kappan, 85*(9), 649–655.

Camerino, C. (2003). Pay to play? *Education Week, 22*(23), 32, 34.

Campbell, D., Cignetti, P., Melenyzer, B., Nettles, D., & Wyman, R. (2007). *How to develop a professional portfolio: A manual for teachers* (4th ed.). Boston: Allyn & Bacon.

Campbell, J., & Beaudry, J. (1998). Gender gap linked to differential socialization for high achieving senior mathematics students. *Journal of Educational Research, 91,* 140–147.

Canter, L. (1988). Let the educator beware: A response to Curwin and Mendler. *Educational Leadership, 46*(2), 71–73.

Canter, L., & Canter, M. (1976). *Assertive discipline: A take-charge approach for today's educators.* Santa Monica, CA: Canter.

Canter, L., & Canter, M. (2001). *Assertive discipline: Positive behavior management for today's classroom.* Bloomington, IN: Solution Tree.

Carbo, M. (1997). Reading styles times twenty. *Educational Leadership, 54,* 38–42.

Carnegie Forum on Education and the Economy. (1986). *A nation prepared: Teachers for the 21st century.* Washington,

DC: Author. (ERIC Document Reproduction Service No. ED268120)

Carnegie Learning. (2005). *Success stories and case studies.* Retrieved March 16, 2005, from *http://www.carnegielearning.com*

Carnine, D., Silbert, J., Kameenui, E., Tarver, S., & Jongjohann, K. (2006). *Teaching struggling and at-risk readers: A direct instruction approach.* Upper Saddle River, NJ: Merrill/Prentice Hall.

Carnoy, M., Jacobsen, R., Mishel, L., & Rothstein, R. (2005). *The charter school dust-up: Examining the evidence on enrollment and achievement.* New York: Teachers College Press.

Carpenter, D., & Finn, C. (2006). *Playing to type.* Washington, DC: Thomas Fordham Foundation. Retrieved June 22, 2006, from *www.edexcellence.net*

Carr, N. (2003). The toughest job in America. Education vital signs [Supplement.]. *American School Board Journal, 190*(2), 14–19.

Casey, J., Andreson, K., Yelverton, B., & Wedeen, L. (2002). A status report on charter schools in New Mexico. *Phi Delta Kappan, 83,* 518–524.

Cassady, J. (1999, April). *The effects of examples as elaboration in text on memory and learning.* Paper presented at the annual meeting of the American Educational Research Association, Montreal.

Cavanagh, S. (2004). Online teacher training courses win converts. *Education Week, 23*(23), 20.

Cavanagh, S. (2006a). Perkins bill is approved by Congress. *Education Week, 25*(44), 1, 27.

Cavanagh, S. (2006b). Possible road map seen in Dover case. *Education Week, 25*(10), 1, 10, 11.

CDW Government. (2005). *Teachers talk tech.* Retrieved December 21, 2005, from *www.cdwg.com/ttt*

Center on Addiction and Substance Abuse. (2001). *Malignant neglect: Substance abuse and America's schools.* New York: Columbia University.

Certo, J., Cauley, K., & Chafen, C. (2002, April). *Students' perspectives on their high school experience.* Paper presented at the annual meeting of the American Educational Research Association, New Orleans, LA.

Chalk v. U.S. District Court Cent. Dist. of California, 840 F.2d. 701 (9th Cir. 1988).

Chance, P. (1997). Speaking of differences. *Phi Delta Kappan, 78*(7), 506–507.

Charles, C. M. (2005). *Building classroom discipline* (8th ed). Boston: Allyn and Bacon.

Charner-Laird, M., Watson, D., Szczesuil, S., Kirkpatrick C., & Gordon, P. (2004, April). *Navigating the "Culture Gap": New teachers experience the urban context.* Paper presented at the annual meeting of the American Educational Research Association, San Diego, CA.

Charter Connection. (2006). *Charter school facts.* Center for Education Reform. Retrieved June 22, 2006, from *http://edreform.com/charter_schools*

Chekles, K. (1997). The first seven . . . and the eighth: A conversation with Howard Gardner. *Educational Leadership, 55*(1), 8–13.

Christie, K. (2005). Providing the facts. *Phi Delta Kappan, 86*(5), 341–342.

Ciofalo, J., & Wylie, C. (2006). Using diagnostic classroom assessment: One question at a time. *Teachers College Record.* Retrieved March 20, 2006, from *http://www.tcrecord.org* ID Number: 12285.

Clandinin, J., & Connelly, M. (1996). Teacher as curriculum maker. In P. Jackson (Ed.), *Handbook of research on curriculum* (pp. 363–401). New York: Macmillan.

Clark, R. C., & Mayer, R. E. (2003). *E-learning and the science of instruction: Proven guidelines for consumers and designers of multimedia learning.* San Francisco: Pfeiffer/Wiley.

Cochran-Smith, M. (2005). The new teacher education: For better or for worse? *Educational Researcher, 34*(6), 1–17.

Cognition and Technology Group at Vanderbilt. (1992). The Jasper Series as an example of anchored instruction: Theory, program description, and assessment data. *Educational Psychologist, 27,* 291–315.

Cognition and Technology Group at Vanderbilt. (1997). *The Jasper Project: Lessons in curriculum, instruction, assessment, and professional development.* Mahwah, NJ: Erlbaum.

Cohen, J. (2006). Social, emotional, ethical, and academic education: Creating a climate for learning, participation in democracy, and well-being. *Harvard Educational Review, 76*(2), 201–237.

Coleman, J. (2005, November 15). California Latinos to reach parity with Anglos by 2010. *Salt Lake Tribune,* p. C5.

Coleman, J., Campbell, E., Hobson, D., McPortland, J. Mood. A., Weinfield, F., & York, R. (1966). *Equality of educational opportunity.* Washington, DC: U.S. Department of Health, Education and Welfare.

Coley, R. (2001). *Differences in the gender gap: Comparisons across racial/ethnic groups in education and work.* Princeton, NJ: Educational Testing Service.

Colgan, C. (2004). The controversy over charter school scores reinforces a partisan split. *The American School Board Journal, 191*(10), 6–8.

Colgan, C. (2005). The new look of school safety. *The American School Board Journal, 192*(3), 11–13.

Collis, B., Peters, O., & Pals, N. (2001). A model for predicting the educational use of information and communication technologies. *Instructional Science, 29,* 95–125.

Comer, J., Joyner, E., & Ben-Avie, M. (Eds.) (2004). *Six pathways to healthy child development and academic success.* Thousand Oaks, CA: Corwin Press.

Commonwealth of Pennsylvania v. Douglass, 588 A.2d 53 (Pa. Super. Ct. 1991).

Compayre, G. (1888). *History of pedagogy* (W. Payne, Trans.). Boston: Heath.

Conant, J. (1959). *The American high school.* New York: McGraw-Hill.

Conoley, J., & Goldstein, A. (2004). *School violence intervention: A practical handbook.* New York: Guilford Press.

Cook, G. (2006). What's a teacher worth? Houston joins the push for merit pay. *The American School Board Journal, 193*(3), 4–6.

Cooper, D., & Snell, J. (2003). Bullying—not just a kid thing. *Educational Leadership, 60*(6), 22–25.

Cooper, H., Robinson, J., & Patall, E. (2006). Does homework improve academic achievement? A synthesis of research, 1987–2003. *Review of Educational Research, 76*(1), 1–62.

Cooper, H., Valentine, J., Nye, B., & Lindsay, J. (1999). Relationships between five after-school activities and academic achievement. *Journal of Educational Psychology, 91*(2), 369–378.

Cooper, L. (2001). A comparison of online and traditional computer applications classes. *T.H.E. Journal, 28*(8), 52–58.

Cooperman, S. (2003). A new order of things. *Education Week, 22*(38), 30, 32.

Coppola, E. (2004). *Powering up: Learning to teach well with technology.* New York: Teachers College Press.

Cornelius, L. (2002, April). *Legal implications of school violence.* Paper presented at the annual meeting of the American Educational Research Association, New Orleans, LA.

Corno, L., Cronbach, L. J., Kupermintz, H., Lohman, D. F., Mandinach, E. B., Porteu, A. W., & Talbert, J. E. (2002). *Remaking the concept of aptitude: Extending the legacy of Richard E. Snow.* Mahwah, NJ: Erlbaum.

Corporation for Public Broadcasting. (2003). *Connected to the future: A report on children's Internet use from the Corporation for Public Broadcasting.* Retrieved February 2004, from *http://www.cpb.org/Ed/resources/connected*

Coughlin, E. (1996, February 16). Not out of Africa. *Chronicle of Higher Education,* pp. A6–A7.

Council for Exceptional Children. (2005). Retrieved May 17, 2005, from *http://www.CEC.sped.org.IDEALaw&resources*

Council of Chief State School Officers. (2003). Chief state school officers method of selection. Retrieved February 2004, from *http://www.ccsso.org/chief_state_school_officers/method_of_selection/index.cfm*

Coyle, K., Kirby, D., & Robin, L. (2006). All4You! A randomized trial of an HIV, other STDs, and pregnancy prevention intervention for alternative school students. *AIDS Education and Prevention, 18*(3), 187–203.

Craig, D. (2003). Brain-compatible learning: Principles and applications in athletic training. *Journal of Athletic Training, 38*(4), 342–350.

Crick, N. R., Grotpeter, J. K., & Bigbee, M. A. (2002). Relationally and physically aggressive children's intent attributions and feelings of distress for relational and instructional peer provocation. *Child Development, 73,* 1134–1142.

Crockett, C. (2004). What do kids know—and misunderstand—about science? *Educational Leadership, 61*(5), 34–37.

Cross, T. (2005). *The social and emotional lives of gifted kids: Understanding and guiding their development.* Austin, TX: Prufrock Press.

Cuban, L. (1993). *How teachers taught: Constancy and change in American classrooms: 1890–1980* (2nd ed.). New York: Teachers College Press.

Cuban, L. (1996). Curriculum stability and change. In P. Jackson (Ed.), *Handbook of research on curriculum* (pp. 216–247). New York: Macmillan.

Cuban, L. (2005). *Growing instructional technology in U.S. classrooms.* J. George Jones & Velma Rife Jones Lecture: University of Utah, Salt Lake City.

Cunningham, W., & Cordeiro, P. (2000). *Education administration.* Boston: Allyn & Bacon.

Cushman, K. (2003). *Fires in the bathroom: Advice for teachers from high school students.* New York: The New Press.

Cushman, K. (2006). Help us care enough to learn. *Educational Leadership, 63*(5), 34–37.

Dance, L. J. (2002). *Tough fronts: The impact of street culture on schooling.* New York: Routledge Falmer.

Darling-Hammond, L. (1997). *The right to learn.* San Francisco: Jossey-Bass.

Darling-Hammond, L. (2000). How teacher education matters. *Journal of Teacher Education, 51,* 166–173.

Darling-Hammond, L., & Baratz-Snowdon, J. (Eds.). (2005). *A good teacher in every classroom: Preparing the highly qualified teachers our children deserve.* San Francisco: Jossey-Bass/Wiley.

Darling-Hammond, L., Berry, B., & Thoreson, A. (2001). Does teacher certification matter? Evaluating the evidence. *Educational Evaluation and Policy Analysis, 23,* 57–77.

Darling-Hammond, L., & Bransford, J. (Eds.). (2005). *Preparing teachers for a changing world: What teachers should learn and be able to do.* San Francisco: Jossey-Bass.

Darling-Hammond, L., Chung, R., & Frelow, F. (2002). Variation in teacher preparation: How well do different pathways prepare teachers to teach? *Journal of Teacher Education, 53,* 286–302.

Darling-Hammond, L., & Hammerness, K. (2005). The design of teacher education programs. In L. Darling-Hammond & J. Bransford (Eds.), *Preparing teachers for a changing world: What teachers should learn and be able to do* (pp. 390–441). San Francisco: Jossey-Bass.

Datnow, A., Hubbard, L., & Conchas, G. (2001). How context mediates policy: The implementation of single gender public schooling in California. *Teachers College Record, 103,* 184–206.

Davis, G. (2003). Identifying creative students, teaching for creative growth. In N. Colangelo & G. Davis (Eds.), *Handbook of gifted education* (3rd ed., pp. 311–324). Boston: Allyn & Bacon.

Davis, G., & Rimm, S. (2004). *Education of the gifted and talented* (5th ed.). Boston: Allyn & Bacon.

Davis, M. (2003). Title IX panel deadlocks on critical change. *Education Week, 22*(21), 24–25.

Davis, M. (2006). Drug-free-schools grants targeted by Bush. *Education Week, 25*(25), 21, 23.

DeAngelis, T. (2004). Size-based discrimination may be hardest on children. *Monitor on Psychology, 35*(1), 62.

DeBray, E., McDermott, K., & Wohlstetter, P. (2005). Introduction to the special issue on federalism reconsidered: The case of No Child Left Behind Act. *Peabody Journal of Education, 80*(2), 1–18.

DeMeulenaere, E. (2001, April). *Constructing reinventions: Black and Latino students negotiating the transformation of their academic identities and school performance.* Paper presented at the annual meeting of the American Educational Research Association, Seattle, WA.

Denig, S. J. (2003, April). *A proposed relationship between multiple intelligences and learning styles.* Paper presented at the annual meeting of the American Educational Research Association, Chicago.

DeRoche, E., & Williams, M. (2001). *Character education: A guide for school administrators.* Lanham, MD: Scarecrow Press.

Dewey, J. (1902). *The child and the curriculum.* Chicago: University of Chicago Press.

Dewey, J. (1906). *Democracy and education.* New York: Macmillan.

Dewey, J. (1923). *The school and society.* Chicago: University of Chicago Press.

Dewey, J. (1938). *Experience and education.* New York: Macmillan.

Diamond, J. (1999). *Guns, germs and steel: The fates of human societies.* New York: Norton.

Dickinson, G., Holifield, M., Holifield, G., & Creer, D. (2000). Elementary magnet school students' interracial interaction choices. *Journal of Educational Research, 93,* 391–394.

Dill, V., & Stafford-Johnson, D. (2002). A different road. *American School Board Journal, 189*(11), 44–46.

Dillon, D. (1989). Showing them that I want them to learn and that I care about who they are: A microethnography of the social organization of a secondary low-track English reading classroom. *American Educational Research Journal, 26,* 227–259.

Dillon, S. (2006, July 25). Most states fail demands set out in education law. *New York Times,* p. A14.

Dimick, A., & Apple, M. (2005). Texas and the politics of abstinence-only textbooks. *Teachers College Record.* Retrieved June 29, 2005, from *http://www.tcrecord.org* ID Number 11855.

Dodge, K. A., Lansford, J. E., Burks, V. S., Bates, J. E., Pettit, G. S., Fontaine, R., & Price, J. M. (2003). Peer rejection and social information-processing factors in the development of aggressive behavior problems in children. *Child Development, 74,* 374–393.

Doe v. Renfrow, 635 F.2d 582 (7th Cir. 1980).

Doll, B., Zucher, S., & Brehm, K. (2004). *Resilient classrooms: Creating healthy environments for learning.* New York: Guilford Press.

Donovan, M. S., & Bransford, J. D. (2005). Introduction. In M. S. Donovan & J. D. Bransford (Eds.), *How students learn: History, mathematics, and science in the classroom* (pp. 1–26). Washington, DC: National Academies Press.

Dowling-Sendor, B. (1999). Struggling with set-asides. *American School Board Journal, 186*(4), 20, 22, 63.

Doyle, D. (1999). De facto national standards. *Education Week, 18*(42), 56, 36.

Doyle, W. (1986). Classroom organization and management. In M. Wittrock (Ed.), *Handbook of research on teaching* (3rd ed., pp. 392–431). New York: Macmillan.

Drajem, L. (2002, April). *Life stories: Successful White women teachers of ethnically and racially diverse students.* Paper presented at the annual meeting of the American Educational Research Association, New Orleans, LA.

Drake, S., & Burns, R. (2004). *Meeting standards through integrated curriculum.* Alexandria, VA: Association for Supervision and Curriculum Development.

Drevitch, G. (2006). Merit pay: Good for teachers? *Instructor, 115*(5), 21–23.

Duke, N. (2000). For the rich it's richer: Print experience and environments offered to children in very low- and very high-socioeconomic status first-grade classrooms. *American Educational Research Journal, 37,* 441–478.

Dulude-Lay, C. (2000). *The confounding effect of the dimensions of classroom life on the narratives of student teachers.* Unpublished manuscript, University of Utah, Salt Lake City.

Durst, A. (2005). "The union of intellectual freedom and cooperation": Learning from the University of Chicago's Laboratory School community, 1896–1904. *Teachers College Record, 107*(5), 958–984.

Dworkin, R. (1998, October 23). Affirming affirmative action. *New York Times Review of Books,* pp. 91–102.

Dynarski, M., & Gleason, P. (1999, April). *How can we help? What we have learned from evaluations of federal dropout-prevention programs.* Paper presented at the annual meeting of the American Educational Research Association, Montreal.

Echevarria, J., & Graves, A. (2007). *Sheltered content instruction* (3rd ed.). Boston: Allyn & Bacon.

Echevarria, J., Powers, K., & Short, D. (2006). School reform and standards-based education: A model for English-language learners. *Journal of Educational Research, 99*(4), 195–211.

Economic Policy Institute. (2002). *Inequality at the starting gate: Social background differences in achievement as children begin school.* Washington, DC: Author.

Economic Policy Institute. (2005). *Wage trends.* Retrieved July 14, 2006, from *http://www.epinet.org*

Education Vital Signs. (2005, February). Poverty. *American School Board Journal Supplement,* pp. 22–23.

Education Vital Signs. (2006a, February). School finance. *American School Board Journal Supplement,* pp. 20–21.

Education Vital Signs. (2006b, February). Student health. *American School Board Journal Supplement,* pp. 12–13.

Educational Testing Service. (2005). *The Praxis series 2005–2006: Information and registration bulletin.* Available online at *http://www.ets.org/praxis/prxtest.html*

Educational Testing Service. (2006). *The Praxis series 2005–2006: Information and registration bulletin.* Retrieved August 23, 2006, from *http://www.ets.org/praxis/prxtest.html*

Edwards, V. (2003). Techs answer to testing. *Education Week, 22*(35), 8, 10.

Eggen, P. (1998, April). *A comparison of urban middle school teachers' classroom practices and their expressed beliefs about learning and effective instruction.* Paper presented at the annual meeting of the American Educational Research Association, San Diego, CA.

Eggen, P., & Kauchak, D. (2006). *Strategies and models for teachers: Teaching content and thinking skills* (5th ed.). Boston: Allyn and Bacon.

Eggen, P., & Kauchak, D. (2007). *Educational psychology: Windows on classrooms* (7th ed.). Upper Saddle River, NJ: Merrill/Prentice Hall.

Ehlenberger, K. (2001/2002). The right to search students. *Educational Leadership, 59*(4), 31–35.

Eide, E. R., & Goldhaber, D. D. (2005). Grade retention: What are the costs and benefits? *Journal of Education Finance, 31*(2), 195–214.

Eisner, E. (1993). *The educational imagination: On the design and evaluation of school programs* (3rd ed.). New York: Macmillan.

Eisner, E. (2003). Questionable assumptions about schooling. *Phi Delta Kappan, 84,* 648–657.

Emmer, E., Evertson, C., & Worsham, M. (2006). *Classroom management for secondary teachers* (7th ed.). Boston: Allyn & Bacon.

Emmer, E., & Stough, L. (2001). Classroom management: A critical part of educational psychology with implications for teacher education. *Educational Psychologist, 36,* 103–112.

Engel, B., & Martin, A. (Eds.). (2005). *Holding values: What we mean by progressive education.* Portsmouth, NH: Heinemann.

Engle v. Vitale, 370 U.S. 421 (1962).

Epstein, J. (2001). *School, family, and community partnership: Preparing educators and improving schools.* Boulder, CO: Westview Press.

Ertmer, P. (2005). Teacher pedagogical beliefs: The final frontier in our quest for technology integration? *Educational Technology Research and Development, 53*(4), 25–39.

Essex, N. (2006). *A teacher's pocket guide to school law.* Boston: Allyn & Bacon.

Evans, C., Kirby, U., & Fabrigar, L. (2003). Approaches to learning, need for cognition, and strategic flexibility among university students. *The British Journal of Educational Psychology, 73,* 507–528.

Evans, G. W., & English, K. (2002). The environment of poverty: Multiple stressor exposure, psychophysiological stress, and socioemotional adjustment. *Child Development, 73*, 1238–1248.

Evertson, C., Emmer, E., & Worsham, M. (2006). *Classroom management for elementary teachers* (7th ed.). Boston: Allyn & Bacon.

Evertson, C., & Smithey, M. (2000). Mentoring effects on protégés' classroom practice: An experimental field study. *Journal of Educational Research, 93*, 294–304.

Fagen v. Summers, 498 P.2d 1227 (Wyo. 1972).

Fairchild, T. (2006). Race and class: Separate and not equal. *Education Week, 26*(3), 35, 36.

Faject, W., Bello, M., & Leftwich, S. A. (2005). Pre-service teachers' perceptions in beginning education classes. *Teaching and Teacher Education, 21*(6), 717–727.

Farkas, R. (2003). Effects of traditional versus learning-styles instructional methods on middle school students. *Journal of Educational Research, 97*(1), 42–51.

Federal Interagency Forum on Child and Family Statistics. (2005). *Family structure and children's living arrangement.* Retrieved April 23, 2006, from *http://www.childstats.gov/americaschildren/pop6.asp*

Federation of Tax Administrators. (2006). *State comparisons.* Retrieved March 21, 2006, from *http://www.taxadmin.org*

Feiman-Nemser, S. (2001). From preparation to practice: Designing a continuum to strengthen and sustain teaching. *Teachers College Record, 103*, 1013–1055.

Feinberg, W., & Soltis, J. (2004). *School and society* (4th ed.). New York: Teachers College Press.

Feldman, A., & Matjasko, J. (2005). The role of school-based extracurricular activities in adolescent development: A comprehensive review and future directions. *Review of Educational Research, 75*(2), 159–210.

Feldman, J., López, L., & Simon, K. (2006). *Choosing small: The essential guide to successful high school conversion.* San Francisco: Jossey-Bass.

Feller, B. (2006, August 17). Support for new high school graduation tests is waning, study says. *Salt Lake Tribune,* p. A4.

Ferguson, J. (2002). Vouchers—an illusion of choice. *American School Board Journal, 189*(1), 42–45, 51.

Ferrero, D. (2005). Does "research based" mean "value neutral"? *Phi Delta Kappan, 86*(6), 425–432.

Fine, L. (2002). Writing takes a digital turn for special-needs students. *Education Week, 21*(20), 8.

Finkelstein, E. (2005). Making PowerPoint quizzes. *Presentations, 19*(1), 18–20.

Finn, J., Gerber, S., & Boyd-Zaharias, J. (2005). Small classes in the early grades, academic achievement, and graduating from high school. *Journal of Educational Psychology, 97*(2), 214–223.

Finn, J., Pannozzo, G., & Achilles, C. (2003). The "why's" of class size: Student behavior in small classes. *Review of Educational Research, 72*(3), 321–368.

Finn, K., Willert, H., & Marable, M. (2003). Substance use in schools. *Educational Leadership, 60*(6), 80–85.

First Amendment Center. (1999). *The Bible and public schools: A First Amendment guide.* Nashville, TN: Author. Retrieved February 2004 from *http://www.freedomforum.org/publications/first/BibleAndPublicSchools/bibleguide_reprint.pdf*

Fischer, L., Schimmel, D., & Kelly, C. (2003). *Teachers and the law* (6th ed.). New York: Longman.

Fischer, L., Schimmel, D., & Stellman, L. (2006). *Teachers and the law* (7th ed.). New York: Longman.

Fisher, D. (2006). Keeping adolescents "alive and kickin' it": Addressing suicide in schools. *Phi Delta Kappan, 87*(10), 784–786.

Fiske, E. (2001). *Learning in deed: The power of service-learning for American schools.* Battle Creek, MI: W.K. Kellogg Foundation.

Fiske, E., & Ladd, H. (2000). A distant laboratory. *Education Week, 19*(56), 38.

Flanagan, A., & Grissmer, D. (2002). The role of federal resources in closing the achievement gap. In J. Chubb & T. Loveless (Eds.), *Bridging the achievement gap* (pp. 199–226). Washington, DC: Brookings Institution Press.

Flanagan, A., & Murray, S. (2004). A decade of reform: The impact of school reform in Kentucky. In J. Yinger (Ed.), *Helping children left behind* (pp. 195–214). Cambridge, MA: MIT Press.

Flanagan, K., & Park, J. (2005). *American Indian and Alaska Native children: Findings from the base year of the early childhood longitudinal study, Birth Cohort (ECLS-B).* Washington, DC: National Center for Education Statistics.

Flanigan, R. (2003). A challenging year for schools. Education Vital Signs [Supplement]. *American School Board Journal, 190*(2), 21–25.

Fleischfresser v. Directors of School District No. 200, 15 F.3d 680 (7th Cir. 1994).

Florida Department of Education. (2005). *Sunshine State standards, mathematics preK–2.* Retrieved June 27, 2006, from *http://www.firn.edu/doe/menu/sss.htm*

Florida Department of Education. (2007). *Florida comprehensive assessment test: Mathematics sample test book* (2007). Retrieved October 1, 2006, from *http://www.firn.edu/doe/sas/fcat/pdf/sample/0607/math/FL07_STM_G3M_TB_Cwf001.pdf*

Forcier, R., & Descy, D. (2005). *The computer as an educational tool: Productivity and problem solving* (4th ed.). Upper Saddle River, NJ: Merrill/Prentice Hall.

Francis, B., & Skelton, C. (2005). *Reassessing gender and achievement*. New York: Routledge Falmer.

Franek, M. (2005/2006). Foiling cyberbullies in the new wild west. *Educational Leadership, 63*(4), 39–43.

Frankenberg, E., & Lee, C. (2003). *Charter schools and race: A lost opportunity for integrated education*. Retrieved February 2004 from Harvard University, Civil Rights Project Website: *http://www.civilrightsproject.harvard.edu/research/deseg/Charter_Schools03.pdf*

Franklin, W. (1997, March). *African-American youth at promise*. Paper presented at the annual meeting of the American Educational Research Association, Chicago.

Fredericks, J. A., & Eccles, J. S. (2006). Is extracurricular participation associated with beneficial outcomes? Concurrent and longitudinal relations. *Developmental Psychology, 42*(4), 698–713.

Freedman, M. (2004). A tale of plagiarism and a new paradigm. *Phi Delta Kappan, 85*(7), 545–548.

Freeman, J., McPhail, J., & Berndt, J. (2002). Sixth graders' views of activities that do and do not help them learn. *Elementary School Journal, 102*(4), 335–347.

Freiberg, J. (1999a). Consistency management and cooperative discipline. In J. Freiberg (Ed.), *Beyond behaviorism: Changing the classroom management paradigm* (pp. 75–97). Boston: Allyn & Bacon.

Freiberg, J. (1999b). Sustaining the paradigm. In J. Freiberg (Ed.), *Beyond behaviorism: Changing the classroom management paradigm* (pp. 164–173). Boston: Allyn & Bacon.

Furlan, C. (1999). States tackle Internet-filter rules for schools. *Education Week, 17*(43), 22, 28.

Furlan, C. (2000). Satellite broadcasts seek to enliven study of history. *Education Week, 19*(26), 8.

Furrer, C., & Skinner, E. (2003). Sense of relatedness as a factor in children's academic engagement and performance. *Journal of Educational Psychology, 95*, 148–162.

Gall, M., Gall, J., & Borg, W. (2003). *Educational research: An introduction* (7th ed.). Boston: Allyn & Bacon.

Galley, M. (2003). Despite concerns, online elementary schools grow. *Education Week, 22*(16), 1, 12.

Galley, M. (2004). Court blocks school ban on weapons images. *Education Week, 23*(16), 6.

Garcia, D. (2004). Exploring connections between the construct of teacher efficacy and family involvement practices: Implications for urban teacher preparation. *Urban Education, 39*(3), 290–315.

Garcia, R. (2006). Language, culture, and education. In J. Banks, *Cultural diversity and education* (5th ed., pp. 266–291). Boston: Allyn & Bacon.

Gardner, H. (1983). *Frames of mind: The theory of multiple intelligences*. New York: Basic Books.

Gardner, H. (1999). The understanding pathway. *Educational Leadership, 57*(3), 12–17.

Gardner, H., & Hatch, T. (1989). Multiple intelligences go to school. *Educational Researcher, 18*(8), 4–10.

Gay, B. (2000). Educational equality for students of color. In J. Banks & C. Banks (Eds.), *Multicultural education: Issues and perspectives* (4th ed., pp. 195–228). Boston: Allyn & Bacon.

Gay, G. (2005). Politics of multicultural teacher education. *Journal of Teacher Education, 56*(3), 221–228.

Gay, Lesbian, Straight Education Network. (2005). *National school climate survey*. Retrieved July 14, 2006, from *http://www.glsen.org*

Gaziel, H. (1997). Impact of school culture on effectiveness of secondary schools with disadvantaged students. *Journal of Educational Research, 90*, 310–318.

Gee, J. P. (2005). *Learning by design: Games as learning machines*. Retrieved April 23, 2006, from *http://labweb.education.wisc.edu/room130/papers.htm*

Gehring, J. (1999a). Displays entangle Ten Commandments, First Amendment. *Education Week, 19*(15), 7.

Gehring, J. (1999b). Groups endorse guidelines on using the Bible in instruction. *Education Week, 19*(12), 7.

Gehring, J. (2000). Schools' Bible courses "taught wrong," report says. *Education Week, 19*(19), 10.

Gehring, J. (2002a). Benefit of Illinois credit misses needy, study says. *Education Week, 22*(8), 11.

Gehring, J. (2002b). Vouchers battles head to state capitols. *Education Week, 21*(42), 1, 24, 25.

Gehring, J. (2005). Researchers say girls thrive in single-sex gym classes. *Education Week, 25*(1), 13.

Gewertz, C. (2000). Wisconsin study finds benefits in classes of 15 or fewer students. *Education Week, 19*(31), 10.

Gewertz, C. (2002). Edison buffeted by probe, loss of contracts. *Education Week, 22*(1), 3.

Gewertz, C. (2003a). Study: No academic gains from vouchers for Black student. *Education Week, 22*(30), 13.

Gewertz, C. (2003b). Vallas calls for cuts to private companies. *Education Week, 22*(29), 3.

Gewertz, C. (2006a). Groups accuse Fla. districts of harsh discipline approaches. *Education Week, 25*(34), 7.

Gewertz, C. (2006b). L.A. mayor steps up bid to control schools. *Education Week, 25*(16), 3, 9.

Gewertz, C. (2006c). H.S. dropouts say lack of motivation top reason to quit. *Education Week, 25*(26), 1, 14.

Gewertz, C. (2006d). Race, gender, and the superintendency. *Education Week, 25*(24), 1, 22, 24.

Gilbert, L. (2005). What helps beginning teachers? *Educational Leadership, 62*(8), 36–39.

Gill, B. (2005). School choice and integration. In J. Betts & T. Loveless (Eds.), *Getting choice right: Ensuring equity and efficiency in education policy* (pp. 130–145). Washington, DC: Brookings Institution Press.

Gill, S., McLean, M., & Courville, M. (2004). A tale of two professions. *Phi Delta Kappan, 86*(1), 63–64.

Gillies, R. (2000). The maintenance of cooperative and helping behaviours in cooperative groups. *British Journal of Educational Psychology, 70,* 97–111.

Gilman, D., & Kiger, S. (2003). Should we try to keep class sizes small? *Educational Leadership, 60*(7), 80–85.

Ginsberg, A., Shapiro, J., & Brown, S. (2004). *Gender in urban education: Strategies for student achievement.* Portsmouth, NH: Heinemann.

Ginsberg, M., & Murphy, D. (2002). How walkthroughs open doors. *Educational Leadership, 59*(8), 34–36.

Girard, K. (2005). Lost in translation. *Edutopia, 1*(8), 36–38.

Gladden, J. E. (2003). Where have all the reading groups gone? *Education Week, 22*(36), 33.

Gladding, M. (2007). *A guide to ethical conduct for the helping professions* (2nd ed.). Upper Saddle River, NJ: Merrill/Prentice Hall.

Glanzer, P. (2004). In defense of Harry . . . but not his defenders: Beyond censorship to justice. *English Journal, 93*(4), 58–63.

Glanzer, P. (2005). Moving beyond censorship: What will educators do if a controversy over "His Dark Materials" erupts? *Phi Delta Kappan, 87*(2), 166–168.

Goddard, R., Hoy, W., & Hoy, A. (2004). Collective efficacy beliefs: Theoretical developments, empirical evidence, and future directions. *Educational Researcher, 33*(3), 3–13.

Goldhaber, D. (1999). School choice: An examination of the empirical evidence on achievement, parental decision making and equity. *Educational Researcher, 28*(9), 16–25.

Goldhaber, D., & Hyde, E. (2002). What do we know (and need to know) about the impact of school choice reforms on disadvantaged students? *Harvard Educational Review, 72,* 157–173.

Goldstein, D. (2006, May 6). Upset over anthem translation? Change your tune; it's old news. *Salt Lake Tribune,* pp. A1, A4.

Goldstein, L. (2002). Election results boost special ed. vouchers. *Education Week, 22*(14), 21, 24.

Goldstein, R. A. (2004). Who are our urban students and what makes them so different? In S. R. Steinberg & J. L. Kincheloe (Eds.), *19 Urban questions: Teaching in the city* (pp. 41–51). New York: Peter Lang.

Gollnick, D., & Chinn, P. (2006). *Multicultural education in a pluralistic society* (7th ed.). Upper Saddle River, NJ: Merrill/Prentice Hall.

Gonzales, P., Guzmán, J., Partelow, L., Pahlke, E., Jocelyn, L., Kastberg, D., & Williams, T. (2004). *Highlights from the trends in international mathematics and science study (TIMSS) 2003 (NCES 2005–005).* U.S. Department of Education. Washington, DC: National Center for Educational Statistics.

Good, T., & Brophy, J. (2003). *Looking in classrooms* (9th ed.). Boston: Allyn & Bacon.

Goodlad, J. (1984). *A place called school.* New York: McGraw-Hill.

Goodman, J. F. (2005). How bad is cheating? *Education Week, 24*(16), 32, 35.

Gordon, R. (2006). The federalism debate: Why the idea of national education standards is crossing party lines. *Education Week, 25*(27), 48, 35.

Gordon, R., Della Piana, L., & Keleher, T. (2001). Zero tolerance: A basic racial report card. In W. Ayers, B. Dohrn, & R. Ayers (Eds.), *Zero tolerance* (pp. 165–175). New York: New Press.

Grant, L. W. (2006). Persistence and self-efficacy: A key to understanding teacher turnover. *The Delta Kappa Gamma Bulletin, 72*(2), 50–54.

Gratz, D. B. (2005). Lessons from Denver: The pay for performance pilot. *Phi Delta Kappan, 86*(8), 569–581.

Gray, T., & Fleischman, S. (2005). Successful strategies for English language learners. *Educational Leadership, 62*(4), 84–85.

Greene, J. (2000). Why school choice can promote integration. *Education Week, 19*(31), 72, 52.

Greene, J. P., & Winters, M. A. (2006). Getting ahead by staying behind: An evaluation of Florida's program to end social promotion. *Education Next, 6*(2), 65–69.

Greifner, L. (2006). National PTA aims to restore time for recess. *Education Week, 25*(28).

Gresham, A., Hess, F., Maranto, R., & Milliman, S. (2000). Desert bloom: Arizona's free market in education. *Phi Delta Kappan, 81*, 751–757.

Griffith, J. (2002). A multilevel analysis of the relation of school learning and social environments to minority achievement in public elementary schools. *The Elementary School Journal, 102*, 349–366.

Gronlund, N. (2004). *Writing instructional objectives for teaching and assessment* (7th ed.). Upper Saddle River, NJ: Merrill/Prentice Hall.

Grove, K. (2002). The invisible role of the central office. *Educational Leadership, 59*(8), 45–47.

Gruhn, W., & Douglass, H. (1971). *The modern junior high school* (3rd ed.). New York: Ronald Press.

Grunbaum, J., Kann, L., Kinchen, S., Williams, B., Ross, J., Lowry, R., & Kolbe, L. (2002). Youth risk behavior surveillance: United States, 2001. *Morbidity and Mortality Weekly Report, 51*(SS-4), 1–64.

Guarino, C., Santibañez, L., & Daley, G. (2006). Teacher recruitment and retention: A review of the recent empirical literature. *Review of Educational Research, 76*(2), 173–208.

Guest, A., & Schneider, B. (2003). Adolescents' extracurricular participation in context: The mediating effects of schools, communities, and identity. *Sociology of Education, 76*, 89–109.

Gunderson, L., & Siegel, L. (2001). The evils of the use of IQ tests to define learning disabilities in first- and second-language learners. *Reading Teacher, 55*(1), 48–55.

Gurian, M., & Stevens, K. (2005). What is happening with boys in school? *Teachers College Record.* Date Published: May 02, 2005. Retrieved June 21, 2005, from *http://www.tcrecord.org* ID Number: 11854.

Gutek, G. L. (2005). *Historical and philosophical foundations of education: A biographical introduction.* Upper Saddle River, NJ: Pearson/Prentice Hall.

Gutherie, J. W., & Springer, M. G. (2006). Teacher pay for performance: Another fad or sound and lasting policy. *Education Week, 25*(30), 52, 42.

Gutiérrez, K., Asato, J., Pacheco, M., Moll, L., Olsen, K., Horng, C., Ruiz, R., Garcia, E., & McCarthy, T. (2002). "Sounding American": The consequences of new reforms on English language learners. *Reading Research Quarterly, 37*, 328–343.

Gutiérrez, R. (2002). Beyond essentialism: The complexity in teaching mathematics to Latino students. *American Educational Research Journal, 39*, 1047–1088.

Haas, M. (2005). Teaching methods for secondary algebra: A meta-analysis of findings. *NASSP Bulletin, 89*(642), 24–46.

Haberman, M. (2004). Can star teachers create learning communities? *Educational Leadership, 61*(8), 52–56.

Hallahan, D., & Kauffman, J. (2003). *Exceptional learners: Introduction to special education* (9th ed.). Needham Heights, MA: Allyn & Bacon.

Hamilton, L., Berends, M., & Stecher, B. (2005). *Teachers' response to standards-based accountability.* Paper presented at the annual meeting of the American Educational Research Association, Montreal.

Hammack, F. (Ed.). (2004). *The comprehensive high school today.* New York: Teachers College Press.

Hammack, F. (2005). High school reform, again. *Teachers College Record.* Retrieved August 30, 2005, from *http://www.tcrecord.org* ID Number 11853.

Hammerness, K., Darling-Hammond, L., & Bransford, J. (2005). How teachers learn and develop. In L. Darling-Hammond & J. Bransford (Eds.), *Preparing teachers for a changing world: What teachers should learn and be able to do* (pp. 358–389). San Francisco: Jossey-Bass.

Hanushek, E. (1996). A more complete picture of school resource policies. *Review of Educational Research, 66*, 397–410.

Hardman, M., Drew, C., & Egan, W. (2005). *Human exceptionality* (8th ed.). Needham Heights, MA: Allyn & Bacon.

Hardman, M., Drew, C., & Egan, W. (2006). *Human exceptionality: IDEA 2004 update edition* (8th ed.). Boston: Allyn & Bacon.

Hardy, L. (2002). A new federal role. *American School Board Journal, 18*(9), 20–24.

Hardy, L. (2005). A place apart: How rural schools are tackling the twin problems of isolation and poverty. *American School Board Journal, 192*(4), 18–23.

Harris, S., & Lowery, S. (2002). A view from the classroom. *Educational Leadership, 59*(8), 64–65.

Harris Interactive Inc. 2005. *Nearly two-thirds of U.S. adults believe human beings were created by God.* Retrieved November 8, 2006, from *http://www.harrisinteractive.com/harris_poll/index.asp?PID=581*

Hartman, C. (2006). Students on the move. *Educational Leadership, 63*(5), 20–24.

Hassel, B., & Hassel, E. (2004). Parents take choice driver's seat, but few have a map. *Education Week, 24*(3), 34, 36.

Hasselbring, T., & Bausch, M. (2005/2006). Assistive technologies for reading. *Educational Leadership, 63*(4), 72–75.

Haycock, K. (2001). Closing the achievement gap. *Educational Leadership, 58*(6), 6–11.

Hazelwood School District v. Kuhlmeier, 484 U.S. 260 (1988).

Heath, S. (1982). Questioning at home and at school: A comparative study. In G. Spindler (Ed.), *Doing the ethnography of schooling* (pp. 102–131). New York: Holt, Rinehart & Winston.

Heath, S. (1989). Oral and literate traditions among Black Americans living in poverty. *American Psychologist, 44,* 367–373.

Hecht, E. (2006). There is no really good definition of mass. *Physics Teacher, 44*(1), 40–45.

Hendrie, C. (1999). Harvard study finds increase in segregation. *Education Week, 18*(41), 6.

Hendrie, C. (2002). New scrutiny for sponsors of charters. *Education Week, 22*(12), 1, 18.

Hendrie, C. (2003a). California charter-funding fight hits home. *Education Week, 22*(18), 18–19.

Hendrie, C. (2003b). States target sexual abuse by educators. *Education Week, 22*(33), 1, 16–18.

Hendrie, C. (2005a). Court: Class strip searches unconstitutional. *Education Week, 24*(3), 3, 22.

Hendrie, C. (2005b). Legislation tightens fiscal oversight of California charters. *Education Week, 25*(7), 18.

Hendrie, C. (2005c). T-shirts on gay issues spur lawsuits. *Education Week, 24*(16), 1, 16.

Henry, G., Gordon, C., & Rickman, D. (2006). Early education policy alternatives: Comparing quality and outcomes of Head Start and state prekindergarten. *Educational Evaluation and Policy Analysis, 28*(1), 77–99.

Herbert, B. (2006, July 4). Minimum-wage earners suffer while the rich just get richer. *Salt Lake Tribune,* p. A9.

Herszenhorn, D. (2006, April 19). New York offers housing subsidy as teacher lure. *New York Times,* pp. A1, C15.

Hess, F. (2004a). *School boards at the dawn of the 21st century.* Alexandria, VA: National School Boards Association.

Hess, F. (2004b). The political challenges of charter school regulation. *Phi Delta Kappan, 85*(7), 508–512.

Heward, W. (2006). *Exceptional children* (8th ed.). Upper Saddle River, NJ: Merrill/Prentice Hall.

Hewitt, T. (2006). *What we teach and why.* Thousand Oaks, CA: Sage.

Hiebert, J., Gallimore, R., & Stigler, J. (2002). A knowledge base for the teaching profession: What would it look like and how can we get one? *Educational Researcher, 31*(5), 3–15.

Hinkel, E. (2005). *Handbook of research on second language teaching and learning.* Mahwah, NJ: Erlbaum.

Hirsch, E. (1987). *Cultural literacy: What every American needs to know.* Boston: Houghton Mifflin.

Hirsch, E. (2000). The tests we need and why we don't quite have them. *Education Week, 19*(21), 40–41.

Hirsch, E. (2001). Seeking breadth and depth in the curriculum. *Educational Leadership, 59*(2), 22–25.

Hirsch, E. (Ed.). (2005). What your fourth grader needs to know: Fundamentals of a good fourth-grade education. New York: Dell.

Hirsch, E. (2006). *Knowledge deficit: Closing the shocking education gap for American children.* Boston: Houghton Mifflin.

Hoff, D. (2000). Gap widens between Black and White students on NAEP. *Education Week, 20*(1), 6–7.

Hoff, D. (2003a). KERA: In midlife crisis or golden years? *Education Week, 23*(2), 18, 21.

Hoff, D. (2003b). Math education panel issues long-range plan for action. *Education Week, 22*(33), 11.

Hoff, D. (2005). Schools feel pressure of efforts to increase fiscal responsibility. *Education Week, 24*(39), 1, 24.

Hoff, D. (2006). Texas proposes classroom costs per "65 percent" plan. *Education Week, 25*(32), 23, 24.

Hoff, T. (2002). A fresh approach to sex education. *American School Board Journal, 189*(11), 60–61, 66.

Hofferth, S., & Januniene, Z. (2001). Life after school. *Educational Leadership, 58*(7), 10–23.

Hoffman, L. (2003). *Overview of public elementary and secondary schools and districts: School year 2001–02 (NCES 2003–411).* U.S. Department of Education, National Center for Education Statistics. Washington, DC: U.S. Government Printing Office.

Holloway, J. (2001). Grouping students for increased achievement. *Educational Leadership, 59*(3), 84–85.

Holloway, J. (2001/2002). Research Link: The dilemma of zero tolerance. *Educational Leadership, 59*(4), 84–85.

Holloway, J. (2004). Family literacy. *Education Leadership, 61*(6), 88–89.

Holmes, C. (2006). Low test scores + high retention rates = more dropouts. *Kappa Delta Pi Record, 42*(2), 56–58.

Home School Legal Defense Association. (2004). *Survey of home schooling parents.* Retrieved June 26, 2006, from *http://www.hslda.org*

Honawar, V. (2005). Smoking in movies spurs youth to try it, Dartmouth study says. *Education Week, 25*(13), 15.

Honawar, V. (2006). Md. Lawmakers fight school takeover plan. *Education Week, 25*(31), 25, 28.

Hong, S., & Ho, H. (2005). Direct and indirect longitudinal effects of parental involvement on student achievement: Second-order latent growth modeling across ethnic groups. *Journal of Educational Psychology, 97*(1), 32–42.

Honora, D. (2003). Urban African American adolescents and school identification. *Urban Education, 38*(1), 58–76.

Hopkins, A. (2006). Evolution debate rears head again in Ohio. *Pew Forum on Religion and Public Life.* Retrieved October 1, 2006, from *http://pewforum.org/news/display.php? NewsID=11246*

Hopkins, J. (2006). All students being equal. *Technology & Learning, 26*(10), 26–28.

Horn, I. (2005). Learning on the job: A situated account of teacher learning in high school mathematics departments. *Cognition and Instruction, 23*(2), 207–236.

Howell, W. (2005). School boards besieged. *Education Week, 24*(26), 44.

Howley, C., & Howley, A. (2004). School size and the influence of socioeconomic status on student achievement: Confronting the threat of size bias in national data sets. *Education Policy Analysis Archives, 12*(52). Retrieved September 26, 2006, from *http://epaa.asu.edu/epaa/v12n52/*

Hulse, C. (2006, May 16). Senate passes a bill that favors English. *New York Times,* p. A19.

Hunsader, P. (2002). Why boys fail—and what we can do about it. *Principal, 82*(2), 52–54.

Hurst, M. (2004). School lunchrooms take digital twists and turns. *Education Week, 24*(9), 8.

Hutton, T. (2005). The charter option: 5 big questions your board should ask before authorizing a charter school. *American School Board Journal, 192*(5), 16–20.

Hyland, N., & Noffke, S. (2005). Understanding diversity through social and community inquiry: An action-research study. *Journal of Teacher Education, 56*(4), 367–381.

Ilg, T., & Massucci, J. (2003). Comprehensive urban high schools: Are there better options for poor and minority children? *Education and Urban Society, 36*(1), 63–78.

Illig, D. (1996). *Reducing class size: A review of the literature and options for consideration.* Sacramento, CA: California Research Bureau.

Imazeki, J., & Reschovsky, A. (2004). School finance reform in Texas: A never-ending story? In J. Yinger (Ed.), *Helping children left behind* (pp. 251–282). Cambridge, MA: MIT Press.

Imber, M., & van Geel, T. (2005). *A teacher's guide to education law* (3rd ed.). Mahwah, NJ: Lawrence Erlbaum.

Individuals with Disabilities Education Act of 1997. Pub. L. No. 105–17. C.F.R. 3000 (1997).

Individuals with Disabilities Education Act of 2004. Pub. L. No. 108–446. (2004).

Ingersoll, R., & Smith, T. (2003). The wrong solution to the teacher shortage. *Educational Leadership, 60*(8), 30–33.

Ingersoll, R., & Smith, T. (2004). What are the effects of induction and mentoring on beginning teacher turnover? *American Educational Research Journal, 41*(3), 681–714.

Ingraham v. Wright, 430 U.S. 651 (1977).

INTASC. Interstate New Teacher Assessment and Support Consortium. (1993). *Model standards for beginning teacher licensing and development: A resource for state dialogues.* Washington, DC: Council of Chief State School Officers.

Jackson, A., & Davis, G. (2000). *Turning points 2000: Educating adolescents in the 21st century.* New York: Teachers College Press.

Jackson, P. (1968). *Life in classrooms.* New York: Holt, Rinehart & Winston.

Jacobsen, D. (2003). *Philosophy in classroom teaching: Bridging the gap* (2nd ed.). Upper Saddle River, NJ: Prentice Hall.

Jacobsen, D., Eggen, P., & Kauchak, D. (2006). *Methods for teaching* (7th ed.). Upper Saddle River, NJ: Merrill/Prentice Hall.

Jacobson, L. (2004). Research updates lives of Perry preschoolers. *Education Week, 24*(4), 6.

Jacobson, L. (2005). E-mail opens lines of communication for teachers. *Education Week, 24*(30), 8.

Jencks, C., & Phillips, M. (Eds.). (1998). *The Black–White test score gap.* Washington, DC: Brookings Institution Press.

Jennings, M. (2000). Attendance technology easing record-keeping burden. *Education Week, 19*(35), 7.

Jetton, T., & Alexander, P. (1997). Instructional importance: What teachers value and what students learn. *Reading Research Quarterly, 32,* 290–308.

Jimerson, S., Pletcher, S., & Graydon, K. (2006). Beyond grade retention and social promotion: Promoting the social and academic competence of students. *Psychology in the Schools, 43*(1), 85–97.

Johnson, B., & Christensen, L. B. (2004). *Educational research: Quantitative and qualitative approaches* (2nd ed.) Boston: Allyn & Bacon.

Johnson, D. (2004). Plagiarism-proofing assignments. *Phi Delta Kappan, 85*(7), 549–552.

Johnson, D., & Johnson, R. (1999). The 3 C's of school and classroom management. In R. Freiberg (Ed.), *Beyond behaviorism* (pp. 119–145). Boston: Allyn & Bacon.

Johnson, D., & Johnson, R. (2004). The three Cs of promoting social and emotional learning. In J. Zins, R. Weissberg, M. Wang, & H. Walberg (Eds.), *Building academic success on social and emotional learning* (pp. 40–58). New York: Teachers College Press.

Johnson, D., & Johnson, R. (2006). *Learning together and alone: Cooperation, competition, and individualization* (8th ed.). Needham Heights, MA: Allyn & Bacon.

Johnson, J. (2004). What school leaders want. *Educational Leadership, 61*(7), 24–27.

Johnson, J. (2005). Isn't it time for schools of education to take concerns about student discipline more seriously? *Teachers College Record.* Retrieved March 22, 2005, from *http://www.tcrecord.org/* ID Number: 11739.

Johnson, L., Bachman, J., & O'Malley, P. (2001). *Monitoring the future: Questionnaire responses from the nation's high school seniors, 1997.* Ann Arbor, MI: Institute for Social Research.

Johnson, S., & Birkeland, S. (2003, April). *Pursuing a "sense of success": New teachers explain their career decisions.* Paper presented at the annual meeting of the American Educational Research Association, New Orleans, LA.

Johnson, S., & Birkeland, S. (2006). Fast track certification. *Education Week, 25*(23), 48, 37.

Johnston, J. (2004). Authority, inquiry, and education: A response to Dewey's critics. *Educational Studies, 35*(3), 230–247.

Johnston, R. (1994). Policy details who paddles students and with what. *Education Week, 14*(11), 17–18.

Jonassen, D. (2000). *Computers as mindtools for schools* (2nd ed.). Columbus, OH: Merrill/Prentice Hall.

Jonassen, D., Howland, J., Moore, J., & Marra, R. (2003). *Learning to solve problems with technology.* Upper Saddle River, NJ: Merrill/Prentice Hall.

Jones, S. (2005). More discipline? *Teachers College Record.* Retrieved March 29, 2005, from *http://www.tcrecord.org* ID Number: 11746.

Jones, S., & Dindia, K. (2004). A meta-analytic perspective on sex equity in the classroom. *Review of Educational Research, 74*(4), 443–471.

Jones, V., & Jones, L. (2004). *Comprehensive classroom management: Creating communities of support and solving problems* (7th ed.). Boston: Allyn & Bacon.

Jordan, W. (2001, April). *At-risk students during the first year of high school: Navigating treacherous waters.* Paper presented at the annual meeting of the American Educational Research Association, Seattle, WA.

Jordan, W., & Brooks, W. (2000). *Mending the safety net: A preliminary analysis of the twilight school.* Paper presented at the annual meeting of the American Educational Research Association, New Orleans, LA.

Joseph, P., & Efron, S. (2005). Seven worlds of moral education. *Phi Delta Kappan, 86*(7), 525–533.

Juvonen, J., Le, V., Kagonoff, T., Augustine, C., & Constant, L. (2004). *Focus on the wonder years: Challenges facing the American middle school.* Retrieved September 28, 2006, from *http://www.rand.org/pubs/monographs/2004/RAND_MG138.pdf*

Kahlenberg, R. (2000). *Economic school integration* (IDEA Brief No. 2). Washington, DC: The Century Foundation.

Kahlenberg, R. (2006). Integration by income. *American School Board Journal, 193*(4), 51–52.

Kain, D. (2003). *Problem-based learning.* Boston: Allyn & Bacon.

Kaiser Family Foundation. (2004a). *Sex education in America: Principals survey.* Retrieved March 20, 2005, from *http://www.npr.org/programs/morning*

Kaiser Family Foundation. (2004b). *Survey snapshot: The digital divide.* Retrieved June 19, 2006, from *www.kff.org*

Karten, T. (2005). *Inclusion strategies that work: Research-based methods for the classroom.* Thousand Oaks, CA: Corwin Press.

Kauchak, D., & Eggen, P. (2007). *Learning and teaching: Research-based methods* (5th ed.). Needham Heights, MA: Allyn & Bacon.

Kaufman, F. (2005). Diabesity. In P. Menzel, *Hungry planet: What the world eats* (pp. 242–243). Napa, CA: Material World Press.

Kedar-Voivodas, G. (1983). The impact of elementary children's school roles and sex roles on teacher attitudes: An interactional analysis. *Review of Educational Research, 20,* 417–462.

Keller, B. (2002). Report urges experimentation with teacher-pay schemes. *Education Week, 21*(39), 11.

Keller, B. (2005). Teachers flocking to online sources to advance and acquire knowledge. *Education Week, 24*(43), 22, 24.

Keller, B. (2006). Study for NBPTS raises questions about credential. *Education Week, 25*(37), 1, 16.

Keller, J. (2004). Just their type. *Technology and Learning, 25*(2), 12–18.

Kennedy, M. (2006). Knowledge and vision in teaching. *Journal of Teacher Education, 57*(3), 205–211.

Kerman, S. (1979). Teacher expectations and student achievement. *Phi Delta Kappan, 60*, 70–72.

Kids Health for Parents. (2006). *About teen suicide.* Retrieved March 21, 2006, from *http://www.kidshealth.org/sui_fact.htm*

Kilbane, C., & Milman, N. (2003). *The digital teaching portfolio handbook: A how-to guide for educators.* Boston: Allyn & Bacon.

Kincheloe, J. (2004). Why a book on urban education? In Steinberg, S., & Kincheloe, J. (Eds.), *19 Urban questions: Teaching in the city* (pp. 1–27). New York: Peter Lang.

King, K. P. (2007). *Integrating the national science education standards into classroom practice.* Upper Saddle River, NJ: Pearson/Prentice Hall.

Kitzmiller et al. v. Dover Area School District, 04cv2688 (U.S. District Court for the Middle District of Pennsylvania, 2005).

Kleiman, C. (2001, October 30). Internet helps parents keep an eye on kids [Electronic version]. *Chicago Tribune.* Retrieved May 17, 2005, from *http://www.chicagotribune.co*

Klein, P. (2003). Rethinking the multiplicity of cognitive resources and curricular representations: Alternatives to "learning styles" and "multiple intelligences." *Journal of Curriculum Studies, 35*, 45–81.

Kober, N. (2006). *A public education primer: Basic (and sometimes surprising) facts about the U.S. education system.* Washington, DC: Center on Education Policy.

Kohn, A. (1993). *Punished by rewards: The trouble with gold stars, incentive plans, A's, praise, and other bribes.* Boston: Houghton Mifflin.

Kohn, A. (1997). How not to teach values. *Phi Delta Kappan, 78*, 429–439.

Kohn, A. (1999). Direct drilling. *Education Week, 18*(30), 43.

Kohn, A. (2000). Burnt at the high stakes. *Journal of Teacher Education, 51*(4), 315–327.

Kohn, A. (2006). Abusing research: The study of homework and other examples. *Phi Delta Kappan, 88*(1), 9–22.

Konheim-Kalkstein, Y. (2006). A uniform look. *American School Board Journal, 193*(8), 25–27.

Koppich, J. E. (2005). All teachers are not the same. *Education Next, 5*(1), 13–15.

Kosar, K. (2005). *Failing grades: The federal politics of education standards.* Boulder, CO: Lynne Rienner.

Kounin, J. (1970). *Discipline and group management in classrooms.* New York: Holt, Rinehart & Winston.

Kozol, J. (1991). *Savage inequalities.* New York: Crown.

Kozol, J. (2005). *The shame of the nation: The restoration of apartheid schooling in America.* New York: Crown.

Krashen, S. (1996). *Under attack: The case against bilingual education.* Culver City, CA: Language Education Associates.

Kristoff, N. (2006, May 14). The model students. *New York Times,* Sect. 4, p. 13.

Kroesbergen, E. H., & van Luit, E. H. (2002). Teaching multiplication to low math performers: Guided versus structured instruction. *Instructional Science, 30*, 361–378.

Kroesbergen, E. H., van Luit, E. H., & Maas, C. J. (2004). Effectiveness of explicit and constructivist mathematics instruction for low-achieving students in the Netherlands. *Elementary School Journal, 104*, 233–251.

Krueger, A., & Whitmore, D. (2002). Would smaller classes help close the Black–White achievement gap? In J. Chubb & T. Loveless (Eds.), *Bridging the achievement gap* (pp. 11–46). Washington, DC: Brookings Institution Press.

Kuh, D., & Vesper, N. (1999, April). *Do computers enhance or detract from student learning?* Paper presented at the annual meeting of the American Educational Research Association, Montreal.

Kuhn, D. (2005). *Education for thinking.* Cambridge, MA: Harvard University Press.

Kunzman, R. (2006). *Grappling with the good.* Albany, NY: State University of New York Press.

Labaree, D. (2004). *The trouble with ed schools.* New Haven, CT: Yale University Press.

Labaree, D. (2005). Life on the margins. *Journal of Teacher Education 56*(3), 186–191.

LaChausse, R. G. (2006). Evaluation of the positive prevention HIV/STD curriculum. *American Journal of Health Education, 37*(4), 203–209.

Laczko-Kerr, I., & Berliner, D. (2003). In harm's way: How undercertified teachers hurt their students. *Educational Leaderhip, 60*(8), 34–39.

Ladson-Billings, G. (2005). Is the team all right? Diversity and teacher education. *Journal of Teacher Education, 56*(3), 229–234.

Lafee, S. (2005). Another weighty burden. *School Administrator, 62*(9), 10–16.

LaMorte, M. (2005). *School law: Cases and concepts* (8th ed.). Boston: Allyn & Bacon.

Land, D. (2002). Local school boards under review: Their role and effectiveness in relation to students' academic achievement. *Review of Educational Research, 72*, 229–278.

Lashley, C. (2001, April). *Performance-based licensure: Developing support systems for beginning teachers.* Paper presented at the annual meeting of the American Educational Research Association, Seattle, WA.

Lau v. Nichols, 414 U.S. 563 (1974).

Lee, H. (2004). Understanding and assessing preservice teachers' reflective thinking. *Teaching and Teacher Education, 21,* 699–715.

Lee, J., & Doolittle, P. (April, 2003). *Social studies teachers' uses of non-digital and digital historical resources.* Paper presented at the annual meeting of the American Educational Research Association, Chicago.

Lee, S. (2006). The learner-centered paradigm of instruction and training. *Tech Trends, 50*(2), 21–23.

Lee, V. (2000). Using hierarchical linear modeling to study social contexts: The case of school effects. *Educational Psychologist, 35,* 125–141.

Lee, V., & Smith, J. (1999). Social support and achievement for young adolescents in Chicago: The role of school academic press. *American Educational Research Journal, 36,* 907–946.

Lee v. Weismann, 112 S. Ct. 29649 (1992).

Lei, J. (2003). (Un)necessary toughness?: Those "loud Black girls" and those "quiet Asian boys." *Anthropology & Education Quarterly, 34*(2), 158–181.

Leinhardt, G. (2001). Instructional explanations: A commonplace for teaching and location for contrast. In V. Richardson (Ed.), *Handbook of research on teaching* (4th ed., pp. 333–357). Washington, DC: America Educational Research Association.

Leinhardt, G., & Steele, M. (2005). Seeing the complexity of standing to the side: Instructional dialogues. *Cognition and Instruction, 23*(1), 87–163.

Lemke, M., Sen. A., Pahlke, E., Partelow, L., Miller D., William, T., Kastberg, D., & Jocelyn, L. (2004). *International outcomes of learning in mathematics literacy and problem solving: PISA 2003 results from the U.S. perspective* (NCES 2005–003). U.S. Department of Education. Washington, DC: National Center for Education Statistics.

LePage, P., Darling-Hammond, L., Akan, H., Guitierrez, C., Jenkins-Gunn, E., & Rosebrock, K. (2005). Classroom management. In L. Darling-Hammond & J. Bransford (Eds.), *Preparing teachers for a changing world* (pp. 327–357). San Francisco: Jossey-Bass.

Lever-Duffy, J., McDonald, J., & Mizell, A. (2003). *Teaching and learning with technology.* Boston: Allyn & Bacon.

Lew, J. (2004). The "other" story of model minorities: Korean American high school dropouts in an urban context. *Anthropology and Education Quarterly, 35*(3), 303–323.

Lewin, T. (2006, July 9). At college, women are leaving men in the dust. *New York Times,* July 9, pp. A1, A18, A19.

Lewis, A. (2005). More than just cute kids. *Phi Delta Kappan, 87*(3), 179–180.

Lewis, A. C. (2006). Redefining what high school students learn. *Phi Delta Kappan, 87*(8), 564–565.

Lichter, D., & Johnson, K. (2006). Emerging rural settlement patterns and the geographic distribution of America's new immigrants. *Rural Sociology, 71*(1), 109–131.

Lindeman, B. (2001). Reaching out to immigrant parents. *Educational Leadership, 58*(6), 62–66.

Liston, D. (2004). The lure of learning in teaching. *Teachers College Record, 106*(3), 459–486.

Lou, Y., Abrami, P., & Spence, J. (2000). Effects of within-class grouping on student achievement: An exploratory model. *Journal of Educational Research, 94,* 101–112.

Louis, B., Subotnik, R., Breland, P., & Lewis, M. (2000). Establishing criteria for high ability versus selective admission to gifted programs: Implications for policy and practice. *Educational Psychology Review, 12,* 295–314.

Luekens, M., Lyter, D., & Fox, E. (2004). Teacher attrition and mobility: Results from the teacher following-up survey. *National Center for Education Statistics Quarterly, 6*(3), 40–46.

Lustick, D. (2002, April). *National Board certification as professional development: A study that identifies a framework and findings of teachers learning to manage complexity, uncertainty, and community.* Paper presented at the annual meeting of the American Educational Research Association, New Orleans, LA.

Lyman, R. (2006, September 30). In many public schools, the paddle is no relic. *New York Times,* pp. C1, C2.

Lynch, R. L. (2000). High school career and technical education for the first decade of the 21st century. *Journal of Vocational Educational Research, 25*(2). Retrieved September 3, 2006, from *http://scholar.lib.vt.edu/ejournals/JVER/v25n2/lynch.html*

Lynn, R. (2003, June 9). State fears teacher flight. *Salt Lake Tribune,* pp. D1–D2.

Ma, X. (2001). Bullying and being bullied: To what extent are bullies also victims? *American Educational Research Journal, 38*(2), 351–370.

Macionis, J. (2006). *Society: The basics* (8th ed.). Upper Saddle River, NJ: Prentice Hall.

Macionis, J., & Parillo, V. (2007). *Cities and urban life* (4th ed.). Upper Saddle River, NJ: Merrill/Prentice Hall.

Maeroff, G. (2003). The virtual school house. *Education Week, 22*(24), 40, 28.

Mager, R. (1962). *Preparing instructional objectives.* Palo Alto, CA: Featon.

Mager, R. (1998). *Preparing instructional objectives: A critical tool in the development of effective instruction* (3rd ed.). Atlanta, GA: Center for Effective Performance.

Magnet Schools of America. (2006). Retrieved June 2, 2006, from *http://www.magnet.ed*

Magnuson, K., Meyers, M., Ruhm, C., & Waldfogel, J. (2004). Inequality in preschool education and school readiness. *American Educational Research Journal, 41*(1), 115–157.

Mailloux v. Kiley, 323 F. Supp. 1387 (D. Mass 1971), 448 F.2d 1242 (lst Cir. 1971).

Mandel, S. (2006). What new teachers really need. *Educational Leadership, 63*(6), 66–69.

Manning, M. (2000). A brief history of the middle school. *The Clearing House, 72*(4), 190–195.

Manning, M., & Bucher, K. (2003). *Classroom management.* Upper Saddle River, NJ: Merrill/Prentice Hall.

Manouchehri, A. (2004). Implementing mathematics reform in urban schools: A study of the effect of teachers' motivation style. *Urban Education, 38,* 472–508.

Manzo, K. (2004). Reading programs bear similarities across the states. *Education Week, 23*(21), 1, 13.

Manzo, K. (2005). N.C. backs lottery to fund school projects. *Education Week, 25*(3), 28, 30.

Manzo, K. (2006a). Scathing report casts cloud over "Reading First." *Education Week, 26*(6), 1, 24.

Manzo, K. (2006b). Young adults don't think world knowledge is vital. *Education Week, 25*(36), 8.

Margolis, J. (2004). A response to "The National Board Hoax." *Teachers College Record.* Retrieved February 2004 from *http://www.tcrecord.org/Collection.asp?CollectionID=72*

Marsh, C., & Willis, G. (2007). *Curriculum: Alternative approaches, ongoing issues.* Upper Saddle River, NJ: Merrill/Prentice Hall.

Marsh, H., & Kleitman, S. (2005). Consequences of employment during high school: Character building, subversion of academic goals, or a threshold? *American Educational Research Journal, 42*(2), 331–369.

Marttunen, M., & Laurinen, L. (2001). Learning of argumentation skills in networked and face-to-face environments. *Instructional Science, 29,* 127–153.

Marzano, R. (2003). *What works in schools.* Alexandria, VA: Association for Supervision and Curriculum Development.

Marzano, R., & Kendall, J. (2003). *Designing standards-based districts, schools, and classrooms.* Alexandria, VA: Association for Supervision and Curriculum Development.

Maslow, A. (1968). *Toward a psychology of being* (2nd ed.). New York: Van Nostrand.

Maslow, A. (1970). *Motivation and personality* (2nd ed.). New York: Harper & Row.

Mathews, J. (1999, March 24,). A home run for home schooling. *Washington Post,* p. A11.

Mathis, W. (2005). The cost of implementing the federal No Child Left Behind Act: Different assumptions, different answers. *Peabody Journal of Education, 80*(2), 90–119.

Maxwell, L. (2006a). L.A. mayor seeks role in district. *Education Week, 25*(33), 1, 25.

Maxwell, L. (2006b). Web systems help schools screen visitors. *Education Week, 25*(32), 5, 16.

Mayer, R. (2002). *The promise of educational psychology: Volume II. Teaching for meaningful learning.* Upper Saddle River, NJ: Merrill/Prentice Hall.

Mayer, R. (2004). Should there be a three-strikes rule against pure discovery learning? *American Psychologist, 59,* 14–19.

Mayes, C., & Ferrin, S. (2001). Spiritually committed public school teachers: Their beliefs and practices concerning religious expression in the classroom. *Religion and Education, 28*(1), 75–94.

McAllister, G., & Irvine, J. (2002). The role of empathy in teaching culturally diverse students: A qualitative study of teachers' beliefs. *Journal of Teacher Education, 53,* 433–443.

McCabe, M. (2006). State of the states. *Education Week, 25*(17), 72–96.

McCaslin, M., & Good, T. (1996). The informal curriculum. In D. Berliner & R. Calfee (Eds.), *Handbook of educational psychology* (pp. 622–670). New York: Macmillan.

McCombs, B. L. (2001, April). *What do we know about learners and learning? The learner-centered framework.* Paper presented at the annual meeting of the American Educational Research Association, Seattle.

McCombs, J. (2005). *Progress in implementing standards, assessment for highly qualified teacher provisions of NCLB: Initial finding from California, Georgia, and Pennsylvania.* Paper presented at the annual meeting of the American Educational Research Association, Montreal.

McDermott, J. (1994). Buddhism. *Encarta* [CD-ROM]. Bellevue, WA: Microsoft.

McDevitt, T., & Ormrod, J. (2004). *Child development: Educating and working with children and adolescents* (2nd ed.). Upper Saddle River, NJ: Merrill/Prentice Hall.

McDevitt, T., & Ormrod, J. (2007). *Child development and education* (3rd ed.). Upper Saddle River, NJ: Merrill/Prentice Hall.

McDougall, D., & Granby, C. (1996). How expectation of questioning method affects undergraduates' preparation for class. *Journal of Experimental Education, 65,* 43–54.

McMahon, S., Rose, D., & Parks, M. (2004). Multiple intelligences and reading achievement: An examination of the Teele Inventory of Multiple Intelligences. *Journal of Experimental Education, 73*(1), 41–52.

McMillan, J. (2004). *Educational research: Fundamentals for the consumer* (4th ed.). New York: Longman.

Meier, D. (2002). Standardization versus standards. *Phi Delta Kappan, 84,* 190–198.

Merrow, J. (2002). The failure of Head Start. *Education Week, 22*(4), 52, 38.

Michener, J. A. (2006). Sex education: A success in our social-studies class. *Clearing House, 79*(5), 210–214.

Milanowski, A., & Kimball, S. (2005). *The relationship between teacher expertise and student achievement: A synthesis of three years of data.* Paper presented at the annual meeting of the American Educational Research Association, Montreal.

Mills, G. (2002, April). *Teaching and learning action research.* Paper presented at the annual meeting of the American Educational Research Association, New Orleans, LA.

Mishel, L. (2006). The exaggerated dropout crisis. *Education Week, 25*(26), 40.

Mishel, L., Bernstein, J., & Allegretto, S. (2006). *The state of working Americans, 2004/2005.* Washington, DC: Economic Policy Institute.

Molnar, A., Percy, S., Smith, P., & Zahorik, J. (1998). *1997–98 results of the Student Achievement Guarantee in Education (SAGE) program.* Milwaukee: University of Wisconsin–Milwaukee.

Molnar, A., & Reeves, J. (2001). Buy me! Buy me! *Educational Leadership, 59*(2), 74–79.

Monitoring the Future. (2006). *Teen drug use down but progress halts among youngest.* University of Michigan: Michigan Institute for Social Research.

Monke, L. (2005/2006). The overdominance of computers. *Educational Leadership, 63*(4), 20–23.

Moreno, R. (2004). Decreasing cognitive load for novice students: Effects of explanatory versus corrective feedback in discovery-based multimedia. *Instructional Science, 32,* 99–113.

Moreno, R., & Duran, R. (2004). Do multiple representations need explanations: The role of verbal guidance and individual differences in multimedia mathematics learning. *Journal of Educational Psychology, 96,* 492–503.

Morris v. Douglas County School District No. 9, 403 P.2d 775 (Or. 1965).

Morrison v. State Board of Education, 461 P.2d 375 (Cal. 1969).

Morrison, G., Kemp, J., & Ross, S. (2007). *Designing effective instruction* (5th ed.). Hoboken, NJ: John Wiley & Sons.

Morrison, G. R., & Lowther, D. L. (2002). *Integrating computer technology into the classroom* (2nd ed.). Upper Saddle River, NJ: Merrill/Prentice Hall.

Mosenthal, J., Lipson, M., Torncello, S., Russ, B., & Mekkelsen, J. (2004). Contexts and practices of six schools successful in obtaining reading achievement. *Elementary School Journal, 104*(5), 343–368.

Mostow, J. (2005). Personal website. Retrieved August 27, 2006, from *http://www-2.cs.cmu.edu/~mostow*

Mozert v. Hawkins County Public Schools, 827 F.2d 1058 (6th Cir. 1987), cert. denied, 108 S. Ct. 1029 (1988).

Mulrine, A. (2002, May 27). Risky business. *U.S. News & World Report,* pp. 42–49.

Muñoz, M., & Portes, P. (2002, April). *Voices from the field: The perceptions of teachers and principals on the class size reduction program in a large urban school district.* Paper presented at the annual meeting of the American Educational Research Association, New Orleans, LA.

Murphy, M. (2006). *History and philosophy of education: The voices of educational pioneers.* Upper Saddle River, NJ: Pearson/Prentice Hall.

Murphy, P., DeArmond, M., & Guin, K. (2003). A national crisis or localized problems? Getting perspective on the scope and scale of the teacher shortage. *Education Policy Analysis Archives, 11*(23). Retrieved September 27, 2006, from *http://epaa.asu.edu/epaa/v11n23*

Murray, F. (1986). *Necessity: The developmental component in reasoning.* Paper presented at the 16th annual meeting, Jean Piaget Society, Philadelphia.

Nakagawa, K., Stafford, M., Fisher, T., & Matthews, L. (2002). The "city migrant" dilemma: Building community at high-mobility urban schools. *Urban Education, 37*(1), 96–125.

Nathan, J. (2005). Charters "Yes!" Vouchers "No!" *Educational Horizons, 83*(2), 110–124.

National Association of Elementary School Principals. (2002). What you might not know about vouchers. *Education Week, 22*(1), 10.

National Association of Elementary School Principals. (2006). *Principal salaries 2004–2005.* Retrieved February 14, 2006, from *http://www.naesp.org*

National Association of State Boards of Education. (2004). *State education governance at-a-glance.* Retrieved February 27, 2004, from *http://www.nasbe.org/Educational_Issues/Governance/Governance_chart.pdf*

National Board for Professional Teaching Standards. (1995). *An invitation to National Board certification.* Detroit: Author.

National Board for Professional Teaching Standards. (2006). Retrieved August 16, 2006, from *http://www.nbpts.org*

National Campaign to Prevent Teen Pregnancy. (2004). *Teen pregnancy—so what?* Retrieved July 31, 2006, from *http://www.teenpregnancy.org/whycare/sowhat.asp*

National Center for Education Information. (2000). *Alternative teacher certification: A state by state analysis.* Washington, DC: Author.

National Center for Education Statistics. (1997). *Characteristics of American Indian and Alaska native education.* Washington, DC: U.S. Department of Education.

National Center for Education Statistics. (2002). *Digest of education statistics.* Washington, DC: U.S. Department of Education.

National Center for Education Statistics. (2004). Characteristics of private schools in the United States: Results from the 2001–2002 Private School Universe survey. *National Center for Education Statistics Quarterly, 6*(4), 39–45.

National Center for Education Statistics. (2005a). *Federal expenditures for education.* Washington, DC: Author. Retrieved July 1, 2006, from *http://nces.ed.gov/ubs2005/2005074.pdf*

National Center for Education Statistics. (2005b). *Indicators of school crime and safety: 2005.* Retrieved July 27, 2006, from *http://nces.ed.gov/programs/crimeindicators/index.asp*?

National Center for Education Statistics. (2005c). *Public school enrollments.* Washington, DC: U.S. Government Printing Office.

National Center for Education Statistics. (2005d). *The condition of education 2005.* Washington, DC: U.S. Department of Education.

National Center for Education Statistics. (2006a). *Internet access in U.S. public schools and classrooms: 1994–2003.* Retrieved January 3, 2006, from *http://nces.ed.gov*

National Center for Education Statistics. (2006b). *The condition of education 2006.* Washington, DC: U.S. Department of Education.

National Commission on Excellence in Education. (1983). *A nation at risk: The imperative for educational reform.* Washington, DC: Government Printing Office.

National Council of Teachers of Mathematics. (2000–2004). *Principles and standards for school mathematics.* Retrieved October 1, 2006, from *http://standards.nctm.org/document/appendix/numb.htm*

National Education Association. (1995). *Code of ethics of the education profession, NEA Representative Assembly.* Washington, DC: Author.

National Education Association. (1997). *Status of the American public school teacher, 1995–1996.* Washington, DC: Author. Retrieved February 3, 2004, from *http://www.nea.org/neatoday/9709/status.html*

National Education Association. (2002a). *Status of the American public school teacher, 1999–2000.* Washington, DC: Author.

National Education Association. (2002b). *School vouchers: The emerging track record.* Washington, DC: Author.

National Education Association. (2003). *Status of the American public school teacher, 2000–2001.* Washington, DC: Author. Retrieved March 14, 2004, from *http://www.nea.org/edstats*

National Education Association. (2005). *Weighted student formula (WSF).* Washington, DC: Author. Retrieved January 30, 2006, from *http://www.nea.org/index.html*

National Education Association. (2006a). *Rankings and estimates.* Retrieved January 30, 2006, from *http://www.nea.org/index.html*

National Education Association. (2006b). *Status of the American public school teacher, 2003–2004.* Retrieved August 16, 2006, from *http://www.nea.org*

National Joint Committee on Learning Disabilities. (1994). Learning disabilities: Issues on definition. A position paper of the National Joint Committee in Learning Disabilities. In *Collective perspectives on issues affecting learning disability: Position papers and statements.* Austin, TX: Pro-Ed.

National Law Center on Homelessness and Poverty. (2006). Retrieved June 1, 2006, from *http://www.nlchp.org*

National Research Council. (1996). *National science education standards.* Washington, DC: National Academy Press.

National School Boards Association. (2000). Education vital signs: Leadership. *American School Board Journal, 187*(2), 32–37.

Neill, M. (2003). High stakes, high risk. *American School Board Journal, 190*(2), 18–21.

Neisler, O. (2000). How does teacher education need to change to meet the needs of America's schools at the start of the 21st century? *Journal of Teacher Education, 51,* 248–255.

Neville, K., Sherman, R., & Cohen, C. (2005). *Preparing and training professionals: Comparing education to six other fields.* New York: The Finance Project.

New Jersey v. T.L.O., 105 S. Ct. 733 (1985).

New York State Board Association. (2006). *Board members top 3 concerns: Academics, academics, academics.* Retrieved February 1, 2006, from *http://222.nyssba.org*

Newby, T., Stepich, D., Lehman, J., & Russell, J. (2006). *Instructional technology and teaching and learning* (3rd ed.). Upper Saddle River, NJ: Merrill/Prentice Hall.

Newman, J. (2006). *America's teachers* (5th ed.). Boston: Allyn & Bacon.

Nichols, S., & Berliner, D. (2005). *The inevitable corruption of indicators and educators through high-stakes testing.* Tempe, AZ: Education Policy Studies Laboratory.

Nietfeld, J., Cao, L., & Osborne, J. (2004). *Effect of distributed monitoring exercises and feedback on performance and monitoring accuracy.* Paper presented at the annual meeting of the American Educational Research Association, San Diego, CA.

Nieto, S. (2004). *Affirming diversity* (4th ed.). New York: Longman.

Nikitina, S. (2006). Three strategies for interdisciplinary teaching: contextualizing, conceptualizing, and problem-centering. *Journal of Curriculum Studies, 38*(3), 251–271.

No Child Left Behind Act of 2001, Pub. L. 107–110 (8 January 2002). Washington, DC: U.S. Government Printing Office.

Noblit, G., Rogers, D., & McCadden, B. (1995). In the meantime: The possibilities of caring. *Phi Delta Kappan, 76,* 680–685.

Noddings, N. (2001). The caring teacher. In V. Richardson (Ed.), *Handbook of research on teaching* (4th ed., pp. 99–105). Washington, DC: American Educational Research Association.

Noguera, P. (2003a). *City schools and the American dream: Reclaiming the promise of public education.* New York: Teachers College Press.

Noguera, P. (2003b). The trouble with black boys: The role and influence of environmental and cultural factors on the academic performance of African American males. *Urban Education, 38*(4), 431–459.

Norris, N. (2004). *The promise and failure of progressive education.* Landham, MD: Scarecrow Press.

Nye, B., Hedges, L., & Konstantopoulos, S. (2001). Are effects of small classes cumulative? Evidence from a Tennessee experiment. *Journal of Educational Research, 94,* 336–341.

Oakes, J. (2005). Keeping track: How schools structure inequality (2nd ed.). New Haven, CT: Yale University Press.

Oakes, J., & Saunders, M. (2004). Education's most basic tools: Access to textbooks and instructional materials in California's public schools. *Teachers College Record, 106*(10), 1967–1988.

Oakes, J., & Wells, A. S. (2002). Detracking for high student achievement. In L. Abbeduto (Ed.), *Taking sides: Clashing views and controversial issues in educational psychology* (2nd ed., pp. 26–30). Guilford, CT: McGraw-Hill Duskin.

Odden, A. (2003). Leveraging teacher pay. *Education Week, 22*(43), 64.

Odden, A., Borman, G. D., & Fermanich, M. (2004). Assessing teacher, classroom, and school effects, including fiscal effects. *Peabody Journal of Education, 79*(4), 4–32.

Odden, A., Monk, D., Nakib, Y., & Picus, L. (1995). The story of the education dollar: No academy awards and no fiscal smoking guns. *Phi Delta Kappan, 77,* 161–168.

Oder, N. (2005). Oklahoma legislators urge limits on kid's books with gay themes. *Library Journal, 130*(11), 16–17.

OELA (Office of English Language Acquisition). (2004). *National clearinghouse for language acquisition and language instruction programs.* Retrieved March 2, 2006, from *www.NCLE.gwu.edu/languages*

Ogbu, J. (1992). Understanding cultural diversity and learning. *Educational Researcher, 21*(8), 5–14.

Ogbu, J. (1999). Beyond language: Ebonics, proper English, and identity in a Black-American speech community. *American Educational Research Journal, 36,* 147–184.

Ogbu, J. (2003). *Black American students in an affluent suburb: A study of academic disengagement.* Mahwah, NJ: Erlbaum.

Ogbu, J., & Simons, H. (1998). Voluntary and involuntary minorities: A cultural-ecological theory of school performance with some implications for education. *Anthropology & Education Quarterly, 29*(2), 155–188.

Olivia, P. (2005). *Developing the curriculum* (6th ed.). Boston: Allyn & Bacon.

Olson, J., & Clough, M. (2004). *What questions do you have? In defense of general questions: A response to Croom. Teachers College Record.* Retrieved August 20, 2004, from *http://www.tcrecord.org/content.asp?content* ID Number: 11366.

Olson, L. (1999a). A closer look: What makes a good report card. *Education Week, 18*(17), 29.

Olson, L. (1999b). Report cards for schools. *Education Week, 18*(17), 28–36.

Olson, L. (2000). Finding and keeping competent teachers. *Education Week, 19*(18), 12–18.

Olson, L. (2003). The great divide. *Education Week, 22*(17), 9–20.

Olson, L. (2005a). In hearing, poll, PEN finds support for the goals of NCLB. *Education Week, 24*(27), 6.

Olson, L. (2005b). Nationwide standards eyed anew. *Education Week, 25*(14), 1, 24.

Olson, L. (2005c). Impact of paper and pencil, online testing is compared. *Education Week, 25*(11), 14.

Olson, L. (2006a). A decade of effort. *Education Week, 25*(17), 8–16.

Olson, L. (2006b). The down staircase. *Education Week, 25*(41S), 5, 6, 10, 11.

Opdenakker, M. C., & Van Damme, J. (2006). Teacher characteristics and teaching styles as effectiveness enhancing factors of classroom practice. *Teaching and Teacher Education, 22*(1), 1–21.

Ormrod, J. (2006). *Educational psychology: Developing learners* (5th ed). Upper Saddle River, NJ: Merrill/Prentice Hall.

Ornstein, A., & Hunkins, F. (2004). *Curriculum: Foundations, principles, and issues* (4th ed.). Boston: Allyn & Bacon.

Orr, A. (2003). Black–white differences in achievement: The importance of wealth. *Sociology of Education, 76* (October), 281–304.

Ortiz, F. (2004). Essential learning conditions for California youth: Educational facilities. *Teachers College Record, 106*(10), 2015–2031.

Osborne, J. (1996). Beyond constructivism. *Science Education, 80,* 53–81.

Ozmon, H. A., & Craver, S. M. (2007). *Philosophical foundations of education* (8th ed.). Upper Saddle River, NJ: Pearson.

Park, C. (1997, March). *A comparative study of learning style preferences: Asian-American and Anglo students in secondary schools.* Paper presented at the annual meeting of the American Educational Research Association, Chicago.

Patrick, H., Anderman, L. H., & Ryan, A. M. (2002). Social motivation and the classroom social environment. In C. Midgley (Ed.), *Goals, goal structures, and patterns of adaptive learning* (pp. 85–108). Mahwah, NJ: Erlbaum.

Patterson, F. (2001/2002). Teaching religious intolerance. *Rethinking Schools, 16*(2), 6, 7.

Paxson, R. (2003). Don't know much about history—never did. *Phi Delta Kappan, 85,* 265–273.

Payton, J., Munro, S., O'Brien, M., & Weissberg, R. (2006). Common ground. *Edutopia, 2*(6), 53–55.

Pecheone, R. L., & Chung, R. R. (2006). Evidence in teacher education: The performance assessment for California teachers. *Journal of Teacher Education, 57*(1), 22–36.

Pedulla, J., Abrams, L., Madaus, G., Russell, M., Ramos, M., & Miao, J. (2003). *Perceived effects of state-mandated testing programs on teaching and learning: Findings from a national survey of teachers.* Boston: Boston College.

Peevely, G., Hedges, L., & Nye, B. A. (2005). The relationship of class size effects and teacher salary. *Journal of Education Finance, 31*(1), 101–109.

Peregoy, S., & Boyle, O. (2005). *Reading, writing, and learning in ESL* (4th ed.). New York: Longman.

Perkins-Gough, D. (2005a). Fixing high schools. *Educational Leadership, 62*(8), 88–89.

Perkins-Gough, D. (2005b). The perils of high school exit exams. *Educational Leadership, 63*(3), 90–91.

Petroska, J., Lindle, J., & Pankratz, R. (2000). *Executive summary: 2000 Review of research on the Kentucky Education Reform Act.* Retrieved February 17, 2004, from *http://www.kier.org/2000Research.html*

Pew Hispanic Foundation. (2003). *Latinos in higher education: Many enroll, too few graduate.* Retrieved April 27, 2004, from *http://www.pewhispanic.org/site/docs/pdf*

Piaget, J. (1952). *Origins of intelligence in children.* New York: International Universities Press.

Piaget, J. (1970). *The science of education and the psychology of the child.* New York: Orion Press.

Picciano, A. (2001). *Distance learning.* Upper Saddle River, NJ: Pearson.

Pintrich, P., & Schunk, D. (2002). *Motivation in education: Theory, research, and applications* (2nd ed.). Upper Saddle River, NJ: Merrill/Prentice Hall.

Pittman, M., & Frykholm, J. (2002). *Turning points: Curriculum materials as catalysts for change.* Paper presented at the annual meeting of the American Educational Research Association, Seattle, WA.

Pogrow, S. (2006). The Bermuda Triangle of American education: Pure traditionalism, pure progressivism, and good intentions. *Phi Delta Kappan, 88*(2), 142–150.

Popham, W. (2004a). A game without winners. *Educational Leadership, 62*(3), 46–50.

Popham, W. (2004b). *America's failing schools: How parents and teachers can cope with No Child Left Behind.* New York: Routledge Falmer.

Popham, W. (2005). NAEP: Gold standard or fool's gold? *Educational Leadership, 68*(8), 79–81.

Porter, A. (2002). Measuring the content of instruction: Uses in research and practice. *Educational Researcher, 31*(7), 3–14.

Portner, J. (2000). Fearful teachers buy insurance against liability. *Education Week, 19*(20), 1, 18.

Pressley, M., Raphael, L., & Gallagher, J. G. (2004). Prodience-St. Mel School: How a school that works for African American students works. *Journal of Educational Psychology, 96*(2), 216–235.

Princiotta, D., Bielick, S., & Chapman, C. (2004). 1.1 million homeschooled students in the United States in 2003. *National Center for Education Statistics: Education Statistics Quarterly, 6*(3), 23–26.

Probst, R., Anderson, R., Brinnin, J., Leggett, J., & Irvin, J. (1997). *Elements of literature: Second course.* Austin, TX: Holt, Rinehart & Winston.

Proefriedt, W. (1999). Sorry, John. I'm not who you thought I was. *Education Week, 29*(15), 28, 30.

Public Agenda. (2000). *Just waiting to be asked? A fresh look at attitudes on public engagement.* Retrieved July 27, 2003, from *http://www.publicagenda.org/research/research_resports_details.cfm?list=23*

Public Agenda. (2002). *Sizing things up: What parents, teachers and students think about large and small high schools.* Retrieved June 15, 2004, from *http://www.publicagenda.org/research/research_reports_details.cfm?list=21*

Public Agenda. (2003). *Stand by me: What teachers really think about unions, merit pay, and other professional matters.* Retrieved May 15, 2006, from *http://www.publicagenda.org/specials/standbyme*

Public Agenda. (2004). *Teaching interrupted.* Retrieved June 12, 2004, from *http://www.publicagenda.org*

Pulliam, J., & Van Patten, J. (2003). *History of education in America* (8th ed.). Upper Saddle River, NJ: Merrill/Prentice Hall.

Pulliam, J., & Van Patten, J. (2007). *History of education in America* (9th ed.). Upper Saddle River, NJ: Merrill/Prentice Hall.

Pullman, P. (2002). *His dark materials* (trilogy). New York: Knopf.

Quick, P., & Normore, A. (2004). Moral leadership in the 21st century: Everyone is watching—especially the students. *Educational Forum, 68*(4), 336–347.

Quinlan, T. (2004). Speech recognition technology and students with writing difficulties: Improving fluency. *Journal of Educational Psychology, 96*(2), 337–346.

Quiocho, A., & Ulanoff, S. (2002, April). *Teacher research in preservice teacher education: Asking burning questions.* Paper presented at the annual meeting of the American Educational Research Association, New Orleans, LA.

Raider-Roth, M. (2005). *Trusting what you know: The high stakes of classroom relationships.* San Francisco: Jossey-Bass.

Rainwater, L., & Smeedings, T. (2003). *Poor kids in a rich country.* New York: Russell Sage Foundation.

Ramirez, A. (2001). How merit pay undermines education. *Educational Leadership, 58*(5), 16–20.

Raths, J., & Lynman, F. (2003). Summative evaluation of student teachers. *Journal of Teacher Education, 54,* 206–216.

Ravitch, D. (1990, October 24). Multiculturalism yes, particularism, no. *Chronicle of Higher Education,* p. A44.

Ravitch, D. (2000). *Left back: A century of failed school reforms.* New York: Simon & Schuster.

Ravitch, D. (2006). National standards. *Education Week, 25*(17), 54–58.

Ray v. School District of DeSoto County, 666 F. Supp. 1524, (M.D. Fla. 1987).

Ready, D., Lee, V., & Welner, K. (2004). Educational equity and school structure: School size, overcrowding and schools-within-schools. *Teachers College Record, 106*(10), 1989–2014.

Rebell, M. (2004). Why adequacy lawsuits matter. *Education Week, 23*(44), 40.

Recruiting New Teachers. (2006). *Teacher shortage areas.* Retrieved July 3, 2006, from *http://www.recruitingteachers.org/channels/clearinghouse*

Reeves, E., & Bylund, R. (2005). Are rural schools inferior to urban schools? A multi-year analysis of school accountability trends in Kentucky. *Rural Sociology, 70*(3), 360–386.

Reeves, J. (2004, January 30). Riley proposal would eliminate tenure panel [Electronic version]. *The Decatur Daily News.*

Regents of the University of California v. Bakke, 438 U.S. 265 (1978).

Reich, R. (2002). The civic perils of home schooling. *Educational Leadership, 59*(7), 56–59.

Reid, K. (2005). Sharing the load. *Education Week, 25*(12), 27–30.

Reis, S. M., Colbert, R. D., & Hébert, T. P. (2005). Understanding resilience in diverse, talented students in an urban high school. *Roeper Review, 27*(2), 110–120.

Remillard, J. (2005). Examining key concepts in research on teachers' use of mathematics curricula. *Review of Educational Research, 75*(2), 211–246.

Reys, B., Reys, R., & Chávez, O. (2004). Why mathematics textbooks matter. *Educational Leadership, 62*(5), 61–66.

Rhee, M., & Levin, J. (2006). Staffing urban schools. *Education Week, 25*(16), 52, 30.

Richard, A. (2000a). L.A. board taps Romer for top job. *Education Week, 19*(40), 1, 12–13.

Richard, A. (2000b). Studies cite lack of diversity in top position. *Education Week, 19*(25), 3.

Richard, A. (2003). Colorado voucher measure appears certain. *Education Week, 22*(29), 24, 30.

Richard, A. (2004). W. Va. eyes softer stand on school mergers. *Education Week, 23*(21), 16, 20.

Richard, A. (2005). Fla. board seeks social-promotion ban in all grades. *Education Week, 24*(20), 22, 27.

Richardson, J., & Newby, T. (2005, April). *The role of students' cognitive engagement in online learning.* Paper presented at the annual meeting of the American Educational Research Association, Montreal.

Richardson, P., & Watt, H. (2005). "I've decided to become a teacher": Influences on career change. *Teaching and Teacher Education, 21,* 475–489.

Richardson, V. (2003, April). *Preservice teachers' beliefs.* Paper presented at the annual meeting of the American Educational Research Association, Chicago.

Riordan, C. (2004). *Equality and achievement: An introduction to the sociology of education* (2nd ed.). Upper Saddle River, NJ: Merrill/Prentice Hall.

Ritter, G. W., & Lucas, C. J. (2005). Choosing the lesser of two inequalities. *Education Week, 24*(37), 31, 33.

Rittle-Johnson, B., & Alibali, M. (1999). Conceptual and procedural knowledge of mathematics: Does one lead to the other? *Journal of Educational Psychology, 91*(1), 175–189.

Robelen, E. (2006a). D.C. schools that take vouchers found to be less racially isolated. *Education Week, 25*(20), 13.

Robelen, E. (2006b). Disputes over charter closures winding up in court. *Education Week, 25*(16), 1, 11.

Robelen, E. (2006c). No test-score edge for Cleveland voucher students. *Education Week, 25*(24), 18.

Robelen, E. (2006d). Reanalysis of NAEP scores finds charter schools lagging. *Education Week, 26*(1), 26.

Robelen, E. (2006e). Small schools' ripple effects debated. *Education Week, 25*(34), 1, 20.

Roberts, W. (2006). *Bullying from both sides.* Thousand Oaks, CA: Corwin Press.

Roblyer, M. (2006). *Integrating educational technology into teaching* (4th ed.). Upper Saddle River, NJ: Merrill/Prentice Hall.

Rocha, A. (2006, March 1). The sex education controversy. *The Palo Alto Weekly: Online Edition.* Retrieved June 13, 2006, from *http://www.paloaltoonline.com/weekly/story.php?story_id=461*

Rodgers, C. (2002). Seeing student learning: Teacher change and the role of reflection. *Harvard Educational Review, 72,* 230–253.

Roffman, D. M. (2005). Lakoff for sexuality educators: The power and magic of "framing." *SIECUS Report, 33*(4), 20–25.

Rogers, C. (1967). Learning to be free. In C. Rogers & B. Stevens (Eds.), *The problem of being human.* Lafayette, CA: Real People Press.

Rogers, J., & Oakes, J. (2005). John Dewey speaks to Brown: Research, democratic social movement strategies, and the struggle for education on equal terms. *Teachers College Record, 107*(9), 2178–2203.

Romano, L. (2006, January 6). Fla. voucher system struck down: Court's ruling could affect programs in other states. *Washington Post,* p. A05. Retrieved April 23, 2006, from *http://www.washingtonpost.com/wp-dyn/content/article/2006/01/05/AR2006010501983.html*

Romboy, D., & Kinkead, L. (2005, April 14). Surviving in America. *Deseret Morning News, 155*(303), pp. 1, 11, 12.

Rose, L., & Gallup, A. (1998). The 30th annual Phi Delta Kappa/Gallup Poll of the public's attitudes toward the public schools. *Phi Delta Kappan, 80,* 41–56.

Rose, L., & Gallup, A. (2000). The 32nd annual Phi Delta Kappa/Gallup Poll of the public's attitudes toward the public schools. *Phi Delta Kappan, 82,* 41–58.

Rose, L., & Gallup, A. (2004). *The 36th annual Phi Delta Kappa/Gallup poll of the public's attitude toward the public schools.* Online version. Retrieved February 2005 from *http://www.pdkintl.org/kappan/k0409pol.htm*

Rose, L., & Gallup, A. (2005). *The 37th annual Phi Delta Kappa/Gallup poll of the public's attitude toward the public schools.* Online version. Retrieved March 2006 from *http://www.pdkintl.org/kappan/k0409pol.htm*

Rosenshine, B. (2006). The struggles of the lower-scoring students. *Teaching and Teacher Education, 22,* 555–562.

Ross, K. (2005). Charter schools and integration: The experience in Michigan. In J. Betts & T. Loveless (Eds.), *Getting choice right: Ensuring equity and efficiency in education policy* (pp. 146–175). Washington, DC: Brookings Institution Press.

Rother, C. (2005). Teachers talk tech. *Technological Horizons in Education, 33*(3), 34–36.

Rothman, R. (1997). KERA: A tale of one school. *Phi Delta Kappan, 79,* 272–275.

Rothstein, R. (1998). What does education cost? *American School Board Journal, 85*(9), 30–33.

Rothstein, R. (2004a). *Class and schools: Using social, economic, and educational reform to close the black–white achievement gap.* New York: Teachers College Press.

Rothstein, R. (2004b). The achievement gap. *Educational Leadership, 62*(3), 40–43.

Rowe, M. (1986). Wait-time: Slowing down may be a way of speeding up. *Journal of Teacher Education, 37*(1), 43–50.

Rubinson, F. (2004). Urban dropouts: Why so many and what can be done? In S. R. Steinberg & J. L. Kincheloe (Eds.), *19 Urban questions: Teaching in the city* (pp. 53–67). New York: Peter Lang.

Rutter, M., Maughan, B., Mortimore, P., Ouston, J., & Smith, A. (1979). *Fifteen thousand hours: Secondary schools and their effects on children.* Cambridge, MA: Harvard University Press.

Ryan, K. (1992). *The roller coaster year: Essays by and for beginning teachers.* New York: HarperCollins.

Sabo, D., Miller, K., Farrell, M., Barnes, G., & Melnick, M. (1998). The women's sports foundation report: Sport and teen pregnancy. *Volleyball, 26*(3), 20–23.

Safer, N., & Fleischman, S. (2005). How student progress monitoring improves instruction. *Educational Leadership, 62*(5), 81–83.

Saha, L., & Biddle, B. (2006). The innovative principal: Research in action. *Principal, 85*(5), 28–31.

Saltman, M. (2005). *The Edison schools: Corporate schooling and the assault on public education.* New York: Routledge/Falmer.

Saltpeter, J. (2005). Telling tales with technology. *Technology & Learning, 25*(7), 18–24.

Samuels, C. (2006a). Flexibility detailed for testing students with disabilities. *Education Week, 25*(16), 20.

Samuels, C. (2006b). Stricter school soda limits offered. *Education Week, 25*(36), 1, 18.

San Antonio, D. (2006). Broadening the world of early adolescents. *Educational Leadership, 63*(7), 8–13.

Sandham, J. (2000). Home sweet school. *Education Week, 19*(20), 24–29.

Sandholtz, J., & Reilly, B. (2004). Teachers, not technicians: Rethinking technical expectations for teachers. *Teachers College Record, 106*(3), 476–512.

Sattler, J. M. (2001). *Assessment of children: Cognitive applications* (4th ed.). San Diego, CA: Jerome M. Sattler.

Sax, L. (2005). The promise and peril of single-sex public education. *Education Week, 24*(25), 48, 34.

Schibsted, E. (2006). Fighting for fitness. *Edutopia, 1*(9), 30–37.

Schiever, S., & Maker, C. J. (2003). New directions in enrichment and acceleration. In N. Colangelo & G. Davis (Eds.), *Handbook of gifted education* (3rd ed., pp. 163–173). Boston: Allyn & Bacon.

Schlesinger, A. (1992). *The disuniting of America: Reflections on a multicultural society.* New York: Norton.

Schlozman, S. (2002). The shrink in the classroom: Fighting school violence. *Educational Leadership, 60*(2), 89–90.

Schnaiberg, L. (2000). Charter schools: Choice, diversity may be at odds. *Education Week, 19*(35), 1, 18–20.

Schoen, H., Fey, J., Hirsch, C., & Coxford, A. (1999). Issues and options in the math wars. *Phi Delta Kappan, 80*, 444–453.

Schon, D. (1983). *The reflective practitioner: How professionals think in action.* New York: Basic Books.

School Board of Nassau County, Florida v. Arline, 480 U.S. 273 (1987).

Schrimpf, C. (2006). This is me. In E. Keefe, V. Moore, & F. Duff (Eds.), *Listening to the experts* (pp. 87–90). Baltimore, MD: Paul H. Brookes.

Schult, C. A. (2002). Children's understanding of the distinction between intentions and desires. *Child Development, 73*, 1737–1747.

Schunk, D. (2004). *Learning theories: An educational perspective* (4th ed.). Upper Saddle River, NJ: Merrill/Prentice Hall.

Schutz, A. (2004, April). *Home is a prison in the global city: A critical review of urban school–community relationships.* Paper presented at the annual meeting of the American Educational Research Association, San Diego, CA.

Sears, J. (1993). Responding to the sexual diversity of faculty and students: Sexual praxis and the critically reflective administrator. In C. Capper (Ed.), *Educational administration in a pluralistic society.* Albany, NY: SUNY Press.

Selingo, J. (2004). The cheating culture. *Prism, 14*(1), 24–30.

Sergiovanni, T. (2004). *Educational governance and administration* (5th ed.). Boston: Allyn & Bacon.

Sergiovanni, T. (2006). *Principalship: The reflective practitioner perspective* (5th ed.). Boston: Allyn & Bacon.

Serrano v. Priest, (1), 96 Cal. Rptr. 601, 487 P.2d 1241, Calif. (1971).

Sewall, G. (2000). History 2000: Why the older textbooks may be better than the new. *Education Week, 19*(38), 36, 52.

Shakeshaft, C., Mandel, L., Johnson, Y., Sawyer, J., Hergenrother, M., & Barber, E. (1997). Boys call me cow. *Educational Leadership, 55*(2), 22–25.

Shaunessy, E. (2003, Summer). State policies regarding gifted education. *Gifted Child Today Magazine.* Retrieved March 14, 2004, from *http://www.findarticles.com/cf_dls/m0HRV/3_26/106290404/p1/article.jhtml*

Shay, S., & Gomez, J. (2002, April). *Privatization in education: A growth curve analysis of achievement.* Paper presented at the annual meeting of the American Educational Research Association, New Orleans, LA.

Shaywitz, S. E., & Shaywitz, B. A. (2004). Reading disability and the brain. *Educational Leadership, 61*(6), 7–11.

Shelley, A. (2003). Vanishing heritage. *Education Week, 22*(38), 24–29.

Shepard, L., & Smith, M. (1990). Synthesis of research on grade retention. *Educational Leadership, 47*(8), 84–88.

Shuell, T. (1996). Teaching and learning in a classroom context. In D. Berliner & R. Calfee (Eds.), *Handbook of educational psychology* (pp. 726–764). New York: Macmillan.

Silver-Pacuilla, H., & Fleischman, S. (2006). Technology to help struggling students. *Educational Leadership, 63*(5), 84–85.

Simonson, M., Smaldino, S., Albright, M., & Zavacek, S. (2006). *Teaching and learning at a distance* (3rd ed.). Upper Saddle River, NJ: Pearson.

Sincero, P., & Woyshner, C. (2003). Writing women into the curriculum. *Social Education, 67,* 218–225.

Siris, K., & Osterman, K. (2004). Interrupting the cycle of bullying and victimization in the elementary classroom. *Phi Delta Kappan, 86*(4), 288–291.

Skiba, R., & Peterson, R. (1999). The dark side of zero tolerance. *Phi Delta Kappan, 80,* 372–376, 381–382.

Slavin, R. (2006). *Educational psychology* (8th ed.). Boston: Allyn & Bacon.

Slavin, R., & Cheung, A. (2004). *Effective reading programs for English language learners: A best-evidence synthesis.* Baltimore: Center for Research on the Education of Students Placed At Risk, Johns Hopkins University. Retrieved April 23, 2006, from *www.csos.jhu.edu/crespar/techReports/Report66.pdf*

Slavin, R., & Cheung, A. (2005). A synthesis of research on language of reading instruction for English language learners. *Review of Educational Research, 75*(2), 247–284.

Slavin, R., Karweit, N., & Madden, N. (Eds.). (1989). *Effective programs for students at risk.* Needham Heights, MA: Allyn & Bacon.

Sleeter, C. (2005). *Un-standardizing curriculum: Multicultural teaching in the standards-based classroom.* New York: Teachers College Press.

Smally, S., & Reyes-Blanes, M. (2001). Reaching out to African American parents in an urban community: A community–university partnership. *Urban Education, 36*(4), 518–533.

Smith, F. (2005). Intensive care. *Edutopia, 1*(9), 47–49.

Smith, F. (2006). Learning by giving. *Edutopia, 2*(1), 54–57.

Smith, J., Brewer, D. M., & Heffner, T. (2003). Using portfolio assessments with young children who are at risk for school failure. *Preventing School Failure, 48*(1), 38–40.

Smith, P., Molnar, A., & Zahorik, J. (2003). Class-size reduction: A fresh look at the data. *Educational Leadership, 61*(1), 72–74.

Smith, T., Desimone, L., & Ueno, K. (2005). "Highly qualified" to do what? The relationship between NCLB teacher quality mandates and the use of reform-oriented instruction in middle school mathematics. *Educational Evaluation and Policy Analysis, 27*(1), 75–109.

Smith, T., Polloway, E., Patton, J., & Dowdy, C. (2004). *Teaching students with special needs in inclusive settings* (4th ed.). Boston: Allyn & Bacon.

Smith v. Board of School Commissioners of Mobile County, 827 F.2d 684 (llth Cir., 1987).

Snider, J. (2006). The superintendent as scapegoat. *Education Week, 25*(18), 40, 31.

Sommers, C. (2000). *The war against boys: How misguided feminism is harming our young men.* New York: Simon & Schuster.

Sonnenberg, W. (2004). Federal support for education: Fiscal years 1980 to 2003. *National Center for Education Statistics: Education Statistics Quarterly, 6*(3), 65–68.

Spring, J. (2005). *The American School 1642–2004* (6th ed.). Boston: McGraw-Hill.

Spring, J. (2006). *American education* (12th ed.). Boston: McGraw-Hill.

Stabiner, K. (2003, January 12). Where girls aren't [Electronic version]. *New York Times.* Retrieved April 15, 2005, from *http://www.nytimes.com*

Stahl, R., DeMasi, K., Gehrke, R., Guy, C., & Scown, J. (2005, April). *Perceptions, conceptions and misconceptions of wait time and wait time behaviors among pre-service and in-service teachers.* Paper presented at the annual meeting of the American Educational Research Association, Montreal.

Stahl, S. A. (1999). Why innovations come and go (and mostly go): The case of whole language. *Educational Researcher, 28*(8), 13–22.

Starnes, B. (2006). What we don't know *can* hurt them: White teachers, Indian children. *Phi Delta Kappan, 87*(5), 384–392.

Steches, B., Hamilton, L., & Scott-Naflet, S. (2005). *Introduction to first-year findings: Implementing standards-based accountability (ISBA) project.* Paper presented at the annual meeting of the American Educational Research Association, Montreal.

Steele, C., Spencer, S., & Aronson, J. (2002). Contending with group image: The psychology of stereotype and social identity threat. In M. Zanna (Ed.), *Advances in experimental social psychology* (Vol. 34, pp. 379–440). San Diego: Academic Press.

Steering Committee on Science and Creationism. (1999). Science and creationism: A view from the National Academy of Sciences (2nd ed.). Washington, DC: National Academies Press.

Stefkovich, J., & O'Brien, G. (2001, April). *The courts, school governance, and students' rights: A meta-analysis of educators' knowledge of Fourth Amendment law.* Paper presented at the annual meeting of the American Educational Research Assoication, Seattle, WA.

Stiggins, R. (2005). *Student-centered classroom assessment* (4th ed.). Upper Saddle River, NJ: Merrill/Prentice Hall.

Stigler, J., Gonzales, P., Kawanaka, T., Knoll, T., & Serrano, A. (1999). *The TIMSS videotape classroom study: Methods and finding from an exploratory research project on eighth-grade mathematics instruction in Germany, Japan, and the United States* (NCES 990074). Washington, DC: U.S. Department of Education, National Center for Educational Statistics.

Stipek, D. (2002). *Motivation to learn: Integrating theory and practice* (4th ed.). Boston: Allyn & Bacon.

Stone v. Graham, 449 U.S. 39 (1981).

Strong, J., & Hindman, J. (2003). Hiring the best teachers. *Educational Leadership, 60*(8), 48–52.

Summers, J., Woodruff, A., Tomberlin, T., Williams, N., & Svinicki, M. (2001, April). *Cognitive processes of cooperative learning: A qualitative analysis.* Paper presented at the annual meeting of the American Educational Research Association, Seattle, WA.

Swaim, S. (2004). Strength in the middle. *Education Week, 23*(32), 32.

Swanson, C. (2004). *The real truth about low graduation rates: An evidence-based commentary.* Washington, DC: Urban Institute. Retrieved March 30, 2006, from *http://www.urban.org*

Swanson, C. (2006a). Bigger district size gives superintendents earnings edge. *Education Week, 25*(43), 18–19.

Swanson, C. (2006b, May). Tracking U.S. trends. *Education Week, Technology Counts,* pp. 50–52.

Swidler, S. (2004). *Naturally small.* Greenwich, CT: Information Age Publishing.

Sykes, S. (2006, July 31). College recruitment efforts will raise tuition. *Salt Lake Tribune,* p. B5.

Szczesiul, S. (2004, April). *Urban definitions, urban differentials: Implications for how new teachers locate the urban school problem.* Paper presented at the annual meeting of the American Educational Research Association, San Diego, CA.

Tallent-Runnels, M., Thomas, J., Lan, W., Cooper, S., Ahern, T., Shaw, S., & Liu, X. (2006). Teaching courses online: A review of the research. *Review of Educational Research, 76*(1), 93–135.

Taxman v. Board of Education of Township of Piscataway, 91 F.3d 1547 (3rd Cir., 1996).

Taylor, B., Pressley, M., & Pearson, P. (2002). Research-supported characteristics of teachers and schools that promote reading achievement. In B. Taylor & D. Pearson (Eds.), *Teaching reading: Effective schools, accomplished teachers* (pp. 361–374). Mahwah, NJ: Erlbaum.

Terwel, J., Gillies, R., van den Eeden, P., & Hoek, D. (2001). Cooperative learning processes of students: A longitudinal multilevel perspective. *British Journal of Educational Psychology, 71,* 619–645.

Thiers, N. (2006). Do single-sex classes raise academic achievement? *Educational Leadership, 63*(7), 70.

Thirunarayanan, M. O. (2004). National Board certification for teachers: A billion dollar hoax. *Teachers College Record.* Retrieved May 24, 2005, from *http://www.tcrecord.org*

Thompson, G. (2000). The real deal on bilingual education: Former language-minority students discuss effective and ineffective instructional practices. *Education Horizons, 78*(2), 80–90.

Thornton, S. (2003). Silence on gays and lesbians in social studies curriculum. *Social Education, 67,* 226–230.

Thornton, S. (2005). *Teaching social studies that matters: Curriculum for active learning.* New York: Teachers College Press.

Tiedt, P., & Tiedt, I. (2005). *Multicultural teaching* (7th ed.). Boston: Allyn & Bacon.

Tinker v. Des Moines Community School District, 393 U.S. 503 (1969).

Tobin, K. (1987). Role of wait-time in higher cognitive level learning. *Review of Educational Research, 57,* 69–95.

Tomlinson, C. (2003). *Fulfilling the promise of the differentiated classroom: Strategies and tools for responsive teaching.* Alexandria, VA: Association for Supervision and Curriculum Development.

Tomlinson, C., & Callahan, C. (2001, April). *Deciding to teach them all: Middle school teachers learning to teach for academic diversity.* Paper presented at the annual meeting of the American Educational Research Association, Seattle, WA.

Tompkins, G. (2006b). *Literacy for the 21st century: A balanced approach* (4th ed.). Upper Saddle River, NJ: Merrill/Prentice Hall.

Tonn, J. (2005a). First amendment attitudes found troubling. *Education Week, 24*(21), 6.

Tonn, J. (2005b). Sexual behavior. *Education Week, 25*(9), 15.

Trotter, A. (1999a). Preparing teachers for the digital age. *Education Week, 19*(4), 37–43.

Trotter, A. (1999b). Technology and its continual rise and fall. *Education Week, 18*(36), 30–31.

Trotter, A. (2000). Home computer used primarily for learning, families say in survey. *Education Week, 19*(30), 6.

Trotter, A. (2001). Channel One drops cash-incentive plan aimed at teachers. *Education Week, 21*(2), 17.

Trotter, A. (2002). Tech firms land privatization role. *Education Week, 22*(4), 1, 11.

Trotter, A. (2003). Simulated driver's ed. takes virtual twists and turns. *Education Week, 22*(19), 8.

Trotter, A. (2004). Digital games bring entertainment into learning realm. *Education Week, 23*(44), 8.

Trotter, A. (2005). Technology turns test-prep into clicking experience. *Education Week, 24*(36), 8.

Trotter, A. (2006a). Diversity on the docket. *Education Week, 26*(6), 27.

Trotter, A. (2006b). U.S. court backs school's decision to bar student's anti-gay T-shirt. *Education Week, 25*(34), 9.

Trotter, A. (2006c). Minorities still face digital divide. *Education Week, 26*(3), 14.

Tschannen-Moran, M., Woolfolk-Hoy, A., & Hoy, W. (1998). Teacher efficacy: Its meaning and measure. *Review of Educational Research, 68*(2), 202–248.

Turnbull, A., Turnbull, R., Shank, M., Smith, S., & Leal, D. (2007). *Exceptional lives: Special education in today's schools* (5th ed.). Upper Saddle River, NJ: Merrill/Prentice Hall.

Tyack, P., & Cuban, L. (1995). *Tinkering toward utopia.* Cambridge, MA: Harvard University Press.

Tyre, P. (2006). "The trouble with boys." *Newsweek, 147*(5), 44–52.

Tyson, H. (1999). A load off the teachers' backs: Coordinated school health programs. *Phi Delta Kappan, 80*(5), K1–K8.

U.S. Bureau of Census. (1990). *Statistical abstract of the United States* (110th ed.). Washington, DC: U.S. Government Printing Office.

U.S. Bureau of Census. (2000). *Educational attainment in the United States: March 1999* (pp. 20–528). Washington, DC: U.S. Department of Commerce.

U.S. Bureau of Census. (2001). Nation's household income stable in 2000. Retrieved June 13, 2006, from *www.census.gov/Press-Release/www/2001/cb01-158.html*

U.S. Bureau of Census. (2003). *Statistical abstract of the United States* (123rd ed.). Washington, DC: U.S. Government Printing Office.

U.S. Bureau of Census. (2004). *The foreign-born population in the United States: 2003.* Washington, DC: U.S. Government Printing Office.

U.S. Bureau of Census. (2005). *Income, poverty, and health insurance coverage in the United States, 2004.* Washington, DC: U.S. Government Printing Office.

U.S. Bureau of Census. (2006). *Effects of government taxes and transfers on income and poverty: 2004.* Washington, DC: U.S. Government Printing Office.

U.S. Bureau of Indian Affairs. (1974). Government schools for Indians (1881). In S. Cohen (Ed.), *Education in the United States: A documentary history* (Vol. 3, pp. 1734–1756). New York: Random House.

U.S. Department of Education. (1995). *Digest of education statistics, 1994.* Washington, DC: U.S. Government Printing Office.

U.S. Department of Education. (1999a). *Digest of education statistics, 1998.* Washington, DC: U.S. Government Printing Office.

U.S. Department of Education. (1999b). *Teachers' guide to religion in the public schools.* Washington, DC: Author.

U.S. Department of Education. (2000). *Digest of education statistics.* Washington, DC: Author.

U.S. Department of Education. (2001). *The longitudinal evaluation of school change and performance (LESCP) in Title I schools: Final report.* Washington, DC: Author.

U.S. Department of Education. (2002). *Press release on Title IX,* June 27. Washington, DC: Author.

U.S. Department of Education. (2003a). *Digest of education statistics, 2002.* Washington, DC: U.S. Government Printing Office.

U.S. Department of Education. (2003b). Title I—Improving the academic achievement of the disadvantaged. *Federal Register, 68*(236). Washington, DC: U.S. Government Printing Office.

U.S. Department of Education. (2004a). *A guide to education and No Child Left Behind.* Washington, DC: U.S. Government Printing Office.

U.S. Department of Education. (2004b). Individuals with Disabilities Education Act (IDEA) data (Table AA3). Washington, DC: Author. Retrieved August 23, 2005, from *http://www.ideadata.org/PartBdata.asp*

U.S. Department of Education. (2005a). *Education for homeless children and youth.* Washington, DC: U.S. Printing

Office. Retrieved July 12, 2006, from *www.ed.gov//programs/homeless/index.html*

U.S. Department of Education. (2005b). *The condition of education in 2005 in brief.* Washington DC: National Center for Education Statistics.

U.S. Department of Education. (2006a). Fact sheet on Title I. Retrieved August 15, 2006, from *http://www.ed.gov/title1*

U.S. Department of Education. (2006b). Magnet schools assistance program. Retrieved June 13, 2006, from *http://www.ed.gov/programs/magnet*

U.S. Department of Education. (2006c). *Statistics of state school systems: Revenues and expenditures to public elementary and secondary education, 2001–2002.* Washington, DC: National Center for Education Statistics.

U.S. Department of Health and Human Services. (2006). *AIDS info.* Retrieved July 31, 2006, from *http://www.aidsinfo.nih.gov/*

U.S. English. (2006). Retrieved August 13, 2006, from *http://www.us-english.org*

U.S. Government Accounting Office. (2006). *No Child Left Behind Act: Additional assistance and research on effective strategies would help small rural districts.* Washington, DC: Government Printing Office.

U.S. Government Printing Office. (1975). *Historical statistics of the United States: Colonial times to 1970* (Vol. I). Washington, DC: Author.

Ubben, G., Hughes, L., & Norris, C. (2001). *The principal: Creative leadership for excellence in schools* (4th ed.). Boston: Allyn & Bacon.

Ubben, G., Hughes, L., & Norris, C. (2004). *The principal: Creative leadership for excellence in schools* (5th ed.). Boston: Allyn & Bacon.

UCLA Center for Communication Policy. (2001). *Surveying the digital future: Year two.* Retrieved March 14, 2005, from *http://www.ccp.ucla.edu*

Underwood, J., & Webb, L. (2006). *School law for teachers.* Upper Saddle River, NJ: Pearson.

Vail, K. (2002). Same-sex schools. *American School Board Journal, 189*(11), 32–35.

van den Berg, R. (2002). Teachers' meanings regarding educational practice. *Review of Educational Research, 72,* 577–625.

Vander Ark, T. (2002). It's all about size. *American School Board Journal, 89*(20), 34–35.

Vander Ark, T. (2003). America's high school crisis: Policy reforms that will make a difference. *Education Week, 22*(29), 52, 41.

van Gelder, T. (2005). Teaching critical thinking: Some lessons from cognitive science. *College Teaching, 53,* 41–46.

Vergon, C. (2001, April). *The exclusion of students of color from elementary and secondary schools: A national dilemma and some research-based suggestions for its resolution.* Paper presented at the annual meeting of the American Educational Research Association, Seattle, WA.

Viadero, D. (1996). Middle school gains over 25 years chronicled. *Education Week 16*(8), 7.

Viadero, D. (1999). Education Department is set to release its list of recommended math programs. *Education Week, 19*(6), 1, 14.

Viadero, D. (2000). Lags in minority achievement defy traditional explanations. *Education Week, 19*(28), 1, 18–19, 21.

Viadero, D. (2003a). Nice work: The growing research base for character education programs shows benefits for students' social—and academic—skills. *Education Week, 22*(33), 38–41.

Viadero, D. (2003b). Staying power. *Education Week, 22*(39), 24–27.

Viadero, D. (2003c). Tormentors. *Education Week, 22*(18), 24–27.

Viadero, D. (2003d). Two studies highlight links between violence, bullying by students. *Education Week, 22*(36), 6.

Viadero, D. (2005a). Key data on charter achievement missing as policy questions mount. *Education Week, 25*(13), 6.

Viadero, D. (2005b). Smoking-prevention programs in schools found ineffective for teens. *Education Week, 24*(26), 6.

Viadero, D. (2006a). Debate over dropouts renewed as scholars issue dueling reports. *Education Week, 25*(33), 18.

Viadero, D. (2006b). Rose reports influence felt 40 years later. *Education Week, 25*(41), 1, 21–24.

Villegas, A. (1991). *Culturally responsive pedagogy for the 1990s and beyond.* Princeton, NJ: Educational Testing Service.

Wadsworth, D. (2001). Why new teachers choose to teach. *Educational Leadership, 58*(8), 24–28.

Walberg, H. (2003). Accountability helps students at risk. *Education Week, 22*(33), 42, 44.

Wallace, J., & Wildly, H. (2004). Old questions for new schools: What are the students doing? *Teachers College Record, 106*(4), 635–650.

Wallace, R. (2004). A framework for understanding teaching with the Internet. *American Educational Research Journal, 41*(2), 447–488.

Walsh, M. (1998). Religious freedom amendment fails in house vote. *Education Week, 17*(39), 22.

Walsh, M. (2000a). Church–state rulings cut both ways. *Education Week, 19*(42), 1, 40–41.

Walsh, M. (2000b). Voucher initiatives defeated in Calif., Mich. *Education Week, 19*(11), 14, 18.

Walsh, M. (2002a). Admissions case could have impact on K–12 education. *Education Week, 20*(15), 1, 24.

Walsh, M. (2002b). Charting the new landscape of school choice. *Education Week, 21*(42), 1, 18–21.

Walsh, M. (2002c). Peer grading passes muster, justices agree. *Education Week, 21*(24), 1, 28, 29.

Walsh, M. (2003a). Justices give K–12 go-ahead to promote diversity. *Education Week, 22*(42), 1, 28, 30.

Walsh, M. (2003b). Private management of schools. *Education Week, 22*(29), 17.

Walsh, M. (2003c). Reports paint opposite pictures of Edison achievement. *Education Week, 22*(25), 5.

Walsh, M., & Hendrie, C. (2003). High court upholds law on Internet filtering in libraries. *Education Week, 24*(42), 24.

Wang, J., & Odell, S. (2002). Mentored learning to teach according to standards-based reform: A critical review. *Review of Educational Research, 72,* 481–546.

Wang, M., Haertel, G., & Walberg, H. (1993). Toward a knowledge base for school learning. *Review of Educational Research, 63,* 249–294.

Warren, J., Jenkins, K., & Kulick, R. (2006). High school exit examinations and state-level completion and GED rates, 1975 through 2002. *Educational Evaluation and Policy Analysis, 28*(2), 131–152.

Wartofsky, A. (2001, February 19). The last word: Philip Pullman's trilogy for young adults ends with God's death and remarkably few critics. *Washington Post,* p. C–1.

Washington, B. (1932). *Selected speeches of Booker T. Washington.* New York: Doubleday.

Watch Me! Read (2005). Reinventing education. Retrieved March 20, 2005, from *http://IBM.com*

Watkins, W. (2001). *The White architects of Black education: Ideology and power in America, 1860–1954.* New York: Teachers College Press.

Waxman, H., Huang, S., Anderson, L., & Weinstein, T. (1997). Classroom process differences in inner-city elementary schools. *Journal of Educational Research, 91*(1), 49–59.

Wayne, A., & Youngs, P. (2003). Teacher characteristics and student achievement gains: A review. *Review of Educational Research, 73,* 89–122.

Wayne, A., Youngs, P., & Fleischman, S. (2005). Improving teacher induction. *Educational Leadership, 62*(8), 76–77.

Weaver-Hightower, M. (2005). *Dare the school build a new education for boys?* Retrieved June 7, 2005, from *http://www.tcrecord.org/Content.asp?ContentID=11743*

Wechsler, D. (2003). *Wechsler Intelligence Scale for Children* (4th ed.) San Antonio, TX: Psychological Corporation.

Weiner, L. (2002, April). *Why is classroom management so vexing to urban teachers? New directions in theory and research about classroom management in urban schools.* Paper presented at the annual meeting of the American Educational Research Association, New Orleans, LA.

Weiner, L. (2006). *Urban teaching: The essentials.* New York: Teachers College Press.

Weinstein, C. (2007). *Middle and secondary classroom management* (3rd ed.). Boston: McGraw-Hill.

Weinstein, C., & Mignano, A., Jr. (2003). *Elementary classroom management: Lessons from research and practice* (3rd ed.). New York: McGraw-Hill.

Weinstein, C., Woolfolk, A., Dittmeier, L., & Shankar, U. (1994). Protector or prison guard? Using metaphors and media to explore student teachers' thinking about classroom management. *Action in Teacher Education, 16*(1), 41–54.

Weinstein, R. (2002). *Reaching higher: The power of expectations in schooling.* Cambridge, MA: Harvard University Press.

Weiss, C., & Kipnes, L. (2006). Reexamining middle school effects: A comparison of middle grades students in middle schools and K–8 schools. *American Journal of Education, 112,* 239–272.

Weiss, I., & Pasley, J. (2004). What is high-quality instruction? *Educational Leadership, 61*(5), 24–28.

Weiss, L. (2005). Book battle in Fayetteville, AR, rages on. *School Library Journal, 51*(11), 20.

Weiss, S., DeFalco, A. A., & Weiss, E. M. (2005). Progressive = permissive? Not according to John Dewey . . . Subjects matter! *Essays in Education, 14,* 1–21.

Wessel, K. (2005). Campus leaders: Why this gender discrepancy? *Lessons, 7*(1), 16–19.

West, E. (1972). *The Black American and education.* Upper Saddle River, NJ: Merrill/Prentice Hall.

West, M., & Manno, B. (2006). The elephant in the reform room. *Education Week, 25*(34), 44, 36.

Whalen, S. (2002). *The Polk Bros. Foundation's Full-Service Schools-Initiative: Synopsis of evaluation findings.* Retrieved June 1, 2006, from *http://www.polkbrosfdn.org/full_service_schools_initiative.htm*

Whitson, J. (2006). *The Dover (PA) evolution case: A true win for education? Teachers College Record.* Published January, 4, 2006. Retrieved January 18, 2006, from *http://www.tcrecord.org* ID Number 12271.

Wiersma, W., & Jurs, S. G (2005). *Research methods in education: An introduction* (8th ed.) Needham Heights, MA: Allyn & Bacon.

Wiggins, G., & McTighe, J. (2005). *Understanding by design* (2nd ed.). Upper Saddle River, NJ: Pearson.

Wilder, M. (2000). Increasing African American teachers' presence in American schools: Voices of students who care. *Urban Education, 35*(2), 205–220.

Wiles, J., & Bondi, J. (2007). *Curriculum development: A guide to practice* (7th ed.). Upper Saddle River, NJ: Pearson.

"Will KERA come to PA?" (2003). *Education Advocate, 4*(3), 1–2. Retrieved August 14, 2005, from *http://www.ceopa.org/documents/Page1–4_001.pdf*

Willard, N. (2006). Cyberbullying. *Education Week, 25*(30), 41, 43.

Williams, J. (2003). Why great teachers stay. *Educational Leadership, 60*(8), 71–75.

Williams, S., Bareiss, R., & Reiser, B. (1996, April). *ASK Jasper: A multimedia publishing and performance support environment for design.* Paper presented at the annual meeting of the American Educational Research Association, New York.

Wilson, B. L., & Corbett, H D. (2001). *Listening to urban kids: School reform and the teachers they want.* Albany, NY: State University of New York Press.

Wilson, H., & Donenberg, G. (2004). Quality of parent communication about sex and its relationship to risky sexual behavior among youth in psychiatric care: A pilot study. *Journal of Child Psychology and Psychiatry and Allied Disciplines, 45*(2), 387–395.

Winitzky, N. (1994). Multicultural and mainstreamed classrooms. In R. Arends (Ed.), *Learning to teach* (3rd ed., pp. 132–170). New York: McGraw-Hill.

Winn, I. (2005). *The education mirage: How teachers succeed and why the system fails.* New York: iUniverse.

Winn, W. (2002). Current trends in technology research: The study of learning environments. *Educational Psychology Review, 14,* 331–351.

Winograd, K. (1998). Rethinking theory after practice: Education professor as elementary teacher. *Journal of Teacher Education, 49,* 296–303.

Wong, H., Britton, T., & Ganser, T. (2005). What the world can teach us about new teacher induction. *Phi Delta Kappan, 86*(5), 379–384.

Wood, K. (2005). *Interdisciplinary instruction* (3rd ed.). Upper Saddle River, NJ: Pearson.

Wood, M. (2005). *High school counselors say they lack skills to assist gay, lesbian students.* Retrieved July 14, 2006, from *www.bsu.edu/news*

Wood, T., Cobb, P., & Yackel, E. (1992). Change in learning mathematics: Change in teaching mathematics. In H. Marshall (Ed.), *Redefining student learning: Roots of educational change* (pp. 177–205). Norwood, NJ: Ablex.

Woodward, T. (2002, June 20). *Edison's failing grade. Corporate Watch.* Retrieved November 23, 2005, from *http://www.corpwatch.org/issues/PID.jsp?articleid=2688*

Wynne, E. (1997, March). *Moral education and character education: A comparison/contrast.* Paper presented at the annual meeting of the American Educational Research Association, Chicago.

Yan, W., & Gong, Y. (2003, April). *Who selects teaching as a career? An analysis of Hispanic American high school students' career aspiration of teaching.* Paper presented at the annual meeting of the American Educational Research Association, Chicago.

Yecke, C. (2006). Mayhem in the middle. *Education Week, 25*(21), 44.

Yinger, J. (Ed.). (2004). *Helping children left behind.* Cambridge, MA: MIT Press.

Young, B. (2002). *Characteristics of the 100 largest public elementary and secondary school districts in the United States: 2000–01* (NCES 2002–351). U.S. Department of Education, National Center for Education Statistics. Washington, DC: U.S. Government Printing Office.

Young, M., & Penhollow, T. (2006). The impact of abstinence education: What does the research say? *American Journal of Health Education, 37*(4), 194–202.

Young, M., & Scribner, J. (1997, March). *The synergy of parental involvement and student engagement at the secondary level: Relationships of consequence in Mexican-American communities.* Paper presented at the annual meeting of the American Educational Research Association, Chicago.

Zahorik, J. (1991). Teaching style and textbooks. *Teaching and Teacher Education, 7,* 185–196.

Zehr, M. (1999). Moving teachers along a competency continuum. *Education Week, 19*(4), 41.

Zehr, M. (2000). National standards on technology education released. *Education Week, 19*(31), 18.

Zehr, M. (2002a). Early bilingual programs found to boost test scores. *Education Week, 22*(1), 6.

Zehr, M. (2002b). Voters courted in two states on bilingual ed. *Education Week, 22*(2), 1, 22.

Zehr, M. (2004). Va. plan would ease standards for home school parents. *Education Week, 23*(34), 26.

Zehr, M. (2006). More home schoolers taking Advanced Placement tests. *Education Week, 25*(33), 12.

Zeldin, A., & Pajares, F. (2000). Against the odds: Self-efficacy beliefs of women in mathematical, scientific, and technological careers. *American Educational Research Journal, 37*, 215–246.

Zhao, Y. (2002, August 5). Wave of pupils lacking English strains school [Electronic version]. *New York Times*. Retrieved March 24, 2005, from *http://www.nytimes.com*

Zins, J., Bloodworth, M., Weissberg, R., & Walberg, H. (2004). The scientific base linking social and emotional learning to school success. In J. Zins, R. Weissberg, M. Wang, & H. Walberg (Eds.), *Building academic success on social and emotional learning* (pp. 3–22). New York: Teachers College Press.

Zirkel, P. (1999). Urinalysis? *Phi Delta Kappan, 80*, 409–410.

Zirkel, P. (2001/2002). Decisions that have shaped U.S. education. *Educational Leadership, 59*(4), 6–12.

Zollars, N. (2000). Schools need rules when it comes to students with disabilities. *Education Week, 19*(25), 1, 46, 48.

Glossary

A

Ability grouping. The practice of placing students of similar aptitude and achievement histories together in an attempt to match instruction to the needs of different groups.

Academic freedom. The right of teachers to choose both content and teaching methods based on their professional judgment.

Academic learning time. Combining engagement and success, this is the amount of time students are successful while engaged.

Academy. A secondary school that focused on the practical needs of colonial America as a growing nation.

Acceleration. A program for gifted and talented students that keeps the regular curriculum but allows students to move through it more quickly.

Accountability. The process of requiring students to demonstrate understanding of the topics they study as measured by standardized tests, as well as holding educators at all levels responsible for students' performance.

Action research. A form of applied research designed to answer a specific school- or classroom-related question.

Administrators. Individuals responsible for the day-to-day operation of a school.

Advanced placement classes. Courses taken in high school that allow students to earn college credit.

Affirmative action. A collection of policies and procedures designed to overcome past racial, ethnic, gender, and disability discrimination.

Allocated time. The amount of time a teacher designates for a particular content area or topic.

Assessment. How student understanding is measured.

Assimilation. A process of socializing people so that they adopt dominant social norms and patterns of behavior.

Assistive technology. A set of adaptive tools that support students with disabilities in learning activities and daily life tasks.

Autonomy. The capacity to control one's own professional life.

Axiology. The branch of philosophy that considers values and ethics.

B

Behavior disorders. Exceptionalities involving the display of serious and persistent age-inappropriate behaviors that result in social conflict, personal unhappiness, and school failure.

Between-class ability grouping. Grouping that divides all students in a given grade into high, medium, and low groups.

Block grants. Federal monies provided to states and school districts with few restrictions for use.

Buckley Amendment. A federal act that makes school records open and accessible to students and their parents.

Bulletin board. An electronic message center for a given topic.

C

Career technical. A term used to identify programs designed to provide students with education and job skills that will enable them to get a job immediately after graduating from high school.

Caring. A teacher's investment in the protection and development of the young people in his or her classes.

Categorical grants. Monies targeted for specific groups and designated purposes.

Censorship. The practice of prohibiting the use of objectionable materials, such as certain books used in libraries or in academic classes.

Certification. Special recognition by a professional organization indicating that an individual has met certain requirements specified by the organization.

Character education. A curriculum approach to developing student morality suggesting that moral values and positive character traits, such as honesty and citizenship, should be emphasized, taught, and rewarded.

Charter schools. Alternative schools that are independently operated but publicly funded.

Chat room. A site on the Internet where many people can simultaneously communicate in real time.

Classroom climate. The emotional and psychological environment of a classroom.

Classroom management. Teachers' strategies that create and maintain an orderly learning environment.

Closure.   A form of review occurring at the end of a lesson.

Cognitive learning theories.   Explanations for learning that focus on changes in the ways people think that result from their efforts to make sense of the world.

Collaboration.   Joint communication and decision making among educational professionals to create an optimal learning environment for students with exceptionalities.

Collective bargaining.   Process that occurs when a local chapter of a professional organization negotiates with a school district over the rights of the teachers and the conditions of employment.

Common school movement.   A historical attempt to make education available to all children in the United States.

Communication disorders.   Exceptionalities that interfere with students' abilities to receive and understand information from others and to express their own ideas or questions.

Compensatory education programs.   Government attempts to create more equal educational opportunities for disadvantaged youth.

Comprehensive high school.   A secondary school that attempts to meet the needs of all students by housing them together and providing curricular options (e.g., vocational or college-preparatory programs) geared toward a variety of student ability levels and interests.

Computer-mediated communication (CMC).   Telecommunication between people via electronic mail (e-mail).

Cooperative learning.   A set of instructional strategies used to help learners meet specific learning and social interaction objectives in structured groups.

Copyright laws.   Federal laws designed to protect the intellectual property of authors, including printed matter, videos, computer software, and various other types of original work.

Corporal punishment.   The use of physical, punitive disciplinary actions to correct student misbehavior.

Creationism.   A religious view suggesting that the universe was created by God as described in the Bible.

Credentials file.   A collection of important documents teachers need to submit when they apply for teaching positions.

Cultural diversity.   The different cultures that you'll encounter in classrooms and how these cultural differences influence learning.

Culturally responsive teaching.   Instruction that acknowledges and accommodates cultural diversity.

Culture.   The knowledge, attitudes, values, customs, and behavior patterns that characterize a social group.

Curriculum.   The knowledge and skills that teachers teach and students are supposed to learn.

D

Database program.   A computer program that allows users to store, organize, and manipulate information, including both text and numerical data.

Decision making.   Problem solving in ill-defined situations, based on professional knowledge.

Development.   The physical, intellectual, and social changes in children that occur as a result of experience.

Developmental programs.   Programs that accommodate differences in children's development by allowing them to acquire skills and abilities at their own pace through direct experiences.

Digital portfolio.   A collection of materials contained in an electronic file that makes the information accessible to potential viewers.

Direct instruction.   An instructional strategy designed to teach well-defined knowledge and skills that are needed for later learning.

Disabilities.   Functional limitations or an inability to perform a certain act, such as hear or walk.

Discipline.   Teachers' responses to student misbehavior.

Distance learning.   Organized instructional programs in which teachers and learners, though physically separated, are connected through technology.

Drill-and-practice programs.   Software designed to provide extensive practice with feedback.

E

Early childhood education.   A general term encompassing a range of educational programs for young children, including infant intervention and enrichment programs, nursery schools, public and private prekindergartens and kindergartens, and federally funded Head Start programs.

Educational technology.   A combination of the processes and tools involved in addressing educational needs and problems.

Effective instruction.   Instruction that builds on principles of learning to maximize learning in the classroom.

Effective school.   A school in which learning for all students is maximized.

Emphasis.   Verbal and vocal cues and repetition used to alert students to important information in a lesson

Engaged time.   The time students actually spend actively involved in learning activities. Also called *time on task*.

English as a second language (ESL) program.   Language program that emphasizes rapid transition to English.

English classical school.   A free secondary school designed to meet the needs of boys not planning to attend college.

English language learners (ELLs).   Students whose first language is not English and who need help in learning to speak, read, and write in English.

Enrichment.   A program for gifted and talented students that provides richer and varied content through strategies that supplement usual grade-level work.

Epistemology.   The branch of philosophy that examines questions of how we come to know what we know.

Equitable distribution.   The practice of calling on all students—both volunteers and nonvolunteers—as equally as possible.

Essential teaching skills.   Abilities that all teachers, including those in their first year, should have in order to maximize student learning.

Essentialism.   An educational philosophy suggesting that a critical core of knowledge and skills exists that all people should possess.

Establishment clause.   The clause of the First Amendment that prohibits the establishment of a national religion.

Ethics.   Sets of moral standards for acceptable professional behavior.

Ethnicity.   A person's ancestry; the way individuals identify themselves with the nation from which they or their ancestors came.

Existentialism.   A traditional philosophy suggesting that humanity isn't part of an orderly universe; rather, individuals create their own realities.

Explicit curriculum.   The curriculum found in textbooks, curriculum guides, standards, as well as other planned formal educational experiences.

Extracurriculum.   Learning experiences that extend beyond the core of students' formal studies.

Extrinsic rewards.   Rewards that come from outside oneself, such as job security and vacations.

F

Fair-use guidelines.   Policies that specify limitations in the use of copyrighted materials for educational purposes.

Feedback.   Information about existing understanding that we use to enhance future understanding.

Focus.   Activities or materials used to attract and maintain attention during lessons.

Formative evaluation.   The process of gathering information and providing feedback that teachers can use to improve their practice.

Free exercise clause.   The clause of the First Amendment that prohibits the government from interfering with individuals' rights to hold religious beliefs and freely practice religion.

Full-service schools.   Schools that serve as a family resource center to provide a range of social and health services.

G

Gender-role identity.   Differences in expectations and beliefs about appropriate roles and behaviors of the two sexes.

Gifted and talented.   A designation given to students at the upper end of the ability continuum who need special services to reach their full potential.

Giftedness.   Abilities at the upper end of the continuum that require support beyond regular classroom instruction to reach full potential.

Grievance.   A formal complaint against an employer alleging unsatisfactory working conditions.

Guided discovery.   An instructional model designed to teach concepts and relationships among them through the use of examples.

H

Head Start.   A federal compensatory education program designed to help 3- to 5-year-old disadvantaged children enter school ready to learn.

High collective efficacy.   The belief by teachers that their school can make a difference in students' lives.

High-quality examples.   Representations of content that ideally have all the information in them that students need in order to reach teachers' learning objectives.

High-stakes tests.   Assessments that states and districts use to determine whether or not students will advance from one grade to another, graduate from high school, or have access to specific fields of study.

Homeschooling.   An educational option in which parents educate their children at home.

Hypermedia.   A linked form of multimedia that allows learners to make connections to different points in the program based on their background knowledge and learning progress.

I

Icons.   Pictures displayed on computer screens that act as symbols for some action or item.

Idealism.   A traditional philosophy asserting that ideas are the only reliable form of reality.

Immersion program.   Language program that emphasizes rapid transition to English.

Implicit curriculum.   The kinds of learning children acquire from the nature and organization of the classroom and school as well as the attitudes and actions of their teachers.

In loco parentis.   A principle meaning "in place of the parents" that requires teachers to use the same judgment and care as parents in protecting the children under their supervision.

Inclusion.   A comprehensive approach to educating students with exceptionalities that advocates a total, systematic, and coordinated web of services.

Individualized education program (IEP).   An individually prescribed instructional plan devised by special education and general education teachers, resource professionals, and parents (and sometimes the student).

Induction programs. Professional experiences for beginning teachers that provide systematic and sustained assistance to ease the transition into teaching.

Instruction. The strategies teachers use to help students reach learning goals in the curriculum.

Instructional alignment. The match between learning objectives, learning activities, and assessments.

Instructional time. The amount left for teaching after routine management and administrative tasks are completed.

Integrated curriculum. Curriculum in which concepts and skills from various disciplines are combined and related.

Intelligence. The capacity to acquire knowledge, the ability to think and reason in the abstract, and the ability to solve problems.

Intelligent design. A theory suggesting that certain features of the universe and of living things are so complex that their existence is best explained by an intelligent cause, rather than an undirected process such as natural selection.

Internet. The complex web of interconnections among computers that allows people to communicate and share information worldwide.

Intrinsic rewards. Rewards that come from within oneself and are personally satisfying for emotional or intellectual reasons.

J

Junior high schools. Schools that were originally designed in the early 1900s to provide a unique academic curriculum for early adolescent youth.

L

Language clarity. Teacher talk that omits vague terms in questions and explanations.

Language disorders (or **receptive disorders**). Problems with understanding language or using language to express ideas.

Latchkey children. Children who go home to empty houses after school and who are left alone until parents arrive home from work.

Latin grammar school. A college-preparatory school originally designed to help boys prepare for the ministry or, later, for a career in law.

Learning communities. Classrooms in which the teacher and all the students work together to help everyone learn.

Learning disabilities. Exceptionalities that involve difficulties in acquiring and using listening, speaking, reading, writing, reasoning, or mathematical abilities.

Learning objectives. Statements that specify what students should know or be able to do with respect to a topic or course of study.

Learning styles. Students' personal approaches to learning, problem solving, and processing information.

Least restrictive environment (LRE). The placement of students in as normal an educational setting as possible while still meeting their special academic, social, and physical needs.

Lecture-discussion. An instructional model designed to help students acquire organized bodies of knowledge and understand the relationships of ideas within them.

Licensure. The process by which a state evaluates the credentials of prospective teachers to ensure that they have achieved satisfactory levels of teaching competence and are morally fit to work with youth.

Local school board. A group of elected lay citizens responsible for setting policies that determine how a school district operates.

Logic. The branch of philosophy that examines the processes of deriving valid conclusions from basic principles.

Looping. The practice of keeping a teacher with one group of students for more than a year.

Lower class. Socioeconomic level composed of people who typically make less than $25,000 per year, have a high school education or less, and work in blue-collar jobs.

M

Magnet schools. Public schools that provide innovative or specialized programs that attempt to attract students from all parts of a district.

Mainstreaming. The practice of moving students with exceptionalities from segregated settings into regular education classrooms.

Maintenance language programs. Language programs that place the greatest emphasis on using and sustaining the first language.

Mental retardation. An exceptionality that includes limitations in intellectual functioning, as indicated by difficulties in learning, and problems with adaptive skills, such as communication, self-care, and social ability.

Mentors. Experienced teachers who provide guidance and support for beginning teachers.

Merit pay. A supplement to a teacher's base salary intended to reward superior performance or work in a high-need area.

Metacognition. Students' awareness of the ways they learn most effectively and their ability to control these factors.

Metaphysics (ontology). The branch of philosophy that considers what we know.

Middle class. Socioeconomic level composed of managers, administrators, and white-collar workers who perform nonmanual work.

Middle schools. Schools, typically for grades 6–8, specifically designed to help students through the rapid social, emotional, and intellectual changes characteristic of early adolescence.

Models of instruction.   Prescriptive approaches to teaching designed to help students acquire a deep understanding of specific forms of knowledge.

Moral education.   A curriculum approach to developing student morality that emphasizes students' moral reasoning.

Multicultural education.   A general term that describes a variety of strategies schools use to accommodate cultural differences in teaching and learning.

Multimedia.   Combinations of media, including text, graphics, pictures, audio, and video that are designed to communicate information.

Multiple intelligences.   A theory that suggests that overall intelligence is composed of eight relatively independent dimensions.

N

Negligence.   A teacher's or other school employee's failure to exercise sufficient care in protecting students from injury.

Normal schools.   Two-year institutions developed in the early 1800s to prepare prospective elementary teachers.

Normative philosophy.   A description of the way professionals ought to practice.

Notoriety.   The extent to which a teacher's behavior becomes known and controversial.

Null curriculum.   Topics left out of the course of study.

O

Old Deluder Satan Act.   Early colonial law designed to create scripture-literate citizens who would thwart Satan's trickery.

Organization.   The set of teacher actions that maximizes the amount of time available for instruction.

Organized bodies of knowledge.   Topics that connect facts, concepts, generalizations, and principles, and make the relationships among them explicit.

P

Perennialism.   An educational philosophy suggesting that nature—including human nature—is constant.

Personal development.   The growth of enduring personality traits that influence the way individuals interact with their physical and social environments.

Personal teaching efficacy.   A teacher's belief in his or her ability to promote learning in all students regardless of their prior knowledge or experiences.

Perspective taking.   The ability to understand the thoughts and feelings of others.

Philosophy of education.   A framework for thinking about educational issues, and a guide for professional practice.

Philosophy.   The study of theories of knowledge, truth, existence, and morality.

Positive teacher expectations.   Teachers' beliefs in students' capabilities to learn.

Postmodernism.   An educational philosophy contending that many of the institutions in our society, including schools, are used by those in power to control and marginalize those who lack power.

Poverty thresholds.   Household income levels that represent the lowest earnings needed to meet basic living needs.

Pragmatism.   A traditional philosophy that rejects the idea of absolute, unchanging truth, instead asserting that truth is "what works."

Principal.   The individual who has the ultimate administrative responsibility for the school's operation.

Problem-based learning.   An instructional strategy that uses a problem and the data gathered in attempts to solve it as the focal point of a lesson.

Procedures.   Management routines students follow in their daily learning activities.

Productive learning environment.   A classroom that is orderly and focuses on learning.

Professional ethics.   A set of moral standards for acceptable professional behavior.

Professional portfolio.   A collection of representative work materials to document developing knowledge and skills.

Professionalism.   An occupation characterized by a specialized body of knowledge with emphasis on autonomy, decision making, reflection, and ethical standards for conduct.

Progressivism.   An educational philosophy emphasizing curricula that focus on real-world problem solving and individual development.

Prompt.   A teacher question or directive that elicits a student response after the student has failed to answer or has given an incorrect or incomplete answer.

Property taxes.   The major source of educational funding, determined by the assessed value of a home or property.

Q

Questioning frequency.   Refers to the number of times a teacher asks questions during a given period of instructional time.

R

Realism.   A traditional philosophy suggesting that the features of the universe exist whether or not a human being is there to perceive them.

Reduction in force.   The elimination of teaching positions because of declining student enrollment or school funds. Also known as "riffing."

Reflection.   The process of teachers' thinking about and analyzing their work to assess its effectiveness.

Reforms.   Suggested changes in teaching and teacher preparation intended to increase the amount students learn.

Resilient students.   Students placed at-risk who have been able to rise above adverse conditions to succeed in school and in other aspects of life.

Résumé.   A document that provides an overview of an individual's job qualifications and work experience.

Review.   A summary that helps students link what they have already learned to what will follow in the next learning activity.

Rules.   Guidelines that provide standards or norms for acceptable classroom behavior.

S

School district.   An administrative unit within a state, defined by geographical boundaries, and legally responsible for the public education of children within those boundaries.

School principal.   The individual having the ultimate administrative responsibility for a school's operation.

Separate but equal.   A policy of segregating minorities in education, transportation, housing, and other areas of public life if opportunities and facilities were considered equal to those of nonminorities. In education, the policy was evidenced by separate schools with different curricula, teaching methods, teachers, and resources.

Service learning.   An approach to promoting ethical and moral development that combines service to the community with content-learning objectives.

Sexual harassment.   Unwanted and/or unwelcome sexual behavior that interferes with a student's sense of well-being.

Simulations.   Programs, either in software or Web-based form, that model a system or process.

Single-gender classes and schools.   Classes and schools where boys and girls are segregated for part or all of the day.

Site-based decision making.   A school management reform movement that attempts to place increased responsibility for governance at the individual school level.

Social development.   The advances students make in their ability to interact with and get along with others.

Social institution.   An organization with established structures and rules designed to promote certain goals.

Social problem-solving skills.   The ability to resolve conflicts in ways that are beneficial to all involved.

Socioeconomic status (SES).   The combination of family income, parents' occupations, and the level of parental education.

Special education.   Instruction designed to meet the unique needs of students with exceptionalities.

Speech disorders (or **expressive disorders**).   Problems in forming and sequencing sounds.

Spreadsheet programs.   Computer programs that are used to organize and manipulate numerical data.

Standards.   Statements specifying what students should know and what skills they should have upon completing an area of study.

Standards-based education.   The process of focusing curricula and instruction on predetermined standards.

State board of education.   The legal governing body that exercises general control and supervision of the schools in a state.

State office of education.   Office responsible for implementing a state's education policy on a day-to-day basis.

State tuition tax-credit plans.   A variation on school voucher programs in which parents are given tax credits for money they spend on private-school tuition.

Stereotype.   A rigid, simplistic caricature of a particular group of people.

Students placed at-risk.   Students in danger of failing to complete their education with the skills necessary to survive in modern society.

Students with exceptionalities.   Learners who need special help and resources to reach their full potential.

Summative evaluation.   The process of gathering information about a teacher's competence, often for the purpose of making administrative decisions about retention and promotion.

Superintendent.   The school district's head administrative officer, along with his or her staff, responsible for implementing that policy in the district's schools.

T

Teacher modeling.   The tendency of people to observe and imitate others' behaviors and attitudes.

Teaching contract.   A legal employment agreement between a teacher and a local school board.

Technician.   A person who uses specific skills to complete well-defined tasks.

Tenure.   A legal safeguard that provides job security by preventing teacher dismissal without cause.

Thematic lessons.   Lessons in which all parts of a teacher's instruction are related, so that the lesson leads to a specific point.

Theory.   A set of related principles that are based on observation and are used to explain additional observations.

Title I.   A federal compensatory education program that funds supplemental education services for low-income students in elementary and secondary schools.

Tracking.   The practice of ability grouping that places students in a series of different classes or curricula on the basis of ability and career goals.

Transition programs.   Language programs that maintain the first language until students acquire sufficient English.

Transition signals.   Verbal statements within a lesson that indicate one idea is ending and another is beginning, and suggest connections between the two ideas.

Tutorial.   A software program that delivers an entire integrated instructional sequence similar to a teacher's instruction on the topic.

U

Underclass.   People with low incomes who continually struggle with economic problems.

Upper class.   The socioeconomic class composed of highly educated (usually a college degree), highly paid (usually above $170,000) professionals who make up about 5 percent of the population.

URL (uniform resource locator).   A series of letters and/or symbols that acts as an address for a site on the Internet.

V

Voucher.   A check or written document that parents can use to purchase educational services.

W

Wait-time.   The amount of time a teacher pauses after asking a question both before and after calling on a student to answer.

War on Poverty.   A general term for federal programs designed to eradicate poverty during the 1960s.

Website.   A location on the World Wide Web identified with a uniform resource locator (URL).

Weighted student formula.   A means of allocating resources within a district to schools on an individual basis based on student needs.

Within-class ability grouping.   Grouping that divides students within one classroom into ability groups.

Withitness.   A teacher's awareness of what is going on in all parts of the classroom at all times and the communication of this awareness to students, both verbally and nonverbally.

Working class.   Socioeconomic level composed of blue-collar workers who perform manual labor.

World Wide Web.   A system on the Internet that allows people to access, view, and maintain documents that include text, data, sound, and video.

Z

Zero-tolerance policies.   Policies that call for students to receive automatic suspensions or expulsions as punishment for certain offenses, primarily those involving weapons, threats, or drugs.

Name Index

Subject Index